The Waning of the Green
Catholics, the Irish, and
Identity in Toronto, 1887–1922

Most historical accounts of the Irish Catholic community in Toronto describe it as a poor underclass of society, ghettoized by the largely British, Protestant population and characterized by the sectarian violence between Protestants and Catholics that earned Toronto the title "Belfast of Canada." Challenging this long-standing view of the Irish Catholic experience, Mark McGowan provides a new picture of the community's evolution and integration into Canadian society.

McGowan traces the evolution of the Catholic community from an isolated religious and Irish ethnic subculture in the late nineteenth century into an integrated segment of English Canadian society by the early twentieth century. English-speaking Catholics moved into all neighbourhoods of the city and socialized with and married non-Catholics. They even embraced their own brand of imperialism: by 1914 thousands of them had enlisted to fight for God and the British Empire.

McGowan's detailed and lively portrait will be of great interest to students and scholars of religious history, Irish studies, ethnic history, and Canadian history.

MARK G. MCGOWAN is associate professor of history, St Michael's College, University of Toronto.

McGILL-QUEEN'S STUDIES IN THE HISTORY OF RELIGION

Volumes in the McGill-Queen's Studies in the History of Religion have been supported by the Jackman Foundation of Toronto.

SERIES ONE
G.A. Rawlyk, Editor

The Waning of the Green

Catholics, the Irish, and Identity in Toronto, 1887–1922

MARK G. MCGOWAN

McGill-Queen's University Press
Montreal & Kingston · London · Ithaca

© McGill-Queen's University Press 1999
ISBN 0-7735-1789-8 (cloth)
ISBN 0-7735-1790-1 (paper)

Legal deposit first quarter 1999
Bibliothèque nationale du Québec

Printed in Canada on acid-free paper

This book has been published with the help of a grant
from the Humanities and Social Sciences Federation of
Canada, using funds provided by the Social Sciences
and Humanities Research Council of Canada.

McGill-Queen's University Press acknowledges the
financial support of the Government of Canada
through the Book Publishing Industry Development
Program for its activities. We also acknowledge the
support of the Canada Council for the Arts for our
publishing program.

Canadian Cataloguing in Publication Data

McGowan, Mark George, 1959–
   The waning of the green: catholics, the Irish, and
   identity in Toronto, 1887–1922
   (McGill-Queen's studies in the history of religion,
   ISSN 1181-7445)
   Includes bibliographical references and index.
   ISBN 0-7735-1789-8 (bnd)
   ISBN 0-7735-1790-1 (pbk)
   1. Catholics – Ontario – Toronto – History. 2. Irish
   Canadians – Ontario – Toronto – History. I. Title.
   II. Series.
   FC3097.9.I6M33 1999   305.6'20713541
   C98-901105-4   F1059.7.I6M33 1999

This book was typeset by Typo Litho Composition Inc.
in 10/12 Palatino.

For Eileen and
Erin, Patrick, Brendan, Kathleen, and
John-Francis

In memory of
Albert G. Giesler (1905–1991), and
Douglas G. McGowan (1933–1973)

Contents

Acknowledgments

One accumulates considerable personal debts over the span of a twelve-year project. My greatest regret is that George Rawlyk of McGill-Queen's University Press did not live to see this project come to fruition. His support and encouragement gave me great hope at times when I thought this study would be buried among a myriad of academic duties and projects. My sincerest thanks to Donald Akenson and Philip Cercone of McGill-Queen's, who have ushered this project along with skill and kindness. Susan Kent Davidson used her masterful editing skills to enhance the clarity and readability of this book. Additional thanks to Joyce Williams and Kristin Perry of St Michael's College, who worked diligently smoothing out the rough edges of the manuscript and provided technical knowledge well beyond my competence. I would also be remiss if I did not thank my daughter Erin, who helped to sort and file five volumes of newspaper notes.

I owe a considerable debt to the many archivists who assisted me as I gathered historical fragments. Sister Frieda Watson, CSJ, retired archivist of the Archdiocese of Toronto, and her staff, past and present – Marc Lerman, Linda Wicks, Suzanne Lout, Marie Daly, Ray Marshall, Anne Brimmicomb – offered gracious assistance and sincere friendship as I ferreted my way into their superbly catalogued collection. For the many times I sent Marc, now chief archivist, in hot pursuit of a crazy hunch or some archival grail, my sincerest apologies, gratitude, and congratulations; invariably, he would make some discovery that engendered new questions. I also wish to thank Glenn Wright, formerly of the National Archives, and Tim Wright and Ray Hébert of the National Personnel Records Centre in Ottawa, for their invaluable assistance with materials relating to the First World War. In Rome and at the Vatican, Dr Matteo Sanfilippo provided me with document inventories for the Vatican Archives and made arrangements for hundreds of photocopies.

I am also grateful for the support of many colleagues and mentors who each influenced the preparation of this book. Brian Loring Villa of the University of Ottawa shared his insights and his great love of the discipline of history with me; Joseph F. Kenkel, formerly of that institution, kept my interest alive; and their colleague Robert Choquette introduced me to the study of Canadian religious history. John S. Moir, professor emeritus of the University of Toronto, directed my dissertation, upon which this book is based – and for that I am ever thankful. John constantly challenged me with his formidable Socratic style, cheered me with his wit, and demonstrated great patience; in the Scottish tradition of hospitality he and Jacqueline opened their home many times to my family. I would like to thank Brian Clarke of Emmanuel College, Toronto, and Michael Cottrell of the University of Saskatchewan – two fellow travellers who became invaluable and very generous sounding-boards for my questions and discoveries regarding the Catholics of Toronto and who made this journey much more pleasurable. More recently, I am grateful to Elizabeth Smyth, who shared with me her considerable insights into women's religious orders and their role in Catholic education. Several of my colleagues in the Canadian Catholic Historical Association also offered constructive criticism and helpful questions over the years: Brian Hogan, CSB, Michael Power, Terrence Murphy, Gerald Stortz, Jeanne Beck, Terence Fay, SJ, Vicki Bennett, Duff Crerar, and Edward Jackman, OP.

I am very thankful to my colleagues at the University of St Michael's College, who have given me personal support and cleared the pathways towards financial assistance: Richard Alway, Maria "Mimi" Marrocco, Joseph Boyle, Mechtilde O'Mara, CSJ, and Mariel O'Neill-Karch. David Wilson offered me sound advice and marvellous *craic*. The Social Sciences and Humanities Research Council assisted this study in its preparatory stage. My thanks as well to the Aid to Scholarly Publications Program and its anonymous assessors. Their comments helped to sharpen the manuscript. Any errors and omissions in the book, however, are entirely my doing.

Finally, on a personal note, my own family supported this study through twelve years, which for some must have seemed like a century. Betty Anne and Roddie MacDonald and Mary Beth and Robert Starkey gave me shelter, sustenance, and good company on my many research trips to Ottawa, as did Betty and Evan Patrick. The late Albert Giesler shared with me his oft-told, colourful tales of a young farm lad's visits to "Toronto the Good" in the days of King George V.

I am no match for my grandfather's ability to set a scene or cast a character, but I have recently come to realize the influence he had on my love of history. Perhaps when put in this light, my children – Erin, Patrick, Brendan, Kathleen, and John-Francis – will understand some of the reasons for dad's spending late nights at the computer or days away from home in places whose names, sometimes, could barely be pronounced by toddlers. My wife Eileen has been the most patient of all. From the birth of the question to the final printing of the tome, she has offered much support, love, and sacrifice. The words thank you can only begin to express my gratitude to her.

The Growth and Location of Catholic Parishes in Toronto 1822–1920

Lawrence

•15

Eglinton

Bayview

10•

St Clair

•26 21

•25

11 • Keele Dufferin Dovercourt Bathurst Avenue Rd Yonge

•27 12• Bloor

17

High Park

•23 6

•14 •22

College 4

16•

•20 5•

•8

Carlton

•13 3• Queen

24•

Danforth

29•

Woodbine

19

Kingston Rd

Victoria Park

Don River

•18

Leslie

7•

1•9

•2

28

TORONTO BAY

⧄ The Ward

LEGEND

1 St Paul's 1822
2 St Michael's Cathedral 1848
3 St Mary's 1852
4 St Basil's 1856
5 St Patrick's 1861
6 St Helen's 1875
7 St Joseph's 1878
8 Our Lady of Lourdes 1886
9 Sacré Coeur 1887
10 Holy Rosary 1892
11 St Cecilia's 1895
12 St Peter's 1896
13 Holy Family 1900
14 St Francis of Assisi 1903
15 St Monica's 1906

16 Our Lady of Mt Carmel 1908
17 St Anthony's 1909
18 St Ann's 1909
19 St John's 1909
20 St Stanislaus' 1911
21 St Clare's 1913
22 St Agnes's 1914
23 St Vincent de Paul 1914
24 Holy Name 1914
25 St Mary of the Angels 1915
26 St Mary's Polish 1915
27 St Joan of Arc 1919
28 Corpus Christi 1920
29 St Brigid's 1920

Source: Mark G. McGowan and Brian P. Clarke, eds., *Catholics at the "Gathering Place": Historical Essays on the Archdiocese of Toronto, 1841–1991* (Toronto: Canadian Catholic Historical Association 1993), xii.

The Wearing of the Green

Oh Paddy dear and did you hear the news that's going round,
The Shamrock is forbid by law to grow on Irish ground.
No more St Patrick's Day we'll keep, his colours can't be seen
For there's a cruel law against the wearing of the green.

I met with Napper Tandy and he took me by the hand
And he said, "How's poor old Ireland and how does she stand?"
She's the most distressful country that ever yet was seen
For they're hangin' men an' women for the wearing of the Green.

And if the colour we must wear is England's cruel Red
Let it remind us of the blood that Ireland has shed
Then pull the shamrock from your hat, and throw it on the sod
And never fear, 'twill take root there, tho' under foot 'tis trod.

When the law can stop the blades of grass from growing as they grow
And when the leaves in summer-time, their colour dare not show
Then I will change the colour, too, I wear in my caubeen
But 'till that day, please God, I'll stick to the wearing of the Green.

Introduction

William O'Brien stepped out from the side entrance of the Rossin House Hotel to catch a breath of fresh air. Within minutes he and his colleagues were being chased by an angry mob of young men hurling fruits, vegetables, and stones in their direction while they screeched, "To hell with the Pope and O'Brien." The quarry scampered through a bicycle shop and, breathless, took refuge in the workshop of a local tailor. The shop was stormed by the hollering assailants, and only the delay provided by his shillelagh-wielding supporters allowed O'Brien his escape back to his hotel without serious injury. A small riot ensued, causing hundreds of dollars in damage to the shop and serious injury to at least one man who caught a brick in the head. The O'Brien in question was William O'Brien, Irish radical, Home Rule advocate, and president of the Irish Land League. The occasion was his speaking tour of North America in 1887, which, by mid-May, had landed in Toronto. To the rest of the world this incident was to be expected from the more fanatical Irish Catholics and Protestants of Ontario's capital. After all, thought most observers, Toronto was the Belfast of North America.[1]

Historically, Toronto's notorious reputation as a hotbed of sectarian bigotry has been difficult to shake. Certainly, in the middle of the nineteenth century this moniker had been well earned. The public face of Protestant-Catholic relations was characterized by periods of ritualized violence on St Patrick's Day and on the Glorious 12th of July, by articulate and sometimes outrageous sectarian sniping by the religious and secular newspapers, and by a shameful display of blood-letting during the Jubilee pilgrimages of 1875. At times this public face of sectarian bitterness was reflected in the behaviour of Catholic and Protestant clerics and politicians. Squabbles over political patronage, points of theology, and separate Catholic schools only tended to sour attempts at peaceful coexistence, and jaded the private day-to-day relationships between Toronto's Protestant and Catholic neighbours. Indeed, in the nineteenth century Toronto, "the city of Churches," was scarcely the home of the blessed peacemakers of which the Christian gospel speaks.

At face value, the O'Brien visit and the ensuing riot would seem to have been just one more episode in a string of confrontations between Toronto's Catholics and their Protestant fellow citizens. If only history were so simple. On the contrary, the O'Brien visit offers less a glimpse of robust Irish nationalism and sectarian division in the city than it does a Catholic community undergoing significant change and internal cleavage.[2] In the spring of 1887 O'Brien's visit to several Canadian and American cities was intended to rouse support among the Irish of the diaspora for the plight of the impoverished and abused tenant farmers of Ireland. The Toronto visit, however, coincided with the visit to the Queen's City by Lord Lansdowne, Canada's governor general. Lansdowne, or Henry Charles Petty-Fitzmaurice, was himself an absentee Irish landlord, a fact not lost on O'Brien, who was travelling with one Denis Kilbride, one of Lansdowne's tenants, who would expose Lansdowne's oppression firsthand.

Instead of rousing Toronto's Catholics, most of whom were of Irish descent, to O'Brien's cause, the visit exposed serious divisions within the Catholic community. Archbishop John Joseph Lynch opposed the visit, as did numerous clergy, Catholic lay leaders, and the more conservative and clerical *Catholic Weekly Review*. While there was sympathy for the plight of Irish tenants, there was also concern that Lansdowne was the representative of the Crown and as such deserved respect and loyalty. Catholic leaders feared the public "disruption" the visit would likely cause, and they were anxious about having to choose sides between Irish political activists and the representative of Canada's head of state. Lynch and leading laymen attempted to divert O'Brien from the Toronto leg of the tour. For Senator Frank Smith the choice was clear: "I still think it is a mistake to let the politicians of Ireland interfere with the Catholic people of Canada … We should as Catholics and as true subjects of Canada discountenance and endeavour to continue the good feeling that now exists between all classes of Canadians."[3] The Irish nationalists, including some clergy, openly participated in the visit, while many other Catholics, less sure of their position, were conspicuous by their absence.

When one penetrates beyond the violent veneer of the O'Brien visit, a very different portrait of the Catholics of Toronto begins to emerge. This was a community that was in the process of transferring

Catholic Europeans, depict the host English-speaking Catholics as no better than the American "Irish" assimilationists when it came to welcoming Italian, German, or Polish Catholics.[13] In short, Canadian English-speaking Catholics appear in our histories as little more than clones of their Irish Catholic American cousins.

Ironically, Canadian Catholics themselves have perpetuated this image because it underscores profoundly the adversity faced by Catholics as they emerged to become one of the most influential groups in contemporary Canada. The image of the poor, downtrodden, and oppressed "Irish" Catholic has become a historical image worn as a badge of pride, evidence of struggle to success despite overwhelming odds. No matter the source, the end result is the same. English-speaking Catholics in Canada have rarely been understood on their own terms. The "Belfast of North America" label has been particularly obstructive to those scholars wanting to probe beyond the myth and fantasy enveloping the English-speaking Catholics of Toronto after the 1890s.

This book argues that, from 1887 to 1922, English-speaking Catholics in Toronto submerged their overt ties to Ireland, embraced many of the values of Canadian society, and allowed their faith life to make some needed adjustments to the North American environment. It is a community study of a religious group that shared a common language although it comprised a variety of ethnic origins. While the vast majority of Toronto's English-speaking Catholics were of Irish descent,[14] there were Catholics of Scottish, English, American, Dutch, and German origin, and converts from Protestantism, who entered the community and emerged as leaders, entrepreneurs, clergy, and religious. These minorities joined "Irish" associations, attended the same schools, participated in the same religious societies, and worshipped at the same churches. Consequently, for the purposes of this study the term English-speaking Catholic refers to all these constituents, although the focus will often shift to those of Irish descent and their adaptation to Canadian society. Nevertheless, by the end of the First World War these cultural subgroups of English-speaking Catholicism in Toronto were generally indistinguishable.

Toronto provides an excellent laboratory for the study of English-speaking Catholics for several reasons. Since the "Queen's City" was the largest city in English-speaking Canada and a fortress of the Orange Order in Ontario,[15] the growth and development of Catholic culture in the context of a "Protestant" city could suggest patterns to be tested in Catholic communities elsewhere in English Canada. If Catholics were able to succeed socially, economically, and religiously in the heart of Protestant Ontario, serious questions must be directed

at the long-standing historical stereotypes of Catholic underachieve-
ment across Canada.[16] Similarly, as one of the principal administrative, political, and industrial centres in central Canada, Toronto offers
the historian the opportunity to examine an ethno-religious group
coping with change at all levels of a modern industrial society and at
the heart of decision-making in both the secular and ecclesiastical
spheres. The Archdiocese of Toronto was clearly the most important
Roman Catholic see in English Canada, and its metropolitan influence was felt throughout Ontario, the prairies, and even the Maritimes in the late Victorian and Edwardian periods.[17] Although there
has been considerable historiographical debate over whether or not
Irish Catholics in nineteenth-century Ontario were primarily urban or
rural, these demographic questions have little bearing on this study.[18]
By the turn of the century Canada had experienced a significant
rural-to-urban shift as families and youths of all religious denominations migrated from small towns and the agricultural hinterlands to
such centres as Toronto in hopes of sharing in the economic boom of
the Laurier era. Consequently, it is entirely appropriate to study English-speaking Catholics in this urban context, although a contrary
case may be made for an earlier period.[19]

Low levels of Irish immigration to Toronto and the decreasing
numbers of Irish-born inhabitants in the city also give the historian an
excellent opportunity to scrutinize an English-speaking Catholic population that was primarily Canadian born. After the surge of famine
migrants in the late 1840s and early 1850s, British North America received fewer newcomers from Ireland.[20] In addition, many of these
arrivals throughout the nineteenth century were Protestant Irish,
which in itself narrowed the scope of Irish Catholic domination in
Ontario's cities and rural hinterlands. By 1911 most of the English-
speaking Catholics in Toronto were the children, grandchildren, and
perhaps great-grandchildren of pre-Confederation Irish and Scottish
immigrants. Although place of birth is only one of many factors contributing to identity, and a limited one at that,[21] the overwhelming
preponderance of Canadian-born Catholics in Edwardian Toronto is
an excellent basis for initiating a study of Catholic integration into
Canadian society.

The dates that historians choose to narrow the frame of reference of
their research can be as arbitrary as the interpretations offered by the
studies themselves. Despite these idiosyncracies of the profession, the
dates selected for this study – 1887 to 1922 – incorporate a period of
profound change for Toronto's English-speaking Catholics. We have
already noted that 1887 marked a distinctive tearing in the Catholic
community over the O'Brien visit and the Queen's Jubilee. Within a

year Archbishop Lynch was dead, and the old clerical-nationalist politics of an earlier era were pretty much entombed with him. In December 1889 John Walsh, a major proponent of the Canadianization of the Church, began his tenure as archbishop of Toronto.[22] It was under Walsh's leadership in the 1890s that Toronto's Catholics began to resolve this confusion of identity, and found that they could be the most loyal of Canadians and still retain an active interest in Irish politics. This interest in Irish affairs, however, would wane with each succeeding generation and each passing year.

The First World War marked a distinct end to the Victorian and Edwardian periods. The "roaring twenties" brought new concerns to the attention of all Canadians – the fractured political scene, moral upheaval, and economic recession. The war and its social, economic, and politic repercussions had effectively ushered Canada into a new phase of its history. Internationally, the war, and then civil war, also changed the course of Irish and imperial history. While the "de-Hibernization" of English-speaking Catholics was well under way before 1922, certainly the winning of Irish Home Rule in that year effectively ended any lingering public interest in Irish affairs on the part of Toronto's Catholics.[23] The return of Roman Catholic Torontonians from the blood-soaked fields of France and Belgium in 1919, the dedication of plaques and memorials in churches to war's fallen heroes, and the outpouring of patriotism and religious confidence during the celebration of Archbishop Neil McNeil's episcopal Silver Jubilee in 1920 confirmed the pre-eminence of a Canadian identity among English-speaking Catholics in Toronto; if anything, the creation of the Irish Free State in 1922 merely removed one last distraction.[24]

Classical sociological definitions of acculturation and assimilation are not easily applied to the experience of Toronto's English-speaking Catholics after 1887. Of the seven classifications of assimilation advanced by Milton Gordon, the behaviour of Toronto's anglophone Catholics from 1887 to 1922 resembles some types of assimilation but defies any one particular categorization.[25] There are numerous indications that Toronto's English-speaking Catholics were integrating themselves into the city's English Canadian milieu: the rise of interfaith marriages; the more even distribution of Catholics in the socioeconomic structures of the city; increased political participation by Catholics; Catholic adoption of Canadian nation-building ideals and stronger imperial sentiment; and sustained fraternization among all denominations in non-sectarian clubs and events. Despite such strong levels of acculturation to the world around them, English-speaking Catholics still retained their distinctive creed, although they found ways to adapt and shape it according to their needs. Anglophone Catholic identity in Toronto was itself a product of the group's "double minority status" – as a linguistic minority in Canadian Catholicism and a religious minority within Canada as a whole.[26] In the thirty-five years following O'Brien's visit Toronto's English-speaking Catholics created for themselves a unique Canadian identity that borrowed from the national vision and nation-building agenda of Protestant Canada while preserving the Roman Catholic beliefs held in common with French Canadians. That the Catholic subculture[27] combined elements from both Canadian "majorities" without fully succumbing to either suggests that Carl Berger is correct when he writes: "There have been many varieties of Canadian nationalism, and, while all have been inspired by the same nation, the manner in which the character and interests of Canada have been interpreted vary enormously."[28]

Those readers familiar with historical developments in the Irish Catholic communities of the United States will identify many similarities in the English-speaking Catholic experience in Toronto. The embrace of American ideals and values by Boston's Irish community, as described by Paula Kane, has many parallels in Toronto in the same period.[29] Catholics in both Toronto and Boston experienced significant integration in terms of their flight to the suburbs, embrace of contemporary political ideologies, occupational upward mobility, and participation in the First World War. In Toronto, however, the persistence of a separatist subculture was not as evident as in Boston. Indeed, English-speaking Catholics continued to hold on dearly to their distinctive faith, but the lay community demonstrated syncretic tendencies in their worship and flexibility in their application of the moral canons. Similarly, bishops and clergy exhibited a pastoral flexibility that was sensitive to the realities of a small Catholic minority living the daily realities of Canada's largest non-Catholic city. Toronto had no equivalent of Boston's William O'Connell to advance Catholic "separatist tendencies"; Toronto's only comparable bishop, Denis O'Connor, was compelled to resign his see.

Another difference between the Canadian and American experiences was the absence in Toronto of an "anti-British" and "exile" mentality among its English-speaking Catholics. Kerby Miller's landmark study of the American Irish, *Emigrants and Exiles*, asserts that American Irish Catholics created a subculture that, through subsequent generations, was remarkably persistent in retaining an ethos of "exile" in a new world, of antagonism to bourgeois ideals, and of easily aroused hostility towards Britain, the oppressor of Ireland.[30] Such a model cannot be applied to the English-speaking Catholics of Toronto, most notably, to its overwhelming Irish majority. As this study will demonstrate, Canadian-born generations of Catholics, while retaining their creed, would acculturate willingly to English Canadian society. The predominance of pre-famine migration in the Canadian Irish experience, the differences in the migration and settlement experiences of the Irish generally in Ontario and the United States, differences in clerical leadership, or the aforementioned "double minority status" of English-speaking Catholics in Canada may account for the absence of an "exile" motif in Toronto.

Discovering how English-speaking Catholics created this unique identity is by no means simple. Until Brian Clarke's recent exploration of the Toronto Irish Catholic laity in the nineteenth century, most studies of Catholics in the city had been institutional and political in their orientation and limited in their ability to assess the social impact of Catholic accommodation in the city.[31] Views from the pulpit, initiatives from the parson's desk, and the careers of notable laypersons tell only half of the story. It is only when we enter the classroom of the separate school and peer into a child's textbook, or follow a family as they purchase a new home and seek better employment, or engage in the dance of Catholic ritual and congregate with the parish fraternal societies that we are able to gauge more accurately the process of Catholic social integration in Toronto. This multilevel examination of English-speaking Catholicism demands the rigour of the quantitative social historian and the sensitivity of the scholar attracted to more traditional source materials.

This book attempts to reach behind the "Belfast" motif and provide a needed social portrait of Catholic social and religious life, often missed in the examination of Catholic elites and institutions. While Clarke's scholarship has shed much light on lay Catholic initiatives in the nineteenth century, this book will bring the study of English-speaking Catholics into the twentieth century, offering a view of change within the Catholic community from the inside in.[32] Too often the growth and development of the Catholic community has been measured with reference to the social and political pressure applied upon it, directly or indirectly, by the host Protestant community.[33] So viewed, Catholic development becomes little more than knee-jerk reactions to groups in competition with Catholics: the Catholic story, and the internal forces at work, are forgotten or relegated to a secondary role. While Protestant-Catholic relations are a recurring subtheme in this study, more emphasis is placed on the Canadianizing impulses arising among those in the pulpit and the people in the pews than on the pressures allegedly exerted by the Protestant host community.

This book argues that the integration of English-speaking Catholics into the mainstream of Canadian life in Toronto occurred at many levels. In a sense this community study is really a composite of a number of stories demonstrating economic, occupational, and ideological integration. Throughout, the Catholic faith appears less and less a barrier to embracing Canadian citizenship than a vehicle for encouraging full Catholic participation in Canadian life. Curiously, the English-speaking Catholics of Toronto moved in the shadow of second-century Christian apologists who argued that Catholics, by their very faith, were loyal citizens of the Empire. In time, and sometimes to the chagrin of local church leaders, religious life responded to the ebb and flow of the Canadian society in which it found itself.

By the time we reach the Edwardian period the traditional scholar's image of Catholics as the underclass of the Belfast of North America has become fallacious. Catholics participated fully in the economic upswing of the late Victorian and Edwardian periods, and by their adaptability to industrial capitalism and their social mobility Catholics cultivated a sense of rootedness in Toronto. Furthermore, investigation of Catholic settlement patterns, movement into white-collar occupations, and the increased extent of Catholic property ownership demonstrates how far the city's English-speaking Catholics had shed their nineteenth-century heritage of poverty, limited skills, and the ghetto. Given these demographic and economic foundations, the liturgical, ideological, and communal changes in Catholic life can be contextualized appropriately.

After the death of Archbishop John Joseph Lynch in 1888 the majority of the bishops serving in Toronto departed from the policy of isolating Catholics from the non-Catholic world and encouraged their flock to build Canada side by side with Protestant Canadians but to retain their faith in the process. This change in attitude was complemented by the rise of a home-grown clergy and male and female religious communities. From 1887 to 1922 the dominance of Irish-born and Irish-educated priests and religious in the Archdiocese of Toronto was overturned by a new generation of Canadian-born and Canadian-educated men and women. This process was facilitated by Archbishop John Walsh's call for a priesthood "rooted" in the Canadian soil, and by the creation of St Augustine's Seminary, where English-speaking Catholic candidates for the priesthood could be educated in Toronto, independently of the Catholic Church in Quebec.

Similarly, the devotional life of the laity showed signs of change and adaptability to the North American environment. Localized devotions were adopted, and passive resistance was employed by both clergy and laity in order to retain local customs when some Church leaders attempted to bring the archdiocese into rigid conformity with canon law. This deviance from strict interpretations of Church law and pious practices was both an assertion of local custom and insurance that Catholics would not abandon the Church because of inflexible regulations on such common activities as mixed marriage. At the same time, however, Toronto's Catholics were confident that they could win a significant number of converts from Protestantism. Despite the many interfaith marriages in the city, Catholics were self-assured that their religiosity would prevail.

The fusion of Catholicism and a growing appreciation for Canada was also reflected in the curriculum and proliferation of Catholic separate schools. Catholic integration at its most basic level – the inculcation in Catholic youth of a love for "God and country" – became the benchmark in Toronto's separate schools, as did the efforts of teachers to prepare Catholic children for life in all areas of Canadian society. Similarly, the Catholic impulse to pursue higher education after 1910 exemplified the lofty aspirations of a new generation of English-speaking Catholic Canadians. It was hoped that the Catholic community might provide more doctors, nurses, teachers, engineers, and lawyers to the ranks of the Canadian professions and the halls of Canadian leadership.

New Catholic voluntary associations also attempted to foster Catholic spirituality while promoting pride in Canadian and imperial citizenship. In the 1890s the older Irish Catholic nationalist associations faded, for reasons of both Irish and Canadian making, and new North American organizations filled the gaps. In these religious, insurance, ritualistic, and ethnic societies the English-speaking Catholic laity cultivated their own sense of Canadian patriotism, a patriotism that did not work at cross purposes with their Catholicity. Within these associations Catholics of all economic and social backgrounds were able to forge a common identity based on loyalty to the Church and to Canada. Voluntary associations for men and women soon became crucibles of Canadian patriotism and Catholic confidence in their full and equal citizenship. By the 1920s the growing class orientation of some of these Catholic fraternal associations reflected the depth to which Catholics had blended into all levels of the local social structure. Catholic workers joined unions with non-Catholics and accrued insurance benefits there, while perhaps joining a devotional society for its spiritual and fraternal benefits. As such, Catholics became more notable as social chameleons who could wear the cap of Catholicism on Sundays but could also wear a different hat while socializing on other days of the week. This was a far cry from the more rigid lines of sectarian division that some historians claim was traceable through every walk of life in the city.[34]

Catholic weekly newspapers also reflected a waning of the green and a growing embrace of a Canadian Catholic identity. These Catholic papers, through distribution, circulation, and advertisements, served as a significant barometer of Catholic thought in Toronto. The Catholic press shed its Irish image after 1892, although reporting on events in the Old Country did not cease entirely. Even the periodic reports on Ireland lost their former emotional edge, and hard news from the Emerald Isle diminished in the face of rising Catholic interest in affairs of the British Empire, the state of the Catholic Church worldwide, and Canadian issues. The Catholic press began to formulate a vision of an autonomous Canada within the context of the British Empire, and implanted in its constituents a pride in Canada hitherto rarely acknowledged by English-speaking Catholics. Furthermore, the press's invocation to build and support Canada was accompanied by pleas for more Catholic participation in Canadian political life. By the 1920s the press had become a mouthpiece of Catholic Canadian identity and reflected the extent to which Toronto's English-speaking Catholics had adapted themselves to contemporary Canadian nationalist movements.

Toronto's English-speaking Catholics also came to an awareness of themselves by realizing how different they were from their co-religionists in Quebec and from those recently arrived from eastern and southern Europe. The problems surrounding the formation of "national" parishes in Toronto and the creation of the Catholic Church Extension Society to aid Catholic immigration revealed the double-edged sword of English-speaking Catholic home-mission policy: immigrants were to be Catholicized and Canadianized. The latter policy, of anglicization and acculturation to the values and traditions popular in English Canada, widened the existing gulf between anglophone and francophone Catholics. Anglo-Celtic Catholics came to understand that their vision of implanting the Catholic faith in Canada through the medium of the English language was completely at odds with the nationalism of French-Canadian Catholics. At the same time, the similarities between anglophone Protestant and Catholic missionary rhetoric and activity underscore how closely English-speaking Catholics had come to identify with Canadian institutions, Canadian law, Canadian opportunities, and the dream of an English-speaking nation where religious affiliation was not an inhibiting or divisive factor.

Much of this adaptation was put to the test when Canada went to war in 1914. The reactions of Catholic leaders, the press, women, and the young men who volunteered for service illustrate the extent to which English-speaking Catholics had come to recognize that their primary political loyalties were to Canada and the British Empire. The war gave them an opportunity to exhibit this loyalty and offered a unique opportunity for Catholic-Protestant co-operation in Toronto. Loud demonstrations of patriotism, shared responsibilities with non-Catholic Canadians, and the large numbers of Catholics who paid the supreme sacrifice all confirmed in the Catholic mind that English-speaking Catholics were indeed full and equal citizens of Canada.

The Catholic community we witness in May of 1922 was a far cry from those who had agonized over their attendance at O'Brien's rally thirty-five years before. Many of the Irish-born generation were dead and gone. Leadership and rank and file Catholics, both clerical and lay, were second-, third-, and even fourth-generation Canadians. They belonged to a group whose members could not immediately be assumed to live in Cabbagetown, wield a sledgehammer or haul water, refuse to toast the monarch, or be barely able to read or write. The English-speaking Catholics of 1922 had few of these among their ranks in Toronto. Rather than refer to their life in Toronto as toiling in the Belfast of North America, they would more likely have identified with the words of D.A. Carey when he proclaimed, "The time has gone past when a man's religion should determine his fitness or unfitness for any position be it high or low, we are all Canadians, and as Canadians, loving our country and honouring her laws, do we desire to be judged."[35] The degree to which English-speaking Catholics in Toronto implanted Canadian values, material culture, and political ideologies within their own Catholic ethos is a testament to the proposition that these English-speaking Catholics were forerunners of Canadian pluralism.

CHAPTER ONE

Life in the Queen's City

It is alleged that Armand de Charbonnel, the second Roman Catholic Bishop of Toronto, was so distressed by the situation in his new diocese in 1850 that he wrote to Rome praying for God's blessing in his work among these barbarians near Lake Ontario: "Venio de Toronto / Apud Lacum Ontario / In populo barbaro / Benedicamus Domino."[1] Charbonnel had reason to be concerned. His new flock were spread throughout the forests, farms, and towns from present-day Oshawa in the east to Georgian Bay in the north, west to Sandwich, and south to the Niagara frontier. The headquarters of his see was Toronto, a burgeoning colonial town that was slowly expanding its influence over much of central and western Upper Canada. The Catholics in the urban headquarters of his diocese were primarily Irish, many of whom had settled there between 1820 and 1845. They were joined after 1846 by a conspicuous minority of Irish who were refugees of the Great Famine.

Although they were a minority among even the Catholic Irish of Toronto, the famine migrants quickly became the most identifiable group of Catholics under Charbonnel's care. Ironically, despite their ragged and diseased appearance upon arrival in Toronto Bay, these Irish refugees had been among the more fortunate of the famine's victims, having sufficient capital to make the expensive trip to British North America, then to travel hundreds of miles by barge and sailing-craft into the interior of the colonies. Upon arrival these Irish were weakened from their harrowing trans-Atlantic journey, malnourished, vermin-infested, and susceptible to communicable disease. Such physical infirmities, in addition to the scarcity of cheap agricultural land, made it difficult for famine migrants to leave the port of Toronto quickly. An outbreak of typhus further delayed their settlement as they languished in sheds, dying by the dozens along Toronto's waterfront.[2] Even Charbonnel's predecessor, Bishop Michael Power, succumbed to the disease as he administered to the stricken.

Heartfelt feelings of charity towards these migrants among the local population, and reactions of horror at their struggle, turned to hostility as this needy Catholic community remained fixed in Toronto.[3] In time the appearance and plight of these faminites became a lens through which local Torontonians came to view most Catholics: poor, semi-literate, dirty, diseased, and criminal. In 1858, as it struggled to interpret the rise of international Catholicism and the power of French Canadian Catholic politicians, the *Globe* warned its readers that the Catholic problem was on their very doorstep in Toronto: "Irish beggars are to be met everywhere, and they are as ignorant and vicious as they are poor. They are lazy, improvident and unthankful; they fill our poor houses and our prisons, and are as brutish in their superstition as Hindus."[4] This image of the poverty-stricken Irish Catholic has weathered the test of time and has been adopted without question by many Canadian historians and journalists.[5] While one scholar has dismissed such stereotypes as racist, there remains a huge body of evidence attesting to the poverty of English-speaking Catholics in mid-nineteenth-century Toronto.[6]

However vivid and compelling these early images of Toronto's Catholics, they are not applicable to the development of English-speaking Catholics in the city by the 1890s. The real failing of many scholars and journalists has been to engage in a kind of historical projection: somehow the ghettos, poverty, and hardship of Charbonnel's day have been accepted as normative for generations of English-speaking Catholics in Toronto.[7] Peter Goheen has argued the relative poverty of Catholics when compared to other religious denominations in Toronto, but has cautioned that there was no substantial correlation between Catholicism and any particular economic class.[8] Unfortunately, Goheen did not pursue his socio-economic analysis of the city past 1900, but his caution suggests that, by the late nineteenth century, social change among Toronto's Catholics was well under way. Recent studies of the 1871 census should also warn us against stereotyping Irish Catholics as an ethclass[9] on the bottom rung of Ontario's social ladder. Furthermore, Brian Clarke has pointed out that Irish Catholic ghettos were probably less evident than previously assumed. In the 1860s one would have been hard pressed to find a neighbourhood dominated by Irish Catholics, although there were significant concentrations in St David's and St Lawrence wards.[10] Such assertions challenge the long-standing "stories" and some scholarly accounts of Irish Catholic life and work. They also raise questions about how such stereotypes were able to persist well into the twentieth century, burdening subsequent generations of "dogan" Catholics in Edwardian Toronto with resisting the clichés of their ghettoization and penury.[11]

All the evidence argues that, between 1887 and 1922, English-speaking Catholics in Toronto adopted three behaviours that defy traditional stereotypes. First, they did not physically separate themselves from the rest of the community by means of ghettos, ethnic enclaves, or even distinctive streets. Despite the legend of "Cabbagetown" – which in reality was primarily English and Protestant[12] – there was no Toronto equivalent of the Irish wards so characteristic of Boston, New York, or Chicago. In the late Victorian period Toronto's English-speaking Catholics began to migrate from their traditional inner-city parishes[13] to the suburbs, forming new parish communities, while rarely exhibiting a tendency to establish a distinct Catholic neighbourhood.

Secondly, in the same period there was no correlation whatsoever between English-speaking Catholics and class. Catholics of Anglo-Celtic Catholic origin integrated themselves into all of the city's occupational classifications. In the Edwardian era the number of English-speaking Catholic unskilled workers declined sharply, while Catholic men and women made substantial gains in the clerical, supervisory, and skilled sectors of Toronto's labour market. Thirdly, as English-speaking Catholics ventured into a stunning variety of jobs and took up residence in nearly every neighbourhood of Toronto, many laypersons demonstrated a greater sense of rootedness in the city and displayed more openly the evidence of their newly acquired wealth. Between 1890 and 1910 many Catholics had sufficient economic means to share in the city's housing boom.[14] In some parishes the percentage of English-speaking Catholic home-owners greatly exceeded the general trend of home-ownership for the entire city. Record numbers of Catholics bought their own homes and, in the process, confirmed their rising occupational and economic status, as well as their belief that so-called Orange Toronto was their city too. Much of this social mobility was encouraged by the clergy and the Catholic press, who saw education and civic involvement as keys to Catholic success and full citizenship.

This study is a description of how English-speaking Catholics in Toronto actively integrated themselves into the social structures around them. The assimilation of Catholics into local social and economic life not only reflected an enhanced sense of Catholic rootedness in Toronto; it facilitated stronger English-speaking Catholic identification with Canada, its institutions, its opportunities, and its promise. This growing awareness of a Canadian identity was complemented by the demise of Irish nationalism in Toronto and by the economic boom in which Catholics of Celtic descent shared. By 1922, although there were still Catholic poor in Toronto, the city's English-speaking Catholics, buoyed by their own success and displaced from unskilled jobs by European immigrants, no longer occupied the lowest rungs of the social ladder.

Until very recently Catholics have not made up a significant proportion of Toronto's population. Prior to the Irish famine of the late 1840s, Catholics comprised less than 17 per cent of Toronto's people. The numbers of famine migrants between 1846 and 1848 boosted this proportion temporarily to about 25 per cent. It should be remembered, however, that many of these migrants were transient, leaving Toronto for rural areas or other towns in western Upper Canada, or securing passage to the United States. Of the 38,000 Irish immigrants who arrived in Toronto during "Black '47," only about 2,000 settled in the town permanently.[15] With a dramatic drop in Irish migration after the famine, and high levels of population mobility generally, the proportion of Catholics in Toronto's population dropped significantly. By the time of Confederation, Catholics counted for only about 20 per cent of Toronto's population, and by 1891, the first recorded census for the present study, Catholics made up little more than 15 per cent of the local population. This proportional decline is stunning given the fact that in real numbers, in the fifty years between 1841 and 1891, the total number of Catholics had actually increased nearly tenfold, from 2,401 to 21,830.[16] Despite an increase in live births, rural depopulation, and increased migration from continental Europe and the United States, Catholics did not keep pace with the rapidly increasing numbers of Toronto's citizens.[17]

The years between 1891 and 1921 were marked by this same paradox: the total numbers of Catholic Torontonians increased while the proportion of Catholics in the general population decreased. In real terms, from 1891 to 1921 the Catholic population tripled from 21,830 to 64,773, although its percentage of the city population dropped marginally from 15 per cent to 12.4 per cent (see Table 1.1).[18] Despite the meagre proportional increase, Catholics were the fastest-growing single denomination in the city in terms of actual numbers, increasing by 11.3 per cent between 1914 and 1918 alone.[19] Quite simply, Catholics in Toronto were a relatively small group whose cohesion was perhaps affected by the increased numbers of non-anglophone Catholics entering the city after 1900, and the city-wide diffusion of the Anglo-Celtic core group.

Table 1.1
Catholic Population of Toronto and Suburbs, 1891–1921

Year	Total pop.	Catholics	%	Irish birth	% of total pop.
1891	144,023	21,830	15.2	13,252	9.2
1901	208,040	28,994	13.9	–	–
1911	327,753	43,080	13.2	14,740	4.5
1921	521,893	64,773	12.4	97,361	18.7

Source: Census of Canada, 1891, vol. 1, Table 4, 282–3, and Table 3, 174–5; Census of Canada, 1901, vol. 1, Table 14, 554–5; Census of Canada, 1911, vol. 2, Table 2, 80–1, and vol. 1, Table 4, 402–4; Census of Canada, 1921, vol. 1, Table 28, 542–3, and Table 39, 756–7. The figures for 1911 include Toronto North, South, East, West, and Centre. The 1921 figures include all persons living within the city limits. The "Irish birth" figure for 1921 is actually a figure representing those who claimed Irish "origin."

Throughout much of its history the Catholic community was dominated numerically and administratively by the Irish-born and their descendants. In 1891 perhaps as many 90 per cent of the community could trace their Irish origins through a parent or grandparent, while a declining number could do so by merit of their own Irish birth. The Irish-born segment of the Catholic population was in continual decline as the Victorian era gave way to the Edwardian. By 1911 only 5 per cent of Toronto's population could claim Ireland as a place of birth. This figure may also be misleading in terms of describing the indigenous nature of the Catholic population by the time of the Great War. Contrary to popular belief, to be Irish in Toronto in the nineteenth and early twentieth centuries did not necessarily mean one was Catholic. When ethnic origin or birth was included on the census, the total number of people claiming Irish birth often exceeded (sometimes doubled) the number of declared Catholics in the city. This confirms the contentions of contemporary scholars that, for Ontario, Irish Protestant migrants outnumbered Irish Catholics by a margin of nearly two to one.[20]

Clearly, by the turn of this century most Catholics in Toronto were Canadian-born but of Irish ancestry. Most were the descendants of famine and pre-famine Irish who had migrated to Toronto in hopes of participating in the city's growing employment opportunities in factories and service industries. The English-speaking population of Catholics was rounded out by small numbers of Scottish Highlanders, English, converts from Protestantism, and some Catholics of northern European descent who, in this urban environment and in a sea of Irish Catholics, had thoroughly assimilated into the anglophone milieu. Foreign immigration, especially from Ireland, had little impact on the numbers of foreign-born English-speaking Catholics in Toronto after 1880. There was a small influx of young Catholics from Scotland and England, but these other British groups were a significant minority who blended in with the largely Canadian-born Catholic population by the eve of the First World War.[21] Collectively the Canadian-born majority, with a strong Irish component and small British, American, and German constituencies, constituted the English-speaking Catholic population of the city in the early twentieth century. Their dominance in numbers in the local Church was impressive, close to 90 per cent of Catholics in 1901, but was steadily eroding in the face of pre- and post-war arrivals of Catholics from Quebec and continental Europe. By 1921 English-speaking Catholics probably made up about 80 per cent of the local Catholic population.[22]

Small in number when compared to Toronto as whole but significant in their influence in the local Church by the Edwardian period, English-speaking Catholics could not be defined by any particular neighbourhood. Unlike their co-religionists in major American and British cities, Toronto's English-speaking Catholics had no North End, South Side, or Falls Road to call their own. In the mid-nineteenth century the majority of Toronto's Catholics had been living in five inner-city parishes south of Bloor Street and between Dovercourt Avenue in the west and the Don River in the east.[23] The combination of employment opportunities, new housing facilities, a yearning for better living conditions, and the arrival of increasing numbers of European immigrants in the inner city prompted many English-speaking Catholics to seek new homes in the suburbs of Toronto. By the end of the Great War, Catholics had built parishes in every area of the city, to such an extent that suburban Catholics constituted an influential and financially secure majority within the local Church.

Those neighbourhoods traditionally identified as Irish Catholic enclaves certainly bore no relationship to a "Corktown" or "Slabtown" between 1887 and 1922. Careful scrutiny of city directories and assessment rolls reveals that there were no significant English-speaking Catholic enclaves in the period. Cabbagetown, the alleged home of the Irish,[24] was more a ghetto for working-class Irish and English Protestants than for Catholics. Catholics had established a little "Corktown," south of Queen Street and east of Sherbourne to the Don, in the early nineteenth century, but their influence in the neighbourhood dwindled within a generation of the Irish famine. By 1891 only 3,992 (22.8 per cent) of 17,535 inhabitants of the area were Roman Catholic, and a small number of these were French Canadian.[25]

By 1890 Catholics were so broadly distributed in the city that one historical geographer could only locate two significant clusters: along the central and eastern waterfront and in the western portion of the city around the Toronto Junction.[26] Closer scrutiny of municipal records reveals that the Catholic population of 21,830 was spread fairly evenly throughout the city's ten wards, with the highest proportional representation in St Andrew's and St George's wards south of Queen Street.[27]

This Catholic diffusion throughout Toronto continued into the early decades of the twentieth century. The rapid industrialization of the city created a veritable Catholic diaspora to areas of employment and industrial development. Although one scholar has noted that, in 1899, there were three nodes of Catholic settlement – the streets west of the mouth of the Don River, the area surrounding the confluence of Bathurst and King Streets, and the Junction in West Toronto[28] – these areas contained only four of the city's twelve Catholic parishes. Assessment and parish records indicate that Catholics were far more widespread, as parish communities sprouted up and flourished in the eastern, western, and northern extremities of the city. In a city on the move, growing and reaching its entrepreneurial tentacles over a wide hinterland, people, including Catholics, were highly transient, and physical segregation between religious groups was negligible.[29]

The dispersal of Catholics throughout the city was seen most vividly in the growth of Catholic parishes after 1887. For Toronto's Catholics, like their co-religionists elsewhere, the parish was the primary focus of cultural, recreational, spiritual, organizational, and social life.[30] Between 1887 and the 1920s parish growth was a barometer of Catholic expansion, population growth, and the acknowledgment of cultural diversity arising from the arrival of non-English speaking Catholics from Europe and Quebec. Church buildings were constructed in response to the need to service a large Catholic population living some distance from an older parish; once erected, they became magnets for new Catholic settlers. The construction of a parish church in the suburbs offered Catholics the assurance of sacraments and pastoral care as they ventured out to the frontiers of the city in search of new jobs, or a home within commuting distance of their place of work yet nestled well away from the hubbub of the downtown core.

The dramatic expansion and growth of Catholic settlement at the turn of the century would be most evident to the traveller who ventured on foot from the eastern extremity of Toronto to the western wards. With a sturdy pair of legs and a strong heart, the traveller's promenade through the streets of the suburbs and inner city would expose him or her to the variety of houses and neighbourhoods in this Edwardian city. Catholic churches would be spotted in new neighbourhoods being carved out of farmers' fields, pastures, and woods; the spires would be noted among the soot-encrusted and dilapidated housing of the Don Flats and in the tenements of "the Ward"; and distinctive Italian and Gothic sacred structures would peer through the thickets of trees near the Rosedale ravines or by Clover Hill.

Beginning in the extreme eastern portion of Toronto, between Scarborough Township and the Don River, a traveller would note that, in 1900, English-speaking Catholics were served by two very small parishes, both lying along the Queen Street–Kingston Road axis that pierced through the heart of what had been forest and farmland. St Joseph's, Leslieville, founded in 1878, and St John's, in the Beaches district, established in 1895, were the foci of Catholic life in the area. In the late Victorian period St Joseph's parish served 220 families, who were employed in the brickyards, commercial outlets, and market gardens in the area around Broadview and Queen Streets. Crisscrossed by dirt roads that turned to mud in inclement weather, and dotted by farms, pasture land, and summer cottages, the portions of the city incorporated by St Joseph's and St John's parishes were undoubtedly part of Toronto's settlement frontier in addition to being the future home of numerous Catholic migrants from inner-city Toronto and other parts of Ontario.[31] In the 1890s the introduction of the street railway to the area facilitated new settlement and gave men and women who worked in the downtown core an opportunity to reside in less congested and well-connected suburban areas.[32] Thousands of new Catholic settlers would prompt the creation of four additional parishes in the area by 1920 (see Table 1.2).

As the traveller crossed the Queen Street bridge over the soupy Don River, he would enter the bustling and sometimes filthy inner city of turn-of-the-century Toronto. English-speaking Catholics who lived on the west bank of the Don were served by the city's oldest Catholic parish, St Paul's, founded in 1822. Rebuilt by 1889 in a Romanesque style reminiscent of its namesake outside the walls of Rome, St Paul's included the downtown area bounded on the north and south by Carlton Street and Lake Ontario and on the east and west by the Don and Sherbourne Street.[33] Given its extensive boundaries, St Paul's was one of the largest parishes in the city, serving nearly four thousand parishioners by 1905.[34] Contrary to the images of an Irish Catholic Cabbagetown ghetto, Catholics distributed themselves throughout the expanse of St Paul's parish, with occa-

Table 1.2
Catholic Population by Parish, 1887–1922

Parish	Date	1887	1895	1905	1914	1918	1922
St Paul's	1822	4000	–	3926	2870	2700	2800
St Michael's Cathedral	1848	4100	–	3654	2000	1000	2400
St Mary's	1852	6000	6000	4500	–	2400	2100
St Basil's	1856	2000	–	1780	1840	1850	–
St Patrick's	1861	2200	2600	3023	–	1400	1100
St Helen's	1875	900	–	1673	2760	2750	3874
St Joseph's	1878	800	1000	1386	1650	1912	1920
Lourdes	1886	–	–	757	1724	–	2100
Holy Rosary	1892	–	–	400	400	500	–
St Cecilia's	1895	–	–	830	1500	2410	3150
St John's	1895	–	–	245	–	600	700
St Peter's	1896	–	1950	695	2000	–	–
Holy Family	1902	–	–	685	1275	1690	2256
St Francis's	1903	–	–	1826	2380	2672	2600
St Monica's	1909	–	–	–	240	460	600
St Anthony's	1909	–	–	–	2275	2030	2434
St Ann's	1909	–	–	–	1400	–	–
St Clare's	1913	–	–	–	–	1200	1800
Holy Name	1914	–	–	–	512	1513	–
St Vincent's	1914	–	–	–	1182	1513	1788
St Brigid's	1920	–	–	–	–	–	1300
Corpus Christi	1920	–	–	–	–	–	1430

Source: ARCAT, J.J. Lynch Papers, AG 09.30, Churches; Parish Spiritual and Financial Statistics, 1887–1922; Holograph Collection, 29.93. GABF, O'Connor Papers, box 1, file 3, Draft of Quinquennial Report to Rome, Dec. 1905.

sional concentrations along Queen, Sackville, Power, and Front Streets. Power Street, for example, where both the church building and the House of Providence were located, was one of the most concentrated settlements, with just under half its residents Catholic.[35]

This very short side-street, however, was an exception rather than the rule for Catholic settlement in the parish. On the whole, Catholics lived side by side with Protestants of all denominations and income levels, from the rich brick houses of River Street to the decrepit, rough-cast and frame shacks at the mouth of the Don.

The traveller turning north off Queen Street on to Sherbourne would find the clustered housing, shops, and businesses giving way to tree-lined streets and larger residences. Here, north of St Paul's, the more affluent residents of St David's ward were served by the archbishop's parish of residence, Our Lady of Lourdes. Founded in 1886 to commemorate the Silver Jubilee of archbishop Lynch's elevation to the episcopacy, Lourdes served the smaller Catholic population living between Carlton Street on the south, Park Road on the north, the Don Valley on the east, and Church Street on the west. Modelled elegantly on the domed church of Santa Maria del Populo in Rome, the parish church was the principal place of worship for the most powerful and influential Catholics in the city.[36] Judging from assessment data spanning thirty years, Catholics were well interspersed with non-Catholics in the area and inclined to no significant clustering, either by entire street or single city block.[37]

Much the same could be said of the composition of Lourdes' equally affluent neighbour, St Basil's parish, just a short walk to the west, near where Wellesley Street was lost in the arboretum of Queen's Park. Founded by the Congregation of St Basil in 1856, this parish served St Michael's College, Rosedale, Yorkville, and the lightly settled section of the city north of present-day Dupont Street to Eglinton Avenue. St Basil's drew a great many wealthy and influential Catholics from all areas of the city. It became notable for spectacular musical liturgies, fiery parish missions, and fashionable weddings.[38] St Basil's constituted part of the intermediary zone between the inner-city parishes and suburban areas. As such it attracted Catholics from within and outside the city, both those who wished to build homes in the forested northern frontier of Toronto and those who aimed to settle among the wealthy scions of Jarvis Street or those nestled along the sides of the Rosedale ravine. In 1892, when the Basilians founded Holy Rosary parish at Deer Park, now the area of Bathurst Street and St Clair Avenue, St Basil's parish jurisdiction in the north of the city was greatly diminished.

From St Basil's, a sharp turn south along University Avenue would bring our ambler to the centre of the city. Here Catholics were served by St Michael's, the fashionable Cathedral parish, and by St Patrick's Church, perhaps the poorest parish in the city. As the foci of worship for the working classes of central and southern Toronto, St Patrick's and St Michael's each contained slightly smaller numbers of parishioners than St Paul's. St Patrick's was situated near "the Ward," a shabby neighbourhood of tenements and manufacturers that became a haven for European migrants early in the century. The Ward would become an urban polyglot, including Catholics from a variety of ethnic backgrounds who would soon form their own "national" parishes in the area. Recently arrived German Catholics and English-speaking Catholics would share the facilities of St Patrick's throughout the early twentieth century. The parish also retained the working-class constituency of its neighbourhood. Unlike St Patrick's, however, the Cathedral, by merit of its central location and its prestige as the episcopal seat in Toronto, attracted a great variety of Catholics, from wealthy elites to blue-collar believers, many of whom travelled regularly to the Cathedral from outside the parish boundaries.[39] Situated in an area of high commercial, retail, and manufacturing activity, the Cathedral had a large constituency of its own, although little potential for residential expansion from within its boundaries.

As he turned to the west along Dundas Street, the walk would take our traveller into the neighbourhoods served by several burgeoning Catholic parishes, the oldest and largest of which was St Mary's, founded in 1852. From its imposing Gothic presence at the corner of Adelaide and Bathurst Streets, St Mary's parish served the large Catholic population in the western portion of St Andrew's and St George's wards, from St Patrick (later Dundas) Street to the lake on the north and south, and from Peter Street and Spadina Avenue to Dovercourt Avenue, east to west. In 1887 it consisted of nearly 5,500 Catholics, including those from St Peter's parish at Bloor and Markham Streets, which separated from its mother parish in 1896. Potential for growth was so good that, in 1903, St Francis of Assisi parish was created in the north-central portion of old St Mary's, an area that had been transformed from forest and pasture into a residential suburb. The existence of these three parishes in the western portion of the city demonstrates the extent to which English-speaking Catholics had migrated and settled over a large chunk of territory, from St Clair Avenue down to Lake Ontario. Furthermore, the fact that Catholic settlement in the district was diluted further by the arrival of large numbers of Jews and Eastern European Catholics confirms that Irish Catholic neighborhoods such as Claretown had passed into history.[40]

If our traveller had any breath left, and his legs were not too swollen, a walk along Dundas Street beyond St Mary's parish would reveal the extent of Catholic expansion by 1900. Catholics in the extreme west of Toronto worshipped at either St Helen's Church

(1875), at the corner of Lansdowne and Dundas, or at St Cecilia's (1895), at Toronto Junction. Collectively both parishes served the area east to west between Dovercourt Avenue and Mimico, and south to north from the village of Parkdale to the city limits. In 1890 St Helen's contained 316 households and was considered to be in one of the least desirable areas of the city in terms of homes, industry, and public transportation. This soon changed. Prospective employment in the railway yards, factories, foundries, and such food-processing plants as Neilson's Chocolate, and the construction of numerous inexpensive single-family dwellings, attracted those looking for work, investment opportunity, or a home to own.[41] English-speaking Catholics, imbued with the work ethic and lured by economic opportunity, migrated by the hundreds to the western suburbs. By 1920 St Helen's and its sister parish, St Cecilia's, became the largest and most prosperous of Toronto's parishes, with nearly seven thousand souls between them.[42]

Despite this dramatic increase of Catholic settlement in the Junction and environs, assessment rolls and city directories indicate no significant Catholic concentrations of settlement between the 1890s and the 1920s. As with St Paul's, however, one can discern occasional tiny Catholic clusters on streets near the parish church, forming perhaps the closest thing to an urban village.[43] In St Helen's parish, St Claren's Avenue and Margueretta Street, both residential thoroughfares, were heavily populated by Catholics over this thirty-year period. On St Claren's, for instance, some city blocks contained a Catholic majority, many of whom owned their homes and remained rooted for several decades.[44] Yet these clusters do not approximate the ghettos examined in studies of North American Little Italies[45] or the self-contained Corktowns to which some historians repeatedly refer. These were residential streets of single-family dwellings, lacking a commercial or service zone to make them closed communities. Shopping and services had to be sought from Catholic and non-Catholic businesses on neighbouring arteries such as College, Dundas, or Bloor Streets. In addition, Protestants were well interspersed on St Claren's and Margueretta, to the extent that no city blocks were the exclusive domain of Catholic residents. Our traveller, perhaps disappointed, would not be able to distinguish a Catholic home from a non-Catholic one or a Catholic street from a non-Catholic one.

At the turn of the century these dozen or so city parishes provided the focus of English-speaking Catholic life and offered the principal bases from which new parishes would be created as the Catholic population expanded and relocated between 1900 and 1920. Most significantly, however, the scattering and the size of the older parishes indicate that in the 1890s, and more so in the decades that followed, Catholics branched out from their original homes and rooming-houses in the downtown core. Moreover, even in the largest parishes, St Mary's and St Paul's, Protestants and Catholics were generally well integrated, thus preventing the formation of ghettos.

The rapid expansion of the city between 1900 and the 1920s confirms this pattern. Catholics were very much part of the general movement of Torontonians to the western, eastern, and northern frontiers of the city and the recently annexed portions of York County.[46] The suburbs provided Catholics with a chance to build and own a house in the "open air and sunshine" unavailable in the inner-city parishes, which had recently been congested by the arrival of Eastern and Southern European Catholic immigrants.[47] Expansion necessitated new parishes: in the east St Ann (1909), Holy Name (1914), St Brigid (1920), and Corpus Christi (1920); in the north St Monica (1909), St Anthony (1909), and St Clare (1913); and in the west St Francis (1903), Holy Family (1902), St Vincent de Paul (1914), and St Joan of Arc (1919). The construction of the Prince Edward Viaduct over the Don at the end of the Great War and the extension of city transportation routes to the suburbs facilitated Catholic movement to these areas. Moreover, by 1922 the new parishes accounted for 46 per cent of the city's English-speaking Catholic population, which indicates how dramatically English-speaking Catholic settlement had shifted away from the inner city.[48]

Holy Name parish, established in 1914 at the corner of Danforth and Carlaw avenues, provides a good case study of many of the difficulties faced by Catholics during the great rush to the suburbs. Many of the founders of the parish came from inner-city parishes and brought their Catholic customs, loyalties, and ties of kinship with them. As hundreds of Catholics moved into the vicinity of the parish, north of Bain Avenue and between Broadview Avenue in the west and Greenwood Avenue in the east, some migrants attempted to cluster settlement on the streets closest to the church site.[49] This proved to be troublesome for the earliest settlers when the original site of the church on Fulton Avenue was sold in 1914 and a new site was purchased at Danforth and Carlaw, several blocks to the south. A delegation representing some angry parishioners complained to Archbishop Neil McNeil about the change, claiming that they had purchased their properties because of their convenience and proximity to the prospective parish church building.[50] The change in venue ensured a more thinly spread Catholic population at Holy Name, and despite the intent of some of the earliest residents, no Catholic clustering would occur in the parish.[51] In fact, when the farmlands north of the city limits in what is now East York became available, Catholics in the parish were further dispersed. In addition to complaints about the diffusion of Catholics in the area, some parishioners lamented that a cohesive parish family at Holy Name was further hampered by the fact that parishioners traced their origins to so many different parishes, which ultimately tended to divide rather than unite them in their new setting.[52]

The spread of Catholics to the suburbs also meant significant de-population of the inner-city parishes. In the process of this out-migration, English-speaking Catholics were displaced south of Queen Street by hundreds of European Catholics and French Canadians who came to work in local factories. In 1890, 96.5 per cent (908) of the Catholic household heads living within the boundaries of St Paul's parish were English-speaking. The rest were French Canadian or Eastern and Southern European in origin. By 1920 English-speaking Catholic household heads had declined to 733, or only 82 per cent of Catholics in the area, as French Canadians and European Catholics increased their presence in the area exponentially.[53] Many French-speaking Catholics settled below Queen Street in order to be within walking distance of the cigar factories and the Gendron Manufacturing Company, their two principal employers.

The decline of English-speaking Catholics in St Mary's parish was more dramatic. In 1890 St Mary's contained 1,054 English-speaking Catholic household heads, or roughly 97 per cent of the assessed Catholic households within the parish. By 1920 only 64 per cent of Catholics in the parish had Anglo-Celtic surnames. The combination of heavy Italian and Polish immigration to Wards 4 and 5, English-speaking Catholic out-migration, and the erection of St Francis of Assisi and St Peter's parishes in St Mary's northern territory was primarily responsible for this decline.[54] Curiously, some of the young English-speaking Catholic families and couples who remained in both St Mary's and St Paul's from 1910 to 1920 were recent immigrants from England and Scotland, some of them of Irish descent.[55] It appears that second-, third-, and fourth-generation English-speaking Catholic out-migrants from inner-city parishes were being replaced, in part, by new Anglo-Celtic Canadians who themselves contributed to the growing immigrant flavour of Toronto's oldest parish communities.

It is difficult to accept the imposition of a "ghetto" life on Toronto's English-speaking Catholics in the early twentieth century. Extreme caution should be roused by the view of one historian who, in 1985, wrote that Irish Catholics were an alien population whose social mobility was slow and who remained in ghettos for decades. He added, "it took generations for any sizeable middle class to form, and when it did, it operated within the confines of a specific Irish society."[56] Our walking tour through the streets and parishes of Toronto and through the pages of the city's assessment rolls confirms the dispersion of English-speaking Catholics throughout the Queen's City. Patterns of clustering – if indeed they existed even in the mid-nineteenth century – were not a factor in Catholic living by the early twentieth century. Tiny clusters of Catholics along streets close to churches were evident in some areas, and probably for very practical reasons: proximity to place of Sunday worship, closeness to the separate school, and nearness to Catholic friends. On the whole Catholics were well distributed both within the parish boundaries and throughout parishes that cut across every socio-economic zone in the city. They lived among non-Catholics, seeming to prefer neighbourhoods of similar class to ones of similar religion. In some instances, as was the case at the affluent Our Lady of Lourdes and the blue-collar St Paul's, entire parishes took on the appearance of class enclaves rather than ethno-religious ghettos. The physical integration of Toronto's English-speaking Catholics was a fact of life by 1922.

English-speaking Catholic dispersion throughout Toronto was accompanied by a second important development: the increased integration of Catholics into the occupational structure of the city. Between 1887 and 1922 significant numbers of English-speaking Catholics found themselves in occupations and vocations that demanded more skill, expertise, and education, and yielded a better pay-cheque. This observation seems startling considering some of the well-worn interpretations of Catholic life in the city. It has become almost a cliché to talk about the poverty, landlessness, and illiteracy of Irish Catholics in nineteenth-century Toronto, a growing industrial centre whose factories were sustained by the sweat and brawn of semi- and unskilled Irish-Catholic labourers.[57] Study upon study has carped on the existence of an urban Irish Catholic ethclass that dominated the lowest-skilled and lowest-paying jobs in Ontario's labour market. Somehow Irish Catholicism and poverty walked arm in arm; as one historian has observed, "Being Irish and Catholic increased the probability of one's being poor, but it is less clear that it was *per se* a cause of poverty."[58]

This image of the Irish Catholic navvy may be substantiated by Father Jean Jamot's two censuses of Toronto's Catholics in the early and late 1860s. Jamot discovered that just under half of the Catholic males of the city were unskilled labourers, while a little over 70 per cent were blue-collar workers.[59] Only in St Lawrence ward was the percentage of Catholics in the unskilled sector lower than 30 per cent, whereas all other wards had rates in excess of 40 per cent. More recent studies of St David's ward for 1861 have estimated the proportion of unskilled workers among Catholics at a whopping 65 per cent, well in excess of the levels indicated by Jamot's census.[60] Although Father Jamot's records took no account of specific unskilled tasks or the seasonality of labour, the image of the Irish Catholic male as labourer in mid-nineteenth-century Toronto appears grounded in the contemporary sources.

When referring to English-speaking Catholics by the late Victorian period, however, we should avoid the temptation to perpetuate this image of "Paddy," and even "Sandy," as hewers of rock, loaders of freight, and washers of floors. Judging from recent analysis of the census of 1871 by A. Gordon Darroch and Michael Ornstein, there appears to be no correlation between ethnicity and occupational status in late nineteenth-century Canada. They found no grounds for a "vertical mosaic" wherein "knowledge of an individual's ethnicity effectively predicts individual occupational status."[61] Even Peter Goheen, reporting on Toronto in 1899, could find no substantial correlation between class and Catholicism in the city.[62] It appears that, contrary to the worn stereotypes, English-speaking Catholics in mid- to late-nineteenth-century Toronto had overcome the hurdles of the migrating generations and were now experiencing greater choice in the labour market and greater occupational diversity.

It is clear that, by the late nineteenth century, the enthusiasm for and advocacy of such diversification and upward mobility were emanating from church leaders and Catholic journalists. In a more practical sense, the Catholic response to this encouragement was facilitated by better educational institutions within the Catholic community and greater employment opportunities in the boom economy of the Laurier-Borden period. In 1900 Patrick F. Cronin, editor of the *Catholic Register*, called upon Catholics to abandon the remnants of a lackadaisical character and to pursue hard work, learning, and occupational mobility as keys to successful Canadian citizenship:

Our present employment should always be looked upon as a stepping stone to something higher, and the only way in which that can be done is to throw ourselves energetically and enthusiastically, so that our supervisors may readily see that we are capable of something better ... Canadian air seems to have changed the buoyant care-for-nothing air of the Irishman ... Education has developed traits in the Irish-Canadian character that are unknown in the Old Land. The more self reliance, the more determination, the more push we can stir up among our people, the more progress will our race make in this new land ... what we want is the education of bashfulness, of timidity out of our nature. [63]

Such pleas continued through the subsequent decade and beyond, encouraging thrift, temperance, and home-ownership for a better life. The *Register* even suggested that the spread of Catholic "moderation and helpfulness" had permeated "all grades of society," soothing relations between capital and labour and creating an air of religious toleration.[64]

Even more vehement in their advocacy of Catholic advancement were Archbishop Neil McNeil (1912–34) and the *Catholic Register*'s labour columnist Henry Somerville (1915–18). A blacksmith by trade, McNeil was a strong advocate of trade unionism, workmen's compensation, education for advancement, and the rights of the Catholic worker. Early in his episcopate he advocated co-operation between the classes as a means to end social unrest and to bridge economic disparities. To any businessman who might ask what he must do to be saved, MacNeil said he would answer: "Pay your men current wages, give your men an equitable share in your profits, and give them also the care and fellowship you owe them as fellow-men and Christians."[65] Somerville, recruited by McNeil from the Catholic Social Guild in England, recognized the correlation between better education and better jobs. Somerville advised Catholic leaders that "in English-speaking Canada to-day our chief lack is not opportunities for higher education, but ... lack of desire ... lack of appreciation of its value and power."[66] The promotion of upward mobility by Catholic leaders was complemented by educational reform in Toronto's separate schools, more varied programs for young women at St Joseph's Academy and Loretto College, and improvement in the liberal arts program offered at St Michael's College.[67]

Encouragement by Catholic leaders, educational reform, and favourable economic conditions locally engendered significant results. A glimpse of the occupations of household heads in five sample parishes – St Paul's, St Mary's, St Helen's, Our Lady of Lourdes, and Holy Name – between 1890 and 1920 reveal startling changes in the occupational alignment of Catholics in the city.[68] Over this thirty-year period Catholics made significant inroads into clerical and supervisory jobs while leaving the unskilled occupations in droves. Although there was a marginal increase in Catholic professionals, the number of lawyers, doctors, architects, and dentists remained short of 4 per cent of Catholic household heads by 1920. Catholics were well represented in all other occupational classifications, remaining surprisingly stable in skilled jobs – fluctuating between 11 and 13 per cent – despite the high levels of general underemployment in several skilled trades over the period.[69]

The most significant decrease for Catholics was in their stereotypical classification: unskilled labour. In 1860, 45 per cent of Catholic
household heads were classified as unskilled, but by 1890 this total
had dropped significantly to 33.5 per cent. In 1920 22.6 per cent, or
slightly more than one in every five of Catholic household heads,
was classified as unskilled. As remarkable was the evaporation of
Catholics designated by the ill-defined term "labourer." In the early
1860s Catholics classified as "labourers" represented about three-
quarters of all unskilled Catholic workers. By 1890 only about 20
per cent of all Catholic household heads were so assessed, and by
1920 this figure was halved to a mere 10 per cent. Instead, the majority of unskilled English-speaking Catholics came to be employed in
such service occupations as teamster, carter, driver, porter, baggageman, and railroader.[70]

As fewer English-speaking Catholics could be counted in the ranks
of Toronto's unskilled workers, the number of Catholic men in clerical and supervisory jobs increased substantially. In 1860 less than
3 per cent of Catholic household heads found work as clerks, sales-
persons, foremen, bookkeepers, police officers, and travellers. Thirty
years later the assessment rolls reveal that 8 per cent of Catholics
were engaged in clerical and supervisory roles. By 1920 over 16 per
cent were so employed. This rapid growth in the clerical sector attests
to the occupational diversification of Catholics over the later thirty-
year period and demonstrates the better level of education reached
by Catholics in order to fill jobs requiring a high degree of literacy,
such as accounting or secretarial work (see Table 1.3).

The general trend of Catholic mobility and diversity in Toronto did
not materialize the same way in each parish. Catholics seem to have
blended in with the character of class stratification established in each
of the city's distinctive neighbourhoods. Among Catholics living in
industrialized areas of the city we are apt to discover a preponderance of "blue-collar" workers. In the suburbs, the trend was to
"white-collar" labour or the professions. Thus, English-speaking
Catholics appear to have adapted to the occupational behaviour of
their Protestant neighbours throughout the city. In two larger inner-
city parishes such as St Paul's and St Mary's, for instance, there was
little significant change in occupational distributions except for a
small decline in the unskilled sector and marginal increases in the
clerical. Both parishes, however, served the industrial core of the city
along the lakeshore, Front, King, and Queen streets, and as such it
only stands to reason that they would contain a high proportion of
blue-collar workers. In addition, each had a highly transient popula-

Table 1.3
Occupations of Catholic Household Heads in Sample Parishes:
St Paul's, St Mary's, Our Lady of Lourdes, Holy Name, and St Helen's

Category	1890	%	1900	%	1910	%	1920	%
Professional	28	1.2	26	1.0	21	0.9	49	1.8
Private	45	1.9	9	0.3	0	0.0	8	0.3
Widow/spinster	299	12.6	407	14.9	388	15.7	448	16.7
Clerical	184	7.7	280	10.2	318	12.9	438	16.4
Business	263	11.0	253	9.3	247	10.0	257	9.9
Skilled	270	11.3	376	13.8	308	12.5	305	11.4
Semi-skilled	396	16.6	447	16.3	425	17.2	472	17.6
Unskilled	802	33.7	806	29.5	681	27.6	604	22.6
None/no data	95	4.0	131	4.8	77	3.1	97	3.6
Total	2382	100	2735	100	2465	100	2678	100
Labourer*	500	21.0	439	16.1	333	13.5	272	10.2

* The figures for Labourers are already included in the categories of Skilled, Semi-skilled, and Unskilled, and thus are already included in the totals.

Source: CTA, Assessment Rolls, 1891, 1901, 1911, 1921.

tion that seems to have flowed through without significantly changing the occupational grid of the area. In St Paul's parish less than one in five Catholics could be expected to remain in the parish for ten years or more.[71] In each case Catholics who wanted to move up the occupational ladder, in terms of skill or education, generally moved out of the parish.

Male parishioners in suburban parishes were vivid examples of the social change taking place generally in the Catholic community. Catholics in such parishes as St Helen's and Holy Name demonstrated little desire to move out of their homes and were less inclined to engage in unskilled work. Increasing numbers of suburban Catholics chose clerical and supervisory jobs for their daily bread.[72] In fact, when the suburban Catholic is placed within a broader context, the continued use of nineteenth-century stereotypes appears rather foolish. The Catholic tendency to seek out clerical, supervisory, business, and professional careers corresponded with strong desires to own their homes, build new school facilities, and send their children to secondary schools and beyond. These were also areas where English-speaking Catholics remained unchallenged by new Catholic migrants of European origin. When all these factors combined, it is not surprising that our traveller could not have distinguished Catholic from Protestant in the neighbourhoods outside the inner city.[73]

Occupational diversity was shared by Catholic men and women alike. In the nineteenth century Catholic women earned pittances as seamstresses, shirtmakers, charwomen, and landladies. The inadequate wages of workingmen, notable decline in real wages, and sometimes the untimely death of a male household head required women to work in order to feed the family.[74] In the thirty-five years after 1887 young Catholic women continued to be employed in the manufacturing and textile industries in Toronto,[75] and some widows still operated grocery stores or small millinery shops. Similarly, city tax-assessment rolls indicate that a few Catholic widows still continued the decades-old custom of taking in boarders to supplement their meagre incomes and help to pay the mortgages on their homes. Much as in the nineteenth century, some Catholic women were reported to be subject to abusive bosses, poor wages, and long hours in the workplace.[76]

Such conditions, however, were not universal among Catholic women in the workplace on the eve of the Great War. After 1900 many Catholic women in Toronto entered the clerical and professional sectors. By 1920 one-third of the thirty-three Catholic women who celebrated their nuptials at St Helen's parish identified themselves as clerks, secretaries, and bookkeepers; others recorded in the marriage register that they were telephone operators. Only ten of the brides at St Helen's claimed that they had chosen to stay home with their parents as an alternative to choosing a job in the marketplace.[77] Young Catholic laywomen at St Helen's and in other parishes also sought employment as teachers in the separate schools, invading a profession that had, in practice, been the exclusive domain of men's and women's religious orders.[78] While many of these young women would cease their public careers after marriage, their increased presence in the clerical and supervisory sector of the economy further attests to the occupational diversity of Toronto's Catholic community.

The changing interests of Catholic women, however, were not always appreciated in official Catholic circles. In 1900 the *Catholic Register* regarded the increase of women in clerical and factory jobs as a threat to the Catholic home: "Many of the works in which women are engaged, and which they are eager to undertake, are not so nearly suited for them, morally and physically as for household duties."[79]

Even the progressive Archbishop McNeil regarded day nurseries for the children of working women as a necessary evil, fearing that, without them, Catholic children might be placed in the care of proselytizing agencies. Above all he and others believed that "the best place for babies is with the mother in the home."[80] Yet neither the protests nor threats of moral decay from Catholic male leaders arrested the advance of Catholic women into the workplace, whether in blue- or pink-collar jobs.

Another feature of Catholic occupational diversification was their accession to jobs previously considered reserved for the city's Protestants and, in some cases, members of the Orange Order. The Toronto Fire Department and the Toronto Police Department were two such Orange bastions where Catholics made small but symbolic inroads.[81] In 1907 roughly 9 per cent of the police force were Catholic, most of whom were Canadian-born. By 1911 the number of Catholics had increased as the force expanded, constituting over 10 per cent of the officers and ranks. In the 1920s a record number of Catholics were employed by the police department, and although their percentage remained below that of their overall proportion of Toronto's population, their presence marked a significant toehold in what had traditionally been an Protestant bastion.[82] Many of the Catholic constables gained entry to the force by merit of their military, militia, and other policing experience. Catholic recruits from the Royal Irish Constabulary were the single largest group of Catholic policemen by 1924.

In the Edwardian period a few Catholics could even be found in the Toronto Fire Department, whose stations sometimes shared a mailing address with a local Orange lodge.[83] In 1911 the numbers of Catholic firemen rose in some suburban parishes, especially in neighbourhoods where Catholics were well integrated with the non-Catholic and where the influence of the Orange Order was less pronounced. St Helen's parish claimed at least six fire-fighters by 1911, and James C. Hurst of Our Lady of Lourdes parish had risen to the rank of captain after serving for over twenty years with the TFD.[84] Admittedly, Catholic fire-fighters were few, but the fact that some Catholics entered this Orange domain freely and, in the case of Hurst, actually rose in the ranks, indicates a growing tolerance between Catholics and Protestants in the workplace. In 1908 even the *Register* proudly reported that "the day … when a Catholic would be rejected on account of his religion is rapidly passing, even in Toronto, and our young men and women are given places of trust wherever honesty and capability are recognized."[85]

Middle- and upper-class Catholics also showed signs of entering the circles of Toronto's non-Catholic elite. When he arrived in Toronto in the late nineteenth century Timothy Warren Anglin, despite his political fame, felt that Catholics were unable to move in elite social or business circles.[86] Anglin's children, however, would have found things improved for Catholics in the Edwardian period. The 1907 edition of Dau's *Blue Book* lists at least sixteen prominent Toronto Catholic families, and the 1920 edition includes at least 25. Moreover, Catholic men and their wives are listed as members of the Albany Club, Empire Club, Canadian Club, and the very exclusive Royal Canadian Yacht Club.[87] The children of leading Protestant and Catholic families intermarried, which resulted in a new generation of Catholic children emerging from such leading Protestant families as the MacKenzies, Falconbridges, and Mulocks. Thus, interfaith marriages and the increased participation of Catholics in the elite circles of Toronto's well-heeled and monied classes complemented the ongoing integration of blue-, white-, and pink-collar Catholics into non-Catholic circles.

The gradual movement of Catholic workers and elites into previously near-forbidden territory underscores the manner in which issues of class outweighed creed as Catholics chose where to live, where to work, and with whom they would associate. At times the fissures between social classes in Toronto's Catholic community were pronounced. Successful Catholic entrepreneurs and politicians – Thomas Long, Eugene O'Keefe, the Elmsleys, and Senator Frank Smith – lived and worked in a very different social world from that of their co-religionists. In 1886 Frank Smith, owner of the Toronto Street Railway, locked out his workers – many of whom were Catholic – in an effort to resist their unionization. A second confrontation between Smith and his workers in May of the same year illustrates vividly the way in which issues of class could sever the bonds of Catholic solidarity in some circumstances.[88] As we reach the Edwardian period, it becomes increasingly difficult to accept the view of one historian that Irish Catholics eschewed participation in a working-class culture.[89] Catholic skilled workers appear to have prefered the benefits accruing from trade unions to the fraternity and insurance offered by Catholic societies. Despite inexpensive mutual benefit plans offered by the Knights of Columbus and the Catholic Mutual Benefit Association, the two largest Catholic fraternal organizations in Edwardian Toronto, skilled workers remained underrepresented in these friendly societies. Even contemporaries were aware that cleavages between different classes had become more a fact of life. When the Holy Name Society attempted to establish a city-wide Catholic boys' club, wealthy parishes were warned not to exclude poorer parishes from their activities:

Another objection was that boys of one social class would not be allowed by their parents to mix with poorer boys. In those parts of the city where there is something like equality of social circumstances of the families in the parish, as for instance in West Toronto ... the difficulty would not exist; but there are wide differences between such adjoining parishes as St Basil's and St Patrick's, or Our Lady of Lourdes and St Paul's. Of course social differences exist between children of families in the same parish without making parish institutions impossible, and there is room for considerable co-operation between parishes. [90]

Catholic diversification among all occupational groups greatly facilitated this growing awareness of class among Catholics. Recognizable differences in lifestyle and work were reinforced by the disparities evident between the upward mobility of Catholics in the suburbs and the penury experienced by some Catholics in the older inner-city parishes.

Toronto's English-speaking Catholics of the late Victorian and Edwardian periods had become as occupationally varied as their Protestant neighbours. Second and third generations of Catholic Irish, Scots, and some English had made their way into all sectors of the labour market, even in jobs traditionally viewed as being off-limits to Catholics. If such a thing as a correspondence between Catholic (particularly Irish Catholic) and common labourer had existed in the 1850s, it was not a notable feature of Catholic life after 1890. The east end "Corktown" of old was now a new "Quebec" or a "Little Europe," and the west end's "Claretown" was on the verge of being "New Cracow" or "Little Lwiw." The image of the Irish Catholic navvy was an anachronism.

Although the years 1887 through 1922 were marked by their greater occupational and residential diversity, some English-speaking Catholics still struggled to make a living and escape the burdens of poverty. Poverty among working-class Catholics was still much in evidence in the depression years of the early 1890s, so much so that, in 1890, Archbishop John Walsh informed Rome that collections for the Holy See would be temporarily suspended across the Archdiocese of Toronto because "the calls made upon [the people] for Church purposes and local charities are such as to tax their scanty means to the greatest extent."[91] Walsh argued that the operating costs of diocesan charities and institutions and the payments on parish debts were burden enough for Catholics, whom he identified as "chiefly labourers, mechanics, small shopkeepers, and farmers." Papal collections did not resume until later in the decade.

In the context of this depression Walsh established several social service agencies. All the new projects – St Michael's Hospital in 1892;

St Vincent de Paul Catholic Children's Aid Society in 1894; and St John's Industrial School in 1893 – were designed to relieve poverty and the conditions for crime among the faithful, and to provide a distinctly Catholic environment for those in economic distress. Walsh, among others, believed that Catholics were in danger of losing their faith if exposed to the public agencies established for poor relief. When he established an industrial school for delinquent boys at Blantyre Park, he justified the venture in terms of charity and as a means to prevent the "shipwreck" of their "Catholic faith – the most precious gift of God."[92] The proliferation of such social service agencies indicates the two-pronged intentions of Catholics in the city: providing respite to the destitute during the "bust" years of the economic cycle, all the while preserving the faith among the Catholic poor.

It would be a serious misreading of history to view Catholic life in Toronto exclusively through Walsh's experiences in the depression of the early 1890s. By the early twentieth century social and economic conditions for English-speaking Catholics in Toronto could be characterized in three distinct ways. First, poverty was never a condition exclusive to the city's Catholics: it was shared by working-class Torontonians regardless of religious persuasion. Secondly, the composition of the Catholic poor changed during the Edwardian period, and there emerged a notable disparity between the English-speaking Catholic poor of the inner city and their co-religionists in the growing suburban parishes. Finally, and perhaps most significantly, English-speaking Catholics became aware that the numbers of their own poor were diminishing but the numbers of destitute Catholic immigrants from Eastern and Southern Europe were rising. English-speaking Catholics seized the opportunity to preserve the Catholicism of these newcomers while at the same time offering them the linguistic and cultural tools necessary to succeed in Canadian society.

Between 1887 and 1922 at least 50 to 60 per cent of English-speaking Catholic household heads were working class, susceptible to similar levels of the underemployment, low wages, and poverty evident among other blue-collar workers in Toronto. Hard times knew no creed. The three major depressions after the 1890s – 1907, 1913, and 1919[93] – affected Catholic and Protestant workers alike. In January 1908 the *Catholic Register* offered a Catholic perspective on the lean conditions facing many Torontonians:

There is unhappily no doubt that distress of a widespread and severe character exists in Toronto at the present time. Our charitable organizations have not had for many years so much misery clamouring for relief. And the unpleasant truth is well known to all interested in succoring distress, that the misery which clamours for relief is only the advance guard of the suffering which endures in silence and seeks rather to hide than reveal itself ... we find ourselves plunged into hard times with almost the suddenness of a railroad train rushing from high noon into the gloom of a tunnel.[94]

Similar reports of destitution were reported during the depressions immediately before and after the Great War. In the latter crisis the St Mary's Conference of the St Vincent de Paul Society exhausted its resources on tools, food, bedding, and medicine for numerous unemployed Catholics.[95]

Poverty among the working classes was not restricted to these specific depression years. Despite the economic upswing of the early twentieth century, some groups of working people in Toronto and Montreal suffered a relatively static standard of living. Workers faced a crisis in real income – the ability to produce a living wage, earned over an uninterrupted term of work, that could keep a family abreast of regular increases in the cost of living.[96] Unfortunately, the seasonal character of work and low wages made it difficult for workers to keep pace with rents or the cost of food and other necessities of life. Most working-class families could only rise above the poverty line if several family members worked, and even this was no guarantee of security, since the wages for women and children were less than half those for an adult male.[97] There is little contrary evidence to suggest that English-speaking Catholic workers were immune to this constant struggle engendered by declining real wages.

Keeping a family well fed, clothed, and warm, at a time of high prices and inflation, was a problem for all of the working class in Toronto at the turn of the century.[98] Staples, such as bread, eggs, milk, sugar, bacon, and cheese, rose in price dramatically between 1900 and 1920, some of the steepest increases coming during the inflationary spiral after the Great War. In 1918 Father P.J. Bench, president of Catholic Charities, declared that "75¢ has not the purchasing power of 60¢ of a few years ago."[99] Similarly, the *Catholic Register* observed that some families could only manage one serving of meat per week, and others were surviving on stew that consisted of beef cuttings and carrots. By 1920 Bench was appalled that prices of food and clothing had risen 102 and 110 per cent respectively, while wages between 1917 and 1920 had been augmented less than 50 per cent.[100]

Under normal working conditions and with constant employment the working class might have been able to meet budgetary expectations. Reality for most working families was steady employment for an average of only 40 to 43 weeks per year. The duration of seasonal work and the wages offered varied, however, from occupation to occupation. In 1921, for example, transportation workers had the highest average wage and the longest number of weeks worked. In contrast, construction workers, while making a wage of $25.60 per week, worked about six fewer weeks per year than their counterparts in transportation. The average blue-collar wage by 1921 was $24.05 per week, which compared unfavourably to $32.11 per week for white-collar workers.[101] More alarming is the fact that this average wage had to cover an estimated weekly budget, excluding clothing and emergencies, for a family of five of $25.47 per week.[102] This may have been more critical for some Catholic households, which tended to be slightly larger than the city average.[103] Under such circumstances women and children entered the labour force to keep families afloat.

The question at hand is: how did English-speaking Catholics fit into this general scenario? Are we to believe, as stereotypes would suggest, that the descendants of the Irish-Catholic community were conspicuous for generations on the long breadlines of the poor? Did every working "Pat" and "Sandy" have "hard times" as a permanent house-guest? In which sectors of the labour market could one find Catholics, and did this make a difference to their standard of living? When we examine working-class Catholics in our five sample parishes – St Paul's, St Mary's, Lourdes, St Helen's, and Holy Name – we discover only a small group employed in the most lucrative of the blue-collar sectors, transportation. City-wide, only about 10 per cent of Catholic workers engaged in railway transportation and related work, although Catholics in suburban parishes tended to be better represented in these jobs than their co-religionists in the inner-city parishes. Catholics in St Helen's parish, with neighbourhoods conveniently located near the yards of the Canadian Pacific and Canadian National Railways, had twice as many Catholic transport workers as the city-wide Catholic average. This uneven distribution of Catholics in the transportation occupations underscores once again the danger of generalizing about the social and economic life of Catholics in the city, and emphasizes the distinctive economies from parish to parish.

Railways offered the most lucrative incomes and lengthy terms of work, but they provided employment for only about half of Catholic workers in the transportation sector. Other Catholic transportation workers, particularly in the inner-city parishes, held jobs as teamsters, carters, drivers, cabmen, coachmen, and hackmen. Although the number of weeks worked in these occupations was high, wages fell below those in the railway-related jobs.[104] In some cases drivers, lacking the skills of others in the transportation sector, probably made little more than $20 per week. In such circumstances families would require wages earned by older children, mothers, or relatives to remain at an income on or above the poverty line. This scenario would also help to explain the growing economic disparity between the blue-collar workers of St Helen's and St Paul's parishes.

English-speaking Catholic participation in the manufacturing sector stood in sharp contrast to transportation. By 1921 over one-quarter of Catholic blue-collar household heads were employed in this sector, sharing an average wage of $24.37 per week, fourth highest among the working class. These Catholics could anticipate at least 43 weeks of work per year. Wages within this sector varied, although the high numbers of Catholic printers could expect weekly wages in excess of $27 per week and at least 47 weeks of work. Catholic iron and steel workers and highly skilled employees could expect higher than the $24 average weekly wage.[105]

Less fortunate than these manufacturing workers were the 17 per cent of English-speaking Catholics employed by the building trades. The numerous Catholic bricklayers, stationary engineers, carpenters, and plasterers earned between $27 and $35 per week. Despite the relatively high wage, the weeks of expected work were among the lowest, at an average of a little over 40 per year. From 1900 to 1920 unemployment in the construction sector was a constant fear, even though Toronto experienced a housing boom in the first ten years of this century. The recession of 1907 hurt the building trades, as did the near halt in construction in the early stages of the Great War.[106] Nevertheless, the number of Catholics in the building trades rose significantly, particularly between 1900 and 1910, thereby demonstrating the willingness of some Catholics to tolerate seasonal unemployment in exchange for the substantial wages that could accrue when housebuilding in Toronto experienced temporary peaks between recessions (see Table 1.4).[107]

The most dramatic change among Toronto's Catholic workers came from the sharp decline of those described as unskilled labourers. Catholic "labourers" dropped from a high of one-third of blue-collar workers in 1890 to a low of less than one-fifth by 1920. The move out of unskilled work was more significant in the midtown and suburban parishes than in the inner-city ones, where the percentage of labourers dropped only slightly between 1890 and 1920: in contrast, St Helen's and Holy Name parishes had few "labourers" by 1920. Most important, the Catholic departure from positions as labourers signalled a movement away from jobs that paid as little or less than $20 per week. In general, this shift out of unskilled occupations demonstrated the degree to which Toronto's English-speaking Catholics,

Table 1.4
Working-Class Sectors and Percentage of Parish Blue-Collar Labour Force

	1890	%	1900	%	1910	%	1920	%
TRANSPORTATION								
St Paul's	83	14.4	87	15.8	103	19.6	57	13.4
St Mary's	90	14.1	106	15.1	57	13.4	38	11.8
St Helen's	23	10.4	58	17.7	77	23.2	47	13.9
Lourdes	7	21.2	3	6.1	16	19.8	15	12.3
Holy Name	–	–	–	–	8	16.3	17	9.9
Total	203	13.8	254	15.6	261	18.5	174	12.6
CONSTRUCTION								
St Paul's	72	12.5	61	11.1	80	15.2	72	16.9
St Mary's	109	17.1	96	13.7	69	16.2	45	13.9
St Helen's	54	24.3	46	14.1	67	20.2	60	17.7
Lourdes	6	18.2	11	22.4	16	19.8	16	13.1
Holy Name	–	–	–	–	12	24.5	32	18.6
Total	241	16.4	214	13.1	244	17.3	235	17.0
MANUFACTURING								
St Paul's	146	25.3	184	33.4	183	34.8	84	19.8
St Mary's	122	19.2	165	23.5	125	29.3	80	24.8
St Helen's	41	18.5	89	27.2	91	27.4	119	35.1
Lourdes	8	24.2	8	16.3	26	32.1	32	26.2
Holy Name	–	–	–	–	10	20.4	40	23.3
Total	317	21.6	446	27.4	335	23.7	355	25.7
LABOURER								
St Paul's	197	34.2	158	28.7	146	27.8	81	19.1
St Mary's	223	35.0	206	29.3	120	28.2	106	32.9
St Helen's	76	34.2	65	19.9	48	14.5	54	15.9
Lourdes	4	12.1	10	20.4	9	11.1	16	13.1
Holy Name	–	–	–	–	10	20.4	15	8.7
Total	500	34.1	439	26.9	333	23.4	272	19.7

Table 1.4 (continued)

	1890	%	1900	%	1910	%	1920	%
TOTAL BLUE-COLLAR AS PERCENTAGE OF PARISH HOUSEHOLD HEADS								
St Paul's	576	63.4	551	61.9	526	60.0	425	58.0
St Mary's	637	60.4	702	61.2	426	60.7	323	61.8
St Helen's	222	70.2	327	61.5	332	58.1	339	49.4
Lourdes	33	31.7	49	29.7	81	33.5	122	32.8
Holy Name	–	–	–	–	49	66.2	172	47.3
Total	1468		1629		1414		1381	

Source: CTA, *Assessment Rolls*, 1891, 1901, 1911, 1921. All calculations are mine.

as a group, had changed in their relationship to the city's industrial complex. With greater earning power in more skilled occupations and in the white-collar sector, English-speaking Catholics, particularly those in midtown and suburban parishes, could enjoy a higher standard of living than that known by their predecessors in the city.

It becomes increasingly clear in the exploration of Catholic life in Toronto that the Catholic community was a complex web of economically and socially distinct neighbourhoods. The most distinctive cleavage in working-class Toronto did not run along a Catholic-Protestant axis but along lines of occupation and neighbourhood. A loose relationship existed between English-speaking Catholic income levels and parish of residence. Inner-city Catholics appear to have fared less well than their suburban co-religionists when it came to mobility, wages, and underemployment. Given the high numbers of Catholics involved in manufacturing, the highest-paying jobs in the construction trades, and the decreasing levels of labourers, it is not unreasonable to conclude that Catholic workingmen outside of the downtown area were holding their own compared to those in parishes like St Patrick's, St Mary's, or St Paul's. Levels of labourers and blue-collar workers in low-wage seasonal industries were far more prevalent in the inner-city parishes than in parishes like St Helen's, where the labour force was buoyed by a larger number of workers in the railway occupations and in high-paying construction and manufacturing jobs, such as stationary engineers and machinists.[108] It was also in the midtown and suburban parishes like St Helen's or Holy Name where the growth of white-collar work was substantial between the 1890s and the end of the Great War.

The disparity between the inner-city and suburban parishes was also evident in general living conditions and the rates of crime. Between 1890 and 1926 there was a general decline in the numbers of English-speaking Catholic felons across Toronto. Juvenile delinquency in 1926, for instance, was far more prevalent in the inner-city parishes bounded by Dovercourt Avenue and the Don on the west and east and by Bloor Street and the lakeshore on the north and south. While accounting for only about half of the Catholic population, these parishes produced in excess of 60 per cent of English-speaking Catholic delinquents. Moreover, the declining English-speaking Catholic populations of St Paul's and St Mary's parishes alone provided 31.1 per cent of all the city's English-speaking Catholic delinquents.[109] Similarly, reports from the chief constable, dating from as early as 1890, indicate that Catholic "waifs" held in police custody declined from 27.4 per cent of the total number arrested in 1890 to 20.4 per cent in 1924.[110] While the figure for 1924 was still in excess of the proportion of the Catholic population in the city, and there may have been some waifs who avoided police apprehension, the decline in arrests may indicate a decline in the social ills that caused child homelessness and delinquency in some sectors of the Catholic community.

As with our survey of wages and jobs, police reports on criminal activity tend to confirm the growing disparity between inner-city and suburban parishes after 1900. At the turn of the century only 19.4 per cent of all Catholic waifs arrested in Toronto were sheltered in police stations on the periphery of the inner city. More important, as the Catholic population of the suburban parishes began to increase, the number of waifs from these same parish areas remained lower than in the inner-city parishes. By 1924 only 10.1 per cent of the Catholic waifs sheltered by the police came from outside police stations serving the parishes of St Mary's, St Francis's, St Patrick's, St Michael's, and St Paul's.[111]

The problem of inner-city youth and delinquency was not lost on Catholic leaders. After 1916 Big Brothers, Big Sisters, and the Boy Scouts were introduced to save delinquent youths "and make them grow up good Christians and good citizens."[112] The Big Brothers of Toronto were operated by the Holy Name Union, who considered the task of "the reclamation of underprivileged Catholic boys" among "the highest of the spiritual works."[113] By 1922 the Brothers were part of the Catholic Boy Life Council, organized primarily to co-ordinate the building of clubhouses and the founding of scout troops, and to provide Catholic boys with the opportunity to go to summer camps outside of Toronto.[114]

The statistics offered by the Big Brothers regarding the "reclama-tion" of Catholic boys also indicate that the poverty among Catholics was concentrated in the inner city. In 1920, 62.4 per cent of the male delinquents handed over to the Big Brothers from juvenile court were from the inner-city parishes, and at least one-third of all the cases came from St Mary's and St Paul's alone. By contrast, St Helen's, Our Lady of Lourdes, and Holy Name parishes claimed only 11.2 per cent collectively. These data, when combined with the reports from the po-lice department and the Catholic Children's Aid Society, clearly indi-cate that poverty and the problems frequently associated with impoverished circumstances were not endemic to Toronto's English-speaking Catholics as a whole. One was more likely to find poor Catholics in the downtown parishes.

Housing was another tell-tale sign of the general betterment of so-cial and economic conditions for English-speaking Catholics, and a confirmation of the growing disparity between the suburbs and the inner city. Rates of home-ownership are a fairly good index of social mobility within the Victorian city.[115] In contrast to Montreal and many other North American urban areas, Toronto was primarily a city of single-family dwellings. In 1861 the home-ownership level in Toronto was at roughly 10 per cent, whereas by 1899 the level had more than doubled to just over 26 per cent.[116] Between 1900 and 1911 home-ownership jumped in the city from 26.4 to 47.1 per cent, indi-cating, perhaps, that real wages may actually have increased in the first decade of this century.[117] In addition, the construction of new homes occurred when the gross rents of existing property exceeded the desired rents of landlords, thus providing capital and incentive to engage in more residential construction.[118] Consequently, home-own-ership in Edwardian Toronto would appear to have been less static than has been claimed, and by 1900 ownership itself was a normative condition for all classes of Catholics (see Table 1.5).[119]

Toronto's English-speaking Catholics did remarkably well in terms of home-ownership. In 1890 Catholics in the city kept pace exactly with the 24 per cent rate of home-ownership for the entire city. The percentage of parishioners who owned houses in St Mary's and St Paul's was lower than the city trend, while Catholics in St Helen's and Our Lady of Lourdes exceeded the general rate with levels of 31 and 36 per cent respectively. After dipping below the general rate of home-ownership in 1900, Catholics bounced back in 1910. The widen-ing economic gap between the inner city and suburbs, however, is once again noticeable. While the general city-wide home-ownership rate for all Torontonians stood at 47.1 per cent, English-speaking Catholics in St Paul's and St Mary's parishes managed ownership of

Table 1.5
Rates of Home-Ownership in Five Sample Parishes, 1890–1920

Parish	1890	%	1900	%	1910	%	1920	%
ST HELEN'S								
Household heads	316		532		571		686	
Owner	97	30.7	152	28.6	303	53.1	331	48.3
Householders	200	63.3	380	71.4	268	46.9	355	51.7
Tenants	19	6.0						
LOURDES								
Household heads	104		165		242		372	
Owner	38	36.5	49	29.7	95	39.6	142	38.2
Householder	66	63.5	116	70.3	147	60.4	230	71.8
HOLY NAME								
Household heads					74		364	
Owner					46	62.2	255	70.1
Householder					28	37.8	109	29.9
ST PAUL'S								
Household heads	908		890		876		733	
Owner	192	21.1	185	20.8	202	23.1	168	22.9
Householder	716	78.9	705	79.2	674	76.9	565	77.1
ST MARY'S								
Household heads	1054		1148		702		523	
Owner	269	25.5	304	26.5	199	28.4	125	23.9
Householder	785	74.5	844	73.5	503	71.6	398	76.1

Source: CTA, Assessment Rolls, 1891, 1901, 1911, 1921.

only 23.1 and 28.4 per cent respectively. At St Helen's and Holy Name parishes, however, the level of home-ownership was an impressive 52.5 and 62.2 per cent respectively, well above the city-wide levels. Much the same pattern was repeated in 1920.[120]

The rates of home-ownership in the suburbs deserve particular attention because they demonstrate a notable rootedness and the economic stability of the Catholic population. In St Helen's parish, for example, home-ownership steadily rose among those who remained in the parish in excess of ten years. Nearly 30 per cent of the resident Catholics in St Helen's remained in the parish from 1890 to 1900. Of these, only about half owned their homes in 1890. By 1900, however, close to 60 per cent were home-owners, despite minimal movement among occupational classifications. A more startling pattern emerges when home-owners in 1900 and 1910 are compared. Of those who lived in the parish in 1900 and remained until 1910, only 46.2 per cent owned their homes in the former year. By 1910, however, 82.4 per cent of this same group of Catholics owned their own homes.[121]

Catholics in midtown and suburban parishes were able to participate fully in the housing boom. Here, Catholics seemed to have earned a steady incomes, some modest savings, and the resultant ability to invest what they had earned. While clerical workers at St Helen's seem to have benefited more than other groups from the wealth generated in the period, all classes of Catholics were well represented among home-owners outside of the inner city. In fact, half were blue-collar workers, obviously benefiting from occupations that provided living wages and reasonable regularity in terms of weeks of employment. With home-ownership came rootedness and stability,[122] and rootedness engendered feelings of pride and belonging in the community. Therefore, home-ownership is not only evidence of greater Catholic mobility but also of the Catholic community's claim on Toronto as their home.

The issue of home-ownership not only challenges the notions of Catholics and their mobility in Toronto society; it reaffirms the perception of growing differences within the Catholic community. Fewer English-speaking Catholics were staying in the inner city, and many were building and buying their own homes in the suburbs. A sample of twenty families living in Holy Name parish in 1921 demonstrates this point clearly. Fully 80 per cent of these families owned their own homes in their new parish, and at least one-third of these had been renters in their old parish.[123] The same could not be said of those Catholics who remained in St Paul's, St Mary's, St Patrick's, or in, parts of the Cathedral parish. Some English-speaking Catholics experienced hardship and poverty, but it is also true that many owned their own homes and, by 1920, had acquired a stability their forebears had not known. That the *Catholic Register* began to advertise high fashion, expensive furs, excursions, and diamonds indicates the thickening of many a Catholic's pocketbook.[124]

The benefits of home-ownership, however, were not shared uniformly among all of Toronto's English-speaking Catholics. Hundreds of Catholics in Toronto's inner-city parishes had neither the dispos-

able income for the down payment on their own house nor the security of employment to settle permanently in the same dwelling. For
those who did not own their own houses, rents were high, increasing
gradually after 1896 and making a formidable jump of nearly 71 per
cent between 1900 and 1905. In fact, Toronto's rents increased a
whopping 123 per cent between the turn of the century and the Great
War.[125] High rents, when combined with the scarcity of adequate
housing, paint a bleak picture of the Toronto housing market for
working people of all denominations.[126]

The preponderance of slums and substandard living conditions in
the inner city made the housing situation in Toronto even more discouraging for Catholics and non-Catholics alike. In his famous report
of 1911 Dr Charles Hastings, the medical health officer for Toronto, lamented the appalling slum conditions in the inner city, characterized
by "rear houses, dark rooms, tenement houses, houses unfit for habi-
tation, inadequate water supply, unpaved and filthy yards and lanes,
sanitary conveniences so-called which … have become a public nui-
sance, a menace to public health, a danger to public morals, and, in
fact, an offence against public decency."[127] He added that slum conditions and high rents had forced some workers to build a "Shacktown"
to the west of Toronto Junction, thus spreading slum conditions to
some parts of the suburbs.[128] Hastings cast much of the blame for
privy pits and overcrowded housing on the recently arrived immigrants from Southern and Eastern Europe and on shameful landlords
– native and foreign – who exploited the newcomers.[129] In this light
Hastings' report reveals as much about the host society's impressions
of European immigrants as it does about Toronto's slums.

Between 1890 and 1920 English-speaking Catholics could be counted
among both slum-dwellers and home-owners, and occasionally both.
Considering that Hastings' six case-study slums cut across four large
Catholic inner-city parishes – St Paul's, St Patrick's, St Mary's, and the
Cathedral – it is not surprising that some Catholics were identified as
being among the poorest persons in the city. Frequently the *Register*
complained about dirty streets, the gap between good and bad housing, and the inadequacy of decent accommodation in Toronto and
warned that "Toronto the Good bids fair to become a city of slums
where heretofore poverty in its extreme sense was almost unknown
and where our smiling homes gave us a continental reputation."[130] As
a remedy, columnists and editors proposed state-financed housing,
along the lines of British public-housing programs.

Hastings' discoveries also unsuspectingly confirmed the growing
disparity between comfortable and poor Catholics, typified by the
gap between suburban and inner-city Catholics and by local dispari-

ties within individual parishes. Two of Hastings' surveyed areas fell within the boundaries of St Paul's parish, accounting for close to 59 per cent of the assessed Catholic households in the parish. The "slum strip" within St Paul's differed significantly from the other portions of parish surrounding it. Nearly 60 per cent of parish home-owners lived on very highly assessed property outside of Hastings' slum strip. In 1911 the average assessed value of property (dwelling and land) was $1,069.21 inside the strip, whereas Catholics elsewhere in St Paul's held property with a mean value of $1,415.61.[131]

Similar internal disparities were evident in St Mary's parish, although the overall property values were slightly higher than in St Paul's. Hastings' two slum strips in St Mary's accounted for just over 55 per cent of the assessed Catholic homes in the parish, and contained only about 46 per cent of the home-owners. Like St Paul's, property values in the zones at St Mary's were over $400 lower on average than the value of houses and land outside the zone. A report by Catholic Children's Aid on one home was fairly typical of these strips within the inner-city parishes: "Home is not comfortable. In a rather crowded and factory district. Family occupies lower floor. Rooms are dark and appear to be a little damp." Outside of the strip, conditions were much better. Inner-city parishes indeed appear to have been studies in contrast, where at least half of the assessed Catholic households were doing considerably better than those who were considered poor slum-dwellers by city officials.[132] On the whole, however, parishes like St Mary's or St Paul's had lower property values and more pressing problems of urban blight than suburban parishes like St Helen's and others, where homes were described as "comfortable," "tidy," and "nicely furnished."[133]

It should not be forgotten that some Catholics in the inner city were part of the spatial and economic mobility of the Catholic population as a whole. In St Paul's and St Mary's the overall proportion of Catholics living in the slum streets, such as Niagara or Eastern Avenue, decreased between 1911 and 1921, and there were more home-owners in both parishes. It is clear that, by 1921, more and more Eastern and Southern European Catholics were replacing Anglo-Celtic Catholics in the slum strips formerly outlined by Hastings.

Slum housing and the poor sanitary conditions that affected some of the city's Catholics spurred clergy and lay leaders into action. In 1908 a group of wealthy Catholic women, with the encouragement of Archbishop Fergus P. McEvay, founded the St Elizabeth's Visiting Nurse Association, which provided a Catholic alternative to the Victorian Order of Nurses as well as home care for the infirm and chronically ill. In 1910 four nurses made over 5,000 calls on 645 patients. Ten years later up to eight nurses accommodated over 1,300 patients in over 9,000 visits, of which 26 per cent were made to non-Catholics.[134] Obstetrical cases were the most common, with attendance on over 600 births recorded by 1920.

For numerous Catholics poor living conditions and high infant mortality were grim partners. As late as 1910 Catholic children were lucky if they survived their first year.[135] Upon his accession to the See of Toronto in 1913, Neil McNeil was appalled by the high rate of mortality among Catholic infants under twelve months of age. In 1912 the rate had reached 47 per cent of registered births. He found the maternity and infant's facilities at St Vincent's home to be crowded, unsanitary, and too near the inner-city slums to be a healthy environment. In 1914 he founded St Mary's Infants' Home in Bond Street and placed it under the care of the Sisters of Misericorde from Montreal. By 1919 the new maternity hospital boasted a death rate of only 6.9 per cent.[136] One unwed mother was so grateful for the life of her child that she named him Neil after the archbishop.[137]

By 1910, however, Catholic leaders and pundits increasingly identified poverty among Catholics as an immigrant problem. Henry Somerville, labour columnist for the *Catholic Register*, admitted that there were a large number of poor Catholics, but qualified this by asserting: "Most of the poverty in this City is amongst the foreign immigrants, especially Italian and Polish, and nearly all of these are Catholics."[138] By 1917 three-quarters of the waifs and delinquents cared for by the St Vincent de Paul Catholic Children's Aid Society were "foreign" Catholics.[139] Likewise, the Sacred Heart Orphanage, operated by the Sisters of St Joseph at Sunnyside, recorded a significant rise in immigrant orphans after 1910. In 1914, 76.4 per cent of the 161 inmates were English-speaking Catholic children, but by 1918 the numbers at the orphanage had swollen to 253, of which only 49 per cent were Canadian-born and anglophone. The rest were immigrant children, many of whom were Italian, Polish, French, and English.[140]

The increase of Catholic immigrants on the rolls of the police juvenile-delinquency files confirms the contemporary impression that more and more of the Catholic poor in Toronto were foreign-born. Reports on Catholic juvenile delinquents submitted to Archbishop McNeil in 1926 reveal that Eastern and Southern European children were represented in excess of their proportional representation in the Catholic community. Foreign-born Catholic children accounted for half of juvenile crime, despite the fact that they constituted probably less than 20 per cent of the Catholic population.[141] If there was a correlation between crime and poverty, these figures would suggest that Catholic immigrants were indeed a fast-growing proportion of the city's Catholic poor, whereas English-speaking Catholics, especially in the suburbs, were quickly shedding their mid-nineteenth-century stereotype.

In Victorian Toronto crime statistics had frequently been used to highlight poverty and moral degeneracy among Irish Catholics. The Toronto daily press delighted in publishing the most recent crime statistics that dramatized the overrepresentation of Catholics among the city's malefactors and felons.[142] These expositions continued into the Edwardian period, and the Catholic response was a predictable defence of Catholic virtue, citing appropriate statistics. By 1902, however, the old arguments against Catholics had worn thin. Charles Fitzpatrick, Wilfrid Laurier's Catholic minister of Justice, demonstrated that the ratio of Catholics in Canadian prisons was lower than that of any other religious denomination.[143] By 1920 English-speaking Catholic youths appearing in juvenile court constituted 15.5 per cent of total cases, just slightly higher than the proportion of Catholics in the city.[144] English-speaking Catholics could no longer be singled out as the city's chief breeders of criminals.

The proliferation of Catholic charities in Toronto reflected the rising number of poor Catholic immigrants and new approaches to poverty and disease. By 1913 Archbishop McNeil had united all the Church's hospitals and charitable organizations under the umbrella group "Catholic Charities."[145] All Catholic social services in the city fell under its aegis, including the House of Providence, orphanages, infants' homes, industrial schools, Big Brothers and Big Sisters, Catholic Children's Aid, St Elizabeth's Visiting Nurses, and St Michael's Hospital.

The new charitable structures were committed to updated approaches to the causes and treatment of poverty. Although articles in the *Register* sometimes blamed poverty on a "lack of initiative, industry, efficiency and thrift," or on the "unfitted" condition of some immigrants, the Catholic approach to poverty did become more sophisticated.[146] Leadership provided by McNeil and Somerville indicates that Catholics were keeping pace with contemporary developments in social work and sociology. As early as 1913 McNeil wrote: "There is now running a strong reaction against industrial individualism. Not liberty, but co-operation is the watchword of to-day. Poverty has to be studied in its causes as well as in its effects. Today Christian charity grapples with the economic and social ills which underlie poverty, and is, therefore, largely social in its operations."[147] Likewise, Somerville advocated the training of more Catholic social workers, claiming that lay Catholics had fallen behind in charitable and social work because they depended too heavily on religious orders. He also advised Catholics that the new social work would have to be adopted within the context of Catholic principles, hence social Catholicism.[148]

Poverty in Toronto, however, produced a far more dramatic effect on Protestant–Roman Catholic relations. With the poverty in the city shared between Catholics and non-Catholics alike, Catholics such as Somerville and McNeil called for greater ecumenical co-operation in the area of social work. Although little happened in the wake of their suggestions, Catholic-Protestant co-operation during the Great War acted as a catalyst for rapprochement in charitable works. In 1919 the Catholic Charities joined the Federation for Community Service of Toronto, a fund-raising umbrella organization for public charities in the city.[149] The federation of non-Catholics and Catholics was hailed as a major triumph, especially its first joint fund-raising drive in December of that same year: "Never was an army of Christian workers animated by a more lofty purpose and were more determined efforts made to realize the goal ... the people of Toronto are developing a unity-of-purpose attitude against disease, poverty, degradation, accident, ignorance, delinquency and all social enemies."[150] Even the editor of the *Register* commented: "It will be well for the people of Ontario and of Canada to watch Toronto's effort ... for in the movement and the men may be found the beginning of a better day for the Province and the Dominion."[151]

By 1922 the English-speaking Catholics of Toronto had undergone significant social and economic development that clearly undermines the stereotypes applied to their Irish forebearers. No longer could they be designated by a particular neighbourhood or ghetto in the city. Demographically, Catholics spread out over the entire city, filling up the new suburbs while leaving their traditional inner-city parishes to generations of new Canadians. Similarly, the days when English-speaking Catholics predominated in the unskilled urban proletariat were over. Now, they were entering the work force better educated and better prepared to assume jobs in all occupational classifications. The Edwardian period witnessed the diversification of Catholic labour and its successful attempts to enter the clerical and professional sectors of Toronto's labour market.

Amid the poverty of many areas of the inner city, Catholics on the whole experienced progress in their standard of living. Despite low wages, underemployment, and slum conditions, many Catholics, especially those who migrated to the new suburban parishes, displayed a remarkable degree of social mobility. Catholic living was now characterized by lower rates of crime and delinquency, higher participation in clerical occupations, consistent working-class employment, a drop in unskilled labourers, and phenomenal increases in home-ownership outside the inner-city. Even within some of the large inner-city parishes, English-speaking Catholics enjoyed an improved living standard, often just blocks away from the crowded tenements of new Catholic Canadians.

While Catholic charities expanded from 1890 to 1920, after 1900 much of their attention was focused on the Eastern and Southern European immigrants. Catholic charities, however, were distinguished by two significant developments: the incorporation of the language and practices of social work, and, more important in terms of the city's history, a growing co-operation with non-Catholics in the fight against poverty. Perhaps this latter development indicates the extent to which the Catholic community had stepped up its fight against poverty and its members were prepared to enter civic life as full partners and equal citizens. As older generations of English-speaking Catholics became more rooted in Toronto's capitalist culture, the visible disparities and growing class differences between Catholics themselves became more pronounced; there were several Catholic worlds – the comfortable and the destitute, the suburban and the inner city, and the English-speaking Anglo-Celts and the "foreigners." Catholics came to resemble the urban world around them, and established the foundations of Catholic life and Church politics for the decades following the Great War.

CHAPTER TWO

Prelates, Priests, and Professors: The Rise of a Home-Grown Church

Father John Read Teefy's pen skipped quickly over the small notepaper that rested in front of him. He had been preaching retreats for six weeks straight, and on this Monday evening, 20 August 1906, he was the guest of the sisters at the Hôtel Dieu in Kingston. Within a week he would be travelling to Ottawa and then on to Alexandria. Despite his absence from St Michael's College in Toronto, whose students were now enjoying summer vacation, Teefy was never distant from the troubles in his native archdiocese. His mail was forwarded to him, so the problems at home followed him wherever he sojourned. The nature of his epistle tonight was so important he would label it "Confidential" and beg its recipient to keep his name "perfectly secret." The letter was to be sent with due speed to Ottawa, to the office of Donatus Sbarretti, Apostolic Delegate to Canada – the eyes and ears of the Pope in British North America. Teefy's task was most unpleasant. There were few ways one could sugarcoat the abuse of episcopal authority, the demoralization of religious communities, the frustration of local priests, and the open resistance of lay Catholics to their archbishop. Nevertheless, Teefy worked on, documenting how religion in Toronto suffered from "rigorous, severe, and narrow interpretation" of Church law and practice. At the same time, whether he knew it or not, Teefy had provided a rarely seen glimpse of religious leadership and pastoral challenges in early twentieth-century Toronto.[1]

Between 1887 and 1922 the Archdiocese of Toronto experienced significant change in the character and style of its leadership. In the nineteenth century Bishops Armand de Charbonnel and John Joseph Lynch attempted to create a parallel Catholic world in an effort to nurture the faith, control the faithful, and preserve their flock from the "insult" of Protestantism. With the assistance of priests and religious, Charbonnel and Lynch laid the foundations for a Catholic network of schools, devotional associations, and social services; in this distinctive society Catholic men, women, and children would be neither distracted nor "corrupted" by the Protestant world around them. Arguably the laity also played a pivotal role in the establishment of clubs and confraternities that bore an Irish nationalist flavour and, later, a Catholic devotional ethos.[2] While lay initiative is not to be underestimated, it fell to the clerical and episcopal leadership to put in place a centralized, hierarchical, and truly Catholic institutional framework. Inspired by the ultramontane spirit of the Catholic world of the nineteenth century, the institutional completeness of the Church in Toronto was so evident that Bishop Lynch, in a moment of bravado, could boast to Sir John A. Macdonald: "I must acknowledge that I lead them [Catholics] in all matters concerning faith and religion."[3] Although he hastily equated his presumed authority with the effectiveness of such authority in reality, the image of strong hierarchical control over Toronto's Catholics has been a indelible image in local history until very recently.[4]

Episcopal domination of Catholic institutions and lay religious life, and the image of Catholic exclusiveness and isolation in a Protestant world, ought not to be presumed for the late Victorian and Edwardian periods. Between 1887 and 1922 the economic and social changes inherent in Catholic life in Toronto were complemented by changes in personnel and in the character of the leaders of the institutional Church. After the 1880s bishops, clergy, and leaders of religious orders in Toronto became increasingly aware that the Catholic Church could coexist comfortably with non-Catholic denominations in the city, and could even make valuable contributions to civic life without endangering the faith. From within the Catholic community itself there emerged a desire to put a Canadian face on the Church and to engage in the work of "nation-building." This shift in leadership style and vision was characterized by several factors: the individual initiatives of Lynch's episcopal successors to emphasize patriotism as a Catholic virtue; the emergence of Canadian-born and Canadian-educated priests, brothers, and sisters; and the assertiveness of clergy and religious to protest inappropriate episcopal policies, particularly in matters related to shaping the public image of the Church, fostering devotional and associational life, and regulating Catholic morality.

The three decades after the 1880s produced a new generation of Church leaders who were as vociferous in their Canadian patriotism as they were protective of their Catholic piety. By 1922 the archdiocese was no longer under the control of the "Hibernarchy" – Irish-born priests, bishops, and religious – and no longer was clerical formation dependent on facilities provided by the Church in Quebec. A distinctive anglophone Canadian leadership had emerged, and the Church in Toronto established itself as a community that embraced the promise and potential of Canada. Far from being a community that was stereotypically imprisoned in mortal combat with the Equal Rights Association, the Orange Lodge, or the Protestant Protective Association, Catholic leaders trumpeted denominational peace and greater Catholic participation in Canadian life.[5] Catholics maintained their distinctive institutions but were in no way restricted to them. Indigenized leadership, in combination with increased lay assertiveness, ensured that separate schools, voluntary associations, and pious practices might insulate Catholics and preserve the faith but would not isolate Catholics and exclude them from being builders and leaders in Canadian society.

From the 1890s to the Great Depression the archbishops of Toronto contributed greatly to the acculturation of English-speaking Catholicism in central Ontario. Although not the only force at work in the adaptation and integration of Catholics in the Queen's City, the hierarchy provided an example that trickled down through the subordinate layers of the Church's institutional structures. The death of John Joseph Lynch in 1888 marked the beginning of the end of the rule of foreign-born bishops in Toronto and signalled distinct changes in the way Catholic prelates approached Canadian society and attempted to instil a sense of Canadian identity in their flock. Lynch's successors, John Walsh, Fergus McEvay, and Neil McNeil, were all acutely aware that the Catholic Church in Canada had to be Canadian in its concerns and loyalties in non-spiritual matters. These three bishops challenged, encouraged, and even chastised the clergy and laity into being good Catholics, and active and patriotic Canadians. Their colleague Denis O'Connor (1899–1908), endured a torturous tenure as bishop when he promoted a policy of extreme isolation that prompted a near revolt of clergy, laity, and religious in the Archdiocese of Toronto. Not even the fiat of this archbishop could arrest English-speaking Catholic participation and integration into the world around them.

On 12 May 1888 Archbishop John Joseph Lynch breathed his last. Born in the parish of Clones, County Monaghan, Ireland, in 1816, Lynch was a member of the Congregation of the Mission (Vincentian Fathers) who began his priestly career in 1846 as a missionary in Texas. After contracting malaria, he was moved to Missouri, and later arrived at the Niagara frontier in western New York State, where, in 1857, he founded Our Lady of the Angels Seminary.[6] Attracted by his reputed administrative acumen, and encouraged by reports from the

superior of the Vincentians, in 1859 Armand de Charbonnel consecrated Lynch bishop of Echinus and coadjutor to the bishop of Toronto.[7] Shortly thereafter, in 1860, Lynch succeeded Charbonnel as
bishop of Toronto. Ten years later, in 1870, Lynch became archbishop
of Toronto and, in the public mind, the most prominent Catholic
bishop in Ontario.

Lynch's career was marked by significant paradoxes. Although he
frequently preached on the subject of religious tolerance and circulated amiably with some of the city's leading Protestants, he managed to irritate both the city's non-Catholics and many members of
his own flock.[8] Part of Lynch's problem was his innate talent for
sending out mixed messages to the community. Despite his public
preaching of religious toleration and his urging of Catholics "to endure what they cannot cure" (Protestant bigotry), Lynch had the
knack of enraging local Protestants by his overt political activities, his
well-attended and sometimes inflammatory public lectures on Catholic doctrine and Protestant error, and his blunt manner in facing
down his enemies.[9] Frequently associated with Irish nationalist
causes and the fight for Home Rule, Lynch succeeded in creating an
impression among his detractors that his primary loyalties lay any-
where but in Canada. Unfortunately, such impressions came at a time
of great linguistic and sectarian strain throughout Canada. Lynch's
tenure was marred by major riots in 1864, 1875, and 1877, in addition
to frequent public skirmishes between Protestants and Catholics on
12 July and 17 March .[10] Much as he tried to deny it, Lynch was partially responsible for the enduring image of Toronto as the "Belfast of
Canada."

Lynch's social and spiritual concerns were typical of his ultramontane episcopal colleagues elsewhere in North America.[11] As the Catholic population increased in the city and the archdiocese as a whole,
Lynch initiated and supported programs to strengthen separate
schools, expand the network of Catholic charitable organizations, and
generate services to invigorate the visible Catholic subculture in Toronto. His reinforcement of a parallel Catholic society adds strength
to George Grant's comment that in Canada, "the two currents of religious life flow side by side as distinct from each other as the St
Lawrence and the Ottawa after their junction. But the two rivers do
eventually blend into one. The two currents of religious life do not."[12]
Protecting the integrity and insularity of the Church and its faithful
was a hallmark of Lynch's career; he blocked the incorporation of the
Orange Order in Ontario, had a hand in censoring the curriculum of
public schools, and attempted to broker the Catholic vote to the political party friendliest to Catholic interests. Protestant Torontonians

were not amused, and they made Lynch the target of theological attack, political rebuke, and the subject of amusing, and biting satirical cartooning.[13]

The local population was particularly frustrated by the fact that Lynch's primary focus of loyalty was never entirely clear. In terms of allegiance to Canada or Ireland, Lynch's heart was with his homeland, and he considered himself the natural leader of Irish nationalists in Toronto.[14] At the time of his death the *Catholic Weekly Review* eulogized him as a "great Churchman" and a "true Irishman" who, although "a Canadian Archbishop – he remained an Irish patriot at heart and in act, the benefactor of an ignorant and exiled Irish people, and an unwavering believer in the apostolic mission of the Irish race among the nations of the earth."[15] Prominent at St Patrick's Day celebrations, and a vocal supporter of Home Rule, Lynch promoted the vision of the Irish North American as an exile, driven by poverty and oppression from his/her homeland yet blessed by the hand of Providence to be an instrument of conversion to the true faith throughout the world.[16] Lynch's Irish nationalism stood in stark contrast to the attitudes of such contemporaries as Thomas D'Arcy McGee or Nicholas Flood Davin, who focused on the duties and responsibilities of the Irishman as a Canadian as opposed to dwelling upon the tragedies, tribulations, and trauma of the Irish past.[17]

Even those who shared Lynch's burning desire for justice in Ireland and the defence of the faith did not always agree with the archbishop that he was the obvious leader of the nationalist movement. Lynch's claim to spiritual and nationalist leadership of Toronto's Irish Catholics collided with the aspirations of some nationalist laymen who, in 1887, renewed demands for the secret ballot in separate school elections. For lay nationalists the ballot would ensure the amelioration of the quality of education while limiting clerical control. Lynch's battle against the nationalist trustees, whom he regarded as "anti-clerical," seriously eroded his nationalist power-base and demonstrated his inability to enforce every dimension of ultramontane Catholicism in the archdiocese.[18] The laity's demands engendered both a rejection of his leadership and a desire for greater Catholic respectability in the eyes of the city's non-Catholics.[19]

By the time William O'Brien stepped off the train to blitz Toronto in 1887, Lynch's effective power among the laity and his brother bishops was seriously weakened. Despite his efforts to divert O'Brien away from the archdiocese, Lynch had failed and was conveniently absent from the city for the duration of the visit.[20] He had won a temporary victory in the ballot question and seen the election of his candidate, Timothy Anglin, to the Toronto Separate School Board, but lay radical

nationalists remained at arm's length from his leadership. While doing battle with lay radicals like Remigius Elmsley, Lynch faced increased competition from Bishop James Vincent Cleary of Kingston.
In 1884 Lynch had approved of a text of Bible readings to be used in
Ontario's public schools. Cleary led the opposition to the use of the
"Ross Bible," named appropriately after the minister of Education, on
grounds that it endangered the faith of Catholic students in the public
school system.[21] Lynch's influence waned as Cleary's prominence
was enhanced by his fierce confrontation with Ontario Conservative
leader William Meredith and George M. Grant, principal of Queen's
College. Lynch became increasingly alienated from other bishops,
and Cleary emerged with reliable support from John Walsh of London and even Timothy Mahoney, Lynch's auxiliary bishop in Toronto.[22] Lynch's lay detractors had seen him as not radical enough,
while his brother bishops second-guessed his judgment in political
matters pertaining to Catholics in Canadian society.

John Lynch's Irish nationalism and political activism differed
greatly from the views and actions of his successors to the See of Toronto. Those who assumed control of the archdiocese after his death –
John Walsh, 1889–98; Denis O'Connor, 1899–1908; Fergus Patrick
McEvay, 1908–11; and Neil McNeil, 1912–34 – would facilitate the
shift in Catholic loyalties from Irish to Canadian issues. Their official
speeches, legislation, and unofficial encouragement would help the
city's English-speaking Catholics to reformulate their sense of identity. Although they shared Lynch's primary loyalty to the Church,
these bishops would be far more forthright in their demand that a
Catholic's duties as a Canadian citizen superseded any allegiance to
Ireland.[23] For Walsh, McEvay, and McNeil, a good Catholic was by
very definition a good Canadian. In many ways, when the city's
Catholics entombed Lynch in the north wall of St Michael's Cathedral, they buried the first and last of the "Irish" archbishops and cler-
ico-nationalism in Toronto.

John Walsh's understanding of the Catholic community represents
a historical shift from Lynch's. Born 24 May 1830 in the parish of
Mooncoin in County Kilkenny, Walsh was the last Irish-born bishop
of Toronto. Walsh came from a comfortable and prominent farming
family and was educated at St John's College in Waterford.[24] Raised
in the Pale, the most anglicized region of Ireland, Walsh, unlike the
Ulster-born Lynch, cultivated a much more moderate position on the
famed "Irish question," and as a cleric he resisted the temptation of
becoming too prominent in political struggles, whether Irish or, later,
Canadian.[25] Walsh completed his seminary education at the Grand
Séminaire in Montreal and was recruited for Toronto by Armand de

Charbonnel. He was ordained in 1854 and served the diocese in numerous capacities until 1867. During these early years in Toronto, Walsh earned a reputation for eloquence, political moderation, and conciliation in terms of Catholic-Protestant relations, no mean feat considering the sectarian tension and violence that marked the city in the 1850s and early 1860s. In the year of Confederation, Walsh was elected bishop of Sandwich (later London, Ontario), a post that he held with distinction until August 1889, when he was translated to the Archdiocese of Toronto.[26]

Although Irish-born, Walsh was convinced that the Irish immigrants and their descendants had to make Canada the primary focus of their loyalty. Walsh had lived in Canada since 1852, which may account for his greater sensitivity to the changes taking place in Canadian society, especially among second- and third-generation Irish Canadians. His desire for Catholics to live in peace with non-Catholics and for his flock to cultivate a loyalty to Canada was eulogized in 1898 by the *Catholic Record*: "He administered his important charge with great recognized ability and endeared himself to all his flock, while outside his bounds his ability, fairness and moderation caused him to be held in the highest esteem and respect."[27] Such accolades, from all religious groups, appear somewhat ironic considering that upon his return to Toronto in 1889, his carriage was stoned by a rowdy gang of Orange Young Britons.[28]

From the moment of his installation Walsh requested that the clergy and laity take a greater interest and pride in things Canadian. Throughout his career he encouraged Catholics to work to build the Church in "this free and noble country," a description of Canada he used frequently.[29] In 1889, at a meeting of students at De La Salle College, he was unequivocal about his primary loyalty to Canada and her institutions, and implied this should be the attitude of Catholic youth as well:

I am a Canadian in heart and sympathy. I admire the country, I admire its constitution, I admire its people. We should inculcate in our boys the best sentiments of patriotism and love of country, for this is their country ... Let us love our country despite the injustice preached against us at the present time – an injustice which will not, which cannot prevail in a free country.[30]

In this spirit he encouraged young men to join with Protestant Canadians in the building of Canada, to be socially and economically mobile, to seek public office, and, most importantly, to embrace the priestly vocation. Walsh was convinced that the Catholic Church would never be Canadian until it had a native-born clergy.[31]

In making his appeals on behalf of Canada, however, Walsh never completely abandoned the cause of Ireland; in fact he saw the two dreams as complementary. As a young priest in Toronto he had been an articulate moderate Irish nationalist, advocating a constitutional settlement as opposed to violence.[32] In 1895 he suggested that Irishmen from every continent meet to resolve the Home Rule problem in Ireland and heal the painful rift among the members of the remnants of Parnell's Parliamentary Party. A year later his idea bore fruit in the form of the Irish Race Convention, held in Dublin.[33] Yet, despite his on-going concern about Irish politics, Walsh was cautious about the limits of involvement in Irish affairs; he warned members of Toronto's Irish associations: "I say to you stand by the old land and its memories and traditions; but at the same time stand by Canada as your home and country."[34] Walsh's premise was fairly clear: any man who was loyal to the land of his birth would be, by nature, loyal to the land of his adoption, but the latter should never be in doubt. For Walsh the quality of loyalty was inborn; once a person had demonstrated loyalty, it was easily called upon throughout life.

John Walsh provided the bridge between the assertive Irish leadership of his predecessor and the profound attachment to Canada espoused by his episcopal successors. While Lynch held up Canada's Dominion status as a model for Irish independence,[35] Walsh praised the country itself, its people, and its promise, inviting his flock to take pride in their citizenship. These words were reinforced by his co-operation with the Protestant community and the air of toleration engendered by his episcopate. In 1896, at the opening of St Cecilia's Church in the west end of Toronto, and in the presence of the mayor of the city, Walsh called for sectarian peace a prerequisite for nation-building:

This country wants peace and good feeling in our social life, in our relations with one another as citizens of a common country. Let us strive for it as men, as Christians, as neighbors; let us strive to build up a great country; let us strive to make this country of ours what it ought to be and what it shall be – the home of millions of prosperous, free and happy citizens. This is what should be done by Protestants and Catholics, and this is what the Protestant people of this town have done – as Christian men they have shown an example of tolerance and liberality.[36]

Through Walsh's example, the laity and clergy were given reason to concentrate their energies on the new land, Canada, whose laws offered them freedom and equality. At the same time, Toronto's Protestants were so impressed with Walsh that the *Canadian Churchman*, an

Anglican weekly, eulogized: "Being what you are, we wish you were ours."[37]

Walsh's death in 1898, appears to have provoked some unusual behaviour among the clergy of southern Ontario. In English Canada the tradition of nominating successor bishops was now fairly well established. One could be elevated to a see by merit of being the duly ordained coadjutor of a diocese. This was how Lynch succeeded Charbonnel. In the absence of a coadjutor, the surviving bishops of the ecclesiastical province normally drew up a list of three names, or a terna, in which the prospective candidates were listed in descending order, from the "dignissimus" (the most worthy) down to the "dignus" (the worthy). The terna was then submitted to other archbishops for opinion, and frequently to selected priests and heads of religious orders who might have pertinent information on the candidates. The terna was ultimately submitted to Rome, with comments attached, and the Pope made the final decision. After the appointment of an Apostolic Delegate to Canada in 1899, the selection process was co-ordinated by the Pope's representative.

The vacancies that arose in 1898 with the deaths of Walsh in Toronto and Cleary in Kingston released a growing movement among Canadian clergy to nominate Canadian-born men to the vacant sees in Canada. Both clergy and laity had expressed hostility to the continued appointment of Irishmen who had little knowledge of Canadian culture and local traditions. Father P. Corcoran from Parkhill went so far as to appeal to Sir John A. Macdonald for help in securing Canadian-born bishops. He argued that the priests of Ontario wanted an end to the appointment of bishops from other countries. The selection of an indigenized episcopacy "would conduce to the welfare of our Dominion" by providing leaders who "would better understand the manners and customs and wants of the clergy and laity, and would work more harmoniously with the general population of the country."[38] Corcoran's plea was by no means isolated. When it was rumoured, in 1898, that Cleary of Kingston was to be succeeded by the Bishop of Waterford, Ireland, the *Catholic Record* remarked: "This is not home rule exactly."[39] In a historic moment, the priests in the Diocese of Kingston met and selected the terna for Cleary's successor themselves. True to the wave of anti-foreign feeling, they chose Charles Hugh Gauthier of Trenton, Ontario. Such electoral practices, although rare in Ontario, were commonplace in England, Ireland, and, more recently, the United States.[40]

Priests in the Archdiocese of Toronto were by no means unaware of the new spin put on the term "Home Rule." When Walsh's successor Denis O'Connor abruptly resigned in 1908, local priests were enraged that they had never been informed about either the resignation or the selection of a successor. Relieved that the "melancholy, peevish and incapable" O'Connor was gone, they were furious that they had been ignored in the process to appoint a successor.[41] When Fergus McEvay, O'Connor's successor, died in 1911, Toronto's priests distributed a circular among themselves asking for the local clergy to present three names as candidates for the see. The three names with "the highest number of votes" would be submitted to the Apostolic Delegate under the pretext that "this mode is nearest to canonical election which the Holy See will recognize."[42] Some priests gathered in clandestine meetings to discuss suitable candidates, and continued to do so, defiant of the strong warnings from the Apostolic Delegate that such meetings had no official sanction and were not the custom of the country.[43] It appears that the priests were willing to risk censure in order to free themselves from bishops who had little sensitivity to the traditions and precarious history of the Catholic minority in Ontario. The experiment in democratic home rule was short lived; in June 1911 the bishops of the province of Toronto met in Berlin, Ontario, and submitted an official terna to the Apostolic Delegate.[44] Undeterred by earlier warnings, a large body of priests gathered again to submit their own terna, consisting of three "home-grown" pastors. Their suggestions were met with a glacial rebuke from the Apostolic Delegate.[45]

The growing assertiveness of Toronto's priests had come as a result of the desire for "home rule" and their wish to avoid the selection of bishops like Denis O'Connor. On paper, the appointment of O'Connor had seemed to be in tune with the times. Born in Pickering, Ontario, in 1841, he was the first native-born bishop of the archdiocese and, as such, was a shining example of Canadians taking hold of their own ecclesiastical affairs. As a Basilian Father he was a member of one of the most prominent religious orders in southwestern Ontario. The Basilians had founded Toronto's St Michael's College in 1852 and had been responsible for the preparatory education of many of Ontario's priests. O'Connor himself resurrected the floundering Assumption College in Windsor, and in his twenty years as its superior, from 1870 to 1890, he had garnered a reputation as an excellent teacher, builder, and administrator.[46] When the shy O'Connor was nominated to succeed Bishop Walsh in London in 1890, the appointment was hailed by Catholic clergy and lay leaders as inspired.[47] After a quiet sojourn in London he was elevated to the Archiepiscopal See of Toronto in 1899, shortly after the death of Walsh. There is a note of foreshadowing, or impending doom, in the sentiments passed on to him by his sister Lizzie. She offered no congratulations, because she knew he would work in Toronto until he could "work no more."

All she could offer him was her prayers. Similarly, when reflecting upon his arrival in the Queen's City, the *Catholic Register* reminisced that he seemed to be "a person weighted down with a sense of responsibility, unsought and somewhat dreaded."[48]

O'Connor's leadership style was antithetical to Walsh's. The latter's openness to all Torontonians and especially his "nation-building" rhetoric appear to have been foreign to O'Connor's temperament. He eschewed cultural events, did not mingle with the business and social elites of the city, resisted any temptation to involve himself in politics, and retreated from the public appearances that Walsh had used to increase the public profile of the Catholic community. O'Connor felt that such activities were incompatible with Christian humility.[49] The new bishop was so modest and shy that he allowed himself to be photographed only once, in 1883, when he was superior of Assumption College. For the remaining years of his life this was the only photograph used for public purposes – after 1890 a pectoral cross had to be airbrushed into the original photograph to denote his episcopal office.[50] Walsh's leadership style, which emphasized piety and patriotism, was abandoned by O'Connor. The public presence of the Church waned; the laity began to grumble; and priests were near revolt.

Denis O'Connor's singular preoccupation as bishop was his insistence on liturgical uniformity and strict obedience to the canons of the Church. His ecclesiology stressed unfailing orthodoxy and orthopraxy.[51] He was disgusted by what he witnessed among the city's Catholics, whom he felt mingled too freely with the Protestant elements of the city. In 1900 he reported to Diomede Falconio, the Apostolic Delegate, that Catholics in Toronto were in danger of losing their faith because of their attendance in public schools, their habit of seeking the "good society" in clubs and associations, their acquiescence to ideas generated in the local press, and, most distressing of all, their intermarriage with non-Catholics. For O'Connor these circumstances produced "tepid Catholics, who without living as Catholic, like to die as such."[52] If there was any leadership needed in Toronto, it was that of the shepherd who would preserve his flock from the wolves of modernity that lay ready to pounce upon them.

In this sense O'Connor was reflecting the fears that characterized the pontificate of Pius x (1903–14). Integrist Catholics under Pius x girded themselves for battle against secularism, rationalism, and anticlericalism, and the dissent generated by the alleged Americanist and Modernist heresies. Pius x, whose motto was "Instuare omnia in Christo" (Restore all things in Christ), emphasized the authority of the Church's magisterium, recodified canon law, condemned the so-called Modernist theologians, regularized Catholic marriage, and reformed liturgical music.[53] In the same spirit O'Connor set about restoring the Church in Toronto in the hope of isolating Catholics from the excesses of North American life, even to the extent of encouraging Catholics to cluster their settlement around local churches.[54] He was categorical in his obedience to Rome, applying Church regulations and canons to the letter.

There was little emphasis in O'Connor's leadership of Toronto's Catholics on social mobility, economic security, political activism, or patriotism. On the contrary, he discouraged a high degree of Catholic assertiveness in Canadian society:

We must all learn to bear and forebear – to bear our share in everything that tends to the well-being of the country, and at the same time to forebear, that is to say, to be ready to sacrifice occasionally some of our rights, because by doing this ... we show how ready we are to produce the good which is expected of us. As it is proper we ought to insist upon our rights, let us not forget that rights pushed too far become wrongs, grievous wrongs. [55]

While admitting a love of his country, he was insistent on the primacy of a Christian's duty to God, claiming "only in that country in which religion is respected, in which God always stands first, that there can be prosperity."[56]

What is significant about O'Connor's term of leadership is the resistance of Toronto's Catholics to his ideas of isolationism and canonical rigidity. His attempts to reform the life of the clergy, religious, and laity backfired, and perhaps revealed the great extent to which Catholics were prepared to acclimatize themselves to the rhythms of English Canadian life. Prominent priests like John Teefy and J.L. Hand complained to Rome that O'Connor's "repression" bred "indifference in both priests and people."[57] His insistence on orthopraxy – especially in matters of parish social activities and mixed marriages – forced the Catholics of Toronto to choose between strict adherence to Church law and a flexible response, conditioned by the reality of being a small minority in a non-Catholic city. They chose the latter, thereby formalizing, in a religious sense, their greater willingness to participate more actively in the urban world around them. Near rebellion by the priests and laity, and his failure to turn the clock back to an isolated Catholicism, prompted O'Connor's resignation from Toronto in 1908.[58]

By contrast, Fergus Patrick McEvay, O'Connor's immediate successor, was an attractive and well-loved leader. Born in Lindsay, Ontario, in 1856, he was raised in Ennismore Township, although much of his early education was pursued at the separate school in Lindsay. In

1874 he entered St Michael's College in Toronto, where he earned high honours in history and English.[59] After a brief sojourn at St Francis de Sales Seminary in Milwaukee, McEvay returned to Toronto for a pre-seminary year at St Michael's. Between 1880 and 1882 he completed his licence in theology at the Grand Séminaire in Montreal. Thus, McEvay spent his entire academic preparation in North America, quite the opposite of O'Connor, who was weaned in the rigidly ultramontane environment of Basilian colleges in France.[60]

On 9 July 1882 McEvay was ordained in Trenton, Ontario, by Bishop James Vincent Cleary of Kingston, and was loaned immediately to the new diocese of Peterborough. There he was pastor at Fenelon Falls, in his native Victoria County, an apostolate that included mission churches scattered throughout the lake-filled highlands, serving a predominantly Irish and French Canadian Catholic population of between 1,000 and 1,800.[61] In 1889 he accompanied his bishop, Thomas Dowling, to Hamilton, where McEvay had a better opportunity to display his pastoral and administrative talents. Described as a "progressive and broad-minded Hamiltonian,"[62] he was appointed Bishop of London in 1899, succeeding O'Connor, who was translated to Toronto. Within a decade McEvay would follow O'Connor again.

Although he served in Toronto for only three years, from 1908 to 1911, McEvay provided a welcome relief from O'Connor's "strong and austere personality."[63] His infectious personality and well-hewn pastoral skills made him extremely popular among clergy and laity both, to the extent that he was praised highly, even in O'Connor's obituary: "Everyone felt the magnetic thrill of a strong, kindly, tactful, progressive personality, and there was sunshine in the hearts as well as around them."[64] To Toronto he brought a wealth of experience derived from a Catholic education in a non-Catholic environment, and impressive pastoral credentials that included administering to Catholic minorities in Ontario's rural Orange heartland in Victoria County and in the bustling urban centres of London and Hamilton. This first-hand experience of meeting the challenges of Catholic life in a Protestant world better prepared McEvay for the pressing task of being chief Catholic pastor in the alleged Belfast of North America. McEvay knew the enormity of this appointment. "Toronto is a difficult city to manage both for the Church and the State," he confessed to Sir Wilfrid Laurier, "and while I hope to be conciliatory no doubt there will be local religious storms sometimes."[65]

McEvay was essentially the first "Canadian" bishop of Toronto whose national vision and model of episcopal leadership eclipsed that of Walsh. Catholic journalists in Toronto considered McEvay's insistence that Catholics fully participate in national life one of the most important contributions of his episcopacy:

He loved the country, and on all occasions strove to induce the best good feeling amongst all classes and creeds within its borders. He used to say "Canada will be a great country. The Church of God must do its part to make a good country, or what will it all avail?" ... he had a statesman's view in public matters, and a patriot's heart in promoting the common good. There was nothing narrow or sectional about him. He detested race bickerings and despised national agitators ... The Catholic Church was his model. What she accepted he accepted, and Canadian nationality he believed was good enough for all.[66]

His accommodation of new immigrant Catholic groups and their liturgies into the Church in Toronto, his establishment of an English-speaking Catholic seminary, and his founding of the Catholic Church Extension Society – to bring the Catholic faith in the medium of the English language to home missions[67] – clearly demonstrated McEvay's Canadian orientation. In all of these efforts McEvay called upon English-speaking Catholics to be Canadian nation-builders and leaders of the Catholic Church outside of Quebec.

The importance of McEvay's unabashed Canadianism cannot be overemphasized. Buoyed by his personality and sustained by his vigorous expansion of Church structures both in and out of Toronto, McEvay provided his flock with an example that Church membership did not preclude participation in the life of the nation. His work with immigrants in the inner city made English-speaking Catholics realize they had a large role to play in the integration of newcomers into Canadian society. This alone provided them with a greater sense of their own Canadian identity. Institutions such as St Augustine's Seminary helped to reinforce this ethos as well as Toronto's independence from the French Canadian arm of the Church, which for centuries had dominated Catholic life in central Canada.

With a similar intent McEvay moulded the Ontario episcopate into a better-co-ordinated cadre of Catholic leaders. He considered the unity of Ontario's bishops to be essential for arguing the cause of separate schools in Ontario and thwarting the influence of French Canadian nationalism in the Church outside of Quebec. His vision was of a vibrant Church, of Catholics actively engaged in the life of the nation, and of the paramount importance of the use of English if Catholics were to achieve their potential as Canadian citizens. McEvay was resolute that French Canadian control of the Church in Ontario be limited. He informed Pope Pius x that the Ontario hierarchy had been and would continue to be generous to the interests of Ontario's francophone Catholics, but that the work of the bishops had been hampered by a group of prelates and politicians, mostly from Quebec, "who seem to place race before religion and language before faith."[68] In the course of the debates over language, schools, and missions McEvay not only quietly established himself as the English-speaking Catholic leader; he renewed the episcopal prominence of the Archdiocese of Toronto as English Canada's most influential see. He also created a more tightly knit network among the ecclesiastical provinces of English Canada, and in 1909 secured their position in Rome when he and Archbishop Edward McCarthy of Halifax hired an agent or procurator to represent them in the Vatican.[69] Under McEvay's unassuming leadership the archbishop of Toronto and his fellow bishops became more effective players in ecclesiastical politics and respected voices in the civil arena.

McEvay undertook these many tasks despite the fact that he was plagued by recurring battles with pernicious anaemia. On 10 May 1911 he lost his fight with this blood disorder, and local priests and bishops scrambled to find a successor. After one failed terna, the Vatican finally selected Vancouver's Archbishop Neil McNeil. Toronto's new bishop was no stranger to the Canadian Church. Born in the Scottish hamlet of Hillsboro, Mabou parish, Nova Scotia, in 1851, McNeil was educated in the local public school, and later at St Francis Xavier University in Antigonish and in the Urban College, Rome, where, in 1879, he earned his doctorate. In his varied career he served as pastor to the Acadians of Cape Breton Island (1880, 1891–95), vice-rector and then president of St Francis Xavier University (1880–91), and editor of the Casket (1890–92), the widely read Catholic weekly in eastern Nova Scotia. In 1895 he was consecrated titular bishop of Nilopolis and Apostolic Vicar to St George's, Newfoundland. His reputation as pastor and pioneer prompted his transfer, in 1910, to the Archiepiscopal See of Vancouver.[70] Upon assuming the mantle of archbishop of Toronto, McNeil had trod far from his anticipated career – to follow in the footsteps of his blacksmith father, with whom he had apprenticed as a boy.[71]

McNeil's initial ambition in Toronto was to complete the programs initiated by McEvay. If McEvay was the first "Canadian" bishop of Toronto, McNeil was surely the first twentieth-century bishop. He completed McEvay's seminary, reformed the Catholic Church Extension Society, expanded the structures of Catholic charitable work, and increased the number of ethnic parishes.[72] McNeil, however, went well beyond the foundations laid by his immediate predecessor. He was the first bishop in the city to come to terms with the side-effects of the mushrooming urban-industrial complex. He founded hostels for immigrants and working women, infant's homes and orphanages, new parishes for suburban dwellers, and further soothed the traditional tensions between Catholics and Protestants in the city. McNeil, the former blacksmith, became an advocate for working people, supporting unions, social justice, and a broadening of education. Like his fellow Cape Bretoners of the Antigonish Movement – Fathers Moses Coady and James Tompkins – McNeil saw education as the key to social and economic advancement. "What we must aim at," he told his nephew John R. MacDonald, "if as Canadians we have any public spirit, and as Catholics have the interest of the Church at heart, is to place high school education within the reach of any family desirous of raising children above their own level of education."[73] At his Silver Jubilee, in 1920, the clergy referred to his first eight years in office as "a Golden Age in development in the Archdiocese."[74]

In several respects McNeil's leadership was marked by renewed attempts to reconcile the city's Catholics with English Canadian society. McNeil was renowned for his Canadian patriotism by both Catholics and Protestants, as was made clear in the tribute paid him by his priests during his jubilee: "Your zeal for education, your patriotism, your charity and your unselfishness have won for Your Grace the reputation of being one of the most admired and best beloved Churchmen in Canada."[75] Such adulation was not restricted to the Catholic community. That a group of local Presbyterians referred to him as "the best Presbyterian in Toronto" underscores the esteem in which McNeil was held by some Protestants in the city.[76] This rapprochement was reinforced by his active endorsement of the Canadian war effort from 1914 to 1918, and his toning down of the sometimes bigoted editorials of Alfred Burke in the *Catholic Register*. McNeil recognized what Denis O'Connor could not: "that a policy of isolationism is impossible and would be deadly for English-speaking Catholics in Canada."[77]

By 1922 the Toronto hierarchy no longer encouraged Catholic isolationism in the city. The policy of openness, initiated by Walsh, took formal shape under McEvay and McNeil. While the formation of separate Catholic institutions was still encouraged in order to foster and nurture the faith, bishops no longer looked at non-Catholic English Canada, or non-Catholic Torontonians, for that matter, with hostile suspicion. Catholics were encouraged to be less parochial and more national in their vision, creating in the process a greater identification of the advancement of Catholicism with the progress of the nation. As the head of the Catholic body, the archbishops, in becoming "Canadian," offered a sound precedent and clear direction to similar developments by the rest of the Church.

The bishops' encouragement of a greater openness to Canadian society was reflected in the men who were to carry out the episcopal will at the grass roots. In the ecclesiology of the period, in Toronto and elsewhere, the parish was the focus of local Catholic life, and the priest was to be the undisputed leader of the parish. "The success of the parish," argued Monsignor Alfred E. Burke, "is largely due to the executive ability of its spiritual head."[78] Few of his colleagues would have argued the point when he added that the priest was "the first necessity of the Church," who could take an area populated with "degenerate men" and "make it blossom as the rose."[79] Given such weighty expectations, it is not surprising that Canadianization of Toronto's priests would have a significant effect on the life of the Catholic community in the city. The priest's ability to understand and respond to the cultural, political, and social traditions of his flock, given his birth and education, is not to be underestimated. Local writer and pastor Dean William Richard Harris explained that while "the freedom accorded the Catholic Church by the laws of our country, and to the liberal and progressive spirit of a people and a land blessed by God" contributed to expansion of the Church, it was really the devotion and zeal of priests and bishops that made these advantages "operative" for Ontario's Catholics.[80] Reflecting the policies of Walsh, McEvay, and McNeil, and prominent in their rejection of O'Connor, the increasingly Canadian clergy of Toronto provided leadership that facilitated the integration of Catholics into their community.

The indigenization of the clergy in Toronto, however, was far more dramatic than that of the hierarchy. From 1887 to 1922 the composition of the archdiocesan clergy underwent significant transformations in terms of place of birth, education, discipline, and attitudes regarding Catholic isolation from Canadian society. At the end of the period, secular clergy in Toronto were generally Canadian born and educated, and often flexible in the way they approached some points of Church legislation in the context of a pluralistic Canadian environment. They were a distinct body, reinforced by their own seminary and no longer dependent on French Canadian institutions for their training. Moreover, they did not form a class independent of the laity but bore a great affinity to their roots and a remarkable degree of empathy for their parishioners.

In the nineteenth century the origins and education of priests in Toronto reflected the fact that this was still a pioneer diocese populated by immigrants. In 1873 nearly 80 per cent of the archdiocesan clergy had been born in Ireland.[81] By 1890 this figure had decreased to just over half the total number of priests in the archdiocese (see Table 2.1).

Table 2.1
English-speaking Catholic Secular Clergy, Archdiocese of Toronto, 1890–1920

Birthplace	1890	1895	1900	1905	1910	1915	1920	1930	1940
Toronto	3	4	3	5	7	11	18	31	42
	5.8	6.8	5.0	8.2	9.6	12.9	18.2	25.4	30.7
Archdiocese	6	10	13	17	24	30	32	42	43
	11.5	16.9	21.7	27.8	32.9	35.3	32.3	34.4	31.4
All other Canadian	7	10	8	7	10	12	13	12	8
	13.5	16.9	13.3	11.5	13.7	14.1	13.1	9.8	5.8
Total Cdn	16	24	24	29	41	53	63	85	93
	30.8	40.7	40.0	47.5	56.2	62.3	63.6	69.6	67.9
Ireland	28	29	30	27	25	22	24	19	15
	53.9	49.2	50.0	44.3	34.2	25.9	24.3	15.6	10.9
Other	7	4	6	5	7	8	9	10	12
	13.4	6.7	10.0	8.2	9.6	9.4	9.1	8.2	8.8
Unknown	1	2	0	0	0	2	3	8	17
	1.9	3.4			2.4	3.0	6.6	12.4	
Total	52	59	60	61	73	85	99	122	137

Sources: ARCAT, Priests' Files; Father Edward Kelly Papers; *Sadlier's Catholic Almanac and Ordo*, 1890–95; *Hoffman's Catholic Almanac*, 1896–1900; *The Official Catholic Directory, Almanac and Clergy List Quarterly* (Milwaukee: M.H. Wiltzius 1901–11); *The Official Catholic Directory* (New York: P.J. Kennedy and Sons 1912–13, 1921); *The Ontario Catholic Year Book and Directory* (Toronto: Newman Club 1914–20).

Most of these Irish-born priests were educated at the missionary seminary of All Hallows in Dublin, or in such local schools as St Patrick's, Maynooth, or St Brendan's, Killarney.[82] They bore the distinct imprint of the Irish ultramontane revival of the 1850s and its emphasis on unquestioned obedience to Rome, doctrinal orthodoxy, and devotional purity.[83] When we consider that these secular priests were added to the Basilians of St Michael's College and St Basil's parish, who were predominantly French and Irish by birth, it is clear that the 60,000 Catholics of the archdiocese were in the hands of a clergy that was overwhelmingly foreign.[84]

At the beginning of his episcopacy Archbishop Walsh realized the importance of cultivating a Canadian-born clergy that would be able to lead future generations of Canadian-born Catholics. That there were only three Toronto-born priests in the archdiocese at Walsh's succession in 1888 indicates the serious uphill fight that faced the new Metropolitan. In a pastoral issued in 1890, Walsh asserted:

It can truly be affirmed that the Church will never be firmly established in this country until it possesses a native Priesthood – until it is interlaced with the feelings, affections, and national habits and traditions of the people – until, in fine, it is made "racy with the soil," like some giant oak that has grown gradually up in our forests, spreading its roots abroad, and driving them deep into the soil and deriving therefrom its sap and nourishment, until it has acquired the sturdy strength and magnificent proportions that bid defiance from the fiercest storms.[85]

Walsh encouraged local Catholic parents to send their sons to parochial schools and seminaries to ensure the growth of a priesthood that was indigenously Canadian. As was the custom, the archbishop promised to pay all of the candidates' tuition fees and board at the seminary.[86]

After 1895 the numbers of native-born secular priests grew rapidly. In that year the Irish-born clergy were still a majority, although Canadian-born men represented 40 per cent of the archdiocese's priests. Ten years later Canadians, of whom at least one-third were born in the archdiocese, had overtaken the Irish-born clergy. Finally, by 1920, the composition of Toronto's Catholic priests had completely reversed itself from what it had been in 1890. Well over 60 per cent of the clergy were Canadian born, and the majority had been born in the city of Toronto and other deaneries in the archdiocese. The Irish-born priests, once the mainstay of the front-line clergy, were less than one-quarter of the total and were usually over fifty years of age. New recruits no longer came from Ireland but from the ranks of the city's own Catholic young men. By the 1920s clerical home rule in Toronto was clearly a fact.

Similar patterns can be detected among some of the religious orders in the city. The Congregation of St Basil, by far the most important and largest male congregation in the city, became increasingly indigenized over the period. While there was a high percentage of French priests serving at St Michael's College and in St Basil's and Holy Rosary parishes, Canadians constituted the largest English-speaking component in the congregation. Because of the high rate of mobility and transfer among Basilians, it is difficult to isolate the growth of Canadian membership in the city. Although over half of the congregation serving in Toronto at any given time were Canadian born, the number of Canadian-born Basilians serving in Ontario between 1887 and 1922 topped

Table 2.2
Congregation of St Basil,
Birthplace of Members Serving in North America, 1887–1922

Birthplace	No.	%
Toronto, city	8	7.4
Toronto. rural archdiocese	12	11.1
Other Ontario	42	38.9
Other Canada	3	2.8
Ireland	9	8.3
United Kingdom & Nfld	5	4.6
United States	14	13.0
France	15	13.9
Other	0	0.0
Total	108	100

Source: *Dictionary of Basilian Biography,* ed. Robert Scollard, CSB (Toronto: Basilian Press 1969). All calculations are mine.

60 per cent (see Table 2.2).[87] These Canadians challenged the leadership of Father Victorin Marijon, the North American Provincial of the congregation (1890–1907), and advocated a more open and democratic administrative structure within the order. The strains between the new English-speaking Canadian-born Basilians and their French colleagues came to a head in 1922, when the congregation split and a distinctive North American community was created.[88]

The assumption of a new leadership style had been evident among the Basilians long before the split. The education offered to Catholic men at St Michael's College changed dramatically in 1910, when this Basilian College became federated with the liberal arts program at the University of Toronto.[89] The formal federation of St Michael's with its giant secular neighbour prompted the tiny Catholic college to change its curriculum from a narrow classical program, copied from the Basilian schools in France, to a more comprehensive North American liberal arts education. Subsequently the college offered students a much broader education, for which they could receive official accreditation. The availability of good secondary and post-secondary education, as well as an English-Canadian seminary, provided important catalysts for the growth of an indigenized clergy.

Promoting the ordination of Canadian-born men was only the first step in the Canadianization of the clergy. Acquiring a native-born clergy was of only minimal value if they were trained outside Ontario, as was the case for Toronto's priests prior to the First World War. In the late nineteenth century Archbishop Lynch relied heavily on his alma mater, All Hallow's College in Dublin, for the education of his priests.[90] Occasionally priests were sent to American seminaries, and the most gifted men were sometimes sponsored by the archdiocese to study in Rome or enrol in the five-year program at Brignole Sale Seminary in Genoa, Italy.[91] In general, however, Lynch and all his successors except McNeil also depended on the Grand Séminaire of Montreal, run by the Sulpician Fathers, for the preparation of Toronto seminarians for ordination.[92] In an effort to make Toronto more independent in clerical formation Lynch had founded the diocesan Seminary of St Mary and St John at Our Lady of Lourdes parish in 1885, but this was only a minor seminary and its candidates were still required to attend the Grand Séminaire if they desired ordination (see Table 2.3).[93] Logically, English-speaking Catholic independence from Irish and French Canadian seminaries would only be achieved if Toronto had its own major seminary, both to prepare priests for ordination and to reinforce priestly discipline among young men who had been recently ordained.

In 1899, and without investing in a major seminary, Denis O'Connor took a significant step towards the goal of upgrading the education of Toronto's youngest priests. Although he was a firm believer in the rigorous training offered by the Sulpicians in Montreal, O'Connor believed that younger priests became lazy and undisciplined in the archdiocese after only a few short years out of the seminary.[94] Consequently, he instituted semi-annual meetings of the diocesan clergy at which all priests ordained for less than four years would be examined on all aspects of their vocation. The idea was by no means unique; O'Connor was influenced by his own Basilian training in France and the recommendations of the Council of Toronto in 1875.[95] Earlier, in 1882, Archbishop Lynch had instituted similar exams for the clergy at St Mary's and St John's Seminary, but the program fizzled within six months.[96] O'Connor's intentions were inspired less by a desire for independence from the control of the Grand Séminaire than by his firm belief in clerical discipline and obedience to the magisterium, particularly its decree for the establishment of a seminary in every diocese. This dimension of O'Connor's effort to approximate the disciplinary and liturgical regeneration in Rome failed to outlive his episcopate, and in the end only created near-revolt among his priests.

Table 2.3
Education of Priests in Toronto, 1890–1920

Birth/education	1890	%	1900	%	1910	%	1920	%
CANADIAN-BORN	16	100.0	24	100.0	41	100.0	63	100.0
St Michael's*	10	62.5	14	58.3	30	73.2	49	77.8
Grand Seminary	10	62.5	17	70.8	31	75.6	27	42.9
Brignole Sale	3	18.8	5	20.8	5	12.2	5	7.9
Rome	0	0.0	0	0.0	1	2.4	2	3.2
St Augustine's	0	0.0	0	0.0	0	0.0	26	41.3
Other Canada	2	12.5	1	4.2	0	0.0	0	0.0
Other foreign	1	6.2	1	4.2	4	9.8	3	4.7
No data	0	0.0	0	0.0	0	0.0	0	0.0
IRISH-BORN	28	100.0	30	100.0	25	100.0	20	100.0
St Michael's*	7	25.0	7	23.3	3	12.0	4	20.0
Grand Seminary	7	25.0	11	36.7	5	20.0	4	20.0
All Hallows (Dublin)	6	21.4	9	30.0	5	20.0	4	20.0
St Patrick (Maynooth)	0	0.0	1	3.3	1	4.0	1	5.0
St Brendan (Killarney)	1	3.6	0	0.0	0	0.0	0	0.0
Rome	2	7.2	3	10.0	3	12.0	3	15.0
Brignole Sale	3	10.7	3	10.0	3	12.0	1	5.0
Other Canada	0	0.0	0	0.0	0	0.0	2	10.0
Other foreign	6	21.4	3	10.0	6	24.0	5	25.0
No data	3	10.7	0	0.0	2	8.0	0	0.0
OTHER-BORN	7	100.0	6	100.0	7	100.0	9	100.0
St Michael's*	4	57.1	4	66.7	4	57.1	3	33.3
Grand Seminary	5	71.4	5	83.3	4	57.1	2	22.2
Rome	0	0.0	0	0.0	0	0.0	0	0.0
Other Canada	0	0.0	0	0.0	0	0.0	1	11.1
Other foreign	0	0.0	1	16.7	1	14.3	2	22.2
No data	2	28.6	0	0.0	2	28.6	4	44.5

* The figures for priests educated at St Michael's are also included in the figures for the other seminaries following.

Source: ARCAT, Priests' Files.

On 28 November 1899 O'Connor's first examination of priests was held at St Michael's Cathedral. At that time the curates were required to present a written sermon on a pre-arranged topic and then attempt written and oral examinations on scripture, dogmatic theology, moral theology, church history, canon law, catechism, and liturgy.[97] Senior clergy presided over each session, and junior clergy (ordained more than four years but less than eight) served as auxiliary examiners. The final evaluations, however, were made by the more experienced priests, a professional theologian, and O'Connor himself.

In the short term the examination process proved to be a humiliating experience for many priests. Evaluations of the priests' work were frequently blunt and coldly impersonal. In 1904, for example, the prepared sermons on "The Immaculate Conception" exposed the weaknesses of the younger clergy in dogmatic theology, organization, and defining terminology. Typically, examiners chastised one fellow for excessive verbosity: "This sermon covers ten and a half pages before we reach the Immaculate Conception. Such a portico would lead one to look for an edifice of far vaster proportions than the one we have here."[98] Results on some scripture examinations were worse; in 1902 the class average was a meagre 61.1 per cent.[99] On other occasions, however, the priests proved equal to the task: in 1903 the candidates shone in Church History, with a class average of over 80 per cent, and sermons on Guardian Angels and expositions on the Sacrament of Confirmation brought comparable marks.[100] These inconsistent examination results, from subject to subject and from year to year, underscore the ineffectiveness of O'Connor's program.

In the long term O'Connor's effort to reassume his persona of schoolmaster, dating from his presidency of Assumption College,[101] destroyed good relations between him and his youngest priests. The clergymen involved left no record describing their reaction to the examination experience, but judging from O'Connor's own reminiscences, the examinations did not reverse his growing unpopularity among the clergy. O'Connor had banned parish picnics, removed women from church choirs, and stymied parish fund-raising door-to-door. Priests were forbidden to ride bicycles on account of his belief that it would "lower the dignity of the priest who rides them."[102] For the many priests who could not afford horses, the bicycle ban hampered their ability to make emergency sick calls and visit with regularity the far reaches of their parishes. Leading priests like John Teefy and J.L. Hand complained to Rome of the low morale among the priests and the fussy and abusive behaviour of the bishop. "I am not well regarded by one third of the clergy," wrote O'Connor to the prefect of the Propaganda Fide, "and the others are not all zealous friends."[103]

Throughout his career O'Connor clashed with a succession of local priests who openly defied him. In 1903 Father Lancelot Minehan of St Peter's parish mobilized parishioners to protest O'Connor's failure to provide a salary for Minehan's brother, the "alleged" assistant pastor. The Apostolic Delegate resolved the matter, admonishing the Minehans for "unpriestly conduct" but also ordering O'Connor to pay the salary.[104] Similar disagreements erupted between O'Connor and other priests over their support for parish socials and leniency in mixed marriages, two practices O'Connor vehemently opposed. Many priests appealed directly to the Vatican to overturn O'Connor's intransigence on the mixed marriages.[105] With respect to other sacraments O'Connor, who favoured monthly reception of the Eucharist, chided Father John Mary Fraser for his endorsement of weekly reception. When Father Hugh Canning, the locally born director of religious education, agreed with Fraser, and Pope Pius x later encouraged daily reception for all Catholics, O'Connor was further alienated from some of his priests.[106]

O'Connor's personal rigour and literalism in the application of canon law widened the gulf between him and his priests. But one could also ask whether something was happening to Toronto's Roman Catholic priests. In the early twentieth century Toronto's priests were more and more the products of a rapidly changing North American environment, and, while no less devout in their adherence to the theology and teachings of the Church, they were more sensitive to the Church's place within the Canadian context. What O'Connor and some others might interpret as laxity was perhaps the emergence of a concerted effort by Canadian priests to respond more pastorally than litigiously to life in Toronto. Unlike O'Connor, who was raised and educated in French Basilian seminaries, renowned for their rigid ultramontanism and hostility to the modern world,[107] Toronto's priests were increasingly sons of the soil who had been educated in Canadian high schools – some of them public schools – and in Canadian minor and major seminaries. This indigenous clergy had been raised and educated as a minority in a predominantly Protestant province and realized that compromise was needed in order to ensure Catholic survival. Doctrinaire positions on marital, religious, and social matters were potentially harmful to the Catholic community. Such sensitivity to the plight of the Catholic minority, especially in marital cases, was foreign to O'Connor's vision of Catholic isolationism, nor was it universally appreciated by Catholic leaders. Father Hugh Canning, listed as the dignissimus on the terna to succeed Archbishop Gauthier of Kingston, was dismissed by one adjudicator because he came from a Protestant background (his father) and he still bore the imprint of that upbringing.[108] Similarly, Victorin Marijon, csb, admitted to Rome that he could not trust the local priests who had attended public schools because they were never able to rid themselves of the taint of Protestantism.[109] O'Connor's solution, isolation from the world and the re-education of young clergy, was rejected by the local clergy – perhaps the most compelling reason for his resignation in 1908.[110]

McEvay changed this approach to the clergy and clerical education and, in so doing, hastened the process of the Canadianization of the clergy. When the wealthy Catholic brewer Eugene O'Keefe wanted to erect a church dedicated to St Augustine in addition to his previous donation of a church in honour of St Monica, Father Martin Whelan convinced him to redirect his funds to establish a seminary. McEvay agreed that a seminary would honour the decree of the First Canadian Plenary Council (1909) that a seminary be established for each ecclesiastical province, as part of an effort to recruit priests for the dioceses and to meet the needs of the home missions in the prairie west. Initially O'Keefe donated $400,000 to the project, adding another $100,000 by the time the seminary was completed in 1913.[111] O'Keefe's generosity made it possible for the archdiocese to purchase land near the Scarborough Bluffs and to build a large structure, housing a chapel, sleeping quarters, library, classrooms, and recreation facilities.

The new seminary was central to the changing ethos of English-speaking Catholics of Toronto for three reasons: it offered them independence from the French Canadian Church for the education of clergy; it became a focus for the national vision of Toronto's Catholics to build the Church in Canada under English-speaking auspices; and it became a source of triumphalism, holding out the possibility of the conversion of Protestant Canada. Its English-speaking character and national role was unmistakable from its very beginning. At the seminary's opening a prominent layman, Michael J. Haney, emphasized the importance of the location of St Augustine's in the centre of English-speaking Canada as "God's work." The Catholic Register argued that the "hopes and ideals" of the Church in Canada focused on St Augustine's, where "an army of self-sacrificing men are preparing for the mission field, equipping themselves to carry the message of the cross to all parts of this country."[112] McEvay affirmed that the seminary was not to be strictly diocesan but open to all candidates from across the nation.[113] Only an institution with a national focus could provide priests for Toronto while also tending to the needs of the Maritimes and the mission fields of the west.[114]

This dual religious and patriotic vision for the seminary was brought into sharper focus by Archbishop Neil McNeil. Shortly after his arrival in Toronto in 1912, McNeil emphasized the contribution St Augustine's could make to Canadian nation-building:

Students will come from distant parts of Canada and the United States. Our students will have the benefit of association with various racial elements which make up the population of Canada, with resulting enlargement of mind, and of Catholic sympathies ... A Seminary can do much to harmonize the many elements of Canada's population. Our Church and our Country are both vitally interested in securing this harmony. We have it in our power to do a great work for the Church and for Canada by means of St Augustine's Seminary, and the Catholic laity of this Archdiocese will respond to the call of duty and of patriotism. [115]

Later, in 1917, McNeil reaffirmed this patriotic commitment, explaining to the Propaganda Fide that the seminary accepted students from across Canada because "Nous chérissons l'espoir que le Séminaire ... contribuera en quelque mesure à l'unification nationale du Canada, en réunissant les élèves de toutes les patries du Canada."[116]

In its early years St Augustine's lived up to the local expectation that it would be an English-speaking Catholic training centre of national importance. In fact, the seminary eventually became an important component of an English-speaking Catholic clerical network that linked the Maritime provinces, Ontario, and the mission territory of the prairies and Pacific slope. With his strong ties to eastern and western Canada, McNeil was able to encourage bishops in eastern Nova Scotia, Newfoundland, Alberta, Manitoba, and British Columbia to send candidates for the priesthood to Toronto. Surpluses of priests in Atlantic Canada, and the lure of the frontier, made it easy for western Canadian bishops, many of whom were expatriate Maritimers, to cull prospective priests from St Augustine's for the mission dioceses of the west.[117] From 1913 to 1934, the year McNeil died, the Diocese of Antigonish alone sent forty-two students to St Augustine's. Several of these chose to serve in a diocese or apostolate other than that of Antigonish.[118] For a young John R. MacDonald, the future bishop of Peterborough and later his native Antigonish, St Augustine's provided both a valuable centre for priestly formation and a place where young men could develop a spirit of "fellowship and co-operation in Canada." His passion for Catholic unity in Canada was sufficient reason for him to apply to the seminary as a professor in 1921.[119]

In its formative decades St Augustine's provided theological and pastoral formation for seminarians from nearly every diocese in Canada, for missionaries in the China Mission Society, and, for a time, candidates for holy orders in the Byzantine Catholic rite.[120] J.T. Kidd, the first rector of the seminary, linked St Augustine's English-language character with the role of the school as a missionary college. Claiming that European Catholic immigrants were in need of clergy, he affirmed that "the English language would receive due attention" among the seminarians who would serve among new Canadians.[121] Hence the new seminary became both an expression of English-speaking Catholic independence in the area of clerical formation and an assertion of new confidence among Canadian clergy that the English-speaking Catholic Church, centred in Toronto, had a mission that extended "a mari usque ad mare."

There was yet a third significant dimension to the founding of St Augustine's: the conversion of all Canada. Such hopes that the legions of Canadian priests would evangelize the land were expressed without subtlety in Catholic literature at the time of the seminary's opening. In this spirit the Catholic literary magazine published quarterly by St Joseph's College, *St Joseph's Lilies*, likened the future of the institution to the life of its patron saint: "May St Augustine's Seminary, like its glorious patron, become a light and oracle of the faithful among English-speaking Canadians, and a peculiar object of Catholic love! The illustrious penitent by his wonderful conversion proved to the world that no crimes are too great for the God of all mercy to pardon, no heart too corrupt for his love to purify, no obstacle too great for his love to overcome."[122] The presence of St Augustine's boosted English-speaking Catholic confidence that not only would they secure a "Canadian" clergy of their own but that English-speaking Canadian priests were the vanguard of a Catholic apostolate to non-Catholic Canadians. This was no pipe-dream. The Vatican acknowledged the value of a strong English-speaking Catholic presence in Canada when, in 1909, it shocked the Church by appointing Michael Francis Fallon bishop of London. For Donatus Sbarretti, the Apostolic Delegate, not only was the English language destined to dominate Canada; men like Fallon were in the best position to convert the Protestants of Canada by means of their shared language.[123]

Language issues and national dream aside, McNeil's and the Catholic community's hopes for clerical formation at St Augustine's were generally fulfilled. Its first faculty included a mixed teaching staff of Canadians, Irishmen, and one Ukrainian who were responsible for executing a program that included moral, dogmatic, and pastoral theology, church history, liturgy, catechism, patrology, canon law, Greek, Latin, and French.[124] In 1916, 78 per cent of the seminarians at St Augustine's were Canadian-born, and represented thirteen dioceses from all regions of the country except Quebec. Seventeen Ukrainian men were being prepared for ordination in the Byzantine Catholic rite, thereby demonstrating St Augustine's commitment to immigrant constituencies within the Church.[125] Furthermore, to keep pace with the clerical training given to Protestant ministers in Canada, Toronto's priests convinced McNeil to ensure that all candidates had sufficient background in the liberal arts, at the university level. The new generation of priests felt that only a sound background in the humanities could make "Toronto priests leaders of thought and action in Ontario."[126]

By the early 1920s Toronto's Catholic community had attained Walsh's hope of a clergy rooted in the soil. The erection of St Augustine's ensured that the training of native-born clergy would be done in Toronto, under English-speaking Catholic auspices. With the apparatus in place to ensure clerical home rule, it is not surprising that, by 1940, over 70 per cent of the serving clergy in Toronto were Canadian. The importance of the indigenization of Toronto's priests cannot be overestimated. Given their roots, and consequent empathy with the laity in the disciplinary battles under Archbishop O'Connor, the affinity between priest and parishioner is clear. Even the foreign-born but Canadian-raised priests demonstrated a significant degree of accommodation to North American society and aspects of Canadian nationalism. Francis Ryan, rector of the Cathedral, and William Harris, the dean of St Catharines, both attended the Pan-American Congress of Religion in Chicago in 1895, despite the claims of some ardently conservative Catholic bishops that Catholic participation might be seen as condoning "heretical" Christian groups.[127] At a meeting of the "Old Boys' Club" in 1900 Harris waxed eloquent that prejudice was dying in Canada, and a strong nation was being built:

For never was there in the settlement of nations found such a splendid material for the building up of a great Dominion that which Providence has placed upon our territory. Here the daring sons of Japhet, the sons of liberty-loving races, have from the forests carved out their homes and hewed for themselves an abiding place. The stalwart and broad-shouldered Scotch, the slow-thinking but irresistible English, the imaginative and high spirited Irish, with the cheerful and hospitable French Canadian, are daily coalescing and from their loins there is begotten a race that, if true to itself, must be the greatest the world has ever seen.[128]

The Canadianized priesthood in Toronto, steeped in the traditions and peculiarities of a Catholic minority in a Protestant city, was an important component in the overall maturation of the entire Catholic community.

Between 1887 and 1922, women in religious orders shared in the transformation of Catholic leadership in Toronto. From the time of their foundations in Toronto in the late 1840s and early 1850s the two largest and most important religious orders in the archdiocese, the Institute of the Blessed Virgin Mary (Loretto Sisters) and the Congregation of St Joseph, witnessed dramatic growth in the number of their recruits. By 1911 the mere handful of CSJs and Lorettos who had arrived in Toronto in the wake of the Great Famine had flourished, growing to communities of 148 and 266 members respectively. Proportionally, these two orders constituted over 80 per cent of the women religious serving in the Archdiocese of Toronto.[129] Unfortunately, the leadership of the "nuns" has often been overshadowed by the men, clerical and lay, who dominated the most powerful and highest-profile administrative and deliberative positions in the Catholic Church. In reality the sisters, in their roles as teachers and professors, had a profound influence on the Catholic men and women in the pews. As the single largest group among separate school teachers in Toronto, the examples set, lessons taught, and cultural ambience nurtured by the sisters were an important part of the formation of new generations of Catholic Canadians. The actual work in the schools will be treated in detail later, but it is important to establish that the process of indigenization that characterized the personnel and training of the episcopacy and clergy was also a significant factor among the women religious of Toronto in this period.

The Loretto Sisters and Sisters of St Joseph contributed to the building of a home-grown Church in several ways. The most obvious development within these two orders by the 1920s was their overwhelming Canadian character. Their recruits were largely Ontario-born and educated. Secondly, recent studies by Elizabeth Smyth argue that the sisters defied the stereotype that they were conducting "finishing schools" led by "mothers inferior." In reality the Lorettos and Sisters of St Joseph provided Catholic women with a varied, multi-faceted, and challenging curriculum that not only easily met provincial standards but launched many Catholic women into professional, post-graduate, and religious careers. Finally, in their own right both orders adapted to their North American environment and, when the need arose, challenged internal dissent and episcopal disapproval of straying too far from the letter of the old rule. By the 1920s the Lorettos and CSJs were providing tools and a living example of how Catholics could nurture their faith and emerge as leaders in Canadian society.

The largest order of women religious in Toronto, the Congregation of St Joseph, or Sisters of St Joseph, traced their origins to the Catholic devotional revival in France in the seventeenth century. Devastated by the French Revolution, the order reconstituted itself in 1807 under the leadership of Mother St John Fontbonne. In 1835 Bishop Joseph Rosati of St Louis invited a group of these missionary sisters to St Louis, Missouri, where they established a school and orphanage for local native peoples. By 1847 the CSJs had expanded their apostolate to Philadelphia, which in turn provided the first recruits for their mission in Toronto.[130] In 1851, at the invitation of Armand de Charbonnel, the first group of CSJs arrived in Toronto and within a year began teaching, in addition to administring of an orphanage. In 1854 the order opened St Joseph's Academy, which initiated the Sisters' historical position as one of the dominant forces in Catholic education, not only in Toronto but throughout much of Ontario. It is ironic that the act incorporating the Sisters in 1855 made no mention of "education as a work of the order," when in reality the CSJs became the bone and sinew of the teaching profession in the Toronto and District Separate School Board, so much so that by the 1890s they constituted 80 per cent of the teaching sisters in Toronto's Catholic schools.[131]

The sisters of the Institute of the Blessed Virgin Mary, or Loretto Sisters, pre-dated the arrival of the Sisters of St Joseph. Invited to Toronto by Bishop Michael Power, the Loretto sisters came directly from the motherhouse at Rathfarnham, Ireland. The institute was originally founded in Belgium, in 1609, by English Catholic expatriate Mary Ward. Intended to be an order oriented to teaching, it was reconstituted in 1821 by Mother Teresa Ball in Ireland. In accordance with their chrism and in keeping with Power's request, in 1847 the four original Lorettos established a school in downtown Toronto within a week of their arrival.[132] A generation later their educational establishments had expanded to include a girls' school in St Paul's parish, a new abbey (1862) at Dundas and Bond Street, close to the Cathedral, a school at Niagara Falls, and several others outside of the archdiocesan boundaries.[133] What is remarkable about the expansion is that it happened at all, considering that the Lorettos' patron, Bishop Michael Power, died so suddenly after their arrival; two of the originals, Mother Bonaventure Phelan and Sister Gertrude Fleming, died in 1849 and 1850 respectively; and the superior, Mother Ignatia Hutchinson, passed away shortly thereafter, in 1851. The fate of the fledgling institute, and a handful of recent arrivals from Ireland, was left in the care of thirty-one-year-old Teresa Dease.[134] Mother Teresa's administrative expertise and ability to adapt the rule contributed to the growth of the Lorettos in terms of school establishments and recruits. By the 1920s there were 311 Loretto Sisters serving in schools in Canada and the United States.

Part of the remarkable growth of both the Lorettos and the Sisters of St Joseph was their ability to recruit young women who were born in Canada. The rise in the Canadian born and educated within these two religious congregations occurred at a much faster rate than among the secular clergy. Elizabeth Smyth has asserted that close to 76 per cent of the women who entered the Congregation of St Joseph between 1851 and 1920 were Canadian born.[135] Of these a whopping 92 per cent hailed from the province of Ontario. Canadian recruits to the order were clearly the overwhelming group after 1891, with rates of recruitment as high as 96 per cent of the total.[136] Recruitment among Canadian-born women for the Lorettos was comparable, and, as with the CSJs, dependence on women born in Ireland decreased dramatically. In 1891 Irish-born women had constituted nearly one-quarter of the active sisters in the institute, whereas thirty years later they numbered less than 7 per cent. By 1921 over 75 per cent of the Lorettos were Canadian, most of whom hailed from Ontario. In both cases the Canadianization of the order can likely be attributed to the sisters' role as the educators of young women in Ontario (see Table 2.4). Elementary and secondary institutions operated by the sisters became the best nurseries for future recruits. In this way both orders were able to recruit much more effectively, through their day-to-day example, than were the diocesan clergy, who, apart from the Basilians at St Michael's and Christian Brothers at De La Salle, had few ready-made clerical role-models who were so visible so often.[137]

The kind of education that both the Lorettos and the Sisters of St Joseph offered not only created an environment for recruitment but also a sound preparation for young women poised to enter Canadian society in the early twentieth century. Canadian-born Catholic girls, some of whom eventually embraced the religious life, received an education at St Joseph's Academy and Loretto Abbey well beyond the stereotypical courses designed to "finish" a young Victorian lady. The sisters at St Joseph's Academy had kept abreast of the latest innovations in pedagogy in North America. By the turn of the century the curriculum offered at the academy made ridiculous the notion that "Catholic institutions for women are behind the times." St Joseph's offered three streams for their students: a collegiate department that prepared women for university honours programs and the professions; a commercial section affiliated with local Toronto business schools; and an academic department, which offered a liberal arts education, some sections of which were affiliated with the University of Toronto and the Toronto School of Art.[138] Both the CSJs and the Loret-

Table 2.4
Institute of the Blessed Virgin Mary in North America,
Sisters Serving between 1887 and 1922 by Birthplace

Archdiocese	1891	%	1901	%	1911	%	1921	%
Toronto, city	16	7.8	23	8.7	25	8.7	24	7.7
Rural	18	8.9	25	9.4	24	8.3	30	9.7
Other (archdiocese)								
Ontario	82	40.0	129	48.7	151	52.3	165	53.1
Quebec	15	7.3	13	4.9	15	5.2	13	4.2
Other Canada	0	0	0	0	1	0.4	2	0.7
Ireland	49	23.9	41	15.5	30	10.4	21	6.8
USA	13	6.3	21	7.9	31	10.7	47	15.1
UK and Nfld	3	1.5	4	1.5	5	1.7	5	1.6
Other	2	1.0	3	1.1	3	1.0	3	1.0
Incomplete	7	3.4	6	2.3	4	1.4	1	0.3
Total	205		265		289		311	

Source: Sister Mary Aloysius Kerr, IBVM, *Dictionary of Biography of the Institute of the Blessed Virgin Mary in North America*. Toronto: Mission Press 1984. Sisters included are those who were received prior to 1922 and served between 1887 and 1922. The sample includes 471 sisters in total. Of this number the following are not included in the table: 6 received after 1921 but before 1922; 7 died before 1891; 11 were received and died between samples; and 12 had incomplete entries in the dictionary. Percentages are rounded off to the nearest tenth of a point. All calculations are mine.

tos offered up-to-date programs, current with the expectations of the Ontario Ministry of Education and serviced by texts approved by the ministry.[139] As such, the schools under the professorial care of the sisters provided Catholic women with the tools needed to pursue professional, clerical, or religious careers. Such advances in the curriculum of the Catholic colleges run by the Lorettos and CSJs help to explain how Catholic laywomen in Toronto entered the clerical, teaching, and nursing professions in greater numbers, and how an individual like Gertrude Lawlor became a leader in public education, or Teresa Korman emerged as a leader during recruiting drives during the First World War and as Regent in the IODE.[140]

The adaptation of the CSJs and Lorettos in a Canadian environment, and the evolution of the sisters into a cadre of Canadian-born,

Canadian-educated women, sometimes worked at cross purposes to the image of "women religious" held by the local bishop. Instead of the absolute compliance he expected from these women, Denis O'Connor encountered resistance to many of his proposed plans for the CSJs in his archdiocese. Unlike the Loretto Sisters, who, as of 1877, were an institute that reported directly to Rome, the Congregation of St Joseph was organized by diocese and answered ultimately to the local bishop. As part of his Catholic restoration program in Toronto, O'Connor attempted to tighten the discipline within the CSJs. He insisted that the rule be applied to the letter, which meant he enforced the wearing of a heavy veil when the sisters were on the street, and he curtailed the more liberal practice of permitting them to visit ill relatives.[141] During pastoral visits to St Joseph's Convent he was blunt in his criticism of the discipline and intelligence of some of the sisters. Given his heavy hand, he should not have been surprised that during one visit one sister "told him his business."[142] Clearly, the CSJs, many of whom were Ontarians born and educated, had adapted the rule to life in a Canadian environment, and as such resented the meddling of the local ordinary.

Although less troubled by the whim of the local bishop, the Lorettos also struggled to adapt their rule to a Canadian environment. Their aspirations to be a more cloistered order had been dashed earlier in their history, when they discovered that their activities in local parochial schools, the distances between their establishments, and even the city block between their Bond Street Convent and the Cathedral necessitated their public appearance in the streets of the city. "We had unfortunately lost our repugnance to going out," commented Teresa Dease. "We had to do it by necessity, and afterwards, the habit made it a little too easy in the end."[143] Ironically, it was Mother Teresa Dease who became primarily responsible for adapting the rule of the institute to the North American environment, embracing a more academic focus for the institute's schools and permitting the professionalization of its teachers. For her efforts Dease had to contend with criticism from some of her own sisters regarding the divergence of the rule in Canada from its practice in Ireland.[144] The Canadianization of the order did not settle well with some of the Irish expatriate sisters.

What appears clear is that by 1920 the Loretto Sisters and Sisters of St Joseph were in step with the changes in Catholic leadership throughout the city. At even a greater pace than their male colleagues the major religious orders were being staffed and led by women who were Canadian born and educated. The pressures of government and the marketplace also ensured that the education and leadership they offered served two purposes: to cultivate the sacred mysteries of the Catholic faith in young women, and to prepare these same women for the complexities of the industrial capitalist world they inhabited. In the process the sisters adapted their own lifestyle and resisted opposition from within – and, on occasion, from the local bishop – when it appeared that the original rules were not being applied with vigour. Throughout, however, the sisters offered a model of Canadian Catholic leadership that complemented the emergent pastoral objectives of the Canadian-born priesthood, and the confident and encouraging programs of such bishops as McEvay and McNeil.

By the 1920s the sisters, priests, and bishops in Toronto engendered remarkable changes in the style and substance of the leadership of the local institutional church. At the highest levels of power, priests and bishops showed a remarkable receptiveness to the Dominion, its traditions, and its potential. The days of the Irish "Hibernarchy" were over, as all levels of clergy and male and female religious became increasingly Canadian born and trained. While the impetus to embrace North American society and make the Church a leader in Canadian life came from the strong insistence of Walsh and two of his successors, McEvay and McNeil, the mechanics of creating a Catholic yet Canadian community were worked out on a day-to-day basis by the priests in the parishes and the sisters in the schools. While they differed little from other Catholic priests in terms of devotions and orthodoxy, Toronto's priests, many of whom were themselves locals, empathized with the precarious existence of a Catholic minority in a Protestant province, and often moderated their dogmatism accordingly. The rather frosty response by clergy and religious to Denis O'Connor's reforms demonstrated that many Canadian-born and -educated priests – men like Father John Teefy – realized the need for more flexibility when dealing with a Catholic minority in a Protestant land. Rigidity and legalism, in their experience, would only make Catholics more amenable to other choices offered in a religiously pluralistic society. Collectively, the statements of bishops and priests and the "annalists" and writers from among the religious orders express an ethos of confidence: assurance that English-speaking Catholic men and women were coming of age and had the potential to become leaders in the city, the province, and the nation.[145]

CHAPTER THREE

A View from the Pew:
Lay Initiative in Toronto

Denis O'Connor's life as the archbishop of Toronto was a personal misery. For much of his professional career as a priest he had been accustomed to the disciplined life as rector of a small Catholic college and minor seminary in a rather quiet town that rarely garnered much public attention. When he spoke, his staff and students listened. When he laid down rules, he was unquestioningly obeyed. In his ultramontane Catholic way of thinking, all of this was to be expected. Those situated lower in the hierarchy were to defer without question to those who, by the grace of the Holy Spirit, occupied the upper echelons of the pyramid of authority. Just as all those in a school were subject to the schoolmaster, so too the Catholic laity were to look to their priests for direction, who, in their turn, deferred to the bishop – master of the diocese. O'Connor would have applauded the popular Jesuit writer Edward J. Devine when he instructed the laity to obey the priest: "He can command with an authority which comes to him in an unbroken line, through pontiffs and bishops, from the Saviour Himself, who said 'Go teach all nations ... He who hears you hears Me.' "[1] In Toronto the theory would not translate into practice. When O'Connor resigned after less than nine years as bishop, in 1908, his spirit was broken and his patience exhausted. "I have not done," he lamented to Cardinal Gotti, "and cannot do the good that a bishop is expected to do."[2]

The English-speaking Catholic community that frustrated O'Connor in this end, and the one that endured his canonical litigiousness, was a group in the process of religious change. O'Connor encountered a community of lay Catholics who were adapting their faith life to a Canadian environment and giving their Catholic prayers, devotions, and moral life a Canadian flavour. Lay initiative among the English-speaking Catholics of the city took many forms after 1887, some of which had their origins in the period of Irish nationalist fervour of the mid-nineteenth century. In the late Victorian and Edwardian periods, however, lay Catholics in Toronto, often in concert with their Canadian-born pastors and "nuns," developed forms of pious expression, liturgical celebration, sacramental behaviour, and associational life that wedded the devotional aspects of nineteenth-century ultramontanism with the rhythms and expectations of life in English Canada.

Between 1887 and 1922 English-speaking Catholics still bore elements of Irish piety and devotion, but had melded this with sacred spaces and moral expectations that were germane to the community at large. One problem that arises as we reflect upon the spirituality of a people in the past is the lack of tangible records – conscious efforts of men and women in the pews to record the inner dynamics of their religiosity. Echoes of their devotional life are heard in the Catholic periodicals, minutes of their sodalities, or their devotional manuals. Religious objects and art also bear the fingerprints of their religious culture. In the case of Toronto's Catholics, expressions of devotional and moral life often surfaced when they were challenged by Church authorities, particularly during the O'Connor years.

In the period leading up to and immediately following the Great War, the English-speaking Catholic community in Toronto was characterized by three significant initiatives.[3] First, while laymen and women attended Sunday mass, venerated the saints, and thumbed their beads, their public devotions, especially pilgrimages, assumed a distinctly Canadian flavour as the number of shrines in the Toronto area increased. Secondly, the laity had also grown accustomed to liturgies in which popular music was enjoyed, Communion was more frequent than the expected monthly reception, and women and children took an active role in the liturgical celebrations. When the "Catholic restoration," begun by Pius x and complemented by the episcopate of Denis O'Connor, was launched in Toronto, clergy and laity protested in favour of the liturgies to which they had come accustomed. Finally, in terms of the sacraments and moral life, young Catholics married non-Catholics at an unprecedented rate. These "mixed marriages," as they were called, were symptomatic of the increased fraternization and integration taking place between young Catholics and Protestants in Toronto. Tolerated by the more pastorally oriented clergy, who feared the apostasy of the youth if harshness and rigour were the Church's posture on such unions, mixed marriages in the eyes of O'Connor and others became a symbolic of the complete breakdown of the Catholic community. In reality the marriage question was a sign of the times, that English-speaking

Catholics were adapting their religious life to exigencies of the larger English-Canadian world. Their Church was becoming Canadian.[4]

The nineteenth century was characterized by a militant and triumphant resurgence of Catholic piety, Church life, and papal power. When Napoleon abdicated his imperial throne in 1814, Pope Pius VII was released from his captivity in France, where he had been incarcerated for refusing to involve the Papal Sates in Napoleon's "Continental System." After the fall of France, there arose a resolve among the most zealous of Catholic leaders that neither pope nor Church would be humiliated in such a fashion again. These "zelanti" soon held sway in Rome, as did their objections to the evils of modernity, liberalism, and rationalism – all "step-children" of the French Revolution.[5] For those in Catholic Europe, caught in the maelstrom of local struggles between the remnants of the *ancien régime* and the tribunes of liberalism, the renewed and refreshed Vatican was increasingly viewed as an island of stability in an age of revolution. Harking back to loyalties once observed in the Middle Ages, some Catholics looked over the Alps to Rome – hence the re-emergence of the label "ultramontane."[6] For these Catholics, the rock upon which the Saviour had built his Church, embodied in the leadership of the successors of Peter, would become the primary focus of their loyalties.

The ultramontane resurgence was marked by several developments, two of which were the increasing centralization of Church authority under the Pope and the Church's ordinary magisterium, and the renewal, romanization, and proliferation of Catholic devotions. In terms of the former, the hierarchical pyramid of the Church was reinforced, with every level of power limited by the one above it and all levels ultimately subordinate to the authority of the pontiff himself. In this period the charismatic and pervasive personality of Pope Pius IX (1846–78) reinforced the cult of the papacy.[7] During his pontificate the Catholic hierarchy was re-established in Protestant Great Britain (1850) and Calvinist Holland (1853);[8] concordats were negotiated with the Catholic monarchies in Spain (1851) and Austria (1855), thereby restoring lustre and prominence to the Church there after a period of tarnish under the "enlightened despots" of the eighteenth century; the evil "isms" of the modern period – liberalism, rationalism, materialism – were condemned by the famous Syllabus of Errors attached to the encyclical *Quanta Cura* (1864); and the Vatican Council (1869–70) proclaimed the doctrine of papal infallibility.[9] Across the globe, in national churches and mission territories, Catholics became aware that, in matters spiritual, the teaching of Holy "Mother Church" was supreme;[10] and where the interests of the church and the state collided (education, censorship, marriage, to name a few), dutiful Catholics were to follow the lead of the Holy See.

The ultramontane revolution was far more than just a challenge of the Church militant to the forces of modernity. It was also a popular movement, replete with prayers, devotions, and pious practices – vehicles of sanctification and salvation. Through such devotions the sacred world of Catholicism was made immediate, personalized, and portable to the laity. The renewal of such devotions as the Sacred Heart and the Immaculate Heart of Mary, the rosary, and the use of scapulars, manuals of prayer in the vernacular, pictorial prayer cards, and medals of various saints allowed Catholics to individualize their worship, carve out their own sacred space, and personalize their prayer life while still maintaining a strong link to the Catholic "world."[11] This grass-roots ultramontane renewal also had a distinctive Italian flavour, with standards and norms frequently set in Rome. Nevertheless, the irony of such devotions was that, while they drew the laity into a renewed and approved Catholic spirituality, including its sacraments, they also allowed Catholics the opportunity to individualize their piety outside the watchful eye of the priesthood and daily mass. Parish and diocesan associations and confraternities for men and women helped to popularize devotions further. Yet, although founded by clergy and conveniently situated within the hierarchical structures of the institutional church, devotional organizations could become avenues of lay activism at the parish level.[12] Devotional practices and religious confraternities also had far-reaching appeal because they stir the emotions of men and women, cultivate religious sentimentality, and transform laypersons into active participants in the life of the Church.

In the Victorian and Edwardian periods Toronto's Catholics were strikingly similar to Catholics elsewhere in terms of their pious practices. Marian devotions, such as the rosary and the celebration of the feast of the Immaculate Conception, were an integral part of Catholic devotional life in the city. The month of May was consistently kept as "Our Lady's Month," with a litany of prayers, devotions, and hymns dedicated to the "Mother of God."[13] Similarly, the veneration of the Sacred Heart as a means of honouring the divine love of Jesus was one of the most common devotions in the city.[14] The St Basil's Hymn Book, prepared by the Basilian Fathers at St Michael's College, included at least sixteen hymns dedicated to the Sacred Heart and sixty-seven devoted to the Blessed Virgin Mary. In contrast, only one hymn commemorated St Patrick, patron of Ireland, and only one honoured St Michael, the patron of the archdiocese.[15] The popular ultramontane devotions to the Sacred Heart and to Mary were also supplemented by written intentions in local newspapers and charitable gifts that requested the intercession of St Joseph, St Anne, St Jude, and St Teresa, the Little Flower of Jesus.[16]

Nevertheless, by the turn of the century the devotion to the Sacred Heart of Jesus had emerged as perhaps the most popular pious practice among the Catholic men and women of Toronto. The Heart of Christ was symbolic of the burning love of Christ for God the Father and for all humankind. This devotion dated to St Bernard of Clairvaux, in the eleventh century, although its popularity was revived in the seventeenth century by St Margaret Mary Alacoque and, later, the Society of Jesus.[17] The Jesuits instituted the Apostleship of Prayer, which became the primary vehicle for lay participation in the devotion. Through meditation on the Sacred Heart – by means of morning exercises, the recitation of prayers, and keeping the Holy Hour – Catholics touched the sacred humanity of Christ, and sought to be enriched by the burning love of Jesus, who surrendered his life for the sins of humanity. At a time when God the Father and God the Son were characterized as remote and judging, the Devotion to the Sacred Heart put prayerful Catholics in communion with the humanity of a loving Jesus, while at the same time providing a means to "promote God's glory and the salvation of souls."[18] Between 1888 and 1896 "centres" of the devotion in the archdiocese had increased from 11 to 53, and the total membership of the Apostolate swelled from 4,088 to 15,701, or at least one-quarter of the entire archdiocesan population.[19]

In addition to private devotional exercises, Toronto's Catholics were conspicuous in their participation in the celebrations in the liturgical calendar. The notable liturgies during the Church year, such as the Easter Triduum and Christmas, Sunday masses in ordinary time, and holy days of obligation, in addition to extraordinary parish events, were generally well attended. Between 1887 and 1922 Toronto's Catholics usually kept Lent strictly, and the "Forty Hours" devotion, commemorating the length of time Jesus' body lay in the tomb, was celebrated annually in every parish.[20] In addition to regular liturgies, significant crowds of local Catholics were drawn to "revival-style" parish missions, which usually featured a visiting priest from a religious order, and "fire-and-brimstone" homiletics each day for a week.[21] The object of the mission was to enliven the parish community, instruct the laity in matters of faith and morals, and corral the loose and lapsed Catholics back into the fold. In 1906, for example, a mission for women at St Mary's, St Paul's, and St Helen's parishes drew in excess of five thousand women and girls. A similar mission for men, which included early morning mass before work and sermons every evening, brought comparable results.[22]

In addition to high rates of attendance at special events like missions, the fragmentary evidence available indicates that Toronto's Catholics may have had a higher rate of regular church participation than other Christians in the city. In 1901 the Canadian census, as a supplement to its usual tabulations of religious statistics, included a table on religious membership derived from information solicited directly from Canada's churches. Mainline Christian denominations provided information on the number of church buildings and their seating capacity, communicants, Sunday schools, teachers, and pupils. What became evident to readers of the census, and perhaps to the embarrassment of Canada's churches, was that the number of people who professed some religious affiliation was far higher than the official number of communicants and Sunday school scholars actually registered in the denominations themselves. In other words, there were those who spoke of affiliation, and a much smaller number whom the churches knew were in attendance or at least on communion rolls and parish registers. In Toronto, 86 per cent of the Catholics who claimed religious affiliation were actually acknowledged as communicants and scholars by the Catholic Church. This rate far exceeded the levels of all other Christian churches in the city; the Church of England, for instance, could only claim a rate of registered communicants and scholars of 37.2 per cent of those who actually claimed to be Anglican. In fact, Toronto's level of "participant" Catholics was among the highest in the province, both for rural and urban areas.[23] Though fraught with problems, this unique census indicates that either the Catholic clergy were experts at including every warm body they ever saw in their churches – perhaps by using large numbers of laity making their obligatory Easter duty as the official number for communicants – or suggests that perhaps Toronto's Catholics were active participants in the life of the local Church.

Catholic men and women in Toronto appear to have been regular churchgoers and fairly diligent in their devotional exercises and pious practices. Although Irish nationalism and its associations had been a point of entry into the world of devotions, particularly for laymen,[24] English-speaking Catholics in the early twentieth century seem to have been less inclined to emblazon their public piety with an overt Irishness. The evolution of the feast of St Patrick, the patron of Ireland, is one case in point. In the mid-nineteenth century St Patrick's Day had been celebrated by a parade, mass, and various secular "banquets," all of which blurred the lines between the religious and nationalistic nature of the feast.[25] By the 1890s the religious dimension of St Patrick's Day and the orgy of nationalistic sentiment were better distinguished. The Catholic press reminded readers that the day was primarily a religious feast and, perhaps, the closest thing to a holy day of obligation. Mass became the primary focus of Catholic attention in the daylight hours of 17 March, and the Cathedral was often "packed from wall to wall."[26] There were no parades after 1893, perhaps indicating the declining strength of Irish Catholic nationalist voluntary associations.[27] In the evenings, concerts sponsored by the Irish Catholic Benevolent Union at St Andrew's Hall, and the Ancient Order of Hibernians at Massey Hall, became the primary vehicles for the community's outpouring of emotion for Ireland, although the Catholic clergy held a high profile at these concerts – strong enough to have vaudeville acts banned from the evening program. These soirées eventually attracted a more ecumenical constituency, as Irish nationalists, Protestant and Catholic, began to work more closely in the city, as they often had prior to Confederation.[28] There was no better sign of this than the St Patrick's Day concert at Massey Hall in 1920, when the keynote address was given by Grattan Mythen, an Episcopalian minister and descendant of Henry Grattan.[29] On that occasion, Professor Thomas O'Hagan's glowing remarks on Protestant leadership in the cause for Irish self-government accentuated how little Toronto's St Patrick's Day celebrations had become exclusively Catholic.

In the late nineteenth century the public dimension of Catholic piety and devotion increasingly took on a local persona. Pilgrimages to shrines and holy places offer a glimpse of the Catholic community embracing sacred spaces and foci that were Canadian. This had not always been the case. In the 1880s Archbishop Lynch had been a devoted traveller to the Shrine of Mary at Knock, Ireland. Renowned for his veneration of this Marian apparition, Lynch was petitioned by Catholics from Toronto and other parts of North America for pieces of plaster from Knock, which were believed to have special medicinal powers.[30] Because travel costs were prohibitive, however, most of Toronto's Catholics were unable to visit Christian shrines in Palestine, Italy, France, Spain, or Ireland. As a result, at the turn of the century more convenient and less costly Canadian "holy places" became the focus of local pilgrimages. Every July a pilgrimage was made from Toronto and other Ontario dioceses to the popular shrine of Ste Anne de Beaupré near Quebec City. Interest in this Quebec shrine and another, at Notre-Dame-de-Cap near Trois Rivières, was heightened by numerous stories of miraculous healings there reported by local Catholic papers in their summer issues.[31] In 1909 the Ste Anne de Beaupré shrine was so popular in Toronto that the new St Ann's Church, east of the Don, was modelled architecturally on the French Canadian holy place.[32] Also of great importance to Catholic devotional life in the 1890s were the regular pilgrimages from Toronto to the shrine of Our Lady of Mount Carmel in Niagara Falls, again bearing visible testimony to the prominence of Marian piety among the city's Catholics.[33]

Processions and pilgrimages within the archdiocese itself also grew in popularity in the late nineteenth century. In 1887, when workers were renovating St Mary's parish, they encountered a sight of supernatural proportions. They moved the tomb of Father Louis Della Vagna, a Capuchin friar, who had died in 1857 while serving the parish. When the workers opened his tomb, some thirty years after it had been sealed, they found the body to be in "a remarkably good state of preservation."[34] Quickly, this discovery of the "incorruptible" stirred up great excitement among local Catholics, who began to flock to the tomb of Father Della Vagna, praying for the miraculous intercession of this local "saint." Similarly, the charismatic Father Francis McSpiritt, known throughout the archdiocese since the 1870s for his faith-healing powers, attracted numerous afflicted and curious Catholics to him. Archbishop Lynch, however, took a dim view of McSpiritt's displays and threatened the priest with charges of "charlatanry" if the healing demonstrations continued.[35] Nevertheless, testimonies to the priest's healing power took on a life of their own, and faithful from the city and elsewhere continued to seek cures from McSpiritt right up until his death in 1895.[36] As late as the 1930s there was a request for soil from his grave at Wildfield because of its alleged healing powers.[37]

The establishment of the shrine to the Canadian martyrs at Midland, in the northernmost reaches of the archdiocese, however, best symbolizes how pilgrimages in the archdiocese took on an increasingly Canadian ambiance. In 1907, 2,500 people attended the dedication of the martyrs' shrine by Archbishop O'Connor, and shortly thereafter, reports of miracles and cures began to emanate from the Midland area.[38] By 1913 both the Grand Trunk Railway and the Canadian Pacific Railway had regular train service between Toronto and Midland to handle the large number of pilgrims in the summer and autumn.[39] English-speaking Catholic interest in the Martyrs' Hill shrine indicates the extent to which Toronto's Catholics had begun to draw on their own religious heroes, history, and immediate surroundings as objects of public piety. This was a shrine they could call their own, with a special historical connection to the diocese, and a testament to the Catholic pioneering spirit in the region. It was a reminder that the Church was universal, but it also had a particular regional character – in this case made even more powerful by the blood of intrepid Jesuits who were martyred while preaching the gospel.

Thus Catholic piety in Toronto was both international and local in character. English-speaking Catholics bore the imprint of the ultramontane devotional revolution of the time, while adapting their piety to local circumstances. Regional sacred spaces became Canadian prisms of the "universal" faith. Local shrines and their saints also offered Toronto's Catholic laity a strong sense that their Church had both a history and an investment in Canada. Mass excursions and individual pilgrimages to such holy places could energize local Catholic communities, which were already experiencing spiritual and social change.

The parish was the hub of Catholic spiritual and community life in Toronto. The parish church was a locus for Sunday worship and devotional activities. In addition, the parish hall and parochial school became meeting-places for a variety of social activities, which usually bore some religious imprint. Lay involvement in parish life ranged from men and women of all ages participating in the choir, boys serving at daily masses, regular gatherings of devotional sodalities and confraternities, monthly meetings of insurance societies, literary clubs, and athletic associations, and the convening of parish socials and picnics. The breadth and regularity of these activities varied from parish to parish, as did the kinds of facilities that were available. Parish activities involved all social classes, as such things as parish societies – spiritual and insurance – were open to laypersons from all walks of life. What is clear is that Toronto's English-speaking Catholics placed a significant investment of their time in parish activities and, by the early twentieth century, had imbued their social and liturgical activities with a local flavour. Some parishes, like St Basil's and Our Lady of Lourdes, were noted for their liturgical music. St Joseph's had a strong youth group and literary association. St Mary's, in addition to being a focus of local pilgrimages, boasted an excellent debating society and an accomplished children's choir. Parishes, their associations, and their schools were the foundations of lay life in the city; when trifled with by bishops or ambitious clergy, they became bastions of lay resistance.

The laity's liturgical, devotional, and social practices in Toronto did not always jibe with the expectations of the hierarchy. The episcopate of Denis O'Connor, from 1899 to 1908, was punctuated by numerous disputes over liturgy, parish recreational activities, associational life, and Catholic marital behaviour. Concurrent with his enforcement of discipline among the clergy, O'Connor precipitated a period of rigorism in Church law, liturgical practices, and Catholic social mores in the archdiocese. His vision of the Catholic life was twofold: strict adherence to the doctrinal authority of the magisterium, and punctilious obedience to all the regulations prescribed by Rome. At his installation O'Connor threw down the episcopal gauntlet, thereby setting the tone of his attempt to restore order and purity to Catholic faith and practice in the archdiocese. Identifying all church regulations as integral to the "doctrine of the word," O'Connor's plans were crystal clear: "The discipline of the Church my dear brethren, is an essential part of her teaching, as well as the articles of faith; and just as a strict compliance with the teaching of Jesus Christ brings the graces of God upon those who believe, so also ... those who observe these disciplines of the Church, her regulations in all things, obtain ... those blessings."[40] He intended to apply the laws of the Church rigorously, and, in the manner to which he had become accustomed as a schoolmaster, he expected the full co-operation of both clergy and laity.

In March 1900 O'Connor clarified his plan for the regeneration of the archdiocese in the circular letter "Regulations to be Observed to Ensure Uniformity and Good Order." This document contained thirty-four regulations covering four broad areas that soon became the principal battlefields of his episcopate: clerical discipline, liturgical uniformity, effective catechesis, and adherence to Church law by the laity in sacramental and social matters. His message to Catholics was unequivocal: "Exemptions from Church Laws are to be much discouraged."[41] O'Connor's program concentrated on strengthening existing structures; no plans were made to expand the Church to accommodate the growing Catholic population.[42]

O'Connor's strict abolition of all forms of popular liturgical music cut to the core of parish devotional life. In 1895 North American dioceses had not been included in the Congregation on Sacred Rites' directive to the Italian bishops to ban musical performances inappropriate to the liturgy.[43] In 1903, however, one of Pius x's first acts as pope was to issue a *Motu Proprio* standardizing liturgical music throughout the Church by prohibiting what he considered profane classical compositions in favour of Gregorian chant. Also forbidden were performances by orchestras and most soloists, and singing in the vernacular. Furthermore, women were banned from choirs and other musical roles on grounds that singers held a real liturgical office and "women, as being incapable of exercising such office, cannot be admitted to any part of the choir or of the musical chapel."[44]

The musical traditions of the archdiocese of Toronto, and the expectations of Catholics in the pews, were definitely at odds with the *Motu Proprio*. Compositions by Mozart, Haydn, Weber, Gounod, Dvorak, Farmer, and Millard were used frequently in all the city's Catholic churches, during regular Sunday liturgies and on feast days.

The Catholic press praised the "splendour" and "pomp and ceremony" of masses celebrated with a full orchestra and a mixed choir.[45] Before Christmas 1895, for example, advertisements for the liturgies and their musical accompaniment appeared in the *Catholic Register*, suggesting a competition for the souls and ears of local parishioners. The two principal rivals seemed to be Our Lady of Lourdes Church, with Glionna's Orchestra playing Dvorak's Mass, and St Paul's parish, featuring Farmer's Mass in B-flat, as performed by the Neapolitana Orchestra.[46] Classical compositions and popular tunes, however, were not exclusive to the liturgies of feast days. Popular music entered the liturgy at other times. A wedding celebrated at Our Lady of Lourdes, for instance, included a soloist's rendition of the popular tune "A Dream In Paradise."[47] That Gregorian chant was used regularly in only three parishes prior to 1903 is evidence of the strength of popular music in the diocese.[48]

Unhappy with what he considered sloppy liturgies in his new diocese, O'Connor initiated sweeping reforms in the spirit of Pius x's *Motu Proprio*. In 1904 he issued a circular demanding that "all profane music, particularly if it savors of theatrical motives, variations and reminiscences, is absolutely forbidden."[49] Press reports of musical liturgies abruptly stopped, as the city's pastors struggled to conform to the new rules. The toughest task was trying to remove women from all parish choirs. At St Mary's, for example, the children's choir that had won the praise of the *Register* the previous Christmas was purged of its girls.[50] At St Basil's, once considered to have the finest liturgical celebrations in the city, the choir was reduced to half its strength when the women were forced to leave.[51] Rural parishes complained that there were not enough young boys to replace the sopranos. The rhythms of parish life had been interrupted, and there was considerable grumbling.

Nevertheless, O'Connor's actions won immediate praise from some of his brother bishops and an obedient element in the local Catholic press. Toronto, along with Cincinnati, Montreal, Newport, and New York, were some of the few dioceses in North America to apply Pius's directives to the letter.[52] In 1904 O'Connor began the second stage of his reform by creating the Choral and Athletic Society at the Cathedral, and hiring a music director to teach and conduct Gregorian chant. A few pundits who had described some of the local liturgical music as "flippant" and "a medley of sounds and disjointed words without sense and without reverence," lauded O'Connor's scrupulousness.[53] By 1908 Patrick Cronin, editor of the *Catholic Register*, beamed, "Toronto is par excellence the musical centre of Canada on general claims."[54]

The *Register's* ebullition was not shared by laypersons who struggled with the changes, particularly the imposition of Gregorian chant, in parish liturgies. Lay leaders and some clergy killed the restoration by their slowness to enact the reforms. Even in 1908 one journalist was forced to admit that "the period of transition is not yet passed, and in a few instances the initial stage of change is not yet attained."[55] At Easter in 1905, for example, St Mary's parish continued its use of the forbidden music, featuring compositions by Mercadante and Lembillotte.[56] Mary Hoskin, a scion of St Basil's parish, remarked that the loss of women from the choirs was lamented by both the choir leaders and the congregation, to such an extent that the choir director resigned.[57] Acknowledging that there was much bitterness and resistance from the faithful regarding the changes, Patrick Cronin at the *Register* criticized any and all Catholics who protested the bishops' directives concerning liturgical music.[58]

Neither criticism from Cronin nor O'Connor's vigilance were able to win the approval of the vast majority of the laity. In the long term the quiet resistance and even open defiance to the *Motu Proprio* at the parish level ensured its failure. When O'Connor resigned the see, in 1908, there was no uniformity: some parishes used the Gregorian exclusively; others sought a mixture between the plainchant and popular compositions. By 1909 Archbishop McEvay witnessed a variety of musical styles at the Cathedral, although the remarkable performance of the choir at McEvay's installation prompted one local lay expert to seek the Apostolic Delegate's "imprimatur" on the Cathedral's musical selections.[59] Other parishes, such as St Vincent de Paul's in Parkdale, continued to use the "prohibited" masses by Mozart.[60] Toronto was not alone in its resistance to the changes. In 1909 the Vatican, at the request of the American hierarchy, permitted female participation on the condition that they be separated from the men and away from the altar.[61] The most cutting indictment of the general failure of musical reform in Toronto, however, came from a supporter of the O'Connor program, who complained to Archbishop Neil McNeil of the dearth of proper congregational singing in the city parishes:

it makes the evening service more attractive especially to non-catholics in some parishes priests take no interest in it whatever, hymn cards are not given out, and in St Francis and some other parishes it has never been started; Pope Pius x reforms in church music are a dead letter in this city; we usually have a very poor performance of high mass by a lot of untrained usually screechy sopranos or mixed choir, instead of uniformity of a boy or male choir.[62]

While the purists and musical aficionados lamented, local parishes once again assumed control of their parish liturgies and customs.

Lay Catholics resisted other attempts to change parochial life with equal resolve. Lay behaviour was characterized by strategies similar to those evident in the battle over liturgical music. There was open defiance of episcopal fiats, procrastination in applying new legislation, and sometimes passive acquiescence of a people merely biding their time until an opportunity to "backslide" came their way. In 1900 O'Connor was convinced that Catholics in the city were in serious danger of losing their faith. When asked by Rome about levels of Protestant proselytization in the archdiocese, O'Connor admitted that there was nothing overt. He was more dismayed, however, that the influence of Protestantism was being felt in more subtle ways. "The greater number [of 'perversions']," he reported, "is due to mixed marriages, public schools, newspapers and Protestant company."[63] O'Connor's solution to the problem was to cut Catholics off from the community around them and to recreate a pious, active, yet strictly disciplined and canonical Catholic parish life. The laity, however, would not follow.

O'Connor initiated a serious of regulations for parishes in the city and rural areas. He regarded parish picnics, public processions, parish excursions, entertainments, and semi-philanthropies as denigrating to the truths of the Church. Picnics, in his mind, were the playgrounds of political hacks who had little regard for religion and used the Church for their own selfish purposes.[64] He categorically refused his own participation in them and recommended his flock do the same. His ban on religious processions kept Catholics temporarily off the streets; associations that did not comply might risk ecclesiastical censure and perhaps expulsion from the archdiocese. His disfavour of picnics, however, was openly ignored by laity and clergy. Local parishes continued to hold these community gatherings successfully. The House of Providence annual picnic sponsored by the Sisters of St Joseph, for example, was the highlight of the spring; in 1903 alone it netted $3,700 for the city's poor, and by 1907 the crowds at the event numbered in excess of ten thousand people.[65]

O'Connor's policy on public devotions and socials crumbled after his resignation; the picnics continued as they always had, and the processions resumed. In 1909, within a year of O'Connor's departure, the Holy Name Society – the largest male Catholic fraternity in the city – resumed its annual parade, with episcopal approval from Fergus McEvay. By 1913 over ten thousand Holy Name Society members marched openly through the streets of the city, without molestation from non-Catholics and free from ecclesiastical censure.[66] O'Connor's fears of a Protestant backlash were unrealized. The spectre of the Jubilee procession and riots of 1875 had been exorcized.[67]

The success and survival of picnics and processions, despite O'Connor's hostility, demonstrated the importance these religious and social gatherings held for the laity. A minority in a Protestant city, Catholics had few social activities in which they could rally together and celebrate their common creed. Thus, as the foci of faith, charity, and recreation, parish socials were far too important to the Catholic community to be eradicated by O'Connor's rigorism. Local priests knew that if these events were eliminated, Catholics would seek their entertainments elsewhere, perhaps at Protestant church halls.[68] Women also offered resistance. O'Connor's prohibitions seriously limited their role in the life of the parish. Without the network of parochial social activities, women were designated to participate only in the Mass and in sodalities concerned largely with prayer or altar beautification. Unwilling to surrender their vital social role in the parish, women in many parishes simply ignored the new directives from the episcopal palace. Finally, local pastors were unwilling to pay the financial price of paring down parish activities. The loss of picnics and the like put serious financial strains on parishes and institutions, which otherwise would have had to resort to frequent special collections during the mass to cover debts. For revenue-poor parishes, such as St Joseph's in east Toronto, O'Connor's prohibitions meant increased debts for a community that could not balance its accounts by relying exclusively on the collection plate.[69] Collectively, the priests and the people defeated the prelate.

O'Connor's dealings with fraternal associations demonstrate another dimension of lay resistance to his reforms of parish social life. When the Knights of Columbus, a rapidly growing American Catholic fraternal association, requested permission to establish a council in Toronto, O'Connor flatly refused. Although the society was gaining thousands of members elsewhere in the province, he felt "that there were all too many societies already, and one more would only tend to weaken all." Even a special plea from their state chaplain, Father Michael F. Fallon, future bishop of London, did not change O'Connor's mind.[70] The laymen would not relent. In "contempt" of episcopal authority, at least two hundred Toronto Catholics joined councils from neighbouring dioceses, biding their time until O'Connor either changed his policy or departed the see.[71] The waiting game was shorter than even the dissenters had anticipated. After O'Connor's resignation in 1908 a delegation of leading Toronto laymen recommended that the Supreme Knight, Edward Hearn, approach O'Connor's successor for approval to establish a Toronto council. In

February 1909 Archbishop McEvay granted the Knights permission to establish in the archdiocese, on the condition that he and not the council appoint the chaplain.[72] One month later McEvay's secretary was appointed chaplain, and the Knights were formally established in Toronto, thus overturning O'Connor's earlier ruling. Within a decade the Toronto council, over six hundred strong, was the largest in Ontario.[73]

The whole episode illustrates how O'Connor had seriously miscalculated the need for new fraternal associations in Toronto. Old societies, such as the Irish Catholic Benevolent Union (hereafter ICBU) and the Emerald Benevolent Association, had an Irish nationalist agenda that was anachronistic to new generations of Catholics by the turn of the century. By 1900 the Emeralds were moribund, and the ICBU was recruiting women to fill its depleted ranks.[74] O'Connor had assumed that the restoration of these societies, among others, merely required restrictions on competing societies. He failed to recognize that second- and third-generation Irish Catholics in Toronto had a more developed sense of their Canadian identity – forged in part by their common language and shared environment with non-Catholics – which undermined the applicability of the old Irish associations.

O'Connor's rigorous behaviour did not seem to alter significantly the social behaviour of the Catholics in the pews. They continued their socials, excursions, door-to-door collections, and interaction with local Protestants despite episcopal warnings to desist. Some observers might read this lay resistance as secularization, anti-clericalism, or evidence of tepid Catholicism. In reality, a group of local Catholics were simply insisting that their local Catholic traditions be respected. Being less rigorous in canonical discipline, in their eyes, did not necessarily make them the tepid Catholics that O'Connor thought them to be. On the contrary: many of these same pastors and laypersons who resisted O'Connor's tightening up of parochial life were the same ones encouraging interaction with local Protestants, not because they aspired to be children of Luther, Calvin, or Knox but because they felt they could facilitate the conversion of local Protestants to Catholicism.

In fact, English-speaking Catholics in Toronto had become more confident of their place in the nation, and triumphalist in believing that such things as musical rites, as they existed, attracted Protestants to Catholic worship. The desire to convert the city's Protestants to Catholicism was very much alive in Edwardian Toronto, as the many conversion narratives in the *Catholic Register* bear testimony. Furthermore, the arrival in Toronto of the Paulist Fathers, an American order of priests dedicated to the conversion of Protestants,[75] added lustre to this triumphalism.[76] In 1912 the Paulists held a mission at Our Lady of Lourdes Church at which five hundred non-Catholics were present for each of seven nights. The *Register* commented that such meetings helped both to dissipate "prejudice" and provided an occasion to inform "fair- minded" Protestants "searching for the truth": "The Protestants of Canada, as a class are still deeply religious ... This deeply religious spirit is the certain guaranty that missionary effort along this line will be productive of lasting benefits in many ways. We have here and now in Canada a great opportunity for the most effective kind of missionary work."[77] Catholics in Toronto seemed satisfied that they could prevail in the "ecumenical" dialogue and even impress others with their theological discourse and, of course, the richness, vitality, and ceremony of a orchestrated musical liturgy. Local clergy and laity appeared impressed with the possibilities produced by a more public Catholic character in the city; O'Connor saw only the risks of denominational interaction and poor discipline in the parishes.[78]

The conflict between O'Connor and his clergy, and the defiant initiatives of the laity, emerged most clearly in the "mixed-marriage" question. In the Catholic tradition, the valid marriage of a man and a woman is considered a sacrament, an occasion when the grace of God is conferred by the partners on each other.[79] Marriage between man and woman is an example of the mystical union of Christ and his Church. As a holy estate, Christian marriage is considered the foundation of family life, as the marital partners pledge to accept offspring and to nurture these children in the faith. Given the belief in the family as the foundation of society, respect for the sacrament of matrimony and honouring the responsibilities of the married life have been acknowledged as among the highest callings of the laity.[80] Catechisms remind the laity that marriage is to be entered into only with parental consent and with notice to their pastor; and once solemnized, the marital bond can never be broken.[81] Not only has the valid marriage been considered permanent, subject to clerical scrutiny, and essential for the Christian family, but marriage itself became a means to define the boundaries between Protestant and Catholic communities.[82] In order to ensure the integrity of the Catholic family in the present and secure the preservation of the "true faith" among future generations, Catholics were obliged to marry only Catholics. Interfaith marriage, or "mixed marriage," as it was often called, was considered a threat to the Catholic family, the fabric of the faith, and the very life of the Church.

From the time of the Reformation the Catholic Church eschewed the practice of mixed marriage. At the twenty-fourth Session of the

Council of Trent, in 1563, the bishops passed a decree to safeguard against invalid marriages and abuses in clandestine marriages. Henceforth, from the proclamation of the "Tametsi" decree, valid marriages were to be announced by the publication of marriage banns in advance of the nuptials, and the ceremony itself was to take place in the presence of a parish priest, two witnesses, and within a prescribed liturgy.[83] "Tametsi" imposed clerical control over marriage where it had rarely existed before. Clerical involvement to protect against the occasion of interfaith marriage became more acute as Catholic and Protestant populations intermingled in parts of Europe and the newly settled territories in North America. Renewed arguments against mixed marriages were summarized with vehemence by Pope Leo XIII in his encyclical *Arcanum*, "On Christian Marriage," published in 1880:

when minds do not agree as to the observances of religion, it is scarcely possible to hope for agreement on other things. Other reasons also providing that persons should turn with dread from such marriages are chiefly these: that they give occasion to forbidden association and communion in religious matters; endanger the faith of the Catholic partner; are a hindrance to the proper education of the children; and often lead to a mixing up of truth and falsehood, and to the belief that all religions are equally good.[84]

The urgency of *Arcanum* was translated into the unequivocal statements of school catechisms and the fiery sermons of anxious pastors throughout the Catholic world. Thus, mixed marriage was regarded as dangerous, "unlawful and grievously sinful," and something that the Church mourned, for it was "neither a Communion in faith nor in grace."[85]

As has been the case with many of the canons of the Church, there were circumstances that permitted a relaxation of the rules of marriage by means of a special "dispensation." In the Netherlands in 1740, for example, the Church permitted Catholics to be married by Calvinist ministers of the state church because it was the only legal marriage permissible in that state. This "Dutch precedent" was sometimes invoked in other Protestant territories, particularly England until 1837, where the decrees of the Council of Trent had never been promulgated and the civil rights of Catholics might be jeopardized otherwise.[86] In other cases an interfaith marriage might be permitted if the Catholic and non-Catholic parties were able to consent to four criteria: that all children of the marriage be baptized and raised in the Catholic faith; that the Catholic party have full liberty in the practice of his/her faith; that no marriage ceremony take place other than in a

Catholic church; and, finally, that the Catholic attempt to convert the other party to Catholicism. It was then customary for each to sign a written agreement in the presence of the local parish priest.[87] Faculties to grant the dispensation for a marriage either *mixtae religionis* (between a Catholic and a non-Catholic Christian) or *dispiratus cultus* (between a Catholic and a non-Christian) were conferred on the local bishop by the Vatican, although it was really up to individual bishops whether this extraordinary power was exercised. If the dispensation was granted, the ceremony normally took place privately in the rectory, with two witnesses, no music, and without the Mass or any fanfare.[88] Although permitted by the Church, the dispensed mixed marriage was still not considered a joyful occasion.

For Catholics living in the predominantly Protestant province of Ontario, the right to marry and the "rite" of marriage were subject to considerable controversy. When the province of Upper Canada was established in 1791, it had been the intent of Lieutenant-Governor John Graves Simcoe to create a "new" England in the image of the old, complete with class privileges, including the establishment of a state church. By the Marriage Act of 1793, only the Church of England was permitted to officiate at marriages unless one lived outside an eighteen-mile radius from the nearest Anglican minister. In these cases, magistrates could officiate and collect the fee for the marriage licence. Given that there were only three Anglican clergy in the colony at the time, the Church of England was frequently circumvented and deprived of marriage licence revenues.[89] Given the ludicrous situation the law presented, and the outcry from other Protestant denominations who actually formed the vast majority of the colonists, the Marriage Act was revised in 1798 to allow ministers from churches that were "established" elsewhere – Presbyterians, Baptists, Quakers, and Lutherans – the right to perform marriages and collect the fees.[90] Methodist clergy, who were mistrusted because of their "dissent" from the English church and their strong ties to American Methodist Episcopals, were excluded from legally marrying their adherents – even though they were clearly the majority in the province – until 1829, when the Marriage Act was revised and made more inclusive.[91]

Catholics found themselves in the grey areas of the colonial Marriage Act. They were not alone in this legal fog. Presbyterians, who openly pressed their claims of co-establishment by merit of their status as an extension of the Church of Scotland, won the right to officiate at marriages.[92] The Catholic case was a tad more subtle, if not testy in this Protestant territory. The Quebec Act of 1774 had recognized the rights of the Catholic Church in the old province of Quebec, out of which Upper and Lower Canada had been carved. Thus there was a case to be made that Catholics retained the right to officiate at marriages. Although not evident in the documents, this seems to have been the accepted practice. Since English canon law recognized Roman Catholic holy orders, there appeared to be no canonical or theological impediment to Roman Catholic priests officiating at marriages.[93] In fact, there is little in the episcopal correspondence to suggest that Catholics were penalized, although "a friend to the good cause" warned Bishop Alexander Macdonell in 1833 that some Catholics were allowing themselves to be married by Protestant clergy and magistrates.[94] Nevertheless, through the nineteenth century Toronto's bishops appear to have gained control of the legal apparatus of marriage and, although opposed to interfaith unions, were not averse to granting dispensations when warranted.[95] One of their concerns, apparently unique to Ontario, involved the frequency of marriage between Catholic women and non-Catholic men. Given that these families did not have a Catholic head of household, they were ineligible to forward taxes to the local separate school board. Given the obvious spiritual conundrums created by such liaisons, in addition to lost revenue for the struggling Catholic schools, the dating practices of Catholic girls were of particular concern to Toronto's Catholic leaders.[96]

By the 1890s unions between Catholics and Protestants had become more common in Toronto, as the Catholic youth increasingly worked alongside and fraternized with non-Catholics. While Archbishop Lynch had been rather stingy in granting dispensations, John Walsh grudgingly acknowledged that sometimes dispensations were a necessary evil to keep young Catholics in the fold.[97] Walsh petitioned Rome for fifty additional dispensations over the fifty originally granted him, on grounds that, if he denied young Catholics their request to marry non-Catholics under the eyes of a Catholic priest, it was highly probable that Catholic youth would just be absorbed by the overwhelming Protestant majority in the city.[98] For Walsh, the risk of saying yes to interfaith unions was less than the risk of saying no. During his episcopate mixed marriages increased from one in every twenty valid Catholic marriages in 1890 to one in every five by the time of his death. When O'Connor arrived in 1899, mixed-marriage dispensations were granted liberally in the city, although they varied in frequency according to parish.[99]

The liberality in granting dispensations would be buried with Walsh. Denis O'Connor was appalled by what greeted him in Toronto. "Let me say," he complained to the Propaganda Fide in Rome, "that when I first arrived in the Diocese little respect was shown the sacrament of marriage." He was deeply offended that the banns of marriage were rarely published, that sometimes Protestant clergy officiated over the marriage of Catholics, and that "the ceremony of the marriage rarely took place at a mass, and frequently in the evening as Protestants do."[100] O'Connor's restoration soon included a complete overhaul of marital practices in the archdiocese. He applied the canons strictly: three calls for banns, ceremonies before noon, and a nuptial mass for all Catholic weddings were made mandatory. These directives were neither popular nor evenly enforced. In several parishes, priests dispensed up to a third of couples from announced banns, thereby reducing the red tape for those who wanted to marry quickly.[101]

O'Connor's assault on the practice of interfaith marriage in Toronto was particularly poignant. He regarded Walsh's flexible policy on mixed marriages as "deplorable" and blamed all such unions as the cause of what he thought was the erosion of Catholicism in the city. "In this Diocese," he told Bishop Diomede Falconio, "the advance of evil is due to mixed marriages, which in my judgement have been tolerated to readily."[102] As had been his custom on other issues regarding parish life, he blamed the secular press, public schools, and non-Catholic associations as the first steps to mixed marriage and loss of Catholics to the Church. Deep down, O'Connor saw the real problem as rooted in the laxity of the clergy and indifference of the laity: "the asking of a dispensation," he lamented, "seems to have been sufficient reason for granting it."[103] His opinions were shared by a few priests and journalists, one of whom commented, "A mixed marriage is as bleak as a windswept moor, and as joyous as a funeral."[104]

O'Connor's attack on mixed marriages was decisive. In his Regulations of 1900 he rigorously applied the canons on marriage and demanded that all applications for dispensations be sent, in writing, to him with the fee enclosed. Moreover, agreements would have to be signed by the Protestant parties, promising that they would not impede the practice of Catholicism of their spouse or their prospective children. Furthermore, he doubled the fee for mixed marriage from five to ten dollars, adding a significant economic deterrent to seeking a dispensation, particularly for lower- and middle-income Catholics. Unlike Walsh, O'Connor never waived payment of fees on grounds of "in pauperes" – the inability of the applicants to pay.[105] To deliver themselves from the temptation of such marriages, he even suggested that Catholics might segregate themselves from Protestants by moving into tightly knit urban villages around the city's churches.[106] This was a throw-back to the isolationism that Catholics were in the process of rejecting as they moved into all of Toronto's neighbourhoods and into the broad spectrum of the city's labour market.

O'Connor's strict enforcement of the canon law brought dramatic results in the city parishes. By the end of 1899, his first year in office, O'Connor reduced the numbers of dispensed mixed marriages to 5 per cent of all Church marriages, the same level as in 1890. By 1907 he had further reduced this figure to 2.5 per cent (see Table 3.1). It is little wonder that his biographer, the Reverend Francis O'Brien, claimed by the end of O'Connor's episcopate that "a dispensation Mixtae Religionis was almost unheard of. The plan had succeeded; mixed marriages could be abolished."[107]

A more careful examination of the reaction of the laity to O'Connor's policy and its long-term significance, however, reveals the superficiality of O'Brien's assessment. Although there was no violent reaction to the archbishop's strict application of marriage laws, there was active disobedience by the laity. Marriage dispensations from O'Connor's successors reveal that some couples opted to leave the Church rather than not marry at all. Later they were reconciled to the Church, and their mixed marriages were regularized under the terms laid out by the new *Ne Temere* decree from the Vatican.[108] Some laypersons took their case to the *Register*, but the rather conservative editor, Patrick Cronin, offered a decidedly frosty response.[109] Others, with the aid of sympathetic priests, appealed to the Apostolic Delegate to overturn decisions made by O'Connor. In this way Fathers John Cruise and Frederick Rohleder, of Our Lady of Lourdes and the Cathedral respectively, incurred the wrath of O'Connor. In 1904, ill will between the pastors and O'Connor intensified when Donatus Sbarretti, the Delegate, granted several appeals for dispensation.[110]

Catholics of wealth and higher education fought openly with the archbishop. They had the status, public profile, and knowledge of canonical procedures to challenge O'Connor within the parameters of the canon law. Families like the Mulocks, Falconbridges, and Thompsons (the widow and children of Prime Minister Sir John Thompson) appealed for dispensations through the normal channels. Most of these cases involved Catholic young adults requesting marriage to Protestants of high social rank and influence in Toronto. Such unions were evidence of the integration of Catholics and Protestants at the highest levels of Toronto society. O'Connor, however, regarded them as "a plague," a denigration of the sacrament of marriage, and "society" weddings, particularly in the homes of the elites, were a "great scandal to the less pretentious members of the Church."[111] When O'Connor, rejected these requests, the families appealed to a higher court – the desk of Donatus Sbarretti, the Pope's representative in Canada. In one case Sir William Mulock, the postmaster general, secured the successful intervention of Prime Minis-

Table 3.1
Dispensed Interfaith Marriages in Toronto's English-speaking Parishes, 1887–1920

Year	All marriages	Interfaith	Percentage
1887	186	7	3.8
1888	165	9	5.5
1889	162	6	3.7
1890	175	10	5.7
1891	166	4	2.4
1892	170	14	8.2
1893	136	10	7.4
1894	148	14	9.5
1895	160	22	13.8
1896	114	24	21.1
1897	143	29	20.3
1898	153	22	14.4
1899	145	8	5.5
1900	151	6	4.0
1901	131	8	6.1
1902	179	12	6.7
1903	216	16	7.4
1904	222	13	5.9
1905	228	15	6.6
1906	205	6	2.9
1907	245	6	2.5
1908	248	20	8.1
1909	310	37	11.9
1910	337	47	13.9
1911	365	47	12.9
1912	419	74	17.7
1913	453	74	16.4
1914	417	52	12.5
1915	405	87	21.5
1916	454	111	24.5
1920	640	199	31.1

Source: ARCAT, Marriage Registers, 1887–1920; Dispensation Stub Books, 1887–1920. Note: Denis O'Connor granted only 3 dispensations prior to his resignation in May 1908. McEvay granted the 17 others that year.

ter Sir Wilfrid Laurier, who contacted the Apostolic Delegate on behalf of the younger Mulock and his Catholic bride-to-be.[112] Such actions made O'Connor even more intransigent because they violated the accepted chain of command in the Catholic hierarchical pyramid. When he said no, he expected obedience, not appeals to higher authorities who might interfere with his proper jurisdiction. "I am much ashamed," spoke the miffed O'Connor to Sbarretti, "to be summoned so often by your Excellency to give an account of my administration of the Diocese."[113] O'Connor was beside himself when Sbarretti urged moderation, or actively intervened on behalf of leading Catholic families.[114]

Resistance from prominent Catholics, the alienation of O'Connor from his priests, and the public humiliation of the archbishop were all evidenced in the Thompson cases. After Sir John Thompson's tragic death, Annie Affleck Thompson moved the remnants of her family to Toronto, where they became members of St Basil's parish at Clover Hill. The Thompson children were well educated in Catholic academies; the boys had attended the Jesuits' Stoneyhurst College in England, and the girls had graduated from the Ursuline College in Quebec. As a family they had socialized freely with the politicos in Ottawa, regardless of religion. The Thompsons also had a history of interfaith relationships of a sort; Sir John himself had converted to Catholicism with the aid of Archbishop Thomas Connolly of Halifax, a fact that perhaps slowed his succession to the post left vacant by Sir John A. Macdonald.[115] In 1903, supported by Father J.M. Cruise of Our Lady of Lourdes parish, Joseph Thompson applied for a dispensation to marry an Anglican, Mary Maude Teeple. O'Connor refused, despite the fact that both signed the agreement and suggested that, in the event of a refusal, they would go to a Protestant minister to officiate.[116] Lady Thompson swung into action, secured the support of Archbishop Cornelius O'Brien of Halifax, and appealed to Sbarretti, who in turn advised O'Connor that there were sufficient grounds for a dispensation. O'Connor buckled under the pressure and reversed his decision.[117] In 1905, however, Joseph's sister Mary Thompson and a Protestant fiancé signed the agreement through the help of Father M.V. Kelly at St Basil's parish and applied for a dispensation. O'Connor had had enough. They were flatly refused, partly on grounds that there were already too many mixed marriages in the family. Mary Thompson eventually married outside of the Church.[118] Toronto circles were abuzz with gossip of yet another entanglement between Catholics and their bishop. Both Thompson cases had tarnished O'Connor's public image and estranged him from Catholic leaders, clerical and lay.

Catholics of more modest means could not call upon prime ministers, archbishops, or even the Apostolic Delegate for help. There were simpler solutions for those who were discouraged by the unavailability of dispensations, or lacked the knowledge of the canons, or perhaps preferred to follow their hearts rather than the regulations. Ordinary Catholics simply married non-Catholic partners outside of the Church. While O'Connor could boast of a policy that virtually eliminated mixed marriages among the solemnized Catholic marriages, the truth was that mixed-marriage levels were not really diminished. Even during the more liberal Walsh years, only about one-third of interfaith marriages took place in the presence of a priest. It was more common for Catholics to avoid strangulation in canonical red tape and simply marry their Protestant partners in front of a minister or a magistrate. O'Connor's rules only worsened the situation and lessened the Church's opportunity to stop the "leakage" out of the Church. The total numbers of mixed marriages in York County nearly doubled between 1899 and 1905, while the number at which a Catholic priest officiated fell dramatically. Of the 718 interfaith marriages contracted, only 83 (11.6 per cent) were validated by the Church (see Table 3.2). Ordinary Catholics resisted O'Connor's rules by leaving the fold in droves.

Whether O'Connor and other Church authorities liked it or not, interfaith marriage was quickly becoming a popular option among Toronto's Catholics. After O'Connor's resignation in 1908 the number of dispensations granted rose sharply. During Archbishop McEvay's short episcopate the number of validated interfaith marriages increased from O'Connor's low of 2.5 per cent of all Catholic marriages in 1907 to nearly 14 per cent in 1910. From 1912 to 1934, during the episcopate of Neil McNeil, the levels reached an all-time high: in 1913 nearly one in every eight marriages was mixed; by 1915 over one in four; and in 1920, nearly one in three.[119] The general trends were even more startling. When we take into consideration all interfaith marriages, valid in the eyes of the Church or not, by 1920 they constituted over 40 per cent of all marriages involving Catholics.[120] While this interfaith-marriage phenomenon was common to most Catholic dioceses outside of Quebec, Toronto's rates of valid and invalid interfaith marriages were among the highest in Canada (see Table 3.3).[121] In one sense O'Connor was correct: English-speaking Catholics in the city were integrating more completely with the Protestant community around them; one of the results was the "mixed marriages" he feared. A French Canadian observer agreed, blaming the "déplorable" rate of mixed marriage among English-

Table 3.2
John R. Teefy's Report on Mixed Marriages in York County, 1894–1905

Year	All mixed marriages	Before a Priest	%	Before a minister	%
1894	55	18	32.7	37	67.3
1895	70	17	24.3	53	75.7
1896	81	24	29.6	57	70.4
1897	82	27	32.9	55	67.1
1898	74	25	33.8	49	66.2
1899	76	11	14.5	65	85.5
1900	82	12	14.6	70	85.4
1901	98	8	8.2	90	91.8
1902	96	7	7.3	89	92.7
1903	107	11	10.3	96	89.7
1904	126	21	16.7	105	83.3
1905	133	13	9.8	120	90.2
Total	1,080	194	18.0	886	82.0

Source: ASV-DAC, 89.4, John R. Teefy to Donatus Sbarretti, 10 June 1906, 11 July 1906. All calculations are mine.

speaking Catholics on the "community of language, of sentiments, of patriotism and ideas" that they shared with Protestants. Steadfast in their culture, claimed the author, French Canadian Catholics did not cause such disintegration in the Church.[122]

Throughout the battles over mixed marriage, the local clergy were not inactive. While sharing the common belief among the hierarchy and theologians that such unions were not desirable, pastors realized that risks of not granting a dispensation were far greater to the faith of the Catholic party than granting one. Making pastoral decisions, priests assisted parishioners, rich or poor, through the canonical thickets to receive dispensations. When faced with episcopal intransigence, clerics like Michael Kelly, John Cruise, Lancelot Minehan, Francis Rohleder, and John Teefy challenged the archbishop, advocating flexibility and prudent moderation.[123] Teefy himself supplied the statistics from the municipalities and province to sustain the case that mixed marriages outside of the Church were on the increase, despite

Table 3.3
Rates of Interfaith Marriage in Toronto and Ontario, 1911-20

Year	Place	RC groom	RC bride	Total unions	RC union	Mixed union	% mix
1911	Ont	3305	3438	4131	2612	1519	36.8
	Tor	371	417	494	294	200	40.5
1912	Ont	4250	4526	5346	3430	1916	35.8
	Tor	384	519	534	369	165	30.9
1913	Ont	4415	4588	5160	3843	1317	25.5
	Tor	640	689	806	523	283	35.1
1914	Ont	3836	3973	4374	3435	939	21.5
	Tor	561	584	701	444	257	36.7
1915	Ont	na	na	na	na	na	na
	Tor	541	590	696	435	261	37.5
1916	Ont	3907	4030	4494	3443	1051	23.4
	Tor	557	577	710	424	286	40.3
1917	Ont	4111	4156	4677	3590	1087	23.3
	Tor	676	654	824	506	318	38.6
1918	Ont	3429	3428	3957	2900	1057	26.7
	Tor	662	668	844	486	358	42.4
1919	Ont	4626	4587	5227	3986	1241	23.7
	Tor	708	682	881	509	372	42.2
1920	Ont	5100	5135	5837	4930	1447	24.8
	Tor	775	777	984	568	416	42.3

Source: AO, Provincial Secretary, Registrar General's Office, Report Relating to Registration of Births, Marriages and Deaths in the Province of Ontario, Reports 42–51 (1911–20). Calculations are mine.

O'Connor. He and several colleagues knew well that limiting dispensations did not solve the marriage question. It was also recognized that in cases where dispensations were refused, the children of the marriage were "lost." One priest was so adamant about granting dispensations that he threatened to marry a couple himself if his brother priest balked.[124] It became clear that the pastors who lived and breathed with their parishioners on a daily basis understood the difficulties of Catholic life in a Protestant town. To them, pastoral solutions outweighed canonical literalism.

The marriage question crushed O'Connor, and he tendered his resignation to Rome. The public explanation – that he was in ill health – was merely a veneer covering his real reasons. Writing to the Propaganda Fide, he complained:

From the first [I] called attention to the sanctity of marriage ... by discouraging mixed marriages unless for very grave reasons. These increase because, in my opinion, of the interference of the Delegate, who instead of sustaining me, grants dispensations without consulting me and without my knowledge. Naturally I know the state of the diocese better than he, and I am better able to judge how a dispensation will affect not only the parties concerned but on Catholics in general.[125]

O'Connor also protested the private correspondence between the Delegate and his priests, and acknowledged "un ésprit critique des mes activités soumis ... trop commun parmi les laïcs."[126] The Delegate retorted that his few interventions were intended to save the parties in question from leaving the Church. Rome had rejected O'Connor's earlier attempts to resign in 1904 and 1905, reassuring him that his vigilance was generally appreciated.[127] By 1907, however, the resistance from clergy and laity on so many issues prompted Rome to comply. On 4 May 1908 O'Connor terminated his episcopal duties, becoming titular Archbishop of Laodicea, and retreated to a semi-monastic life at St Basil's novitiate in Toronto, where he died 30 June 1911.

Neither McEvay nor McNeil continued O'Connor's rigorist program, electing instead to promote the expansion of Church facilities and institutions to meet the needs of the growing Catholic population. These two men concentrated on relieving the social ills and poverty that came as a result of the rapid industrialization and urbanization of Toronto. While they shared O'Connor's concern about mixed marriages, they deferred to Walsh's wisdom in dealing with the problem.[128] If morality was to be legislated, they were more interested in eliminating prostitution, the evil effects of theatres, and promiscuity in the cinema.[129] Few of O'Connor's programs survived him.

The reaction of the laity underscores the extent to which lay Catholics in Toronto had carved out a place for themselves in the greater community. They were neither isolated nor citizens of a closed community. Living in integrated neighbourhoods, working in religiously pluralistic surroundings, and coming to share, in varying degrees, the ideas and expectations of life in Canada with their Protestant neighbours made it much easier to consider marrying a non-Catholic. Some passed through the canonical hurdles and tried to live up to their pre-nuptial agreements as best as they could. While evidence is fragmentary, the children of interfaith unions do show up in parish registers, school ledgers, and even in the seminary.[130] Many were not prepared to acquiesce to the litigious application of the canons and sever their ties with their Protestant lovers. While some returned and had their marriages validated after the fact, by a canonical procedure known as *sanatio in radice*, most have vanished from the routinely generated records of the Church.[131]

Between 1887 and 1922 the laymen and women of Toronto were active in the process of recreating their faith within a Canadian context. While they were conspicuous in their embrace of several forms of ultramontane piety and devotion, they were also adept at recasting their devotional exercises and pilgrimages with a Canadian flavour. The overt trappings of their Irish and Scottish parentage gradually gave way to a piety that found its expression in Canadian heroes, Canadian associations, Canadian shrines, and in the local parish communities. In conjunction with their clergy, Catholics adapted their clubs, societies, and liturgies to the rhythms of their own lives. The Church of Toronto bore the distinct imprint of international ultramontanism, but its expression was increasingly of a local character.

When faced with dramatic changes to their parochial and devotional life imposed from above, the laity resisted, vigorously defending what they, in part, had created. Denis O'Connor's devotional and moral reform in Toronto was a faint echo of Pius x's "restoration" throughout the Church. Having no identifiable "modernists" or "Americanists" in the city, O'Connor's integrism[132] was directed at keeping Catholics disciplined in their faith and devotions, and segregated from non-Catholic influences. It was suggested by contemporary observers that some of the old devotional intensity of the laity was gone. Some Catholics began to excuse themselves from holy days because they worked in a non-Catholic establishment. Similarly, the *Register* complained that "the strenuous spirit of commercialism and the rush of business activities" in Toronto were killing Catholic family devotions such as the rosary, the display of holy pictures, grace at meals, and the use of domestic holy-water fonts.[133] O'Connor's rigorous "restoration" of parish discipline, devotional purity, and Catholic marriage was designed to arrest such acculturation and apostasy.

The resistance of the laity was neither surprising nor without precedent. Both Bishops Lynch and de Charbonnel, prior to O'Connor, had faced stiff opposition to their devotional and moral reforms, as well as their efforts to isolate Catholics from the influence of their neighbours.[134] It was not a case of Catholics being irreligious or disrespectful; perhaps theirs was the sin of not measuring up to a "Roman" or European standard, against which Catholic life had to be measured. O'Connor's restrictions on female choirs, fraternal associations, religious parades, and parish picnics, however, seriously curtailed some of the laity's only means of religious and social participation outside of the Mass. Neither clergy nor laity were willing to surrender activities that had become so integral to parish life.

The laity seem to have been confident that their faith could be maintained even if they worked and lived in an environment that was not Catholic. Maintaining the balance was no mean feat. More frequent social intercourse with the non-Catholic world around them diminished the psychological barriers that had once isolated Catholics from Protestants. The opportunities extended to them in Canadian society could be balanced with the interests of living a good Catholic life. The real dilemma for younger Catholics came when choosing marriage partners. Here the fiancé from the Protestant city had to be reconciled with the dictates of Church law. For some, the reconciliation was made possible by attempting the risky path of dispensation, usually aided by a sympathetic pastor. Others made the decision far more easily. When faced by Church law and its rigorous application, they simply left the Church for the city. The life of English-speaking Catholics in Toronto was filled with such challenges as they carved out their own place in Canadian society and forged a Canadian identity. The Catholic isolationism offered by O'Connor and the integrists was rejected as new generations of Catholics cultivated a lifestyle that embraced the world around them.

CHAPTER FOUR

Nurseries of Catholics and Canadians: Toronto's Separate Schools

When children filed back into Toronto's Catholic schools in September 1899, something new awaited them. In many senior classrooms the Sisters had stacked neat piles of a new reader. Auburn-covered and smelling of fresh, unfingered paper, the *Canadian Catholic Readers* greeted students for the first time. At the appointed hour the children of the fourth form snapped the spines of the little books and peered through the collection of poems, stories, and prayers, which reflected both Catholic and Canadian themes. The book's unavoidable opening selection set the tone for what was to come: "Then hail to the broad leaved Maple! / Wither her fair and changeful dress – / A type of our youthful country / In its pride and loveliness."[1] H.F. Darnell's syrupy ode to Canada, "The Maple," offered an unmistakable metaphor for the young Dominion, standing proud, strong, and beautiful among the nations of the world. It also symbolized the direction in which Catholic schools were now charting their course in the city of Toronto. The days when Catholic schools were nurseries of Irish culture and Catholic catechetics were coming to a close. Like the textbooks they now brandished, Toronto's Catholic separate schools aimed to inculcate youth with a strong Catholic faith and a spirited Canadian patriotism.

Between 1887 and 1922 Catholic schools in Toronto changed in several ways. Initially, physical facilities, faculty, and enrolment grew apace with the increase in the city's Catholic population. Improvements to school property, closer adherence to the Ministry of Education's curriculum, and better qualified teaching personnel helped to raise Catholic pride in the quality of education offered by their "separate" schools. The improvement of Catholic schools at several levels underscored the English-speaking Catholic community's growing concern that their educational institutions be better equipped to produce graduates fitted to take their place in Canadian society and in the Toronto labour market.

At the same time Catholic schools became crucibles of Canadian patriotism and nurtured new generations of Catholics who identified closely with Canada and with her place in the British Empire. Although it has been argued that separate schools in Victorian Toronto served primarily to preserve Irish and Catholic identity in the hope of shielding children from "the pressures of assimilation into the charter English Protestant society,"[2] by the turn of the century much of the Irish flavour in the children's studies had been supplanted by a Canadian and British imperial ethos. This better-developed sense of Canadian identity was facilitated by alterations to the Ontario school curriculum and by attitudinal changes among the clergy, religious, and laity, who became more favourably disposed to a Canadian-oriented education. Separate schools were still primarily concerned with the preservation of the Catholic faith in a Protestant environment, but they varied little from their public-school counterparts in terms of inculcating children with the principles of patriotism and good citizenship. Catholic bishops and educators alike considered strong and intelligent Catholicism, by its very definition, to be the stuff of which good citizens were moulded.

The quest for learning did not end after the fourth form. Toronto's Catholics began to regard the pursuit of higher learning as a necessity if Catholic youths were to pursue opportunities and create livelihoods in Toronto's urban-industrial complex. In their faith that higher education was the stepping-stone to advancement and success in Canadian society, clergy, religious, and leading laymen redoubled their efforts to recruit larger numbers of Catholics into high schools and universities. By 1922 the efforts of Toronto's Catholic leaders began to show positive results, as greater numbers of Catholics from the city entered the fourth and fifth forms, and later enrolled in baccalaureate programs at the University of Toronto, St Michael's College, and its women's affiliates. This combination of changing attitudes towards higher education and educational improvement marked the further development of Toronto's English-speaking Catholics in their quest to entrench themselves as full and equal Canadian citizens.

The schools provided one of the principal engines of transformation for English-speaking Catholics in Toronto. It was in the rejuvenated Catholic classroom where new generations of Catholics learned basic and technical skills that helped to fuel the white-collar revolution in the community. The lessons, exercises, and classroom devotions added further energy to the spiritual formation of students. Here they learned of the Catholic contribution to Canada's history, and of the exploits of Canadian Catholic heroes – saints, explorers, and politicians. The separate schools' adoption of public school history books, geography texts, and readers, all of which were imbued with imperial and Canadian themes, also made it possible for English-speaking Catholic children to cultivate a deeper identification with Canada and the British Empire. The teaching cadre of sisters, male religious, and laywomen were increasingly Canadian born, directing a curriculum that developed along Canadian lines, with Canadian concerns. When the teaching sisters were joined by a generation of laywomen, many of whom were products of the school board in which they taught, the Canadian ambiance of the schools was made permanent. In the three decades after Archbishop Lynch's death, Toronto's Catholic schools became the nurseries of Canadian Catholics who would lead the Church into the twentieth century.

Between 1887 and 1922 Toronto's separate schools experienced one of the longest periods of sustained growth and expansion in their history. Catholic elementary schools increasingly became the foci of community attention as facilities, teaching personnel, and services were improved in an effort to promote excellence in elementary school education and to enhance their rather shabby public image. Lay initiative in the introduction of the secret ballot in separate-school-board elections, the imposition of provincial standards of teacher qualifications on religious orders, and the gradual laicization of teachers all garnered a greater degree of respectability for the Toronto Separate Board. Better-qualified teachers and improved facilities established the Toronto Catholic schools as parish centres where children could be informed of their responsibilities as Catholics and as Canadian citizens.

Established in law, constitutionally protected, and publicly funded, the numbers of Catholic separate schools in the Toronto area grew steadily.[3] Considered integral to Catholic community life, most Catholic schools in the city of Toronto were intimately tied to specific parishes, the name of which was usually adopted by the school. By the 1920s nearly every city parish had its own school, while more heavily populated parishes often had two.[4] Several of the larger inner-city schools were segregated by gender. St Paul's, St Mary's, St Helen's, St Michael's, and St Patrick's parishes had schools with segregated classes, although the girls and boys frequently occupied the same school building. In some instances parish schools with low enrolments shared students of specific grades with neighbouring separate schools. In the 1890s, for instance, St Ann's and St Joseph's shared facilities, with all children going to the former for second and fourth form and all to the latter for third form. Both schools were too small for a full complement of grades.[5] By the twentieth century, however, ever-rising student enrolment ensured that every school had all the required grade levels and sufficient faculty. In 1895 Toronto had 13 Catholic elementary schools and 3 "high" classes, which offered courses beyond the four elementary forms. In addition, the Toronto Separate School Board employed 82 teachers to instruct the 3,341 registered students. By 1919 the board had more than doubled to 29 schools, serving 8,500 pupils and employing 208 teachers. This growth, which corresponded to the rise in Toronto's Catholic population, continued well into the "roaring" twenties, as the number of officially registered students surpassed 10,000 (see Table 4.1).[6]

This proliferation of school buildings and students reflected the overall demographic growth and diffusion of Catholics in all of Toronto's neighbourhoods. While the population in the downtown schools remained constant due to the influx of immigrants into classes formerly filled entirely by English-speaking Catholic children,[7] the absolute school growth in the suburban parishes was impressive. In 1907 Catholic school inspector William Prendergast was astounded by the rapidly increasing enrolments in midtown and suburban areas:

A new school, St Anthony's was opened ... last September to meet the needs of the north and west of the city; a fourth teacher was added to the staff of Holy Family school in November making a total of 105 teachers in charge of class rooms ... The growth of school attendance in the Northwest part of the city may be noted at a glance from reports from three schools: St Anthony's, St Peter's and St Helen's; the former with a registered attendance of 112 now serves the district formerly served in part by St Peters but chiefly by St Helen's school; notwithstanding the opening of the new school the attendance at St Helen's is practically the same as it was a year ago while St Peters shows an increase.[8]

The shift to suburban parish schools was so extensive by the early part of this century that Prendergast suggested that De La Salle School, which offered a course of study similar to a high school, should be relocated from the industrial district along Duke Street to a new site closer to the suburban Catholic population. Given the movement of Catholics, he added, the "downtown school" in general was bound to disappear.[9]

The predominance of teaching orders of sisters, brothers, and priests, another seemingly timeless feature of Toronto's Separate School Board, also began to change by 1910. Since the 1850s the Con-

Table 4.1
Attendance in Toronto's Catholic Schools Operated by the Sisters of St Joseph,
1895–1912

Year	Total	Form 1	2	3	4	5	Studying hist.	% studying hist.
1895	2,815	1,403	665	442	237	88	701	24.9
1897	3,030	1,698	600	450	171	111	732	24.2
1898	2,964	1,521	615	506	205	117	668	22.5
1899	3,039	1,591	667	460	214	107	781	25.7
1900	3,053	1,637	667	413	239	97	540	17.7
1901	3,033	1,618	612	462	236	105	572	18.9
1903	2,915	1,338	712	503	271	91	865	29.7
1904	3,004	1,382	687	491	319	125	NR	NR
1905	3,231	1,484	750	460	379	158	NR	NR
1906	3,108	1,391	696	539	347	135	1,021	32.9
1907	3,225	1,483	700	545	374	123	NR	NR
1908	3,314	1,557	714	543	356	144	NR	NR
1909	3,287	1,315	799	564	438	171	NR	NR
1910	3,385	1,457	747	546	426	209	NR	NR
1911	3,610	1,610	755	635	428	182	NR	NR
1912	3,530	1,596	796	577	378	183	NR	NR

Note: The table indicates enrolment in each form, junior and senior sections, and the total number of students taking lessons in Canadian history. Roughly 350 students per year took British history as well. Schools included in the sample are St Paul's Girls, St Mary's, St Patrick's, St Francis's, St Basil's, St Joseph's, St Peter's, St Ann's, Sacre Coeur, Sunnyside Orphanage, and St Joseph's College. NR = No record.

Source: ACSJ, Separate School Reports, 1895–1912.

gregation of St Joseph, the Basilian Fathers, the Institute of the Blessed Virgin Mary (Loretto Sisters), and Brothers of Christian Schools had virtually monopolized teaching in Catholic elementary and secondary schools. During this period the Sisters of St Joseph assumed the burden of nine or more elementary schools, an orphanage, and a high school. In 1890, 90 per cent of the teachers employed by the board were clergy or religious. Six young women comprised the entire lay personnel, and four of these taught at the same school.[10] The first two decades of the twentieth century, however, witnessed a significant decline in the dominance of the teaching clergy and religious. During the 1915–16 school year alone, 57, or over one-third of the teachers in the board, were laypersons. In less than six years this figure jumped to 89, most of whom were young unmarried Catholic women.[11] Ironically, many of these women had been educated by the same women religious whom they were now beginning to replace.

This process of laicization of the teaching corps was one of the features of a general increase in the numbers of Catholic women entering the white-, perhaps pink-collar labour force. The teaching sisters had made every effort to prepare young women for such employment. St Joseph's Academy and Loretto Academy offered several modern programs of study to prepare Catholic women for "post-secondary education and the world of work."[12] Catholic women were thoroughly prepared academically for their second- and third-class teaching certificates at the academies, and many furthered their education at the Normal School in order to acquire first-class certificates.[13] Rising student enrolment, new suburban schools, and new immigrant children made it necessary for the board to hire more teachers. In the first decades of this century these well-trained Catholic teachers were graduating just when their skills were most needed. The increase in separate school registrations, coupled with strict provincial guidelines for teacher certification after 1907 opened up employment opportunities for Catholic laywomen.[14] To penny-pinching trustees, the added attraction was that, at a salary of $200 per year, young Catholic laywomen earned a wage comparable to the Sisters of St Joseph and far less than the $500 paid to the Christian Brothers.[15]

Directives from the Ministry of Education regarding teacher certification also facilitated the hiring of better-qualified laywomen. In 1907 John Seath, Ontario's superintendent of Education, introduced a bill requiring that all teachers from religious orders be properly certified by the Ministry of Education. Ironically, Seath was responding to demands from the Catholic laity that their teachers be fully qualified. A local squabble between anglophone and francophone Catholics in Ottawa led to Judge Hugh MacMahon's ruling, in 1904, that only those members of religious orders who had taught in Ontario prior to 1867 were considered exempt from provincial regulations regarding teacher certification. The implications of the MacMahon decision were staggering for Catholic schools, which depended on the tireless and inexpensive religious orders to sustain their underfunded schools. The bishops, particularly in eastern Ontario, were near-apoplectic at the thought of losing the Sisters and Brothers, many of whom came from Quebec and would sooner return to their home province than attend Ontario's normal schools for certification.[16] The episcopates' defence of the status quo continued with an even greater sense of urgency.[17]

At the same time, lay leaders, Catholic schools inspectors, and Toronto's elite Canadian Catholic Union considered the proper certification of Catholic teachers a means to refute public suspicions that Catholic schools were inferior institutions directed by poorly trained teachers.[18] Such lay initiative should not come as surprise, given the agitation of some TSSB trustees who, in the 1870s and 1880s, argued for the introduction of the secret ballot in school board elections. Buoyed by concern for the quality of Catholic education but imbued with a pointed hostility to episcopal control of the board, the lay trustees' persistence eventually resulted in the passage of the Conmee Act in 1894, which established the secret ballot in separate school board elections across Ontario.[19] While the lay leaders of 1907 proved to be less confrontational with their bishops than their predecessors – they did not have to contend with the likes of Cleary or Lynch – they were quietly confident that the Seath Bill might be a blessing in disguise.

Fergus Patrick McEvay, Bishop of London and soon to be Archbishop of Toronto, struck a moderate tone on the issue of certification, suggesting that he was more sympathetic to the position of lay leaders than to some of his episcopal colleagues. Like the lay leaders, he had been outspoken on the need to improve pedagogy in the separate schools. McEvay may also have sensed that the dice had been rolled on the issue and that public pressure from Catholics and non-Catholics on certification had made the bishop's chances of blocking Seath remote. He credited Premier James Pliny Whitney with doing his utmost for Catholics and, instead of "agitation," sought concessions for the religious orders "on account of their experience, permanency and zeal in promoting the interests of children." He also reminded Whitney that Ontario should not pale in comparison to the way in which Quebec treated its minorities.[20] When negotiations failed to meet the demands of the bishops, McEvay was inclined to accept the inevitability of certification, promising the premier that the Church would do its best to "comply" with the terms of the bill.[21] The Seath Bill passed in April 1907, with provisions that ministry certificates would be awarded in relation to the number of years of a Sister's or Brother's teaching experience. Permanent certificates would be offered to members of religious orders who had seven years' experience, provided that they took summer sessions at the Normal School. Second- and third-class certificates required less teaching experience and the obligatory summer-school course.[22] Toronto's women religious responded quickly. By 1909 school inspector J.F. Power reported that in Toronto, "all the teachers are legally qualified except four and these are teaching on temporary certificates."[23]

The certification issue was a significant step in the professionalization and laicization of Catholic teachers. The new law put religious and lay on the same professional footing for the first time, requiring the former to achieve the same provincially recognized qualifications as the latter. Furthermore, the law put some restraints on the freedom of various orders to import uncertified reinforcements from out of the province. With a wealth of young, eager, inexpensive, and well-trained Catholic women close at hand, it is little wonder that the laity carved out a greater place for itself in the rapidly growing board.

The rising number of lay Catholic teachers entering Toronto's schools, however, created salary problems unknown prior to 1900. The Toronto separate board saved money by hiring religious orders to operate the Catholic schools in the city. Having taken vows of personal poverty, and living in communities offering all the necessities of food, shelter, and companionship, members of religious orders received salaries that were neither competitive on the open market nor compatible with the cost of living. The board's frugality regarding nuns and brothers spilled over to the lay teachers; layperson's salaries ranged between $200 and $350 per year in the 1890s, a level that fell far below the provincial average of $425 for urban female teachers.[24]

As the number of lay teachers in the board rose, so did their demands for a wage that could meet the rising cost of living. In 1917 one female teacher complained to the *Catholic Register* that she earned only $11.52 per week, or roughly $600 per year. She seriously questioned the board's inability to pay Catholic teachers a fair wage when, she remarked, a factory girl at Eaton's in Toronto earned $12.00 per week. In 1919 a male teacher commented that, after rent was paid, his weekly take-home pay was only $5.54 of $11.54. Furthermore, the rising cost of clothing and food and his personal medical expenses easily wiped out the remainder of his weekly pay-cheque. Few teachers made more than $600 per year in 1917, in a city where barest survival required at least $1,000. It was also well below the provincial average of $1,637 for male teachers and $795 for women.[25] By 1920 these demands for better pay forced the board to raise teacher salaries.

The condition of schools in which teachers served varied, but on the whole more care was taken to keep facilities in order than to do the same for teacher's salaries. Although some buildings were labelled monuments "to the bad taste of the Board," Toronto's separate schools were in far better physical shape than the frame "shacks" being used in other parts of the province.[26] In the early 1890s school buildings were wooden or brick, and were commonly heated by coal stoves. This method of heating frequently blackened the walls of the classroom, creating an unsightly sooty mess, not to mention the assault it made on the nostrils and lungs of children and teachers. In 1903 black walls and ceilings prompted inspector William Prendergast to observe wryly: "Many class rooms are in need of decoration."[27] By 1910, however, many of the older buildings had been replaced by newer brick ones with central heating, thus relieving teachers and students from the stuffy and sooty environment to which they had grown accustomed.[28]

The most pressing problems discussed by inspectors in Toronto were those of inadequate washroom facilities, lighting, and ventilation. Janitors were frequently criticized for their poor cleaning practices. As early as 1888 Daniel Cahill, candidate for the school board, complained that St Paul's School lacked running water in the summer, and St Patrick's School reported several cases of diphtheria, resulting, apparently, from a school cellar "reeking with stagnant water."[29] The movement for better public health in the schools in the late Victorian and Edwardian period brought the whole issue of washroom conditions to prominence. In the 1890s Catholic schools in Toronto fared poorly at inspection time. Poor lighting in water closets was cited as a major reason for improper cleaning, thereby inviting the spread of disease. Some schools still had outdoor privies, which the inspector described as filthy, malodorous, and too close to the schoolhouses.[30] Older buildings were singled out for having poor water closets, and those with adequate stalls were frequently reminded that they were in "need of cleaning and disinfecting regularly."[31] Prendergast had high expectations when he added: "I see no reason why school closets – especially in a city – should not be as clean and comfortable as those of a first class hotel."[32] In the early twentieth century new school buildings helped to remedy the privy problem.

Perhaps the most pressing concern for the separate school inspectors was the overcrowding that came as a result of increased student enrolment and inadequate school facilities. Aggregate figures for the board for the years from 1888 to 1921, however, indicate a general decline in the student-to-teacher ratio. In 1888 there was 1 teacher per

Table 4.2
School Population, Faculty, and Class Size in Toronto's Separate Schools, 1888–1921

	Faculty	Registered	Attendance	Classes	Student-to-teacher
1888	–	4232	–	65	65.1:1
1895	82	3341	–	–	40.7:1
1896	–	3791	3321	–	–
1897	–	3952	3369	–	–
1903	–	3910	3383	–	–
1904	–	5297	–	101	52.4:1
1905	–	4328	3872	–	–
1907	102	5753	3826	–	56.4:1
1914	–	6761	5842	147	46.0:1
1915	–	7165	6218	160	44.8:1
1916	–	6821	–	167	40.8:1
1919	187	8222	7202	–	44.0:1
1920	194	8819	–	–	45.5:1
1921	225	9666	8579	–	43.0:1

Note: Provincial ratios for the same period are: 1892 (59:1), 1902 (49:1), 1912 (45:1), and 1917 (41:1). The student-to-teacher ratio on this table has been computed by dividing the registered number of students by the number of teachers or classes, assuming that in most cases one teacher is assigned per class. Statistics for 1920 do not include 246 pupils from St John's Industrial School, St Mary's Industrial School, and Sunnyside Orphanage. Neither teacher nor classroom numbers were available for these three institutions.

Source: *Irish Canadian*, 14 Feb. 1889; MSSBA, Board Minutes, 3 Nov. 1896, 7 Feb. 1905, 4 Feb. 1908, 7 Mar. 1921; *Catholic Register*, 9 Dec. 1897, 18 May 1905, 13 Feb. 1908, 18 Mar. 1915, 9 Dec. 1915, 13 May 1916; ARCAT, Education Papers, 1914, Report of Attendance 1919, and Report of Attendance 1920; Robert Stamp, *The Schools of Ontario* (Toronto: University of Toronto Press 1982), 280.

65 students in the city's Catholic schools, slightly higher than the Ontario average. With the hiring of additional teachers to keep pace with rising student registration, the student-to-teacher ratio dropped modestly in the twentieth century, from over 52 to 1 in 1904 to 46 to 1 by 1914. Both these rates were comparable to the province-wide ratio for the same period. In 1921 there was 1 teacher to every 43 registered pupils in the Toronto Catholic board, again comparable to the public-school average in Ontario (see Table 4.2).[33]

A school-by-school analysis of attendance figures and student-teacher ratios demonstrates that congestion in the Catholic classroom, while still by no means eliminated by 1919, had improved significantly in some of the older schools since the 1890s. Some Catholic schools demonstrated overall student-to-teacher ratios comparable to the provincial average, although overcrowding could vary from grade-level to grade-level, especially in the sprawling suburban areas of the city. In 1896, at St Francis School, upper forms had class sizes under 40 pupils, while one Sister of St Joseph was forced to teach a first-form class of 107 registered students, of whom 88 regularly attended. Similarly, at St Ann's school, Inspector White commented, "order is excellent in the senior department, but weak in the junior." This was not surprising, since the junior teacher had a class of 70, while the senior teacher supervised 25.[34] Overcrowded junior classes were commonplace and continued to be singled out by critical inspectors well into the twentieth century (see Table 4.3).[35]

Catholics usually laid much of the blame for inadequate facilities, overcrowding, and low salaries on the minuscule revenue base allowed the Catholic schools in comparison to the non-sectarian public schools. The dollar per student allotment to separate schools was far lower due to the ineligibility of Catholic schools to receive corporate taxes.[36] Catholics even lost tax revenue through mixed marriages and the failure of Catholics to register themselves as separate school supporters. In such cases Catholics, who were entitled to direct their taxes to the separate board, often neglected to indicate their preference to the city assessors, thus depriving Catholic schools of needed tax dollars.[37] At the same time, non-Catholic men with Catholic children attending separate schools were legally bound to direct their taxes to the public board. The potential double tax burden was too overwhelming for many of these families. Nevertheless, by 1919, 8 per cent of Catholic children in the Toronto Separate School Board had Protestant fathers who paid fees to the separate schools in addition to their obligatory taxes to the public school board.[38]

Limited finances, overcrowding, and modest facilities do not appear to have detracted from the quality of education received by some Catholic children. Separate school inspectors offered copious praise of the discipline and intelligence of the students. From 1890 to 1910 students inspected scored "good" and "middling" evaluations on their work in reading, arithmetic, history, spelling, and other elementary school subjects. In 1890 Sister Martha's fourth class at St Francis school was considered "one of the best of that grade in the city."[39] Comparable reports were filed for high school classes throughout the period. "Bad" inspections were few, and negative

Table 4.3
Attendance, Faculty, and Class Size by School, 1895–1919

School	1895			1907			1919		
	Staff	Pupils	Ratio	Staff	Pupils	Ratio	Staff	Pupils	Ratio
St Helen's	6	316	52.7	8	409	51.1	12	528	44.0
St Cecilia's	2	119	59.5	4	182	45.5	7	337	48.1
St Mary's	15	584	38.9	13	578	44.5	15	655	43.7
St Francis's	6	331	55.2	6	313	52.2	13	716	55.1
St Peter's	2	69	34.5	4	227	56.8	9	387	43.0
St Basil's	4	193	48.3	4	173	43.3	4	170	42.5
St Patrick's	9	428	47.6	10	380	38.0	10	426	42.6
St Paul's	14	638	45.6	13	566	43.5	16	669	41.8
St Joseph's	2	98	49.0	2	122	61.0	9	421	46.8
St Ann's	2	95	47.5	4	195	48.8	6	317	52.8
St John's	2	83	41.5	3	126	42.0	5	234	46.8
St Michael's	8	301	37.6	8	304	38.0	6	271	45.2
De La Salle	5	78	15.6	5	98	19.6	6	209	34.8
Loretto HS	2	32	16.0	NR			NR		
St Joseph's HS	3	59	19.7	4	76	19.0	6	132	22.0
Holy Family	NR			2	165	82.5	7	328	46.9
Sunnyside	NR			5	233	46.6	5	185	37.0
St John's Ind	NR			2	81	40.5	3	114	38.0
St Mary's Ind	NR			1	36	36.0	1	43	43.0
St Anthony's	NR			NR			8	368	46.0
Holy Name	NR			NR			7	348	49.7
St James's	NR			NR			6	256	42.7
St Charles's	NR			NR			1	20	20.0
Lourdes	NR			NR			4	198	49.5
St Monica's	NR			NR			3	103	34.3
St Vincent's	NR			NR			3	197	65.7
Others	NR			NR			7	266	38.0
Total	82	3424	41.7	98	4264	43.5	179	7898	44.1

Note: Ratios indicate the number of students per teacher.

Source: AO, Ministry of Education, Separate School Inspector's Reports, 1895, 1907; ARCAT, Education Papers, Report of Attendance, 1919. All calculations are mine.

comments were usually reserved for overcrowded classes reported to
have had poor discipline.[40] That so many young women from St Joseph's Academy easily met the requirements of the normal school for
teaching certificates also attests to the high standards set by the Sisters in their schools.[41] Despite ongoing gossip about the inferiority of
Catholic schools, inspectors consistently acknowledged the steady
improvement in the classrooms of the TSSB.[42]

The fight for quality can better be measured in terms of the Catholic schools' adaptability to the "new education." In the 1880s and
1890s middle-class Ontarians had demanded a more practical education beyond the traditional three "r"s. New programs in agricultural,
technical, and commercial training were added to Ontario schools. In
addition, the innovative teaching ideas of Friederich Froebel became
popular, resulting in the establishment of kindergarten classes, where
children could learn through play.[43] After 1900 the number of voca-
tional schools increased, as did high school attendance, and by 1905
Premier Whitney adopted "the new education" as the Conservative
Party's education policy.[44]

Catholic educators in Toronto did not ignore the "new education."
In 1890, 49 five-year-old children were registered in the board's first
kindergarten. Columns by Emma O'Sullivan in the *Register* offered
strong support for the ideas of Froebel, and urged more kindergar-
tens in Catholic schools.[45] Also innovative was the Christian Brothers' establishment, in 1893, of St John's Industrial School for Boys at
Blantyre Park. St John's offered homeless, destitute, delinquent, and
orphaned boys an open and community-style environment where
they could learn agricultural skills, floriculture, baking, tailoring, car-
pentry, typewriting, and printing.[46] St John's also ensured that Catholic waifs and strays would aquire useful skills and become good
citizens under a humane "Catholic" influence.[47] Precedents for technical and commercial education had been pioneered by the brothers
at De La Salle Institute. In 1890 Inspector J.F. White commended the
Brothers for their "highly creditable" programs and the "exception-
ally good" technical drawing exhibited by the students.[48] Catholic
high schools also offered courses in typewriting, bookkeeping, business, phonography, and sewing as supplements to the basic liberal
arts and sciences program.[49]

Generally, the twentieth century witnessed greater interest among
Ontarians in having their children enter high school. Catholic parents
and educators shared this concern. In 1904, 235 students were registered in local Catholic high schools. By 1916 over 1,115 Catholics
could be found in classes above the fourth form, and of these 59 were
in attendance at public high schools.[50] Catholic students were also

passing high school entrance examinations in greater numbers. In 1908 only 115 passed the annual examination. Six years later, 207 of the 244 children who attempted the examination passed it.[51] On several occasions separate school students passed the examinations in proportionately higher numbers than students leaving public schools.[52] Furthermore, the numbers of students entering even the fourth form increased significantly prior to the Great War. Greater numbers entering high school are evidence not only of greater interest in higher learning but also a credit to the high standards set by Catholic schools.

Improvements in facilities, teacher qualifications, and basic curriculum satisfied many in the Catholic community, but not all. Numerous Catholic children were still sent to the neighbourhood public school. Sometimes it was just a matter of proximity: the public school was closer to home. At other times the trouble of double taxation for interfaith families was a factor. Some prominent Catholic families supported the Catholic elementary schools but preferred to enrol their children in more prestigious non-Catholic academies later on. Businessman and merchant John Mallon, for example, was a pillar of St Helen's parish, and his children attended the local parochial school. Nevertheless, when they were of age, two of his sons, Edward and Michael Patrick, were enrolled in Upper Canada College.[53] Others, like Thomas Mulvey, an aspiring public servant from St Mary's parish, were disgusted by the intermingling of their children with the "unwashed" or the "border-line criminal classes." In the dying days of O'Connor's episcopate, Mulvey complained directly to the Vatican that, due to the lack of an education that could provide "culture and refinement" to Catholic young men, some families were sending their lads to boarding schools in the United States, or to "protestant" schools. For those of Mulvey's ilk, the local schools had not progressed fast enough to "produce men of learning and culture to lead us on."[54]

For the majority of the English-speaking Catholic community, both washed and "unwashed," the early twentieth century brought greater confidence in their schools. Separate schools were able to provide training adequate to permit and encourage Catholic students to continue their studies beyond the elementary level. Moreover, Catholic schools provided both the necessary religious indoctrination and ever-improving secular programs, thereby enabling Catholic children to live and work fully in the society around them. Ongoing development of facilities, personnel, and services made good the attempts by new generations of clergy, laity, and religious to exorcise the demons of second-class status.

Fresh coats of paint, larger schools, a professional corps of teachers, and some of those "new Yankee frills" in curriculum provided the broad context for a significant transformation in the Catholic schools. By the early twentieth century Toronto's separate schools produced a new breed of Catholic child – one who was thoroughly immersed in matters of faith and in the qualities of upstanding Canadian citizenship. At times, the older generations of Irish Catholics tut-tutted in disapproval of the new, of how they discarded "dear old mothers native tongue" and declared "themselves against everything Irish."[55] What must have come as even more of a shock to the "old timers" was that the separate schools had a hand in redirecting the minds and loyalties of their children and grandchildren. The schools cultivated the young English-speaking Catholic child's growing identification with all things Canadian. Each day, children imbibed the British and Canadian themes that flowed from the poems, stories, and histories printed in their readers and textbooks. Their little minds soaked up tales of Catholic heroes like Jean de Brébeuf and Thomas More in addition to the sagas of secular saints like Isaac Brock, Lord Nelson, and General James Wolfe. As their imaginations trod the earth with such saints, soldiers, and statesmen, Catholic children learned that they were part of the largest and most powerful Empire in the world, one upon which the sun never set. The generation gap between the "old timers" and the new generations of Catholic Canadians was widening indeed.

Between 1887 and 1922 Catholic schools in Toronto were committed to produce virtuous Christians and good citizens of Canada and the Empire. William Prendergast's comment's regarding St John's Industrial School could have been made with equal force for any other school in the board: "Every effort is made to strengthen the character of the boys, to make them good men and good citizens."[56] Clergy and leading lay educators consistently reminded Catholic teachers of their onerous duties in upholding these two pillars of piety and patriotism. In 1890 Archbishop John Walsh instructed teachers "to fit them [children] as far as possible for their future duties, and at the same time deposit in their young minds the seeds of virtue."[57] That same year George Ross, minister of Education, reminded a convention of Toronto's Catholic educators that character formation and "thoroughly trained" citizens were the goals of all Ontario's teachers.[58]

Catholic commitment to character building and citizenship training were intensified over the three decades between Ross's speech and the First World War. Basilian Father and educator M.J. Oliver was convinced that Catholic schools were responsible for preparing Catholic youth to take their place in the home, the Church, and the state.

"The school is the servant of this trio," wrote Oliver. "Their needs must be considered and their commands obeyed."[59] Taking this responsibility of his schools seriously, Archbishop Neil McNeil, when arguing in 1919 for the extension of government funding to Catholic high schools, asserted that "Separate Schools are an efficient instrument for the training of Ontario citizens. We have passed the test of war. No one can claim, and I do not know of any who do claim, that the graduates of Separate Schools in Ontario lacked either patriotism in enlisting or courage in battle."[60] Catholic schools flew the Union Jack, commemorated the arrival of United Empire Loyalists, and made "The Maple Leaf Forever" a feature at school concerts. Such was the outward testimony of schools engaged in "the careful inculcation of religion and patriotism."[61]

While patriotic education gained an unheralded prominence in Catholic schools, religious instruction was the chief pillar upon which all else in the curriculum rested. Catholic leaders and educators alike sought a school system wherein all facets of education and all knowledge fitting for practical life would be informed by and "under the holy influence of religion."[62] The connection, however, between a Catholic education and national loyalty was self-evident to many Catholic leaders.[63] McNeil emphasized the patriotic role of the school and more so the fact that "a good Catholic cannot be a bad citizen. Goodness of character is the foundation of good citizenship."[64] C.J. Foy, a leading Catholic layman, reaffirmed this when he noted that the purity, frequency of sacraments, and "divine knowledge" taught in separate schools made better men and women, and certainly a better country.[65]

The foundations of religious teaching rested on two cornerstones: Butler's *Catechism* and Gilmour's *Bible History*.[66] Butler's provided a formulaic question-and-answer exploration of the principal tenets of Catholic belief. Students were required to read and memorize the questions in order to prepare for semi-annual examinations supervised by Father Hugh J. Canning, diocesan inspector of Religious Education. Examination results were mixed, frequently leaving one to doubt how much "purity" and "divine knowledge" was getting through to Catholic students. St Helen's girls' classes consistently scored higher than 80 per cent from 1902 to 1911, while classes from such inner-city schools as St Patrick's, St Paul's, and St Mary's rarely exceeded averages of 65 per cent. Canning attributed the disparity to "careless and slovenly work" and "vague answers" by students, and implied that some teachers were "half-hearted" in their work.[67]

In 1914, however, Archbishop McNeil blamed the weakness in religious education and catechetics on the texts themselves. He was extremely critical of Butler's, with its emphasis on rote learning and mouthing the prepared answers to questions of faith and morals. To McNeil such methods did less to inculcate a love of the Church than they engendered "distaste for religious principles and pious practices, a distaste which often grows with age and manifests itself in religious indifference."[68] These criticisms were substantiated by teachers themselves, one of whom commented that rote learning did not help the child's understanding of religion. Sister M. Ernestine (Margaret Pierce) of the Loretto Sisters echoed McNeil's criticism, claiming that when teaching with Butler's "the answer comes back in a monotonous blank verse sort of way (lest one word slip and thereby the whole meaningless answer be lost)."[69] By 1918 the Butler was updated, although McNeil kept searching for a better catechism that approached Christian doctrine more historically. In that year McNeil found a more developmental approach in the catechisms of Father Roderick McEachen of the Catholic University of America, and made arrangements for Canadian publication and distribution rights.[70]

Attempts by the provincial government to interfere with religious education in Toronto's separate schools were uniformly rebuffed. In 1913 and 1914 John Seath approved the preparation of a series of texts in moral education. A faulty line of communication between Seath and separate school inspector J.F. Power led the minister to believe that these *Golden Rule Books* would be adopted in both public and separate schools. McNeil quickly dispelled the misinformation, claiming that the books would be acceptable to Catholic students within the public system but would in no way be used in separate schools. "Catholics," he said, "have no idea of allowing their church to be the subject of the State in the sphere of moral teaching." That this view was upheld by other Ontario bishops underscores the fiercely guarded nature of Catholic religious education.[71]

Spiritual education provided the foundation for the education of the Catholic child in the secular disciplines. Catholic educators were less jealous of complete control in these matters, which meant that Catholic schools borrowed and adapted the resources and materials used in the public common schools. In spelling, arithmetic, history, geography, hygiene, and algebra the public school texts were used widely in the TSSB. More importantly, the use of public school readers, history texts, and geography books brought Catholic students into direct contact with prevailing attitudes, ideas, and prejudices relevant to Canadian society. There is little doubt that Toronto's Catholic schools exposed students to stories and ideas designed to inculcate loyalty, honour, patriotism, and good citizenship in both a Canadian and a British imperial context.

Readers for phonics and literature were central to the curriculum. As such, Catholics often demanded some control over the types of readers used in their schools. In the late nineteenth century Catholic schools in the city had used a variety of readers, many of them published by Sadlier's of Montreal and none of them authorized by the Ontario Ministry of Education. In 1886 the Toronto Separate School Board approved the use of Sadlier's readers in all Catholic schools, although several experts levied criticism at the often "too childish" selections in the fourth book.[72] The readers themselves, especially the third and fourth books designed for senior grades, were markedly Catholic in tone, including as they did Catholic prayers, Bible stories, lives of saints, and episodes from the history of the Catholic Church. Noticeably absent were poetry or prose that might instil a sense of Irishness among children. Stories and poems were based on historical events and activities common to Canada and Britain. Among the dozen selections on Canadian themes in the fourth book were included "The Winter Carnival," "First View of Montreal," "Jacques Cartier," "Dominion of Canada," "The Canadian Rebellion," and "Toronto." The latter praised the police and fire brigades of the city, and mentioned that sectarian tensions were on the wane and "a fuller national sentiment on the rise."[73]

The 1886 editions of Sadlier contained no poems or prose on Irish themes. Instead, the reader included numerous selections from British and American writers such as Dickens, Bulwer-Lytton, Tennyson, Gray, Hawthorne, Longfellow, Southey, and Oliver Wendell Holmes. In the 1890s the revised Sadlier series included selections on "Daniel O'Connell," "The Cross and the Harp," and "The Exile of Erin," but there is no evidence, from either the school board records or autographs within existing readers, that suggests these texts were adopted in Toronto.[74] The new books, however, contained a plethora of Canadian and British items, indicating once more the extent to which Catholic schools had departed from former attempts to imbue new generations of children with a sense of Irishness at the expense of their Canadian citizenship.[75]

In 1899 the Toronto board replaced the Sadlier series with the new Canadian Catholic Series published by Copp Clark. The pedagogical flaws of the Sadlier series had become too noticeable by the 1890s, and the bishops of Ontario invited the province's leading Catholic teachers to submit proposals for a new series. Father John Teefy, superior of St Michael's College, was appointed editor of the five readers in the new series. By the end of the decade the inspector of Catholic schools gave approval to the final product, and for the first time the Ministry of Education authorized distinctive readers for Catholic schools. The Canadian Catholic Series quickly replaced all unauthorized readers in Toronto's separate schools.[76]

The quality of the new series was quickly recognized. Teachers commented on their superior treatment of phonics, the quality of the Catholic material, and the overall physical durability of the books themselves.[77] The *Catholic Record*, however, was far more pointed in its praise of the "character-building" aspects of the fourth reader, in particular its selections from "the best English, American and Canadian writers ... whose influence in molding character is so great."[78] The *Record* added that the series was easily up to the standard of the readers used in public schools. That there was only one selection on an Irish theme in the fourth book – "The Exile of Erin" – raised no noticeable outcry against the readers.

The pattern of the selections was similar to the Sadlier readers, although the Copp Clark readers had a greater quantity of Canadian and British selections than the Sadlier. In the third and fourth Books children were exposed to numerous religious pieces interspersed among some overtly patriotic selections. In the third book, Teefy's own "Early Settlers in Canada" was prefaced by an incantation of thanks for the many comforts and conveniences in this "rich and fair" country.[79] Close by one finds Agnes M. Machar's stirring ode to the Dominion, "Canada Forever":

> Saxon and Celt and Norman we:
> Each race its memory keeps,
> Yet o'er us all from sea to sea
> One Red Cross Banner sweeps.
> Long may our "Greater Britain" stand
> The bulwark of the free;
> But Canada, our own dear land,
> Our first love is for thee.
>
> God bless our own Canadian land
> Of mountain, lake and river;
> The chorus ring from strand to strand
> Of "Canada Forever."[80]

Such verse sent a clear message to the reader: Canada first. The rest of the book seemed to follow suit, with nineteen other pieces related to Canada, her history, people, and landscape. After their encounter with Darnell's "The Maple" at the beginning of the text, children set off for adventure in "The Great Fur Land," were thwarted by "The Forest Fire," and challenged in their imaginations by "The Climbing of Percé Rock." They learned of the "glorious" exploits of General James Wolfe on the Plains of Abraham and were called, by John Schultz, to recognize their membership in "a northern race ... ruled by a northern Queen." Such was their heritage, they were told; such was their privilege.[81] In contrast to this gushing of Canadian patriotism, only two Irish selections were offered.

Added to the Canadian content were a considerable number of selections from English history and literature. Poems and stories from Dickens, Wordsworth, Shakespeare, Browning, Conan Doyle, Coleridge, and Gray not only exposed Catholic students to the finest in English literature but sensitized them to British culture and the historical events that made Britain the great power she was. The inclusion of Walter Scott's "Love of Country" in the book, although not particularly directed to Canada, called upon students to "love their native land" and honour their roots.[82] Collectively, the English pieces, when combined with the Canadian and American selections, offered Catholic children a powerful portrait of a young, rich country with a glorious heritage and a promising future. Canada was a nation of which a Catholic student was to be proud.

The Catholic readers clearly illustrated the double-edged intent of Catholic schools. Numerous pieces on the Virgin Mary, saints, Church history, Bible stories, and Catholic heroes put children in touch with the current Catholic devotional ethos. Canadian- and British-flavoured poetry and prose, some of it stridently nationalist in tone, provided students with the raw materials from which civic pride and strong citizenship could be cultivated. For children in Toronto's separate schools, the traditional inculcation of Irish Tridentine Catholicism was quickly being replaced by a new partnership between Catholic orthodoxy and English-Canadian patriotism. Although a sense of the Irish past was never completely lost, it was definitely eclipsed by the Canadian present.

The demise of the Copp Clark readers by 1910 opened up new avenues for religious and patriotic instruction. Archbishop Charles Hugh Gauthier of Kingston, and later of Ottawa, reported that most of the teachers in his diocese found the books inferior in quality to the public school readers, and that they were more costly to purchase in classroom sets.[83] Gauthier was one voice of dissent among many. In 1909 the bishops agreed that a series of separate school readers would be retained if financially possible. Archbishop McEvay, Bishop David Scollard of Sault Ste Marie, and Bishop Narcisse Lorrain of Pembroke pushed hard for revisions. McEvay even commissioned Teefy and Hugh Canning to proceed with examination of the new *Public School Reader* and supervision of the revisions of the Catholic readers.[84]

These plans collapsed, however, in May 1909, when Copp Clark announced that the new venture would be too expensive. A set of revised Catholic readers would cost $1.20, while the cost of a comparable set of newly revised *Public School Readers* was only 49¢.[85] Although the publishers lowered the cost estimates, the lack of available funds in Catholic schools across the province forced the termination of the project by 1910.[86]

This failure to revise the Catholic readers left two options open to the hierarchy: continue the use of the old series or adopt the new series of *Public School Readers*. The latter choice was not extraordinary; in 1890 at least 84 per cent of Catholic schools in the province were using public school readers on a full-time or partial basis.[87] The new readers, however, troubled some Catholic examiners. Teefy, having examined the books for McEvay, thought that the readers were generally good, save for some items of dubious moral and religious value, and several sections of "excessive militarism," which he claimed would "excite antagonism" so far as "our French-Canadian citizens are concerned."[88] What Teefy did not mention was whether he thought the "militarism" appropriate for English-speaking Catholic Canadians. Other evaluators shared some of Teefy's concerns. Catholic school inspector Michael O'Brien of Peterborough considered much in the *Public School Readers* to be excellent. He approved of patriotism in the texts, "but when the patriotism savours of militarism or jingoism there is not the same defence to be offered." In the final analysis he recommended to McEvay that the Catholic readers be retained but that the public school texts could be used as supplementary reading.[89]

Regardless of this reluctance to adopt texts in which patriotism was twisted into militarism, the bishops were prepared to adopt *Public School Readers* for the separate schools. By January 1909 Gauthier had already stated his preference for them because they made better financial and pedagogical sense.[90] The Ontario Catholic hierarchy met in Peterborough and discussed the possibility of using the adoption of public school textbooks as a bargaining chip with the government in order to win greater concessions for separate schools. Reporting on the meeting to Premier Whitney, Bishop Scollard asserted:

Uniformity we understand is one of the great aims of your Department of Education. By this concession we have made a great stride towards this goal ... It is we say it advisedly, almost the *surrender* of a principle. Catholic schools and Catholic readers have ever gone hand in hand. Such readers were considered indispensable to us because of the moral and religious knowledge inculcated in them, and because of the exemplary ideals of the noblest virtues set forth in them, to impress and mould the tender plastic minds of the pupils. With no small reluctance then, we have consented to this compromise, and have done so with the belief that some concessions for the well-being of our Separate Schools will be forthcoming. [91]

In return the hierarchy demanded a fair share of corporate school taxes, an equitable system of municipal grants, and the right of Catholic ratepayers to declare their notice of school support orally. While the official minutes of the 13 January meeting make no reference to the bishops' surrender, Ontario's episcopate was willing to adopt "jungoistic" readers if tax concessions were forthcoming from Whitney's government.[92]

The *Public School Readers* made their way into Toronto Catholic schools after 1910.[93] There had been no concessions at the bargaining table to warrant their use, just the practical necessity of having updated texts in the schools. The new textbooks were clearly the most imperialistic readers to be introduced to date.[94] The portrait of King Edward VII and a print of the Union Jack bearing the inscription "One Flag / One Fleet / One Throne" at the beginning of the fourth book essentially set the tone for the entire series. Catholic children followed the exploits of the British Army and Navy to all corners of the globe. They witnessed the rugged pioneering spirit of the "makers" of Canada. They were stirred by the hymns of the Empire composed by the likes of Rudyard Kipling, F.G. Scott, and W.E. Henley.[95] Catholic teachers would have been sensitized to this orgy of imperial nationalism by the precedent set by the Copp Clark Catholic series. It was difficult for teachers and students to avoid the "patriotic" selections – they were just too numerous, and crafted in much too interesting a fashion to be ignored. The combined use of the new *Public School Readers* and the old *Catholic School Readers* helped awaken Catholic youth to a love of Canada, and for the Empire of which they were happily a part.[96]

The nationalistic sentiment engendered by public and Catholic school readers was fortified by the history and geography texts used by older students. According to the teacher's manual, "History may be made, in several ways, an important factor in informing intelligent, patriotic citizens."[97] By means of history, it continued, teachers could "correct the prejudices – social, political, religious – of communities."[98] In Ontario educators had long regarded history as a subject that could develop a child's appreciation for Canada, assimilate the foreigner, and project qualities of good citizenship. To this end Education Minister George Ross (1883–1904) had put increased emphasis on history and geography in elementary schools.[99]

Prior to 1900 the Catholic press and hierarchy had been critical of the anti-Catholic prejudices of public school history textbooks. The *Catholic Weekly Review* protested that the unfair treatment given Mary Queen of Scots in school histories was offensive to Catholic students.[100] Nevertheless, the Sisters of St Joseph, who operated the majority of separate schools in Toronto, claimed in 1895 that one-quarter of their students were enrolled in either British or Canadian history. By 1906 this number had increased to nearly one-third. According to Toronto Separate School Board minutes after 1900, all the history texts being used were the public school histories.[101]

Other Catholic educators attempted to remedy the problem of Protestant "bias" by creating histories of their own that would promote "the whole truth in regard to Catholic interests."[102] In 1888 the Sadlier Company published *The Outlines of Canadian History*, a very brief survey of the nation's political history from New France to the Riel Rebellion of 1885. It was decidedly inferior to its public school rival, W.J. Robertson's *History of England and Canada*, in length, depth, and breadth. The Catholic bias of the Sadlier text was clear:

The pioneers of America were almost exclusively Catholic. The importance of this remark may not fully appear in referring to the era of Columbus and the Cabots, because then all Europeans were Catholics. Its real significance is seen in a later period. During the sixteenth century, while the nations of northern Europe were distracted by the disorders caused by the heretical doctrines of Luther, the daring sons of Catholic France, Spain, and Portugal were traversing this continent in all directions ... sounding the praises of God amid regions that hitherto echoed only to the cries of wild beasts and savage men.[103]

This Catholic version of Canadian history was neither authorized on Circular 14 nor used as the exclusive history text in separate schools. By October 1893 the public school texts were the principal ones used in Toronto's Catholic schools.[104]

By the 1890s the public school British and Canadian history texts offered greater balance when broaching issues sensitive in Catholic-Protestant relations. Contentious issues in British history – the English Reformation, "Bloody" Mary Tudor, the reign of Elizabeth I, the "gunpowder plot," the Battle of the Boyne, and the conquest of Canada – were treated in an even-handed manner, with even Mary Tudor and Thomas More garnering surprisingly sympathetic portrayals.[105] Much more prevalent in the texts was the argument and style of the "National School" of Canadian historical writing, a variant of the "whig" historiographical tradition. Far from Catholic-baiting, whig-gish authors extolled their faith in English institutions, religious toler-ation, and the progress of individual liberty through British constitutional development since the Glorious Revolution.[106] When focused on Canada, these books trumpeted the idea of progress and the historical milestones that, in an upward and linear fashion, had culminated in the great achievement of responsible government.[107] Catholic students, like their counterparts in public schools, learned how Canadian self-government was the necessary precursor to full partnership within an imperial federation, in which Canada would share power with other Dominions and Britain itself.[108] Transcending the rather narrow and jaded sectarian flavour often evident in the his-tory texts of previous generations, these new school texts took a high moral tone, exuding pride in the young Dominion and confidently advocating Canadian patriotism and duty to the British Empire as a common focus of loyalty for all Canadian children.[109] After 1910 the geography texts used in the schools claimed that this confidence in being a northern people was grounded in scientific "truth." Unlike the "backward tribes" of the "brown race" or the "childlike" mem-bers of the "black race," the British peoples were among the most progressive in the world: "they have won where others have failed; and their colonies ... have grown great and wealthy, and have be-come powerful and important members of the British Empire."[110]

The receptiveness and sensitivity of Catholic children to the bar-rage of nationalistic sentiment was evident in their school activities, especially after 1900. The "Maple Leaf Forever" outflanked "The Wearing of the Green" as the principal anthem sung by Catholic stu-dents. The *Catholic Register*'s criticism of the "Maple Leaf's" narrow conception of Canada did not hinder its use by Catholic children in the classroom or on Dominion Day.[111] Patriotic music in the schools was accompanied by the flying of the Canadian Ensign at each school, the drawing of the Union Jack in art classes, and topical reso-lutions of import to Canada and the Empire debated by students in the Catholic Debating League.[112] After 1899 Catholic schools also par-ticipated in the province-wide celebrations of Empire Day, held one day in advance of Victoria Day (24 May). The *Register* supported the festivity as an important means to cultivate British patriotism among Canadians and to foster "high national sentiment in youth."[113] The flag-waving, writing contests, patriotic singing, cadet corps drills, and allegiance-pledging all associated with the day drew Catholic children ever more completely into the vortex of imperial nationalism that was sweeping across English-speaking Canada.[114] The children of Catholic schools, particularly the cadets who shouldered their replicas of rifles in the early 1900s, were putty in the hands of the recruiter during the First World War.

In the early twentieth century the Catholic classroom became a curious blend of the sacred and the secular. While the crucifix and portraits of the Sacred Heart and Immaculate Heart of Mary still adorned the classroom walls as testaments of the faith, they were now joined by drawings of flags and the odes to Empire – and, for those who could afford it, that world map, shaded in British red in a broken pattern that enveloped the earth. On special occasions even red, white, and blue bunting might appear.[115] Catholic children learned their twofold obligations: to be obedient servants of Christ and his Church, and to be loyal citizens of Canada and the Empire. School activities, readers, history books, and geography lessons left their indelible imprint on the minds, hearts, and souls of young Catholics. There was reason for the "old timer" to be shocked. For many students pride in Canada lodged in their head and heart, and in doing so further distanced them from the Irish heritage of their parents, grandparents, and great-grandparents. Quite simply, between 1887 and 1922 the separate elementary schools in Toronto produced new generations of Canadianized English-speaking Catholics.

While Catholic elementary schools expanded and refined their programs, Catholic higher education in Toronto at the turn of the century advanced at a snail's pace. A minority of Catholics went to high school, and even fewer pursued university or college training. Blame for this situation was cast in all directions. Rationalizations for the slow integration of Catholics into circles of higher learning included inadequate high school facilities, the lack of a Catholic university in the city, Protestant bigotry, the godlessness of secular universities, and parental neglect.[116] In the 1890s Archbishop Walsh lamented the fact that clergy and professionals had to be imported from abroad because young men in Toronto chose not to attend St Michael's or any other Catholic college. In that decade nearly half of the students at St Michael's were Americans lured by low fees and the school's "good tradition."[117]

The most poignant criticism laid at the door of Toronto Catholics themselves was the lack of an "Irish Catholic" tradition of higher education. Although Catholics of Irish descent in the city had steadily improved their economic and social standing, and increasingly identified with Canadian customs and a English Canadian patriotism, they often lacked an appreciation for higher learning. At the *Catholic Register* Patrick F. Cronin commented bluntly:

The old type of Irishman was careless in seeing to it that his children received the advantages of an education: as a rule he came to this country with absolutely no school training, and failed to see the necessity of it in his children. They went to school when they liked and were invariably taken away in the early spring. It was a system of winter education, of education that profited him little or nothing because of its shortness. As soon as the boy had grown strong enough to work, he was set at it. Poverty was pleaded as an excuse for this injustice to the children. There is scarcely any necessity now-a-days to show the fallacy of such shortsightedness.[118]

In order to reverse this trend, clergy, the press, and the hierarchy encouraged Catholics to fund their college scholarship programs adequately and direct their children to a high school and university education as the surest means of advancement in Canadian society.[119]

This plea for higher education was accelerated during the episcopate of Neil McNeil, himself a former president of St Francis Xavier University. McNeil tirelessly promoted university education for Catholics, as did his friend and ally Henry Somerville, whom McNeil brought to Toronto from England. In 1918 Somerville reminded Catholics that technical education, even if it was in a public high school, was strongly urged and approved by Archbishop McNeil. Such an admission that learning beyond fourth form was a necessity, be it in a public or Catholic institution, was a revolutionary stance for Catholic leaders. On the one hand it demonstrated the high value placed on education by English-speaking Catholics of non-Irish origin, and on the other marked a departure in thinking about the need for denominational segregation in higher learning.[120]

McNeil also counted himself among the many English-speaking Catholics who eagerly sought the establishment of a Canadian version of the Catholic University of America. Even prior to his arrival in Toronto, some English-speaking Catholic laymen suggested that if young Catholic men wanted to raise their status in Canadian society, more would have to enrol in professional programs – law, medicine, engineering – which were unavailable in Ontario's Catholic colleges. These same Catholics, however, were reluctant to endanger their faith by attending classes at secular universities.[121] In 1906 the *Register* suggested the facilities at the University of Ottawa could be converted into a national English-speaking Catholic institution. The *Register*, however, warned its constituents that a separate English-speaking Catholic university would have to depend on a scattered English-speaking Catholic population, many of whom had limited means.[122]

The practicality of converting the University of Ottawa was complicated by the vicious backbiting between Ottawa's French- and English-speaking Catholics over control of the university. In 1901 prominent English-speaking Catholics in the Ottawa area petitioned the Oblate Order, who operated the University of Ottawa, to transform that institution into an English-speaking school.[123] Within a year Cardinal Gerolamo Gotti of the Propaganda Fide rejected the petition on grounds that the university was intended for all Catholics regardless of "language, race, or nationality."[124] This rebuke, combined with the earlier removal of Michael Francis Fallon, OMI, the champion of the English cause on faculty, signalled a temporary defeat for the English takeover at the University of Ottawa.

The dream of a Canadian version of the Catholic University of America took much longer to die. In 1914 McNeil broached the subject with the Apostolic Delegate, who agreed to resume discussions in Rome.[125] A magnificent campus was planned for the tiny Ottawa resort community of Britannia, northeast of the capital, at the end of the street-railway line.[126] Economic restraints during the war, however, and the fear of losing too much money on the venture caused considerable re-evaluation of the proposal by Catholic leaders. A takeover of the University of Ottawa was judged by some bishops to be impractical, considering that the school lost roughly $3,000 per month. In addition, the shaky financial status of the model Catholic University of America, despite its huge endowments from wealthy American Catholics, confirmed earlier fears that a Canadian university would be forever in dire financial straits. In a confidential letter to McNeil, Father J.W. McIsaac of St Francis Xavier wondered if some Catholics were "sufficiently removed from barbarism" to be ready for their own university.[127] By 1922 the National English-speaking Catholic University project was temporarily on hold, as local initiatives provided more workable and immediate solutions for English-speaking Canada's bishops and leading laymen.[128]

In Toronto, leadership in transforming Catholic higher education came from three sources: Archbishop Neil McNeil; Basilian priest and Oshawa native Henry Carr; and several women associated with St Joseph's and Loretto Colleges, particularly Gertrude Lawlor, Sister Austin MacKay, CSJ, and Mother Ignatia Lynn, IBVM. For his part, in 1913 McNeil arranged for the Paulist Fathers to establish a Catholic chaplaincy at the University of Toronto. They soon founded the Newman Club, a Catholic clubhouse and chapel that provided room and board, social activities, daily mass, and spiritual counselling for Catholic men at the university. McNeil thought that the presence of these priests would preserve the faith of Catholics on campus, and perhaps encourage other Catholics to attend the university without fear of losing their faith.[129] Prior to the establishment of the Newman Club, Catholic men attending the degree-granting University College depended entirely on St Michael's College for the satisfaction of their spiritual and social needs within a Catholic context.[130]

St Michael's had long been the largest Catholic presence at the University of Toronto. Founded by the Basilian Fathers in 1852, St Michael's offered theological and classical training to young men, many of whom aspired to the priesthood. In 1881 St Michael's affiliated with the University of Toronto, thereby allowing its students in the history section to be evaluated by the university. Its five-year classical program was still operative, however, and graduates were not eligible for a university degree.[131] Only its philosophy and history programs were recognized by the university.

By 1900 St Michael's was little more than a "stagnant" Catholic backwater that was probably as much a hindrance as a help to Catholics aspiring to higher education. Its program of studies was well out of date for Catholic men seeking careers other than the priesthood. Even for those interested in the liberal arts it offered no degrees on par with the province's secular universities. According to Edmund McCorkell, it was more American than Torontonian in composition: "It was a mere ghetto of Catholic boys, mostly American, in a growing Canadian city with which it had little or no contact ... It prepared its students adequately for the priesthood of the time, which was its original purpose, and it was for that reason that practically all the American boys came, attracted by the lower fees."[132] St Michael's offered no incentive to Catholic men in the city to aspire to college education close to home, and this may have been one of the reasons for the absence of Toronto's Catholics from institutions of higher learning. Boys who did not want to become priests but aspired to secular training without fear of losing their Catholicity found no solace at St Michael's.

The coming of Father Henry Carr to St Michael's dramatically altered the state of Catholic higher education in the city. In 1906 he negotiated the full integration of St Michael's into the arts program at the University of Toronto. In the 1907–08 academic year St Michael's had two classes ready for the university's entrance examinations. By 1910 St Michael's graduated its first class of men through University College, marking the official integration with the university.[133] One year later Catholic men were able to graduate directly from St Michael's. Now Catholic Torontonians at last had a degree-granting institution under Catholic auspices, thus opening the doors to potentially greater Catholic access to higher education.

Catholic women also recognized the potential benefits of affiliation with the University of Toronto. Graduates of the academies run by the Sisters of St Joseph and the Loretto Sisters normally had to pursue university degrees by enrolling at University College. By the end of the first decade of this century both religious orders were seeking affiliation independently for their academies. The Sisters of St Joseph had strong ties to the University of Toronto community. Sister Austin MacKay was an award-winning student in first year "moderns," and the Catholic Women's Club of the university met at St Joseph's Convent nearby.[134] With the federation between St Michael's and the university completed in 1910, the overtures of the Sisters of St Joseph and Mother Ignatia Lynn of the Lorettos were rebuffed by university President Robert Falconer. A compromise was reached whereby the two women's colleges would access the university indirectly by means of an affiliation with St Michael's College. In 1911 St Joseph's and Loretto agreed to this plan, thus enabling Catholic women to be examined by the University of Toronto for their bachelor's degrees without having to enrol at University College. One year later Agnes Murphy, later Sister Mary Agnes, IBVM, transferred from University College to St Joseph's, becoming the first Catholic woman to attempt a degree through St Michael's.[135] Noting the significance of higher education for women, *St Joseph's Lilies*, the alumni magazine of St Joseph's College, commented: "as our new nation has developed and advanced all the interests that make for a nation's greatness, and not least among, them its educational standards and ideals, so we have come to the Women's College, and to meet the demands of those who desire that their girls have academic degrees, where academy medals and diplomas not so long ago sufficed, this progressive institution has made provision."[136] The promotion of higher education for Catholic women underscores both the gradually shifting attitudes in the Catholic community towards higher education and a new confidence among Catholics that higher education was the passport to greater leadership and participation in Canadian society.

This new Catholic confidence and aspiration to post-secondary studies was evident in the changes in Catholic enrolment at the University of Toronto. In 1902 the *Catholic Register* reported that there were only 67 Catholics enrolled at the university. Two years later James F. Kenney, a Catholic student from Marysville, Ontario, who enrolled at University College, could find only 12 other Catholics registered in the institution.[137] By the 1910–11 academic year the number of Catholic students had more than doubled the 1902 total. Approximately 138 Catholics were registered, of which one-third were from the city of Toronto. By 1920 the reforms at St Michael's College and the shift in Catholic attitudes towards higher education had irreversibly altered the Catholic presence at the University of Toronto. Catholics counted 644 students at the institution, including 232 at St Michael's, 107 in theology, 67 in medicine, and 70 in dentistry.[138]

This greater participation of Catholics in the University of Toronto did not stop Catholic leaders' vigilant promotion of higher education. Both McNeil and writers for the *Register* repeated their demands for more scholarships and donations from rich Catholics to keep interest in a college education alive. Moreover, Catholic children were told repeatedly that if they chose to enter the labour force instead of attending high school or college, Catholics would fail to attain the roles of civic leadership awaiting them. The problems of securing higher education were by no means solved by 1920: the lure of the American labour market, paucity of scholarships in comparison to other universities, and the lack of Catholic secondary school facilities provided serious hurdles to higher education.[139]

The twenty years between 1900 and 1920, however, did mark some significant changes in the Catholic outlook on higher education. Leadership and encouragement from the Catholic hierarchy and press stimulated interest in higher education where there had previously been little. Reforms at St Michael's College and the accessibility of degree programs under Catholic auspices further enabled Catholics to venture into the secular University of Toronto without fear of compromising their faith.[140] Equally important, the ever-increasing wealth of Toronto's Catholics facilitated the payment of college fees.[141] Although their embrace of higher education was by no means complete by 1920, English-speaking Catholics had developed a new confidence in themselves and a sense that they could take leadership roles in Canadian society if only they possessed the desire to educate themselves better.

By the 1920s Catholic education in Toronto had undergone significant change. Schools had expanded city-wide, growing as the Catholic community stretched out east along the Danforth, north into the wooded Deer Park, and west past the railyards of the Junction. New facilities, the rising number of lay teachers, and the increased enrolment of children in the higher forms were hallmarks of a revitalized system of Catholic education in the city. Accompanying these physical changes were massive alterations in the orientation of the schools. Separate schools became crucibles of a new type of Canadian citizenship. Catholic children were still taught the devotions, practices, and doctrines of Tridentine Catholicism, but now these were fused to a sense of membership in Canadian society. Readers, social studies, and extra-curricular activities encouraged children to identify with Canada and the nation's role in the British Empire. Even the smallest reminders of one's Irish heritage were subordinated to a higher duty: loyalty to Canada and service to the Empire.

For those Catholic children who passed through their parochial schools there was now strong encouragement from Catholic leaders to pursue Catholic post-secondary education. In their quest for a university degree these young Catholics were confident that leadership in society was certain and that they would assume their rightful place and share in the wealth of their rich and expanding motherland. These new generations of Catholics developed well-defined ideas of loyalty, social values, and economic desires that were already influencing the adult community. Above all, education offered them some assurance that they could rise above their own historical preoccupation with their "second-class" citizenship and aspire to be full, and the most loyal, participants in Canadian society.

CHAPTER FIVE

For God and Country: Lay Associations and Catholic Identity

Times had changed. In October 1875, rocks, bottles, and various projectiles strafed the crowd of Catholic pilgrims as they snaked from church to church in Toronto's inner city. Neither police nor militia had much success containing the Catholic and Protestant thugs who periodically duked it out while women and children ran for cover. Coming at a time of heightened sectarian tensions, locally and nationally, the Jubilee year pilgrimages were symbolic of Catholics pressing their religious rights in the city, and Protestants attacking what they considered to be both a desecration of the Sabbath and a brazen Catholic claim to "their" streets.[1] Thirty-six years later, one warm June Sunday afternoon in 1911, the scene was startlingly different as six thousand members of the Holy Name Society marshalled at St Michael's Cathedral and then marched with military precision up Yonge Street, with banners and flags unfurled, en route to Benediction at Clover Hill.[2] These men came together, pledged to refrain from taking the Lord's name in vain, dedicated their manhood to the Sacred Heart of Jesus, and swore "loyalty to the flag ... And to God-given principles / Of freedom, justice and happiness for which it stands."[3] The huge crowds of peaceful spectators testified to the fact that English-speaking Catholics were no longer to be treated as pariahs of the nation. The success of the parade revealed new levels of restraint and toleration among Toronto's Protestants, while it also underscored the renewed confidence of the Catholic community and the remarkable ability of their associations to harness the piety and patriotism of the laity.

Voluntary associations, religious confraternities, and mutual aid societies were the most effective vehicles of lay participation and expression in the Church in Toronto. Nearly every Catholic parish had one or more associations from which parishioners could choose. In sodalities and confraternities laypersons could engage in the rituals, prayers, and devotions popularized during the ultramontane revolution. In fraternal benevolent societies Catholic men could combine acts of charity and piety with participation in life-insurance or death-benefit programs. These societies – the devotional, charitable, and benevolent – also provided laity with the opportunity to meet and discuss other issues of the day. In the nineteenth century Toronto's Catholic fraternal benevolent societies had been crucibles of Irish nationalism. After 1887 new associations emerged that blended a strong sense of Catholicity with a growing appreciation of Canada, its institutions, and its potential. As such, parish and diocesan associations not only became critical to lay spiritual life but emerged as important nurseries of Canadian sentiment among the city's English-speaking Catholic men and women.

Since the mid-nineteenth century Toronto's Irish Catholics had created associations to preserve their culture, foster a sense of community, and defend themselves in a sometimes hostile environment. These organizations provided group solidarity, security, a common devotional focus, and, at times, a communal voice that could be used to advance the rights of the Irish in the city.[4] In Toronto, Catholic associations also propelled laypersons into positions of community leadership, fostered a generation of lay activists, and cultivated a sense of Irish Catholic ethnicity.[5] Several voluntary associations were steeped in Irish nationalist politics, and, although deeply imbued with Catholicism, they were resistant to clerical control.[6] The disarray in the constitutional movement for Home Rule in Ireland after the Parnell scandal, and the Church's ability to co-opt the nationalist movement in the late 1880s deflated the power of lay nationalist leadership and their associations.[7] In the early 1890s these Irish nationalist organizations and their rhetoric were superseded by new fraternal benevolent societies that focused upon Catholic piety, insurance benefits, and loyalty to Canada.

Interest in the Catholic associations went far deeper than just giving up on the failing remains of the old ethnic associations. As Toronto became more industrialized, heavily populated, and complex, Catholic workingmen, both blue- and white-collar, sought security and comfort by joining clubs and fraternities where they could associate with others who shared similar ideas and class interests. It is not surprising that, in a time when the government offered paltry assistance to the poor, no workmen's compensation, and little hope for families stricken when the principal bread-winner died, many Catholic men joined organizations that offered life insurance and paid funeral costs. While the Vatican forbade Catholics to join "secret societies" that smacked of freemasonry and its "deism" – the Oddfellows, Independent Order of Foresters, or Knights of Pythias[8] – they were encouraged to establish their own associations that were "founded upon religion" and "encouraged the peaceful living and prosperity" of members. Leo XIII regarded such groups as contributing to the relief of the poor and promoting the "prosperity of the state."[9]

Arising from the needs of the laity to adapt to their ever-changing urban world, and encouraged by the Vatican and local clergy, new voluntary associations took root in every parish of the city.[10] Each variety of association – Catholic devotional, insurance/religious, fraternal, charitable, or intellectual and literary – expressed a new sense of peoplehood emerging among the English-speaking Catholics of the city. Irish nationalism and ethnic separatism gave way to a new appreciation and identification with English Canada and its values. Most societies of the period shared an impulse to enrich and defend their Catholic faith while extolling the virtues of Canadian citizenship, and in this sense complemented the endeavours of the Catholic schools in the city. The growth and the varied social activities of the Holy Name Society, Canadian Catholic Union, the Catholic Mutual Benevolent Association, the Knights of Columbus, and the Catholic Women's League all bear witness to the further acculturation of the English-speaking Catholic laity into English Canadian society.

By the 1890s Irish Catholic nationalist associations were dying. Sustained interest in these organizations began to falter for a number of reasons: the advent of moderate constitutional nationalism in Ireland, the failure of the Home Rule bills in the 1880s, the aging of the Irish-born community in Toronto, and the bitter schism in the Irish Parliamentary Party after Parnell's death in 1891. The decline of membership in the Emerald Benevolent Association and Irish Catholic Benevolent Union was compounded when these organizations surrendered their former claims to offer a self-contained social life separated from the larger culture around them. The Irish Catholic "separatism" formerly preached by these associations was supplanted by more moderate approaches to the Irish problem. The Irish National Land League, for example, united Irishmen of all religions behind a coherent constitutional program for Irish Home Rule. Similarly, the Knights of Labor attracted Irish Catholic support by channeling nationalism into a wider fight against oppression and exploitation by the capitalist elites. Societies that promoted ethnic separation were passing away.[11]

The decline and fall of the exclusive nationalist associations was also the product of a return of the Irish male to an active role in the

Catholic Church. In the mid-nineteenth century the Irish associations such as the Hibernian Benevolent Association, the Emerald Benevolent Association, and the Irish Catholic Benevolent Union had been thorns in the side of Archbishop John Joseph Lynch, especially with regard to their marches on St Patrick's Day, their ties to Fenianism, and their involvement in the separate school ballot controversy.[12] The rise of constitutional nationalism and the strong presence of some local priests in the Land League in the 1880s neutralized the more radical elements in the nationalist associations. That these associations increasingly sensitized Catholic men to the devotions of the Church facilitated the submission of moderate and radical nationalists to the leadership and influence of the Church. By 1886 the Emerald Benevolent Association had made its peace with the Church, and henceforth accentuated its Catholicity above all else.[13]

Nationalist exclusiveness and radicalism was further diminished when Irish Catholic leaders began to identify Canada's Dominion status as a model for Irish Home Rule.[14] "The Canadian flag is as precious to our fellow countrymen and co-religionists as it is to any other class of the population of this Dominion," argued Patrick Boyle of the *Irish Canadian*, "because under its folds they enjoy what the 'Union Jack' denied them at home – the right of self government."[15] Recognition that Canada offered Catholics true liberty was taken to heart by the new English-speaking Catholic generations. Separated physically and, in many ways, sentimentally from Ireland, children and grandchildren of Irish immigrants made the "model" of Home Rule their focus and joined associations that were more Canadian in their orientation and activities.

In the 1890s the numbers of Emerald Benevolent Association and Irish Catholic Benevolent Union councils in Toronto and the total membership in Ontario declined dramatically. The efforts of both associations to open up membership to "all Catholics irrespective of nationality" and to Catholic women provided some short-lived gains at the turn of the century, but failed to arrest the long-term decay.[16] In 1890 the Emerald Benevolent Association had six branches in Toronto but only two hundred beneficiaries province-wide. Within ten years there were only three tiny branches left in the city.[17] At the parish level such moderately "successful" branches as St Paul's No. 8 experienced only "fair" attendance at meetings, and were forced eventually to reduce the numbers on their executive.[18] The Irish Catholic Benevolent Union councils fared a little better. Between 1890 and 1900 this association lost three Toronto branches and gained only one new one, largely because of the admission of women from 1895 to 1905. By 1915, however, the total provincial membership was less than half of

Table 5.1
Decline of the Old Associations, Toronto, 1895–1918

Association	Number of Members					
	1895	1900	1905	1910	1915	1918
Emerald Benevolent Association	262	200	–	–	–	–
Irish Catholic Benevolent Union	376	267	407*	259	197	–
Knights of St John	322	380*	199	346	183	–
Ancient Order of Hibernians	629	865	1778	1460	1236	–
Knights of Columbus	–	–	–	–	–	7633

Note: As of 31 Dec. 1909, only 273 of 1,508 (18.1 per cent) Ontario members of the association were from the York County Board. First inclusion of ladies' auxiliaries.

Sources: Detailed Report of the Inspector of Insurance and Friendly Societies (Toronto: Queen's and King's Printer, 1895–1920; ARCAT, Knights of Columbus Papers, Columbiad (Sept. 1918).

the high of 407 achieved in 1905 (see Table 5.1).[19] By 1920 the ICBU and EBA were so small that the registrar of Friendly Societies for Ontario omitted them from his annual report.

The Ancient Order of Hibernians, the youngest Irish nationalist society, was the only such organization to weather the sharp declines of the 1890s and actually increase its membership. Founded in the United States in the late 1820s, the AOH formed its first Canadian branch in 1887 at Woodstock, New Brunswick.[20] The AOH was more of an ethno-cultural insurance society than a vociferous exponent of Irish nationalism. Although it was founded with Catholic principles in mind, as evidenced by its motto – "Friendship, Unity and True Christian Charity" – the AOH was strictly Irish in spirit and personnel. Only those of Irish birth or Irish descent, who were practising Catholics and between the ages of nineteen and forty-five, were considered for membership. Older Catholic men were admitted as honorary members, although they were ineligible for insurance coverage.[21] Full members of the order were entitled to attend regular meetings, participate in recreational activities, and receive funeral benefits, provided that they paid a monthly assessment.[22] In 1889 Catholic men in Toronto formed their first AOH branch, which was soon followed by three more, comprising a total of 350 members in the city. On 27 June 1893 the association was officially incorporated as a friendly insurance society in the province of Ontario. In the next decade Ontario branches of the AOH nearly tripled their membership to nearly 1,800 Catholic men.[23]

Canadian Hibernians had less to do with lobbying the British Parliament for Irish Home Rule than they had with instilling an appreciation of Irish culture in Canada. During a membership drive in 1895, AOH President Hugh McCaffery told the membership that it was the association's duty to "educate her people to a higher realization and appreciation of the patriotism of our forefathers and not forget the hardships and sufferings which they underwent for their country [Ireland] and their religion."[24] The AOH fulfilled its mandate to "guarantee" the race's future by undertaking a number of intellectual projects, including the promotion of the study of Irish history in Catholic schools and the preparation of a history of the Irish people in Canada. Provincial Secretary Charles J. Foy was adamant that "Irishmen have not received their proper measure of credit for all they have done and all they are doing in this Country."[25] In addition to these projects, Toronto branches of the AOH organized the annual St Patrick's Day banquet, followed by a concert at Massey Hall, invited notable speakers on questions germane to Irish culture and the politics of Home Rule, and held regular meetings of members in its five "divisions" throughout the city.[26] Throughout their short history in Toronto the AOH presented themselves as custodians of Irish culture in a country where, they admitted, the descendants of Irish Catholic immigrants were "too apt to forget the land of their forefathers."[27]

In all activities the AOH anchored itself firmly to the Catholic Church. According to Charles Foy, Irishness and Catholicity were so interwoven that, if separated, Ireland's name would disappear from "the worlds annals."[28] The instructions of the clergy were usually obeyed, whether they involved the censoring of acts in the annual St Patrick's Day concert or the exclusion of controversial speakers. In 1910 Archbishop Fergus McEvay demanded that no American lecturers of an anti-British ilk would be permitted to speak at the annual concert. McEvay wanted no doubt of the loyalty of Catholic Canadians, "who enjoy privileges in this country." Local AOH Secretary Frank Walsh agreed to resign if "anything objectionable" took place.[29] McEvay's attention was flattering considering the glacial relations between the AOH and Archbishop Denis O'Connor, who completely disapproved of the group, particularly its effort to establish women's auxiliaries.[30]

The AOH provided the last significant effort to stymie the integration of Irish Catholic youth into the English-speaking Canadian culture that surrounded them. The Hibernian programs, however, bore little fruit. In competition with so many other associations, membership in the AOH plummeted as fast as it had risen. In 1909 only an average of 55 men belonged to an AOH division in Toronto, and between

1907 and 1909 alone, 160 Torontonians suspended their member-ship.[31] Catholic men of Irish descent under the age of forty-five had become more diversified in their interests and less preoccupied with enriching their sense of Irishness or engaging in the political prob-lems of a country few of them had ever seen. The rapid decline of the AOH in Toronto by the time of the First World War suggests once again that the narrowly ethnic ideals for which it stood were becom-ing less relevant to new generations of English-speaking Catholics.

It was also clear that the AOH in Canada had evolved in a very dif-ferent fashion from the American parent organization. When war erupted in 1914, Canadian Hibernians quickly expressed their loyalty to the British Empire's cause. "We feel as Irishmen and descendants of Irishmen domiciled in this Dominion of Canada, an integral part of that great Empire," wrote one AOH board, "fully conscious that par-ticipation of all British subjects in this very unfortunate European war is in the best interests of civilization."[32] The words of the Carleton County members were echoed by AOH boards across Canada, as Hi-bernians worked for the success of the war effort. Provincial chaplain of the order Bishop Michael Francis Fallon of London advocated a public display of Catholic patriotism for the British cause, declaring this fight "for the rights of humanity" to be as much Canada's fight as Britain's.[33] When the AOH in the United States disagreed and ex-pressed anti-British and pro-German sentiments, the Canadian AOH en masse threatened schism in the order.[34] Canadian members even petitioned the federal government to block the Canadian distribution of their official organ, the *National Hibernian*, which was clearly anglo-phobic to the point of suggesting that Ireland use the war to secure her freedom.[35] Across Canada AOH boards declared their loyalty to the Empire, disavowed themselves of the statements made by the *Na-tional Hibernian*, and passed motions of secession from the American order.[36] Some declared that the AOH had always been too American anyway and that it was time for a "Canadian flag side by side with the Harp of Erin."[37] In July 1916 New Brunswick priest C.J. McLaughlin unleashed a blistering attack on the American AOH at their annual convention, extolling the freedoms afforded Catholics in Canada and the fact that thousands of Irish Canadians were now at war with "German aggression from Luther's land." The Americans compromised, toned down the rhetoric, and secession was averted.[38]

The near schism between American and Canadian Hibernians un-derscored how the nature of Irish Catholic ethnic associations had evolved differently in much of Canada. Those Catholic males who still sought membership in Irish ethnic associations came to identify their Irish heritage more closely with their Canadian home and its freedoms, and with membership in the British Empire. Hibernians espoused a love of Ireland, but it was eclipsed by a growing appreciation and love for Canada and for the work the Irish had done to build the country. They acknowledged that as Irish and Canadian partners in the British Empire they were responsible for the Empire's maintenance.

Lay religious associations drew much more successfully from the Catholic ranks than had the fledgling Hibernians. In the nineteenth century the League of the Sacred Heart, the Apostleship of Prayer, the Sodality of the Blessed Virgin Mary, the Holy Angels Society, the Children of Mary, and the St Vincent de Paul Society were pious devotional associations organized at the parish level. With the exception of the St Vincent de Paul Society, all these groups were dominated by women until the last quarter of the century. Irish Catholic men had remained indifferent to devotional societies under the watchful eye of the clergy, preferring instead to associate in the nationalist groups, where clerical interference was minimal. Religious confraternities were usually incorporated into the "separate sphere" of the woman, who was given primary responsibility for the management of the home and the nurturing of children in the religious values and doctrines of the Church.[39] Consequently, the religious ethos of Catholic confraternities in mid-nineteenth-century Toronto was feminine, with many Catholic women seeking to emulate the Virgin Mary, the role-model of Christian faith, virtue, service, and maternalism.[40]

The paucity of available records makes intensive and detailed study of these pious confraternities next to impossible. Religious societies rarely exceeded 150 members in any given parish. The only exception was the League of the Sacred Heart, which included both men and women, and frequently enlisted up to 50 per cent of a parish's population (see Table 5.2).[41] The low costs and demands of the League, and the fact that it did not preclude one's membership in other associations, made it particularly attractive to Catholics. The League crossed class and gender boundaries, charged no fees, and demanded little of a member, save for private individual devotion. The three devotional requirements for the society included a morning offering, reciting a decade of the rosary, and receiving communion monthly.[42]

The most prominent of the male confraternities, and one that actually preserves some of its records, was the St Vincent de Paul Society. Frequently mistaken for a charitable organization pure and simple, the Society was actually founded for the purpose of saving the souls of its own members through their charitable works. According to one

Table 5.2
Parish Confraternities and Sodalities, 1918–22

Parish	League of the Sacred Heart	St Vincent de Paul	Christian Mothers	Sodality of BVM	Holy Angels
C Christi	400	–	81	–	–
Holy Family	765	12	110	43	37
Holy Name	400	–	–	75	–
Holy Rosary	362	–	90	64	–
Lourdes	900	14	150	160	85
St Basil's	250	15	65	52	–
St Brigid's	230	–	155	48	–
St Cecilia's	610	22	387	123	–
St John's	125	–	75	35	140
St Joseph's	1250	–	210	–	80
St Leo's	225	–	67	62	–
St Michael's	250	7	–	–	–
St Patrick's	900	–	–	175	–
St Paul's	600	17	–	–	–
St Vincent's	650	–	150	77	45
St Ann's	650	12	380	125	78
St Anthony's	550	21	350	140	–
St Clare's	–	–	75	30	–
St Francis's	1100	25	215	134	–
St Helen's	853	15	400	150	–
St Mary's	1730	18	302	218	–
St Monica's	56	35	42	26	–
St Peter's	1400	–	275	250	–

Note: The statistics from St Ann's parish through to St Peter's are from 1918.

Source: ARCAT, Parish Spiritual and Financial Statistics, 1918, 1921, 1922. All calculations are mine.

member of the Society, "In the exercise of Charity which covereth a multitude of sins, we could make atonement for the irregularities of our past lives; and labouring for our sanctification ... we escaped the danger of future relapses."[43] Members visited the city's poor door-to-door, evaluated the conditions they found, and then extended help in the form of food, fuel, and clothing. By 1882 the Society's "Particular Council" had opened an employment agency and was aiding migrant workers to Toronto in their quest for employment and lodging.[44] Throughout these activities, however, the main aim of the Society remained not the act of charity itself but the individual salvation of members, with the long-term intent of transforming the religious behaviour of the city's Catholic men.[45]

Society members came from all walks of life, although the majority of members were businessmen, clerks, or skilled workers. The occupational composition of the membership fluctuated according to parish, but there was a general decline in the participation of unskilled labourers by 1890.[46] This decline, however, was not exclusive to class, as the Society's total membership in all parishes fell dramatically during the late nineteenth and early twentieth centuries. Despite the substantial growth in the Catholic population in Toronto generally, between 1884 and 1894 the Society attracted only 41 new members. By 1897 there were only 211 active members in Toronto. Decline at the parish level was more substantial. In St Mary's parish the number of members dropped from 40 in 1895 to only 18 in 1922. Similar losses were recorded in other inner-city and suburban parishes.[47]

In many ways the St Vincent de Paul Society was a victim of circumstance. By the 1890s English-speaking Catholic men were joining Church-based associations in record numbers. In one sense the Irish nationalist societies of an earlier era had been too successful. Groups like the Emeralds had sensitized their members to devotions and Catholic doctrine, thus making it easier for members and their sons to make the jump to parochial and diocesan fraternal associations.[48] As the older nationalist societies decayed and died, Catholic men looked to a variety of new choices, many of which were less costly alternatives to the St Vincent de Paul Society. Its former pre-eminence thus diminished, the Society remained only a small group among many devotional and charitable associations for Catholic males.

In contrast to the struggling svp, the largest, most influential, and most successful devotional association in Toronto was the Holy Name Society. Founded in 1274 by John of Vercelli, a Dominican priest, the hns demanded that its members give reverence to the Holy Name of Jesus and cultivate a life of piety. Proving a successful counterweight to the Albigensian heresy, the Society spread quickly, and gained prominence in 1433, when the city of Lisbon claimed that its special devotion to the Holy Name of Jesus had saved it from an outbreak of the plague. In 1564 Pope Pius iv raised the Society to a confraternity and Emperor Charles v (1519–58) ordered its establishment throughout the Holy Roman Empire. It was not until 1871, however, that the Society was formally established in the United States, and twenty-six years later that Pope Leo xiii permitted individual parishes to establish their own societies, independent of the Dominican order.[49]

The methods used to honour the Holy Name of God and Jesus were both proactive and reactive. On the one hand, members were organized so that they could engage in "practices of piety, in frequent manly prayer and in group action of worship and devotion."[50] To this end, North American members of the Society attended Sunday mass, received the Eucharist at least once per month, distributed Catholic literature, and visited the sick and imprisoned.[51] With this devotional foundation in place, men then curbed their use of profane language, refrained from violating the second commandment (Exodus 20:7), and at all times pledged to respect the name of Jesus. Here the Society was aggressive in its mandate to denounce and destroy "crimes against the sacred name of God," most often committed in acts of "blasphemy, perjury, cursing, swearing, profane language, and all manner of obscene and indecent speech."[52]

The first Holy Name societies in Toronto were established shortly after 1900. Canadians, like Americans before them, formed the new branches of the Society along parish lines and under joint clerical and lay direction. At St Paul's, for example, the Reverend John L. Hand received spiritual privileges for the establishment of a Holy Name Society in 1903, and by December 1905 a senior Holy Name branch for the city was formed under his supervision. At least 132 members attended the first meeting at St Paul's, thus demonstrating the enormous potential for such a society among the city's Catholic men. Within a year the St Paul's branch had increased to 225 members.[53] That there were no insurance premiums, regular charitable obligations, or heavy dues to be paid made the society even more attractive to some Catholic men. Within ten years of the establishment at St Paul's there were 24 adult and 11 junior branches of the Holy Name Society across the archdiocese. Every English-speaking parish in the city had at least one branch of the Society, and sometimes two with the inclusion of a junior group.[54] By 1918, however, Toronto's urban parishes accounted for over 5,000 Society members, or roughly one in six Catholic males. In St Helen's, St Mary's, St Ann's, and St Anthony's parishes over 20 per cent of the entire parish (perhaps as many as half of all men) belonged to the Holy Name Society.[55] In 1910 the incredible growth of the Society prompted the formation of a Holy Name Union or federation, which was responsible for the establishment of new branches, monitoring parish branches, enforcing the Society's constitution, organizing the annual parade, and supervising work among Catholic boys and new Canadians.

The Holy Name Society had become the largest and most pervasive of Catholic religious associations in Edwardian Toronto. The Society also had a marked effect on the preservation and enrichment of the piety of its Toronto members. It brought Catholic men to the heart of the Church's devotional life, encouraging their reception of the sacraments, attendance at mass, and the pious celebration of feast days. Communion at least once every three months was encouraged by the Society, and parish branches sponsored Communion Sundays that brought members, as a group, to the Eucharist. In 1916 the union president reported that "The vision of a man at the altar railing at a time other than Easter is no longer a signal for the immediate female relatives to smooth their wrinkles out of ancestral mourning."[56] Church parades or "communion Sundays" arranged at the parish level drew between 50 to 100 per cent of local Society members. Similarly, masses celebrated on the feast of the Holy Name were well attended. In 1914 alone, 5,000 members attended mass at St Helen's, St Paul's, St Patrick's, and St Mary's, the selected focal parishes in the city's four Holy Name Union zones (see Table 5.3).[57] If it accomplished anything, the Holy Name Society encouraged Catholic men to profess their faith publicly and become more active in parish life.

Holy Name's efforts to draw laymen into an active devotional life was not exclusive to social class. The Society's membership mirrored the growing diversity of Catholics occupationally and the rise of the Catholic middle class as leaders in Toronto. Membership in parish branches reflected the occupational profile of each individual parish, although executive leadership in most parishes was dominated by white-collar workers. In 1918 close to 60 per cent of parish executive members of the Society were either businessmen or clerical employees. Working-class Catholic men made up little more than one-quarter of the city-wide executives, although they formed the majority in the inner-city parishes of St Paul's and St Patrick's (see Table 5.4).[58] The overall dominance of white-collar Catholics in leadership roles in an association as important as Holy Name, however, further indicates the extent to which the rising Catholic middle class was consolidating its control within the Catholic community. One control on lay assertiveness was established from the beginning by Father Hand: in each parish, the lay executives worked under the watchful eye of the pastor.

As it expanded in numbers and diversity of its members, the Holy Name Society began to direct its energies in new directions outside of

Table 5.3
Growth of the Holy Name Society in Toronto Parishes, 1912–23

Parish	1912	1918			1921–23		
	Members	Members	Parish	%	Members	Parish	%
C Christi	–	–	–	–	305	1430	21.3
Holy Family	50	201	1690	11.9	315	2256	14.0
Holy Name	–	235	1513	15.5	385	1900	20.3
Holy Rosary	60	–	–	–	60	–	–
Lourdes	50	–	–	–	250	1800	13.9
St Ann's	180	400	1820	22.0	–	–	–
St Anthony's	261	420	2030	20.7	–	–	–
St Basil's	197	210	1850	11.4	180	1920	9.4
St Brigid's	–	–	–	–	250	1300	19.2
St Cecilia's	70	450	2410	18.7	425	3250	13.1
St Clare's	–	50	1200	4.2	–	–	–
St Francis's	270	360	2672	13.5	–	–	–
St Helen's	290	730	2750	26.5	720	3874	18.6
St John's	40	–	–	–	190	700	27.1
St Joseph's	144	268	1912	14.0	394	1920	20.5
St Leo's	–	68	–	–	70	600	11.7
St Mary's	325	460	2400	19.2	–	–	–
St Michael's	155	–	–	–	320	2400	13.3
St Monica's	–	63	460	13.7	–	–	–
St Patrick's	146	100	1400	7.8	200	1100	18.2
St Paul's	314	210	2700	7.8	380	2800	13.6
St Peter's	176	300	2000	15.0	–	–	–
St Vincent's	–	89	1000	8.9	250	1788	14.0
Total	2728	4614	29807	15.5	4694	29038	16.2

Source: ARCAT, Parish Spiritual and Financial Statistics, 1918, 1921, 1922, 1923; Holy Name Society Papers, Quarterly Meeting, 30 June 1913.

the parish. While it never wavered from its pledge "to protest against unclean and irreverent speech, to assert the divinity of Christ, and the

Table 5.4
Holy Name Executive Members by Occupation and Residence, 1918

Occupational Group	Inner-city parishes		Suburban parishes		Union exec.	Total	
	No.	%	No.	%		No.	%
Professional	2	3.4	3	3.2		5	3.1
Private	1	1.7	0	0.0		1	0.6
Business	14	23.7	16	17.0	1	31	19.1
Clerical	17	28.8	38	40.4	7	62	38.3
Skilled	6	10.2	10	10.6		16	9.9
Semi-skilled	7	11.9	9	9.6		16	9.9
Unskilled	7	11.9	4	4.3	1	12	7.4
No data	5	8.5	14	14.9		19	11.7
Total	59	100.0	94	100.0		162	100.0

Note: The midtown parishes of Our Lady of Lourdes, St Francis's, and St Basil's are included under the Inner-city designation.

Source: ARCAT, Catholic Truth Society Papers, Holy Name Union Executive, 1918. All calculations are mine.

personal sanctification of every member,"[59] the Society widened its mandate to preserve the Catholicity and citizenship of Catholic boys. Members were reminded by Holy Name Union officials that it was their responsibility to spread the Faith "in places and under conditions where it was impossible for the most zealous priests to reach."[60] In this spirit the Society's union organized baseball and hockey leagues, summer camps, junior Holy Name branches, and Catholic Big Brothers, with an aim to offer Catholic youth a "virtuous" environment in which to recreate and grow.[61]

The Holy Name Society lost little time in extending its presence into the world of Toronto's Catholic youths. In 1917 eleven parishes had junior Holy Name branches that attempted to uphold the ideals of the Society in addition to providing prospective recruits to the local adult branches.[62] The Holy Name baseball and hockey leagues took root during the Great War and, by 1924, had 12 and 24 teams respectively.[63] Here, when one fanned on the third strike or hit the goalpost on a breakaway, restraint was expected instead of that usual, more colourful noun or adjective. In addition to the parish leagues, Holy Name Union operated a Catholic summer camp with accommodation for 65 boys at Clarkson on Lake Ontario.[64] Finally, the Holy Name Big Brothers organization monitored all court cases involving Catholic youths and attracted 40 big brothers by 1919 and 52 by 1920.[65]

The spiritual and social activism of the Holy Name Society in Toronto also bore a distinctive patriotic imprint. Although founded primarily as a devotional association in the city, the Society copied its American parent branches in its espousal of the exemplary citizenship of its members. The Holy Name pledge was adapted from the one developed in the United States. In reciting it, the member confirmed his belief in the divinity of Christ, his dedication to the sacred teachings of the Church, his personal duty to exemplify Christian virtue, and his promise of loyalty to "the flag" and "to all lawful authority." The principles of the Society elevated loyalty to one's country and the preservation of the ideals of "freedom, justice and happiness" as sacred duties.[66] Holy Name members were expected to demonstrate ideals of patriotic citizenship, and loyalty to the Crown and to the Dominion.

The patriotic pledge of the Holy Name Society was given its greatest test during the First World War. The Society openly encouraged its members of age to enlist in the Canadian Expeditionary Force, and it advertised the sale of Victory Bonds. In 1917 the Society marched in the Victory Loan parade, with Archbishop McNeil's blessing, and actively purchased bonds. Individual branches raised money for war relief, had mass intentions offered for peace, and provided free breakfasts for soldiers.[67] In terms of actual recruitment, the fifteen city branches of the Society sent 1,385 volunteers to the CEF during the voluntary phases of enlistment. Of these recruits, 48 were killed, 73 wounded, and 2 were listed as missing in action.[68] A branch of the Society was established in the Second Canadian Contingent, and was so well respected that Sir Arthur Currie, the non-Catholic Canadian commander-in-chief, requested membership. Hundreds of Protestant troops followed suit![69]

The popularity of the Holy Name Society among Catholics, and the toleration for it demonstrated by non-Catholics, was most evident in the Society's annual parade in Toronto. The rally and parade was a visible profession of faith by Society members and, as a ritual, dated to the founding of the Society in medieval Europe. "The Holy Name Rally," commented an observer, "is simply a public act of Faith in the great belief of Christ's Divinity ... It is a public protest against perjury, blasphemy, profanity ... It is a public pledge of patriotism and of the support of law and order."[70] A tradition adopted by the American branches of the Society, the parade was initiated in Toronto in 1908 after the resignation of Archbishop Denis O'Connor, who had prohibited such public displays during his nine-year episcopate.

Having secured the support of O'Connor's successor, the ailing Fergus McEvay, the Holy Name Union held its first parade on Sunday, 18 June 1911. At three o'clock in the afternoon members of the local Holy Name branches assembled at St Michael's Cathedral. Members of the Knights of St John, dressed in the regalia of their association, headed the procession of individual branches, each led by the parish priest and members of the branch executive. All of the participating members wore badges of the Society, refrained from smoking, and marched in orderly fashion through the streets of downtown Toronto to St Michael's College at Clover Hill, where they attended benediction and heard a "stirring" sermon. Upwards of 6,000 men from across the archdiocese pierced through the heart of the "Belfast of North America" as they paraded up Yonge Street in the largest public Catholic gathering in a generation. The human train reached its intended destination without molestation of any kind, as the police experienced no difficulties from the crowds that lined both sides of the street along the parade route.[71] The parade set a precedent for more open displays of Catholicity in Toronto and ushered in an era of Catholic confidence in civic life.

With this precedent set, the annual parade continued to grow in numbers and in popularity. In 1912 the parade route had to be lengthened to accommodate the marchers and the crowds. Starting at the House of Providence grounds on Power Street, thousands of men marched four abreast, in eight divisions, to the grounds of St Michael's College, where 25,000 people attended a rally and benediction.[72] A year later an even larger parade meandered through the western neighbourhoods of the city and culminated in a rally headlined by the new archbishop, Neil McNeil. According to the *Register*, the parade had become an event in which all Torontonians could share:

There were at least ten thousand men in line. The streets were lined everywhere to see them pass. It was the best ordered and prettiest procession of men we ever saw, a legion of the Lord to praise and glorify His Name … Then the increased membership, the better singing of the stirring hymns, the spoken word of encouragement, and the ever adorable act of highest religion in the exposing of the Blessed Eucharist make the function the closest to the sublime we can possibly attempt. The reverence of the Protestant community, too, grows apace. The seed is germinating.[73]

Although suspended during the war years, these triumphalist demonstrations resumed with greater vigour after the combatants returned home. In 1921, 20,000 Catholic men marched behind the Canadian Ensign through the city's streets. Hailed as the largest gathering of its kind in Toronto's history, the parade was so long that the *Register* claimed, with some exaggeration, that when "the van was at the House of Providence grounds on Power Street the rear was still in Queen's Park."[74]

First and foremost the Holy Name Society parades were a celebration of the Catholic faith. They were also expressions of the emergent male Catholic Torontonian: an individual swept up in the socio-economic changes of the time and moulded by associations that were sensitive to and complementary of these changes, while nourishing members in the faith. The Society had successfully fused a zealous love and devotion to the Catholic Church, a lay alliance with the local pastors, and expressions of loyalty and Canadian patriotism. In the process it had cultivated men proud of their faith, proud of their country, and assertive enough to wear the badges of faith openly in a supposedly Protestant city.[75] That Holy Name parades and festivities dwarfed St Patrick's Day celebrations offers further proof that the pith of Catholic culture was changing to a less "Hibernized" form. Moreover, peacefully executed and well attended, the parades were also a sign that attitudes in the Protestant community had changed, thus refuting the hasty generalization that given Toronto's Orange legacy, Catholics could not march in the streets and expect to go unharmed.[76] The spiritual and patriotic implications of Holy Name's success were not lost on local leaders. In his address entitled "The Responsibilities of Catholic Laymen" at the Holy Name rally in 1921, Father Francis Pennylegion tackled this issue directly: "You are no more strangers and foreigners," he said, citing St Paul, "but you are fellow citizens with the saints and domestics of God."[77]

Just as the spirituality and patriotism of the Holy Name Society had usurped the older Irish nationalist associations, new Canadian and American mutual aid societies responded to the needs of Catholics requiring sick benefits and life insurance. Organized in 1876 in Niagara Falls, New York, by Bishop Stephen Ryan of Buffalo, the Catholic Mutual Benefit Association, or CMBA, quickly became the largest Catholic mutual aid society on the continent. Its three aims were both spiritual and financial: to bring Catholic men together for the purposes of strengthening their faith; to disseminate and encourage the reading of Catholic literature; and to extend charity and life-insurance benefits to association members.[78] Practising Catholics between the ages of eighteen and fifty who had passed a thorough medical examination were eligible for one of three insurance policies paying $500, $1,000, or a handsome $2,000, which could be claimed either by families at the time of death or by the member at the end of a thirty-year term.[79] There were no ethnic qualifications for membership, no secret hand-shakes, and no elaborate rituals.[80] In addition to its inexpensive assessments and recreational activities, the CMBA offered what it considered to be a distinctive Catholic alternative to the "dangerous" and "unbelieving" benevolent organizations.[81] Its exclusive Catholic membership, defence of the Catholic home, promotion of charitable works and acts of virtue, and advocacy of reception of communion regularly by its members, won it the ringing endorsement of both the Catholic press and the Canadian bishops. According to London's *Catholic Record*, the CMBA was to be lauded because "its aim is to foster Catholic manhood: its strength comes from its loyalty to the Church."[82]

The rapid growth of the CMBA, like the Holy Name Society, was due in part to close lay-clerical co-operation. Branches were established and managed within parishes and usually included the membership of the local priest. Clergy assumed leadership roles and actively recruited laymen to form association branches. In his earlier days as Bishop of London, Toronto Archbishop John Walsh had actually helped to establish the first Canadian council in 1878 and became the first Canadian prelate to acquire association membership. The initial foundation in Windsor, Ontario, was followed in rapid succession by CMBA branches across the Diocese of London and, by 1882, the Archdiocese of Toronto. By 1890 the first CMBA branch at St Patrick's parish was one among branches in all the major inner-city parishes. Ten years later there were seven branches, claiming over four hundred members. Toronto's potential for association growth was recognized by the CMBA as early as 1888, when the city hosted the first meeting of the Ontario Grand Council, the governing body of all local branches.[83] No doubt the strong clerical endorsement had much to do with the association's expansion. Father Henry McPhillips, branch president at St Helen's parish, enthusiastically endorsed the CMBA because of its ability to exercise "great moral influence" on both association members and the Catholic community as a whole.[84]

CMBA success in Toronto also reflected the fortunes of the association elsewhere in Canada. In 1880, when the Grand Council of Canada was organized, there were only 220 members, all of whom lived in Ontario. By the time of the 1888 convention in Toronto there were 3,220 members nationally. In 1894 the number of members nationally had tripled to over 10,000. The steady growth continued for over a decade, as new branches were established in eastern Canada and new provinces in the west were admitted into the fold. At the height of the association's popularity in 1904 there were 384 branches containing an estimated "membership of 19,056 covering the whole of our great Dominion from the Atlantic to the Pacific."[85] In 1895 the Canadian branches of the CMBA published the *Canadian*, a bilingual monthly newsletter that kept members abreast of changes in insurance rates, recently deceased members, and association news from across the country.

The sliding scale of insurance rates and premiums made membership in the CMBA affordable for Catholic men regardless of class. In 1893, $2,000 insurance could be had for a payment of $14 annually, and $1,000 for $7, both spread over 16 payments.[86] Association organizers warned the more pretentious Catholics in such rich parishes as St Basil's in Toronto: "The labouring man is just as welcome in our Church as the millionaire ... do not try to make any distinction in our membership."[87] Once the $500 policies were made available, even the poorest-paid unskilled workers could afford death benefits. Death claims from semi-skilled and unskilled workers, however, demonstrate that many opted for the higher-priced policies, especially those with a return of $1,000.

No doubt the range of benefits, reasonable rates, and parochial ties made the CMBA attractive to Catholics right across the occupational spectrum. In 1894 over half of the death claims filed were those of blue-collar workers, 40 per cent of whom were workers in unskilled jobs. Catholics in the business and clerical occupations were equally represented, accounting for over one-third of all claims (see Table 5.5). For the next twenty years all classes of Catholic men invested in the CMBA, although white-collar workers, growing in number in the city generally, increased in their proportion of the association's membership. These representatives of the emerging Catholic middle class, with their clerical, business, and managerial skills, could more easily afford the $2,000 policies.[88] In contrast, the proportion of skilled and semi-skilled workers fell. At a time when trade unions were growing in popularity among skilled workers, it is possible that highly skilled Catholic blue-collar workers were attracted more by the fraternal and financial benefits offered to them by the labour movement. Here, perhaps, the CMBA was outflanked by the occupational diversification, shop-floor loyalties, and varying social interests of Catholic men.[89]

Although never intended as such at the outset, the Catholic Mutual Benefit Association in Toronto and elsewhere in the Dominion helped English-speaking Catholics better to articulate their growing identification with Canada. The rapid growth of Canadian branches in the 1880s stimulated interest in a Canadian insurance beneficiary separate from the American parent. On the surface the primary reason for the independence movement was financial. The rate of deaths among

Table 5.5
Occupation and Average Value of Insurance Premiums,
Catholic Mutual Benefit Association, 1894–1918

Group	Year, claims, proportion, and average of claim							
	1894	%	1905	%	Av. claim	1918	%	Av. claim
Professional	44	11.4	12	8.6	$1,666.67	14	11.9	$1,055.08
Private	1	0.3	1	0.7	$2,000.00	5	4.3	$1,451.50
Business	66	17.0	27	19.3	$1,555.56	26	22.2	$1,360.14
Clerical	67	17.3	27	19.3	$1,518.52	25	21.4	$974.42
Skilled	41	10.6	9	6.4	$1,444.44	5	4.3	$1,000.00
Semi-skilled	80	20.7	22	15.7	$1,522.73	17	14.5	$843.41
Unskilled	88	22.7	41	29.3	$1,390.24	25	21.4	$838.21
No data	0		1	0.7		0		
Total	387	100.0	140	100.0		117	100.0	

Note: Given the absence of membership lists, occupational profiles are derived from the claims made by the estates of members in 1894, 1905, and 1918. The *Canadian* is incomplete for the year 1918; therefore, the figures here represent only the first seven months of the year.

Source: *Catholic Register*, 6 Sept. 1894; *Canadian* 11 (1905), and 24 (1918).

Canadian members of the association was significantly lower than that in the United States. That the Canadian Grand Council paid out more beneficiary money to the American Supreme Council than they received to pay off Canadian members' policies left Canadian leaders with the impression that they were subsidizing the higher American death rate. Moreover, the Americans refused Canadian payments at par, charging .25 per cent on all Canadian drafts.[90] By 1889, 99 out of 105 branches in Canada voted for a separate beneficiary financed directly by Canadians. Local branches in favour of separation argued that members had joined the association thinking that separation was inevitable, and that more Canadians would apply for membership once ties with the United States were cut.[91]

The minority opposing the separation proposed by Canadian Grand Council President John A. McCabe was vociferous. Some branches in London, Toronto, and Montreal feared that separation would prohibit transfer of membership if one moved across the border, and more significantly, Canadians might lose their investments in a time of epidemic if there was no access to the American association's reserve funds.[92] Dissenters also claimed that the move for a separate beneficiary was a direct violation of the principle of fraternity upheld in the philosophy of the association. One branch indicated that the "continental Brotherhood of Catholics" ought not to be compromised by national concerns.[93] The executive of St Mary's Parish No. 49, the only anti-separatist branch in Toronto, asserted: "It should always be remembered that a bond of unity of purpose and desire to do good is our connecting link ... disintegration in part leads to disintegration as a whole."[94] Other anti-separatists rejected ideas of an American conspiracy, claiming that the Canadian CMBA had a younger membership than that of the United States and so, demographically, a lower death rate was to be expected.[95]

Such arguments did not dampen the spirit of the Canadian separatists. In fact, the anti-separatist rhetoric, when combined with the American rejection of the Canadian Grand Council's petition for a separate beneficiary, awakened an even more pronounced nationalism in the Canadian majority. American attempts to alter the CMBA constitution to deprive Canadians of the right to separate evoked harsh comment. Grand President McCabe complained bitterly about American arrogance in thinking they knew "better than Canadians what is best for Canadian interests." Grand Secretary O.K. Fraser, however, was more poignant in his allegations that Canadians had been discriminated against by Americans when it came to representation on the Supreme Executive: "We do not seek office because we are Catholics. We do so because we are Canadians and we are set adrift because we are Catholics. So far as nationality is concerned the same may be said of the treatment meted out to us by our American friends. We look for fair play because we are CMBA men and we are left shivering in the cold because we are Canadians."[96] Fraser claimed that, at the Supreme Convention of 1888, influential American delegates caballed in private in order to keep "foreigners" off the new executive. What had begun as a movement for greater Canadian control of its own beneficiary became a full-fledged independence movement.

By August 1891 CMBA delegates passed a motion to create a separate beneficiary. Official confirmation, however, would have to wait until the regular biennial meeting of the Canadian Grand Council of the association, to be held in Hamilton in August 1892. In the meantime, a report by association member W.J. Smith that condemned separation caused considerable in-fighting among the general membership. William M. Moran, a member from the anti-separatist branch No. 49 in Toronto, defied his own council, declaring that the statistics in the report had been "fudged" by Smith.[97] During the next twelve months the backbiting among Canadian members continued, while the Americans plotted to undermine the Canadian separatists. In October 1891 the *Catholic Record* reported that the Americans had secretly gained control of all Canadian medical certificates. The Americans then arranged that Canadian councils who dissented from the separatists could form a new Canadian Grand Council, to the exclusion of the separatists, who in turn would lose all insurance benefits.[98] The American and anti-separatist efforts were all for naught; in October 1892 the Americans, though still anxious to retain the anti-separatist branches, granted the separate Canadian beneficiary, effective 15 January 1893. With the independence of all Canadian branches achieved, Archbishop Walsh implored all Canadian members "to banish disunion and discord."[99]

The separation question had begun as a matter of saving Canadians money on their insurance premiums. Opposition from a minority of Canadian branches and from the American Supreme Council transformed the issue into a Canadian Catholic statement of identity. Under the leadership of the CMBA Canadian men voiced their pride in their Canadian citizenship, stressing their differences from their brothers in the United States. Perhaps for the first time, English-speaking Catholic men in Canada, Toronto included, felt the sting of discrimination, not because they were Irish, German, Scottish, or Catholic, but because they were Canadian. American manoeuvring to deprive Canadian members from executive positions, and their adamant refusal to consider any form of Canadian autonomy in collecting or paying insurance, helped to arouse patriotic sentiment among Canadian members and heightened English-speaking Catholic awareness of their own Canadian identity.

The independent Canadian CMBA founded its own monthly newspaper, appropriately called the *Canadian*, and received an official certificate of registration from the federal government. The new association also began to wear its badge of Canadian identity more openly. By 1904 the installation of officers included toasts to both the Pope and the reigning British monarch, and such affairs were usually closed by the singing of "God Save the King."[100] The national executive and editorial staff of the *Canadian* constantly encouraged members to be loyal citizens and devout Catholics, thereby underscoring the association's confident claim that they were producing the "best men" in the land. "From the far away shores of the calm Pacific through to the shores of the mighty Atlantic, from British Columbia to the fair gem of the ocean," beamed the *Canadian*, "the chosen of the C.M.B.A. came together in the interests of charity, fraternity, and Catholicity. No finer body of men could come together in any land or in any cause."[101] In the wake of independence the CMBA confirmed its pride in being Canadian and advanced the conviction that English-speaking Catholics were among the most active and hardest-working of Canadian citizens.

For the CMBA, assertiveness and hard work was the most appropriate response to the alleged Protestant "bigotry" that prohibited Roman Catholics from advancement. Less inclined to fall into the easy argument of blaming Protestants for Catholic misfortune, by 1919 CMBA leaders identified Catholic "apathy and general ignorance of public issues" as the chief cause of the underrepresentation of Catholics in political life. Citing numerous instances of Catholic mayors in predominantly Protestant locales – Prescott, Lanark, Perth, Morrisburg, and Collingwood – the Canadian refuted notions that Protestants would not share power with Catholics. Going well beyond their original beneficial and religious mandate, the CMBA advised Catholic men to dive into the public arena and community service without the expectation of special rights or privileges.[102]

The strongest manifestation of the association's attempt to end Catholic isolationism and to uphold both Catholic and patriotic aims came during the Great War. The CMBA openly supported the war effort and encouraged the maximum effort by Catholics both at home and overseas. President F.J. Curran publicly went so far as to advocate Catholic acceptance of national registration, calling upon all members to "do all in their power, individually and collectively," to aid in registration as a "valuable aid to the civil and military authorities in the discharge of their patriotic duties."[103] Since the average age of association members was forty-five, and most policy-holders were married with children, the number of recruits from the association was limited to young Catholic men who had recently taken out policies.[104] The Grand Council, however, made it easier for these men to enlist in the army and navy by continually rejecting demands from other members that military volunteers waive their insurance rights prior to active military service. The national executive claimed it was unfair to place the responsibility of the association's insurance losses during the war "on those who 'support the colors' and make the supreme sacrifice."[105]

The Great War, and the association's support for the Canadian war effort, however, cost the insurance fraternity dearly. Throughout the hostilities the CMBA maintained the insurance benefits of soldiers, many of whom had paid few premiums on their policies. It honoured the policies of those who were killed or declared missing in action, often without having accumulated complete payments from the policy holder.[106] Worse yet, a nationwide influenza epidemic in 1918 and

1919 caused numerous premature deaths among association members, costing the CMBA thousands of dollars. In November 1918 alone, 17 of the 35 deaths among policy holders were caused by influenza, and 11 of the dead were under the age of forty-five. As a result of the war and the epidemic the CMBA amassed a deficit of over $500,000 by 1919.[107] In response to this worsening situation, policies were reduced: $2,000 benefits were cut by as much as $180, and $1,000 policies were lessened proportionately.[108] In an effort to maintain solubility, though articulated as a response to the "insurable value" of the "economically independent and self supporting" Catholic woman, the society admitted women to its ranks as policy holders.[109] While the response from women was positive, with the inclusion of women's auxiliaries of 25 or more women to many councils, the effort was too little and too late to save the CMBA.

The CMBA tumbled further despite the innovations. In Toronto the number of branches fell from 11 in 1915 to 6 in 1920, and only 4 in 1922. Of those 4, only St Mary's No. 49 experienced a significant increase of members, but this was undermined by the high rate of expulsions for unpaid premiums.[110] The aging membership of the association cost it up to $16,000 per month in 1919, and by 1920, the organization had only $600,000 in its reserve fund to cover $8 million in outstanding certificates.[111] In 1920 the American parent body relinquished its remaining policies to the American Insurance Union of Columbus, Ohio, but the Canadians disavowed any connection with the American move and stayed in business, consistently professing their association's health until the Great Depression.[112]

Despite its difficulties during and after the Great War, the Catholic Mutual Benefit Association, over three decades, had demonstrated its ability to gather Catholics together to share religious fellowship and to express confidence in their common citizenship. From its inception the CMBA was never designed to become a society that inculcated with nationalistic sentiment in its members. The separation question of the 1890s and ensuing battle between Canadian and American Catholics heightened the Canadian Catholic's sense of his national identity. Toronto's Catholics, save for Council No. 49, shared with other Canadians a growing appreciation for the fact that as Canadian Catholics they were different from their co-religionists south of the border. After separation in 1893 the CMBA in Canada was exuberant in its assertions of good citizenship and devout Catholicism. It had become more than just a Catholic insurance society – it inspired Catholic men to embrace their Canadian citizenship and claim an equal stake in the Dominion.

The decline of the CMBA in Toronto and elsewhere was due as much to the growing popularity of other Catholic associations as to its own administrative mismanagement. If CMBA men were looking for a villain, they need look no further than the new club on the block – the Knights of Columbus. In one sense the Knights offered Toronto's Catholic men all of the features evident in the associations already discussed: a spiritual focus, charitable work, intellectual stimulation, recreation, insurance and investment opportunities, and a unrepentant patriotism. An added incentive to membership was the manner in which the Knights packaged all their principles and projects in the garb and glamour of medieval knighthood. With its elaborate rituals, colourful costumes, degrees of Knighthood, and historical titles, the Knights offered Catholic men a chance to clad themselves in the trappings of an age when Catholicism had made its presence felt in every aspect of society. Although small, highly ritualized fraternities had existed among Catholics in Toronto in the nineteenth century,[113] none recruited as vigorously, grew as rapidly, or captured the public attention and imagination as did the caped and plumed Knights of Columbus.[114]

Like so many other Catholic fraternal organizations in Toronto, the Knights of Columbus originated in the United States. In 1882 Father Michael McGivney and nine Irish Catholic American laymen founded the Knights in New Haven, Connecticut. The principles of the organization were denoted by the four principal points on the "Compass of Virtue": charity (north), fraternity (east), unity (south), and patriotism (west).[115] The first two principles of charity and unity were actualized by the creation of a benefit fund from which sick and death benefits could be drawn by members of a Knight's family.[116] Member Knights of each council contributed regularly to this fund. Knights themselves were required to be practicing Catholics, as well as able to pay insurance premiums, although by 1892 "associate" memberships were created for those who did not opt for the insurance plan. Ideas of fraternity, unity, and charity were buttressed by programs to preserve and nurture the faith of members. Each council had a chaplain to offer moral assistance to members, and each meeting was prefaced by prayer and hymns. The Knights were to emulate their medieval namesakes, who battled "the enemies of the Church by an intelligent defense of its teachings." The modern defence of the faith included the dissemination of Catholic "truth."[117]

The final point of the compass, the principle of "patriotism," flowed naturally from the Knights' heightened sense of Catholicism. Unlike most other Catholic organizations of its day, the Knights of Columbus placed little emphasis on the ethnic origins of its constituents, "emphasizing not so much Old World ties as loyalties to the new republic."[118] McGivney envisaged a fraternal insurance organization, rich in its devotion to the Catholic faith yet "imbued with a zealous pride in one's American-Catholic heritage."[119] Accordingly, under the banner of charity, unity, fraternity, and patriotism the Knights asserted that Catholic citizenship was the highest form of American citizenship and emphasized both the pluralistic nature of American society and the Catholic's equal claim to the rights of a citizen.[120] The order's adoption of the name "Columbus" reinforced the notion that America's earliest roots were Catholic, and as such the Church had made a contribution to the growth of the nation.[121] The founding of the Fourth Degree of Knighthood, in 1899, provided Knights with an elite section of the order that accentuated patriotism and Catholic citizenship. "Proud in the olden days was the boast; 'I am a Roman Catholic,'" asserted the Knight, "prouder today is the boast 'I am an American citizen'; but the proudest boast of all times is ours to make, I am an American Catholic citizen."[122]

In 1897 the first Canadian branch of the Knights of Columbus was founded in Montreal. "Canada Council 284" was largely anglophone in composition, with only six French Canadian members, although J.J. Guerin, a member of the Quebec legislature, became the council's first Grand Knight. When some Canadian bishops, including Archbishop Paul Bruchési of Montreal, prepared to condemn the order as a "secret society," Cardinal James Gibbons of Baltimore intervened and, by private negotiation, defused the attempt to prohibit the expansion of the Knights in Canada.[123] Cleared of episcopal censure, the Knights grew rapidly, forming new councils in Quebec and Montreal in 1899; Sherbrooke and Ottawa in 1900; Charlottetown, Kingston, Cornwall, Peterborough, and Ottawa in 1903; St John in 1904; and Sydney, Nova Scotia, in 1905. In 1904 the "State" Council of Canada was divided into two separate state jurisdictions: one for Quebec and the other for Ontario and the Maritimes. By 1910 there were 9,000 Knights in Canada organized in 60 councils.[124]

Despite the remarkable growth of the Knights of Columbus across eastern Canada, no council was formed in Toronto. Archbishop Denis O'Connor blocked the efforts to establish a Toronto council on grounds that there were already too many Catholic societies in the city. Little is known of O'Connor's reasoning behind the move, especially considering the deteriorating state of many Irish fraternal organizations in the archdiocese.[125] Given his rigidly conservative positions on doctrine and orthopraxy, O'Connor may have had serious misgivings about the alleged masonic overtones of "Columbian" ritual. The pleas of "state" representatives and of chaplain Michael F. Fallon could not change the archbishop's mind.[126]

O'Connor's resignation in 1908 provided the Knights with an opportunity to establish a council in Toronto. The new archbishop, Fergus McEvay, granted the Knights the permission they needed, provided that it was he, not the Knights themselves, who would appoint the chaplain to the new council. The Knights assented to McEvay's request, and Father James T. Kidd, McEvay's secretary, was appointed chaplain of Toronto Council 1388.[127] A spacious mansion on Sherbourne Street, in Our Lady of Lourdes parish, was converted into a clubhouse to serve all members city-wide. This single location in the east end of town, however, did not seem to hinder membership growth. Within eight years the Toronto council had grown from 131 "charter" members to well over 600 and, as such, constituted the largest council in Ontario, accounting for nearly 10 per cent of the province's Knights.[128]

The 131 charter members of Toronto Council 1388 were overwhelmingly English-speaking, and were also predominantly middle class. Fully 80 per cent of the original members of the council were engaged in either professional, business, or clerical occupations (see Table 5.6). Council 1388's strong constituency of barristers, physicians, retailers, salesmen, and clerks stood in sharp contrast to the humble blue-collar roots of the Knights in New Haven. The dearth of skilled and semi-skilled labourers among the first Knights in Toronto may also confirm the hypothesis of some labour historians who claim that class-consciousness among blue-collar workers transcended denominational affiliation.[129] In 1909 the near absence of blue-collar Catholics in Toronto's Knights of Columbus council suggests perhaps either that the white-collar image of Council 1388 was a deterrent to blue-collar membership or that working-class Catholics found their fraternal insurance and recreation in older Catholic societies and in religiously neutral craft unions. This is not to imply, as others have, that class-consciousness eclipsed religious identification; rather, at a more basic level, it indicates that Catholic workers had several social foci to which they could turn as their needs demanded.

The preponderance of white-collar Catholics in the Knights of Columbus, however, does suggest the consolidation of middle-class control over the new Catholic associations in the city. The parishes of origin of the charter members also confirm the growing social differentiation between the inner-city and suburban parishes. Close to 60 per cent of the founders came from parishes outside the four old inner-city churches south of College Street. Even those members who did hail from St Mary's, St Paul's, St Michael's, and St Patrick's lived in better-developed areas within these parishes. Undoubtedly, the rise of the Knights of Columbus, soon to be the most prominent Catholic society in the city, reflected the dramatic rise of the suburban Catholic middle class.

The rise of the Knights and their ability to attract middle-income and wealthy Catholics may also have contributed to the demise of the Canadian Catholic Union. Founded in 1901 by nineteen of the city's

Table 5.6
Occupational Background and Residence of Knights of Columbus,
Council 1388,and Canadian Catholic Union, 1909–10

Occupational Group	Charter Knights		Catholic Union	
Professional	22	16.8%	13	21.9%
Private	3	2.3%	2	3.2%
Business	26	19.8%	10	16.1%
Clerical	60	45.8%	33	53.2%
Skilled	11	8.4%	1	1.6%
Semi-skilled	3	2.3%	0	
Unskilled	2	1.5%	0	
None/no data	4	3.1%	3	4.8%
Total	131	100.0%	62	100.0%
Total white-collar	108	82.4%	58	93.6%
Total blue-collar	16	12.2%	1	1.6%
RESIDENCE				
Inner-city parishes	49	37.4%	11	17.7%
Midtown parishes	25	19.1%	26	49.1%
Suburban parishes	51	38.9%	18	29.0%
No data	6	4.6%	7	11.3%

Source: *Knights of Columbus, Toronto Council 1388, Seventy-fifth Anniversary, 1909–1984* (Toronto 1984); ARCAT, Other Collections, Canadian Catholic Union, box 1, envelope 2, Membership List, 1909–10; *City of Toronto Directory* (Toronto: Mights 1909, 1910, 1911). All calculations are mine. Percentages have been rounded off to the nearest tenth and may not total 100.

prominent Catholics, the CCU attempted to stimulate Catholic intellectual life in the city and promote excellence in Catholic education.[130] At
the summit of its influence in 1905 it boasted over one hundred members, most of whom were considered to be the leading Catholic men of
Toronto. They met monthly for supper and a lecture on topics that varied from "Early Italian Art" to "Mosquitos and Malaria."[131] Catholic
and Protestant notables often attended the banquets at the posh King
Edward Hotel – Premier George Ross, Mayor Oliver Howland, Henri
Bourassa, Professor Goldwin Smith, Lord Lovat, and even the reserved Denis O'Connor.[132] Upon the Knights' arrival, however, sev-

eral members defected from the union to the new fraternity. By 1910 attendance at the monthly suppers had dropped substantially, as had the paid membership. By 1912 the union was no longer the club of choice for upwardly mobile Catholic men in the city. The Knights of Columbus, situated in the affluent neighbourhood south of Rosedale and offering more services, activities, and financial benefits than the CCU, quickly became their association of choice.

The principles of the Knights as first outlined in the United States were imported wholesale by Canadian members, with few alterations. On Dominion Day 1910 a large group of American and Canadian Knights filled St Michael's Cathedral to hear the aims of the order being trumpeted by Father J.T. Roche of the *Catholic Register*:

The Knights of Columbus came into existence first, in order to bring Catholic men into closer touch with one another, to give them inspiration of numbers and of solidarity. Second, to work unitedly for the furtherance of Catholic interest. Third, to be ready for any emergency which may arise. Fourth, to defend the Catholic cause whenever or wherever attacked. Fifth, to strengthen the weak spots in the Catholic fabric, and to bring to the solution of present-day civic and social problems Catholic ideals of right and justice, and the Catholic viewpoint on public and private morals.[133]

The cry was aggressive and the mood was up-beat. The Knights were seen as those laymen who could successfully defend the Church from external opposition when required and, more importantly, could voice the opinions and teachings of the Church, bringing them to bear on the problems of Canadian society. As such the Canadian Knights, more so than the Holy Name Society, Hibernians, CMBA, or Canadian Catholic Union, promoted active Catholic participation in Canadian society and brought attention to the positive influences of Catholic presence in Canada.

The principle of patriotism was as much a part of the Knight's oath in Canada as it was in the United States. The Canadian version of patriotism, not surprisingly, was altered to suit the British North American context. Pride in Canada was important, as the Honourable Charles J. Doherty told five hundred Knights in Toronto in 1912:

You have within your ranks ... men of all races, and there is no distinction. You are all brothers, labouring for the promotion of our common Faith, and in doing your best for the furtherance of these things which have been a blessing upon this country's welfare. I am sure that every one of you here feel as I do, that Canada has a most glorious future. We are all happy to be the citizens of a great, free and prosperous country. If you could only realize, as I have done, on the occasion of my recent visit to the Motherland, how large Canada looms in the eyes of the world, you would feel more proud than ever to be Canadians. It is a good thing for our country to be made up of different racial elements. We need the genius, the aggressiveness and the industry which has been coming here in recent years from many lands, and which are being fused in the melting-pot of Canada ... in order to bring forth from the crucible a nation which will be heir of all that is best and most progressive in European civilization.[134]

Doherty's words epitomized the sentiments of Canadian Knights, who increasingly regarded the Catholic populace as a key constituent in a pluralistic land and good Catholicism as good citizenship, which in turn made Canada great.[135]

For Toronto's Knights these sentiments had three practical applications: the Canadianization of the Catholic immigrant, the rapprochement between French and English-speaking Catholics, and the categorical promotion of the Canadian war effort. Prior to 1920 these three initiatives, in addition to other activities,[136] provided the focus of the order's effort to thrust to the fore examples of Catholic loyalty and dedication to Canada. There was little if any reference to Irish issues, and there were no public pleas for Home Rule among the Canadian Knights. Their focus was strictly North American, and in this spirit executive officers quickly set about defining English-speaking Catholic identity and the role Catholics would play in the development of the Dominion. To this end Council 1388 established a public affairs committee that was mandated to stimulate Catholic interest in public affairs and political participation.[137]

The arrival of non-English-speaking Catholic immigrants prior to and after the Great War posed new problems for Anglo-Celtic Catholics. Both English- and French-speaking Catholics rallied to the new Catholic Canadians in the hope of preserving the faith of the "foreigners" and securing allies in the struggle between the "Irish" and French Canadians for control of the Canadian Church. Prior to the First World War the Knights established an immigrant aid bureau, and after the war the Knights joined with the fledgling Catholic Women's League in a program of "Canadianization of the Newcomer." Little documentation survives regarding these projects, although fragments indicate that the Knights of Columbus undertook a concerted effort to assimilate new Canadians. Regional "division points" designed to meet and gather information on immigrants were set up by the Knights and CWL across Canada. Contacts were made with the League in England and Scotland, who were to assist

Catholic migrants prior to their departure from British ports. Similar agreements were made with such continental European organizations as Le Société pour la protection de la jeune fille.[138] These activities confirmed the Knights' commitment to Canada, and their earnest desire to bring other Catholics to the same.

The quest for national unity also brought forth patriotic sentiment from the Knights. When the Great War and the conscription crisis divided Canada along linguistic lines, district deputies in Quebec and Ontario, with the encouragement of Archbishops McNeil of Toronto and Paul Bruchési of Montreal, joined forces as an example to the rest of Canada that national unity could be achieved. McNeil regarded the 600,000 English-speaking Catholics of Canada as able to translate the concerns of Canada's two solitudes to one another. United to Protestant Canada by language, and sharing a common faith with French Quebec, McNeil envisaged the English-speaking Catholic Knights as "the connecting link" that could heal the nation's wounds.[139] The first step in solving the age-old unity question could be the melding of French- and English-speaking Knights into one truly national Catholic voice, through which Catholic opinion and influence could be brought to bear on social legislation.[140]

The Knights in Toronto and the rest of Ontario were not as confident as McNeil. Ontario State Deputy J.L. Murray of Renfrew asserted that he was favourable, but was sceptical of French Canadian Knights' willingness to unite with Ontario. Likewise, Quebec State Deputy George Boivin said that Québécois were still too angry over the Ontario government's restrictions of French-language schools to be overly enthusiastic about joining with the Ontarians.[141] Toronto Council 1388, however, proved to be an exception to the mutual suspicions of English- and French-speaking Knights. The council invited George Boivin to speak on national unity at its annual Labour Day banquet in 1917. Boivin was most impressed by the visit, and Knights "applauded loudly every time he emphasized the main point of his speech."[142] This Toronto action, while illustrating keen interest in cultivating national unity, both Catholic and Canadian, was not repeated elsewhere in Ontario. Mutual suspicion and a recent history of "racial" conflict, particularly in the Ottawa Valley, killed the formation of a national administrative body for the Knights.[143]

Such efforts to preserve national unity may have been viewed with suspicion by francophone Knights on account of the whole-hearted support offered by Ontario's Knights to the Canadian war effort. From 1914 to 1919 the Knights of Columbus became involved in practically every facet of the Canadian mobilization, from recruiting young men for the CEF to assisting the returning veterans. After the war some Knights recalled that it was their finest hour as Catholics and Canadians:

For the first time in the history of our young nation, Catholic citizens of Canada, from Prince Edward Island to Victoria, worked together as a body; for the first time the Knights of Columbus were afforded an opportunity of putting fully into practice their two-fold obligation to God and Country; for the first time they had a chance to come out before their Protestant fellow-citizens and give testimony that their oft-repeated protestations were not mere idle mouthings ... No class or creed can justly claim a monopoly of Patriotism; whether we happen to be Catholics or Protestants, we are all Canadians – and ... 'Canadians first.'[144]

True to these sentiments, the Toronto Knights did yeoman work during the war. They sponsored recruiting, signed up for local rifle clubs immediately upon the declaration of hostilities, entertained soldiers, and, most importantly, undertook the building of "Army Huts" – recreation halls for all members of the CEF.[145] In the course of the Army Hut campaign many of Toronto's non-Catholic leaders joined with the Knights to raise funds. This historic campaign not only testified to the fusion of Catholicism and Canadian identity among Catholic laymen but signalled significant changes in Protestant Toronto's acceptance of English-speaking Catholics as loyal citizens.[146]

The Knights' attitudes towards immigration, the *bonne entente*, and the Great War affirm the power of the Catholic voluntary association to nurture the faith of its members at the same time as it provided an expression of members' patriotism. While few membership figures are available for the order's early years' in Toronto, the Knights had the advantage of arriving in a city where change among English-speaking Catholics was already well underway. Catholic assertiveness was already marked by Holy Name marches and by the carefully guarded independence of Canadian CMBA members. The pool from which the Knights could claim healthy, insurable recruits was the same Canadian-born generation of Catholic men who had come to identify less and less with Ireland or with other European countries and were imbued instead with a strong attachment to Canada. The Knights' twin pillars of faith and patriotism captured this sentiment and thrust it openly on to the public stage.[147]

A similar portrait could be painted of what became known as the Knights' female counterpart – the Catholic Women's League of Canada. Although it was barely established in Toronto, in the early 1920s the CWL became the vehicle through which Catholic women could promote Catholic values, charitable works, and Canadian patriotism. Little is known of the emergence of the CWL in Toronto except that, like the Knights, the League grew quickly in nearly all parishes and, in the process, came to dominate women's associational life across the archdiocese.[148] The work of the CWL and rising recruitment overshadowed such older sodalities and women's groups as the Pious Association of the Holy Family, the Sodality of the Blessed Virgin Mary, the Confraternity of Christian Mothers, and the Holy Angels' Society.[149]

Unlike the American-based male associations, the CWL traced its roots to England. In 1906 an English convert to Catholicism, Margaret Fletcher, founded the League "in the spirit of charity, work and loyalty, to promote religious and intellectual interests, as well as social endeavours."[150] Although some interest was stirred in Canada as early as 1910, when Archbishop Bourne of Westminster spoke of it at the Eucharistic Congress in Montreal, the first Canadian branch was not established until 1912 in Edmonton, Alberta. There, prompted by local social problems and the urgent need for immigrant aid, Catholic journalist Katherine Hughes, with the co-operation of Archbishop Emile Legal, forged existing parish women's groups into the first CWL council.[151] League branches were eventually established in Halifax, Montreal, Ottawa, Regina, and Sherbrooke. In 1919 women in Toronto established the first CWL unit in western Ontario.[152] The rapid expansion of CWL units by 1920 prompted Bellelle Guerin of Montreal to invite representatives from the seven local Canadian branches of the League to Montreal, in the hope that a national organization could be formed. In June 1920 the Montreal convention achieved this objective with the encouragement of Archbishops McNeil and Bruchési, who presented the League with a mandate to promote racial harmony in Canada.[153]

The CWL certainly mirrored the Knights of Columbus in terms of its twofold emphasis: Catholicism and patriotism. The League's motto – "love of God and Canada"[154] – was clear evidence that some Canadian Catholic women were as anxious as Catholic men to blend their Catholic piety and social service with patriotic work. This sentiment was reinforced by Bellelle Guerin at the Montreal convention when she asserted:

We may be said to be laying the cornerstone of an edifice that will arise fair and beautifully strong and proud before the eyes of the world. Shoulder to shoulder, heart to heart, let us go forth from this Conference bound by a solidarity that nothing can break, *gentlewomen*, but brave soldiers – holding aloft our banner of patriotism to our beloved country and of invioble fidelity to our glorious faith.[155]

Responding to the signs of the time, the CWL joined many of their Protestant sisters in the pursuit of the diligent and wise use of the ballot in all elections and the promotion of racial and linguistic harmony in Canada. That delegates from twenty-one English-speaking dioceses entrenched this promise in the League's constitution spoke unequivocally of the organization's resolve to create a Catholic and Canadian unity that transcended linguistic and cultural barriers.[156]

League members actualized their dedication to God and country in a plethora of activities. In 1922 they pledged financial support to the Sisters of Service, a newly formed religious congregation dedicated to the preservation of Catholicism among immigrants while instilling in the newcomer "the principles of good Canadian citizenship."[157] Similarly, the League joined with the Knights of Columbus in a program to "Canadianize" Catholic immigrants, greeting them at the time of their arrival and assisting them materially once they were settled. In Toronto, League President Gertrude Lawlor established an influenza "relief depot," contributed to the rebuilding of Louvain University in Belgium, and reaffirmed the local organization's commitment to patriotism. Quoting Tennyson, Lawlor appealed to her colleagues: "Love thou thy land with love far-brought / From out of the storied past."[158] For members of the CWL the advance of Catholicism was tied intimately to the advance of Canada itself. In terms of that principle they took no back pew to their male co-religionists.

It is very clear that in late Victorian and Edwardian Toronto, Catholic voluntary associations like the Catholic Women's League and its male counterparts were crucibles of Canadian Catholic identity. Devotional, mutual aid, charitable, and recreational associations, although often differing in aims and objectives, facilitated the process of self-identification among the city's English-speaking Catholic men and women. On the practical side, Catholic societies developed leadership, organizational, and accounting skills among many of their members. In this way Catholics were better able to meet challenges presented to them in daily life. As such, the associations were an integrative force, breaking down more completely the long-standing myth that Toronto's Catholic community was separated, ignorant, semi-literate, and undisciplined.

Toronto's Catholic voluntary associations gave a visible public presence to the type of Catholic who was an active participant in the social and economic forces at work in the city. Each association in its own way promoted a Catholicity that provided the necessary qualities of citizenship: loyalty, honesty, and morality. Moreover, such associations were advocates of Catholic participation and influence in the community, including co-operation with non-Catholic social service organizations.[159] In the process, Catholic associations became powerful advocates of a new lay identity that fused elements of their Roman Catholicism with a spirited love of Canada, its history, its freedoms, and its potential as a world leader. Members were expected to be devoutly Catholic and self-consciously Canadian. Such developments gave lustre to the prophetic words of D.A. Carey, who in 1893 chimed: "The time has gone past when a man's religion should determine his fitness or unfitness for any position be it high or low ... we are all Canadians, and as Canadians, loving our country and honouring her laws, do we desire to be judged."[160]

CHAPTER SIX

Tribunes of the People:
The Catholic Press,
Politics, and Identity

"The number is all too rapidly dwindling," observed Patrick F. Cronin, editor of the *Catholic Register*, as he mourned the recent death of his rival Patrick Boyle.[1] When his friends, supporters, and detractors gathered around Boyle's casket, many shared Cronin's realization that Boyle's passing marked the end of an era. A generation of Irish Catholic laymen who had been leaders in the community since the days of Charbonnel – Patrick Hughes, Edward Murphy, Sir Frank Smith, Hugh Ryan – were vanishing from the scene. The strained arms that carried Boyle's remains down the centre aisle at St Basil's Church represented the last remnant of the old guard: Eugene O'Keefe, William Burns, and Matthew O'Connor. A one-time Fenian sympathizer in the 1860s, Boyle had spent much of his life changing his political colours as often as he inked the steel plates in his many printing ventures. The one constant in his life was an undying belief in autonomy for Ireland and equal rights for Irish Catholics in Canada. Whenever the people of Ireland were assailed by injustice or the prerogatives of the Catholic laity were curtailed by the clergy, there was neither politician sly enough nor prelate sufficiently sanctimonious to escape the wild thrust of Boyle's pen. Sir John A. Macdonald, George Brown, and Archbishop J.J. Lynch were frequently the targets of Boyle's blunt, acerbic style.[2] At the height of his popularity in the 1870s and 1880s he had built the *Irish Canadian* into one of Canada's most-read Catholic weekly newspapers. By the 1890s, however, his constituency was dwindling; death had claimed many of his staunchest allies, and the new generations were not captivated by Boyle's crusade as their parents and grandparents had been. When Boyle tried to resurrect his beloved *Irish Canadian* in 1900, after a hiatus of eight years, the venture sucked away his savings and likely contributed to his cardiac failure.

Boyle's death in 1901 closed a chapter in the history of Catholics in Toronto. In the decade after the O'Brien visit in 1887, interest in Irish politics and affairs waned among English-speaking Catholics in Toronto. New generations in the city were much more concerned with domestic politics and economics, particularly Canada's role as a principal member of the British Empire. The passion that Catholics of Irish birth and descent had once shown for the "homeland" was replaced by a preoccupation with all things Canadian. This shift in the focus of loyalty was already evident in so many facets of English-speaking Catholic life: the development of new voluntary associations, changes in the separate schools, the Canadianization of clergy and religious, the indigenization of Catholic piety, and the growing white-collar revolution among laymen and women. The Catholic press was an important barometer of this transformation. In the pages of the local Catholic weeklies greater emphasis was placed on the role of Catholics in Canadian life, the need for Catholic participation in Canadian political culture, and the important Canadian contribution that was to be made to the British Empire. Men like Boyle, whose moderate Irish nationalism helped others to cultivate an appreciation for Canadian governance, were left behind as their children and grandchildren set out in new ideological directions.

The pages of local Catholic newspapers and the observations of their editors open an important window on the life of the English-speaking Catholic community. Owners and publishers of such weeklies as the *Catholic Weekly Review* (1887–92), the *Irish Canadian* (1863–92), the *Catholic Register* (1893–present), and the London *Catholic Record* (1878–1954) relied on a small Catholic population in central and southwestern Ontario for their subscriptions. Editors and columnists who ventured too far away from the accepted views of Catholic readers did so at their own peril. There was precious little compensation for too many alienated readers and their cancelled subscriptions.[3] In Toronto the newsprint marketplace was already saturated with several dailies and the rise of the popular "people's press" that pandered heavily to the interests and opinions of their readers.[4] Shrewd Catholic publishers knew that for many Catholics the purchase of a Catholic weekly was made usually in addition to a subscription to the *Star*, the *Globe*, the *Mail and Empire*, the *News*, or the *World*. If Catholics did not like what they were reading in the *Register* or the *Record*, they could save their money and stick to their favourite daily. Thus, the survival of Catholic newspapers in the city after 1887, their reasonably healthy circulation and distribution levels, and the nature of advertising in the journals attest to the wide audience sustained by several Catholic papers as well as to strong reader identification with the papers' editorial content and news selection. In their role as religious and political tribunes and as advocates of loyal and patriotic citizenship, it is most reasonable to regard Catholic weeklies as "the most direct and influential monitor of public sentiment."[5]

By 1922 the evolution of the Catholic press into a vehicle of both Catholic and Canadian values was virtually complete. The Toronto-based *Register* and widely subscribed London *Record* espoused a vision of Canada that included a strong sense of loyalty to the Crown and Empire while maintaining that Canada must be governed exclusively by Canadians. Both papers eschewed "jingoism" and "imperial federation" because both concepts were too badly tainted by Orange "fanaticism " and Joseph Chamberlain's vision of England's dominance over the politics and economy of the Empire. The "imperial" solution proposed by the Catholic press in Toronto offered Catholic readers the ideal of a self-governed Canada within the context of an Empire of equal partners. This variant of Home Rule, the editors suggested, was a model to which even Ireland could justifiably aspire. In this way Toronto's Catholic weeklies clearly articulated the focus of English-speaking Catholic identity for the twentieth century: " 'Canada first' must be our motto and 'Canada a nation' must be our hope."[6]

The tradition of Catholic journalism in Toronto dated to pre-famine times. In June 1825 Francis Collins founded the first Catholic-owned and -operated newspaper in the town of York. More political than religious in its orientation, Collins' *Canadian Freeman* was a vociferous opponent of the colony's ruling Family Compact, a position that landed Collins in jail in 1828 on charges of libel.[7] The paper ceased publication in 1834, when Collins died of cholera. Three years later Charles Donlevy and Patrick McTavey founded the *Mirror*, a newspaper that quickly gained a reputation as a worthy political successor to Collins' demands for responsible government and the voice of Catholic opinion in Toronto. It joined the *Catholic*, established in Kingston in 1830, as the only Catholic tribune in Upper Canada.[8] Issues of the *Mirror* were sporadic in the first decade of the Union of the Canadas, and by 1854 it was superseded by the *Catholic Citizen*, which was owned and operated by Thomas and Michael Hayes.[9] Coming at a time of sectarian discord in the United Province, the *Citizen* offered readers enthusiastic support of Catholicism, the rights of the hierarchy, and separate schools, as well as plenty of Irish news and features for newly arrived famine immigrants.[10] In 1858 it was sold to James G. Moylan and James J. Mallon, who promptly changed its name to the *Canadian Freeman*, although its editorial policies did not change significantly.[11] By 1863 this religious and political weekly was in competition with the nationalistic and sometimes anti-clerical *Irish Canadian*, thus establishing the tradition of at least two points of view available to Catholic readers in the city.

By 1887 Toronto had two Catholic newspapers that varied in tone, political affiliation, and disposition towards the hierarchy: the *Irish Canadian* and the *Catholic Weekly Review* (whose predecessor, the *Tribune*, had succeeded the *Freeman* in the 1870s). The *Irish Canadian* had been founded in 1863 by Patrick Boyle and Michael Hynes, although Boyle eventually assumed full editorial control of the paper.[12] In its quest to defend the political rights of Catholics, the *Irish Canadian* was neither subservient to the hierarchy nor a puppet of any political party, although it supported both Liberals and Conservatives at various stages of its thirty-year history.[13] As late as 1888 Boyle confessed that, although the *Irish Canadian* was not strictly a religious journal, it did take the liberty to "speak on the questions affecting Catholics politically" and mandated itself to "strike a blow" at the "organization" that impeded Catholics' "civil and political rights."[14] As bombastic as he was zealous, Boyle challenged the Church's leadership when it opposed the Fenians in the 1860s, the O'Brien visit of 1887, and the secret ballot in separate school board elections in the 1880s. The paper's often bold defiance of Church "authorities" prompted Archbishop Lynch to exclaim: "See what terrible mischief can be done by false brethren."[15]

As a voice for Catholic interests domestically and in Ireland, the *Irish Canadian* was everything it promised to be. In the 1860s it was pro-Fenian – which landed Boyle in jail – and it consistently advocated Irish independence. While recognizing that loyalty to Canada was important for Canadian Irish, the *Irish Canadian* preferred that Irish Canadians hold "an undying love and sympathy for the Green Island" and join in the fight for Irish self-government. Boyle claimed that those who showed love for their fatherland would "seldom fail in their duty to the land of their adoption."[16] On the home front the *Irish Canadian* scampered like a chameleon through the political thickets of post-Confederation federal and provincial politics. With green as its true colour, the *Irish Canadian* could change to a Liberal red just as quickly as it could don a Tory blue in order to secure a better deal for Irish Catholics. In 1882, for example, Boyle allowed Sir John A. Macdonald's Conservatives to bankroll the paper, temporarily publishing it as a daily. Before the decade was out, however, Boyle, who was up to his apron in red ink, denounced the Orange hues of the Tory party as inimical to Catholic interests and offered cautious praise of the Liberals, regarding them as the best political option for Catholics, federally and provincially.[17]

Table 6.1
Circulation of Local Catholic Newspapers, 1892–1919

Newspaper	1892	1899	1905	1909	1919
Irish Canadian	14,000	–	–	–	–
Catholic Weekly Review	8,000	–	–	–	–
Catholic Register	–	4,250	3,000	NR	13,000
Catholic Record	8,768	9,000	11,837	18,833	31,155

Source: McKim's Directory of Canadian Publications (Toronto: A. McKim 1892–1919).

Table 6.2
Circulation of Newspapers in Selected Toronto Parishes, 1916–22

Year	Parish	Subscriptions	Parish %
1916	St Vincent's	316	26.7
1918	Holy Family	114	6.8
	Holy Name	65	4.3
	St Cecilia's	210	8.7
	St Joseph's	250	13.1
	St Leo's	50	9.5
	St Monica's	56	12.2
1921	St Cecilia's	185	5.7
1922	Lourdes's	250	11.9
	St Brigid's	200	15.4
	St Joseph's	250	13.0
	St Michael's	310	12.9

Note: Percentages indicate the proportion of subscriptions to the parish population. Given that Catholic households averaged between 4.5 and 5.2 persons, one can assume that a paper could actually have been read by at least 2 to 4 family members. Consequently, the percentages indicated here represent only the bare minimum of the regular Catholic readership in the city.

Source: ARCAT, Parish Spiritual and Financial Statistics, 1916–22.

Such assertive Irish nationalism and political advocacy won the *Irish Canadian* a broad readership. The paper was distributed nationally and, by 1892, had a paid circulation of 14,000 (see Table 6.1).[18] At a mere one dollar per year it undersold both its major competitors in the Ontario market – the *Catholic Weekly Review* and the *Catholic*

Record – by 50 per cent. The low subscription price permitted the paper to reach a larger audience that crossed all classes of Catholics (see Table 6.2). Advertisements featured in the *Irish Canadian* from 1888 to 1892 also indicate the breadth of Boyle's audience. Readers were visually assaulted by ads hawking a wide range of goods and services – by grocers, hotel owners, haberdashers, lawyers, insurance companies, and the splendid elixirs and salves of patent medicine manufacturers (see Table 6.3).

What the *Irish Canadian* lacked in religious news was more than compensated for by its chief rival, the *Catholic Weekly Review*. Founded in 1887, the *Review* was intended to be an "efficient auxiliary to the Church in Canada" designed for the "defence of Catholic principles, and the propagation of Catholic thought."[19] Historically, it was the lineal descendent of both the *Canadian Freeman* and the *Tribune* and, as such, served as the countervailing force to Boyle's *Irish Canadian*.[20] In a spirit that reflected its readiness to "submit in all things to the authority of the Church"[21] the *Review* printed news reports of Catholic activities worldwide, papal pronouncements, curial politics, religious stories, and essays on devotions, liturgy, and ecclesiastical history. Above all the paper saw itself as a vital arm of the "Church militant,"[22] teaching, professing, and defending the Roman Catholic faith, thereby enriching Catholic family life and broadening the laity's understanding of the doctrines and practices of the Church.

The *Catholic Weekly Review*, however, was less financially robust than the *Irish Canadian*. In 1892 the *Weekly Review* had a modest 8,000 paid subscribers, mostly in Toronto, Ottawa, and Montreal.[23] Intended primarily as a "literary journal" for the clergy and "the educated among their people," the *Weekly Review* had a much narrower base of support than its chief rival. Subscription lists from Toronto indicate that the paper drew most of its audience from Catholics in the clerical, business, and professional occupational classes.[24] This elite constituency is confirmed by the narrow emphasis in the *Weekly Review*'s advertisements. In stark contrast to the cornucopia of merchandise offered in the commercial notices in the *Irish Canadian*, the *Review* attracted advertisers of patent medicines, religious items, professional services, and books.

Under its editors Gerald Fitzgerald and Philip de Gruchy, the *Weekly Review* rarely strayed from its course as "the organ of [Church] authority."[25] It consistently opposed "assaults" against Catholic rights or the Catholic electorate, and usually remained neutral to official political parties. Nevertheless, the presence of noted Conservative A. Claude Macdonell on the editorial team ensured

Table 6.3
Advertisements in Toronto's Catholic Papers, 1888–93

Advertisement	Irish Canadian	% of total advertising by paper	
		Catholic Weekly Review	Catholic Register
clothing/tailors	10.0	7.2	1.2
education	1.3	4.9	3.7
entertainment	1.3	0.0	0.0
food/household	5.9	4.9	6.1
general merchandise	17.2	2.6	13.4
government	1.0	3.2	2.5
hotels	3.3	0.0	0.0
insurance	6.2	0.0	6.1
lotteries	0.0	3.7	0.0
patent medicines	20.8	19.8	24.4
printing/books	3.9	10.0	1.2
professional	12.6	14.0	23.2
religious items	1.3	11.5	4.9
services	1.8	0.0	2.4
shipping	0.8	4.9	1.2
spirits/tobacco	5.6	0.0	7.3
other	7.0	13.3	2.4
Total	100.0	100.0	100.0

Source: Catholic Weekly Review, 17 May 1890, 14 June 1890, 12 July 1890, 16 Aug. 1890, 18 Oct. 1890, 15 Nov. 1890, 13 Dec. 1890; Irish Canadian, 26 Jan. 1888, 26 Apr. 1888, 13 Jan. 1889, 28 Feb. 1892, 13 Aug. 1892; Catholic Register, 5 Jan. 1893.

that subtle consideration was given to the Tories, much to the chagrin of the rival *Irish Canadian*.[26] When Catholics became the target of a Conservative "No Popery Campaign" in the 1890 Ontario election, however, the *Weekly Review* discouraged Catholics from voting for William Meredith's Conservatives, although it did not formally endorse Premier Oliver Mowat's Liberals.[27] Editors at the *Review* had less trouble with politicians than they had with Boyle and his paper. Each battled the other, spilling litres of ink over such issues as the secret ballot in separate school elections, the annexation of Canada by the United States, and the visit to Toronto by Irish nationalist William O'Brien.[28] On one occasion Fitzgerald fumed about Boyle as "a puissant figure among tap-room politicians" with whom the *Review* would prefer not to engage in open controversy, contending that such would be "altogether demeaning."[29]

Archbishop John Walsh put an end to this squabbling in 1892, when he instructed the papers to merge under a new masthead. Both papers were in financial straits; in 1890 the *Review* had reorganized as a joint stock company, selling shares to prominent clergy and laypersons in Toronto, Ottawa, and Montreal. A dip in advertising revenues and subscribers who were tardy in their payments made the financial underpinnings of the *Review* tenuous, to say the least.[30] Walsh selected the editor of *Saturday Night* as mediator between the two papers, and a deal was struck to take effect in January 1893.[31] Despite their amalgamation into the new *Catholic Register*, the *Irish Canadian* rose again briefly in 1900. Boyle continued his fight for Irish Home Rule and Irish-Catholic representation while claiming political neutrality.[32] The resurrected *Irish Canadian* died with Boyle a year later, prompting the *Register* to comment that the whole enterprise had "dragged Mr. Boyle down in extreme embarrassment" and left his family penniless. After his death, Boyle's friends and rivals set up a trust fund for Harriet Boyle, his surviving daughter.[33]

The demise of both the *Catholic Weekly Review* and the *Irish Canadian* signalled important changes in Toronto's Catholic community. While the loss of the two Irish Catholic newspapers did not indicate the end of the English Catholic–speaking community's interest in Irish issues, it did underscore the erosion of a constituency in Toronto for a distinctly Irish and Catholic newspaper. With Boyle's death the curtain closed on a generation of Irish Catholic leaders, "an old fashioned lovable class of men" who "gave direction to the influence of the lay Catholic body."[34] The *Register* and its chief rival in London, the *Catholic Record*, carved out their niche among the children and grandchildren of famine and pre-famine migrants, whose ties to the "motherland" were tenuous to say the least.

The *Catholic Register*, offspring of the shotgun wedding between the *Review* and the *Irish Canadian*, bore a similarity to both of its parents without being identical to either one. Inaugurated in January 1893, it promised to be "a Catholic journal thoroughly representative of Catholic opinion in Canada."[35] The *Register* was obedient to the hierarchy, particularly Archbishop John Walsh, who had officiated at the union of the two rival papers. The new paper described itself as a "a reliable medium through which [Walsh's] opinions upon religious and other questions of interest could reach the wider bounds of a journal's circulation." In its commitment to these ends, the *Register* claimed the support of the clergy and the "thoughtful of the laity."[36] The new editor, Father John R. Teefy, CSB, of St Michael's College, represented the new breed of Canadian-born and educated priests. A graduate of a public high school and the University of Toronto, Teefy was also an outspoken advocate for improvements in Catholic education. Under his influence Catholic journalism began to resemble the changes engendered by new generations of Catholics in Toronto. From the new journal's inception Teefy the announced that, while the *Register* would support the aims of the Irish parliamentary party on the question of Irish Home Rule, it would be taking an interest in "the institutions, the growth and prosperity of our country [Canada]."[37]

Walsh's efforts to put the city's Catholic papers under episcopal influence was not unprecedented in the history of Toronto's Catholic press. With the notable exception of the *Irish Canadian*, Toronto's Catholic weeklies were regularly guided by the visible hand of the clergy. Archbishop John Joseph Lynch had been generous in his support and use of the *Tribune* in the 1870s; likewise, he gave his blessing to its successor the *Catholic Weekly Review* in 1887.[38] Perhaps more overt in its management by local priests, Walsh's *Catholic Register* numbered three clergymen among its first seven editors. Similarly, the *Register*'s chief rival after 1893, the London *Catholic Record*, had the same number of clergy in the editor's chair prior to 1922.[39] Walsh's successors to the See of Toronto – Denis O'Connor, Fergus McEvay, and Neil McNeil – kept a close watch on the city's papers; in 1908 McEvay actually consolidated clerical control over the *Register*, to prevent the possibility – however remote – of Modernist influence.[40]

The *Register* utilized both the personnel and resources of its two parent papers, in the hope of building a sound organizational and financial foundation. Shares of $25 each were sold to a host of notable Catholic laymen and several clergy, most of whom were residents of the Archdiocese of Toronto, many – including Patrick Boyle with seventy-two shares – former staff members and owners of the *Review* or *Canadian*.[41] The *Register* was printed on the presses of the former *Review*, although it was distributed every Thursday, as had been the case with the *Canadian*. Advertisers in the new paper covered the spectrum of merchandising and services offered by both predecessors, illustrating that the *Register* intended to appeal to the widest possible audience. Moreover, the news and features offered a mélange of Irish and Canadian political news, typical of the *Canadian*, and historical essays, reprints from European journals, and Catholic news reflecting more the tastes of the *Weekly Review*. Most importantly, however, the *Register* declared its only ends to be "Our God's, our country's, and truth's."[42]

The *Register*'s emphasis on local news and its change in format may have hurt circulation. From the few statistics available it appears that the new journal was unable to hold on to the 22,000 subscribers of its predecessors. Given the moneys collected for subscriptions from 1893 to 1895, the paid circulation of the paper may have been as small as 5,000. By 1895 the journal's directors reported that in the first two years 1,400 subscriptions had been discontinued, although 700 new ones were bought in 1895. Directors blamed these fluctuations in subscriptions and commercial printing jobs on "the continued business depression" in Canada. Nevertheless, the paper claimed to be "more profitable" in 1895 than it had been in the two previous years.[43] By 1899, however, the *Register*'s annual paid circulation was only 4,250, and this dropped to 3,000 by 1905.[44]

Changes in ownership and editorship were commonplace in the *Register*'s first thirty years. Between 1893 and 1922 the paper had eight editors and three different owners. By 1900 it had dropped its subscription rates from two dollars to one in hopes of increasing its circulation, which by this point was almost entirely local.[45] This move seems to have succeeded; at the end of 1901 editor Patrick F. Cronin announced that the past year had been "the most successful" in the *Register*'s history."[46] In 1905, however, the paper was sold to George Plunkett Magann, indicating perhaps that Cronin's optimism about the paper remained unrewarded. In 1907 Magann was pleased to report that, in spite of the depression that year, the paper had increased subscriptions. Naturally, the *Register* boasted of success despite the fact that it remained neutral in matters of politics and refused to accept advertisements for alcoholic beverages.[47]

In 1908 the Catholic Church Extension Society purchased the paper and altered its direction permanently. This newly formed Catholic immigrant and frontier aid society gave the *Register* a national audience. Within three years the paid subscriptions grew by 3,000, and by 1919 the paper's paid circulation was 13,000, a figure that did not take into account the numerous copies that were purchased weekly at the doors of Toronto's Catholic churches.[48] Under the editorship of Father Alfred E. Burke, the *Register* now concentrated on missionary endeavour in Canada and abroad, Canadian affairs, literary criticism, and local news.[49] Burke and his successors – J.A. Wall, Father Thomas O'Donnell, and P.J. Coleman – gave the *Register* a national voice, thereby converting it from a mirror of the local church into one of the most influential Catholic weeklies in Canada. Most important, however, fragments from parish records indicate that by the end of the

Great War in some parishes as many as one in every three families subscribed to a Catholic paper.

Part of the *Register*'s problem in attempting to establish a wider circulation outside of the Toronto area was the popularity of the London-based *Catholic Record*. In a survey taken by the *Register* in 1920, five of the forty-eight respondents surveyed claimed that they read the *Catholic Record* and liked it as much as the *Register*.[50] Founded in 1878 by Father George Northgraves, the *Record* focused on news in all of Ontario's dioceses but paid only scant attention to Toronto. Unlike the *Register*'s assumed, but never admitted, sympathy for the Conservative party,[51] the *Record* was openly Liberal. "We were obliged to take a decided stand against the Conservative party in this Province," confessed the *Record*'s editors in 1890, "for the very good reason that the leaders and prominent men in its ranks had departed from the old political lines and sought place and power by pandering to those whose prejudices against the Catholic Church are easily aroused."[52] In 1903 this partisanship paid political dividends when the paper's proprietor, Thomas Coffey, was elevated to the Senate by Prime Minister Wilfrid Laurier.[53] In this period, it was estimated that at least 90 per cent of the *Record*'s subscribers in Ontario were Liberal.[54]

The *Record* clearly had an advantageous position among Catholics in Ontario. By disassociating itself from one locality, it appealed to all, and, in turn, to the advertising dollar in each local market.[55] In 1915 the paper reaffirmed its policy of not reporting local parish picnics, meetings, and the like because of its commitment to be "the national Catholic weekly of Canada." The editor, Father James T. Foley, noted that there were more readers of the paper in St John's, Newfoundland, than in London, added to which there were at least 1,500 American subscriptions. As a result, the *Record*, by the time of the Great War, stuck to matters of "general Catholic interest."[56] Likewise, being openly Liberal in a province where Catholics were supporting the Liberals in increasing numbers did not hurt the *Record*'s circulation. Given the paid subscriptions from Catholics in at least eight dioceses in southern Ontario, American patrons, and Maritime readers, the *Record* grew from a circulation of 9,000 in 1899 to 31,155 in 1919.[57]

In the period leading up to and following the Great War, the *Record* and the *Register* served a large Ontario constituency and acted upon their shared vision of being truly "national" Catholic voices. The road to such prominence was marked by profound changes in the type of news coverage offered by both papers and an ever-diminishing interest in Irish culture or even Irish news, except in times of acute crisis in Ireland. While attempting to provide a rich array of treatises, stories, and news reports on Catholic themes, both papers sought a close alignment to clergy and episcopacy that would have made Patrick Boyle shudder. What became prominent in each paper, however, was the editor's appreciation for the Crown and the progress of the British Empire. Intimate to these sentiments was the belief that Canadians, including Catholic citizens, were destined to play a significant role in the maintenance and governance of the Empire.

The decline of an Irish presence in Toronto's Catholic journals was symptomatic of a general waning of the "green" among Toronto's English-speaking Catholics. There had been a time, in the nineteenth century, when editorials on the Irish question, Irish news, Celtic culture, and updates from the Irish counties were a mainstay in Toronto's Catholic papers.[58] From 1893 to 1922, however, the focus of news reports, features, and editorials in the Catholic weeklies became preoccupied with issues germane to Canadian society, politics, and culture. Front-page news, reports of St Patrick's Day celebrations, and editorial comment on Ireland diminished significantly. It was only when full-scale civil war erupted in Ireland during the First World War that coverage of Irish news increased. Yet even within the context of the bloodshed in Ireland from 1918 to 1922, the comments of Toronto's Catholic editors were more notable for their advocacy of Woodrow Wilson's principles of self-determination than they were for any sentimental outpouring for the "old sod." The readership had changed, and the publishers and editors made the needed alterations to sustain new generations of subscribers.

The demise of the *Irish Canadian* and the *Catholic Weekly Review* in 1892 directly affected the pervasive influence of Irish news and comment in Toronto's Catholic press. The process of "de-Hibernization" had already begun in the *Review* as early as 1889, when Irish news began to take a back seat to issues more Catholic and Canadian in flavour,[59] and the *Catholic Register* continued this trend during its first decade. By 1899 editorial space devoted to Canadian issues clearly outweighed attention given Ireland.[60] Similarly, "From the Motherland," a full-page report from each of the Irish counties, adopted by the *Register* from the *Irish Canadian*, shrunk dramatically between 1893 and 1900. In 1893 "Motherland" was given extensive space near the back of the paper, but over the next three years it declined to a small column renamed "Irish News," a far less sentimental title. In 1895 topical items from England and Scotland were included.[61] By 1901 this feature had disappeared completely from the *Register*.

Interest in Irish affairs in Toronto can also be traced to the waxing and waning fortunes of the Home Rule movement in Ireland. In the late nineteenth century local Catholic papers followed Charles Stewart Parnell's constitutional movement for Irish self-government with keen interest.[62] Toronto's pundits even offered their Irish cousins the Canadian parliamentary system as a model for colonial self-rule within the greater context of the British tie. "If Canada is loyal today," argued the *Catholic Record*, "it is because she has enjoyed self government, and if Ireland enjoyed the same, it would earnestly uphold the honor of the British Empire and the flag."[63] Ironically, the act of proposing Canada as a sterling example of Home Rule was in itself an affirmation of how closely the Catholics of Irish descent were coming to identify with Canada. "We love the old country," mused Senator Frank Smith in 1897; "we love our own too; and we also see the beneficial results of Home Rule would apply to the whole empire."[64]

By the mid 1890s, however, the Home Rule movement, which had once been described by local Catholic journalists as "the Irish Crisis" and the endeavour for "a great natural, a great national, right," had evolved into a forum for internecine warfare between ambitious Irish politicians.[65] The sex scandal of 1890 involving Parnell, and the disarray it engendered in his Irish Parliamentary Party, disillusioned even the most avid observers of Irish politics in Toronto. Local enthusiasm was further deflated in 1893 by the failure of William Gladstone's latest Home Rule bill.[66] Even the great hope held out for the gathering of Irish expatriates at the Irish Race Convention in Dublin in 1896 was dashed when the Irish abroad witnessed, first-hand, the bitter divisions of the Irish at home.[67] As interest in Irish affairs waned, it became difficult to raise money for the Home Rule cause among average Irish Canadians. The fund-raising drives initiated by Edward Blake continued to meet with modest national targets of $7,000 to $8,000 annually, although it was the fat sums provided by individual wealthy Canadians, friends of Blake's, that actually buoyed this success. In Toronto, where donations fluctuated between $6,500 in 1894 to little over $4,700 in 1898, Blake had to depend on a handful of donors. In 1898, however, Frank Smith stopped his hefty donations, and Blake wisely ended the Home Rule fund-raising, recognizing that Irish-Canadian patience and generosity was spent.[68]

With Home Rule forces in chaos, Irish news was drowned in a sea of other issues. The Boer War, the Spanish-American War, anti-clericalism in France, and the Boxer Rebellion in China all stole headlines from Ireland in the *Register* at the turn of the century. Both the Toronto Catholic weekly and its London rival gave infrequent coverage of the Irish land debate and the Irish education question. In 1902, however, full-page coverage of the Irish Home Rule issue ended the ten-year hiatus in the dominance of Irish news. John Costigan's Home Rule resolution to the

Canadian House of Commons in 1903, and a speaking engagement at Association Hall (McGill and Yonge Streets) by Irish Parliamentary Party leader John Redmond, which drew crowds that "overflowed into the streets" in 1904, marked a modest revival in Catholic interest in Irish issues.[69] Similarly, the defeat of the Conservative-Unionist government in Britain in 1905, the reintroduction of a Home Rule bill in 1907, and the eventual reunification of Irish Parliamentarians, gave new cause for hope for Home Rulers and new copy for the Catholic press.[70] In terms of space and frequency on a weekly basis, however, Irish news rarely regained its former pre-eminent position.

Immediately prior to the passage of the Home Rule bill at Westminster in 1914, coverage of Irish and imperial politics increased in local Catholic dailies. Claiming that in "times past it was a movement which appealed to Canadians of all political and religious beliefs," the *Register* and its rival, the *Record*, followed the debates on Home Rule and criticized the increasing agitation among Protestants in the Irish province of Ulster.[71] On 18 September 1914, when the Home Rule bill became law after three attempts in two years, the *Register* rejoiced that "Ireland's glorious fight of more than one hundred years" was "crowned with success."[72] There was little doubt that Toronto's English-speaking Catholics shared the joy of their co-religionists in Ireland, and breathed a sigh of relief that a chapter in Irish history was finally closed. When the outbreak of the Great War cut the revelry short, editors assured all readers that, despite the suspension of Home Rule for the duration of the conflict, Catholics in Ireland were demonstrating through their loyalty and recruitment that they were deserving of self-government.[73]

The relative lull in the coverage of Irish affairs after 1914 was broken again when both the *Register* and *Record* exploded in horror against Easter Rebellion in 1916. Neither journal dwelt on it for any length of time, other than to express contempt for those who had perpetrated this "unspeakable outrage" and "colossal act of folly."[74] The *Record* called the revolt "criminal" and referred to its Sinn Fein participants as "malcontents," "socialists," and "shirkers" who had constantly irritated true nationalists by their "puerile pleadings and insane ebullitions."[75] The *Register* considered the revolt "utterly unjustified and unjustifiable," given the recent positive developments in Anglo-Irish relations and the fact that "Ireland [had] been fairly well governed for a quarter of a century, and a great deal [had] been done in the direction of redressing the grievous and cruel wrongs from which she suffered in times gone by."[76] Editor J.A. Wall went so far as to suggest that Germany had been the "tempter" behind the revolt. Such opposition to the revolt was shared by many of the Irish themselves.[77] More revealing is the paper's praise of good government in Ireland, indicating the moderate tone that had been assumed by some Catholics of Irish descent, conditioned by years of separation from Irish problems and by a greater sensitivity to imperial sentiments brought to the fore by the war.

Disapproval of Sinn Fein disloyalty was soon tempered by the execution of sixteen rebel leaders by British authorities. The response of Toronto's Catholic papers was guarded, but obviously disappointed. The *Register* recognized that under normal circumstances the execution of murderers like the Sinn Fein rebels would not have been overly severe. In the context of the Irish situation, however, editor J.A. Wall found it difficult to differentiate between the actions of the rebels and the "lawless acts" of Hugh Carson's Ulster Volunteers. Wall wondered why the latter were being treated less severely than Sinn Fein.[78] Given the outcry of the Irish people against the executions, Wall feared the worst: "It will take generations to overcome the effects of the evil wrought in a few hours by the brutal hatred furnished with the opportunity of glutting its desire for blood."[79] Perhaps the single greatest casualty of the rebellion and subsequent executions was the unrequited confidence of English politicians and Irish constitutional nationalists who believed that together, in an atmosphere of trust, they could effect Irish autonomy within the context of the Empire.[80]

The *Record* pulled fewer punches. There was no doubt that the rebellion was wrong in the mind of the *Record*'s editor Father James T. Foley, but the principles of freedom for which it was fought were noble. Sinn Fein, in addition to its other faults, was too quixotic: "It was because they were dreamers, visionaries, and not practical men, that they have made themselves appear so ridiculous."[81] Nevertheless, the *Record* deplored the severity of the punishment handed out to the rebels by the British, but felt that the *Register*'s position, especially its reprinting of an anti–Sinn Fein article from the Dublin *Irish Catholic*, was guaranteed to inflame both anti-Irish and anti-English sentiments.[82] These fears were all for naught. Both papers continued to support Redmond's constitutional nationalists.

The Easter Rebellion and its aftermath prompted the local Catholic press to reopen issues such as Home Rule, Ireland and the war, and disunity among Parliamentary and Republican nationalists.[83] While the *Register* never wavered in its coverage and support of the Canadian war effort, it acknowledged that the events of 1916 had made the Irish people indifferent to the war.[84] Ironically, the *Register* gave front-page exposure to the Irish hierarchy's opposition to conscription for Ireland, even though the paper itself, and its constituents, supported the Canadian government's conscription policy.[85] The actions of Canadian Catholic citizens with regard to the defence of the Empire were made separate and distinct from the responsibilities of those living in Ireland. The *Register* made every effort to isolate and distinguish between Catholic duties in Canada and issues germane to Catholics in Ireland; in so doing, it clearly asserted the priority of Canadian issues to English-speaking Canadian Catholic readers.

Such reluctance to overidentify with or sentimentalize the troubles in Ireland typified the *Register*'s and *Record*'s coverage throughout Ireland's bloody civil war. Generally, the Home Rule fight was argued firmly on the basis of Woodrow Wilson's declaration for the self-determination of peoples. There was little sentimentality, and few maudlin declarations of kinship ties with the Irish. One of the most salient features of the Canadian Catholic reporting of the Irish situation was the denunciation of British "Prussianism" in Ireland. Blame for the atrocities was cast neither on the British public nor on the Crown, but squarely on Prime Minister David Lloyd George. In this way the Catholic press did not compromise their loyalty to either the Crown or the Empire. Secondly, the Irish civil war helped to bring the Catholic press closer to understanding Canada's place as a self-governing member of the Empire. Both the *Record* and the *Register* openly supported the Anglo-Irish Treaty, thus verifying the importance that Toronto's Catholics placed upon the independence of Ireland within a British imperial context. This position confirmed that, although Catholics had lost faith in a particular British regime, they had not lost faith in the idea of a community of self-governing nations beneath the British imperial umbrella, under which Canada, Ireland, and all the Dominions could have an equal place.

The new pleas for Irish Home Rule were very different in tone from those that had preceded the war. The liberation of Belgium from German occupation and the Balkans from the Austro-Hungarian Empire offered vivid illustrations of the principle of the self-determination of peoples. For the Catholic press in Toronto, Ireland was the test case for the integrity of the principles for which the British Empire had fought during the long hard campaign in Europe. Accordingly, the *Register* asserted:

The battle for Irish freedom is not only a struggle for Irish independence, but to uphold the right of all nations to live their own lives – self determination. Ireland today is the champion of the ideal of national freedom for all Europe against barbarous militarism; the barbarous militarism so justly and strongly condemned by World Powers when viewed as Prussianism and wreaking its will on a small nation called Belgium ... Deny Ireland the right to live her own life and you admit the principle that might is right and that justice and humanity are cast down from their pedestal.[86]

This call by the official Catholic paper in Toronto, echoed by its London rival,[87] was one for freedom, justice, and "the rights of humanity,"[88] a far cry indeed from the emotion-filled pleas for the "motherland" decades before. That vocabulary was near dead in Canadian Catholic newspapers after the war. The *Register* lamented that soldiers from their graves in Flanders cried out, "Have we died for this that a small nation may be strangled? Woe to you statesmen who have betrayed our blood-sealed trust and faith."[89]

The Catholic press had lost faith in both Wilson and Lloyd George, and no longer expected them to live up to their high principles. The *Register* argued that the wartime allies were all busy in "the old-style grab" of colonies, while "Wilson sulked in his tent" as his "grandiose" plans were destroyed.[90] Even more disappointing, the whole British Commonwealth was sullied by British handling of the Irish question. Worse still, according to the *Register*, the current British government's hypocrisy on the issue of self-determination also extended to Egypt and India, thus tarnishing all the partner nations in the Empire with the same shame – "the hideous scandal of the British family compact is bruited and bellowed abroad among all the nations of the earth!"[91] Likewise, the *Record* called Ireland's plight a "blight on the Commonwealth" since the treacherous "black and tans" were wearing the uniform of the Crown, and the king reigned over "the self-governing nations of the commonwealth."[92] Given that the whole affair soiled the reputation of the Commonwealth partners and unjustly deprived Catholics of their rights in Ireland, the *Register* called upon all Canadians – Catholic and Protestant – to demand a cessation of the outrages committed by the British government in Ireland.[93] Violence committed by all sides was condemned, though particular scorn was reserved for Prime Minister Lloyd George, whose government was vilified as being "un-British."[94] The Catholic press walked a fine line: it upheld the Commonwealth while condemning a specific government; it rejected violent solutions to the Irish question while offering an alternative to the anti–Sinn Fein diatribes launched in several of Toronto's dailies.[95]

Many Catholic readers of the *Register* surveyed in October 1920 agreed with the course taken by both papers. Occasionally they criticized the paper for too much "abuse," but on the whole readers were supportive of Dominion status for Ireland rather than the creation of an Irish republic. Perhaps the most interesting trend revealed by the survey was that women and young men were generally not as interested in the Irish question as were those informants listed as "old."[96]

This emphasizes, in part, the changing values of subsequent generations of English-speaking Catholics in the city, who were more removed from things Irish than the remnants of the generations that
clung to every word printed by the likes of Patrick Boyle.

The signing of the Anglo-Irish Treaty in December 1921, and its rat-
ification by Parliament one year later, allowed the Catholic press to
breath a temporary sigh of relief. It also gave editors a chance to celebrate the advantages of being self-governing within the Empire. The
Record was jubilant:

we welcome Ireland into that great sisterhood of nations to which she yet
may render service as joyous and as loyally as does the Dominion of Canada.
Her status is ours, and should the occasion arise, in defending the common
independence we prize and cherish the Irish Free State may count on every
loyal citizen of every Dominion in the great British commonwealth.[97]

The editors, J.T. Foley and Thomas Coffey, also analysed the external
and internal powers of a Dominion, arguing that absolute independence of a country was not entirely desirable. The Empire, they
averred, was a league of nations, much in advance of the official creation of the Treaty of Versailles, and in this light the "independent
self-governing nations within the British Commonwealth point the
way of salvation to the nations of the world."[98] The *Register* was no
less enthusiastic in its praise for Dominion status and the benefits
therein, although its Irish-born editors, Father Thomas O'Donnell
and Patrick J. Coleman, were careful to add that there was no limit to
the freedom to which Ireland could aspire.[99]

When the Irish civil war erupted, the Catholic press in Toronto
stood squarely behind the Free State forces in their fight against Ea-
monn de Valera's Republicans. When pro-treaty (Free State) forces
led by Michael Collins and Arthur Griffith won the Irish election, the
support of Toronto's Catholic weeklies was solidified.[100] Thereafter
the *Register* and the *Record* were highly critical of de Valera and the
Republicans' violent reaction to the treaty.[101] When Free State forces
emerged victorious in the civil war, the local Catholic papers slipped
Irish issues back into the inner pages, interspersed among other news
items. With Dominion status achieved in Ireland, both papers lost a
sense of urgency about Irish issues. As far as the local Catholic papers
were concerned, the long-standing problem of governance in Ireland
had been favourably resolved and other issues – domestic, international, and ecclesial – regained their former prominence. There was
no reflection on the "motherland"; in fact the periodic rumblings
about Home Rule had forced English-speaking Catholics to reflect

upon their status as Canadians. If anything, in 1922 they emerged even more committed to Canada, her institutions, and her rising profile within the Empire.

Although tensions and triumphs in Ireland gave editors plenty of copy between 1887 and 1922, the Catholic weekly press in Toronto became increasingly concerned with Canadian identity and the role of Canada in the British Empire. This process of soul-searching and discernment of loyalties came at a time when Toronto's Catholics were weaving themselves into the fabric of the city's social and economic life. As English-speaking Catholics came to live in the same neighbourhoods as other Torontonians, and as they found themselves working side by side with Protestants and, later, "foreign" Catholics, it was only natural that they would ponder the questions of identity that were being debated in the country at large. Four distinct trends became evident in the Catholic press: more affection for the Crown; suspicion of imperialism as sponsored by Imperial Federationists; criticism of American imperialism; and ambiguity regarding Canada's military responsibilities elsewhere in the Empire. Catholic papers did not squeeze themselves neatly into either the imperialist-nationalist school, awash with some "Orange" elements, or the nationalist camp, sometimes identified with the likes of Henri Bourassa or John Ewart.[102] Instead, Catholic opinion was a mixture of both, recognizing on the one hand that Canada was part of a larger Empire to which it had constitutional and military responsibilities, and on the other that Canada was self-governing in all internal matters, reserving for the Crown its role as head of the Canadian state.

In the nineteenth century English-speaking Catholics – particularly the Irish – had been indifferent and sometimes hostile to the British Crown. Events in Ireland had tainted Irish Catholic opinion of the Crown in Canada, although tiny pockets of English and Scottish Catholics had long been enthusiastic monarchists.[103] In 1887, when Queen Victoria celebrated fifty years on the throne, neither Toronto's Catholic archbishop nor its Catholic press was disposed to celebrate the event. Given the British government's coercive measures in Ireland, Archbishop Lynch was critical of Catholics in England singing a Te Deum to mark the anniversary, and Bishop Walsh of London concluded that the extent of his celebration would be a prayer for Victoria's conversion.[104] Toronto Separate School board trustees were divided on the issue; the majority opted to march in the Jubilee parade, but the ardent Irish nationalists on the board boycotted the event.[105] With mixed feelings the *Catholic Weekly Review* claimed that, so far as Ireland was concerned, the "past fifty years have seen not her government, but 'slaughter.'"[106] Accordingly, *Review* correspondent D.A. O'Sullivan added that no Catholic was "one whit less loyal" than any Protestant in the Empire, but that he saw little reason to rejoice in "the continued existence of one particular person" other than to render "Caesar" his due.[107]

These anaemic displays of loyalty to the Crown soon dissipated as English-speaking Catholic leadership changed, social interaction in the city increased between Protestants and Catholics, and more hope was held out for Home Rule in Ireland. As early as 1889 the *Review* commented on how Catholic and Protestant militia had marched shoulder to shoulder during Montreal's parade for the Queen's birthday. In fact, by 1892 the *Irish Canadian* was left alone in its indifference to the monarchy when the *Review* extolled the duty of a Christian to be loyal and argued that the Queen was above sectarian politics: "The Queen is not English, not even British. It is well she is blessed with subjects who didn't care what she is, so long as she is the lawful Queen. The Boyne and her crown are thereby kept at a safe distance."[108] Such comments signalled an important shift in Catholic perception: since the Crown was independent of parliamentary policy, loyalty to the monarch did not necessarily imply one's support of any particular government's policies.

By the time of Victoria's Diamond Jubilee in 1897, the Catholic press was swept up in popular enthusiasm for the celebrations. The *Record* highlighted Laurier's visit to England and the Canadian military contingent's sparkling victory over the British Army in a "bayonet contest" marking the festivities in Westminster. The paper used the latter event to demonstrate that Canadians would be second to none as "defenders of the Empire." The *Record* also credited Victoria with efforts to "do good" for Ireland. Ultimately, the *Record* rejoiced in the progress made by Canada, thanking God "for all the blessings we have received during the Queen's reign, and especially for the blessings of civil and religious liberty which we enjoy under the British flag."[109] Likewise, the *Register* called upon all Canadians to "unite cordially" in a "display of loyalty to the Queen."[110] Such jubilation turned to sorrow when, four years later, the same papers dealt with Victoria's death. Even an aged and mellowed Patrick Boyle at the rejuvenated *Irish Canadian* set aside his editorial page to reprint portions from Father Francis Ryan's eulogy at St Michael's Cathedral, including the rector's claims that Victoria had been "a good mother, a model mother."[111]

The attachment between Toronto's Catholic press and the Crown was strengthened during the reigns of Edward VII and George V. Victoria's grandson, George, was praised for his attempts to eliminate the anti-Catholic references in the coronation oath, while Edward VII was lauded for his spirit of toleration towards Roman Catholics within and outside of the Empire. In 1904 the *Record* reported proudly that Edward had even attended religious services with Franz-Josef, the Catholic emperor of Austria. The king was also given favourable press coverage when his niece, Princess Ena, was permitted to marry King Alphonso of Spain, a betrothal that required her conversion to Catholicism.[112] On his death, the *Register* commended Edward as "a good friend of the Catholic Church" who "visited the Pope and showed him every reverence, confidence, and respect," and in many ways earned the loyalty and love of "his Catholic subjects."[113] In bestowing such adulation upon the British monarchs as friends of the Church, the Catholic press made it possible for English-speaking Catholic Canadians to offer allegiance to them as Canadian monarchs without associating their reign too closely with the policies of the British government in Ireland. What resulted was not the near veneration of the Crown, a behaviour exhibited by many ultra-imperialists of the day, but an incorporation of the Crown into a emerging English-speaking Catholic view of Canada.

The growing affection and loyalty of the Catholic press to the Crown was not easily transferred to ideas of imperial federation or the sacrifice of Canadian interests to England. "Friends you cannot eat 'old flag,'" commented the *Irish Canadian* during the 1891 federal election; "you can't drink 'old flag,' nor will 'old flag' pay your debts, or find you employment or a better market."[114] Boyle's attack was aimed squarely at the Conservative Party and imperialists who were playing on Canadian loyalties to the Empire as a bulwark against the Liberal Party's policy of reciprocity with the United States. The *Canadian* backed Laurier, reciprocity, and the hope that Canada would be annexed by the United States.[115] The paper referred to the program of the Imperial Federation League as an "impossible fad" that threatened Canadian liberties. For the *Irish Canadian* the mere suggestion of greater imperial integration perfectly demonstrated Britain's complete lack of understanding of the Canadian needs. Boyle goaded Canadians to think for themselves and to abandon the "prattle" about "love of old England" and reverence for the Union Jack. Later he added that "Canada, as a free state in the American Union," would be the prosperous home of millions of immigrants who would gladly come once the British connection was severed.[116]

Boyle's rivals at the *Catholic Weekly Review* had always been more British Canadian in their sympathies. The *Review's* fierce pride in Canadian autonomy and its fear of "American morals" prompted it to condemn annexation to the United States while at the same time rejecting imperial federation as a possible solution to Canada's problems.[117] The latter was particularly suspect because of the high profile of such anti-Catholic federationists as Dalton McCarthy, William E. O'Brien, and George T. Denison.[118] In 1888 *Review* guest columnist M.W. Casey asked, "Why is not Canada for Canadians?" and he warned against "foreign" advocates of colonialism who act "as leeches or vampire bats upon national glory and the dignity of nature."[119] His frontal assault on the ultra-imperialists and annexationists was rarely repeated by other journalists, who staked out a moderate alternative that advocated Canadian autonomy within a British imperial context.[120] Although Casey's heated comments were his last in the *Review*, they indicated that at least some Catholics were unhappy with Canada's current status, desiring neither the colonialist solution of the Imperial Federation League nor the continentalist impulses of the annexationists.

In the 1890s the *Irish Canadian* was the only Catholic paper in Toronto that envisaged American annexation as the solution to Canada's problems. Other Catholics in the city viewed the United States with a suspicious eye, fearful of American social mores, secular schools, and America's own brand of imperialism. Similar to many Canadian imperial-nationalists of the time,[121] editors and commentators at the *Review*, *Register*, and the *Record* were critical of American society, providing a hefty list of the sins wrought by "Republicanism," which the *Review* regarded as an agent of "godlessness."[122] Toronto's Catholic papers warned their constituents about what awaited Canadians in the United States: liberalized divorce, free love, birth control, irreligion, Mormonism, the separation of church and state, the loss of separate schools, and an "orgie of extravagance."[123] Such criticisms were buttressed by evidence of American jingoism during the Spanish-American war, by the flocking of carpetbaggers to Cuba in the wake of that conflict, and by the desecration of churches and atrocities committed against Catholics by the American conquerors in the Philippines. American expansion into the ruins of the Spanish empire strengthened local suspicions that Catholicism in Canada would have no advantages under American rule.[124] Moreover, Toronto's Catholics came to recognize who they were as Canadians partly by recognizing that they were definitely not Americans. Perhaps little has changed in the quest to come to terms with the Canadian identity. "The fact is," spouted the *Review* in a rare show of patriotic puffery, "that we in Canada, rightly or wrongly, are bold enough to think that we, in our modest way, have the superior civilization."[125]

While criticism of America helped Toronto's Catholics to map out elements of their own identity, it did not necessarily mean that they hated Americans.[126] On a day-to-day basis Toronto's English-speaking

Catholics had rather cordial relations with Americans: bishops, journalists, fraternal associations, and business associates. Nevertheless, having American colleagues, friends, and relatives was one thing; wanting to be American – with the republic's track record regarding separate schools, social morality, civil liberties, and American support of an anti-clerical regime in Mexico – was quite another. Toronto's Catholic papers were adamant that there was nothing to be gained if the Dominion became part of the republic.[127] By the same token, however, there was much to fear from tweaking Uncle Sam's nose with ebullitions of anti-Americanism.[128]

In the 1890s America's rattling of her "big stick" allowed Catholic journalists to take a closer look at Canada's role as an integral member of the British Empire. As Catholic affection for the Crown had deepened, so had recognition of the British connection. By 1900 the *Register* was declaring the death of American annexationist sentiment in Canada and claiming that a "British connection of the closest warmest character, involving an active participation in the great and most important affairs of the Empire, is the predominant wish of the Canadian people as a whole."[129] Important as this Imperial connection was, however, the *Register* cautioned against an excessive imperialism that might impede the development of distinctly Canadian ideals and the national interest. While the *Register* was prepared to "walk" in the country's ways, it was apprehensive of being caught in the brambles of jingoism and militarism that it identified with the Catholic nemesis – the Loyal Orange Lodge.[130] Likewise, while the *Record* referred to Canada as "the chief jewel that adorns the Imperial crown" and hailed the liberties received by Canadians "under the British flag,"[131] it warned sabre-rattling jingoists that Catholics would rally to the defence of the Empire in any time of an emergency as proof that "loyalty is better proved by acts than by words."[132]

The ambiguity of the Catholic press in Toronto on imperial questions was clarified when the long-standing difficulties in South Africa erupted into full-scale war. At first the *Register* criticized Laurier's raising of Canadian volunteers without the consent of Parliament. The *Register* claimed that the engagement of war by British Colonial Secretary Joseph Chamberlain, also without the consent of Parliament, was an affront to responsible government. Editor Patrick Cronin argued that if the Canadian Parliament was deprived of its exclusive jurisdiction in domestic affairs, then "Mr. Chamberlain is the only ruler in Canada. The Canadian people don't count, and don't seem to wish to count."[133] Cronin was also disturbed by the Imperialists' jingoistic rhetoric against the Transvaal, and suggested that perhaps peace could be negotiated without military intervention against the Boer republics. In this spirit Cronin lambasted Imperialist Sam Hughes as "the cheapest talker in Canada ... [who] could never get a corporal's guard to follow him across a potato patch."[134] The *Register*'s apparent anti-war stance embarrassingly conflicted with the pro-war enthusiasm of Father Francis Ryan, rector of the Cathedral in Toronto, and federal Justice Minister Charles Fitzpatrick, who visited Toronto and declared the war to be "an honour to this country."[135] Similarly, the *Record*, tied as it was to Laurier and his policies, supported the voluntary force and even defended the draconian measures taken by British troops against Boer property.[136]

As the war dragged on and was transformed into a costly game of cat and mouse between imperial forces and Boer guerrillas, the *Register* changed its tune.[137] The first signs of editorial moderation came in November 1899, when the *Register* published a poem praising the victory of Irish troops over the Boers at Majuba Hill. Later, in December, the paper sympathetically analysed the cautious support given the war effort by George Grant, principal of Queen's University and a noted exponent of religious tolerance in Canada. That same month Fathers O'Leary and Matthew, Catholic chaplains with the Canadian forces, were touted as "splendid examples" to use against "those men who ridicule the Church and call us unfaithful to the state."[138] Eventually the paper would offer coverage of battles, tributes to the Canadian wounded, and updates on Catholic personnel, including the distinguished service of two local officers who were serving in the expeditionary force.[139] By the end of 1899 the *Register*'s retreat was more evident. The paper feared that criticism of the war effort was contributing to racial and religious trouble domestically, and while he did not adopt the imperialist's arguments, Cronin urged that Canadians act like Canadians and desist from racially based criticism of the war. Pleading with Canadians to accept the country's pluralism, he urged setting ethnic nationalisms aside for the common good: "France is not Quebec, nor is Ireland Canada; but Canada should be Canada to all her people."[140] Herein lay a plea to Canada's charter peoples to lay their linguistic and cultural differences aside lest the social fabric of the country be torn to shreds.

The lesson learned by the Catholic press and its constituents during the war were many. Certainly, the *Register*'s call for all Canadians to be Canadians mapped out the path that the paper would follow for the next two decades – support for the Empire, but Canada first. The waving of the "bloody shirt" of jingoism during the South African conflict also made Catholics in Toronto even more cautious of the motives that lay behind Imperial Federation, and prompted the Catholic press to embrace more developed ideas of Canadian autonomy. In 1902 the

Register warned the government to send to the Imperial Conference delegates "who are loyal to Canada and to her responsible government, who will not turn the hands of the clock back under the 'loyal' pretext that Greenwich time is good enough for the colonies."[141] The same year the *Register* and the *Record* praised Laurier for his defence of Canadian domestic autonomy during his visit to England. The *Register* added that Canada was "a most important factor in the Empire," but she had to be careful that her independence was not swallowed by the "vortex of imperialism" in its most militaristic form.[142] It was not surprising, then, that the *Register* applauded Laurier's firing of Lord Dundonald, the "imperialist" General of the Militia, who had tried to put Canada on a "war footing" with the United States.[143]

In 1903 the *Register* published a series of six editorials that laid out its position on imperialism unequivocally. The paper regarded the imperialistic overtures of British Colonial Minister Joseph Chamberlain with extreme caution. It rejected any changes in the structure of the Empire that would lessen the autonomy of the colonies in respect to the "motherland." The *Register* also repudiated Britain's extension of significant tariff reductions to the colonies if it meant the surrender of colonial political power. Patrick Cronin argued that British officials themselves knew that "the new [trade] policy was intended to modify the liberties of the self-governing colonies."[144] Chamberlain's advances on behalf of imperial unity were further questioned after Britain appeared to sacrifice Canadian interests in the Alaska boundary dispute. Cronin voiced sympathy with Laurier's desire for separate Canadian treaty-making powers, and referred to the status of the Dominions as "silent ready sacrifices upon the exigency of the hour to the diplomacy of England."[145] The *Register*'s own vision of imperialism was clarified: Canada and Australia should "undertake the exercise of perfectly autonomous powers" and negotiate a bond of interdependence with Britain. In this spirit Toronto's official Catholic organ urged all citizens who believed in the fundamental principles of "liberty and self-government" to stand up against Chamberlain's "new imperialism" and to support an Empire of autonomous partners, united under one crown.[146]

The *Register*'s proposal for imperial "interdependence" and safeguards for Canadian autonomy was by no means unique among Ontario's Catholics. With the exception of a few Catholic extremists on either side of the imperialist-nationalist debate, this middle ground appeared to be the most attractive to English-speaking Catholic leaders in Ontario after 1900. Father James Foley, editor of the *Record*, wrote a series of letters on the naval question to Charles Murphy, a Catholic member of Parliament for Russell County, in which he defended "sound Canadianism" as the only "sound" imperialism. "Is it treason to be a Canadian?" asked Foley in a rhetorical flourish; "I think you will find that downright Canadianism is neither treason nor bad politics ... 'A nation within the Empire' is Imperialism enough for most of us who don't relish the tendency to eliminate the first term of the motto."[147] Murphy thought so much of these letters that he wrote to Laurier, informing him that Foley probably spoke for the majority of the Catholics in Ontario, and he added that a platform based on "Canadianism" might guarantee the Liberals re-election in at least thirteen Ontario constituencies where the proportion of the English-speaking Catholic vote was high.[148]

The opinions of Murphy, Foley, and Cronin were close to the mark. By the early twentieth century, theories of Canadian autonomy within an Empire of interdependent partners appeared to jibe with developments in other facets of English-speaking Catholic life. The laity and clergy were increasingly Canadian by birth and the products of local schools, where the curriculum implanted in children strong feelings for Canada and the Empire. Adults received similar doses of patriotism in their religious associations. For their part, Catholic leaders had encouraged laypersons to implant their faith in Canadian soil with the aim of creating a Church that would sink deep Canadian roots and produce a harvest of souls for generations. The press provided the public face for a process of acculturation that was affecting every aspect of Catholic life in the city. The Catholic press recognized that Canadians could be remain loyal subjects of the British Empire, under a common Crown, while seeking self-fulfilment as an autonomous nation.[149] While Catholic editors abjured the Imperialist extremes of the "home-grown jingo" and "colonial-bred jackass," they created important bridges between Catholics and the moderate imperial ideas of their Protestant neighbours.[150]

When readers snapped open their *Catholic Register* or *Catholic Record* they would discover that these papers were the tribunes of virtuous Canadian Catholic citizenship. After 1900, features, travelogues, poetry, and hard news increasingly reflected a concern for and a pride in Canada. Church news was sandwiched between columns that discussed and debated such burning issues as citizenship, Canadian history, pluralism, national unity, and loyalty. Journalists argued that since Canada was the focus of Catholic loyalty, Catholics must engage more actively in Canadian society, politics, and nation-building. Love of God and love of country, according to the Catholic newspapers of the time, were integral to the idea of "Christian patriotism." In reprinting an article from the *New World*, the *Catholic Register* made it clear to readers that "patriotism and piety, or church and state, are of necessity mutual allies. The Church needs the protection of the state, and the state needs the grace and gospel of the Church for its progress."[151] Local Catholics were assured by Father Francis Ryan that by their fidelity to the Church they had the fibre from which the best citizens were made: "A bad Catholic can never be a good Canadian, and a good Catholic must always be a good Canadian."[152] Strength of faith was a prerequisite for patriotism.

It was not difficult to imagine why English-speaking Catholics trumpeted their patriotism so loudly. In the early twentieth century the Liberals were riding the crest of political popularity under a Catholic prime minister; the country was in the midst of an economic boom; and there was considerable optimism about Canada's role at the international level. Catholics were anxious to share in the tub-thumping. The press reprinted the patriotic speeches of such politicians as Charles Fitzpatrick, Laurier's Catholic minister of Justice, because his words best reflected both "the patriotic convictions of Catholics" and the hope that "Canadian citizenship will produce the best fruit of practical Christian liberty."[153] Similarly, the national holiday, Dominion Day, became an additional opportunity for editorialists to remind their readers where their loyalties lay. In 1901 the *Register* insisted that the feelings evoked on 1 July ought to be carried through each day of the entire year. If this was done, the paper envisaged "a full realization of Sir Wilfrid Laurier's aspiration ... 'Canada first, Canada last, Canada all the time, nothing but Canada.'"[154] Catholic newspapers conveyed the clear conviction that God had endowed the Dominion with many gifts – including political equality and a superior constitution under Crown and Parliament – and these gifts were not to be squandered.[155] These sentiments buoyed Catholic patriotism throughout the First World War and remained in place as Canadians prepared to engage in rebuilding the nation and the world after the war was over. In 1921 the *Register* still invoked the memory of Laurier's dream when it called upon Catholics to "cherish the heritage" bequeathed to them and remember that " 'Canada first' must be our motto and 'Canada a nation' must be our hope."[156]

Canadian patriotism became a badge of honour worn by the Catholic press in Toronto. By embracing the idea of Canada "first," Catholic journalists came to advocate a subordination of one's older ethnic ties to a primary identification as a Canadian. The idea of a greater Canadianism was expressed most poignantly when Patrick Cronin editorialized on the issue in 1901:

Canada is a colony now growing to be a fine young lady ... She is no longer an infant and the time has passed when every inhabitant in this land must refer to some old-country centre as his birthplace. The majority of the people of this grand country were born right here; in very many cases their parents are natives of this land too. While none can find fault in a Canadian feeling proud of his English, Irish, Scotch, or French blood, nevertheless we have gotten beyond that stage where we feel that this is an adopted home only. The majority of our people are proud to acknowledge Canada as their native land, and while they always shall have a warm spot in their hearts towards the home of their forefathers, nevertheless there can never be the same feeling in that way there was some fifty years ago. Canada is rapidly becoming the land of Canadians; of Canadians who know no other love than that toward their glorious country. It is as it should be. A country is but a conglomeration of nations that can never attain its full growth until the several races have been assimilated and have merged into one great union ... When we have attained that growth in this country; when the inhabitants of this land know no other, then we shall have come to the stage where Canada will stand ready to declare herself to the world.[157]

In one stroke the editor of the *Register* revealed the full extent of the bonding process that had taken place between his Catholic community and Canada. More importantly, his statement looked beyond loyalty to a Catholic perception of the very essence of Canadian citizenship. He saw all ethnic groups in Canada forming one unified Canadian body, and thus an end to religious and racial disharmony. All in Canada would be Canadians first and nation-builders, a sentiment the *Register* shared with other Catholic leaders and periodicals.[158]

In their enthusiasm for the nation, Catholic editors became advocates for greater Catholic involvement in community affairs and politics. English-speaking Catholics were awakened to their duties as citizens and urged to take their "stand as Canadians interested in the welfare and progress of our country." Catholics were told by the *Record* to get out of their rut and care about building the country, confident that Catholics were "not serfs but citizens."[159] In light of the exodus of Canadian working people to the United States, the *Record* asked that Catholic men stay in Canada and develop the untapped wealth of the country, and, more importantly, educate themselves to ensure that Catholics would always have prominence in the nation's business: "What we want is enthusiastic love for our native heath, confidence in her future and hard work to effect its realization."[160] James Conmee, a Catholic member of the Ontario Legislature (1885–1905), echoed these sentiments in the *Register* when he urged Catholics to act upon their rights of citizenship and enter upon the task of making Canada a great nation.[161]

In its role as the voice of Catholic opinion in secular matters, the press offered several antidotes to the old Catholic fears of second-class citizenship. From 1887 to 1922 editors urged Catholics to participate more fully in civic life, particularly in politics. In the last decades of the nineteenth century Catholic editors in Toronto had targeted Orange bigotry, Catholic disunity, and Catholic apathy as the principal reasons for the lack of Catholic political involvement at the municipal, provincial, and federal levels of government.[162] The *Irish Canadian*, among other papers, argued that political participation would broaden Catholic influence in society and be powerful "armour" against anti-Catholic bigotry.[163] Catholic voter registration, argued the *Register*, was the surest way of enhancing the Catholic position in society, strengthening Catholic citizenship, and terminating sectarian discord because "Catholics who thus enter with spirit and activity into the public concerns of the state are not only appreciated by their non-Catholic fellow citizens, but become a power among their own co-religionists."[164] The *Register* eschewed the establishment of a separate Catholic political party, as had been suggested by the *Irish Canadian* a decade before, but instead suggested more assertive political participation without reference to creed or partisan affiliation.[165]

Determined and enthusiastic Catholic papers went on the offensive particularly on such issues as Catholic rights and the allotment of government patronage. The Catholic press objected to the Orange "reign of class exclusiveness" at Toronto City Hall, which deprived Catholics of a share of city jobs proportionate to their population.[166] The *Register* claimed that, despite composing 15 per cent of the city's population in 1893, Catholics had little more than 3 per cent of municipal jobs. Five years later jobs occupied by Catholics had risen slightly, to 5 per cent.[167] In 1897 such a one-sided division of civic spoils caused the *Register* to howl: "the Belfast of Canada has not changed its colors in the least … the Orangemen of Canada seemed determined to perpetuate the traditions of their Order in its worst form with the government of a Canadian city, that ought to be the centre of civic enlightenment and advancement."[168] These comments were reminiscent of the editorial views of Patrick Boyle, who eight years earlier had raked Orangeism at City Hall over the coals, and with it Catholics who "slavishly" supported the Orange party for menial jobs, "just as a bone is thrown to a dog."[169]

Catholic editors also complained that the allocation of patronage to Catholics by the provincial and federal governments was insubstantial. In 1889 roughly 15 per cent of provincial government jobs were in the hands of Catholics. Despite the protests of the *Irish Canadian* and some members of the hierarchy, Premier Oliver Mowat insisted that the level of Catholic employment was more than fair given the proportion of Catholics in Ontario.[170] In fact, despite protestations to the contrary by both the *Register* and the *Record*, patronage in Ontario for Catholics roughly accorded to their percentage of the population. In 1898, 19 per cent of government jobs belonged to Catholics, a net increase over ten years and slightly in excess of the proportion of Catholics in Ontario.[171]

On the federal scene, the Catholic press seems to have been fairly satisfied with the patronage allowed Catholics by Sir John A. Macdonald. This satisfaction was not at all transferable to the "Old Chieftain's" conservative successors or to Laurier in his first term.[172] By 1899 Catholic Liberals, who by this point represented a significant realignment of the Catholic electorate in Ontario, were making preparations for a Catholic convention designed to force Laurier to be more "liberal" in civil service and judicial appointments to English-speaking Catholics. The convention failed due to internal divisions among Catholic Liberals, but province-wide dissension over patronage underscored Catholic dissatisfaction with their "share" of the political spoils.[173] The criticism levied by the *Catholic Record*, a paper with long-standing Liberal sympathies, against the Laurier government's record on patronage is most notable. Such dissent indicates the extent to which some Catholic papers would lay aside partisan feelings when the "rights" of Catholics were at issue.

A logical extension of calls for greater political participation of Catholics, and a fair allotment of patronage, were calls for Catholics to seek elected office itself. The Catholic press in the city became the chief expositors of the need for a greater number of Catholic city councillors, members of the Ontario legislature, and federal parliamentarians. In 1892 Catholics composed one-sixth of the city's population, argued the *Catholic Weekly Review*, but had only one elected city official, Alderman William Burns in Ward 4. Catholics also had only one sitting member out of ninety-two at Queen's Park, despite the fact that Catholics constituted one-ninth of the province's population.[174] In the federal Parliament in 1895 there were no English-speaking Catholics representing constituencies west of Carleton County. Having assessed the issue of Catholic representation, the *Register* observed: "By being hewers of wood and drawers of water for opposing parties for ... more than a quarter of a century, Catholics have paid the full tribute of their bondage as a minority. The remedy lies within ourselves."[175]

Toronto's Catholic press continually harangued readers on the need for more political representation. Their ongoing demands in this area seemed designed to awaken Catholics from their inactivity and to demand justice from non-Catholics who were sometimes blamed for keeping Catholics out of elected office.[176] The principle of English-speaking Catholic representation in Cabinet was one on which editors were unequivocal. Prior to the election of 1896 the *Register* reminded both parties to transcend growing anti-Catholicism in their ranks and honour the precedent begun by Sir John A. Macdonald when he placed at least one English-speaking Catholic in Cabinet. The editor added, "English-speaking Catholics do not regard the French-Canadian ministers as their representatives" and therefore demanded fair representation.[177] Likewise, Thomas Coffey, editor of the *Record* and a noted Liberal, cautioned Laurier on the importance of having an English-speaking Catholic Cabinet minister from Ontario.[178] Locally, the *Register* urged the city's Catholics to stand for office, pointing out to young men that "a fair amount of prosperity" was causing them to ignore their obligations to others in the community.[179] For the Catholic press, then, adequate Catholic representation required action simultaneously on two fronts: momentum from the Catholic community and fairness from the major political parties.

The words of Catholic editors, journalists, and clergy were not lost on some ambitious young Catholic men. In the late 1890s Catholic men used existing Canadian political parties as a means of personal advancement and, by implication, offered the Catholic community a greater profile in the corridors of power.[180] The election of Laurier, a Catholic if in name only,[181] encouraged Catholic leaders in their hopes that more Catholics might be enticed to enter politics. The *Register* was pleased that Laurier had the choice of at least three English-speaking Catholics for Cabinet portfolios: Charles Fitzpatrick (Quebec County), James Devlin (Wright), and Richard W. Scott (Senate). That Scott and Fitzpatrick were given portfolios but the latter was denied full Cabinet status splashed a little cold water on the dreams of the paper.[182] By 1904 however, P.F. Cronin reported that the political situation was far brighter for Catholics. The creation of the federal riding of Toronto South, where Catholics controlled at least one-fifth to one-quarter of the vote, gave the *Register* hope that elections there would proceed without "religious misunderstanding."[183] In the federal election of October 1904 a record number of English-speaking Catholics stood for office, especially for Laurier's Liberals. Twelve were elected to the Laurier government, and four to Borden's Conservative opposition. In addition, Toronto South was won by Conservative stalwart A. Claude Macdonell, a former board member at the *Catholic Weekly Review* and the first Catholic to represent Toronto federally since the 1870s.[184]

Similarly, the Tory Protestant bastion of Toronto began to crumble at the provincial level. The *Register* changed its tune towards the Ontario Conservatives when, in 1897, new leader James Pliny Whitney abandoned William Meredith's anti-Catholic crusade of the 1890s and invited Catholics into the party rank and file. That year Whitney backed prominent Catholic lawyer James J. Foy for the Conservative nomination in the provincial riding of Toronto South. Despite some jeers and hisses at the local nominating meeting, Foy, with Whitney at his side, won the right to carry the Tory standard in the riding, thus changing the direction of Conservative politics in Toronto.[185] In the subsequent provincial election Foy won the seat handily, and was one of ten Catholics (10.9 per cent of sitting members) elected to the legislature.[186] The election of 1905 was not a mere blip on the Catholic electoral chart; in 1919 twelve Catholics (10.9 per cent) were elected to Queen's Park. In fact, the politicking of Toronto's Catholics in all areas became so widespread that, in 1918, the *Register*'s labour columnist, Henry Somerville, complained that Catholics were "more conspicuous in political activities" than they were in social movements and were more apt to join a political party than the St Vincent de Paul Society.[187]

The advocacy of the Catholic press was only one of several factors that prompted a more visible Catholic presence in politics. Increased levels of literacy among Catholics, the rising number of Catholics in white-collar and professional jobs with better salaries, the weakening of sectarian tension among elites after 1900, and more widespread social integration of Catholics and Protestants in workplaces, neighbourhoods, and family life created an environment that facilitated the movement of Catholics into public office. For tribunes at both the *Register* and the *Record* this religious peace was to be encouraged by all Torontonians, not only as a civic virtue but as a means to promote the progress and prosperity of Canada so that she might attain her "God-given" destiny. "No other policy," argued the *Register*, "is worthy of a great country, a great party or a great statesman."[188] Confidently the papers reported to their readers that relations between Catholics and Protestants were improving to such an extent that the possibilities of Catholic leadership and influence in Ontario were not to be underestimated. The *Register*, for instance, claimed that most of the city's Protestants were moderates and that "sensible" Catholics and Protestants "continue to live in peace with one another" and "laugh heartily" at the appearance of the "badly discredited Protestant Horse."[189] The paper would add that 90 per cent of "the people of Toronto, as a whole, are tolerant, kindly, and there is good feeling between men of all creeds. A priest can walk on the street and be treated just as respectfully as he would in Chicago or New York."[190]

Fanatics and bigots gradually came to be seen as a small minority, an "anachronism" in what was otherwise a city little troubled by sectarian friction.[191]

Spending less time berating the Protestant menace, Catholic papers attempted to build confidence in the Catholic community, insisting that they were essentially masters of their own destiny. One effective means of doing this was by offering frequent copy on the new generation of English-speaking Catholic politicians such as James J. Foy (provincial secretary, Ontario), Charles Murphy (MP Russell), A. Claude Macdonell (MP Toronto South), C.J. Doherty (minister of Justice, 1911–21), and Charles Fitzpatrick (minister of Justice, 1897–1905), praising them as living proof that Catholics could rise to the top and be among Canada's best leaders. This promotion came full circle when the press reprinted the speeches of Catholic politicians who themselves advocated Canadian patriotism and full Catholic participation in all levels of Canadian politics, enterprise, and industry.[192] As political commentators and agents of Canadian identity, Catholic weeklies brought Toronto's Catholics into greater communion with the realities of the world, and never gave Catholics the excuse of retreating or alienating themselves from Canadian political culture, even in the alleged "Belfast of Canada."[193]

By 1922 the content and character of the Catholic newspaper in Toronto had changed significantly since the days of Patrick Boyle. New generations of Canadian-born readers and the Catholic population's overriding concerns with life in Canada had prompted the erosion and eventual disappearance of the Irish flavour of local Catholic weeklies. The general loss of an Irish ethos in the local Catholic community was recognized as late as 1917 by "The Gleaner," a regular commentator in the *Record*, who observed that when looking at Irish Catholic households he found "no evidence of the nationality of the family."[194] The Gleaner lamented that the Irishness and Catholicity he valued was now passing away and that new generations of Canadians had abandoned the old traditions, associated more fully with their Protestant neighbours, and had in some cases left the Church.

By 1922 English-speaking Catholics in Toronto, through their tribunes in the Catholic press, had come to identify themselves as fully Canadian. The dilemma that tore the community apart during the visit of William O'Brien in 1887 – Catholics between competing loyalties – had faded into the recesses of memory. A sense of Irishness had been submerged in a greater sense of being citizens of the Dominion. The English-speaking Catholic vision of Canada was articulated in such a way as to avoid the extremes of autonomy advanced by

French Canadians and the ultra-imperialism of some anglo Protestants. Canada, in English-speaking Catholic eyes, was to be an independent self-governing nation within an empire of equal partners.[195] The press had become the chief exponent of this vision, speaking for Catholics whose vision was being shaped by their birthplace, their political involvement, their improved economic status, their social integration in Toronto, and, by 1918, their blood spilled on the battlefields of Europe. Charles Murphy, Liberal member of Parliament for Russell, affirmed that since Catholics were on an "equal footing" with other Canadians, and "while ever remembering Ireland," Catholics of Irish descent must "be loyal first, last and all the time to Canada, than which a fairer land or one with a greater or nobler future does not exist on earth."[196] One wonders if Patrick Boyle would have agreed.

Newcomers and Nationalists: Defending and Extending an English-speaking Catholic Vision

It was perhaps the strangest religious ceremony these boys had ever seen. The small chapel at St Mary's Church was packed from wall to wall with foreign-looking people – men dressed in drab grey and brown work clothes and kneeling women with their heads wrapped in pretty coloured scarves. A priest the boys had never seen before murmured his sermon in some indecipherable language, although he said the rest of the Mass in the more familiar Latin. The constant creaking of the sacristy door as it opened and shut, so that each altar-boy could have his turn to look, did not go unnoticed by the celebrant. Later, Father Paul would complain bitterly to his superiors in the Resurrectionist Order about the rudeness that he and his flock of Polish and Macedonian immigrants had experienced at the hands of local Catholics. Pastors allowed them space to worship only if it did not inconvenience the regular flow of parish life; their confessions were delayed to after dark on Saturday evenings because St Mary's choir practice could not be disturbed; caretakers locked them out, cutting short their opportunities to receive the sacraments; and those mischievous peeping altar-boys constantly interrupted services as they gathered intelligence on these foreigners of the faith.[1] At St Mary's and elsewhere in the city the arrival of thousands of southern and eastern European Catholics in Toronto in the early twentieth century caught local English-speaking Catholics by surprise and completely unprepared.

In the years leading up to the Great War the "immigrant question" transformed the urban heartland and prairie frontier of Canada into religious battlefields. Judging the "foreigners" to be a threat to the moral and social fabric of the nation, Canadian Christians actively sought to convert the newcomers in hopes that the immigrant would assimilate into Anglo Canadian society.[2] English-speaking Catholics were no less earnest in their efforts to address the needs of the waves of Italian, Polish, Lithuanian, Hungarian, and Ukrainian Catholic migrants who had ventured to Canada with neither clergy nor resources to recreate their familiar religious institutions.[3] Many feared that if they did nothing, the new Catholic Canadians would fall prey to the proselytizing efforts of Protestant churches to wrestle the newcomers from the tyranny of "popery." Such losses, in the eyes of English-speaking Catholics, would be both an embarrassment for the Church and a major setback in terms of their overall numerical power in Toronto and across Canada. The challenge facing the host Catholic community would be to protect the integrity of various Catholic rites and practices without compromising the essentials of English-speaking Catholic devotion or threatening the anglophone leadership and control of the local Church.

The Catholic newcomers prompted English-speaking Catholics to reaffirm their own position in Canadian society and their loyalty to the English language and Canadian customs, laws, and institutions. Faced with the linguistic, cultural, and devotional differences between themselves and these "foreign" Catholics, Toronto's English-speaking Catholics wore their Canadian patriotism more openly, and thereby blended their religious mission to save the newcomers with a national mission to integrate new Catholic Canadians into the anglophone milieu. They were reassured by the remarks of English primate Cardinal John Bourne, who in 1910 reminded Canadian Catholics that the spread of the faith on this continent depended on use of the English language as the medium of conversion.[4] This English-speaking Catholic missionary confidence was extended by patriotic activities in separate schools and voluntary associations, and by the enthusiasm of the press and Church leaders.[5] Each of these features of their community life had prompted English-speaking Catholics to identify themselves more fully with the promised glory awaiting Canada on the world stage and with the strength offered Canadian Catholicism through the conversion of the immigrants. Toronto's English-speaking Catholics came to regard Catholicism as essential to the immigrant soul, and the English language and British Canadian traditions as essential to the foreigner's success in Canadian society. One leader of the Catholic Church Extension Society, a Catholic fund-raising society for preserving the faith of immigrants and native peoples, boldly asserted that "religious duties and patriotic endeavours" would not work at cross purposes.[6]

This double-edged vision of Catholicization and Canadianization among Toronto's hierarchy and lay leadership provided the foundation for a nationwide home mission movement. The Catholic Church

Extension Society, founded in Toronto in 1908, harnessed this religious and patriotic energy and gathered together like-minded Catholics from across Canada for the purposes of immigrant aid. Toronto quickly became the nerve-centre for English-speaking Catholic missionary activity and the urgent call to all Catholics to save the immigrants for the Church and for Canada. While the home mission efforts of the Extension Society met with mixed results, the patriotic dimension of the program deepened the already festering animosity between French- and English-speaking Catholics. For French-speaking Catholics, particularly those with nationalist sympathies, the home mission activities centred in Toronto confirmed francophone fears that their English-speaking Catholic cousins were charting a course too much akin to that of Canada's anglophone Protestants. Thus, by 1910 not only did the allegiance of new Catholic Canadians hang in the balance, but ultimately the question of who would control the Church outside of Quebec was brought to the fore. In their struggle with their French Canadian co-religionists, English-speaking Catholics demonstrated how clearly they had come to identify with English Canadian values and national aspirations.

The arrival of Catholic sojourners and migrants from southern and eastern Europe, particularly Italians, Poles, and Ukrainians, permanently altered the composition of Toronto's Catholic community. The sheer numbers of the newcomers in comparison to waning Irish and Scottish immigration threatened to disrupt the English-speaking Catholic control of the Church in the city. In 1891 less than 5 per cent of the city's Catholics had been born outside the British Empire or the United States. By the turn of the century foreign-born Catholics had increased to approximately 7 per cent of the denomination's strength in Toronto. Within ten years this nearly doubled to 14 per cent, and by 1921 20 per cent of Catholics in the city were of continental European birth.[7] The increasing numbers of non-English-speaking immigrants could no longer be treated by Anglo-Celts as a curious passing fancy.[8] As the numbers of immigrant Catholics steadily increased, so did the pressures for national parishes, priests fluent in the language and culture of the immigrants, and a sound infrastructure of lay associations to preserve the loyalty of these new Canadians to Catholicism.

Until the installation of Archbishop Fergus McEvay in 1908, English-speaking Catholics in Toronto did precious little for European Catholic immigrants. Such inactivity was born of ignorance and possibly the feeling that the immigrants would sojourn in the city temporarily, earn the monies they needed, and then move on. In the meantime English-speaking Catholics regarded these new Canadians of the faith as a rather quaint or exotic oddity with their ancient Eastern rituals, devotional practices, and cultural variants of Catholicism. Prior to the turn of the century Catholics of Irish, Scottish, English, and American descent encountered little variety in local churches. The French Canadians worshippers at Sacré Coeur parish, founded in 1887; the small German congregation administered by the Redemptorists at St Patrick's Church; and the tiny family of Syrians of the Maronite and Melkite rites that communed with their own priest at St Vincent's chapel – these provided the few splashes of colour in what otherwise was a Church dominated by those with Celtic and Anglo-Saxon roots.[9]

The Catholic press offered mixed reviews of the newcomers, at one time offering stories and platitudes regarding the liturgies of the Maronite, Melkite, and Greek Catholics, in other instances warning Canadians of undesirables and criminals among the immigrants. In the first years of the twentieth century English-speaking Catholic contact with immigrants, though infrequent, was generally characterized by one of only a few responses: curiosity about the religious customs brought to the local Church by their strange "brethren"; revulsion at what at times seemed like pagan practice thinly disguised as Catholic; or relative indifference to the financial and social needs of new Catholic Canadians. Local authorities were content to provide English-speaking Catholic diocesan priests or members of local religious orders who had some second-language skills to arrange special liturgies in local parishes when necessary.[10] That so little was being done for the immigrants caused considerable alarm for several local priests, particularly when the numbers of migrants in local parishes steadily increased as sojourning appeared to give way to permanent settlement. In 1908 Father John L. Hand wrote to the Apostolic Delegate explaining that, although the "foreign population" had reached nearly ten thousand souls, local Church leaders had not mobilized sufficiently to address the needs of the newcomers.[11]

The growing presence of Catholic immigrants was felt most acutely in the inner-city parishes, particularly in the central and western parishes of St Patrick's, St Mary's, and the newly created St Francis, founded in 1903. These parishes were in close proximity to the workshops, garment factories, construction jobs, and manual tasks that were the mainstay of immigrant employment. By the end of the Great War the immigrants would become prominent in areas that had once been home to Protestants and Catholics of Anglo-Celtic origins. In 1890 St Mary's parish, at the corner of Bathurst and MacDonell

Square, included an English-speaking Catholic population that accounted for well over 90 per cent of the entire Catholic population. Over the next thirty years, however, these anglophones diminished to little more than 64 per cent of local Catholics as Poles, Ukrainians, and Italians flooded into the neighbourhoods west of Spadina Avenue.[12] The sight and sound of Italian, Lithuanian, and Polish babies screaming at the baptismal fonts of St Patrick's and St Mary's parishes became commonplace, as did the presence of their older brothers and sisters in the gravel and dirt schoolyards of the local Catholic schools.[13]

In the eastern section of the city and in suburban areas, the increase of non-English-speaking Catholics was the exception rather than the rule. In the Cabbagetown district surrounding St Paul's parish, however, the newcomer's presence was felt. In the wake of migration to the St Paul's area by French Canadian cigarmakers and rattan workers[14] and numerous Eastern European labourers, the English-speaking Catholic proportion of the parish population fell to almost 80 per cent in 1920 from its high of nearly 97 per cent thirty years earlier.[15] In other east-end parishes such as Our Lady of Lourdes, where property values were high, and Holy Name parish, which was distant from the factory district, English-speaking Catholics retained an overwhelming dominance.

The distinctive immigrant neighbourhoods of Toronto's southern and western districts were by no means safe havens for preserving the religious traditions of Catholic newcomers. English-speaking Catholics considered Methodist missionaries of Italian origin to be the greatest Protestant threat to the Catholicity of Toronto's new Canadians. A Methodist mission house was established in the heart of each Little Italy in Toronto with the express intent of converting the Italians, whom they considered "not sincere or earnest Roman Catholics."[16] Italian men were believed to be the most promising converts, since their participation in Sunday mass and associated parish activities was perceived as minimal. Responding to the enthusiastic claims of the *Christian Guardian* regarding the conversion of Toronto's Italians, the *Catholic Register* complained that Methodist successes were due in large part to the slow response of anglophone Catholics to the needs of their immigrant co-religionists.[17] Similarly, after the congress of the Protestant "Laymen's Missionary Movement" in Toronto in 1909, the *Register* repeated its warnings to the city's Catholics to look beyond their local parishes to the needs of the Church everywhere in the province and nation. "We are obligated ... whether we be laymen or cleric," argued the editor, "that, there be no portion of our country wherein the blessing of religion is not brought within the reach of all and we are able to procure it."[18] There was a strong sense that, due to their own apathy, Catholics were being outflanked in their own backyard by groups of better-organized and more zealous Protestants. Catholic leaders were resolved to reverse this trend lest Catholics lose the war for souls.[19]

Archbishops Fergus McEvay and Neil McNeil provided the initial impetus for reversing Catholic indifference to the new Canadians in Toronto. Within weeks of his arrival in the archdiocese in 1908 McEvay founded a "national" parish in the city, Our Lady of Mount Carmel Church, for Toronto's Italian Catholics. By 1920 Toronto's Italians had two more parishes, the Poles had two, and the Syrians and Ukrainians each had one.[20] McEvay's successor, Neil McNeil, was so anxious to get immigrant groups established in parishes quickly that he ignored canonical procedures requiring him to seek permission from Rome for the establishment of special national parishes. After his death in 1934 his successor, James McGuigan, applied to the Vatican for recognition of these parishes after the fact.[21] McNeil's omission testifies to both his dislike of ecclesiastical red tape and his burning desire to provide immigrants with familiar places of Catholic worship.

While the Church's immigrant-assistance program was an expression of concern for the faith of new Canadians, it was also conducted in a manner that would not threaten the dominance of English-speaking Catholics in the local Church. Initiatives to establish national parishes and secure "ethnic" clergy would surely preserve the Catholicity of newcomers, but this was not enough. English-speaking Catholics were also intent on shaping their new "foreign" wards in their own image. The newcomer was expected to conform to "Canadian civilization." Staff at the *Catholic Register* were adamant that, "under the aegis of the British flag," Catholics had been blessed with "peace and prosperity, liberty to the individual both in the political and the religious rights of man." All of these things could be had regardless of race or creed. Therefore, immigrants who made Canada their home were expected to "conform themselves to the reasonable demands of Canadian civilization, law, and order."[22] Thus, for English-speaking Catholics, the process of making the "foreigner" strong in the faith was in itself a patriotic endeavour, because Catholics, on account of their spiritual commitment, were by contemporary definition the best kind of Canadian citizens.[23]

Talking the talk of piety and patriotism was one thing; delivering results on both counts was quite another. English-speaking Catholics were advised to be tolerant and restrained in their use of racial slurs to describe their immigrant neighbours.[24] Bishops and lay leaders encouraged the direct participation of the laity in helping the newcomers to acclimatize to Canadian society. One of the most necessary programs, and certainly one that most easily involved laymen and women, was English-language training. Language skills were considered the first step to acquiring decent employment and gleaning an understanding of Canadian laws and traditions. To this end local Catholics set up night schools for adults in their own homes. Prominent in language instruction was the Women's Auxiliary of the Catholic Church Extension Society, which set up classes two evenings per week for Ukrainians living in St Helen's parish.[25] Although they had criticized Protestants for enacting similar policies of "anglicization," Toronto's Catholics used these voluntary language progams as a means to acculturate the "foreigner" both linguistically and behaviourally.

While Ukrainian and Polish adults were welcomed into the parlours of local Catholics, their children were actively recruited for Catholic separate schools. Here they could acquire basic reading and writing skills and learn the catechism while imbibing the patriotism that had become so integral to Toronto's Catholic curriculum. Wearing the hats of chief pastor of Catholic Toronto and educator, Neil McNeil regarded the separate schools as strong agents of the "assimilating power" of the Catholic religion on the many foreign nationalities that constituted the Church in Toronto. Although not promising that the first generation could be assimilated, McNeil was confident that voluntary assimilation could be achieved by the immigrant's exposure in the schools to Canadian art, literature, and religion. "In their homes they speak a similar variety of language," he argued, "but the language of the school is English and the books are Canadian. The teachers know no other language ... there are always large groups of children whose mother tongue is English and the playground is English."[26] For McNeil, the Catholic school held the key to fusing diverse cultural elements together into a unified Canadian citizenry.

From 1905 to 1920 the initiation of Catholic immigrants in to Toronto's separate schools brought mixed results. As early as 1907, 50 per cent of the boys and 60 per cent of the girls in the first form junior class at St Patrick's school were Italian. The inspector of separate schools reported that language difficulties prohibited these students from doing well, and as a result few foreign children reached the fourth classes, equivalent to today's seventh and eighth grades.[27] Over time, however, some immigrant children learned English quickly, conformed to the English-speaking Catholic school environment, and mastered the principal elements of the curriculum. By 1919, at St Patrick's School three of five honours students in the senior class were Italian, while at St Clare's the ratio was two in five.[28] For McNeil, these students constituted the bedrock of immigrant communities who would be devout in their faith and steadfast in their loyalty to Canada.

On the whole, however, McNeil and other English-speaking Catholic leaders met with frustration and less favourable results in their efforts to Catholicize and Canadianize the adult immigrants. The three principal Catholic migrant groups – Poles, Ukrainians, and Italians – taught the host Church valuable lessons regarding cultural persistence, lay control of Church property, and respect for the non-Latin rites and traditions. Faced by problems of immigrant non-conformity to North American Church practices and customs, English-speaking Catholics sometimes resorted to heavy-handedness, or used European priests to advance episcopal interests within the respective ethnic communities. English-speaking Catholic reliance on misinformation about ethnic communities and on the services of unpopular immigrant clergy frequently created tension within ethnic communities, which in turn led either to schism or to immigrant Catholics joining other churches. Ironically, when faced by English-speaking Catholic efforts to consolidate their control over all ecclesiastical institutions in Toronto, the national parishes were more likely to reinforce their cultural distinctiveness than to conform to the demands of their English-speaking co-religionists.[29]

The Italians in the city provided English-speaking Catholics with a formidable challenge. Both McNeil and McEvay were eager to set up national parishes in order to prevent what they envisaged as a mass exodus of Italians to the Methodist missions.[30] Although three parishes were established by the end of the First World War, attracting good Italian priests was always difficult. McEvay enlisted the services of priest and professor Pietro Pisani to help in the acquisition of Italian clergy.[31] Pisani, however, usually recruited priests with questionable reputations who were more than eager to leave Italy. Father Carl Doglio, for example, despite good reviews from the *Catholic Register*, was suspected of having had an affair with his housekeeper; McEvay got rid of him when it was discovered that parishioners were boycotting mass to protest Doglio's alleged indiscretions.[32] Similarly, Guisseppe Longo, who eventually served in Toronto for over twenty-five years, left Italy willingly after being acquitted in an orphanage scandal.[33]

The difficulty in acquiring the most appropriate clergy for the local Italian community was compounded by the English-speaking Catholic unfamiliarity with Italian culture and the regional nature of Italian identity. Among Italian immigrants, loyalty to the *paese*, one's village or region of origin, usually superseded a sense of greater "Italia." This regionally based loyalty was reinforced by the sojourner's tie to the *padrone*, a fellow traveller from a specific *paese* who arranged labour and lodgings for his *paesani* in Toronto. Local rivalries among Toronto's Italians were so entrenched that on one occasion *paesani* from Puglia and Bari battled over the date to celebrate the feast of St Rocco, one of the major religious feasts in the southern Italian Catholic liturgical calendar.[34] Each group wanted the feast on the day corresponding to the date of the harvest in its home villages.

The arrival of priests did nothing to remedy these local rivalries. Most of the clergy that Pisani acquired had been trained in northern seminaries, while the majority of Italians in Toronto hailed from the southern provinces of Basilicata, Abruzzi, Calabria, Apulia, and Sicily. The priests had been trained primarily for the missions in Italy's African colonies, and their approach to the southerners of Toronto reflected both their northern bias and missionary techniques intended to civilize and Catholicize non-Christian Africans. McEvay and McNeil were sent scrambling for replacements when their recruits proved unable to adapt to the cultural ambiance of their southern Italian congregations, or when news of their shady pasts became common knowledge among their less than satisfied parishioners.

English-speaking Catholic lay leaders also found it difficult to entice Italians and other new Catholic Canadians to enter the accepted rhythms of local Church life. The Toronto Holy Name Union attempted to establish branches in all of the new national parishes, for fear that if Italians and others were not integrated into the existing lay Catholic network, they would be easy prey for Protestant proselytizers and socialists. Holy Name members also regarded their organization as an agency that could transmit the principles of Canadian citizenship and remedy the immigrant's ignorance of "our conditions, customs and tongue." "We have the opportunity to make a good start and prepare for the future," argued Union secretary Francis Boylan. "If we can but bring ourselves to realize for a few years that these people are our brothers in the faith and that our responsibilities do not end at the confines of our individual parish then we will with a little zeal and charity be able to accomplish much."[35]

Accordingly, branches of the Holy Name Society were established, albeit tenuously, among most Catholic immigrant groups. As early as 1913 the Italians of Our Lady of Mount Carmel parish formed a branch and sent 5 delegates to the Union's annual meeting. During the Great War the parish had 150 members in the Holy Name Society despite the exodus of many men destined for the Italian army. Similarly, by 1918, 49 Italian men in St Clement's parish and 40 in St Agnes parish claimed membership in the society. Italian executive members tended to reflect the occupational stratification of their community, many being fruiterers, pedlars, labourers, or skilled workers.[36] Small branches of working-class immigrants were also established in the Ukrainian, Lithuanian, Maltese, and Syrian Catholic communities.[37]

The strength of the newly established branches among Catholic immigrants, however, was questionable. Most Italians and other immigrants showed little interest in the society; Holy Name may have been Catholic, but it was foreign to the associational life they had known in their home villages in Europe and the Middle East. Branches failed as quickly as they were formed, due to the sojourning habits of many European migrants. The Maltese branch, for example, disintegrated when most of its members, having earned sufficient money in Toronto's factories, returned to their homes in Malta. The Lithuanian branch was extinct by 1916, as was the first attempt to form an Italian society at St Agnes Church. The society also failed to take hold among Polish Catholics, who were one of the largest Catholic immigrant groups in the city. By the end of the First World War as few as 6 per cent of all Holy Name Society members in Toronto were from ethnic parishes.[38] This proportionately low level of participation on the part of immigrants suggests both the foreignness of the society to their own cultures and perhaps their fear that it was an English-speaking Catholic agency of assimilation.[39] By 1924 vice-president James O'Hagan reported little success in forming permanent branches among the new Canadians.[40]

The existence of national parishes themselves appeared to strengthen the laity's resolve to resist the assimilative policies of the English-speaking Catholic host community. They rejected the imposition of Anglo-Celtic religious and fraternal benevolent associations, preferring to establish their own clubs and mutual aid societies. Despite inroads among the children through the agency of the separate school, Italian adults retained strong ties with their native *paese*, and they continued to send portions of their income back to Italy in order to support the local *feste*. While the English-speaking clergy and lay leaders measured some success by stopping much of the leakage of Italians to the Methodists, their own brand of Catholicism and patriotism was rejected by the first wave of immigrants.[41]

The English-speaking Catholic encounter with Polish immigrants proved to be no easier than relations with the Italians. By 1907 there were at least 150 Polish Catholics and 12 Lithuanian Catholics in the city being served by members of the Resurrectionist order stationed in nearby Berlin and Waterloo. The first missionaries to the Poles complained of how susceptible they were to Protestant missionaries and con artists. Father J.P. Schweitzer reported to Archbishop Denis O'Connor that "a bogus priest" had charged one dollar per head for hearing confessions, and smoked cigarettes liberally while in the confessional.[42] Despite such rumblings, local English-speaking Catholic leaders remained inattentive to the Polish community until late 1908, when Archbishop McEvay recruited Father Bartlomiej Jasiak to minister to the city's Poles from St Michael's Cathedral.[43] Three years later, in 1911, brewer Eugene O'Keefe purchased West Presbyterian Church for the Poles for $28,000, and it was renamed St Stanislaus Kostka.[44] That same year, the sudden departure of Jasiak created an urgent need for another Polish priest. McEvay managed to secure Joseph Hinzmann from Pittsburgh, who became the first pastor of St Stanislaus.[45] By 1915 a second parish, Nativity of the Blessed Virgin Mary of Czestochowa, was opened in Toronto's northwest. Collectively, both parishes served approximately 4,000 Poles and some Ukrainians of the Latin rite.[46]

As with the Italians, problems with clergy and frictions between cultural minorities within the Polish community created immense problems for the English-speaking Catholic plan of Catholicization and Canadianization. In 1919 Father Hinzmann left Toronto after a dispute over control of the parish erupted between two rival groups of parishioners.[47] His successor, Leopold Blum, immediately set out to establish his authority over all aspects of parish life, which led to a serious power struggle between the new pastor and the parish committee. Blum reported to McNeil that the "mob" had moved that "the priests in this parish have no right to rule but the committee," and that the committee recognized his primacy when at the altar but considered that, outside of the Mass, "he is just the same man we are."[48] Nationalistic Poles in the parish felt that Blum, a Russian Pole, was a traitor to Poland for his acts against the Poles of the parish. Poles who left St Stanislaus were pointed in their assessment of him: "You are not the priest, but Judas, cannibal and wild beast."[49]

In an effort to protect the authority of the clergy in parochial life, Archbishop McNeil sided with Blum against the committee. He promised Blum that he would visit the parish to hear confessions, and he issued a stern, and somewhat uncharacteristically heavy-handed warning to the Polish laity that the pastor was in charge of the church. McNeil reminded them that they were bound as Catholics to support the Church financially, as well as the separate schools. He also confirmed Blum as the "acting financial parson" and reiterated

that "THE PASTOR IS A PASTOR FOR HIS PARISHIONERS; THE PA-
RISHIONER IS THIS, WHO FULFILLS THE DUTY OF THE PARISHIO-
NER."[50] Completely dissatisfied by what they regarded as a
usurpation of lay control of parish temporal affairs, in 1922 a group of
parishioners left St Stanislaus to form a Polish National Catholic
Church, prompting, in turn, Blum's resignation.[51] Those who remained in the parish professed their loyalty to the bishop and the
faith but continued to guard against excessive control by the clergy,
particularly in financial matters.[52] In Toronto the Polish national parish became, like the Italian, a vessel of religious and cultural persistence, and a check on the aspirations of the English-speaking Catholic
hosts.

Issues of culture, parish life, and suitable clergy were also central
in the encounter between Toronto's English-speaking Catholics and
the Ukrainians, or Ruthenians.[53] Toronto's Ukrainian Catholics, natives of Galicia and Bukovynya in the Austro-Hungarian Empire,
were overwhelmingly adherents of the Byzantine Greek rite of the
Church. These Eastern rite or "Uniate" Catholics, although in communion with the Holy See, practiced a distinctive Greek liturgy,
were permitted married clergy, and embraced religious customs and
piety that were more akin to Eastern Orthodox Christians than the
Latin rite Catholics of the West. During the O'Connor years the
Ukrainians had worshipped with Poles and Lithuanians, and were
attended by visiting clergy from Buffalo.[54] In 1911 McEvay offered
them the use of the "old" St Helen's Church, which was renamed,
temporarily, in honour of St Nicholas. The parish, eventually renamed St Josphat's, consisted of 1,500 Ukrainian Uniates under the
pastoral care of Father Charles Yermy, and 500 Latin rite Lithuanians
under Father Deleanis.[55]

The acquisition of good Ukrainian priests was the most formidable
task facing English Catholic leaders in Toronto. Byzantine rite priests
were permitted to marry, but due to protests from the Latin rite hierarchy in the United States, in 1894 the Vatican prohibited further emigration of married priests to North America. In Canada, Latin rite
priests complained of the existence of married clergy in the country,
fearing that their presence might disrupt the status quo among celibate Latin rite clergy.[56] Ukrainian celibates were few in number, and
efforts to recruit this small minority to Canada ended in vain. As one
observer commented, the celibate Basilian monks who enlisted
earned little respect from the Ukrainian people because they were
usually drawn from among the lowest ranks of Ukrainian society.[57]
The English-speaking Catholic hierarchy found it nearly impossible
to entice Eastern rite priests to serve the thousands of Ukrainians in

agricultural colonies on the Canadian prairies and for those in urban ghettos. Securing Byzantine rite celibate priests for Toronto, however, was less difficult, due to reasonably strong lines of communication between the hierarchy and well-established Ukrainian settlements in the northeastern United States. When Charles Yermy left Toronto in 1911, after a dispute with his parishioners, he was replaced within the year by Joseph Boyarczuk.[58]

In the long term the enormous difficulties involved in recruiting Ukrainian priests for the home missions and in supervising serving clergy across Canada forced the Canadian bishops to petition Rome for the creation of a separate Ukrainian Catholic jurisdiction for Canada. When Nykyta Budka was appointed the first Ukrainian Catholic bishop of Canada in 1912, the responsibility for providing Ukrainian priests was no longer in the hands of the French Canadian and English-speaking Catholic bishops. Despite their loss of control over recruiting Eastern rite clergy, English-speaking Catholics in Toronto continued other programs to incorporate Ukrainians into the Canadian cultural milieu. Candidates for the Ukrainian priesthood were accepted at St Augustine's Seminary, and evening English-language classes were maintained by Catholic women and actively supported by Father Boyarczuk.[59]

The English-speaking Catholic attempt to Catholicize and Canadianize the newcomer in Toronto was neither a failure nor a total success. The initial thrust of English-Catholic policy towards Catholic immigrants – preserving the faith – was relatively successful. There had been some defections to Methodism, Anglicanism, Presbyterianism, and Russian Orthodoxy, but most Italians, Poles, Ukrainians, and others remained in the Catholic fold. Nevertheless, by 1920 there were at least nine ethnic congregations in the city, housed in seven "national churches," all of which had been established since 1908. The second feature of the program – the gentle assimilation of the immigrant into Canadian life – was far less successful. National parishes proved to be shelters in which the ethnic groups retained their Catholicism while holding on to the traditions, customs, and family networks of the old world.[60] Ironically, the only real evidence of acculturation was that of English-speaking Catholics themselves, who, when dealing with new Catholic Canadians, became more intimately aware of their own identification with English Canada, its institutions, opportunities, and liberties.

In their effort to Canadianize and Catholicize the newcomer Toronto's English-speaking Catholics became the leaders of a Canada-wide home mission movement. Led by Archbishop McEvay, the *Cath-*

olic Register, and prominent laymen, the Catholics of Canada began to recognize that the battle for extending and defending the faith was going to be fought primarily in the Canadian west, the target of much of the Catholic migration from Europe. Given the inability of the church infrastructure as established by French-speaking missionaries to accommodate the increasing volume and variety of European Catholics migrating west, it appeared to easterners like McEvay and Alfred Burke that the future of the Church in Canada lay in the ability of English-speaking Catholics to marshal money, materials, and personnel for the fledgling Church on the prairie frontier. If the Catholics of Toronto and points east failed, it was reasoned, then Canadian Protestants would likely be the chief beneficiaries of immigrant souls. Within months of McEvay's arrival in 1908 Toronto became the nerve-centre of a nationwide movement by English-speaking Catholics to "save" the immigrants and incorporate them into English Canadian life.

The Catholic Church Extension Society became the principal vehicle for English-speaking Catholic endeavours on behalf of the home missions. Founded in 1908 by McEvay, Apostolic Delegate Donatus Sbarretti, Father Alfred Burke, and Sir Charles Fitzpatrick, the CCES drew heavily upon the principles of the American Catholic Church Extension Society, which had been established three years earlier by an expatriate Canadian priest, Francis Clement Kelley. Like its American cousin, Canadian Extension dedicated itself to developing the missionary spirit in the clergy and laity, raising funds for the erection of churches and training of priests, and attending to the material, spiritual, and intellectual needs of Catholic immigrants.[61] Unlike missionary orders of priests and sisters, however, the CCES was intended primarily for intelligence gathering, fund-raising, and publicizing the developments and challenges to the Church in Canada's frontier regions.

The society quickly gained the support of numerous wealthy and influential Catholics, although the dominance of the Church in Toronto was evident from the very beginning. Such local laymen as Michael Haney, George Plunkett Magann, and Eugene O'Keefe were joined by Chief Justice Fitzpatrick, CPR President Sir Thomas Shaughnessy of Montreal, entrepreneur Michael J. Davis of Ottawa, and Alberta Justice Nicholas Beck, each of whom had to pay a "founders" donation of $5,000. The society rooted itself more firmly in Toronto when it purchased the *Catholic Register*, which it hoped would become more national in scope in order to promote home mission activity from sea to sea.[62] In 1910 Pope Pius X granted the society a pontifical constitution, part of which stipulated that the chancellor of the CCES would be the archbishop of Toronto. Although the society's first president, Alfred E. Burke, was a priest from Prince Edward Island, his successors would come to be selected from priests in Toronto with a few exceptions. Backed by prominent laity, many bishops, and the Pope himself, McEvay came to identify the Extension Society as "the only organization in which our home missions can be regularly and effectively aided by the Catholic laity."[63]

While the initial reflection upon the role of Extension was often couched in the language of the salvation of immigrant souls, it became increasingly clear that the CCES had a much more complex agenda. No doubt McEvay and his board of governors were fearful of aggressive Protestant missionary activity among immigrants both in Toronto and elsewhere. "It is our bounden duty ... ," he declared, "to have a watchful eye for all these strangers ... You are aware that gigantic efforts are being put forward by the missionary societies of the sects, not only to maintain their own adherents, but to draw away the faithful who so rightly belong to our Church."[64] Supporters of Extension saw this type of "watchful eye" or defence as a most effective starting-point for spreading the Catholic faith throughout Canada. In his speech to the Second American Catholic Missionary Congress (1914), for instance, Bishop Michael Francis Fallon of London, an ardent society supporter, offered a far wider interpretation of its aims when he asserted, "we propose to make this North American Continent Catholic; to bring America to Jesus Christ through the divine doctrines of the Catholic Church."[65] Such ideas were reiterated by Alfred Burke, society president and editor of the *Catholic Register*, who declared boldly that Canada "should" be Catholic since "the Catholic Church alone can make it what God seems to have intended ... to be the home of a great race destined to achieve the highest ideals of religion and civicism."[66]

Burke's own forceful personality and imperialist ideas left an indelible imprint on the Canadian Extension Society. A native of Georgetown, PEI, Burke was a dilettante who campaigned for the Liberal-Conservative Party on the island, dabbled in local agricultural societies and beekeeping, and lobbied for the construction of a tunnel under the Northumberland Strait.[67] Known thereafter as "tunnel Burke," he gained a reputation as a British imperialist, Catholic zealot, and temperance advocate. As a prominent Catholic figure at a time of racial and linguistic tension within the Canadian Church, Burke's relentless advocacy for more extensive use of the English language in the Church won him few friends among French Canadian Catholics. His lifelong friend and former altar boy, Francis Clement Kelley, recognized that "his opinions were like dogmas of Faith. No wonder Canada split over him. Half of his world swore by him and the other half at him."[68]

Under Burke's leadership from 1908 to 1915 the society extolled the virtues of Canada's Catholic citizenry while it exposed what it regarded as a conspiracy by Protestant "wolves" intent upon "ravaging the sheepfold" in Catholic immigrant communities.[69] More to the point, the society under Burke promised to be one whose endeavours would be "purely and simply Canadian and Patriotic as well as religious"; as such its works would "singly uplift Canadian civilization."[70] There was little doubt among Catholic observers of all ethnic backgrounds that the leadership and supporters of Extension regarded the English language as the best means of preserving and extending the faith. CCES leaders in Toronto recognized that immigrants, many of whom desired to learn English, were easily attracted to Protestant missionaries who were ready to teach English. As a result, English-language instruction by Catholics was intended to keep immigrants out of the hands of proselytizers, prepare new Canadians for the work force, and facilitate the "foreigner's" embrace of Canadian laws and institutions under Catholic supervision.[71] The *Register* made no apologies for its position:

Propinquity to the United States, the preponderance of Britain in the world, the commercial character of this age and of the age to come, will make for a common vehicle of intercourse and that will not be French but English. We may like it or not, but we cannot and would be foolish to shut our eyes to what is coming or fail to prepare for it … The way of our statesmen and Churchmen is bestrewn with difficulty, but it must be kept clear for the advance of British civilization and effective religion.[72]

As a means to this end the Extension Society's leaders sought English-speaking priests, trained in Ontario or the Maritimes, who could introduce the immigrant to Canadian life, thereby securing both the newcomer's loyalty to Canada and the Church and his contribution to the betterment of Canadian society.[73]

Toronto's English-speaking Catholics were staunch supporters of the CCES and its missionary vision for the Canadian west. Father Hugh J. Canning was appointed diocesan director of Extension, and his efforts established Toronto as the most generous diocese in Canada when the annual Extension collection was taken.[74] In addition, branches of the society were established at St Cecilia's, St Helen's, St Patrick's, St Ann's, St Francis's, St Michael's, and Our Lady of Lourdes parishes. Toronto's Catholic women also zealously engaged in the work of the society. In April 1910 they established the CCES

Women's Auxiliary for the purposes of distributing Catholic literature, sending toys to immigrant children, building chapels, making priest's vestments, buying altar plate, and establishing hostels and night schools for Catholic immigrants in Toronto. By 1920 the auxiliary had doubled its number of parish subcouncils and counted six hundred active members in the archdiocese.[75]

In addition to its success in Toronto, the Extension Society brought the "immigration crisis" to a national audience. Burke's national campaign on behalf of "ONE HUNDRED AND FIFTY THOUSAND RUTHENIANS" who were "pouring into our country without any pastors of their own" helped the society to create an impressive trans-Canada Catholic aid network.[76] Assuring his fellow Catholics that Ukrainians, by merit of their thrift, intelligence, and ambition, were "raw materials for the best type of Canadian citizenship," he also warned that they could be lost to Protestant missionaries if Catholics were idle or "criminally" negligent in their duties.[77] His appearances at the first American Catholic Missionary Congress in Chicago in 1908, the first Canadian Plenary Council in Quebec in 1909, and the second American Catholic Missionary Congress in Boston in 1914 gave Burke a pulpit from which he could preach the Extension Society's gospel to the most influential Catholic leaders on the continent. His passionate rhetoric helped to loosen the purse-strings of lay Catholics in Antigonish, Charlottetown, Halifax, Montreal, Peterborough, and Hamilton so that needed dollars could flow to such missionaries as Emile Legal, OMI, Bishop of St Albert, or Redemptorist priest Achille Delaere.[78] Similarly, his appeal to the first Canadian Catholic Plenary Council in Quebec (1909) netted a pledge of $5,000 per Canadian diocese for the fledgling Ukrainian Church.[79]

Burke also piqued national interest in the society by his ongoing efforts to expose the "trickery" and "fraud" used by Protestant missionaries to the Ukrainians, Italians, and Hungarians.[80] By means of Ukrainian informants and the investigations of two Toronto priests – Hugh Canning and J.T. Roche – who were sent west, the *Register* uncovered efforts by the Presbyterian Church to create an "Independent Greek Church" for Ukrainians that was little more than a way station for their formal integration into Protestantism.[81] Burke heaped vitriol on the Presbyterian Home Missions Board, its chairman Dr E.D. McLaren, and the leaders of the Ukrainian schismatics. Burke's talent for name-calling and wild accusations – he claimed Presbyterians bribed some prospective converts with whisky – not only convinced English-speaking Catholics that there was a veritable crisis in their midst but increased the circulation of the *Register* to previously unimagined heights.[82] In 1911, after little more than two years at the helm, Burke and the Extension society witnessed the *Register's* paid subscriptions soar from a modest 3,000 to 17,000.[83] Donations to the society also increased to over $16,000 per year. By 1912 Francis Kelley credited Burke and the society's campaign with the demise of the Independent Greek Church and the subsequent resignation of McLaren from the Presbyterian Home Missions Board. It is more likely, however, that the Independent Greek Church died because of Ukrainian contempt for Protestant innovations in the church's administrative structure and liturgy.[84]

English-speaking Catholic involvement in the home missions, however, was beset by cultural minefields, old and new. English-speaking Catholic relations with communities that were non-English-speaking and, in the case of Ukrainians and some Hungarians, Eastern rite were often tense and frustrating for all parties concerned. Society members soon discovered that the problems they had experienced in the national parishes of Toronto were repeated in the west. English- and French-speaking Catholics, for example, still found it difficult to recruit sufficient clergy for the "New Canadians," especially priests of Eastern European origin. Hungarians in Saskatchewan relied on Hungarian-speaking Germans and Belgians,[85] while Ukrainians were served by a corps of celibate Ukrainian Basilian monks and Belgian and French Canadian priests who had been transferred to the Eastern rite. Vatican prohibitions on married clergy in North America, the Canadian clergy's protest against working with existing married clergy,[86] and the paucity of celibate Ukrainian priests made the CCES job of securing more clergy for Ukrainians acute until the Eastern rite program was established at St Augustine's Seminary.[87] Five years after his installation, Bishop Budka had a net gain of only 2 priests. By the close of the Great War 29 priests, most of whom were non-Ukrainian, served 19 parishes and 139 missions.[88] Given this high incidence of non-native-speaking clergy, it is not surprising that immigrants felt uneasy, fearing assimilation into the "French Church" or into the Latin rite.[89]

In the midst of the crisis to secure clergy for the fledgling immigrant churches, it became increasingly clear that the society and its supporters had an alternate plan. In 1910 McEvay admitted to Archbishop Louis N. Begin of Quebec that, failing to secure priests for immigrants "who speak their own language," the society sought English-speaking clergy. For McEvay the English language was dominant in the west and therefore the one that immigrants would have to learn if they wanted "to procure a livelihood in the places in which they live."[90] In a rather formal way McEvay had tipped his hand and revealed the "Canadianizing" undertones to the home missionary endeavour. In fact Burke had pursued this policy from the outset. As early as 1909 he and Charles Fitzpatrick contacted the Duke of Norfolk, soliciting his help in locating English priests "who would be willing to go over to the Ruthenian Rite" and who "could save the people religiously and conform them to English in a relatively short period."[91] Knowing full well that he was venturing into a cultural minefield, Burke told the duke that such negotiations were reserved for "friendly eyes," fearing that the matter might "arouse the national spirit in some people."[92]

Ukrainian Catholics looked upon the society's implicit anglicization program with grave concern. Ukrainian leaders were generally sympathetic to plans for their people to learn English, although not at the risk of their distinctive religious rite and culture. Ukrainians "have to adapt themselves to Canadian customs, to learn the English language and to work at whatever their hands will do," commented Ivan Komarinzki, president of the Ruthenian Educational Society. "They have come to Canada to stay."[93] In like sentiment, some Ukrainians were busy translating the English classics into Ukrainian, some of which were serialized in the *Kanadyskyi Rusyn*, the Ukrainian Catholic weekly, which was partially funded by the CCES.[94] Ukrainians and the Extension Society also co-operated in the building of bilingual schools where the new generation of Ukrainian Canadians could be educated in English and Ukrainian, all within a Catholic environment.

Nevertheless, these positive signs for English-speaking Catholics were offset by troubling news from the missions. Most immigrants still feared the loss of their linguistic and religious traditions under the ministrations of French and English Canadian churchmen.[95] Priests on the frontier still reported hostility from their flocks, and few children clamoured to get into English or Ukrainian colleges.[96] To make matters worse, journalists and detractors had labeled Bishop Budka a traitor during the war in light of his early support for the Austro-Hungarian Empire, which he withdrew after Britain declared war. These charges, and the bishop's perceived incompetence, seriously discredited the home missions and forced some clerics to entertain the idea of formally abolishing the Eastern rite in Canada.[97] This dissolution never came to pass, although the mere suggestion indicates the despair felt by some English-speaking Catholics after a decade of home mission work.

The English-speaking Catholic vision of a Canada that was English in language, respectful of British law and governance, and Catholic in faith stumbled out of the starting gate. While the society harnessed considerable anglophone support for missionary endeavour, built numerous chapels for immigrants, and funded schools and clergy, new Catholic Canadians remained understandably cautious.[98] Upon closer scrutiny, the society's financial records reveal that the small successes of the first seven years were essentially cosmetic, and the Extension never reached its full potential. Neil McNeil, the society's second chancellor (1912–34), lamented that Protestant fund-raising efforts continued to outstrip the programs initiated by Burke and his supporters at Extension.[99] McNeil went so far as to suggest that the less than substantial collections resulted in part from the fact that five other Canadian English Catholic weeklies ignored the society because of the threat posed to their circulation by the *Register*.[100] The Burke "factor" was not to be underestimated. He had rubbed some bishops the wrong way with his opinionated and overbearing manners and with the "rough and quite too belligerent" tone of the *Register*.[101] Nevertheless, he had loyal supporters on the board of governors and among the auxiliary groups in Toronto's parishes. McNeil's criticism of the society in 1913 led to his being ostracized by Burke and his supporters. For the next two years Extension was severely hindered in its mission work by the stalemate on its board.[102]

The Catholic Church Extension Society's internal problems paled in significance to the society's failure to speak with a national voice for the Canadian Catholic Church. From the society's inception, many French Canadians had regarded it as an anglicizing institution that threatened the French Canadian sense of *Gestae Dei Per Francos*[103] – a perception that Providence had given French Canadians the mandate to spread the faith in the prairies and the northwest. French Canadian fears were confirmed when Extension chose Toronto as its headquarters, stacked its board with lay leaders from English Canada, recruited English-speaking priests, patronized St Dunstan's College as its training school for missionaries, and enveloped itself in the rhetoric of British imperialism and anglophilia. At best French Canadian clergy regarded the Extension Society and its anglophone vision as a rude insult to the bridgehead already established by francophone clergy and religious west of the Great Lakes. At worst the mission program of English-speaking Catholics was perceived as an "Irish" invasion of a sphere of influence already claimed by the sons and daughters of the Church in Quebec and their French and Belgian associates. In reality, however, the festering resentment between English- and French-speaking Catholics in the home missions was symptomatic of a far greater power struggle between Catholicism's two charter linguistic groups in Canada. By 1910 Canadian bishops, clergy, and lay leaders were engaged in open warfare over which linguistic group ought to lead the Church in territories outside of Quebec. The competing visions of the francophone and anglophone factions of the Church led to bitter confrontations over the nominations of bishops, control of Catholic schools, co-operation with the Canadian war effort, and ministering to Catholic immigrants.

Archbishop Adelard Langevin of St Boniface provided the most formidable challenge to the English-speaking Catholic vision of Canada as fostered by the Toronto-based Extension Society. Instead of congratulating the society upon its founding, he expressed shock and horror. "What a revelation it was for me!" he seethed. "It will be easily admitted by any bishop that if an organization is willing to help him by sending him priests, he should be notified of the fact!"[104] For Langevin, Extension was a thinly disguised challenge to his jurisdiction, as well as an implicit suggestion by Ontario's Catholics that he had not done enough for Catholic immigrants in his ecclesiastical province. In short, he regarded Extension as an attempt by the "Irlandais" of Ontario to spread "la rage anti français, francophobie," to the west. He was particularly infuriated that Fathers Hugh Canning and J.T. Roche of Toronto had entered his diocese in his absence and promised financial and material aid to immigrants.[105] He was adamant that did not require the services of English-speaking priests, whom he regarded as merely the vanguard of an English-speaking conquest of the Church in western Canada and its episcopal sees.[106] Pulling no punches, he confided to his successor Arthur Beliveau: "Dieu nous préserve de ce nationalisme étroit et provocateur qui croit tout conquérir avec de l'argent et de beaux discours."[107] His resistance did not stop with mere words; adjudicating the terna for the Archdiocese of Toronto in 1911, he denigrated the candidacy of Canning – who had entered his diocese for Extension – and then coincidently launched into a tirade on how the Church in Toronto was unjust to French Canadians.[108]

Langevin certainly had his own vision of the Church, which focused on the flourishing of immigrant Catholics under the paternal authority of the See of St Boniface. To this end he established national parishes for immigrants, sought celibate clergy for the Ukrainian uniates, and encouraged French Canadian and Belgian priests to transfer to the Byzantine rite when Ukrainian and Hungarian priests could not be found. The latter he deemed preferable to married priests, who "would be a great scandal for Catholics, a triumph for Protestants, and the subject of mockery for the impious, the unfaithful, and those without religion."[109] He also made clear that those French Canadians who translated to the Eastern rite would be subject to his authority, even if there was a distinct Ukrainian bishop or eparch for Canada. In 1913 he informed Josaphat Jean, who had transferred, that the archbishop of St Boniface had a right to intervene when the Ukrainian bishop's actions interfered with his own for the west.[110] Jean himself commented that the French Canadian priests of the Byzantine rite were still ardent in their loyalty to the French Canadian Church, a posture that was resented by the Ukrainians in their care.[111] In an effort to preserve his own control over Catholics in the west Langevin continually opposed the establishment of a separate Ukrainian eparchy, for fear that it would open the door to married clergy and provoke enumerable jurisdictional disputes between Latin and Byzantine rites.[112]

English-speaking Catholic leaders in Toronto and Catholic immigrants in the west appear to have been well aware of Langevin's strategies. Privately, one Ukrainian priest urged the formation of a Ukrainian Catholic newspaper "entirely removed from the French," in addition to the formal establishment of a Ukrainian eparch for Canada.[113] The Austro-Hungarian consul in Winnipeg, however, publicly denounced Langevin for what he termed his efforts "to force French people [priests] upon Ruthenians."[114] Similarly, but in English-speaking Catholic circles, Archbishop McEvay, the *Catholic Register*, and Michael Fallon saw the hand of "francisation" in Langevin's intentions to settle French Canadian priests among immigrant groups. The *Register* identified Langevin as an "ardent Frenchman" who "would make Northwestern Canada French if he could."[115] McEvay more pointedly labelled him a French Canadian nationalist who threatened the unity of the Church in the west.[116] Facing frustration at Langevin's hands, Extension member Father J.T. Roche reported back to Toronto that Langevin was "an overblown archiepiscopal (—)"; this allowed Alfred Burke to fill in his own definition of his prairie nemesis.[117]

The tension and hostility between the Catholic leaders in Toronto's Extension office and Langevin steadily worsened. In 1909, when Burke discovered that Langevin was angry about the society's financial initiatives on behalf of immigrants in the west, he called Langevin's bluff and politely offered to withdraw all funding.[118] Langevin backed down, but Burke and his associates had little time to savour this minor achievement. Not to be outmanoeuvred by his anglophone co-religionists in the east, in 1910 Langevin launched public insults against the *Register* and used a circular letter to question the endeavours of the Extension Society. He and several of his colleagues in Quebec appear to have blocked attempts by Father Leo Sembratowicz, an associate of Extension, to recruit what may have been married clergy for Ukrainian Catholics in Ontario and the west. Back in Toronto, Burke bristled, claiming that given the Pope's blessing and support for the society, it would not countenance "open or veiled attacks from any quarter."[119] In fact, McEvay and Burke made veiled attempts of their own to bypass the difficult Langevin by appealing directly to his suffragan bishops. McEvay encouraged needy bishops like Emile Legal of St Albert to accept home mission funds directly without the mediatorial role of the See of St Boniface, which Langevin demanded. While French-born bishops such as Legal and Albert Pascal of Prince Albert tried to remain respectful of their Metropolitan, it was clear that they did not share Langevin's French Canadian "nationaliste" spirit. Somewhat removed from the cultural ethos of their French Canadian colleagues, and in dire need of money, men, and materials for the swollen ranks of European Catholic immigrants, many of the Oblate bishops of the prairies and British Columbia remained on good terms with Extension and its English-speaking Catholic leadership.[120]

The tension and frustration between English-speaking Catholics and Langevin was heightened when French Canadian bishops and newspaper editors in the east rallied to the aid of their beleaguered colleague in St Boniface. Archbishops Thomas Duhamel of Ottawa and Paul Bruchési of Montreal were so suspicious of Burke and the Extension as "made in Ontario" that neither would permit it to locate its headquarters in his see.[121] Later, Patrick T. Ryan, the auxiliary bishop of Pembroke, a diocese that straddled the Ottawa River, confessed to McNeil that Burke's pleas on behalf of Extension fell on deaf ears in Quebec because the society "was regarded as an organized attempt to forward the interest of the English language and English influence ... in the Canadian West." French Canadian leaders simply viewed Burke and his colleagues in Toronto as trying to discredit the work already done in the west by the sons and daughters of the Church in Quebec.[122] In this spirit, francophone editors at Le Droit and L'Action sociale criticized English-speaking Catholic aggression in the mission fields, regarding these forays as merely part of a general plan to curtail French language rights west of the Ottawa River. In response, the Register acknowledged the "'Gestae Dei per Francos' in the Province of Quebec" as "one of our tenderest memories," but warned its French Canadian critics that the English language, by necessity, would be the most effective vehicle of conversion in the west and would secure the place of the Church in English Canada.[123]

The French Canadian Catholic media and leaders were not far wrong. The involvement of English-speaking Catholics in the immigration question, and the resultant clash with French Canadian interests, was in reality a theatre of a much more extensive struggle between English- and French-speaking Catholics for control over the Church outside of Quebec. After 1900 French Canadian Catholics, who had established fledgling churches and missions outside of Quebec, watched as their francophone flocks were swamped in their congregations and dioceses by Catholics from other cultural backgrounds. While coping with the needs of these English-speaking and immigrant Catholics, French Canadians rapidly became a tiny minority in the population of the provinces west of Quebec. Vulnerable numerically and culturally, French Canadian Church leaders found their power and influence increasingly challenged. In the internecine linguistic struggle that resulted in Canadian Catholicism, the Archdiocese of Toronto emerged as a command-centre for English-speaking Catholics seeking to consolidate their control over the Church in Ontario and to secure a place for the Church in the prairies and British Columbia. In fact, immigrant aid efforts like that of the Extension Society became sucked into the vortex of an extensive and complex series of struggles over the appointment of Catholic bishops in Canada, separate school funding, and the retention of French-language education in Ontario. Only the intervention of the Vatican, on two separate occasions, prevented the battle within the Church from becoming a greater public scandal than it already was.[124]

Bitterness between the linguistic charter groups of the Church was characteristic of the politics surrounding appointments to episcopal sees. Given the authoritarian nature of the Church in the period prior to Vatican II, it should come as no surprise that English- and French-speaking Catholics competed relentlessly for the appointment of their own candidates to some of Canada's most important sees. When Denis O'Connor resigned from the Archdiocese of Toronto in 1908, French Canadians lobbied for David Scollard, bishop of Sault Ste Marie, as a successor. French Canadians were confident that, by moving Scollard to Toronto, they could place their own candidate at the Sault, a largely francophone diocese that had resented the leadership of the "Irish" Scollard, and then have the Sault transferred from the ecclesiastical province of Kingston to the predominantly French Canadian province of Ottawa. Such a move would place the entire north of Ontario under French Canadian control. The scenario failed when the Vatican selected Fergus McEvay, the choice of the English-speaking Catholic lobby.[125] McEvay was thrust into a see regarded by the Vatican as the most important in English Canada, and he soon emerged as backroom leader of the growing English-speaking Catholic forces.[126]

McEvay's appointment left an opening in London, a diocese containing a large and vocal francophone minority located mostly in Essex county. The selection of a successor in London became bogged down in a linguistic battle, at the heart of which lay the emerging power and influence of the Church in Toronto. Knowing that the French were anxious to instal a prelate friendly to the interests of London's francophone minority, McEvay, in concert with Archbishop Edward McCarthy of Halifax, enlisted the services of an agent in Rome, Father Henry O'Leary.[127] McEvay's single aim was to keep the French out of London. When the Vatican rejected the first terna and requested a more bilingual selection of candidates, McEvay complained that English-speaking Catholics in "this Protestant & English speaking" Ontario had "suffered a long time in school & state matters on account of a few Bishops, Priests & Politicians trying to make French the only language in this Country."[128] Bishop Richard O'Brien of Peterborough agreed, claiming that the French were again trying to displace Scollard, who he felt was "doing much good for religion & towards checking [French Canadian] nationalism."[129]

McEvay's submission of the second terna for London, in late March 1909, included a virtual manifesto of English-speaking Catholic vision for the Church in Ontario. In vivid and clear language the Vatican was made aware of English-speaking Catholic claims on the local Church:

The only language recognized by the state is English, and as a result, all the people living in this province are, in their own interests, obliged to speak English ... there is no other diocese in Canada where the relations between clergy and laity are more happy and edifying than there [London]. This same commendable condition of things may be claimed without fear of contradiction for the two Ecclesiastical Provinces of Toronto and Kingston; That we sincerely regret that in the interests of truth and for a proper knowledge of the situation here, we are compelled to say to Your Holiness that our efforts for the spiritual and temporal welfare of our people, especially in the great matter of Christian education, have been greatly hampered and weakened by the injudicious, and, at times, impertinent interference of a few prelates, priests and politicians, largely in the Province of Quebec, who seem to place race before religion and language before faith.[130]

For his part, O'Leary lobbied sympathetic members of the Curia in Rome, including Cardinal Merry del Val, the secretary of State, long considered a supporter of English-speaking Catholic interests.[131] In December 1909 the accession of Michael Fallon to the See of London marked a major victory for McEvay's party. The Apostolic Delegate, Donatus Sbarretti, actually orchestrated Fallon's rise from third on the terna, or "dignus," to eventual leading candidate. Acknowledging the strength of the English-speaking Catholics' arguments, and aware of the need to spread the faith in the medium of the English language, Sbarretti promoted Fallon because he felt that men of Fallon's ilk were more likely to secure the conversion of Canadian Protestants to the Church. Sbarretti believed that the English language was destined to dominate in Canada, and for its own survival the Catholic Church had to accept that fact.[132]

The English-speaking Catholic power-base in Ontario was solidified when Charles Hugh Gauthier, more anglophone in sympathy than his name suggests,[133] was translated from the See of Kingston to Ottawa. His elevation to the traditionally French Canadian–controlled archdiocese left francophones in eastern Canada stunned and demoralized. David Scollard wrote to McEvay: "The Archbishops of the Dominion by being parties to that Ottawa appointment have occasioned a big noise and all kinds of explosions here and there throughout this vast Dominion."[134] Gauthier's appointment was significant in revealing the forces at play in the English-speaking Catholic party. The Delegate, Sbarretti, and Burke had caballed over Gauthier's appointment as early as July 1909. In fact, Gauthier had agreed to move at that time, as long as he could be assured that he had the support of his English-speaking colleagues. The strong backing given the English-speaking Catholics by the Delegate helped to secure for them the See of Ottawa.[135]

Their control in Ontario consolidated, the English-speaking Catholic party and its allies stepped up their plans to displace the French in the western sees. In Rome, O'Leary began to advance the English-speaking Catholic vision for the west and received assurances of support from Merry Del Val, who had the ear of the Pope. Bishops Scollard and Macdonell were already making overtures for English-speaking Catholic control for western sees in Rome; O'Leary, representing the interests of McEvay of Toronto and McCarthy of Halifax, merely sought to forge a united front.[136] By 1910 McEvay's primary concern was that the newly erected Diocese of Regina be headed by an English-speaking Catholic bishop, despite the fact that French Canadians, native peoples, and European immigrants composed over 90 per cent of the local Catholic population.[137] Back in Toronto, McEvay recognized that a victory for his party in Regina would thwart Langevin's attempts to "tie the Catholic Church in this country to one nationality viz French-Canadianism." To him the appointment of someone of Langevin's ilk would be "a victory for this national craze" with the appearance of "a quasi-approval of the Holy See."[138] With the Catholic demographics in Regina in their favour, French Canadians secured the election, in 1911, of Olivier-Elzéar Mathieu, the rector of Laval University. English-speaking Catholic hopes were dampened further when, a year later, Bishop Timothy Casey of Saint John was translated to Vancouver. On the surface Casey's appointment appeared to solidify the English-speaking Catholic leadership in the west. In reality, Casey and his supporters saw the move as a "demotion," particularly when his replacement for the predominantly anglophone diocese in New Brunswick was an Acadian, Edward Albert LeBlanc.[139]

The setbacks in Regina and Saint John for English-speaking Catholic leaders were short-lived. Within the next eighteen years they secured control of most of the principal episcopal sees west of the Ottawa River. In 1913 John McNally, a Maritimer serving in the Ottawa Valley, was appointed to the new Diocese of Calgary.[140] Two years later another Maritimer, Alfred Sinnott, who had served as secretary to the Apostolic Delegation in Ottawa, was elected to the newly created See of Winnipeg, which stared boldly across the Red River at the See of St Boniface. By 1930 the dioceses of Edmonton, Regina, Calgary, and Winnipeg were controlled by English-speaking Catholic prelates, all of whom were originally from Ontario and the Maritimes. Only Prince Albert, St Boniface, and Gravelburg remained under French Canadian control.[141]

English-speaking Catholic intrigues in Rome, pushing for control of sees in both Ontario and the west, sharpened French Canadian fears that they were going to be displaced in the Church outside of Quebec. When dioceses were falling into English hands at an alarming rate, and inroads were being made in the west after 1911, it is little wonder that such ventures as the Extension Society fared so poorly in French Canadian circles, where it was regarded as just one more example of English-speaking Catholic imperialism. Archbishop McEvay's role in the linguistic politics of the Church placed the See of Toronto at the centre of the storm. Although Bishop Fallon has frequently been singled out as the "bête noir" in the assault against the French, McEvay was actually the leader and strategist behind the English-speaking Catholic party until his untimely death in 1911. Overlooked by some contemporaries and by current historians, McEvay was the mastermind of the intrigues and power-plays, although most of his colleagues – Scollard, Gauthier, Fallon, Macdonell, and O'Brien – were of like mind and staunch allies. Even in the early stages of the bilingual schools question McEvay appear to have been in control, though nearly on his deathbed, with Fallon acting as the spokesperson, or perhaps "fall guy." Fallon himself recognized McEvay's leadership and on one occasion described his relationship to him thus: "I have always felt somewhat as a child might feel towards his father."[142] With McEvay and Alfred E. Burke so central to the fortunes of the home mission effort, it is understandable that French Canadians became more detractors than supporters of Toronto's Extension Society.

After 1910 the troubles between the English and French wings of the Church continued to multiply. In September of that year, while addressing the Twenty-first Eucharistic Congress in Montreal, Archbishop John Bourne of Westminster gave his blessing to the English-speaking Catholic vision of Canada. "If the mighty nation of Canada is destined to ... be won and held for the Catholic Church," proclaimed Bourne, "this can only be done by making known to a great part of the Canadian people in succeeding generations, the mysteries of our faith through the medium of our English speech."[143] Bourne's endorsement of the English language as the medium through which Canada would become "in the full sense a Catholic nation" was hailed by English-speaking Catholic leaders and reprinted in its entirety on the front page of the *Register*.[144] It also marked a very public parting of the ways in the Canadian Church. Although encouraged by Henri Bourassa's stirring rebuttal of Bourne immediately after the archbishop's address,[145] the French Canadian Church realized that they were now sandwiched between the interests of Canadian Protestants and English-speaking Catholics, two groups who, through their common tongue, were exhibiting a convergence in their national interests.

The involvement of Toronto's English-speaking Catholics at the epicentre of the Ontario bilingual schools debate further estranged French- and English-speaking Catholics from one another. Through 1909 the English-speaking bishops of Ontario, led by McEvay, engaged in serious negotiations with the provincial government for extended funding of separate schools and the inclusion of a series of Catholic textbooks. In January 1910 James P. Whitney's government halted negotiations in the wake of demands from the French Canadian Educational Congress for the extension of bilingual schools in Ontario.[146] Whitney explained to McEvay that the French Canadian demands had created so much stress among his Cabinet colleagues over issues of language and religion that discussion of the future of separate schools had to be suspended.[147] Whitney's government then turned its attention to bilingual schools and, by means of Regulation 17, limited the teaching of French to the first two years of school. Angry and frustrated, the English-speaking Catholic bishops refocused their attention on language education and, in August 1910, formally opposed the demands of the French Canadian Educational Congress.

Bitter at the failure of their efforts to extend Catholic education, the bishops were more concerned that Franco-Ontarian demands might raise Protestant ire to such an extent that all Catholic schools, regardless of language, might be in jeopardy. If the English-speaking Catholics of Ontario joined the French Canadians on the schools issue, argued McEvay's successor Neil McNeil, "Orangemen would then have their opportunity to inaugurate a real campaign against the whole separate school system."[148] Bishops in the ecclesiastical provinces of Toronto and Kingston also had their doubts about the quality of the bilingual schools, and considered that a third set of schools in Ontario, established along linguistic lines, was unnecessary.[149] When the details of a private meeting between Provincial Secretary H.J. Hanna and Michael Fallon were leaked to the press in October, revealing that the bishop of London had vowed to eliminate bilingual schools in his diocese, fragile linguistic relations in the Church shattered completely. French Canadians now had tangible proof that their English-speaking co-religionists were allied with "les orangistes" in Ontario.[150]

In the heat of the linguistic war, Toronto's *Catholic Register* armed its presses and rushed to Fallon's defence. Given the front pages of the city's official Catholic organ, Fallon openly denied the "false" accusation that he was "unfriendly to the interests of the French-Canadian people" and expounded his view that bilingual schools ought to be abolished because they were inefficient.[151] Editor A.E. Burke was already a believer, having previously asserted both that bilingual schools were impractical and that their "imposition of another language" on the English-speaking Catholic children of Ontario was "unjust, unwise and injudicious."[152] The paper then heaped criticism on the tactics of ACFEO (l'Association canadienne-française d'éducation de l'Ontario), urging French Canadian Catholic leaders to join their anglophone colleagues in the fight for the extension of separate schools in general. Victory for the separate schools held within it the possibility of a more diplomatic solution to the controversy over bilingual schools, many of which fell under the jurisdiction of separate school boards.[153]

The home missions movement, as co-ordinated by the English-speaking Catholics of Toronto, exposed most clearly the links between the "immigration crisis" and the linguistic "warfare" tearing apart the Canadian Church. Whether English-speaking Catholic leaders liked it or not, their efforts to integrate new Catholic Canadians into the predominantly anglophone communities of Ontario and the west were linked by French Canadians to what they thought was a general attack by English-speaking Catholics on the rights and institutions of their French co-religionists. It was not hard to see how such conclusions could be drawn by francophones. English-speaking Catholic leaders who appeared prominent in schools questions and episcopal struggles – McEvay, Fallon, Scollard, Sinnott, and even Mc-Neil – were also active members of the Catholic Church Extension Society and the home mission effort. The anglophile and often imperialistic rhetoric of the *Register*, which served as both a diocesan and a mission newspaper, further blurred the lines between the home mission movement and other hot issues. Even after Burke stepped down as editor in 1915, the *Register* continued to promote an English-speaking Catholic vision of the country, although editors J.A. Wall and Father Thomas O'Donnell kept "Burkean" rhetorical flourishes to a minimum. In the end the immigration question prompted effusions of English-speaking Catholic Canadian identity from home mission advocates in Toronto and elsewhere. Such expressions confirmed what francophones had come to believe of their anglophone co-religionists on a variety of other issues – that language had superseded religion as a badge of identity. They had become like their Protestant neighbours.[154]

As linguistic relations in the Church spiralled into the abyss after 1910, English-speaking Catholics would prove that their francophone co-religionists were only partially correct in their assessment. When French Canadian bishops Louis Nazaire Bégin of Quebec and Joseph Alfred Archambault withdrew from the board of governors of Catholic Extension in November 1910,[155] McEvay intimated that it was the French-speaking Catholics of Canada who put cultural concerns ahead of the advancement of the faith. As chancellor of the CCES, he reminded Bégin and Archambault that the society was in the business of helping Catholic immigrants, noting that its funds were collected from English-speaking Catholics and then given almost entirely to French-speaking clergy. McEvay added that the English language by necessity had to play a role in securing the loyalty of new Canadians, given that English was destined to be the language of the west and one that the immigrants would have to learn if they wanted to succeed in their adopted land. He then warned Bégin of the damage that could be done to the home missions if the Church was subjected to "any narrow, national or sectional ambitions."[156] Ironically, Mc Evay had made clear the English-speaking Catholic ambition: to forward the interests of the Church among the immigrants by means of the English language and the culture of the majority of Canadians. As far as the Toronto Catholic leadership was concerned, the era of the *Gestae Dei per Francos* had come to an end.[157]

Despite the open linguistic schism after 1910, English-speaking Catholics continued their immigrant-aid projects on both the local level and the national scene via Extension. After McEvay's death, Neil McNeil undertook several reforms of the home mission movement, including changes at the *Register* and several ill-fated attempts to bring French Canadian Catholics on side.[158] McNeil's task became easier once the bombastic Alfred Burke resigned as Extension president in 1915, in order to enlist as a chaplain in the Canadian Expeditionary Force. Both the *Register*, under J.A. Wall, and the Extension Society, under its new president, Father Thomas O'Donnell of St Ann's parish in Toronto, devised new fund-raising strategies and intensified the attention paid to the plight of Catholic immigrants. New personnel in Toronto and new financial strategies led to an increase in CCES revenues and increased participation of English-speaking Catholics in Ontario and the Maritimes.[159] Nevertheless, the Toronto-driven home mission effort never achieved its desired result, specifically because the English-speaking Catholic vision that the movement embodied alienated French Canadian Catholics, who composed the majority of Canada's 3.9 million Catholics. Despite McNeil's recognized integrity, persistent efforts at *rapprochement*, and personal fairness on bilingualism and other cultural issues, French Canadian bishops continued to boycott the CCES, preferring to aid Catholic immigrants by means of their own independent diocesan collections.[160] Since neither McNeil nor his colleagues had surrendered on the idea of using English as the medium of evangelization, it comes as no surprise that their efforts at healing the wounds in the national Church were a resounding failure.[161] Only the intervention of Pope Benedict XV, in his pastoral letter of 1916, brought a temporary calm to the cultural hurricane raging in the Canadian Church.[162]

In Toronto the "immigration crisis" had brought forth the expression of an English-speaking Catholic identity that had been decades in the making. Initially, English-speaking Catholics considered it their Christian duty not only to save new Catholic Canadians from the clutches of inner-city Protestant missionaries but to aid in their advancement in a land filled with promise, liberty, and hopes of social betterment. By acclimatizing immigrants to the traditions of the English language, Canadian law, and British constitutional principles, English-speaking Catholics were also attempting to preserve their hold on the levers of the local Church. New Catholic Canadians, even if they chose to retain many of their religious traditions, would be fashioned in the mould of English-speaking Catholics. The entire process, then, depended on English-speaking Catholics affirming that they were loyal and patriotic Canadians. As citizens of the Empire, upholders of the law, and hopeful believers in the strengths of Canadian society, Toronto's English-speaking Catholics came to see themselves as the natural teachers of the immigrants. While such efforts had minimal effects on the immigrants themselves and contributed to linguistic schism within the Church, the entire process confirmed English-speaking Catholics' wilful embrace of English Canadian society.

CHAPTER EIGHT

Wearing England's Red: Toronto's Catholics and the Great War, 1914–1919

Elmer Wadham was "a good everyday boy" in his mother's eyes. In the summer of 1915 Elmer, like many other young Catholic men in Toronto, joined the infantry and prepared himself to fight for "his King and Country." A scrawny lad of eighteen, Elmer had left school in his early teens to work full-time as a riveter, in order to help support his parents and five siblings. The Wadhams lived in St Helen's parish, but unlike the upwardly mobile Catholics of the area they struggled to feed their children and pay the rent. The war had been hard on them. They had moved residence twice since 1914, and Elmer's father, an abusive alcoholic, worked only three days a week.[1] In other ways, however, Elmer Wadham was representative of his generation. He was a young Canadian-born Catholic living in this British Protestant city. A combination of economic hard times, the urges of his manhood, and his zeal to serve his country were mirrored in hundreds of other young Catholic men in Toronto. By the end of the voluntary phase of recruiting in June 1917, over 3,500 of Elmer's fellow English-speaking Catholics in the city had volunteered for the Canadian army, artillery, service companies, and medical corps.[2] Some went for adventure, others to escape the degradation of unemployment, but on the whole Catholic men and women enlisted because they regarded this war as their own.

The First World War provided an opportunity for the Catholic hierarchy, religious press, Church associations, and the Catholic laity of Toronto to demonstrate proudly their loyalty to Canada and the Empire. Their participation, both in the trenches and in the campaigns on the home front, marked the culmination of their community's decades-long process of integration into Canadian society and an effort to come to terms with English-speaking Protestant Canada without surrendering their Catholicity. Like many other English Canadians, Toronto's English-speaking Catholics entered the war with a sense of being part of the British Empire, but ambivalent about the degree to which Canadians were responsible for the maintenance of Empire. Over the course of the struggle Catholic leaders and writers refined their long-standing vision of Canada as a self-governing state and independent component in the Empire. For Catholics as for thousands of other Canadians, the war became more than just an imperial struggle; Canadians soon recognized that the blood spilled in Flanders was shed for Canada and for basic human liberties.[3] The Great War did not solve the socio-economic strains faced by the Wadham family or other Canadian families like them, but it did allow the Catholic clergy and laity to advertise their loyalty to Canada and her institutions. The Catholic war effort in Toronto marked the culmination of decades of change and offered visible proof that English-speaking Catholics, particularly the overwhelming majority of those of Irish descent, were first and foremost loyal Canadians.

Support for the British and Canadian war effort came quickly and enthusiastically from Toronto's Catholic leaders. Although Archbishop Neil McNeil implored his flock to pray for peace, he was unequivocal about the duties of Toronto's Catholics, regardless of the war's duration. His appeal to his flock was a curious mixture of ecumenism, certain tenets of "imperialist nationalism" common to many English Canadians, and some consideration offered to the "defence of Canada alone" bias of many French Canadians.[4] These specific components of his thought, however, were subordinated to his overriding belief that, when the Empire was in mortal danger, Canadians had a responsibility to come to its aid. In his circular letter published in the *Catholic Register* on 20 August 1914 he reminded Toronto's Catholics that Britain's war against the Kaiser's oppression was as much Canada's fight as Britain's: "You do not need to be reminded of the duty of patriotism. You are as ready as any to defend your country and to share in the burdens of Empire."[5] Four days later, when addressing a recruiting meeting for Toronto and York County, the archbishop repeated his plea for patriotism, courage, and economic restraint. Above all, however, McNeil identified religious tolerance as the key to victory: "In the conflict which we are facing – and let us realize we are facing stern conditions – in that conflict there is no difference between Protestants and Catholics."[6]

The archbishop's call for patriotism and interfaith co-operation permeated every layer of the institutional Church in Toronto. With McNeil's approval, the Church actively endorsed the Patriotic Fund for the families of soldiers killed or disabled. He asked his priests for donations of up to forty dollars every six months so that "all the people of Toronto" could see that "our professions of patriotism are genuine." McNeil himself pledged $5,000 from his own savings.[7] Similarly, patriotic sermons encouraged parishioners to donate to the Patriotic Fund as well as to the relief of war-torn Belgium. With the consent of the Apostolic Delegate, McNeil also permitted the clergy to participate in days of prayer with Toronto's other Christian denominations.[8] While Catholic congregations did not meet jointly with Protestants, it was agreed that the city's Catholic churches would honour the same days of prayer as those set aside in Protestant churches. On one such "Supplication Sunday," 3 January 1915, McNeil's stirring, patriotic oratory at St Michael's Cathedral prompted the *Catholic Record* to comment: "True patriotism is a Catholic instinct and the Church ever nurtured it and fostered it."[9] In like spirit, local priests also offered regular Sunday mass intentions for the safety of the troops and for peace, and when not in their pulpits or at their altars these same pastors could be found ministering to the needs of the Catholic recruits who were training at the Exhibition grounds. As early as 15 November 1914 McNeil himself celebrated mass for over three hundred Catholic troops at the Exhibition, reminding them in his sermon that the defeat of the Empire would be a calamity both for the world and for Canada.[10]

With McNeil's approval, Catholic parishes made their basements and halls available to local battalions who required billets and mess facilities.[11] In 1915 the archbishop and Father James Walsh of St Helen's parish permitted the 126th Infantry Battalion from Peel County to use that church and the adjoining buildings for barracks. There was plenty of space at the old church at the corner of Lansdowne and Dundas streets, which had been abandoned by St Helen's parishioners in favour of their new church nearby. In addition, the Mallon family, scions of St Helen's, allowed the battalion officers use of their hotel across the road from the "barracks." The presence of the 126th had some remarkable effects on parish life: at least one dozen parishioners joined the unit, and several Protestant soldiers were converted to Catholicism during their stay.[12] Upon leaving the barracks in May 1916, the battalion commander, Lieutenant-Colonel F.J. Hamilton, thanked McNeil in an open letter, claiming that the Catholic Church's hospitality had hastened the battalion's readiness to the extent that it was "practically the first county regiment to be selected to go to Niagara."[13] Such praise enhanced McNeil's effort to make Catholic patriotism well-known in Toronto.

The archbishop's support of the war effort even included his involvement in local recruitment campaigns. In 1916 McNeil personally endorsed the recruitment of Catholics for a special company in the 198th "Canadian Buffs" Battalion. Handbills were distributed that requested the services of young Catholic men who were interested in work as machine gunners, bombardiers, sharpshooters, scouts, signallers, and drivers. The handbill added that "His Grace, Archbishop McNeill is heartily in favor of this plan and has given his sanction and approval." With episcopal blessings Toronto's Catholic men were invited to "Join the Buffs and Hunt the Huns."[14]

The enthusiasm of the hierarchy and parish clergy for the war effort was echoed by the Catholic press. Toronto's official Catholic weekly, the *Catholic Register*, under the editorship of Tory stalwart Monsignor Alfred E. Burke,[15] took a zealously imperialist position on the crisis, calling for Catholics to defend the British Empire at all cost:

It will prove for us beyond peradventure that we as Canadians are Britishers to the core and that Britain's troubles are our troubles, Britain's shield our safety. We must sacrifice something for this protection. Where would we be today but for the Empire's navy and the Empire's men? Our part is to give generously what is our honest toll, whether it be for the army and the navy ... what we need is to finish the work effectually – so effectually that "Pax Britannica" may rejoice the world for another half century. The God of Armies is great and wonderful in his dispensations.[16]

Throughout the first six months of the struggle the *Register* published voluminously on the war effort, reminding Canadian Catholics of their duties to the Empire and of that link as a source of pride: "We are as British as we always have been, and we will, please God, always be. We cannot well understand how anyone can be too British now."[17] Such imperialistic rhetoric was reinforced by the editor's policy of printing pro-British speeches by a host of well-known and important Catholics, including Sir Charles Fitzpatrick, Cardinal John Bourne of Westminster, Monsignor Robert Benson, and the federal minister of Justice and Montreal Catholic, Charles J. Doherty.[18]

This sense of imperial duty was heightened by the *Register*'s depiction of the allied war effort as holy when compared to the forces of darkness led by Kaiser Wilhelm. Articles on the invasion of Catholic Belgium, the destruction of Louvain, and the plight of Cardinal Désiré Mercier of Malines emphasized that loyal Catholics in Europe were the innocent victims of the evils of "Prussian militarism." Canadian Catholics were called to emulate their cousins in Ireland, who, with Home Rule in hand, provided unqualified support for the war against Germany.[19] Quite simply, according to Burke, Catholic Canadians had a duty to defend the rights of oppressed Catholics everywhere. As editors raised urgent ethical issues relevant to the war, they also identified patriotism with Christian virtue so closely that the death of a Catholic soldier was given a deeply spiritual significance. Mothers of the fallen men ought to take comfort, thought Burke, in the fact that "Christ crowns his [the fallen boy's] military valour, and that death, accepted in this Christian spirit, assures the safety of that man's soul."[20] Thus Catholic parents were reassured that the sacrifice of their sons' bodies in this holy and noble struggle provided certain eternal bliss for their sons' souls.

The success of the *Catholic Register* in blending Catholic spirituality, civic duty, and British imperialism can be attributed to two factors. First and foremost, the editor, Alfred E. Burke, was a renowned imperialist, Conservative, and friend of Prime Minister Borden. His imprint upon the editorials and his influence in selecting the front-page news is unmistakable. For the first time in the paper's fifteen-year history the Canadian Ensign appeared weekly on the front page over the caption "Our Flag." Burke himself resigned from the paper in 1915 in order to take up duties as a chaplain in the Canadian Expeditionary Force. The second reason, and one that is less explicit, was the ideological disposition of the *Register*'s readership. The hierarchy, which had censored Burke's lack of good judgment in the past, refrained from prohibiting the paper's imperialist tone. In fact, the growth in the *Register*'s readership suggested that the 17,000-plus subscribers to the paper were in accord with Burke's pride in being "Civis Britannicus" and his view that "It was a proud day for Canada. Now then she was really a nation."[21] No subscriptions were reported cancelled; no complaints have been discovered either in McNeil's private papers or in the *Register*'s files; and no adverse criticism was offered either in the published letters to the editor or in those to the *Register*'s rival in London.

The *Catholic Record* was more restrained in its enthusiasm than the rather effusive *Register*. Still loyal to Sir Wilfrid Laurier and his Liberals, who now found themselves on the Opposition benches in Ottawa, the editors at the *Record* were measured in their response to the declaration of war and the Borden government's orders for mobilization.[22] Accordingly, the *Record* warned that the war effort should not rest solely on the shoulders of the militia and that Canada might have to re-evaluate its position in the Empire as it engaged in the war.[23] Restrained though it was in its coverage of the war in early 1914, the *Record* stood by the Liberal dictum that Parliament would decide the manner and extent of recruiting an army. Despite its initial caution, the *Record* agreed with the *Register* that Canada should come to the aid of the Empire in its time of need and that the Christian moral imperative of patriotism required that Canadian Catholics do their duty.[24] Editor James T. Foley appeared confident that Canada would distinguish herself among combatants and would "assume her full measure of responsibility as an integral part of the British Empire."[25]

The pronounced support for the Canadian war effort among Toronto's Catholic clergy and editors set a forceful example for local laypersons. Voluntary associations endorsed the war effort through special programs, fund-raising, and continuing the life insurance policies of recruits. Catholic women in Toronto and environs formed sock committees, assisted at recruiting meetings, and participated in victory bond drives. At St Mary's parish, for example, two hundred women reported for work to raise money for the Patriotic Fund.[26] At St Helen's in 1916 the Women's Patriotic League met every Thursday at the separate school to "sew and knit to aid the defenders of the Empire," while at Our Lady of Lourdes parish the twenty-five members of the Patriotic Association knit 662 pairs of socks for the CEF.[27] Rosary Hall, the city's hostel for Catholic working women, reported that its residents had donated 2,800 pairs of socks, 280 hospital shirts, 2,424 "soldier's comforts," and 35,072 units of surgical supplies.[28] Women also volunteered as nursing sisters through the agency of St Michael's Hospital, which in April 1915 sent its first contingent of nurses to Europe.[29] Children in separate schools sustained their enthusiasm for the war in their poetry and prose, patriotic concerts, "Christmas boxes" for soldiers, and lessons from their imperially flavoured textbooks. Students in cadet corps at St Mary's and De La Salle schools shouldered wooden rifles and drilled in tight formations after school hours.[30] All this lay activity was in addition to the efforts of the men and women who engaged in factory work and sustained their support for the war until its conclusion in 1918.

Perhaps the most visible validation of the war effort among the laity was the manner in which young Catholic men volunteered for the Canadian Expeditionary Force. Both the clergy and the press considered enlistment in the CEF a duty to be observed by all able Catholic men. Catholic leaders, from McNeil down, agreed that only strong Catholic recruitment could provide unassailable evidence of Catholic patriotism.[31] Thus, pulpit and press became vehicles for encouraging young men and women to volunteer, while reassuring the Toronto community at large: "Our Catholic people are as eager as others to defend their country; they would not be Catholics if it were otherwise." The premise argued by the *Register* and others harked back to editorials written earlier in the century, when Catholics, by nature of their faith, were considered the best "stuff" of which Canadian citizens could be made.[32] While some Catholic leaders readily admitted that Catholics had not been prominent in the military apparatus of the country in the past, they assured Torontonians that military preparedness would extend even into Catholic separate schools.[33] At the same time Catholics themselves were warned that lukewarm support for recruitment would be seen as a black mark against Catholic loyalty.[34]

Catholic men and women responded to the call to arms for a variety of reasons. Patriotism and "loyalty" may have been the public rallying cry to the laity, but the economy, family, peer-group pressure, occupation, and a host of other factors all had some bearing on the decisions made by the "common Catholics" of Toronto. Yet, when all these factors are considered, the recruiting patterns of Toronto's Catholics still appear remarkable when compared to those of Catholics elsewhere in Ontario, Quebec, or the Maritimes. When we look at the Catholic volunteers from Toronto, we are struck by their overwhelming "Canadianness," their experience in the military life of the country, and the fact that the majority enlisted during a period when jobs were increasingly available in the war industries. There were plenty of temptations to keep them at home: the slowly improving labour market, family ties, the frequent reports of battles and the lists of war dead in the Catholic and secular press, and the possible aversion to fighting for Britain during the Irish Rebellion. The fact that so many Catholic men and women did enlist bears further testimony, perhaps, to their growing sense of themselves as Canadians, and their belief in Canada's obligation to share in the burdens of the Empire. The war was more than a test of Catholic patriotism; it marked the emergence of a new generation of Canadian Catholics.

Elmer Wadham and other Catholic young men like him responded heartily to the calls of the hierarchy, Catholic newspapers, and the national government. In the three phases of voluntary enlistment – August to October 1914, October 1914 to September 1915, and October 1915 to October 1917 – Canadian Catholics contributed 51,426 volunteers for overseas service.[35] Catholics ranked third in the total voluntary contribution at 14.2 per cent, behind the Anglicans (46.8 per cent) and the Presbyterians (19.7 per cent). At face value these figures are somewhat deceptive. Men who were undecided about their "confession" were often assigned to the Church of England on their attestation forms, thereby inflating the actual number of Anglicans in the CEF.[36] Likewise, the number of Catholic recruits in proportion to their representation in the Canadian population appears rather paltry, at 1.8 per cent. When we consider, though, that French-speaking Catholics, who were the majority of Canada's Catholics, constituted less

Table 8.1
Voluntary Enlistment in the Canadian Expeditionary Force by
Religious Denomination, to 1 June 1917

Denomination	Volunteers	% of CEF	Total in Canada	% volunteered
Anglican	165,145	46.8	1,043,017	15.8
Presbyterian	70,671	19.7	1,115,324	6.3
Roman Catholic	51,426	14.2	2,833,041	1.8
Methodist	35,908	10.1	1,079,892	3.3
Baptist	18,458	5.2	382,666	4.4
Jew	851	0.2	74,564	1.1
Other	12,409	3.8	–	–

Source: NA, Militia and Defence Papers, RG 9, III C15, vol. 4673, Memoranda re Religious Statistics.
Figures based on 1911 Census of Canada. All calculations are mine.

than 30 per cent of the Catholic volunteers, it becomes evident that English-speaking Catholic participation in the war effort was substantial. In fact, an estimated 36,512 English-speaking and "ethnic" Catholics enlisted, constituting roughly 4.87 per cent of the total of the entire non-francophone Catholic population and roughly 10.29 per cent of all recruits, regardless of denomination (see Table 8.1).[37] On closer scrutiny, it appears that English-speaking Catholic recruitment has been vastly underrated by historians and by Catholics themselves.

In Ontario the rate of Catholic recruitment varied only slightly from the national level. Given that they were the fourth-largest religious denomination in the province, it is not surprising that the total number of Catholic volunteers from Ontario was less than that of Anglicans, Presbyterians, and Methodists. It is interesting to note, however, that Catholics at 2.9 per cent ranked higher than the Methodists (2.7) in terms of the proportion of recruits to the respective populations of each religious group (see Table 8.2). The English-speaking Catholic figure looms even larger given that the contemporary estimate of the Franco-Ontarian population was about 42 per cent of the Catholic total.[38] Confident in their strong showing in the recruiting depots, the Catholic weeklies beamed proudly: "When we take into account that more than half of all the soldiers were natives of European Protestant countries, and that all or nearly all the Catholics were native Canadians, we can safely infer that the Catholics of Ontario are doing 'their bit' as well as any."[39]

Table 8.2
Ontario Enlistment in the Canadian Expeditionary Force by
Religious Denomination, to April 1917

Denomination	Volunteers	% of CEF	Total in Ontario	% volunteered
Anglican	74,827	51.6	489,704	15.3
Presbyterian	25,224	17.4	524,603	4.8
Roman Catholic	14,198	9.8	484,997	2.9
Methodist	18,070	12.5	671,727	2.7
Baptist/Congregational	7,214	4.9	–	–
Other	5,152	3.5	–	–
Jew	436	0.3	26,727	1.6
Total	145,121	100.0		

Source: *Catholic Register*, 8 Nov. 1917, 28 July 1918.

In the city of Toronto over 3,500 English-speaking Catholics had volunteered for service by late 1917 (see Table 8.3).[40] This amounted to about eight per cent of the Catholic population of Toronto, judging from the 1911 census.[41] Few details are known about the religious composition of the twenty-eight[42] infantry battalions raised in the Toronto area. Catholics volunteered on their own initiative but were also encouraged by the patriotic stances assumed by such Catholic associations as the Holy Name Society, the De La Salle Cadets, St Joseph's Athletic Club, and the Newman Club.[43] Specialty units – based on occupation, recreational affiliation, or ethnicity – were also attractive to some young men. In 1916, one of the peak periods for Catholic enlistment, dozens of Catholic men in Toronto enlisted in the 208th Toronto Irish Battalion.[44] Units with an Irish flavour, however, were not necessarily an irresistible attraction to English-speaking Catholics, who appear to have been drawn in greater numbers to a variety of other battalions with no particular ethnic ambiance. Catholic men were as likely to gravitate to battalions that recruited in their neighbourhoods, to follow brothers of friends into specific units, or to join companies and batteries that required a particular skill, such as engineering, driving, or mechanical knowledge.

Catholic college students, for example, found themselves enlisting in a number of units formed within the University of Toronto's federation. Catholic students of applied science at Varsity were eager recruits for the university's own Sixty-seventh Artillery Battery.[45] In

Table 8.3
Catholic Population of Toronto Parishes, Recruits,
and Donations to Catholic Army Huts, 1917

Parish	Population	Recruits	Recruits as % of parish pop.	Army Hut donations ($)
St Paul's	2,700	660	24.4	$962.55
St Helen's	2,203	270	12.3	687.71
St Joseph's	1,890	210	11.1	456.65
St Basil's	1,800	160	8.9	1,178.50
St Clare's	1,000	110	11.0	228.85
St Peter's	1,950	102	5.2	893.90
St Anthony's	2,016	86	4.3	538.15
St Patrick's	1,500	60	4.0	263.95
St Monica's	408	38	9.3	134.25
St Mary's	2,400	600	25.0	358.55
St Cecilia's	2,201	242	11.0	345.35
St Michael's	1,000	170	17.0	350.90
Sacre Coeur	–	124	–	252.30
Holy Family	1,484	105	7.1	–
Lourdes	1,800	95	5.3	1,378.80
Holy Rosary	480	60	12.5	313.00
St Vincent de Paul	1,222	45	3.7	349.60
St Francis's	2,653	–	–	541.55
St Ann's	1,820	104	5.7	409.85
St John's	600	80	13.3	269.75
Holy Name	1,300	–	–	217.15
Assumption (Maron)	–	–	–	22.00
	31,507	3,321	10.5	$10,117.31

Sources: *Toronto Star*, 26 Jan. 1918; ARCAT, Spiritual Statistics and Financial Records Boxes, 1917 and 1918; *Catholic Register*, 13 Dec. 1917, Donations for Catholic Army Huts. St Anthony's Parish had 100 recruits by 1918; the figures from St John's and St Ann's are taken from parish files.

March 1915 William Joseph "Bill" O'Brien, a student at Osgoode Hall law school, was typical of Catholic and non-Catholic students when he enlisted in the Twenty-fifth Battery of the Seventh Brigade. A native of Lindsay and the son of separate school inspector Michael O'Brien, Bill O'Brien had spent considerable time in Toronto and was well known to students at St Michael's College as a colleague and tutor.[46] Though they were dispersed in a myriad of units, O'Brien kept touch with his chums and former students from St Michael's through his years of service. Although St Michael's Superior, Father Henry Carr, CSB, lamented that perhaps his students were not encouraged forcefully enough to enlist compared to those in other colleges, nevertheless dozens of young Catholics joined the COTC at St Mike's. By war's end 382 students and alumni had enlisted, of whom thirty-two made the supreme sacrifice.[47] Carr himself could take much of the credit for the recruiting at the college; at a rally in March 1916 he heaped praise on college recruits to the university's "E" Company, and made it crystal clear to young Catholics that, so far as recruitment was concerned, "we are bound under pain of sin to co-operate with it."[48] In late 1918 Carr himself would volunteer as a chaplain, although Archbishop McNeil would block the move, considering Carr too valuable to the archdiocese to lose.[49]

Student or not, Toronto's English-speaking Catholics were represented in every unit recruited in the city. The Seventy-fifth Mississauga Horse Battalion, or "Jolly Seventy-fifth," one of the few Canadian units to preserve its register of recruits, provides an interesting glimpse into the nature of Catholic recruitment in Toronto. Raised by the officers of the Ninth Mississauga Horse militia unit, the Seventy-fifth began recruiting in Toronto in the summer of 1915. Ninety-seven Catholics, including four officers, attested out of a total battalion strength of 1,155. As was the case with most Toronto units, Catholics ranked fourth in numbers in the Seventy-fifth, with just over 8 per cent of the total. This was slightly higher than the norm in the other Toronto units whose religious statistics have been preserved.[50] The odd feature of the Seventy-fifth, however, was the disproportionately low number of Presbyterians, Methodists, and Catholics in the unit when compared to the numerical strength of each denomination in Toronto. Conversely, Anglican recruits were disproportionately high, at 67 per cent of the unit, or about double the proportion of Anglicans in the city.[51] The high numbers of recent British immigrants partially accounted for the numerical superiority of Anglicans,[52] whereas the low number of British-born Methodists, errors in declaring one's Methodist affiliation at the time of attestation, and a long-standing ethos of pacifism and social idealism in the Canadian Methodist Church were cited as reasons for that denomination's poor recruitment figures.[53]

While government officials analysed religious participation in the war by battalion or unit, Toronto's English-speaking Catholics measured their war effort at the parish level. Collectively, St Paul's parish in the inner city and St Helen's in the western "Junction" area of Toronto provided 930 volunteers for active service, or nearly one of every three Catholic volunteers from Toronto. While these parish communities were studies in contrast socially and economically, they both demonstrated the curious patterns of recruitment exhibited by local Catholics generally during the war. The predominance of white-collar Catholics at St Helen's was reflected in the high proportion of clerical and professional recruits, among whom was included one of two English-speaking Catholic generals from Toronto – Archibald Hayes Macdonell.[54] St Paul's, by contrast, ranked as one of the poorest parishes in the city, one from which many English-speaking Catholics were departing for suburban areas. Nevertheless, nearly one-quarter of the entire parish population, or 660 men, had volunteered for service by June 1917. In the first year of the war alone 191 St Paul's men were reported to have enlisted, and the *Register* reported that 100 school children from the parish were wearing the "My Daddy's at the Front" button of the Patriotic League.[55] By war's end Archbishop McNeil proudly exclaimed that when the volunteers from the parish were added to the 102 conscripts, St Paul's had the largest number of combatants of any parish, Catholic or Protestant, in the city.[56] For McNeil and the city officials present at the unveiling of the parish monument to its 81 war dead, the wartime sacrifice of Toronto's Catholics was beyond doubt.

In the earliest phases of recruitment, in August and September 1914, St Paul's and St Helen's parishes provided as many as 44 and 47 men respectively.[57] Of those identified through their personnel files, most were Canadian-born, an anomaly at a time when 60 per cent of the recruits were from the British Isles or other colonies.[58] Although patriotic spirit could have laid claim to these Catholic young men, it is more likely that this first wave of Canadian-born Catholic recruits was propelled into military service by the high levels of unemployment in the city. Such may have been the case with Private Charles Wehrle, a twenty-one-year-old lad from St Helen's parish. Born in Toronto, the young machinist left the comforts of the family-owned home on Margu.eretta Street to join the army at Valcartier. As a skilled worker he had little hope of finding a job in depression-ridden Toronto,[59] and perhaps the army's salary of $1.10 per day was sufficient temptation to join the Canadian Army Service Corps.[60] Whatever his reasons, Wehrle never lived to tell. In March 1917, while serving in Belgium, he was ripped to pieces by shrapnel.[61]

Canadian-born Catholics like Charles Wehrle were clearly the majority among Toronto's English-speaking Catholic volunteers throughout

Table 8.4
Catholic Recruits by Place of Birth

Birthplace	St Helen's		St Paul's		75th Bn		208th B		Total	
	No.	%	No.	%	No.	%	No.	%	No.	%
Canada	103	78.0	52	78.8	49	50.5	25	73.5	229	69.6
Ireland	7	5.3	6	9.1	11	11.3	3	8.8	27	8.2
Great Britain	16	12.1	5	3.8	22	22.7	2	5.9	55	16.7
United States	3	2.3	3	2.7	4	4.1	2	5.9	12	3.6
Other	3	2.3	0	0.0	11	11.4	2	5.9	16	4.9
Total sample	132	100	66	100	97	100	34	100	329	100

Source: NA, Militia and Defence Records, RG 9 III, vol. 4220, 75th Battalion, Register of Recruits; NPRC, Attestation Books and Soldiers' files, CEF; St Paul's Parish Memorial to War Dead; ARCAT, St Helen's Parish box, Honour Roll. Availability of birthplace data permitted larger parish samples than evident in the other tables.

the war. Over two-thirds of the Catholic soldiers from Toronto sampled were Canadian by birth. This figure was twice the percentage of Canadian-born among the all recruits for Military District 2 (Central Ontario), and a little less than double the figure for the entire CEF by August 1916.[62] At the unit level, half of the Catholics of the Seventy-fifth were Canadian-born (see Table 8.4); despite this lower figure, they still ranked second only to the Methodists (59.3 per cent) in terms of Canadian birth and well ahead of the Anglicans (20.7 per cent), Presbyterians (36.9 per cent), and Baptists (40.7 per cent; see Table 8.5).[63] Considering that the majority of these Catholics attested at a time when the employment situation had been ameliorated, especially for workers exclusive of the building trades,[64] the high numbers of Canadian-born volunteers indicate that "common Catholics" were ready to claim this war as theirs. That they were natives of Canada and had never seen Britain or Ireland did not hinder their response to the call for volunteers. Painfully, Berta Wadham lamented over her son Elmer's decision: "It is a great and glorious thing to think he is anxious to go serve his King and Country but it is hard for one to let him go."[65]

As new recruitment drives were initiated in 1915 and 1916, unemployment seemed to figure less in the decision-making of young Catholic men than it had in the case of Charles Wherle. Nor would it be accurate to suggest that Catholics enlisted because most were stuck in low-paying, low-skilled, and seasonal jobs. English-speaking Catholic volunteers came from every walk of life, although distribution among occupational classifications naturally varied from parish

Table 8.5
Seventy-fifth Infantry Battalion by Nativity, 1916

Denomination	Total	Tor	Can	GBr	Ire	Oth	Cdn
Catholic	97	23	26	22	11	15	49
%	100	23.7	26.8	22.7	11.3	15.5	50.5
Baptist	28	6	5	16	0	1	11
%	100	21.4	17.9	57.1	0.0	3.6	39.3
Methodist*	113	27	40	38	3	5	67
%	100	23.9	35.4	33.7	2.6	4.4	59.3
Presbyterian	122	18	27	66	11	0	45
%	100	14.8	22.2	55.1	9.0	0	37.0
Other	13	1	0	8	0	4	1
%	100	7.7	0.0	61.5	0.0	30.8	7.7
Anglican	775	–	160	557	41	17	160
%	100	–	20.7	71.8	5.3	2.2	20.7
Congregational	7	1	1	4	1	0	2
%	100	14.3	14.3	57.1	14.3	0	28.6
Total	1155	76	259	711	67	42	335
%	100	6.6	22.4	61.6	5.8	3.6	29.0

* Includes Wesleyan.

Source: NA, Militia and Defence Papers, RG 9 III C15, vol. 4220, 75th Canadian Infantry Battalion, Register of Recruits. All calculations are mine. Some additional personnel appear on the register of recruits analysed here but not on the official sailing list.

to parish. When compared to the occupational categorization of all units from the Eighteenth to Eighty-fifth battalions raised in Military District 2, St Helen's parish had a proportionately higher number of those in clerical jobs and a much lower proportion of manual workers (see Table 8.6). Not surprisingly, at St Paul's, a heavily blue-collar parish, the opposite was true. The Catholics of the Seventy-fifth Battalion, however, closely mirrored the occupational breakdown for the military district, except for a slightly higher level of businessmen and an understandably lower level of farm recruits (see Table 8.7). More interesting is that there was no significant difference between the levels of manual labourers among the Catholics, Baptists, Methodists, and Presbyterians.[66] In light of such figures, the twentieth-century stereotype of Toronto Catholics as poorly skilled urban labourers in

Table 8.6
Catholic Recruits from Toronto by Occupation

Classification	St Helen's		St Paul's		75th Bn		208th Bn		Total Mil. Distr. 2	
	No.	%	No.	%	No.	%	No.	%	No.	%
Professional	7	5.3	1	1.5	2	2.1	0		285	1.7
Business	4	3.0	3	4.5	6	6.2	2	5.9	351	2.1
Clerical	29	22.0	7	10.6	14	14.4	9	26.5	2,192	13.3
Skilled	34	25.8	13	19.7	16	16.5	4	11.8		
Semi-skilled	25	18.9	14	21.2	23	23.7	5	14.7		
Unskilled	27	20.5	26	39.4	36	37.1	14	41.2		
All blue-collar	86	65.2	53	80.3	75	77.3	23	67.7	12,450	75.5
Private		0	2	3.0	0		0			
Unknown	6	4.6	0		0		0			
Total	132	100	66	100	97	100	34	100		

Table 8.7
Occupational Breakdown of Minority Religious Groups
in the Seventy-fifth Infantry Battalion

Classification	Catholic	%	Methodist	%	Presbyterian	%	Baptist	%
Professional	2	2.1	9	8.2	8	6.7	0	0.0
Business	6	6.2	2	1.8	6	5.0	0	0.0
Clerical	14	14.4	14	12.7	15	12.5	5	18.5
Skilled	16	16.5	17	15.5	23	19.2	4	14.8
Semi-Skilled	23	23.7	34	30.9	25	20.8	7	25.9
Unskilled	36	37.1	34	30.9	40	33.3	10	37.1
Total blue-collar	75	77.3	85	77.3	88	73.3	21	77.8
Private Means	–		–		–		–	
Unknown	–		–		3	2.5	1	3.7
	97		110		120		27	
Officers	4		5		8		0	

Sources: NPRC, Soldiers' Files; NA, Militia and Defence Records, RG 9 III C15, vol. 4220, 75th Infantry Battalion, Register of Recruits; Department of National Defence Records, RG 24, vol. 1249, file HQ 593–1–77, Occupations, Military District No. 2, 18–85th Battalions. The latter document is one of the few available records of the soldiers' occupational alignment.

no way correlates with the Catholic men who volunteered for Toronto's Seventy-fifth Battalion. It was not just the Catholic working poor who went to war.

Strangest of all, at a time when unemployment was rapidly dwindling in Toronto, English-speaking Catholic recruitment was steadily on the rise. In the autumn of 1915 the availability of contracts from the Shell Committee (the government's agency for co-ordinating wartime production) and, later, the Imperial Munitions Board sparked a recovery in Toronto's industrial and manufacturing sectors. Jobs became more plentiful, especially for skilled workers, and by October 1915 even workers in the hard-hit building trades were profiting from the economic turnaround in the city. By December of that year the *Labour Gazette* reported that Toronto was experiencing "less unemployment than has prevailed at this season for several years." In early 1916 most industrial sectors, save the building trades, reported good employment. By March even unskilled workers enjoyed employment; the building trades had revived; and there was need for carpenters, stationary engineers, and bricklayers.[67] During this period of economic recovery the federal government was in the midst of yet another phase of voluntary recruitment. Ironically, with the economy rebounding and reasonably safe and secure jobs available to them, English-speaking Catholic men appeared to be enlisting in the CEF in higher numbers than ever before (see Table 8.8). Even when the general enlistment tapered off between January and June 1916,[68] the number of Catholic recruits peaked. If there was a correlation between employment and Catholic military service in this phase, it was negative. Despite the availability of work, many Catholic men, both married and single, opted to fight.

Upon closer scrutiny, it also appears that those Catholic young men who enlisted from 1914 to late 1917 were better prepared and experienced in military matters than even the *Register* had imagined. At least 30 per cent of the recruits from St Paul's and St Helen's had seen previous militia or regular army experience before they enlisted (see Table 8.9). Most of the young Catholic men claimed earlier service, either before the war or immediately in advance of attestation, in local militia units such as the York Rangers, Ninth Horse, and the Queen's Own Rifles. Nearly 80 per cent of these were Canadian-born, unlike many of the immigrant British volunteers, who claimed previous service in the British Army. One of the most battle-scarred of Toronto's Catholics was Corporal Edward Ryan of St Helen's. An auto mechanic by trade, Ryan had served in the United States Army and had seen duty in Mexico, Hawaii, and the Boxer Rebellion in China. Later he served with the British Army in India, Egypt, and Tibet. His expe-

Table 8.8
Attestation of Catholic Soldiers

Date (mo./yr)	St Helen's		St Paul's		75th Bn		Total	
	No.	%	No.	%	No.	%	No.	%
ATTESTATION OF RECRUITS BORN IN CANADA								
8/14–9/14	5	7.0	1	2.3	0		6	3.7
10/14–9/15	27	38.0	17	39.6	39	79.6	83	50.9
10/15–12/15	14	19.7	3	7.0	3	6.1	20	12.3
1/16–6/16	22	31.0	16	37.2	7	14.3	45	27.6
10/15–6/16	36	50.7	19	44.2	10	22.4	65	39.9
7/16–10/17	3	4.3	1	2.3	0		4	2.4
Conscripts	0		5	11.6	0		5	3.1
Total	71		43		49		163	
ATTESTATION OF ALL RECRUITS IN SAMPLE								
8/14–9/14	7	7.7	1	1.8	0			
10/14–9/15	33	36.3	22	40.0	82	84.5		
10/15–12/15	16	17.6	6	10.9	6	6.2		
1/16–6/16	30	33.0	20	36.4	9	9.3		
10/15–6/16	46	50.6	26	47.3	15	15.5		
7/16–10/17	4	4.4	1	1.8	0			
Conscripts	0		5	9.1	0			
Unknown	1	1.0	0		0			
Total	91		55		97			

Source: NPRC, Soldiers' Files; NA, Militia and Defence Records, RG 9 III, vol. 4220, 75th Infantry Battalion, Register of Recruits. All calculations are mine.

rience earned him corporal's stripes, while most of his fellow parishioners remained privates.[69]

This pattern of previous service by Toronto's Catholics is confirmed on examination of the Seventy-fifth Battalion. Nearly half (47.4 per cent) of the Catholics in the unit had militia or regular army experience. This compared favourably with the Presbyterian (50.1) and Methodist (50.1) members of the unit. Anglicans clearly outdistanced the rest,

Table 8.9
Seventy-fifth Infantry Battalion: Religions Affiliation and Previous Record of Service

75TH BATTALION

Religion	Total	Previous service		Canadian-born		Canadian-born with previous service/ Canadian-born in 75th	
		No.	%	No.	%	No.	%
Catholic	97	46	47.4	20	43.5	20 of 49	40.8
Presbyterian	120	61	50.1	20	32.8	20 of 45	44.4
Methodist	110	56	50.1	34	60.7	34 of 64	53.1
Baptist	27	15	55.6	9	60.0	9 of 11	81.8
Anglican	750	482	64.3	103	21.4	103 of 160	66.0

TORONTO Parish	Previous service		Canadian-born		Canadian-born with previous service/ Canadian-born in parish	
			No.	%	No.	%
St Helen's	30		24	80.0	24 of 71	33.8
St Paul's	15		11	73.3	11 of 43	25.6

Source: NPRC, Soldiers' Files; NA, Militia and Defence Records, RG 9 III C15, vol. 4220, 75th Infantry Battalion, Register of Recruits. All calculations are mine.

with at least 65 per cent of their troops having records of previous service. Interestingly, about 50 per cent of all the Canadian-born Catholics in the unit had previous militia experience. This high rate of participation should come as little surprise, considering that the Seventy-fifth was raised by the Ninth Horse during a period of enlistment co-ordinated by local militia units.[70] Such high levels of Catholic service suggest, however, that Catholics were attracted to the military and militia traditions of Ontario and the Empire well before the war. Furthermore, the respectable level of Canadian-born participation, when coupled with these levels of previous service, indicates the strength of the bonding that had occurred between the new generations of anglophone Canadian Catholics and the Dominion of their birth.

Attachment to military traditions and participation in militia and cadet units prior to the war was only one inducement for English-speaking Catholic men. Often the enlistment of an eldest son initiated an "enlistment chain" that drew younger brothers into active service. Groups of brothers frequently enlisted within months of one another.

In St Helen's parish alone, of the 183 listed on the honour roll of 1917, 26 families had sent two or more men, which accounted for one-third of the volunteers on the list.[71] One widow, Mary Anne Cooney, saw four sons, ranging in age from nineteen to twenty-eight, enlist. Her eldest son, James, died as a result of wounds, and two others were seriously injured in battle. One of the latter, John Thomas, was buried alive by a shell and remained "frightened by loud noises" long after his fighting days were over.[72] For many families the sight of sons leaving for war was a burden both emotionally and financially. Some Catholic men arranged for war gratuities after the war, claiming they were the only means of support for their relatives. Berta Wadham probably echoed the feelings of many mothers and wives when she wrote: "This terrible war is making a lot of terrible trouble, and it is so hard for mothers to give up their sons even though it is for a just cause."[73] It became clear that, among English-speaking Catholics in Toronto, when one son went to war, the entire family joined him, physically, emotionally, and spiritually.

Like their non-Catholic comrades, the majority of the Catholic volunteers were single men under the age of twenty-nine. Only about one in five recruits was married, and most of these family men were over thirty (see Table 8.10). It is difficult to fathom why some of these men, with gainful employment and domestic security, ventured into the mud of Flanders and northeastern France if not in the belief that national service was their patriotic duty.[74] Will Pennylegion of St Paul's was one such. A thirty-one-year-old tailor, Pennylegion lived in his own house with his wife and two young children.[75] His family were well known in the area; in fact, his brother Frank was one of the new generation of Toronto-born priests serving in the city. Given his status in life, it is difficult to imagine few reasons other than "doing his bit" to account for his departure with the 123rd Battalion in 1916.

The strain of sending young, single wage-earners and heads of households had mixed effects on family living in Catholic homes. Father K.E. Morrow of St Anthony's parish in the northwestern section of the city was confident that "the family ties have not been weakened but rather a greater affection has been manifested." He also reported that wives had been more prayerful since the departure of their husbands, and there were no cases of infidelity reported to him.[76] Such was not the case across town in St Joseph's parish. The pastor, Father Arthur O'Leary, reported that, although the married men were dutiful in sending their pay home to their wives, he knew of at least two cases of wives being unfaithful, and at least one case of child neglect. On a brighter note, he stated that many single men had been mindful enough to send funds home to their mothers.[77]

Table 8.10
Age and Marital Status at Time of Attestation

| Age Group | St Helen's | | | St Paul's | | | 75th Bn | |
	Recruits	%	Married	Recruits	%	Married	No.	%
18–21	39	42.8	0	17	30.9	2	25	25.77
22–29	22	24.2	4	20	36.4	6	36	37.11
30–35	8	8.8	4	13	23.6	7	18	18.56
36 plus	14	15.4	8	3	5.5	3	18	18.56
Unknown	8	8.8	0	2	3.6	0	0	
Total	91		16	55		18	97	

St Helen's Parish

| Attestation (mo./yr) | Ages of soldiers | | | | | Marital Status | | |
	36+	30–35	22–29	18–21	Unknown	All	Married	Cdns
8/14–9/14	1	1	1	3	1	7	0	5
10/14–9/15	5	3	11	14	0	33	7	27
10/15–12/15	5	2	2	6	1	16	4	14
1/16–6/16	3	2	7	14	4	30	5	22
7/16–10/17	0	0	1	2	1	4	0	3
Unknown					1	1	–	–
Total	14	8	22	39	8	91	16	

Source: NPRC, Soldiers' Files; NA, Militia and Defence Records, RG 9 III C15, 75th Infantry Battalion, Register of Recruits. All calculations are mine.

One often-overlooked feature of the disruption facing family life was the loss of daughters, both to industrial jobs left vacant by the combatants and to nursing positions in the Canadian Army Medical Corps. In April 1915 the St Michael's Contingent of Overseas Nurses, representing St Michael's Hospital, left for Europe. Here they joined other Catholic women from Quebec, Nova Scotia, and other parts of Canada who had attached themselves initially to hospital units sponsored by Laval and St Francis Xavier universities.[78] Like the young men who were enlisting, these young women were generally Canadian by birth and under thirty. Several, like Margaret McEvoy of Phelpston, had come from areas outside of Toronto to study nursing and were essentially using the CAMC as their first job placement.[79]

Those over thirty, like Aimee Mary Christie of Toronto, were single women who were well into their careers as professional nurses. Given their age and experience, Christie and her peers would be invaluable in the field and at convalescent hospitals in England, where they would likely be promoted to matron.[80] When the first blue-clad unit of Catholic women departed St Michael's Hospital for Europe, McNeil reminded them of their patriotic duty and their special work as Catholic sisters to provide spiritual comfort to dying soldiers. "To the dying soldier – non-Catholic as well as Catholic," McNeil said, "you can suggest ejaculations that will excite sorrow for sin."[81]

The stream of Catholic men and women who donned blue or khaki – or, figuratively, "England's Red" – went to war chiefly because they believed it was their duty to do so. When one examines the English-speaking Catholic volunteers from Toronto, one is struck by their overwhelming "Canadianness," their experience in the military life of the country and the fact that the majority of these men enlisted during a period when jobs were opening in war industries. There were plenty of temptations to keep them at home: the improving labour market, family ties, the frequent reports of the horror of battle and the lists of war dead in the Catholic and secular press, and the possible aversion to fighting for Britain overseas. That so many Catholics enlisted bears further testimony, perhaps, to their growing sense of themselves as Canadians and to their belief in Canada's obligation to share in the burdens of the Empire. For the young Catholics of wartime Toronto, the Irish nationalist sentiments that had motivated their forebears, and prompted them to sing the rousing anti-British verses of the "Wearing of the Green," were no longer relevant. Not even the devastating events of the Easter 1916 Rebellion in Dublin dampened recruitment. Young men of Canadian birth and Irish descent, and older men of Irish birth, continued to join units, including the 208th Toronto Irish Battalion.[82] As McNeil had predicted, the war would be the acid test of Catholic patriotism, and its course would mark the emergence of a new Canadian generation.

As the initial euphoria of the opening months of the war was steadily dampened by the realities of the conflict, Catholic leaders like McNeil, his clergy, lay leaders, and editors redoubled their efforts to encourage Catholic participation and maintain a public image of loyalty to the cause. This proved more difficult as reports of battles filtered home, letters from soldiers – sometimes uncensored – reached the public press, and as Canadian casualty lists lengthened with each passing day. Bishops themselves relived the horrors of the front as they sifted through correspondence from lay combatants and the padres they sent overseas. As Lieutenant Bill O'Brien moved from "Blighty" to the front and back, he kept his hometown bishop, Michael O'Brien of Peterborough, apprised of army life.[83] Similarly, McNeil was kept abreast of events by troubled young soldiers like Gilbert A. Sim, somewhat disgruntled chaplains like Bernard Stephen Doyle, or old acquaintances from the Extension Society such as Belgian-born priest Jules Pirot.[84] Correspondence of this kind was the most vivid way of putting local Catholic leaders in touch with the events transpiring so far away. While tales of the carnage forced local Catholics to address the realities of war, some correspondence was reprinted to rekindle enthusiasm, offering hope that "Our men were a credit to Canada ... none of our men will ever have the prejudices again of former years."[85]

Such hope was needed when each new day brought some Catholic families the news they had hoped would never come. Folks back home at St Paul's parish likely beamed upon hearing that local family man Frank Gorman had been elevated to sergeant in the field, and were equally devastated when informed he had been killed in action.[86] All of St Michael's College mourned when, in 1916, John C. Feeney, an all-round athletic star and third-year student, died while serving with the Princess Pats (PPCLI) at Courcellette.[87] Each year brought greater ugliness. By war's end nearly half of the recruits from St Helen's, for example, had been killed or wounded. One out of four soldiers from the parish suffered from shrapnel injuries, gunshot wounds, or shell-shock.[88] Over at St Paul's, 81 of its 762 soldiers, over 10 per cent, were killed in battle or died of wounds or illness. Battle was not the cause of all the casualties; nearly one in five of St Helen's volunteers suffered from everything from scabies to influenza. The latter struck about 10 per cent of the 91 men surveyed. In some instances battle wounds only left the soldiers weakened and susceptible to infections and viruses. The Pennylegion family mourned the loss of Will, who had been so weakened after being gassed at the front that he contracted influenza and died in an English hospital.[89]

The combination of such battlefield tragedy and the politicization of the war at home was a constant challenge to Catholic leaders. Despite disheartening news from overseas, sock committees kept sewing, school children continued to imbibe news of the latest advances and cheered their heroes, and local clergy stepped up their participation in recruitment campaigns. What made these efforts all the more difficult was the trouble brewing in Catholic Quebec and the spectre of conscription that lurked in the shadows surrounding the Borden government in Ottawa. By 1916, given *nationaliste* agitation in Quebec, the pro-German sympathies of American Irish Catholics, the Easter Rebellion in Ireland, Papal neutrality, and lingering doubts about the loyalties of Ukrainian Bishop Nykyta Budka, the secular press was increasingly tarring all Catholics with the common sin of disloyalty. Thus, when the conscription issue boiled over into a national crisis in 1917, Toronto's English-speaking Catholics girded themselves and became even more resolved to demonstrate that they were good citizens dedicated to winning the war.

In 1916 local priests became even more prominent in local recruitment drives, thereby showing that the Church could wave the flag as well as any member of the Orange Lodge. In March, Father John Burke, CSP, the director of the Newman Club at the University of Toronto, was successful in encouraging Catholic students and members of the club to enlist. Later that month Father Henry Carr, CSB, of St Michael's College joined Protestant leaders and military officials at a major recruiting meeting in the city. By 1917 clergy of all denominations were meeting to discuss recruiting and the possibility of conscription.[90] Other priests, such as Father Lancelot Minehan of Holy Family parish, wrote voluminously to city newspapers demanding that the Militia Department be overhauled in order to make the Canadian war effort more efficient. Minehan demanded a complete investigation, promising that it would create "a tornado of flaming indignation" that would sweep the incompetence out of Ottawa.[91] Such activities among the clergy etched the institutional Church's commitment to the war effort into the public record.

The clerical commitment was also evident in the Catholic response to the Victory Loan drive. In 1917 Archbishop McNeil assured Sir Thomas White, the minister of Finance, that Catholics in Toronto and across the country were committed to the Victory Loan: "I write to assure you that we shall use press and pulpit to encourage investment by the purchase of government certificates." He added that the *Catholic Register*, with a weekly subscription of roughly 17,000 nationwide, was advertising the loan in each issue.[92] McNeil himself publicized the appeal in a circular published 6 November 1917, in which he implied that success in the bond drive would show "that Canada is determined to end this horrible war as soon as possible and to end it victoriously free of German domination."[93] The archbishop repeated the appeals well into 1918 and sanctioned the placing of Victory Loan signs in Toronto's churches.[94] He also maintained his earlier commitments to the patriotic fund.

As they had in the first months of the war, the local Catholic press stood shoulder to shoulder with the clergy and bishops. Both the *Register* and the *Record* editorialized and carried advertisements for Victory Loans, food rationing, economizing, patriotic songs, and increased agricultural production through the "Sons of the Soil" program.[95] Editorial policies changed little before the conscription crisis, despite some changes in personnel at the *Register*. In November 1916 Thomas O'Donnell, Burke's successor at the Extension Society, played upon the patriotism of Catholics when he warned that "the man whose heart does not glow and beat for his native land and whose arm is not willing and ready to strike a blow for her weal is void of noble sentiments, is selfish and a craven."[96] Similarly, J.A. Wall, Burke's successor at the *Register*, reflected on Canadian-imperial interdependence in much the same fashion as had his predecessor Patrick Cronin nearly ten years earlier.

Although the rival *Record* similarly attempted to keep Catholics in tune with the war effort by printing the patriotic pleas of Bishop Fallon, the editors were more preoccupied with intellectualizing on the future of Canadian-imperial relations after the war.[97] Its interests had changed little since the summer of 1914. In fairness to the *Record*, however, it should be understood that its focus was far more international than national, and that a column on recent developments at the front was a regular feature at the back of the paper. At the end of 1915 it called upon its readers to "fight to the finish" for "civilization" and "humanity," and claimed that a "victory by Germany … would in the end substitute German repression and exclusiveness for open-handed generous British rule over the myriads of the human race." Anything less than a British victory, claimed the *Record*, would be a "catastrophe" for the world.[98]

Local Catholic leaders used the celebrations marking the silver anniversary of Canadian Confederation in 1917 as a convenient diversion from the nagging doubts in English Caanda about the loyalty of Catholics in Quebec. Even as he beat hard on the tub of Catholic loyalty, it was not difficult to see in the rhetoric of Archbishop McNeil the strain of the conscription crisis. As he had throughout his career as a prelate, McNeil made clear his commitment to English-speaking Catholic patriotism while always attempting to soothe and heal the wounds left by the battle between the nation's two solitudes. His Jubilee circular marked a watershed in its confirmation of the primary focus of loyalty among English-speaking Catholics: "ours is a great country and we are proud of the lustre which the soldiers of Canada have shed upon their country and the battlefields of Europe … In our case there is a great need of careful statesmanship to avoid the deepening and threatening of civil schisms. I ask our Catholic people to pray to God for the future unity of Canada, which means mutual good will between differing groups of citizens."[99] Given the pressure of Quebec's negative response to conscription, the feelings evoked by the Jubilee, and the Catholic sacrifices for the war effort, it is not surprising that the struggle in Europe was regarded as a Canadian one, not just the Empire's.

The *Catholic Register* echoed McNeil's sentiments, and more. The Reverend W.R. Harris of Toronto revelled in the promise of the Dominion and the hope that its institutions extended to all its groups. Henry Somerville, the paper's most articulate writer and committed social commentator, encouraged Catholics to fulfil their civic responsibilities for the good of the Church, of Canada, and for the welfare of the Commonwealth. From a practical point of view he accused Catholics of being too denominational in their service, coaxing them to participate vigorously outside of religious circles so that they might be "as prominent as non-Catholics" in public affairs.[100] Somerville suggested more "patriotic work," enlistment, joining "win the war" committees, fighting oppressive employers, and battling infant mortality as the types of public service that would bring prestige to the Church in Canada. Likewise, Father Lancelot Minehan retold the story of great Catholic contributors to Confederation – D'Arcy McGee and George-Etienne Cartier – and urged readers to strengthen national unity and celebrate freedom. Finally, reflecting on the Jubilee, the *Register* rejected the practicability of imperial federation and seriously questioned the subordination of Canada's domestic sovereignty for the sake of greater political integration of the Empire.[101] Canada's stake in the war, and her risks, were as great as those of the Empire. By 1917 the Dominion's war experience had crystallized the *Register*'s belief in an autonomous Canada, but partnered within an Empire of equals.

All the rhetoric of the Catholic papers, clergy, and bishops had little effect soothing explosive emotions as the debate over conscription became heated. Historians have long underestimated English-speaking Catholic support for conscription.[102] The national debate on the issue placed English-speaking Catholics in an awkward position. The rejection of conscription by Catholics in Quebec and in Ireland, and the ongoing opposition of Archbishop Mannix of Melbourne to conscription in Australia, meant that the loyalty of Toronto's Catholics might, by association, become suspect in the eyes of the city's Protestants. Papal neutrality was difficult enough to deal with, living in a predominantly Protestant city, let alone the vociferous opposition of other Catholics in the Empire. As the official rhetoric during the Jubilee suggests, English-speaking Catholics in Toronto had moved considerably in their role as citizens of Canada. Facing pressures from all sides, they walked a tightrope, attempting to demonstrate their loyalty while appearing sympathetic to their co-religionists elsewhere in the Empire. Conscription was the litmus test of this maturing national sentiment, and although there was no unanimity on non-voluntary service, the already wide chasm between English- and French-speaking wings of the Church opened considerably.

Catholics in Toronto had been co-operating with the federal government's efforts to direct the war effort as early as 1916. When the National Service Board was created in October 1916, local Catholics voiced no opposition. When the government initiated its campaign to register all Canadians, to assess the manpower needs of the country, Catholics in Toronto were very supportive. In December 1916 R.B. Bennett, director-general of the NSB, asked McNeil for his help in making sure that registration was a success in Toronto. Accordingly, McNeil drafted a circular directing the city's Catholics to participate fully in the program, while easing the fears of some that registration would necessarily lead to conscription.[103] It is not known how well Toronto's Catholics complied with this directive, although the federal government praised Brother Rogatien and other separate school teachers in the city for their 100 per cent participation in the registration drive.[104]

Catholic newspapers echoed McNeil's support for the campaign, featuring pledge cards in their papers in January 1917. While assuring its Liberal readers that registration did not mean conscription, the *Record* urged "a cheerful and ready response" to the government's request for information. It added that the government needed this information from Canadians "to organize the country's resources for the supreme effort in the great struggle in which we are now engaged."[105] The *Catholic Register*, however, went further in its support, calling upon Catholic workers to ignore the opposition of their labour organizations towards the registration: "no labour organization can stand between them and their duty as citizens, upon which their religion lays stress." It agreed with its rival journal that registration did not mean conscription, but if need for the latter arose, "there are, we hope, few Canadians indeed who would not prefer it to German rule."[106]

When conscription became a reality in May 1917, Toronto's English-speaking Catholics obeyed the law with varying degrees of enthusiasm. The *Register* endorsed conscription "on the stern grounds of absolute necessity to the life of the Empire and the continued freedom of our own Dominion." It added, as did other papers in Canada, that the safety of civilization depended on it, as well as the defence of Canada: "It is as truly for the defence of Canada as if the German shells were now crashing into Halifax, or Quebec or Toronto."[107] Throughout the debate the *Register* refuted the criticism of Catholic "loyalty" offered by non-Catholic journalists by citing recruitment figures as proof of the resolve of Ontario's Catholics to win the war. The paper also warned opponents of the war that their position was tantamount to wishing "German rule" for Canada.[108] The *Register* appeared to be in step with the changes occurring in the English Canadian press, which had come to view the war less as an imperial affair and more as a veritable defence of Canada, consecrated by the blood of her men at Ypres, the Somme, and Vimy.[109] The response of the *Register* consummated decades of theorizing on Canada's autonomy, and confirmed the extent to which many English-speaking Catholics had come to identify themselves with the aims and aspirations of many English-speaking Protestant Canadians. The trick was in convincing their non-Catholic neighbours that this transformation of identity had indeed taken place.

For their part McNeil, many clergy, and prominent local Catholic lay leaders stepped into the breach to support the government's war effort. McNeil, whose political alliances had never been clear in the past, backed the Union government and urged young men and women to keep up with their education so that, when the call for military service came, they would have their university program behind them.[110] Father Lancelot Minehan, who had advocated conscription as early as February 1916, supported conscription for both Ireland and Canada. His endorsement of the former discredited him among some Irish Canadians who felt that, since Lloyd George had reneged on Home Rule, conscription in Ireland was tyranny. In the Canadian context Minehan saw conscription as the best way of allocating manpower effectively in every sector of the war effort.[111] Minehan's fellow columnist at the *Register*, Henry Somerville, although a supporter of the labour movement,[112] upheld conscription on several occasions. Commenting that patriotism was a Catholic virtue and national service a Catholic duty, Somerville asserted that "we all have the moral duty of helping in every way we can to defend and maintain that association of living souls to which we belong, that social organization to which we are subject, and by which we are a nation."[113] Earlier, in June 1917, he had praised English-speaking Catholics who supported conscription for displaying "true public spirit," adding that those neutral on the issue had failed in their "duty."[114]

In the House of Commons another prominent Catholic from the city, A. Claude Macdonell, was determined in his support for conscription. Macdonell, a Conservative, was the member from South Toronto, a constituency that contained a high percentage of Catholic voters.[115] During the debate on the Military Service Bill, Macdonell called for unity across the country, regardless of race, class, or creed. He refuted members who had criticized Toronto's contribution: "the record speaks for itself ... The total enlistments for No. 2 military district to the 15th of June 1917, were 93,187, very nearly one quarter of the whole force."[116] He added that more men were needed at the front, and that Canada had to aid the troops who had already sacrificed themselves in the trenches. Despite the rather unspectacular and all too worn points made in his speech, Macdonell concluded his remarks with a imperialist's vision of Canada that could only come to pass if Canada pulled her full weight in the war. He envisaged Canada as the bridge between the Anglo-Saxon peoples of Britain and America: "Let us preserve our country intact, but far more important still, let us preserve the honour and respect of our neighbours ... so that we may be considered worthy to take our place side by side with the Old Country and the country to the south, and play our part in whatever may be the ultimate destiny of the great English-speaking nations of the world."[117] Such sentiments resembled the opinions of some Canadian imperialists of the time[118] and marked a growing awareness of Canada's stature, fighting as an ally. Whether Macdonell expressed the opinions of the majority of Toronto's Catholics is hard to say, especially considering the strong support among middle- and working-class Catholics in the city for the Liberal Party. What is certain, however, is that his words were not unique, given the response of the press, the clergy, and leading laymen; moreover, the fact that he represented a significant body of Catholic voters in South Toronto argues that such views were not inimical to some of the city's Catholics.

Individual, clerical, and press support for conscription among Catholics was augmented by the active participation of a number of Catholic voluntary associations and societies. James P. Murray, president of the influential Catholic Truth Society, swung the weight of his group behind conscription.[119] More important; the Catholic Mutual Benefit Association, one of the largest male insurance and fraternal associations in Canada, openly supported conscription. In their bilingual monthly newspaper, *The Canadian*, F.J. Curran, the grand president, encouraged members to register for service in view of the "very serious turn the war has taken" on the Western Front. "I most readily accept the suggestion," Curran announced, "that we should call – and I do now call – upon the members of our association to do all in their power, individually and collectively, to make registration of Canada's manpower an efficient means and valuable aid to the civil and military authorities in the discharge of their patriotic duties."[120] In addition to Curran's instructions to CMBA members, their official organ also included a pro-conscription speech, demanding reinforcement of the overseas forces, the mobilization of labour at home, and the production of food for Britain. For these laymen the emphasis on the war as a British imperial endeavour had shifted to an understanding of it as a national effort in defence of freedom and the values of civilization.

Not all English-speaking Catholics marched to the sound of the same drummer on the conscription issue. The *Record*, with its obvious ties to the anti-conscriptionist Laurier, was lukewarm at best, fearing that religious and political conflict would erupt throughout Canada in the wake of conscription.[121] The editors warned opponents of the Military Service Bill that Parliament had every legal right under the revisions to the Militia Act of 1904 to conscript troops for overseas service, and suggested that Canadians protesting the Military Service Act should direct their arguments "against the expediency, wisdom, the prudence or the necessity of such a measure."[122] Sympathetic to the wishes of Quebec, the *Record* suggested a national referendum on the issue[123] as the course of moderation, and insisted that the sovereignty of the Canadian Parliament be maintained against any undue imperial pressure.[124] Given the readership of the *Record* in Toronto and the strong support for the Liberal Party in parts of the archdiocese, it is plausible that some Catholics were at variance with their local leaders on the conscription issue.

In the short term the overt English-speaking Catholic support for conscription made relations between the Archdiocese of Toronto and the Quebec hierarchy icy, to say the least. McNeil and his colleagues were already smarting from the fallout of the bilingual schools debate and the home missions controversy. Conscription was tantamount to poking at an open sore with a hot needle. If not settled, the conscription debate threatened to make irreparable the linguistic and cultural damage already devastating the Canadian Church. Conscious of the high stakes, McNeil made every effort to demonstrate to the public that opposition to the Military Service Act was racially, not religiously motivated. Furthermore, he argued, Quebec's vision of Canada's military obligation to the Empire was basically undeveloped since the nineteenth century. He likened Quebec's position to Sir Charles Tupper's dated attitude that Canada contributed to the Empire's wars through production and nothing else. Simply, McNeil asked English Canadians for moderation and understanding in dealing with Canadians of non-British origin.[125] The *Record* and the *Register* echoed these sympathies, although both papers condemned the disloyalty shown by certain "hooligans" in Quebec, as well as some nationalist megalomaniacs whom, they felt, did not represent the majority of Québécois.[126]

As he mapped out a plan of moderation in the secular press, Mc-Neil began a concerted effort to bring French Canadians to a better understanding of the English Canadian position and the possibilities for compromise. In a move strikingly in tune with the *bonne entente* movement of the period, McNeil was invited by *La Presse* of Montreal to write a series of articles to help bring Québécois and Ontarians closer.[127] Since hostilities within the Church were rooted in the bilingual schools affair in Ontario, McNeil concentrated his article on removing this as a barrier to unity. He regarded the issue as more the problem of a lack of co-ordination between Catholic groups in 1909–10 than as actual racial animosity, adding that English-speaking Catholics in Ontario had greater sympathy towards their francophone co-religionists than was realized. He reminded French Canadians that the "mutual ill will" between Catholics in the Ottawa Valley was not typical of the rest of the province, where "the great mass of the English-speaking Catholics throughout Ontario do not share these feelings."[128] His article, which appeared in April 1918, won critical acclaim from both English and French Canadians, especially for his appeal for Christian unity in a time of Canadian crisis.[129] While the racial animosity in the Church was not entirely removed, McNeil had at least attempted to better relations in the Church in spite of conscription.

The Union election of December 1917, however, had severely tested the fragile entente between English-speaking Protestants and Catholics that dated from the earliest days of the war. The Unionist Conservatives and "turncoat" Liberals often failed to make a distinction between the protest of certain Catholic groups to conscription and the English-speaking Catholic position in Toronto. Some in the Union coalition considered the Church to be an enemy of the government, and thereby precipitated the last federal election campaign in Canadian history in which anti-Catholicism had a prominent role.[130] Given the plethora of ethnic subcultures and political subgroups within the Canadian Church, it is not surprising that the official Church attempted to maintain a neutral position during the election. Despite opposition in Quebec, the Ottawa Valley, and some parts of the west, many English-speaking Catholic leaders supported the Union government, including McNeil, Bishop Michael Fallon of London, Bishop James Morrison of Antigonish, and Bishop John T. McNally of Calgary.[131] That voters in Toronto and Montreal returned their two Catholic Tory-Unionist candidates, A.C. Macdonell and C.J. Doherty respectively, indicates a display of support for the Unionists, despite the anti-Catholicism of some of the party's candidates.[132]

Both the *Register* and the *Record* navigated the electoral storm with great awkwardness. The *Register* in particular was caught between refuting Unionist anti-Catholicism and distancing itself from the anti-war feeling in Quebec, while trying to be charitable in refusing to adhere fully to Fallon's appeal to Catholics to turn the other cheek and vote Unionist. Given these motives, the *Register* was without hope that many Catholics, so insulted by bigotry, could vote for Unionists, if at all: "Can we expect that every Catholic voter in Canada will be of such heroic and Christian mould that he will turn the other cheek when he is smitten? Do politicians think they can conduct a 'vile and indefensible anti-Catholic propaganda' and alienate no Catholics?"[133] In light of the fierce anti-Catholic diatribes from Horatio Hocken and Newton Wesley Rowell, among others, the Catholic press construed the Unionist campaign as a major insult to the English-speaking Catholic war effort, and editors were bitter that they were caught in the crossfire in Canada's ongoing war of races. Editors were not alone; Father Arthur O'Leary of St Joseph's parish was stunned by the "selfishness and hypocrisy" evident in the campaign. Had local non-Catholics forgotten how "the Archbishop and clergy of Toronto have been second to none in our sincere loyalty" or how "our Churches have emptied themselves of young men overseas"?[134] Clergy and laymen could only shake their heads in disbelief.

The sectarian tension evident in the conscription election, however, did not linger in Toronto. In fact, except for an outburst of bigotry in nearby Guelph, when local extremists raided the Jesuit novitiate looking for slackers,[135] Torontonians appear to have been able to pick up the debris left in the wake of the election and reconstruct the denominational entente that had been created in 1914. Within months of the election Catholics in the city had reason to celebrate the fact that joint projects between themselves and local Protestants had stimulated good relations between the Christian churches in the closing stages of the war. It appeared that the last perquisite of becoming truly Canadian, a modicum of acceptance by the host Protestant community, might be closer at hand than formerly realized.

Once again Neil McNeil tried his hand at consensus building. When local papers attacked the Pope for being pro-German, McNeil prepared a pamphlet, *The Pope and the War*, and ordered it read from the pulpit of every church in the archdiocese. Father James B. Dollard of St Monica's Church went so far as to read it to convalescing soldiers at the Davisville Hospital.[136] The general response to McNeil's pamphlet was positive; even the *Globe* admitted, after months of editorializing to the contrary, that the Pope was neutral.[137] Letters of support from Protestants and Catholics across Canada poured into McNeil's office, and orders for hundreds of pamphlets were filled.

The success of *The Pope and the War*, however, paled in comparison to the ecumenical campaign for Catholic Army Huts. Canadian Catholic chaplains in England and France had lobbied government and Church authorities for recreational clubs that could provide Catholic men with a "safe" alternative to the facilities operated by the oft-proselytizing YMCA.[138] In 1917 Father J.J. O'Gorman, a battle-scarred padre in the CEF, and the Knights of Columbus founded the Army Huts in order to serve better the religious, recreational, and lodging needs of Catholic servicemen overseas. The Knights were no strangers to soldier-aid programs, having pledged as early as 1915 to help in the rehabilitation of veterans.[139] The proposed huts, whether in England or at the front, were intended to provide two basic functions: "chapels for Catholic soldiers and recreation huts for all soldiers, irrespective of creed."[140] In addition to these practical concerns, the official historians of the Catholic huts, writing immediately after the war, saw deeper patriotic motivations behind the campaign. The Knights recognized that the huts were indisputable symbols of Catholic loyalty:

Even under the stress of the Great War, the Catholics of Canada, loyal and patriotic though they were, did not immediately react to the great crisis as a united body ... The Knights of Columbus sensed danger in all this. They felt that in the years to come we would be denied much of the credit that was justly our due and, as Canadians first, they realized that no sacrifice was too great for the defence of liberty and that without some attempt at national cohesion, much of our well-meant (but ill-directed) efforts would be made in vain.[141]

In this sense the Army hut project became a tangible testament to Catholic patriotism – a visible reminder to Protestant Canada that Catholics had a stake in this war and the values for which it was being fought.

In late 1917 the first Catholic Army Huts fund-raising campaign was initiated nationwide, with the hope of raising $100,000 for the building and equipping of huts in the English training camps and at Canadian bases in France. In Ontario the target amount to be raised was $50,000, of which one-fifth was to be contributed by Catholics from Toronto.[142] The campaign was managed by J.J. O'Gorman of Ottawa and J.L. Murray, the state deputy for the Knights in Ontario; these directors felt that the campaign should be restricted to canvassing individual Catholic dioceses. By 1918, however, it had become clear that the huts could not flourish by Catholic support alone.[143] In Toronto as in other centres, Catholic and Protestant leaders and secular and religious voluntary associations co-operated in a second major campaign in the autumn of 1918. In an unprecedented community effort, Catholic associations, the YMCA, the Salvation Army, the Great War Veterans Association, the Rotary Club, Kiwanis Club, and Masonic organizations joined together to raise money for the huts. Mc-Neil marshalled the clergy behind the plan, with the express intent that all parishes "do their share."[144] A notice was read in all Catholic parishes instructing them to work in full co-operation with persons and groups from all denominations who had pledged their assistance. In addition, the *Catholic Register* carried full and half-page advertisements for the campaign throughout September with sketches of soldiers superimposed over slogans such as "Won't you give as freely of your money as he has of his blood?"[145]

Throughout the campaign, emphasis was placed upon tolerance and the fact that all denominations were fighting shoulder to shoulder for the same cause. In a speech prior to the campaign Colonel Dinnick, the Protestant chairman of the drive, commented:

They [American visitors] said: In Toronto there is something on the faces of the people; there is a different expression, that we do not see in our towns ... I do not catch any of this wonderful spirit, but then this campaign came along and it just seemed to be the opportunity to demonstrate to Toronto, to Canada and to the United States that we have got this true spirit of sacrifice and service. Sacrifice without bigotry or prejudice, and service of broad-mindedness ... This campaign is going to go down in history as most unique. Perhaps as the turning point in the bringing together of the people no matter what religion or creed they profess. Money is not the objective, $150,000 – a mere nothing ... we are in it because we believe it is a righteous cause.[146]

Similarly, on 1 October 1918 a meeting at Massey Hall, described as "the largest gathering ever assembled in that auditorium," heard the message of patriotism and tolerance from numerous campaign workers, including Bishop Fallon of London.[147] For the neophyte observer, who might have witnessed the election campaign just months before, the scenes of sectarian co-operation for Catholic Army Huts defied Toronto's torrid reputation as the Belfast of North America.

Nevertheless, in the first week of October fund-raisers, working in small teams composed of equal numbers of Catholics and Protestants, canvassed each district of Toronto. In the end, Torontonians of all denominations contributed $210,000 to Catholic Army Huts,[148] accounting for 40 per cent of the provincial total and over one-fifth of the Canadian grand total. McNeil quickly responded to this generosity by writing to all the non-Catholic campaign directors, thanking them for their effort and expressing his hope that "its effects are enduring in better mutual understanding and good will, not merely in Toronto but wherever Toronto's influence reaches."[149] While the campaign meant coffee, billiards, beer,[150] clean beds, and the Mass for soldiers in Europe, it meant much more to Catholics left at home. The fund-raising drive for war huts gave Toronto's Catholics hope that perhaps the public bigotry of the past could be left there, and that they could be unhampered in their aspirations to live as full and equal citizens.

In 1922 Joseph Lawrence Murray, state deputy of the Knights of Columbus and executive director of the Huts, clearly expressed such hope. At a Knights' banquet in Ottawa he reminisced about the unity achieved during the Army Hut campaign, referring to it as a prerequisite for Canadian development. For Murray it was a call to all people in the Dominion:

a people who will be one in their Canadianism, a people who would be justly proud of their freedom, proud of their civilization, aye, and proud of their Christianity – a people who will be mutually respectful of one another's rights, liberties and beliefs, a people intent about their individual patriotism as they are of the national prosperity, in a word a people, who will ever have as their motto those golden, glorious words: – "For God and Country."[151]

This spirit of co-operation offered precedents for future interdenominational co-operation in Toronto, including McNeil's participation in the Federal War Service Commission of the Churches in Canada, an organization that assisted in the demobilization process. Under FWSCCC auspices, Catholics and Protestants dealt with matters of civil re-establishment of veterans and the provision of employment and land settlement to returning soldiers.[152] In the heat of war, and after three decades of nurturing, their loyalties and sense of citizenship had crystallized for Toronto's English-speaking Catholics. When the aging Irish pastor of St Mary's parish, Father Michael Moyna, dared to remove the British Ensign from the coffin of a dead veteran during the funeral Mass, McNeil, with the approval of the Apostolic Delegate, censured him.[153]

The Great War marked the culmination of decades of change within the English-speaking Catholic community in Toronto. For a century the Protestant majority in the city had questioned Catholic loyalty to the Empire and its values. The First World War offered

Catholics a chance to prove such questions groundless. In fact, their response to imperialism and the war effort illustrates how remarkably they had adapted to life in Canada, and how well their ideas complemented those of the Protestant community around them. By 1918 Catholics, like other English-speaking Canadians, had articulated clearly that the war was being fought not just for Empire but also for liberty and Christianity. Canada's contributions and losses hammered home the lesson that this struggle was Canada's, demanding all that she could give. It is not surprising, therefore, that many English-speaking Catholics in the city supported registration and conscription as measures necessary to winning the war.

Support for the war effort was most pronounced among the laity. The numbers of volunteers indicate the high level of patriotic feeling among white- and blue-collar Catholics of Toronto. For Archbishop Neil McNeil this strong participation was the perfect demonstration of Catholic loyalty to the cause. The sacrifices made by Will Pennylegion, Frank Gorman, John Feeney, Charles Wehrle, Elmer Wadham, and many others marked the coming of age of the city's English-speaking Catholic population. These men paid the price of citizenship with their lives; others paid through Victory Bonds, war loans, sock drives, rationing, taxation, and unemployment. Many others painfully experienced the mutilation of their families: Berta Wadham lost her favourite son; Mary Cooney lost one son and saw two more wounded; and a widowed Mary Pennylegion faced the challenge of raising two infants by herself.

The Great War ushered in a new era for Toronto's English-speaking Catholics. The Irish nationalism that had characterized Toronto's Catholic community in the 1860s and 1870s had passed away, and new generations of Canadian-born Irish, Scottish, and English Catholics, tempered by the war experience, now regarded Canada as the primary focus of their political and cultural loyalties. If the Great War had alienated Quebec and some immigrant Catholics from the mainstream of Canadian society, it had a centripetal effect on English-speaking members of the Church, allying them more closely with other English Canadians. No other image conveys this sense of Catholic Canadianism better than the scene at St Peter's Church, on the first Sunday after the Armistice, when an evening prayer service for peace was held. The Union Jack and Canadian Ensign hung in the sanctuary. The ancient hymn *Salve Regina* echoed through the church. After prayers and a sermon of thanksgiving, the choir stood and sang heartily "O Canada."[154]

Conclusion

There was a time, in nineteenth-century Toronto, when the strains of that "dear old tune" would have been heard whenever Catholics of Irish birth or descent met in social gatherings. Children in schools, directed by "Sister," would mass at the front of the class and cheerfully sing "The Wearing of the Green." No concert would be complete without a rendition of that hymn, either by a special ensemble or by all those gathered in the hall. Meetings of religious, fraternal, or insurance societies might adjourn with a short prayer and the anthem of loyalty to the "motherland." Its words attested to one's kinship with the old sod, and its theme was one of no surrender to the conqueror or the oppressor. Its tune, now made famous by the Irish Rovers in their ballad "The Orange and the Green," was used by Fenians as they "Crossed their Pikes at Midnight," and by their enemies in the Orange Lodge, who celebrated "The Sash My Father Wore." In and of itself "The Wearing of the Green" was an expression of the bitterness and division that had gnawed at Ireland since the sixteenth century.

In the Toronto of the 1920s the strains of that old song were rarely heard. The significance of the banning of the shamrock was lost on new generations of English-speaking Catholics who were pursuing a very different way of life from their Irish and Scottish forbearers. Children would be hard pressed to know who the United Irishman Napper Tandy was, let alone be seduced to take him "by the hand" as the old tune suggested they do. Perhaps the most telling sign of change among English-speaking Catholics in the city was that, between 1914 and 1919, they had donned "England's cruel red," and had done so enthusiastically and with distinction. The invocation of the old tune to wear the green proudly was supplanted by the pride they now expressed in the little red patch they wore on their government-issue khaki. By war's end the "waning" of the green had progressed so far that English-speaking Catholics appeared to have learned a new tune, steeped in the traditions and lore of their new Canadian home. Ask a child in 1922 what might be sung at the upcoming school concert at St Helen's School, and she might well answer "The Maple Leaf Forever."

The old-timers who had seen the troubles surrounding William O'Brien's visit in 1887 might not have recognized the changes that had overcome their English-speaking Catholic community in Toronto by the 1920s. When asked by an outsider where the Catholic ghetto was, the old-timer might reminisce a little about Cabbagetown, but then confess that English-speaking Catholics were found in every neighbourhood of the city. If the stranger probed further, he or she might also learn that the absence of "Paddies" on city road crews and work details was no accident. These Catholics were now as likely to be found in a lawyer's office, classroom, or bank as planing a window lattice, washing laundry, or blasting iron pigs. By the 1920s it was clear that better education, higher levels of literacy, greater encouragement from the clergy and lay leaders, and the adoption of the gospel of work and success had provoked a white-collar revolution among Toronto's English-speaking Catholics. The result was a Catholic community that was no longer stuck in the rut of the ancient stereotype of the semi-literate, lazy, and low-skilled Paddy. In the three decades leading up to the 1920s Catholics had found that they could aspire to better jobs, better living conditions, ownership of their own homes, and, in many cases, a less congested and more peaceful life in the suburbs of Toronto. Living as they did, they became less distinguishable from their Protestant neighbours.

The changes experienced by the city's English-speaking Catholics in their social and economic life were accompanied by a transformation in their spiritual life. Their leaders – bishops, priests, and religious – expressed a sincere desire that Catholics not isolate themselves from the world around them but instead engage in building the nation and become more conspicuous in the corridors of power. Bishops Walsh, McEvay, and McNeil were anxious that English-speaking Catholics work in greater harmony with their Protestant neighbours and build a better Canada. A new generation of locally born and educated priests – men like John R. Teefy – echoed these sentiments, encouraging Catholics to embrace higher education and to bring a Catholic presence to all facets of their life in the city. The sisters in the schools also had a hand in directing young minds not only to the mysteries of the faith but also to the necessities of being fine, upstanding citizens of Canada. Such professed loyalty, it was thought, would yield a bountiful harvest for Catholics: prominence, equality, respectability, and perhaps additional educational rights.

The message, spiritual and civil, was not lost on the Catholic laity of the city, who were already thinking along the same lines. Catholic piety, religious practice, and moral behaviour became acclimatized to a "Canadian" environment. Pilgrimages and the celebration of Catholic saints and heroes – Francis McSpirrit, the Huronia martyrs, or Father Della Vagna – assumed a distinctly Canadian flavour. Choirs and musical liturgies often reflected local styles and a gender inclusiveness that became increasingly unpopular among many integrists and purists at the Vatican. When challenged by a punctilious bishop on their liturgical practices, parish customs, and social behaviour, Toronto's English-speaking Catholics resisted changes to a Catholic faith-life that they had cultivated in a decidedly Protestant milieu. Many laypersons even resisted the archbishop's strict adherence to canonical laws regarding marriage.

In their resistance, laypersons acknowledged that the survival of Catholicism in an non-Catholic environment required adaptations and changes to the cultural forms through which Catholic truths were expressed. Far from abandoning Catholicism, as leaders like Archbishop Denis O'Connor feared, local Catholics were confident that even in mixed marriages the Catholic party would prevail. The continued practice of contracting interfaith marriages in the city was a testament to the clergy and laity's opinion that the strict enforcement of canon law would only damage the chances of Catholic survival in a Protestant city. Catholics were confident that local Protestants might be attracted to the "true" faith.

Lay initiative was also evident in the way lay voluntary associations were reconstituted under Church auspices. Sodalities, fraternities, and mutual benefit societies offered a context for men and women to share their faith, seek much-needed insurance benefits, and demonstrate their Canadian patriotism in a robust fashion. The old-timer would not have recognized these new societies – the Knights of Columbus, the Catholic Women's League, or the Holy Name Society – as vessels of Irish ethnicity. But the old-timer would be forced to admit that the men and women who gathered under the banners of these societies shared two things: joy in their Catholic faith, and pride in their Canadian citizenship. Catholics in such societies as Holy Name became so confident that their faith had a vital role to play in the moral uplift of Canadian society that they enthusiastically took to the streets of Toronto in gargantuan parades. Unmolested as they marched, English-speaking Catholics laid claim to the streets of the alleged Belfast of North America.

If asked how these men and women had embraced these values, the old-timer might scratch his head and then point his finger at the local separate schools. There, it might be claimed, the religious orders and a growing cadre of professional lay teachers were ensuring that new generations of Catholics were thoroughly indoctrinated in the faith, prepared to embrace a wide spectrum of careers in the secular world, and moulded into loyal and upstanding citizens of Canada and the Empire. If one needed proof of how Catholic schools had evolved, the old-timer might pull out a copy of the *Canadian Catholic Reader* (1899), replete with its patriotic and religious selections. He might also snort that there was too much "jingo" trash in it, and not nearly enough poetry and prose that might kindle a flicker of love for dear old Ireland. The schools had changed; they were emerging as Canadianized nurseries of piety, progress, and patriotism.

Just as the old-timer had watched Irish associations and an Irish flavour in schools wane after 1887, he had also witnessed the decline and demise of the Irish Catholic press. Directed by the increasingly indigenized clerical and lay leadership in Toronto, such papers as the *Catholic Register, Catholic Weekly Review,* and *Catholic Record* reflected the waning concern for Irish news and Irish issues in the face of questions more immediate to Catholics in Canada. Even when the Home Rule question was revived after 1916, the Catholic press intellectualized the fight for self-government in terms of Wilsonian principles as distinguished from mounting passionate pleas for the "motherland." "Canada first" became the watchword of Toronto's Catholic weeklies. The old-timer might lament the growing interest manifest in the pages of the *Register* and *Record* in Canadian issues, history, politics, travel, and home-grown personalities. Catholic journalists demonstrated an appreciation for the Crown, Canada's traditions of liberty and opportunity, Canadian responsibilities to the Empire, and Canada's emergence as a great country. Catholic newspapers, although varying in the intensity of their imperialist fervour, envisaged an autonomous Canada within the context of a British Empire of equal partners. In part this Canadianization of Toronto's Catholic press was accompanied by invitations to Catholics everywhere to participate in national affairs and stand for public office. It was felt that Catholic participation in the Canadian political arena was concomitant with full and equal citizenship.

In this spirit many of Toronto's young English-speaking Catholic men and women enlisted in the Canadian Expeditionary Force and Medical Corps after 1914. Although the old-timer might admit that, because of Britain's oppression of Ireland, he was indifferent to the war effort, he would be hard pressed to say that young Catholics in the city felt the same way. Encouraged by clerics and lay leaders, nurtured on a patriotic diet in the schools, and channelled in their enlistment by their clubs and fraternal associations, young English-speaking Catholics like Elmer Wadham and his chums seemed more than willing to respond to Canada's call with a hearty "Ready, aye, ready." Indeed, some were thrust into the service out of peer pressure, dire economic straits, and a lust for adventure, but such motivations cannot account for the timing and intensity of Catholic recruitment. For many it was the opportunity to set the record straight for the rest of Canada: to prove that English-speaking Catholics were loyal and devoted citizens of Canada and the Empire.

This transformation of the English-speaking Catholic community would be most evident in the way they related to their French Canadian and "new Canadian" co-religionists. The arrival of Catholic immigrants prompted the host English-speaking Catholic community to ensure that these "strange" peoples of the faith stayed in the Church and, at the same time, were taught the value of Canadian citizenship. In the process, English-speaking Catholics were forced to come to terms with their own identity as English-speaking Canadians and, having embraced this idea, were ready to mould the Catholic immigrant in their own image if necessary. The fact that, by 1910, English-speaking Catholics were insisting that English be the medium through which immigrants be exposed to Canadian society exacerbated a turf war between English- and French-speaking Catholics that had been festering since the late 1880s. Thus, while English-speaking Catholics, many of whom looked to Toronto for leadership, extended their influence throughout Ontario and western Canada, the Canadian church was torn asunder along linguistic lines. To many French Canadian Catholics, their cousins in Toronto were little more than "les orangistes" in disguise. Increasingly it appeared that language had replaced religion as the primary focus of loyalty in Canada.

The social and religious changes experienced by Toronto's English-speaking Catholics certainly raise perplexing questions for some Catholic observers, both past and present. An ardent ultramontane might ask, as the French Canadians and Denis O'Connor did, whether all this change merely diluted the Catholicism of English-speaking Catholics in the city. A case could be made that the social, economic, marital, and political integration experienced by Catholics in Toronto essentially destroyed the fibre of the faith in the city and ultimately led to a bastardization of the Church. The inquisitor might very well cite the losses to the Church that came as a result of mixed marriages. Catholics fraternized with Protestants – on the shop floor, in political parties, in clubs, and in the marriage bed – and eventually became so like Protestants that they weakened and then lost their faith. The story of the English-speaking Catholics in Toronto may very well be one of the triumph of the "City of Man" over the "City of God."

The response to such a charge is difficult. In order to acclimatize themselves to the rhythms of the non-Catholic culture around them, Catholics did not necessarily need to jettison their faith. English-speaking Catholics in Canada constituted what John Moir once termed a "double minority." In their own Church they were a linguistic minority, while in the country as a whole they were part of a religious minority. Living and surviving as a "double minority" required different strategies from those of other Catholic groups, which often could rely on a close relationship with the state or their weight of numbers to secure their life and health. The clergy, bishops, and lay leaders in Toronto discovered that Catholics could adapt their faith to the cultural contingencies of English Canada without watering down what was essential to the faith. In fact, when quizzed about their liturgies, English-speaking Catholics were forthright in explaining that the character and splendour of their parish liturgies was actually a selling-point to local Protestants, who were seen by many Catholics as potential converts. Far from watering down the faith, by resisting those liturgical changes emanating from Europe local Catholics felt there were far greater benefits to be had for the local Church. Similarly, mixed marriage was seen as the lesser of many evils that could not only arrest some losses suffered by the Church but could ultimately lure non-Catholics into the fold. McNeil and others saw long-term gains for the Church if Catholics participated in the development of their city and country and if they rose in prominence in the community at large. Loyalty, activism, and community leadership could raise the image and respectability levels of the Church immeasurably.

In Toronto, English-speaking Catholics were confronted by the age-old tension inherent in Christian life: how to live in the world yet not be of the world. In response they elected neither to flee from society and live in sealed isolation nor to embrace the world around them uncritically. Instead, they appear to have grown into a healthy engagement of that tension between the sacred and the profane: they would live their lives in the world and, thoroughly imbued with their Catholicism, transform the areas of life that they touched. Events like the Holy Name parade testify to this community's confidence in its faith and the English-speaking Catholic ambition to claim equal citizenship in Toronto. The traveller to Toronto in 1922 would note that much had changed since the visit of William O'Brien thirty-five years before. English-speaking Catholics had now woven themselves into the very fabric of Toronto society, and with it shared some of the assumptions of the communities around them: the myth of the self-made man, cautious anti-Americanism, belief in the primacy of the English language outside of Quebec, love of the Empire, and the vision that Canada would become "His" Dominion. In the process, however, they did not lose sight of the fact that "His" Dominion should be a Catholic one. The old-timer might not have liked the melody, the lyrics, or the choir, but English-speaking Catholics were indeed singing a new song.

Appendices

APPENDIX A

OCCUPATIONAL CATEGORIES OF TORONTO WORKERS, 1850–1900

Unskilled: cab driver, caretaker, carter, dairyman, drover, express man, farmer, gate keeper, housekeeper, huckster, labourer, lamp lighter, mariner sailor, milkman, nursery and seedsman, packer, pedlar, porter, railroad employee, sawyer, seamstress, servant, stuffer, teamster, waiter, warfinger, washerwoman, watchman, whitewasher.

Semi-skilled: apprentice, axemaker, baker, barber, basket maker, blacking maker, blacksmith, boiler maker, brick maker, broom maker, builder,[1] butcher,[2] cabman, carpenter, carriage maker, cook, cooper, cordwainer, dyer, fareman, filemaker, fireman, fisherman, hostler, joiner, mason, mechanic, milliner, motor man, painter, polisher, presser, press man, printer, roofer, rope maker, saw maker, shipwright, signmaker, steam fitter, tallow chandler, tanner, trimmer, turner, upholsterer, wagonmaker, wheelwright, wood worker.

Skilled: armorer, artist, bell hanger, boat builder, book binder, boot maker, brass finisher, brass founder, brewer, bricklayer, cabinet maker, carver, chair maker, chandler, clock or watch maker, coppersmith, cutler, distiller, dressmaker, edge tool maker, engine driver, engraver, finisher, brass founders, founder, gas fitter, gilder, goldsmith, glass cutter, glass stainer, gunsmith, harness maker, land surveyor, lithographer, lock smith, machinist, marble cutter, miller, molder, musician, organ builder, paper hanger, pattern maker, plasterer, plumber, [professional athlete],[3] saddler, shoemaker, silversmith, stone cutter, tailor, telegraph operator, tinsmith, watchmaker, weaver, yardmaster.

Clerical: accountant, assessor, bailiff, bar keeper, bar tender, book keeper, cashier, clerk, collector, commissioner, [conductor],[4] constable, custom collector, [foreman],⁵ forwarder, gaoler, letter carrier, notary public, photographist, policeman, proofreader, salesman, [shipper],⁶ traveller, turnkey.

Business: agent: general and insurance, auctioneer, banker, boardinghouse keeper, bookseller and stationer, broker, cab owner, cattle dealer, chemist or druggist, clothier, confectioner, contractor, fruiterer, furrier, grocer, hatter, hotel keeper, jeweller, jobber, manufacturer, merchant, publisher, shopkeeper, wholesaler.

Professional: architect, attorney, barrister, civil or other engineers, clergy, dentist, editor, medical doctor, professor, solicitor, student, teacher.

Private Means: gentleman, pensioner, retired, unemployed, widow.⁷

Source: Peter G. Goheen, *Victorian Toronto, 1850–1900* (Chicago: University of Chicago, Department of Geography, Research Paper no. 127, 1970), 229–30.

NOTES
1 If not self-employed.
2 If not self-employed.
3 My own addition.
4 My own addition based on required literacy involved in filing reports and collecting money on streetcars.
5 Although often an upwardly mobile skilled worker, the foreman was a representative of management, performed supervisory duties, and frequently filed reports accounting for activity in his section.
6 My own addition based on the literacy involved in keeping shipping ledgers and files.
7 For the purposes of this study, widows and spinsters have been placed in a separate category in order to indicate the changing levels of female household heads.

APPENDIX B

French/foreign names are not included in the calculations except for their percentage of the entire Catholic population within the parish boundaries.

St Helen's Parish

Particular	1890	%	1900	%	1910	%	1920	%
Household head	316		532		571		686	
Home-owners	97	30.7	152	28.6	303	53.1	331	48.3
Householders	200	63.3	380	71.4	268	46.9	355	51.7
Tenants	19	6.0	0	0.0	0	0.0	0	0.0
French name	4	1.3	9	1.6	15	2.6	20	2.9
Foreign name	6	1.9	5	0.9	19	3.3	13	1.9
Children 5–21	494		878		826		847	
Total Persons	1506		2683		2933		3590	
Av. household	4.7		5.2		5.2		5.4	
Professional	4	1.3	3	0.6	6	1.0	10	1.5
Private	10	3.2	5	0.9	0	0.0	4	0.6
Widow/spinster	17	5.4	39	7.3	50	8.8	83	12.1
Business	31	9.8	69	13.0	67	11.7	77	11.2
Clerical	20	6.3	67	12.6	108	18.9	133	19.4
Skilled	43	13.6	79	14.9	83	14.5	97	14.1
Semi-skilled	64	20.2	111	20.8	106	18.6	139	20.3
Unskilled	115	36.4	137	25.8	143	25.1	103	15.0
No data	12	3.8	22	4.1	8	1.4	40	5.8
Total	316	100.0	532	100.0	571	100.0	686	100.0
"Labourers"	76	24.1	65	12.2	48	8.4	54	7.9
All blue collar	222	70.2	327	61.5	332	58.2	339	49.4

Source: CTA, *Assessment Rolls*, 1891, 1901, 1911, 1921.

Our Lady of Lourdes Parish

Particular	1890	%	1900	%	1910	%	1920	%
Household head	104		165		242		372	
Home-owners	38	36.5	49	29.7	95	39.6	142	38.2
Householders	66	63.5	116	70.3	147	60.4	230	71.8
French name	6	5.8	4	2.4	7	2.9	10	2.7
Other foreign	2	1.9	1	0.6	12	5.0	17	4.6
Children 5–21	108		204		267		232	
Total persons	495		788		1275		1868	
Av. household	5.1		4.9		5.4		5.1	
Professional	8	7.7	9	5.4	9	3.7	24	6.5
Private	5	4.8	1	0.6	0	0.0	2	0.5
Widow/spinster	13	12.5	26	15.8	57	23.6	86	23.1
Business	13	12.5	26	15.8	31	12.8	43	11.5
Clerical	26	25.0	49	29.7	53	21.9	75	20.2
Skilled	10	9.6	11	6.7	22	9.1	32	8.6
Semi-skilled	7	6.7	16	9.7	30	12.4	35	9.4
Unskilled	16	15.4	22	13.3	29	12.0	55	14.8
No data	6	5.8	5	3.0	11	4.5	20	5.4
Total	104	100.0	165	100.0	242	100.0	372	100.0
"Labourer"	4	3.8	10	6.1	9	3.7	16	4.3
All blue collar	33	31.7	49	29.7	81	33.5	122	32.8

Source: CTA, *Assessment Rolls*, 1891, 1901, 1911, 1921.

Holy Name Parish

Particular	1910	%	1920	%
Household head	74		364	
Home-owners	46	62.2	255	70.1
Householders	28	37.8	109	29.9
French name	7	2.9	13	3.6
Other foreign	1	1.4	17	4.7
Children 5–21	79		385	
Total persons	327		1760	
Av. household	4.4		4.9	
Professionals	0	0.0	6	1.7
Private	0	0.0	1	0.3
Widow/spinster	4	5.4	35	9.6
Business	6	8.1	39	10.7
Clerical	14	18.9	101	27.8
Skilled	7	9.5	48	13.2
Semi-skilled	19	25.7	66	18.1
Unskilled	23	31.1	58	15.9
No data	1	1.3	10	2.7
Total	74	100.0	364	100.0
"Labourer"	10	13.5	15	4.1
All blue collar	49	66.3	172	47.2

Source: CTA, *Assessment Rolls*, 1891, 1901, 1911, 1921.

APPENDIX C

Social Statistics for St Paul's Parish

Particular	1890	%	1900	%	1910	%	1920	%
Household head	941		947		1024		894	
Anglo-Celts	908	96.5	890	94.0	876	85.5	733	82.0
Home-owners	192	21.1	185	20.8	202	23.1	168	22.9
Householders	716	78.9	705	79.2	674	76.9	565	77.1
French/ethnic[1]	33	3.5	57	6.0	148	14.5	na	na
Professional	4	0.4	4	0.5	2	0.2	6	0.8
Private	21	2.3	2	0.2	0	0.0	1	0.1
Widow/spinster	127	14.0	159	17.9	148	16.9	145	19.8
Business	101	11.1	70	7.9	78	8.9	63	8.6
Clerical	58	6.4	65	7.3	88	10.1	83	11.3
Skilled	94	10.4	116	13.0	95	10.8	67	9.1
Semi-skilled	159	17.5	148	16.6	156	17.8	137	18.7
Unskilled	323	35.6	287	32.2	275	31.4	221	30.2
No data	21	2.3	39	4.4	34	3.9	10	1.4
Total	908	100.0	890	100.0	876	100.0	733	100.0
"Labourer"	197	21.7	158	17.7	146	16.7	81	11.5
All blue collar	576	63.4	551	61.9	526	60.0	425	58.0

Source: CTA, *Assessment Rolls*, 1891, 1901, 1911, 1921.

1 Not included in any calculations.

APPENDIX D

Social Statistics for St Mary's Parish

Particular	1890	%	1900	%	1910	%	1920	%
Households[1]	1054		1148		702		523	
Home-owners	269	25.5	304	26.5	199	28.4	125	23.9
Householders	785	74.5	844	73.5	503	71.6	398	76.1
Total persons	5063		5675		3893		2803	
Av. household	4.8		4.9		5.5		5.4	
Professional	12	1.1	10	0.9	4	0.6	3	0.6
Private	9	0.9	1	0.1	0	0.0	0	0.0
Widow/spinster	142	13.5	183	15.9	129	18.4	99	18.9
Business	118	11.2	88	7.7	65	9.3	35	6.7
Clerical	80	7.6	99	8.6	55	7.8	46	8.8
Skilled	123	11.7	170	14.8	101	14.4	61	11.7
Semi-skilled	166	15.7	172	15.0	114	16.2	95	18.2
Unskilled	348	33.0	360	31.3	211	30.0	167	31.9
No data	56	5.3	65	5.7	23	3.3	17	3.2
Total	1054	100.0	1148	100.0	702	100.0	523	100.0
"Labourers"	223	21.2	206	17.9	120	17.1	106	20.3
Blue-collar	637	60.4	702	61.1	426	60.6	323	61.8

Source: CTA, *Assessment Rolls*, 1891, 1901, 1911, 1921.

1 Only Anglo-Celtic surnames are included here. In 1890, 1,054 of 1,137 (97.3 per cent) of household heads in the parish had Anglo-Celtic surnames. By 1920, only 523 of 813 (64.3 per cent) household heads living within the parish boundaries had Anglo-Celtic surnames.

APPENDIX E

St Paul's Parish, Marriage Partners

	1890	%	1900	%	1910	%	1920	%
PLACE OF BIRTH								
Canada	51	75.0	22	78.6	56	75.7	86	72.9
Ireland	8	11.8	1	3.6	6	8.1	1	0.8
Britain	5	7.3	2	7.1	4	5.4	20	17.0
USA	0	0.0	3	10.7	2	2.7	0	0.0
Other/no data	4	5.9	0	0.0	6	8.1	11	9.3
Total	68		28		74		118	
MARRIAGES	34		14		37		59	
Canadian bride	31	91.2	10	71.4	28	75.7	41	69.5
Both partners Canadian	19	55.9	9	64.3	na	na	33	55.9
Av. age man	26.1		24.7		27.5		26.3	
Av. age woman	23.4		23.7		25.3		23.9	

St Mary's Parish, Marriage Partners

	1890	%	1900	%	1910	%	1920	%
PLACE OF BIRTH								
Canada	46	47.9	50	71.4	83	72.8	37	59.7
Ireland	19	19.8	11	15.7	5	4.4	1	1.6
Britain	0	0.0	0	0.0	7	6.1	13	21.0
USA	0	0.0	0	0.0	0	0.0	0	0.0
Other/no data	31	32.3	9	12.9	19	16.7	11	17.7
Total	96		70		114		62	
MARRIAGES	48		35		57		31	
Canadian bride	24	50.0	27	77.1	41	71.9	18	58.1
Both partners Canadian	16	33.3	19	54.3	34	59.6	15	48.4
Av. age man	31.1		27.6		26.4		29.1	
Av. age woman	25.6		25.7		23.4		25.3	

St Helen's Parish, Marriage Partners

	1890	%	1900	%	1910	%	1920	%
PLACE OF BIRTH								
Canada	20	55.5	25	73.5	21	58.3	54	81.8
Ireland	6	16.7	4	11.8	5	13.9	2	3.1
Britain	8	22.2	1	2.9	4	11.1	9	13.6
USA	1	2.8	4	11.8	0	0.0	0	0.0
Other/no data	1	2.8	0	0.0	6	16.7	1	1.5
Total	36		34		36		66	
MARRIAGES	18		17		18		33	
Canadian bride	10	55.6	11	64.7	10	55.6	29	87.9
Both partners Canadian	10	55.6	9	52.9	9	50.0	21	63.6
Av. age man	26.3		30.7		27.6		30.6	
Av. age woman	23.1		26.9		26.2		26.9	

Our Lady of Lourdes Parish, Marriage Partners

	1890	%	1900	%	1909	%	1920	%
PLACE OF BIRTH								
Canada	5	41.6	6	75.0	32	72.7	51	47.2
Ireland	2	16.7	2	25.0	4	9.1	5	4.6
Britain	3	25.0	0	0.0	5	11.4	6	5.6
USA	2	16.7	0	0.0	1	2.3	6	5.6
Other/no data	0	0.0	0	0.0	2	4.5	40	37.0
Total	12		8		44		108	
MARRIAGES	6		4		22		54	
Canadian bride	2	33.3	3	75.0	16	72.7	25	46.3
Both partners Canadian	2	33.3	2	50.0	13	59.1	16	29.6
Av. age man	26.0		26.3		30.9		na	
Av. age woman	24.0		23.3		28.2		na	

Holy Name Parish, Marriage Partners

	1915	%	1920	%
PLACE OF BIRTH				
Canada	12	60.0	34	63.0
Ireland	1	5.0	0	0.0
Britain	5	25.0	6	11.1
USA	1	5.0	3	5.6
Other/no data	1	5.0	11	20.3
Total	20		54	
MARRIAGES	10		27	
Canadian bride	7	70.0	16	59.3
Both partners Canadian	5	50.0	13	48.1
Av. age man	27.0		28.4	
Av. age woman	24.9		24.1	

Source: ARCAT, Marriage Registers for each parish by years shown.

APPENDIX F

IRISH CATHOLIC OCCUPATIONS, CA 1860

% of total Catholic population

Ward	Prof.	Priv.	Bus.	Cler.	Skl.	ss	Uns.
St David	1.4	6.6	12.8	3.7	12.8	13.1	49.6
St Lawrence	1.4	4.1	36.7	4.6	4.6	21.1	27.5
St James	1.9	11.0	16.4	3.2	18.4	8.9	40.2
St George	1.7	–	29.3	1.7	6.9	5.2	55.2
St Andrews	2.2	7.3	15.9	1.7	8.6	17.7	46.6
St John	2.4	3.9	19.0	1.6	15.7	15.7	41.7
St Patrick	12.2	5.0	–	1.3	11.7	9.5	59.3
Total	3.3	6.6	16.7	2.8	12.1	13.5	45.0
Male only	4.1	0.9	21.0	3.6	15.4	17.0	37.6

Source: ARCAT, Holograph Collection, Jean Jamot, "Census of City Wards," ca early 1860s. Calculations reprinted from Brian P. Clarke, "Piety, Nationalism, and Fraternity: The Rise of Irish Catholic Voluntary Associations in Toronto, 1850–1895," PhD, University of Chicago 1986; with permission.

Key:
Professional	Prof.
Private means	Priv.
Business	Bus.
Clerical	Cler.
Skilled worker	Skl
Semi-skilled	ss
Unskilled	Uns.

APPENDIX G

Parish Residence Linked Decennially

Decade of residence[1]	Number of sedentary household heads by parish					
	St Helen's	%	St Paul's	%	Lourdes	%
1890–1900	93	29.4	180	19.1	32	30.8
1900–10	119	22.4	193	20.4	50	30.3
1910–20	177	31.0	174	17.0	68	28.1
1890–10[2]	32	10.1	64	6.8	19	18.3
1900–20	50	9.4	59	6.2	21	12.7

Source: CTA, *Assessment Rolls*, 1891, 1901, 1911, 1921. All calculations are my own.

1 Those householders or owners who appear in the city assessment within the same parish over a ten-year period. Calculations and percentages are based on the proportion of residents who remained out of all the householders and owners listed in the earlier year. The percentages for 1890–1900, for example, are based on the total number of household heads listed for 1890.

2 The same residents are linked over a twenty-year period.

APPENDIX H

Occupation and Home-ownership Linked Decennially,
St Helen's Parish

Occupational group	Changes in occupation or home-ownership			
	Group in 1890		Same group in 1900	
	Total	Owners	Total	Owners
Professional	–	–	–	–
Private	3	2	1	0
Widow/spinster	3	2	11	7
Business	11	6	11	4
Clerical	9	3	9	5
Skilled	13	7	13	9
Semi-skilled	19	12	21	14
Unskilled	28	14	25	15
None/no data	7	3	2	1
Total	93	49	93	55
Percentage	100	52.7	100	59.1

Occupation and Home-ownership Linked Decennially,
St Helen's Parish (continued)

Occupational group	Changes in occupation or home-ownership			
	Group in 1900		Same group in 1910	
	Total	*Owners*	*Total*	*Owners*
Professional	–	–	1	1
Private	–	–	–	–
Widow/spinster	5	2	3	2
Business	9	5	12	10
Clerical	20	11	21	16
Skilled	19	8	11	7
Semi-skilled	27	11	26	20
Unskilled	34	15	30	20
None/no data	5	3	15	12
Total	*119*	*55*	*119*	*98*
Percentage	*100*	*46.2*	*100*	*82.4*

	Group in 1910		Same group in 1920	
	Total	*Owners*	*Total*	*Owners*
Professional	2	1	3	3
Private	–	–	–	–
Widow/spinster	14	10	22	19
Business	19	13	13	9
Clerical	32	25	38	33
Skilled	29	20	24	19
Semi-skilled	32	22	37	28
Unskilled	47	30	31	21
None/no data	2	2	9	8
Total	*177*	*123*	*177*	*140*
Percentage	*100*	*69.5*	*100*	*79.1*

APPENDIX I

Cost of Food in Toronto, 1891–1920

	Cost in dollars by year		
Item (food)	1891	1914	1920
butter, 1 lb.	.20	.32	–
sack of flour	.90	–	–
rice, 1 lb.	.05	.05	.135
box of biscuits	.25	–	–
salt, 1 lb.	.01	.12	–
eggs, 1 dozen	.16	.25	.85
potatoes, 1 bag	1.40	1.25	7.00
bananas, 1 dozen	.25	–	–
chicken, whole	.50	–	–
steak, 1 lb.	.15	.25	–
bacon, 1 lb.	–	.22	.38
loin veal chop, 1 lb.	.15	–	.28
pork, 1 lb.	.10	.18	–
beef chuck, 1 lb.	.10	.16	.20
cabbage, 1	.08	–	–
celery, 1	.08	–	–
milk, 1 quart	.07	.10	.95
cream, 1 quart	.20	–	.45
lager, 1 keg	1.20	–	–
tea, 1 lb.	.50	.35	.53
bread, 1 loaf	.065	.08	.17
pearl barley, 1 lb.	.075	–	–
prunes, 1 lb.	.10	.12	.185
lard, 1 lb.	.125	.18	–
coffee, 1 lb.	–	.25	.40
cheese, 1 lb.	–	.20	.31
sugar, 1 lb.	–	.045	.147

Source: ARCAT, John Walsh Papers, Invoices, Our Lady of Lourdes Parish, 1891–93; Lourdes Parish box, Accounts; *Labour Gazette* 14 (May 1914): 1328–9; *Catholic Register*, 27 May 1920.

APPENDIX J

Property Values and the Hastings Report, 1911:
A Comparison of Four Parishes

Particular[1]	St Paul		St Mary		St Helen	Holy Name
Property value in slum zone[2]	$1,069.45		$1,214.21		–	–
Property value outside zone	$1,415.61		$1,621.92		–	–
Average value of property[3]	$1,215.60		$1,385.42		$1,698.50	$1,207.59
Households in slum zone	588	(58.4%)	389	(55.4%)	–	–
Households outside zone	436	(42.6%)	313	(44.6%)	–	–

Source: Charles Hastings, MD, *Report of the Medical Health Officer Dealing with the Recent Investigation of Slum Conditions in Toronto* (Toronto, 1911); CTA, *Assessment Rolls*, 1911. Calculations are mine.

1 Large hotels operated or owned by Catholics have been eliminated from this study.
2 This indicates property located within the areas defined as slums by Dr Charles Hastings. Property values are calculated by adding the assessed value of the buildings and land, and dividing the total assessed value of Catholic real estate in the zone by the number of Catholic households.
3 This average value is calculated by combining all Catholic properties, both inside and outside the slum zones.

APPENDIX K

St Paul's Parish

Occupational group	1890	%	1900	%	1910	%	1920	%
Professional	1	0.5	3	1.6	2	1.0	0	0.0
Private	10	5.2	2	1.1	0	0.0	1	0.6
Widow/spinster	31	16.1	44	23.8	42	20.8	41	24.4
Business	35	18.2	22	11.9	31	15.3	19	11.3
Clerical	12	6.3	10	5.4	20	9.9	20	11.9
Skilled	17	8.9	14	7.6	22	10.9	15	8.9
Semi-skilled	21	10.9	33	17.8	35	17.3	29	17.3
Unskilled	52	27.1	39	21.1	39	19.3	35	20.8
None/no data	13	6.8	18	9.7	11	5.5	8	4.8
Total owners	192	100.0	185	100.0	202	100.0	168	100.0

St Mary's Parish

Occupational group	1890	%	1900	%	1910	%	1920	%
Professional	0	0.0	4	1.3	2	1.0	4	3.2
Private	7	2.6	1	0.3	0	0.0	0	0.0
Widow/spinster	45	16.7	52	17.1	51	25.6	30	24.0
Business	35	13.0	30	9.9	17	8.5	9	7.2
Clerical	20	7.4	35	11.5	19	9.6	15	12.0
Skilled	38	14.1	46	15.1	33	16.6	17	13.6
Semi-skilled	37	13.8	29	9.6	23	11.6	15	12.0
Unskilled	65	24.2	75	24.7	46	23.1	23	18.4
None/no data	22	8.2	32	10.5	8	4.0	12	9.6
Total owners	269	100.0	304	100.0	199	100.0	125	100.0

St Helen's Parish

Occupational group	1890	%	1900	%	1910	%	1920	%
Professional	3	3.1	1	0.7	2	0.7	6	1.8
Private	6	6.2	1	0.7	0	0.0	0	0.0
Widow/spinster	5	5.2	16	10.5	31	10.2	40	12.1
Business	12	12.4	24	15.8	40	13.2	32	9.7
Clerical	6	6.2	20	13.2	61	20.2	72	21.8
Skilled	11	11.3	18	11.8	42	13.8	41	12.4
Semi-skilled	24	24.7	35	23.0	57	18.8	65	19.6
Unskilled	27	27.8	30	19.7	64	21.1	49	14.8
None/no data	3	3.1	7	4.6	6	2.0	26	7.8
Total owners	97	100.0	152	100.0	303	100.0	331	100.0

Our Lady of Lourdes Parish

Occupational group	1890	%	1900	%	1910	%	1920	%
Professional	4	10.6	6	12.2	4	4.2	13	9.2
Private	3	7.9	1	2.0	0	0.0	2	1.4
Widow/spinster	7	18.4	7	14.3	17	18.0	36	25.4
Business	7	18.4	14	28.6	23	24.2	23	16.2
Clerical	7	18.4	9	18.4	23	24.2	30	21.1
Skilled	1	2.6	1	2.0	6	6.3	7	4.9
Semi-skilled	3	7.9	6	12.2	8	8.4	9	6.3
Unskilled	3	7.9	2	4.1	8	8.4	10	7.0
None/no data	3	7.9	3	6.2	6	6.3	12	8.5
Total owners	38	100.0	49	100.0	95	100.0	142	100.0

Holy Name Parish

Occupational group	1910	%	1920	%
Professional	0	0.0	5	2.0
Private	0	0.0	1	0.4
Widow/spinster	2	4.4	22	8.6
Business	5	10.9	24	9.4
Clerical	9	19.5	73	28.6
Skilled	5	10.9	30	11.8
Semi-skilled	10	21.7	53	20.8
Unskilled	14	30.4	40	15.7
None/no data	1	2.2	7	2.7
Total owners	46	100.0	255	100.0

Source: CTA, *Assessment Rolls*, 1891, 1901, 1911, 1921. All calculations are mine.

APPENDIX L

Parish Migration, Home-ownership, and Occupation, 1910–1920

Occupation of migrants	In Parish of Origin, 1910	%	At Holy Name, 1920	%
Professional	0	0	0	0
Private	0	0	0	0
Widow/spinster	0	0	0	0
Business	2	10	2	10
Clerical	7	35	12	60
Skilled	2	10	2	10
Semi-skilled	4	20	2	10
Unskilled	5	25	2	10
None/no data	0	0	0	0
Home-owners	5	25	17	85
Householders	15	75	3	15

Source: CTA, *Assessment Rolls*, 1911, 1921. All calculations are mine.

Notes

AAH   Archives of the Archdiocese of Halifax

AAK   Archives of the Archdiocese of Kingston

AAM   Archives of the Archdiocese of Montreal

AAO   Archives of the Archdiocese of Ottawa

AASB   Archives of the Archdiocese of St Boniface

ACSJ   Archives of the Congregation of St Joseph, Toronto

ADA   Archives of the Diocese of Antigonish

ADAC   Archives of the Diocese of Alexandria-Cornwall

ADC   Archives of the Diocese of Calgary

ADH   Archives of the Diocese of Hamilton

ADL   Archives of the Diocese of London

ADP   Archives of the Diocese of Peterborough

ADPK   Archives of the Diocese of Pembroke

AMSSB   Archives of the Metropolitan Separate School Board

AMTBE   Archives of the Metropolitan Toronto Board of Education

AO   Archives of Ontario

ARCAT   Archives of the Roman Catholic Archdiocese of Toronto

ASAS   Archives of St Augustine's Seminary

ASFM   Archives of the Scarboro Foreign Missions Society

ASFXU   Archives of St Francis Xavier University

ASJUCP   Archives of the Society of Jesus, Upper Canada Province

ASMC   Archives of St Michael's College

ASV-DAC	Archivio Segreto Vaticano, Apostolic Delegate, Canada
BIA	Beaton Institute Archives, Cape Breton
CCES	Catholic Church Extension Society
CCHA	Canadian Catholic Historical Association
CHA	Canadian Historical Association
CRCCF	Centre de recherche en civilisation canadienne-française, Ottawa
CTA	City of Toronto Archives
CWR	*Catholic Weekly Review*
DCB	*Dictionary of Canadian Biography*
GABF	General Archives of the Basilian Fathers
IC	*Irish Canadian*
NA	National Archives, Canada
NPRC	National Personnel Records Centre, Ottawa
Record	*Catholic Record*
Register	*Catholic Register*
UCCA	United Church of Canada Archives
UTA	Archives of the University of Toronto

INTRODUCTION

1 The term "Belfast of North America" appears more frequently in current histories of Toronto and Canadian religious life. Several early references can be found in the *Canadian Freeman*, 15 Jan. 1868, and *IC*, 18 Mar. 1868. See also Gregory Kealey, "The Orange Order in Toronto: Religious Riot and the Working Class," in Kealey and Peter Warrian, eds., *Essays in Canadian Working Class History* (Toronto: McClelland and Stewart 1976), 13.

2 Gerald J. Stortz, "An Irish Radical in a Tory Town: William O'Brien in Toronto, 1887," *Eire-Ireland* 19 (Winter 1984): 35–58; and Brian P. Clarke, *Piety and Nationalism: Lay Voluntary Associations and the Creation of an Irish Catholic Community in Toronto, 1850–1895* (Montreal and Kingston: McGill-Queen's University Press 1993), 240–2.

3 ARCAT, John Joseph Lynch Papers, Frank Smith to Archbishop John Joseph Lynch, 9 May 1887. See also Eugene O'Keefe to Lynch, 4 May 1887, and James G. Moylan to Lynch, 30 Apr. 1887. Clerical support of Lynch was required according to ARCAT, Lynch Papers, Father J.F. McBride to Father O'Reilly, 30 Apr. 1887, Lynch Letterbook LB05.149. See also *CWR*, 5 and 19 May 1887; ARCAT, Lynch Papers, telegram from Lynch to Archbishop Croke of Thurles, Ireland, 20 Apr. 1887.

4 Clarke, *Piety and Nationalism*, 224–53.

5 *IC*, 30 June 1887.

6 Terrence Murphy and Gerald Stortz, eds., *Creed and Culture: The Place of English-speaking Catholics in Canadian Society, 1750–1830* (Montreal and Kingston: McGill-Queen's University Press 1993); Clarke, *Piety and Nationalism*; Roberto Perin, *Rome in Canada: The Vatican and Canadian Affairs at the End of the Victorian Age* (Toronto: University of Toronto Press 1990); Mark G. McGowan and Brian P. Clarke, eds., *Catholics at the Gathering Place: Historical Essays on the Archdiocese of Toronto, 1841–1991* (Toronto: CCHA 1993).

7 Mark G. McGowan, "Life outside the Cloister: Catholics and the Writing of Canadian History, 1983–1996," *Historical Studies* 63 (1997): 123–33.

8 Four significant theses on the Irish Catholics of Toronto are Michael Cottrell, "Irish Catholic Political Leadership in Toronto, 1855–1882: A Study of Ethnic Politics," PhD, University of Saskatchewan 1988; Jeanne Ruth Merifield Beck, "Henry Somerville and the Development of Catholic Social Thought in Canada: Somerville's Role in the Archdiocese of Toronto, 1915–1943," PhD, McMaster University 1977; Murray W. Nicolson, "The Catholic Church and the Irish of Victorian Toronto," PhD, University of Guelph 1980; and Gerald J. Stortz, "John Joseph Lynch, Archbishop of Toronto: A Biographical Study of Religious Political and Social Commitment," PhD, University of Guelph 1980.

9 Donald H. Akenson, *Small Differences: Irish Catholics and Irish Protestants 1815–1922* (Kingston and Montreal: McGill-Queen's University Press 1988); Akenson, *The Irish in Ontario: A Study in Rural History* (Kingston and Montreal: McGill-Queen's University Press 1985); Cecil Houston and William Smyth, *Irish Emigration and Canadian Settlement: Patterns, Links and Letters* (Toronto: University of Toronto Press 1990); Terrence Murphy and Cyril J. Byrne, eds., *Religion and Identity: The Experience of Irish and Scottish Catholics in Atlantic Canada* (St John's: Jesperson Press 1987); Robert O'Driscoll and Lorna Reynolds, eds., *The Untold Story: The Irish in Canada*, 2 vols. (Toronto: Celtic Arts of Canada 1988); Marianne MacLean, *The People of Glengarry: Highlanders in Transition, 1745–1820* (Montreal and Kingston: McGill-Queen's University Press 1991); Raymond MacLean, *Bishop John Cameron: Piety and Politics* (Antigonish: Casket Printing and Publishing Company 1991); J.E. Rea, *Bishop Alexander Macdonell and the Politics of Upper Canada* (Toronto: Ontario Historical Society 1974); A.A. Johnston, *A History of the Roman Catholic Church in Eastern Nova Scotia*, 2 vols. (Toronto: Longmans 1960; repr. Academic Press 1970).

10 Akenson, *The Irish in Ontario*, intro.

11 Murray W. Nicolson, "The Irish Experience in Ontario: Rural or Urban?" *Urban History Review/Revue d'histoire urbaine* 14 (June 1985): 39–40.

12 Robert Choquette, "The Archdiocese of Toronto and Its Metropolitan Influence in Ontario," in McGowan and Clarke, *Catholics at the Gathering*

Place, 297–312; Choquette, *Language and Religion: A History of English-French Conflict in Ontario* (Ottawa: University of Ottawa Press 1975); Choquette, *L'Eglise catholique dans l'Ontario Français du dix-neuvieme siècle* (Ottawa: University of Ottawa Press 1984); Choquette, *La Foi gardienne de la langue en Ontario, 1900–1950* (Montreal: Bellarmin 1987).

13 John Zucchi, "The Catholic Church and the Italian Immigrant in Canada, 1880–1920: A Comparison between Ultramontane Montreal and Hibernian Toronto," in *Scalabrini Tra Vecchio E Nuovo Mondo* (Roma: Centro Studi Emigrazione 1989), 491–508.

14 Murray W. Nicolson, "The Other Toronto: Irish Catholics in a Victorian City, 1850–1900," in Gilbert Stelter and Allan Artibise, eds., *The Canadian City: Essays in Urban and Social History*, rev. ed. (Ottawa: Carleton University Press 1984), 341–2.

15 Cecil J. Houston and William J. Smyth, *The Sash Canada Wore: A Historical Geography of the Orange Order in Canada* (Toronto: University of Toronto Press 1980); Gregory S. Kealey, "The Orange Order in Toronto: Religious Riot and the Working Class," in Kealey and Warrian, eds., *Essays in Canadian Working Class History*, 13–34; and Kealey, "Orangemen and the Corporation: The Politics of Class during the Union of the Canadas," in Victor L. Russell, ed., *Forging a Consensus: Historical Essays on Toronto* (Toronto: University of Toronto Press 1984), 41–86.

16 R.H. Tawney, *Religion and the Rise of Capitalism* (Middlesex: Penguin 1948); Kenneth Duncan, "Irish Famine Immigration and the Social Structure of Canada West," *Canadian Review of Sociology and Anthropology* 2 (1965): 19–40; Nicolson, "The Irish Experience in Ontario: Rural or Urban?"; H. Clare Pentland, *Labour and Capital in Canada 1650–1860*, ed. and intro. Paul Phillips (Toronto: James Lorimer & Co. 1981).

17 ASV-DAC, vol. 91.7/1, Rev. Pellegrino Stagni to Cardinal De Lai, Consistorial Congregation, Rome, 7964, 19 Sept. 1911; and Murray W. Nicolson, "Ecclesiastical Metropolitanism and the Evolution of the Catholic Archdiocese of Toronto," *Histoire sociale – Social History* 15 (May 1982): 129–56.

18 Kenneth Duncan, H. Clare Pentland, and Murray Nicolson hold to an urban model for studying the Irish in the Canadian context. This school likens the Canadian experience of the Irish to the American – the Irish were an urban peasantry, living in ghettos, lacking education, job skills, and financial security. Revisionists – Donald Akenson, Glenn Lockwood, Bruce Elliott, and Julian Gwyn – argue that the Irish experience in Canada was rural and dissimilar in almost every way from the life of Irish immigrants in the United States. These scholars also argue that the Canadian Irish were mostly Protestants, and maintain that Irish Catholics did much better economically than has previously been thought. Kenneth Duncan, "Irish Famine Immigration," 19–40; Nicolson, "The Irish Experience in Ontario: Rural or Urban?"; Pentland, *Labour and Capital in Can-*

ada 1650–1860, 96–129; Akenson, *The Irish in Ontario*, 1–47; Bruce S. Elliott, *Irish Migrants in the Canadas: A New Approach* (Kingston and Montreal: McGill-Queen's University Press 1988); Glenn J. Lockwood, "Success and the Doubtful Image of Irish Immigrants in Upper Canada: The Case of Montague Township, 1820–1900," in O'Driscoll and Reynolds, eds., *The Untold Story*, 319–41; Lockwood, *Montague: A Social History of an Irish Ontario Township, 1783–1980* (Smiths Falls: Corporation of Montague 1980); Julian Gwyn, "The Irish in the Napanee River Valley: Camden East Township, 1851–1881," in *The Untold Story*, 355–77.

19 Robert Craig Brown and Ramsay Cook, *Canada 1896–1921: A Nation Transformed* (Toronto: McClelland and Stewart 1974), 2; John Herd Thompson with Allen Seager, *Canada 1922–1939: Decades of Discord* (Toronto: McClelland and Stewart 1985), 3–4; M.C. Urquhart and K.A.H. Buckley, eds., *Historical Statistics of Canada* (Toronto: Macmillan 1965), 5, 14.

20 Kerby A. Miller, *Emigrants and Exiles: Ireland and the Irish Exodus to North America* (New York: Oxford University Press 1985), 469; Cecil J. Houston and William Smyth, "Irish Emigrants to Canada: Whence They Came," in O'Driscoll and Reynolds, ed., *The Untold Story*, 27–35; Helen I. Cowan, *British Immigration before Confederation*, Historical Booklet No. 22 (Ottawa: CHA 1978), 19.

21 Wsevolod W. Isajiw, *Definitions of Ethnicity* (Toronto: Multicultural History Society of Ontario 1979), 4–6, 12–15, 19–22.

22 *IC*, 2 Oct. 1890.

23 Joseph P. O'Grady, *How the Irish Became Americans* (New York: Twayne Publishers 1973), 137, 138–41, 158; Lawrence J. McCaffrey, *The Irish Diaspora in America* (Bloomington: Indiana University Press 1976), 136–7, 152.

24 Edward Kelly, *The Story of St Paul's Parish* (Toronto: private 1922), 173–5; ARCAT, Holograph Collection, 22.79, Address from the Clergy of the Diocese of Toronto to the Most Reverend Neil McNeil, D.D., Episcopal Silver Jubilee, 20 Oct. 1920.

25 Milton A. Gordon, *Assimilation in American Life: The Role of Race, Religion, and National Origins* (New York: Oxford University Press 1964), 70–1.

26 John S. Moir, "The Problem of Double Minority: Some Reflections on the Development of the English-speaking Catholic Church in Canada in the Nineteenth Century," *Histoire sociale-Social History* 4 (Apr. 1971): 53–67.

27 Ibid., 38–40.

28 Carl Berger, *The Sense of Power: Studies in the Ideas of Canadian Imperialism, 1867–1914* (Toronto: University of Toronto Press 1970), 9.

29 Paula Kane, *Separatism and Subculture: Boston Catholicism 1900–1920* (Chapel Hill: University of North Carolina Press 1994).

30 Miller, *Emigrants and Exiles*, 3–10, 235–53, 327.

31 Nicolson, "The Catholic Church and the Irish in Victorian Toronto"; and Stortz, "John Joseph Lynch, Archbishop of Toronto."

32 Michael Kraus, *The Writing of American History* (Norman: University of Oklahoma Press 1968), 366. See also Gene Wise, "The Contemporary Crisis in Intellectual History Studies," *Clio* 5 (Jan. 1975): 55–69; and Robert Skotheim, review of *New Directions in American Intellectual History* by Paul Conkin, in *William and Mary Quarterly* 37 (Apr. 1980): 314–18.

33 Robert Harney, *Toronto: Canada's New Cosmopolite* (Toronto: Multicultural History Society of Ontario 1981), 12. In this article the late Robert Harney stated: "Ethnicity is affected by the rate of immigration, the prejudice a group encounters, the strength and commitment of the group's cultural leadership, and the ways in which the group fits the economic, and now psychic, multicultural needs of the city."

34 Nicolson, "The Irish in Ontario," passim.

33 *Register*, 18 May 1893.

CHAPTER ONE

1 William Perkins Bull, *From Macdonnell to McGuigan* (Toronto: Perkins Bull Foundation 1939), 278. "I come to Toronto, beside Lake Ontario, among the barbaric people, God bless us" was written by Armand de Charbonnel, the second Roman Catholic bishop of Toronto.

2 Joy Parr, "The Welcome and the Wake: Attitudes in Canada West toward the Irish Famine Migration," *Ontario History* 66 (June 1974): 101–14; Cecil Houston and William Smyth, *Irish Emigration and Canadian Settlement: Pattern, Links, and Letters* (Toronto: University of Toronto Press 1990); Gilbert Tucker, "The Famine Immigration to Canada, 1847," *American Historical Review* 36 (1931): 533–49.

3 Glenn Lockwood, "Eastern Upper Canadian Perceptions of Irish Immigrants, 1824–1868," PhD, University of Ottawa 1988.

4 Toronto *Globe*, 11 Feb. 1858. NA, MG 26 A, Sir John A. Macdonald Papers, vol. 188 (1872), "The History of the Roman Catholics in Canada ... ," 78665–86.

5 Murray Nicolson, "Peasants in an Urban Society: The Irish Catholics in Victorian Toronto," in Robert Harney, ed., *Gathering Place, Peoples and Neighbourhoods of Toronto, 1834–1945* (Toronto: Multicultural History Society of Ontario 1985), 47, 53–4, 58–9, 68; Nicolson, "Irish Tridentine Catholicism in Victorian Toronto: Vessel for Ethno-religious Persistence," CCHA, *Study Sessions* 50 (1983): 423, 425, 435. Gerald J. Stortz, "Archbishop John Joseph Lynch of Toronto: Twenty-eight Years of Commitment," CCHA, *Study Sessions* 49 (1982): 9; Barry Dyster, "Captain Bob and the Noble Ward," in Victor Russell, ed., *Forging a Consensus: Historical Essays on Toronto* (Toronto: University of Toronto Press 1984), 333–4; Peter Goheen, *Victorian Toronto, 1850–1900* (Chicago: Research Paper No. 127, Department of Geography, University of Chicago 1970), 151–3; Michael Katz, "Irish and Canadian Catholics: A Comparison," *Canadian Social*

History Project, Interim Report No. 4 (Toronto: Ontario Institute for Studies in Education 1972), 26, 35; James Michael Pitsula, "The Relief of Poverty in Toronto, 1880–1930," PhD, York University 1979, 96; Kenneth Duncan, "Irish Famine Migration and the Social Structure of Canada West," *Canadian Journal of Sociology and Anthropology* 2 (1965): 19–40. D.S. Shea, "Irish Immigrant Adjustment to Toronto, 1840–1860," CCHA, *Study Sessions* 39 (1972): 59, challenges Katz's notion that poverty was the fault of the Irish themselves.

6 Donald H. Akenson, "Whatever Happened to the Irish?" in D.H. Akenson, ed., *Canadian Papers in Rural History* 3 (1982): 204–56.

7 Murray Nicolson, "The Irish Experience in Ontario: Rural or Urban?" *Urban History Review* 14 (June 1985): 37–45; Jeanne Beck, "Contrasting Approaches to Social Action: Henry Somerville the Educator and Catherine de Hueck, the Activist," in McGowan and Clarke, *Catholics at the "Gathering Place,"* 213–31.

8 Goheen, *Victorian Toronto*, 213.

9 Milton Gordon, *Assimilation and American Life: The Role of Race, Religion and National Origins* (New York: Oxford University Press 1964), 13.

10 Brian P. Clarke, *Piety and Nationalism: Lay Voluntary Associations and the Creation of an Irish-Catholic Community in Toronto, 1850–1895* (Montreal and Kingston: McGill-Queen's University Press 1993), 22–3.

11 The prevailing influence of environmental factors as the principal vehicles of social mobility is asserted by D.S. Shea, "The Irish Immigrant Adjustment," 59; Donald Akenson, *The Irish in Ontario, A Study in Rural History* (Montreal and Kingston: McGill-Queens University Press 1984), 45–6; and Gordon Darroch and Michael Ornstein, "Ethnicity and Occupational Structure in Canada in 1871: The Vertical Mosaic in Historical Perspective," *Canadian Historical Review* 61 (Sept. 1980): 314–15, 329. Clarke, *Piety and Nationalism*, 19–28, demonstrates that Catholics were occupationally diversified as early as the 1860s, and takes Nicolson to task for his "overworked stereotype of Irish Catholics as drunken brawlers."

12 J.M.S. Careless, "The Emergence of Cabbagetown in Victorian Toronto," in Robert Harney, ed., *Gathering Place*, 32–40.

13 St Paul's, St Michael's Cathedral, St Patrick's, and St Mary's parishes constitute inner-city parishes for the purposes of this study. The parish boundaries of all four fall between the Don River on the east, Dovercourt Avenue on the west, Lake Ontario on the south and College and Carlton Streets on the north. Boundary parishes include Our Lady of Lourdes, St Basil's, and St Francis of Assisi. All three are located north of College and Carlton Streets, between the Don and Dovercourt Avenue but south of the Belt Line.

14 Richard Harris, "The Unremarked Homeownership Boom in Toronto," *Histoire sociale-Social History* 18 (Nov. 1985): 433–7.

15 Tucker, "The Famine Immigration," 540.

16 *Census of Canada*, 1841–91.

17 Ibid., 1891, 1: 282–3; *CWR*, 4 June 1892; Stortz, "Archbishop John Joseph Lynch of Toronto," 9; Goheen, *Victorian Toronto 1850–1890*, 65–6, 75–6; *Register*, 30 Mar. 1899.

18 *Census of Canada*, 1921, 1: 593–5.

19 *Register*, 6 Feb. 1919. The same report shows that the highest Protestant increase for the same period was the Church of England, with 5.6 per cent growth.

20 Houston and Smyth, *Irish Emigration and Settlement*, 67–78.

21 Murray Nicolson, "The Other Toronto: Irish Catholics in a Victorian City, 1850–1900," in Gilbert Stelter and Allan Artibise, eds., *The Canadian City: Essays in Urban and Social History*, rev. ed. (Ottawa: Carleton University Press 1984), 341–2. Donald Akenson, *The Irish in Ontario: A Study in Rural History* (Montreal and Kingston: McGill-Queen's University Press 1984), 24–5. For an indication of the rising number of English- and Scottish-born Catholics consult ARCAT, Marriage Registers, St Mary's, St Helen's, St Paul's, St Patrick's, St Peter's, Holy Name, and Our Lady of Lourdes Parishes, 1910, 1915, and 1920. The period between 1900 and 1920 witnessed increased British immigration, although Irish newcomers were poorly represented. See Michael Piva, *The Condition of the Working Class in Toronto, 1900–1921* (Ottawa: University of Ottawa Press 1979), 8–10, app. E.

22 Clermont Trudelle et Pierre Fortier, *La Paroisse du Sacre Coeur* (Toronto: La Société d'histoire de Toronto 1987), 22; Enrico Carlson-Cumbo, "Impediments to the Harvest: The Limits of Methodist Proselytization of Toronto's Italian Immigrants," in McGowan and Clarke, *Catholics at the "Gathering Place,"* 176.

23 St Paul's (1822), St Michael's (1848), St Mary's (1852), St Basil's (1856), and St Patrick's (1861).

24 Hugh Garner, *Cabbagetown* (Toronto 1950); Nicolson, "Peasants in an Urban Society," 63; Nicolson, "The Irish Experience in Ontario," 39, 41.

25 Careless, "The Emergence of Cabbagetown," 32, 34.

26 Goheen, *Victorian Toronto*, 186.

27 *Census of Canada*, 1891, 1:282–3. In St David's Ward, which roughly corresponded to Cabbagetown, it is interesting to note that fewer than one in five persons (18.29 per cent) were Catholics. The total number of Catholics in St George's and St Andrew's was 4,761 (21.8 per cent).

28 Goheen, *Victorian Toronto*, 210.

29 Ibid., 220; This corresponds more closely with Shea, "The Irish Immigrant Adjustment," 4; Donald Akenson, *The Irish in Ontario*, 44–7.

30 This is conceded by Nicolson, "The Irish Experience in Ontario," 39; *Register*, 1 Mar. 1917.

31 Margaret McFarlane, *St Joseph's Parish, Toronto, 1878–1968* (Toronto 1968), 3–6.

32 ARCAT, St Joseph's Parish box, Rev. J.A. McDonagh, "The Story of A Mother Parish" (1933); Peter Goheen, "Currents of Change in Toronto, 1850–1900," in Gilbert Stelter and Alan Artibise, eds., *The Canadian City: Essays in Urban History* (Toronto: Macmillan, Carleton Library Series No. 109, 1979), 87. Goheen's map of the street railway indicates that these two eastern parishes were just off the Queen Street railway line.

33 J.R. Teefy, ed., *Jubilee Volume: The Archdiocese of Toronto, 1842–1892* (Toronto: George T. Dixon 1892), 278–308, and ARCAT, James McGuigan Papers, Boundaries box.

34 Teefy, *Jubilee Volume*, 293; Teefy estimates the number of families at 1,000 in 1890, whereas the city assessment rolls reveal 941 Roman Catholic household heads in the area. The difference could be explained by the fact that households in which the husband was Protestant but the wife Catholic would have been listed as public school supporters, with no indication whatsoever of Catholics living in the home. CTA, Assessment Rolls, St David's Ward, 1891. The figure for 1905 is derived from GABF, Denis O'Connor Papers, box I, file 3, Draft of Quinquennial Report to Rome, Dec. 1905.

35 CTA, Assessment Rolls, 1901, 1911, 1921, Wards 1 and 2. In 1900, 19 of 45 household heads on Power Street were Catholic, whereas in 1921 the figure stood at 21 of 45, excluding the church itself and the House of Providence.

36 Ibid., St Thomas and St David's wards, 1891; Teefy, *Jubilee Volume*, 302; Arthur Kelly, *100 Years, Our Lady of Lourdes Church* (Toronto: Our Lady of Lourdes Parish 1986), 12; John Ross Robertson, *Landmarks of Toronto* (Toronto: J. Ross Robertson 1904), 328–32.

37 CTA, Assessment Rolls, St David's, St James's, and St Paul's wards, 1891; Ward 2, div. 2 and 3, 1901; Ward 2, div. 3 and 4, and Ward 3, div. 6, 1911; and Ward 2, div. 3 and 4, and Ward 3, div. 7, 1921.

38 CWR, 18 June 1887.

39 ARCAT, Spiritual and Financial Statistics, St Michael's Cathedral and St Patrick's Church, 1887, Holograph Collection, 14.51, Cathedral Envelope Collection, 1892–94.

40 Stephen Speisman, *The Jews of Toronto: A History to 1937* (Toronto: McClelland and Stewart 1979), 82–92; Nicolson, "The Other Toronto," 343. For a useful study of transience in the Grange area of St Patrick's parish, see Dennis O'Neil, "Residential Transience in Grange Park, Toronto, 1891–1900," *Canadian Social History Project*, Interim Report No. 6 (Apr. 1974): 65–76.

41 Cynthia Patterson, et al., *Bloor-Dufferin in Pictures*, Local History Handbook No. 5 (Toronto: Toronto Public Library Board 1986), 16, 26.

42 CTA, Assessment Rolls, St Alban's, St Stephen's, and St Mark's wards, 1891; ARCAT, Spiritual and Financial Statistics, St Helen's and St Cecilia's parishes, 1922; Goheen, *Victorian Toronto*, 126, 186–8.

43 Herbert Gans, *The Urban Villagers* (New York: Free Press 1962), examines the formation of small urban villages of rural immigrants and their re-creation of kinship ties in an urban context. In the case of English-speaking Catholics in Toronto, small street clusters of Catholics are occasionally noticeable, but there is no evidence indicating that these clusters were based on any sense of kinship.

44 CTA, Assessment Rolls, St Mark's Ward, 1891; Ward 6, div. 2, 1901, 1911, 1921. In 1900, 40 household heads on St Claren's Avenue were Catholic, and by 1921 the figure reached 84.

45 Robert Harney and J. Vincenza Scarpaci, eds., *Little Italies in North America* (Toronto: Multicultural History Society of Ontario 1981).

46 Michael Piva, *The Conditions of the Working Class in Toronto, 1900–1921* (Ottawa: University of Ottawa Press 1979), 12–13.

47 ARCAT, Holy Name Parish box, *Holy Name Parish, 1913–1927* (1927), 2–3. See Appendix L.

48 ARCAT, Spiritual and Financial Statistics, 1922.

49 The boundaries were under dispute for much of the parish's early history. Father James O'Donnell of St Ann's parish, out of which Holy Name was carved, was alarmed by the loss of some of his own parishioners, who, after the division, preferred the new parish because of its proximity to their homes. ARCAT, Holy Name Parish Papers, R.H. Lacour to McNeil, 17 Apr. 1914; James C. Forman, Commissioner of Assessment, to Father M.D. Whelan, 9 Nov. 1912; Father Michael Cline to Father Kernahan, 5 Oct. 1914; and Michael Cline to Monsignor M.D. Whelan, 18 Feb. 1915; St Joseph's Parish Papers, Father Arthur O'Leary to Archbishop McNeil, 15 Dec. 1919, 16 Oct. 1916.

50 ARCAT, Holy Name Parish Papers, Parishioners represented by R.H. Lacour to Archbishop Neil McNeil, 17 Apr. 1914.

51 CTA, Assessment Rolls, Ward 1, divs. 4–6, 1921.

52 ARCAT, Holy Name Parish Papers, *Holy Name Parish, 1913–1927*, 13.

53 French Canadians and other Catholics had increased by 400 per cent. CTA, Assessment Rolls, St David's Ward, 1891; Wards 1 and 2, 1901, 1911, 1921. See Appendix C.

54 Ibid., St Andrew's, St George's, and St Patrick's Wards, 1891; Ward 4, divs. 1 and 2, 1901, 1911, 1921; Ward 5, divs. 1–3, 1901, 1911, 1921. See Appendix D.

55 ARCAT, Marriage Registers, St Paul's, St Mary's, St Helen's, Our Lady of Lourdes, Holy Name, St Patrick's, and St Peter's parishes, 1890, 1900, 1910, 1920. See Appendix E. The registers frequently contain data on the birthplaces of both brides and grooms, but since canon law stipulated that marriages were to take place in the home parish of the bride, only the place of nativity of the bride was used in these figures. As a rule, the registers do not indicate the parish of origin of the groom.

56 Nicolson, "The Irish Experience in Ontario," 39, 41; Nicolson refines his
   argument in "The Other Toronto," 343, when he claims that there were
   no solidly Irish ghettos from 1850 to 1900, although concentrations did
   occur because of the affordability of real estate, proximity to the workplace, and the need of Irish Catholics to band together for security in
   Protestant Toronto. Frequent movings and the creation of Irish Catholic
   enclaves eventually led to a "ghetto of the mind." Similar treatments of
   the urbanization of Irish Catholics are found in Oscar Handlin, *Boston's
   Immigrants: A Study in Acculturation*, rev. ed. (New York: Atheneum
   1968); Lynn H. Lees, *Exiles of Erin: Irish Migrants in Victorian London* (Ithaca: Cornell University Press 1979); Dennis Clark, *The Irish in Philadelphia: Ten Generations of Urban Experience* (Philadelphia: Temple University
   Press 1973); and Stephen Thernstrom, *The Other Bostonians: Poverty and
   Progress in The American Metropolis, 1880–1970* (Cambridge: Harvard University Press 1973). Nicolson's position is substantiated in the
   nineteenth-century Canadian context by Gerald Stortz, "John Joseph
   Lynch," 9; Paul Romney, "A Struggle for Authority," in Russell, ed., *Forging a Consensus* (Toronto: University of Toronto Press 1984), 11; Kenneth
   Duncan, "Irish Famine Immigration," 23–4. In *Victorian Toronto*, 151, Goheen acknowledges some sharp distinctions between Catholics and the
   rest of the population for the 1870s.
57 Murray Nicolson, "Peasants in an Urban Society," 53; Nicolson, "The
   Catholic Church and the Irish in Victorian Toronto," PhD, University of
   Guelph 1980, chap. 9 passim; Shea, "The Irish Immigrant Adjustment,"
   59; Duncan, "Irish Famine Immigration," 20–2, 33; Goheen, *Victorian Toronto*, 151; Katz, "Irish and Canadian Catholics," 26, 33, 36; Katz, *The People of Hamilton, Canada West: Family and Class in a Mid-Nineteenth Century
   City* (Cambridge, Mass.: Harvard University Press 1975), 61–4;
   C.J. Houston and W.J. Smyth, "The Irish Abroad: Better Questions
   through a Better Source, the Canadian Census," *Irish Geographer* 13
   (1980): 10; Paul Romney, "A Struggle for Authority," 11. For material on
   industrialization and the creation of a capitalist labour market, see Gregory Kealey, *Toronto Workers Respond to Industrial Capitalism, 1867–1892*
   (Toronto: University of Toronto Press 1980), 3–5, 18–34; Peter Goheen,
   "Currents of Change in Toronto, 1850–1900," 60–6; H. Clare Pentland,
   Labour and Capital in Canada (Toronto: James Lorimer 1981), 104–6, 145–8;
   Jacob Spelt, *Urban Development in South Central Ontario* (Ansem, The
   Netherlands: Van Gorcum 1955), 71–2, 81–92, 100–8, 114–20.
58 Pitsula, "The Relief of Poverty in Toronto," 96.
59 ARCAT, Holographs 3.19 and 20.64, Census of the Diocese, ca 1860 and
   ca 1869–71. All calculations are from Clarke, *Piety and Nationalism*, 19. See
   Appendix F.
60 Houston and Smyth, "The Irish Abroad," 10.

61 Darroch and Ornstein, "Ethnicity and Occupational Structure in Canada in 1871," 329; Darroch and Ornstein, "Ethnicity and Class, Transitions over a Decade: Ontario 1861–1871," CHA, *Historical Papers* (1984): 115–16; in direct contrast to this type of research see Pentland, *Labour and Capital in Canada, 1650–1860,* and John Porter, *The Vertical Mosaic: An Analysis of Social Class and Power in Canada* (Toronto: University of Toronto Press 1965).

62 Goheen, *Victorian Toronto,* 213–20.

63 *Register,* 18 Oct. 1900.

64 Ibid., 16 Feb. 1905, 28 Feb. 1908, 27 July 1911.

65 Ibid., 14 Nov. 1912; ARCAT, McNeil Papers, Owen Finn to McNeil, 9 Mar. 1914, and *Register,* 26 Feb. 1914, regarding workmen's compensation. McNeil made known his support for organized labour when he addressed the International Convention of Bricklayers, Masons, and Plasters, *Register,* 20 Jan. 1916.

66 *Register,* 20 Mar. 1918; see also 23 Dec. 1915, 20 Jan. 1916, 12 Oct. 1916, 31 Jan. 1918, 28 Feb. 1918, 4 Apr. 1918, 25 Apr. 1918; Jeanne Beck, "Henry Somerville and Social Reform: His Contribution to Canadian Catholic Social Thought," CCHA, *Study Sessions* 42 (1975): 93–4, 100–2.

67 Kathleen McGovern, IBVM, *Something More than Ordinary* (Richmond Hill: I Team Publishers 1989); Elizabeth M. Smyth, "The Lessons of Religion and Science: The Congregation of the Sisters of St Joseph and St Joseph's Academy, Toronto, 1854–1911," PhD, Ontario Institute for Studies in Education 1989; Lawrence K. Shook, *Catholic Post-Secondary Education in Canada, A History* (Toronto: University of Toronto Press 1971).

68 These five parishes were selected on the basis of their size, age, location – whether inner-city or suburban – prestige in the Catholic community, and recognized economic standing. Collectively the sample accounts for 52.7 per cent of Catholics in 1890; 57.5 per cent in 1900; 31.2 per cent in 1910; and 32.7 per cent in 1920. See Appendices B–D. While it is clear that there was occupational diversification among Catholics, the assessment rolls have limited value in determining class and occupation of Catholics other than household heads. Assessment records rarely offer the occupations of adult tenants or family members residing with the owner or leaseholder of a house. Consequently, the occupations of women, unless widows or spinsters, boarders, and labouring adolescents and young adults cannot be ascertained. Only when the census data for 1911 and 1921 are declassified will scholars have a more complete picture of occupational alignment among Toronto's Catholics. Until then the analysis of household heads, although fallible, will have to suffice as the best available evidence.

69 Piva, *The Condition of the Working Class in Toronto,* 30–5.

70 See Appendices A–F. Clarke, *Piety and Nationalism*, 18–19.

71 Katz, *The People of Hamilton*, 42–51, 309–11; see Appendices G–H.

72 See Appendices B, G, and H.

73 Appendix L. A sample of twenty families who migrated from St Paul's and Our Lady of Lourdes parishes to Holy Name Parish from 1910 to 1920 shows six household heads (30 per cent) who had changed occupations within their classification. In three of these cases the men had visibly bettered their occupational description in terms of duties and level of education required: Francis Boylan moved from lineman to clerk; Blandford Green moved from waiter to manager; and Francis Coles moved from clerk to accountant.

74 Clarke, *Piety and Nationalism*, 24, 76–8. Substantially nothing is mentioned about Catholic working women in Murray Nicolson's "Women in the Irish Catholic Family," *Polyphony* 8, nos. 1–2 (1986): 9–12. Piva, *The Condition of the Working Class in Toronto*, 39–40.

75 *Register*, 6 Mar. 1899.

76 Ibid., 16 Mar. 1899.

77 ARCAT, Register of Marriages, St Helen's Parish, 1920.

78 MSSBA, Roman Catholic Separate School Board Minutes, 1885–91, 1891–1900, 1900–12, 1913–21.

Years	Laywomen
1885–91	12
1891–1900	7
1900–12	43
1913–21	89

79 *Register*, 25 Oct. 1900.

80 ARCAT, McNeil Papers, *Diocesan Bulletin* 1 (Nov. 1913); *Register*, 12 Sept. 1918, 5 June 1919, and 27 Nov. 1919.

81 Gregory Kealey, "Orangemen and the Corporation," in Victor Russell, ed., *Forging a Consensus*, 67–70, 72; Nicholas Rogers, "Serving Toronto the Good," in Russell, ed., *Forging a Consensus*, 120; Kealey, *Toronto Workers Respond to Industrial Capitalism*, 113; Cecil J. Houston and William J. Smyth, *The Sash Canada Wore: A Historical Geography of the Orange Order in Canada* (Toronto: University of Toronto Press 1980), 159; and Nicolson, "The Catholic Church and the Irish in Victorian Toronto," 25, 451. *Register*, 29 Oct. 1903.

82 CTA, Annual Reports of the Chief Constable (Toronto: Carswell Co. Printers 1907), 26, 31–53; (1911), 29–55; (1924), 32, 35–93.

Year	All ranks	Catholics	%	% of Canadian-born R.C.s
1907	380	32	8.42	62.5
1911	539	55	10.20	54.54
1924	871	71	8.15	45.07

83 Houston and Smyth, *The Sash Canada Wore*, 158–9.

84 CTA, Assessment Rolls, Ward 6, 1911 and 1921; Ward 2, div. 3, 1901, 1911, 1921; Ward 2, div. 1, Fire Station, 68 Berkeley St, 44. Given that this station was located in a wealthy section of the city, the Orange Order – largely a working-class organization – may not have had a firm hold on the station in which James Hurst served.

85 *Register*, 28 Feb. 1908.

86 William Baker, *Timothy Warren Anglin, 1822–1896: Irish Catholic Canadian* (Toronto: University of Toronto Press 1977), 243.

87 *The Society Blue Book of Toronto, Hamilton and London: A Social Directory* (Toronto: Dau Publishing Company 1906); *The Society Blue Book, Toronto* (New York: Dau's Blue Books Inc. 1920); H.J. Morgan, *Men and Women of Canada* (Toronto: Briggs 1912), 27–8. In 1919 the *Register* complained that Catholic women were far too eager in their aspirations to gain entry into exclusive Protestant social circles (27 Mar.).

88 "Sir Frank Smith," DCB 13:965–8.

89 Nicolson, "The Irish Experience in Ontario," 40: Nicolson's view is challenged by Gregory Kealey and Bryan Palmer, *Dreaming of What Might Be: The Knights of Labor in Ontario, 1880–1900* (Toronto: New Hogtown Press 1987), 116–26, 313–16, 326–9, and their "The Bonds of Unity: The Knights of Labor in Ontario, 1880–1900," *Histoire sociale – Social History* 14 (Nov. 1981): 395, where they state that the Orange and the Green were able to resolve their differences under the aegis of the Knights of Labor, setting them on the road to forming a common working-class culture.

90 *Register*, 18 Jan. 1917. Class division was noted by the *Register*, 5 Jan. 1893, when it asserted: "our people are separated off into distinctly marked classes … There is unfortunately too much of this social separation, and the very best way to bridge over the chasm is by the union and equality that club life gives – equality not of wealth or class, or condition, but a noble equality or friendly rivalry, in talent, industry, energy and skill."

91 ARCAT, John Walsh Papers, copy of letter from Archbishop John Walsh to the Archbishop of Tyre, Secretary of the Propaganda Fide, 1 Dec. 1890. See also CWR, 9 Feb. 1889, which lamented that 3,534 of 5,814 Ontarians seeking public relief in Ontario were Catholic.

92 ARCAT, Walsh Papers, Circular on Blantyre Park, 2 July 1897. Similar reasoning is evident in the founding of other charitable and social services from 1890 through 1920: ARCAT, Letterbook 6, Walsh to J.M. Gilson, Provincial Secretary, 10 Dec. 1894; *Register*, 4 Mar. 1897; ARCAT, Congregation of St Joseph Papers, Archbishop Lynch's circular on St Nicholas' Home for Working Boys, 12 Feb. 1887; P.J. Bench, "Catholic Charities," *Ontario Catholic Yearbook, 1920* (Toronto: Newman Club 1920), 27–34.

93 Robert Craig Brown and Ramsay Cook, *Canada 1896–1921: A Nation Transformed* (Toronto: McClelland and Stewart 1974), 92, 198–201, 323–4.

94 *Register*, 30 Jan. 1908; more general comments about working-class poverty can be found in Piva, *Condition of the Working Class in Toronto*, xii-xiii, 27, 58–9, 171.

95 *Globe*, 20 July 1914; ARCAT, St Vincent de Paul Society Papers, box 1, Correspondence, Conference of St Mary's Report, 1919.

96 Terry Copp, *The Anatomy of Poverty: The Condition of the Working Class in Montreal, 1897–1929* (Toronto: McClelland and Stewart 1974), 30; Piva, *The Condition of the Working Class in Toronto*, 28–59.

97 Piva, *Condition of the Working Class*, 38–40.

98 Ibid., 29. Department of Labour, *Labour Gazette* 1 (Nov. 1900): 98–9. See Appendix I.

99 *Register*, 21 Mar. 1918.

100 Ibid., 7 Feb. 1918, 10 July 1919, 18 Mar. 1920, 27 May 1920.

101 Piva, *Condition of the Working Class*, 30–2. This meant that a blue-collar worker earned an average of $1,053.32 per year while a white-collar could bring home $1,605.33.

102 Ibid., 37.

103 *Census of Canada*, 1921, 3:11; CTA, Assessment Rolls, 1921, Wards 1–6. The following figures indicate the extent of household size and include all assessed residents of the dwelling, which in some cases may have included extended family and borders: St Paul's (5.08), St Mary's (5.27), St Helen's (5.43), Old Lady of Lourdes (5.05), Holy Name (4.90).

104 Piva, *Condition of the Working Class*, 31–2.

105 Ibid., 31, 34.

106 Ibid., 31–2; *Labour Gazette* 15 (1915): 160, 272, 559, 668; 16 (1916): 881, 1084, 1184.

107 Richard Harris, "The Unremarked Homeownership Boom in Toronto," 433–7; *Labour Gazette* 10 (1910): 300, 400, 501.

108 Ten blue-collar jobs were selected using Michael Piva's wage calculations in *Condition of the Working Class*, 31–5. These jobs included plumber, stationary engineer, bricklayer, carpenter, lather, plasterer, brakeman, printer, machinist, and baggageman. Although defined as white collar for this thesis, conductors were included in the sample because Piva was able to indicate wage rates for this group. Disparity is confirmed when the highest-paid blue-collar workers are examined at the parish level. In 1890 St Paul's Parish had only 9.5 per cent of its blue-collar workers in eleven of the highest-paying occupations, whereas St Helen's and St Mary's had just under 20 per cent. By 1921 St Paul's proportion had risen while St Mary's had declined, both reaching a level of nearly 15 per cent of workers in high-pay categories. St Helen's, in a more suburban location, was 6 per cent higher, with fewer members of the blue-collar occupations proportionally within the parish.

109 ARCAT, McNeil Papers, WL 04, 1926; note that this report includes repeat offenders for all parishes.

110 CTA, City Council Minutes, Reports of the Chief Constable, 1890, Appendix C, 36; 1895, Appendix C, 25–8; 1900, Appendix C, 39–42; 1905, Appendix C, 32; 1911, 6; 1924. The aggregate figures are as follows:

Year	Total waifs	Catholics	Catholic percentage
1890	504	138	27.4
1895	717	232	32.4
1899	530	173	32.6
1900	354	124	35.0
1905	635	198	31.2
1911	513	145	28.3
1924	14,531	2,964	20.4

111 Ibid.
112 *Register*, 31 Aug. 1916; see also 12 Dec. 1918, 22 May 1919, 31 July 1919, 7 Aug. 1919. The Boy Scouts were a patriotic boys corps founded by Lord Baden Powell of Gilwell, a hero of the Boer War. Particular emphasis was placed on British imperial values, good citizenship, and loyalty to the Crown. By 1920 St Monica's Parish had their own troop and participated with other non-Catholic troops city-wide. As a mark of their distinctive Catholic flavour, the parish chose the papal colours, yellow and white, as their own: *Register*, 15 Apr. 1920. By 1922 Toronto's Catholics, with active hierarchical support, were eager participants in scouting. ARCAT, McNeil Papers, Catholic Boy Life Council, 1922.
113 ARCAT, McNeil Papers, AE 04.06, Annual Report of the Secretary of the Big Brothers Association of Toronto, 1920.
114 Ibid., AE 04.09, Catholic Boy Life Council Report, 20 Sept. 1922.
115 Goheen, *Victorian Toronto*, 14.
116 Gordon Darroch, "Occupational Structure, Assessed Wealth and Home-owning during Toronto's Early Industrialization, 1861–1899," *Histoire sociale – Social History* 16 (Nov. 1983): 403; Darroch, "Early Industrialization and Inequality in Toronto," *Labour / Le Travailleur* 11 (1983): 8.
117 Harris, "The Unremarked Homeownership Boom in Toronto," 434–6.
118 Chambers, "Rental Cost of Housing," 171–2.
119 Piva, *Condition of the Working Class*, 125; Darroch, "Occupational Structure, Assessed Wealth," 405.
120 Harris, "The Unremarked Homeownership Boom in Toronto," 433–4. See Appendices B–D, H, J.
121 See Appendices H, K.
122 Darroch, "Occupational Structure, Assessed Wealth," 406.
123 Appendix L.
124 *Register*, 5 Sept. 1901.
125 Edward Chambers, "A New Measure of the Rental Cost of Housing in the Toronto Market, 1890–1914," *Histoire sociale – Social History* 17 (May 1984): 168–9.

126 *Labour Gazette* 5 (Oct. 1905): 497–8. In his report on the working conditions in Toronto, the reporter asserts: "In spite of the amount of building,
houses within the means of the working class remain very scarce and
rents continue to increase. This class of investment is not popular with
builders, who prefer to erect houses commanding higher rents." See also
Piva, *Condition of the Working Class*, 137, 142.

127 Charles Hastings, M.D., *Report of the Medical Health Officer Dealing With
the Recent Investigation of Slum Conditions in Toronto* (Toronto 1911), 4; for
more details see Piva, *Condition of the Working Class*, 113–42.

128 *Labour Gazette* 5 (Oct. 1905): 498.

129 Hastings' six areas of investigation were (1) Eastern Avenue district,
from the Don to Parliament Street and from Queen Street to the Bay
(St Paul's); (2) the Central or City Hall district, from Yonge Street to University Avenue and from College to Queen Street (St Michael's and
St Patrick's); (3) Niagara district, from Bathurst to Shaw Street and from
Queen Street to the Bay (St Mary's); (4) Parliament Street to the Don and
from Wilton to Queen Street (St Paul's); (5) Bathurst Street to Bellwoods,
and from Queen to Arthur (St Mary's); and (6) from Spadina Avenue to
Bathurst Street and from Front to King Street (St Mary's). Hastings, *Report*, 3–4, 6–8, 17, 20. These areas appear in much the same light for the
1880s and 1890s in Goheen, *Victorian Toronto*, 163, 168.

130 *Register*, 13 Dec. 1906; see also 12 Aug. 1897, 8 Sept. 1898, 8 June 1899, 27
July 1911, 1 May 1919, 30 Sept. 1920.

131 See Appendix J.

132 Ibid.

133 ARCAT, McNeil Papers, Children Foster and Delinquent, MN WL 04.1,
1912–13, 1917–18; Children's Aid Society Files, AE04.03, 1917; and Catholic Charities Papers, *Annual Report for Year 1920: Division of Housing and
Industrial Hygiene* (Toronto, 11 Jan. 1921).

134 *Register*, 17 Sept. 1908, 26 Nov. 1908, 3 Dec. 1908, 9 Dec. 1909, 15 Dec.
1910, 18 Dec. 1913, 18 Jan. 1917. ARCAT, McNeil Papers, *Diocesan Bulletin*
1 (Mar. 1913): 5; Report of the St Elizabeth Visiting Nurses Association,
1920, AE 26.10.

135 ARCAT, St Michael's Cemetery Register, 1910. Infant deaths constituted
58 per cent of all burials at the cemetery in 1910.

Deaths	No.	%
Stillborn	41	10.3
Less than 1 month	32	8.0
1–6 months	104	26.0
6–12 months	24	6.0
13 mos.–2yrs.	18	4.5
2–5 years	13	3.2
	232	58.0

136 Ibid., McNeil Papers, Social Welfare Files, Statement of Infants for the Past Ten Years, 1913; *Register*, 8 June 1916, 31 Oct. 1918; ARCAT, McNeil Papers, Circular, 22 Nov. 1921; P.J. Bench, "Catholic Charities," *Ontario Catholic Yearbook, 1920*, 30–1.

137 ARCAT, Sisters of Misericorde Papers, May McNeil to Father Walters, 26 Nov. 1920.

138 *Register*, 29 June 1916.

139 Ibid., 19 Apr. 1917; ARCAT, St Vincent de Paul Society Papers, box 1, Correspondence File, Annual Report from "Particular Council" to St Vincent de Paul Bureau of Information, 31 Oct. 1919. In this letter a Mr Boyle reports: "This coming winter, it is feared, may make heavier demands on the Society ... This when combined with the influx of immigrants when Spring opens, will add very largely to the work of this office."

140 ARCAT, Sacred Heart Orphanage Papers, 1914–18; *Register*, 7 Mar. 1918.

141 ARCAT, McNeil Papers, WL 04, Foster and Delinquent Children, 1926; *Census of Canada*, 1921, 1:593–5, 542–3, 2:574–6. All calculations are my own.

142 Nicolson, "The Catholic Church and the Irish in Victorian Toronto," 25–6; and Shea, "The Irish Immigrant Adjustment," 59; Clarke, *Piety and Nationalism*, 26–8. For contemporary accounts and Catholic responses see *Globe*, 2 Aug. 1869, 18 Aug. 1873, 7 Apr. 1881; and CWR, 26 May 1887, 28 Jan. 1888.

143 *Register*, 29 Jan. 1903, 5 Apr. 1906; see also 17 June 1897, 28 Aug. 1902, 19 Feb. 1914, 9 Apr. 1914, 21 Jan. 1915.

144 ARCAT, McNeil Papers, TE 60, "Delinquency." Of the 1,709 children appearing in juvenile court in 1920, 365 were Catholic. Among the Catholics, 265 were non-immigrant, or 72.6 per cent. The percentage of immigrants is still in excess of their percentage of the total population, but even more astounding is that within six years their percentage of Catholic delinquents jumped from 27.4 per cent to 50.8 per cent.

145 P.J. Bench, "Catholic Charities," *Ontario Catholic Yearbook, 1920*, 27–8.

146 *Register*, 28 Feb. 1918, 9 Jan. 1909.

147 Ibid., 27 Nov. 1913.

148 Ibid., 16 Mar. 1916, 30 Mar. 1916, 18 May 1916.

149 Ibid., 2 Nov. 1920; Bench, "Catholic Charities," 28–9; suggestions for cooperation from McNeil and Somerville can be found in *Register*, 13 Feb. 1913, 16 Mar. 1916.

150 *Register*, 16 Dec. 1920, 6 Feb. 1919. The federation accepted the following: Catholic Charities, Sacred Heart Orphanage, St Mary's Infants' Home, House of Providence, Carmelite Sisters Orphanage, Good Shepherd Refuge, St Vincent De Paul Children's Aid Society, St Elizabeth Visiting Nurses' Association, and Catholic Big Brothers and Big Sisters.

151 Ibid., 18 Nov. 1920.

CHAPTER TWO

1 ASV-DAC, 89.20, John R. Teefy to Donatus Sbarretti, 20 Aug. 1906.
2 Brian P. Clarke, *Piety and Nationalism: Lay Voluntary Associations and the Creation of an Irish-Catholic Community in Toronto, 1850–1895* (Montreal and Kingston: McGill-Queen's University Press 1993), passim.
3 NA, Sir John A. Macdonald Papers, Archbishop John Joseph Lynch to Macdonald, 1 Feb. 1872.
4 Murray Nicolson, "The Growth of Roman Catholic Institutions in the Archdiocese of Toronto, 1841–1890," in Terrence Murphy and Gerald Stortz, eds., *Creed and Culture: The Place of English-speaking Catholics in Canadian Society, 1750–1930* (Montreal and Kingston: McGill-Queen's University Press 1993): 152–70; Nicolson, "Irish Tridentine Catholicism in Victorian Toronto: Vessel for Ethno-Religious Persistence," CCHA, *Historical Studies* 50, No. 2 (1983): 415–36; Gerald Stortz, "Archbishop John Joseph Lynch of Toronto: Twenty-eight Years of Commitment," CCHA, *Study Sessions* 49 (1982): 5–23.
5 J.T. Watt, "Anti-Catholic Nativism in Canada: The Protestant Protective Association," *Canadian Historical Review* 48 (Mar. 1967): 45–58; James R. Miller, *Equal Rights* (Montreal: McGill-Queen's University Press 1979); Thomas T. McAvoy, "The Formation of the Catholic Minority in the United States, 1820–1860," *Review of Politics* 10 (1948): 13–34. John Webster Grant, *The Church in the Canadian Era* (Toronto: Ryerson Press 1970), 87; Robert Choquette, "Les Quatres Solitudes en histoire religieuse Canadienne," paper delivered at Comparative Themes in the History of Christianity, joint meeting of the American Society of Church History and the Canadian Society of Church History, Hamilton, Ont., 23 Apr. 1987.
6 Stortz, "Archbishop John Joseph Lynch," 5–7.
7 André Chapeau, et al., *Canadian R.C. Bishops 1658–1979* (Ottawa: Research Centre in the Religious History of Canada, Saint Paul University 1980), 92.
8 *Christian Guardian*, 4 May 1864; Toronto *World*, 12 Dec. 1884; *Globe*, 12 Dec. 1884.
9 ARCAT, Lynch Papers, "The Alleged Doctrine and True Faith of the Catholic Church," 11 Nov. 1874; "The So-Called Reformation and Its Chief Apostles," 13 Jan. 1875; Lynch to Premier Oliver Mowat, 22 Mar. 1873.
10 Mark G. McGowan, "'We Endure What We Cannot Cure': John Joseph Lynch and Roman Catholic-Protestant Relations in Toronto, 1864–1875," Canadian Society of Church History, *Papers* (1984): 89–116; and Martin Galvin, "The Jubilee Riots in Toronto, 1875," CCHA, *Reports* 26 (1959): 93–107.
11 Stortz, "Archbishop John Joseph Lynch," 22; and "John Joseph Lynch, Archbishop of Toronto: A Biographical Study of Religious, Political and

Social Commitment," PhD, University of Guelph 1980, 227–8; Hereward
Senior, *The Fenians in Canada* (Toronto: Macmillan 1978), 67–68, 84–90.
ARCAT, Lynch Papers, Circular for St Patrick's Day, 17 Mar. 1866. *Tribune*,
26 Nov. 1874. Very good studies of Ultramontanism include Nive
Voisine, "L'Ultramontanisme canadien-français au XIX siècle," in Nive
Voisine et Jean Hamelin, eds., *Les Ultramontaines Canadiens-Français*
(Montréal: Boréal Express 1985), 67–104; Emmet Larkin, "The Devotional
Revolution in Ireland, 1850–1875," *American Historical Review* 86 (June
1972): 625–52.

12 George M. Grant, "Canada," in W.D. Grant, ed., *Christendom Anno Do-
mini MDCCCI*, vol. 1 (Toronto: Briggs 1902), 81.

13 The assault on Lynch varied from Sunday evening theological diatribes,
public meetings, political pampleteering, editorializing in the local press,
and the rapier wit of satirist John Wilson Bengough. ARCAT, Lynch Papers, "Popish Doctrines Refuted," L AE 19.02b, handbill, 1875. *Christian
Gaurdian*, 4 May 1864, 10 Jan. 1866, 3 and 24 Mar. 1875; *Tribune*, 26 Nov.
1874; *Globe*, 6 Dec. 1874; *Grip*, 9 and 16 Jan. 1875; *British American Presbyterian*, 1 and 8 Oct. 1875; *Mail*, 12 Dec. 1884; *Sentinel*, 17 May 1888; and
Duncan McLeod, *Archbishop Lynch "Premier of Ontario" Unmasked* (Peterborough 1884), 6–7, 17.

14 Stortz, "John Joseph Lynch, Archbishop of Toronto," 13, 16, 181, 204,
221–7, 230; *Globe*, 18 Mar. 1864; H.C. McKeown, *Life of Archbishop Lynch*
(Montreal and Toronto: James A. Sadlier 1886). McKeown states: "As
man or boy, priest or prelate, he has ever been faithful to the land of his
birth. A Canadian Archbishop, he is yet emphatically an Irish priest at
heart." McKeown's inclusion of selected primary documents, however,
strengthens the idea that Lynch was first and foremost attached to Ireland (224, 226–47).

15 *CWR*, 19 May 1888. These same words had been printed in the *Review* during Lynch's life, without refutation from the prelate. *CWR*, 17 Mar. 1887.

16 *IC*, 23 Mar. 1864, 22 Mar. 1871, 17 Mar. 1875, 19 Mar. 1885.

17 Nicholas Flood Davin, *The Irishman in Canada* (Toronto: Maclear and
Company 1877), 667, 658. See also Robin Burns, "From Freedom to Toler-
ance: D'Arcy McGee, the First Martyr," in Robert O'Driscoll and Lorna
Reynolds, eds., *The Untold Story: The Irish In Canada*, vol. 1 (Toronto:
Celtic Arts of Canada 1988), 474.

18 Clarke, *Piety and Nationalism*, 215–23, 243–7.

19 Stortz, "Archbishop John J. Lynch," 19–20; Brian P. Clarke, "Piety, Nationalism and Fraternity: The Rise of Irish Catholic Voluntary Associations in Toronto, 1850–1895," PhD, University of Chicago 1986, 494–6.

20 He was attending the jubilee of Father O'Dowd in Montreal. Stortz, "An
Irish Radical in a Tory Town," 45.

21 "Christopher Finlay Fraser," DCB 12:332–3.

22 AAK, James V. Cleary Papers, box 2, file 1, c 41. Assorted letters.
23 *Toronto Telegram*, 13 Jan. 1879; Clarke, "Piety, Nationalism and Fraternity," 495.
24 "John Walsh," DCB 12:1083.
25 The Pale was the original area of settlement around Dublin in which the English were able to exert control easily. The province of Leinster was by far the most anglicized area in Ireland. Karl Bottigheimer, *Ireland and The Irish* (New York: Columbia University Press 1982), 72; Robert Kee, *Ireland: A History* (Toronto: Little Brown and Company 1982), 30.
26 James R. Teefy, ed., *Jubilee Volume: The Archdiocese of Toronto, 1842–1892* (Toronto: George T. Dixon 1892), vi–xi.
27 *Record*, 6 Aug. 1898.
28 CWR, 7 Dec. 1889.
29 Ibid., 30 Nov. 1889; Teefy, *Jubilee Volume*, xxiv, xxvii; *Register*, 19 Mar. 1896.
30 CWR, 28 Dec. 1889.
31 Ibid., 4 Oct. 1890, 28 Dec. 1889; IC, 2 Oct. 1890. His invocations for nation-building and upward social mobility can be found in *Register*, 19 Mar. 1896; CWR, 13 Dec. 1890; and IC, 12 Dec. 1889.
32 ARCAT, John Joseph Lynch Papers, AE 06.04, Father John Walsh to Lynch, 8 Nov. 1864.
33 Daniel C. Lyne, "Irish-Canadian Financial Contributions to the Home Rule Movement of the 1890s," *Studia Hibernica* 7 (1967): 195.
34 *Register*, 19 Mar. 1896.
35 ARCAT, Lynch Papers, AE 02.09, copy of letter from Lynch to Bishop Thomas Connolly, 1 Feb. 1866.
36 *Record*, 15 Feb. 1896.
37 "Quoniamtalissis, untinam noster esses"; quoted in *Record*, 3 Sept. 1898. See also *Globe*, 1 Aug. 1898; *Record*, 6 Aug. 1898.
38 NA, Sir John A. Macdonald Papers, letter from P. Corcoran to Macdonald, 13 Jan. 1888, vol. 452, 225141–225143. This letter, in addition to a letter from Charles Tupper to Macdonald, 6 Aug. 1888, 130497–130500, indicates that Macdonald attempted to influence the selection of a successor to John Lynch in Toronto. Using Lord Salisbury, the Duke of Norfolk, and Cardinal Manning, Macdonald sought a candidate who would be favourably disposed to the Liberal-Conservative Party.
39 *Record*, 16 July 1898 (a reprint from the *Buffalo Catholic Union and Times*).
40 Ibid., 2 Apr., 16 July, 3 Sept. 1898.
41 ASV-DAC, 83.22/2, Father J.L. Hand to Donatus Sbaretti, 13 Apr. 1908.
42 Ibid., 91.7/1, Private Circular, ca June 1911.
43 ARCAT, Apostolic Delegate Papers, James T. Kidd to Delegate, 7 June 1911, and Apostolic Delegate to Kidd, 4 June 1911. ASV-DAC, 91.7/2, A.E. Burke to Pellegrino Stagni, 18 Jan. 1912; copy of letter from Stagni to J.T. Kidd, 19 Jan. 1912.

44 ASV-DAC, 91.7/1, Bishop Thomas Dowling to Most Rev. Pellegrino Stagni, 3 July 1911.
45 Ibid., 91.7/2, Lancelot Minehan to Stagni, 21 Jan. 1912; M. Cline to Stagni, 24 Jan. 1912; Stagni to Cline, 25 Jan. 1912.
46 Michael Power, ed., *Assumption College: The O'Connor Years, 1870–1890, A Documentary History of Assumption College*, vol. 2 (Windsor: Assumption College 1986); F.A. O'Brien, *Life Work of a Saintly Prelate, The Most Reverend Denis O'Connor* (Kalamazoo: Kalamazoo Augustinian Print 1914), 3; Robert Scollard, CSB, "Most Reverend Denis O'Connor, CSB, D.D.," *Basilian Teacher* 4 (1938): 89.
47 GABF, O'Connor Papers, box 1, Personal Correspondence, letters from 1890.
48 *Register*, 6 July 1911.
49 Ibid., 11 May 1899. ARCAT, Denis O'Connor Papers, AA01, galley proofs of biography, author and date unknown. SMCA, Denis O'Connor Papers, obituary from Toronto *World*.
50 ADL, O'Connor Papers, biographical information; ARCAT, Photographic Collection; SMCA, O'Connor Papers; Robert Scollard, *Dictionary of Basilian Biography* (Toronto: Basilian Press 1969), 115.
51 Anne Taves, *The Household of Faith: Roman Catholic Devotions in Mid-Nineteenth Century America* (Notre Dame, Ind.: Notre Dame University Press 1986), 89–102.
52 ASV-DAC, 157.37, O'Connor to Diomede Falconio, 20 Nov. 1900.
53 James Hennessey, SJ, *American Catholicism: A History of the Roman Catholic Community in the United States* (New York: Oxford University Press 1982); William Halsey, *The Survival of American Innocence: Catholicism in an Era of Disillusionment* (Notre Dame, Ind.: Notre Dame University Press 1982), 4; Thomas T. McAvoy, *The Great Crisis in American Catholic History, 1895–1900* (Chicago: Henry Regnery 1957), 2, 310, 350; Thomas T. McAvoy, "The Formation of a Minority," in Philip Gleason, ed., *The Catholic Church in America* (New York: Harper and Row 1970), 11; Gabriel Daly, *Transcendence and Immanence: A Study of Catholic Modernism and Integralism* (Oxford: Clarendon Press 1980), 1–7, 12; Alec Vidler, *A Variety of Catholic Modernists* (Cambridge: Cambridge University Press 1970), 15–18; Ellen Leonard, *George Tyrrell and the Catholic Tradition* (New York: Paulist Press 1982), 1–2.
54 ARCAT, Roman Correspondence, draft of letter from O'Connor to Cardinal Gotti of the Propaganda Fide, 20 Nov. 1900. In this letter O'Connor suggests that Catholics be encouraged to move their homes closer to churches and that Catholic landowners in these areas be requested not to sell to non-Catholics.
55 *Register*, 11 May 1899.
56 Ibid.

57 ASV-DAC, 89.22/2, Hand to Sbarretti, 13 Apr. 1908, 89.20, Teefy to Sbarretti, 20 Aug. 1906.

58 ARCAT, Roman Correspondence, O'Connor to Cardinal Gotti, 10 Feb.
1905. Here O'Connor cites the disapproval of the clergy, the hostility of
the laity, and the interference of the apostolic delegate as principal reasons for his wish to resign. A complete biography of O'Connor is forthcoming from this author and Michael Power in vol. 14 of the DCB.

59 Philip Kennedy, in *Fergus Patrick McEvay and the Church in Ontario: A Biography of the Fourth Archbishop of Toronto* (Toronto: unpublished paper,
St Augustine's Seminary 1982), 6. A complete biography is forthcoming
by Mark G. McGowan in vol. 14 of the DCB.

60 NA, H.F. McIntosh Papers, draft of biography of McEvay; ARCAT, Philip
Kennedy, "Archbishop Fergus Patrick McEvay," unpublished under-
graduate paper, 1982; Edmund McCorkell, CSB, *Henry Carr: Revolutionary*
(Toronto: Griffin House 1969), 15–20.

61 ARCAT, McEvay Papers, James Vincent Cleary to McEvay, 25 July 1882,
ME AA02.03, and McEvay's notebook at Fenelon Falls, 1882, ME AA02.04.

62 *Hamilton Times*, 27 June 1899.

63 *Register*, 6 July 1911.

64 Ibid.

65 ARCAT, McEvay Papers, AA02.26, McEvay to Laurier, 20 June 1908.

66 *Register*, 18 May 1911.

67 NA, Sir Charles Fitzpatrick Papers, vol. XIII, copy of letter from Fergus
McEvay to Louis N. Bégin, 27 Dec. 1910, 5816.

68 ARCAT, McEvay Papers, copy of letter to Pope Pius X, undated, ca 1910,
AL08.01.

69 Ibid., Gauthier to McEvay, 12 Feb. 1909, AF04.08; McCarthy to McEvay,
8 Apr. 1909, AF04.28; McEvay to O'Leary, 15 Apr. 1909, AF04.29; McEvay
Papers, McEvay to O'Leary, 24 Apr. 1911, AF06.29.

70 A.A. Johnston, *Antigonish Diocese Priests and Bishops 1786–1925*, ed. Kathleen MacKenzie. (Antigonish: Casket Printing and Publishing [1994]), 88.

71 George Boyle, *Pioneer in Purple: The Life and Work of Archbishop Neil Mc-
Neil* (Montreal: Palm Publishers 1951), 1.

72 ARCAT, Roman Correspondence, "Rapport Financier du Diocèse de Toronto au Canada," 23 Apr. 1920. The report outlines the major problems
faced by McNeil upon his succession to Toronto – the seminary, unifying
Catholic students at the University of Toronto, the provision of church facilities in the suburbs, and the reform of the Catholic Church Extension
Society and the policy of accommodating Catholic immigrants – and
their eventual resolution. ASFXU, A.A. Johnston Collection, MG 75/1,
SGF 18, McNeil to Judge Nicholas Meagher, 16 Dec. 1913.

73 ASFXU, Johnston Papers, MG 75/1 SGF 18, McNeil to John R. MacDonald,
6 July 1918.

74 ARCAT, Holograph Collection, 22.79, Address from the Clergy of the Diocese of Toronto to the Most Rev. Neil McNeil, D.D., Episcopal Silver Jubilee, 20 Oct. 1920.

75 Ibid.

76 ARCAT, McNeil Papers, galley proofs of biography of Neil McNeil by Henry Somerville. Other biographers report the positive response of Protestants to McNeil: NA, McIntosh Papers, rough notes on McNeil; ARCAT, McNeil Papers, galley proofs. George Boyle, *Pioneer in Purple* (Montreal: Palm 1951), 234, 237.

77 ARCAT, McNeil Papers, galley proofs of biography.

78 *Register*, 7 Nov. 1907.

79 Alfred E. Burke, "Need of a Missionary College," in Francis C. Kelley, ed., *The First American Catholic Missionary Congress* (Chicago: J.S. Hyland and Company 1909), 80; *Canadian Messenger of the Sacred Heart* 17 (Feb. 1907): 52–3.

80 Edward Kelly, *The Story of St Paul's Parish* (Toronto: private, 1922), 305.

81 Murray Nicolson, "The Catholic Church and the Irish of Victorian Toronto," PhD, University of Guelph 1980, 117. Although this is a very helpful study, one must be cautious with Dr Nicolson's statistics; his estimate that 24 of 37 priests were Irish in 1898 does not jibe with the archdiocesan personnel files.

82 Kevin Condon, CM, *Missionary College of All Hallows, 1842–1891* (Dublin 1986).

83 Larkin, "The Devotional Revolution in Ireland," 625–52.

84 Derived from Robert J. Scollard, ed., *Dictionary of Basilian Biography* (Toronto: Basilian Press 1969).

85 *IC*, 2 Oct. 1890; *CWR*, 28 Dec. 1889.

86 ARCAT, Priests' Files, Francis J. Riordan Papers, letter from Francis Riordan to Fergus McEvay, 5 Dec. 1908; see also Miscellaneous Seminary box, James A. O'Ryan to Archbishop Walsh, 31 May 1894, 13 June 1894.

87 Scollard, *Dictionary of Basilian Biography,* my own calculations. The indigenization of other male religious orders, however, was far more dramatic. In the period of the "Canada Mission," 1887–1907, 79 per cent of the Jesuits serving in Canada were Canadian born and educated. Terry Fay, SJ, "What Manner of Men Are These? The Inculturation of Jesuits into a Multicultural Canada, 1843–1963," unpublished conference paper, 1988, 9–10.

88 Kevin Kirley, CSB, *The Congregation of Priests of St Basil of Viviers, France, 1922–1955* (Toronto: Basilian Press 1981), 2–59.

89 McCorkall, *Henry Carr*, chaps. 1–3; Laurence Shook, CSB, *Catholic Post-Secondary Education in English-speaking Canada: A History* (Toronto: University of Toronto Press 1971), 155.

90 ARCAT, Lynch Papers, assorted letters to and from All Hallows Seminary.

91 Ibid., Rt Rev. Patrick J. Coyle File, Coyle to Archbishop Walsh, 27 Mar. 1890; Joseph Amoretti, Rector of Brignole Sale, to Walsh, 12 Dec. 1890.

92 Brian Young, *In Its Corporate Capacity: The Seminary of Montreal as a Business Institution* (Montreal: McGill-Queen's University Press 1986), 153–8.

93 ARCAT, Holograph Collection, 22.78, Seminary of St Mary and St John the Evangelist, and Seminary Conference, 16 Feb. 1882.

94 Francis A. O'Brien, *Life Work of a Saintly Prelate* (Kalamazoo: Augustinian Print 1914), [6].

95 ARCAT, O'Connor Papers, Examination of Young Priests, 28 Nov. 1899; Letterbook 3, box 1, Acts and Decrees of the First Provincial Council, 1875, Decree x, "De Seminariis Instituendis."

96 Ibid., Holograph 22.78, Seminary of St Mary and St John the Evangelist, 1881–83.

97 Ibid., O'Connor Papers, AB 16, Examinations, 28 Nov. 1899, 25 Nov. 1903, 12 June 1906.

98 Ibid., Examination on the Immaculate Conception, Nov. 1904.

99 Ibid., Examinations, 1902.

100 Ibid., Examination Results, Nov. 1903.

101 Power, *Assumption College: The O'Connor Years*, passim.

102 *Toronto Evening News*, 1 Aug. 1899.

103 ARCAT, Roman Correspondence, O'Connor to Cardinal Gotti, 10 Feb. 1905. Original: "Un tier du clergé je ne suis pas bien vu, et les autres ne sont pas tous des amis zélés." Roman Correspondence, 8706, O'Connor to Gotti, 22 Oct. 1904.

104 Ibid., Apostolic Delegate Correspondence, O'Connor to Sbarretti, 13 Apr. 1903; Sbarretti to O'Connor, 21 Aug. 1903; Sbarretti to James Minehan, 22 Aug. 1903; Sbarretti to O'Connor, 13 Sept. 1903; Sbarretti to O'Connor, 14 Jan. 1904.

105 Ibid., O'Connor Papers, AA 04.02, O'Connor to Rev. Martin Whalen, 10 June 1901.

106 ASFM, typescript of the autobiography of Monsignor John Mary Fraser, ca 1955, 14–15.

107 McCorkell, *Henry Carr*, 15, 20. McCorkell refers to Basilian education in the nineteenth century as "an arctic night."

108 ASV-DAC, 91.7/1, Toronto – Elezione dell'arcivescovo Mons. Neil McNeil, Father P. Lamarche to Msgr. P.F. Stagni, 12 Sept. 1911.

109 Ibid., 157.37, Affari Generali – Propaganda protestante (1900–01), Victorin Marijon, CSB, to Diomede Falconio, 14 Nov. 1900.

110 ARCAT, Roman Correspondence, 8801, draft of letter from O'Connor to Gotti, 10 Feb. 1905; Donna Merwick, *Boston's Priests, 1848–1910: A Study of Social and Intellectual Change* (Cambridge: Harvard University Press 1973), x–xii. Merwick argues by contrast that Archbishop William Henry

O'Connell was very successful at romanizing the devotional life and clergy in the Archdiocese of Boston.

111 St Augustine's Seminary, *50 Golden Years, 1913–1963* (Toronto: np, 1963), 1; *Register*, 18 May 1916; ARCAT, Judge Hugh T. Kelly Papers, copy of letter from Kelly to Neil McNeil, 5 Oct. 1914, and McNeil to Mrs McLean-French, 6 Oct. 1914.

112 ARCAT, St Augustine's Seminary Papers, box 2, "The Laying of the Cornerstone at St Augustine's Seminary, Sunday, 23 Oct., 1910"; *Register*, 27 Oct. 1910.

113 ARCAT, St Augustine's Seminary Papers, box 2, 1912 file, Reverend Michael Moyna to Neil McNeil, 15 May 1916. Bishop Fallon of London had been denied membership on the seminary's board of management and so claimed that the institution was originally deemed a diocesan institution for Toronto only. Fallon promoted his own Seminary of St Peter in London as the alternative to St Augustine's, claiming that McNeil had given the seminary a more national focus. Ibid., McNeil Education Papers, Michael Francis Fallon to P.F. Stagni, 26 May 1913, 35–6. In his sermon at the laying of the cornerstone in 1910, Fallon exclaimed: "St Augustine's Seminary will, we all hope and trust, come to be a leading and integral part of the one system of Catholic education in this Province, and in many parts likewise of the Dominion of Canada." *Register*, 27 Oct. 1910. This ambiguous statement raises a cloud of doubt over his later remarks concerning the limited role of the seminary. This is confirmed in ARCAT, Judge Kelly Papers, copy of "Letter to the People of the Archdiocese of Toronto" by Neil McNeil, 1914.

114 *Register*, 7 Feb. 1910, 20 Oct. 1910.

115 Ibid., 13 Feb. 1913, 5 June 1913; St Augustine's, *50 Golden Years*, 13–14; ARCAT, Judge Kelly Papers, McNeil to Eugene O'Keefe, 9 Jan. 1913.

116 ARCAT, St Augustine's Seminary Papers, box 1, McNeil to the Cardinal Prefect of the Propaganda Fide, 20 Oct. 1917. The *Register*, 4 Sept. 1913, 10 Feb. 1910, contained comments from both clergy and laity regarding the national scope of St Augustine's mandate.

117 ARCAT, McNeil Papers, J.R. MacDonald to Neil McNeil, 29 Sept. 1921, MN AP05.33.

118 ASAS, Enrolment Register, 1913–93. Also determined by the nominal roll in Karen M. Booth, ed., *The People Cry – "Send us priests": The First Seventy-Five Years of St Augustine's Seminary in Toronto, 1913–1988* (Toronto: St Augustine's Seminary Alumni Association 1988), 41–60.

119 ARCAT, McNeil Papers, MacDonald to McNeil, 4 Dec. 1922, MN AP05.39; 24 Dec. 1922, MN AP05.40; 1 July 1923, MN AP05.44.

120 Ibid., St Augustine's Seminary Papers, box 1, Le Séminaire de St Augustin a Toronto, 2–7.

121 Ibid., Announcement of the Opening of St Augustine's New Seminary, J.T. Kidd, 1913.

122 Editorial, *St Joseph's Lilies* 2 (June 1913), 7.

123 ASV-DAC, 19.10/1, Sbarretti to Merry del Val, 25 May 1909. The entire Fallon episode is handled by Pasquale Fiorino, "The Nomination of Bishop Fallon as Bishop of London," CCHA, *Historical Studies* 62 (1996): 33–46.

124 *Register*, 21 Aug. 1913.

125 Ibid., 11 May 1916, 18 May 1916; ARCAT, St Augustine's Papers, box 1, McNeil to the Propaganda Fide, 20 Oct. 1917; St Augustine's, *50 Golden Years*, 22.

126 ARCAT, St Augustine's Papers, box 2, Report of Meeting of the Clergy of Toronto, 11 Nov. 1919.

127 AAK, James Vincent Cleary Papers, Bishop McQuaid of Rochester to Cleary, 7 July 1895; copy of letter from Cleary to McQuaid, 11 July 1895.

128 St Michael's College Rare Book Room (SMCRB), Dean William Harris, "Our Own Land," *Book Reviews*, 3 Sept. 1900. See also Francis Ryan on loyalty in the *Register*, 24 June 1897.

129 *Le Canada Ecclesiastique*, 1911. I acknowledge the collaboration and expertise of Dr Elizabeth Smyth, who has been a pioneer in the study of women's religious orders and with whom I have collaborated on the subject of the relations between local ordinaries and women's religious orders.

130 Mary Alban Bouchard, CSJ, "Pioneers Forever: The Sisters of St Joseph of Toronto and Their Ventures in Social Welfare and Health Care," in Mark G. McGowan and Brian P. Clarke, eds., *Catholics at the "Gathering Place": Historical Essays on the Archdiocese of Toronto, 1841–1991* (Toronto: CCHA 1993), 107–9; Elizabeth Smyth, "Christian Perfection and Service to Neighbours: The Congregation of the Sisters of St Joseph in Toronto, 1851–1920," in Elizabeth Gillan Muir and Marilyn Fardig Whiteley, eds., *Changing Roles of Women within the Christian Church in Canada* (Toronto: University of Toronto Press 1995), 39–41; Patricia Byrne, CSJ, "Sisters of St Joseph: The Americanization of a French Tradition," *us Catholic Historian* 5 (Summer/Fall 1986): 241–72.

131 Smyth, "Christian Perfection," 49, 44.

132 Barbara Cooper, "Hagiology and History: A Re-examination of the Early Years of the North American Institute of the Blessed Virgin Mary," in McGowan and Clarke, eds., *Catholics at the "Gathering Place,"* 90.

133 Kathleen McGovern, IBVM, *Something More than Ordinary* (Toronto: I Team Publishers 1989), 149–50.

134 Ibid., 97–8; Cooper, "Hagiology and History," 96; and M. Margarita, IBVM, "The Institute of the Blessed Virgin Mary," CCHA, *Reports* 12 (1944–45): 72–3.

135 Elizabeth Smyth, "The Lessons of Religion and Science: The Congregation of the Sisters of St Joseph and St Joseph's Academy, Toronto, 1854–1911," D.Ed., Ontario Institute for Studies in Education 1989, 74–6.

136 Ibid., 253–4.

137 Mary Aloysius Kerr, IBVM, *Dictionary of Biography of the Institute of the Blessed Virgin Mary in North America* (Toronto: Mission Press 1984). Individual biographies, of which 471 were used for this study, reveal a close correlation between Loretto alumni and recruitment. Other recruits had been trained by the CSJs or Grey Sisters, sensitizing them to religious life at an impressionable age. Smyth, "The Lessons of Religion and Science," 99.

138 Smyth, "The Lessons of Religion and Science," 93; and Smyth, "Developing the powers of the youthful mind': The Evolution of Education for Women at St Joseph's Academy, Toronto, 1854–1911," CCHA, *Historical Studies* 60 (1993–94): 117.

139 ASV-DAC, 179.2, Documenti vari-Statistiche sulle scuole elementari in Canada, Sr. M. Eucheria, CSJ, Superior, St Joseph's Academy, to Diomede Falconio, 23 July 1901; M.J. Magdalena, IBVM, to Falconio, 2 Oct. 1901; M. Dorothea, IBVM, Loretto Academy to Falconio, 5 Aug. 1901.

140 Smyth, "Lessons," 230–5.

141 ASV-DAC, 89.20, Teefy to Sbarretti, 20 Aug. 1906.

142 GABF, O'Connor Papers, box 1, file 1, notes on visitation to Sisters of St Joseph.

143 Cited in McGovern, *Something More than Ordinary*, 151.

144 Cooper, "Hagiology and History," 93–5, 97–100.

145 Among the religious orders and their students such statements are evident in two alumni publications, *St Joseph's Lilies* and *The Rainbow*, published at Loretto College.

CHAPTER THREE

1 E.J. Devine, SJ, "Our Parish Clergy," *Canadian Messenger of the Sacred Heart* (hereafter CMSH) 17 (Feb. 1907): 52.

2 ARCAT, Roman Correspondence, 8706, draft of letter to Cardinal Gotti, 22 Oct. 1904.

3 For American examples of lay initiative see Timothy L. Smith, "Lay Initiative in the Religious Life of American Immigrants, 1880–1950," in Tamara Herevan, ed., *Anonymous Americans: Explorations in Nineteenth-Century Social History* (Englewood Cliffs: Prentice Hall 1971): 214–49.

4 Ann Taves, *The Household of Faith: Roman Catholic Devotions in Mid-Nineteenth Century America* (Notre Dame, Ind.: University of Notre Dame Press 1986); see chap. 6, "Devotions in the American Context," 113–33.

5 E.E.Y. Hales, *The Catholic Church in the Modern World* (New York: Doubleday 1960), 82–106.

6 Nive Voisine et Jean Hamelin, *Les Ultramontanes Canadiens-français* (Montreal: Boréal Express 1985).

7 Marvin O'Connell, "Ultramontanism and Dupanloup: The Compromise of 1865," *Church History* 53 (June 1984): 200–17.

8 J. Derek Holmes, *More Roman than Rome: English Catholicism in the Nineteenth Century* (London: Burns and Oates 1978); Edward Norman, *The English Catholic Church in the Nineteenth Century* (New York: Oxford 1985): 110–52.

9 O'Connell, "Ultramontanism," 200–17.

10 Roger Aubert, *La Pontificat de Pie IX* (Paris: Blound and Gay 1963), 465.

11 Taves, *The Household of Faith*, 21–46; Bill McSweeney, "Catholic Piety in the Nineteenth Century," *Social Compass* 34 (1987): 203–10; Emmet Larkin, "The Devotional Revolution in Ireland, 1850–1875," *American Historical Review* 77 (1972): 625–52.

12 Brian P. Clarke, *Piety and Nationalism*, 63.

13 *CWR*, 12 May 1887, 26 July 1890, 9 May 1891; ARCAT, Walsh Papers, pastoral letter on devotion to the Blessed Virgin, 25 Apr. 1891; *Register*, 4 Oct. 1894, 26 Apr. 1906, 1 Apr. 1915; ARCAT, McNeil Education Papers, "Public Devotions," *Diocesan Bulletin* 1 (Mar. 1913).

14 *Register*, 30 May 1907; *CWR*, 26 July 1890. In 1896, 15,701 Catholics from Toronto were registered members of the League of the Sacred Heart, an international organization dedicated to prayer, good works, and devotion to the Sacred Heart of Jesus. *CMSH* 7 (Jan. 1897): 39, 45–7; 7 (Mar. 1897): 119.

15 *St Basil's Hymn Book* (Toronto: Oxford Press 1888), 99–113, 125–80, 186–7, 191.

16 *Register*, 30 Oct. 1919; *CMSH* 8 (Apr. 1898): 159. Most interesting is a survey of the *Register* from 1910 to 1930, where it is evident that Catholics actively requested the intercession of saints and that one of the growing objects of devotion was St Teresa, whose feast was celebrated every 1 October.

17 John A. Hardon, SJ, *Pocket Catholic Dictionary* (New York: Image Books 1985), 383–4; McSweeney, "Catholic Piety," 209.

18 *CMSH*, 7 (Jan. 1897): 45–6.

19 Ibid., 7 (Mar. 1897), 119; Hoffman, *The Catholic Almanac*, 1897, 41. The latter gives a rounded figure for the city and counties of the archdiocese as 60,000.

20 *CWR*, 1 Mar. 1890, 26 Mar. 1892; ARCAT, Walsh Papers, Lenten Pastoral, 15 Feb. 1898; McNeil Papers, Circular, PC 07, 8 Mar. 1919.

21 Louis Rousseau, "Les Missions populaires de 1840–42: acteurs principaux et conséquences," La Société Canadienne d'Histoire de l'Eglise Catholique, *Sessions d'Étude* 53 (1986): 7–22.

22 *Register*, 1 Nov. 1906.

23 *Census of Canada*, 1901, Tables 9, 20. All calculations are my own. The numbers of communicants and scholars indicated in Table 20 were

added and the sum was compared to totals for the religious groups in Table 9. In Toronto the results (per cent) were as follows: Catholics, 86; Anglicans, 37.2; Presbyterians, 41.9; Methodists, 57.3; Baptists, 66.2. Toronto's Catholics compared favourably to other Catholics (per cent) in Ontario: Brockville, 83.2; Carleton County, 40.2; Essex County, 69.2; Hamilton, 98.6; Hastings County, 82.8; Lanark County, 73.9; Nipissing District, 44.7; Ottawa, 49.9; Oxford County, 60.7; Peterborough, 68.3; Renfrew County, 83.2; Simcoe County, 77.9; and Wellington County, 65.

24 Clarke, *Piety and Nationalism*, chaps. 8 and 9.

25 ARCAT, Lynch Papers, Circular on St Patrick's Day, 17 Mar. 1866; Report of the Diocesan Council, 30 Sept. 1869; *IC*, 14 Mar. 1866, 21 Mar. 1866; Senior, *The Fenians in Canada*, 63–8; *Globe*, 18 Mar. 1864, 19 Mar. 1866. By 1869 Lynch had disassociated the Church from any part of the parade by Irish Catholic nationalist societies. Michael Cottrell, "St Patrick's Day Parades in Mid-Nineteenth Century Toronto: A Study of Immigration Adjustment and Elite Control," *Histoire sociale – Social History* 24 (May 1992): 57–74.

26 *CWR*, 21 Mar. 1891, 24 Mar. 1888; *Register*, 23 Mar. 1893, 5 Mar. 1903, 14 Mar. 1907; *Record*, 27 Mar. 1897, 26 Mar. 1898.

27 *Register*, 23 Mar. 1893; *Record*, 26 Mar. 1898.

28 *Record*, 27 Mar. 1897; *Register*, 16 Mar. 1905.

29 *Register*, 25 Mar. 1920.

30 ARCAT, Lynch Papers, P.H. Quinn to Lynch, 2 Sept. 1887; Edward Power to Lynch, 2 Sept. 1887; Anna M. Cotter to Lynch, 14 Sept. 1887; notation to Miss Sarah, Port Credit, Ont., nd; copy of letter from Lynch to Bishop John Walsh, 13 June 1882; William Clune to Lynch, 16 Sept. 1887; Bernard Fallon to Lynch, 18 Sept. 1887; *CWR*, 3 Sept. 1887.

31 *CWR*, 17 Sept. 1887; *Record*, 17 July 1897; *CMSH* 11 (Aug. 1901): 363–4.

32 *Register*, 19 Aug. 1909.

33 Laurence Shook, "Marian Pilgrimages in the Archdiocese of Toronto," CCHA, *Report* 20 (1953): 56–9.

34 H.F. McIntosh, *The Life of Father Louis Della Vagna, Capuchin Friar* (Toronto: Catholic Weekly Review 1888), 4, 20–1, i–ii.

35 William Perkins Bull, *From Macdonell to McGuigan* (Toronto: Perkins Bull Foundation 1939), 331–3.

36 ARCAT, Lynch Papers, testimonial to Lynch regarding McSpiritt, 1887, AH 32.83.

37 Cited in John Moir, ed., *Church and Society: Documents on the Religious History of the Roman Catholic Archdiocese of Toronto from the Archives of the Archdiocese* (Toronto: Archdiocese of Toronto 1991). "Francis McSpiritt," *DCB* 12:689–90.

38 *Register*, 19 Aug. 1909, 22 Aug. 1907, 29 Aug. 1907; *CMSH* 17 (Oct. 1907): 462–6.

39 *CMSH* 18 (June 1908): 272–4; 23 (June 1913): 264–7.

40 *Register*, 11 May 1899.

41 ARCAT, O'Connor Papers, AA 03.03a, Regulations to be Observed to Ensure Uniformity and Good Order.

42 NA, McIntosh Papers, rough notes on history of the Archdiocese of Toronto; O'Brien, *Life Work*, [5].

43 *Record*, 23 Mar. 1895.

44 ARCAT, O'Connor Papers, Circular Letters, AA 03.06, The Pope and Church Music, 1904 (original 22 Nov. 1903); *Register*, 21 Jan. 1904. For a list of forbidden compositions see *Register*, 1 May 1919.

45 *Register*, 4 Apr. 1891, 23 Mar. 1893, 8 June 1893, 28 Dec. 1893, 29 Mar. 1894, 17 Jan. 1895, 11 Apr. 1895, 23 Dec. 1897, 22 Dec. 1898.

46 Ibid., 19 Dec. 1895.

47 Ibid., 30 June 1898.

48 Ibid., 11 July 1907. St Helen's, St Mary's, and St Michael's Cathedral were the three parishes that made occasional use of Gregorian chant.

49 ARCAT, O'Connor Papers, Circulars, Notice, AA 03.07.

50 *Register*, 25 Dec. 1902, 20 Oct. 1904.

51 Mary Hoskin, *History of St Basil's Parish* (Toronto: Catholic Register and Canadian Extension 1912), 83–4; NA, James F. Kenney Papers, vol. 7, file 21, Diary, 22 Aug. 1903. The young James Kenney commented that the singing of the St Basil's children's choir was "beautiful."

52 *Register*, 19 Oct. 1905, 11 July 1907, 19 Sept. 1907, 28 May 1908; *Record*, 18 May 1901. Archbishop Elder of Cincinnati held a conference on Gregorian chant to encourage its use in the United States. See *Register*, 19 Sept. 1907. Similar moves to plainchant were made in the Archdioceses of Ottawa, Dublin, and Westminster. See *Register*, 7 Apr. 1904, 14 July 1904. The *Australasian Catholic Record* lamented that the debate over Church music had polarized into an either-or situation between Gregorian and classical compositions. Quoted in *Record*, 7 Oct. 1899.

53 *Register*, 13 Dec. 1903; *Record*, 20 Apr. 1901.

54 Ibid., 9 Jan. 1908.

55 Ibid.

56 Ibid., 27 Apr. 1905.

57 Hoskin, *History of St Basil's*, 84.

58 *Register*, 17 Jan. 1907; *CMSH* 22 (Aug. 1912): 349–51.

59 ASV-DAC, 89.31, John E. Lyons to Sbarretti, 19 June 1908, 2 July 1908.

60 *Register*, 4 Feb. 1909, 24 Apr. 1919.

61 Ibid., 25 Feb. 1909.

62 ARCAT, McNeil Papers, AH 08.103, a "Catholic" to McNeil, 31 Oct. 1919. See also *St Joseph's Lilies* 3 (Dec. 1914): 49, for Reverend J.P. Tracy's praise of Mozart, Handel, and Gounod. He claimed that the use of their compositions was proof of the Church's recognition "that man not only has a

head, but he has a heart," and great music could convey to the latter the eternal truths.

63 ASV-DAC, 157.37, O'Connor to Falconio, 20 Nov. 1900.

64 SMCA, O'Connor Papers, clipping from *Catholic Record*, quoting the *Toronto World*, June 1911; ARCAT, O'Connor Papers, AA 04.02, O'Connor to Rev. Martin Whalen, 10 June 1901, clipping attached.

65 *Register*, 9 July 1903, 1 June 1905, 23 May 1907.

66 Ibid., 14 Jan. 1909, 5 June 1913. More picnics are reported 19 Aug. 1915 and 5 July 1917.

67 In 1864 and 1875 Catholic processions in Toronto were attacked by Protestants. The Jubilee Riots of 1875 were among the biggest demonstrations of violence in the city's history, reaffirming Toronto's popular nickname the "Belfast of Canada." Martin Galvin, the "Jubilee Riots in Toronto, 1875," CCHA, *Reports* 26 (1959): 93–107; for background regarding episcopal involvement in the sectarian tension see Mark G. McGowan, "'We Endure What We Cannot Cure': John Joseph Lynch and Roman Catholic-Protestant Relations in Toronto, 1864–1875," *Canadian Society of Church History Papers* (1985): 89–116.

68 ASV-DAC, 89.20, Teefy to Sbarretti, 20 Aug. 1906.

69 ARCAT, St Joseph's Parish box, Financial Report, 1902.

70 O'Brien, *Life Work*; ARCAT, O'Connor Papers, galley proofs of biography, AA01.01; William Macdonell, Bishop of Alexandria, to O'Connor, 16 Sept. 1907, AB 08.13.

71 ASV-DAC, 89.20, John R. Teefy to Donatus Sbarretti, 20 Oct. 1906.

72 ARCAT, Knights of Columbus Papers, Edward Hearn, Supreme Knight, New Haven, Conn., to Archbishop McEvay, 19 Feb. 1909; J.T. Kidd, Archdiocesan Secretary to Edward Hearn, 24 Feb. 1909.

73 Ibid., W.H. Leacock, District Deputy, to Archbishop Neil McNeil of Toronto, 16 Mar. 1917.

74 *Might's City Directory* (Toronto: J.M. Might 1900), 1043; *Detailed Report of the Inspector of Insurance and Registrar of Friendly Societies* (Toronto: Queen's Printer 1895–1921), six reports used.

75 Sidney Ahlstrom, *The Religious History of the American People*, vol. 1 (Garden City: Image Books 1975), 662–5; Hennessey, *American Catholics*, 103, 178–9, 198.

76 *Register*, 3 Aug. 1893, 5 Sept. 1895.

77 Ibid., 22 Feb. 1912, 17 Aug. 1911. The Paulists took up permanent residence at St Peter's Parish in 1914 in addition to their duties as chaplains to the Newman Club at the University of Toronto.

78 ASV-DAC, 89.20, Teefy to Sbarretti, 20 Aug. 1906.

79 "Tametsi," in *New Catholic Enclopedia* 13 (1967): 929; *Decrees of the Council of Trent*, Session 29, Canon 1.

80 *Arcanum*, 10–13.

81 *Butler's Catechism*, Lesson 29 (1947 ed.), 81–2. *Le Catéchisme des provinces ecclésiastiques de Québec, Montréal, Ottawa* (Montréal: par les Archevêques et Évêques de ces provinces, 1888), 58–61. Indissolubility of marriage was derived from Matt. 19:4–9.

82 Peter Ward, *Courtship, Love and Marriage in Nineteenth-Century Canada* (Montreal and Kingston: McGill-Queen's 1990), 15–31. Donald Akenson, *Small Differences: Irish Catholics and Irish Protestants, 1815–1922* (Montreal and Kingston: McGill-Queen's 1988), 108–26.

83 Arthur, Devine. *The Law of Christian Marriage* (New York: Benzinger 1908), 3–4; and "Tametsi," *New Catholic Encyclopedia*, 929.

84 *Arcanum*, 43.

85 Devine, *Law of Christian Marriage*, 150, 153.

86 Francis J. Schenk, *The Matrimonial Impediments of Mixed Marriage and Disparity of Cult* (Washington: Catholic University of America Canon Law Series no. 51, 1929), 56–60; Matthew Ramstein, OFM (conv.), *The Pastor and the Marriage Cases* (New York: Benzinger Brothers 1938), 78; Akenson, *Small Differences*, 108–26; Devine, *Law of Christian Marriage*, 158.

87 Devine, *Law of Christian Marriage*, 155–6; ASV-DAC, 89.15, Agreement, Mary Thompson and S.C. Wragge, 12 July 1905.

88 Ramstein, *The Pastor*, 80.

89 John S. Moir, *The Church in the British Era* (Toronto: McGraw Hill-Ryerson 1972), 89.

90 Ibid.; Moir, ed., *Church and State in Canada, 1627–1867: Basic Documents*, Carleton Library no. 33). (Toronto: McClelland and Stewart 1967), 140–8; Curtis Fahey, *In His Name: The Anglican Experience in Upper Canada, 1791–1854* (Ottawa: Carleton University Press 1991), 9, 22–3.

91 William Renwick Riddell, "The Law of Marriage in Upper Canada," *Canadian Historical Review* 2 (Sept. 1921): 226–48. Although passed in 1829, the revised act is listed as 1830, 11 George IV, cap. 36.

92 Ibid., 229–30.

93 Raymond J. Lahey, "Catholicism and Colonial Policy in Newfoundland, 1779–1845," in Terrence Murphy and Gerald Strotz, eds., *Creed and Culture: The Place of English-speaking Catholics in Canadian Society, 1750–1930* (Montreal and Kingston: McGill-Queen's University Press 1993), 59–64.

94 ARCAT, Alexander Macdonell Papers, "A Friend" to Macdonell, 23 Mar. 1833, MD 0101.

95 Ibid., Michael Power Papers, Power to Michael Robert Mills, LB 02.026; Armand de Charbonnel Papers, Circular, 28 Dec. 1852; Lynch Papers, Circular to Priests, 25 May 1887, L AA1325.

96 Ibid., McNeil Papers, Christian Unity, Feb. 1921, 11. See Table 3.3.

97 ARCAT, Lynch Papers, Lynch to Mr Murray, 11 Sept. 1882, L AH2727.

98 Ibid., Roman Correspondence, Walsh to the Propaganda Fide, 24 Feb.
    1893, 7605; and Walsh to Pope Leo XIII, 14 Mar. 1898, 8113.

99 In 1905 census-takers found that Holy Family Parish in Parkdale had a
    rate of one mixed marriage in ten, whereas the rate was one in four in the
    Earlscourt district, the future home of St Clare's parish. The latter parish
    was populated by English Catholics, many of whom would have easily
    married other English men and women in spite of obvious religious dif-
    ferences. Holy Family Parish was new, relatively small, and in a predom-
    inantly Protestant district, although its former ties to St Helen's Parish
    were sufficiently strong that it was in contact with a large Catholic com-
    munity in which numerous marital partners could be found. ARCAT,
    Holy Family Parish microfilm, Parish Census, 1905; St Clare's Parish box,
    Remarks on Earlscourt District, 26 Aug. 1908. Given O'Connor's policy
    on the subject, most of these unions probably predated his arrival.

100 Ibid., Roman Correspondence, O'Connor to Cardinal Gotti, 22 Oct. 1904,
    8706.

101 Ibid., Parish Marriage Registers, 1899–1900, passim.

102 Ibid., Apostolic Delegate Papers, draft of report from O'Connor to Apos-
    tolic Delegate, 20 Nov. 1900. ASV-DAC, 157.37, O'Connor to Falconio,
    20 Nov. 1900. The draft and final copies are very close.

103 ARCAT, Apostolic Delegate Papers, draft of O'Connor to Apostolic Dele-
    gate, 20 Nov. 1900.

104 Record, 18 Sept. 1915. Other similes used for mixed marriages included
    "the contamination of doctrine," an irreconcilable mix of "oil and water,"
    and "no concord, no true happiness." See Register, 6 Sept. 1900, 30 Nov.
    1919, 25 Jan. 1900.

105 ARCAT, O'Connor Papers, Circulars, Regulations; Dispensation Stub
    Books. For publication of banns see ibid., Roman Correspondence, draft
    of letter from O'Connor to Cardinal Gotti, 22 Oct. 1904.

106 ASV-DAC, 157.37, O'Connor to Falconio, 20 Nov. 1900.

107 O'Brien, Life Work.

108 ARCAT, Marriage Dispensation Stubs, 1908–20. For more information on
    Ne Temere, see John Moir, "Canadian Protestant Reaction to the Ne Temere
    Decree," CCHA, Study Sessions 48 (1981): 78–80.

109 Register, 21 May 1908.

110 ARCAT, Roman Correspondence, rough draft of letter from O'Connor to
    Cardinal Gotti, 22 Oct. 1904, 8706.

111 ASV-DAC, 89.1, Thompson-Teeple Case, O'Connor to Sbarretti, 13 Apr.
    1903; Mulock-Falconbridge Case, O'Connor to Sbarretti, 8 June 1903,
    28 Nov. 1903;

112 Ibid., 89.3, Laurier to Sbarretti, 2 June 1903.

113 Ibid., 89.1, Documenti Evidenziati, O'Connor to Sbarretti, 3 June 1903.

114 Ibid., 89.3, Sbarretti to O'Connor, 6 June 1903.

115 Peter B. Waite, *The Man From Halifax* (Toronto: University of Toronto Press 1985), 10–33.
116 ASV-DAC, Documenti Evidenziati, 89.2, J.M. Cruise to O'Connor, 13 Apr. 1903.
117 Ibid., Annie Thompson to Sbarretti, 8 Apr. 1903; Sbarretti to O'Connor, 8 Apr. 1903, 16 Apr. 1903.
118 Ibid., 89.15, John Thompson, Jr., to Sbarretti, 8 Dec. 1905; Joseph Thompson memorandum, 9 Nov. 1905; O'Connor to Sbarretti, 19 Sept. 1905.
119 ARCAT, Apostolic Delegate Papers, letter from Rev. J.T. Kidd, Archdiocesan Administrator, to Delegate, 1 Sept. 1912. Kidd reported: "The number of applications for such dispensations made of late has been rapidly increasing. Although many of Catholic girls who keep company with a protestant young man will threaten to go to a protestant or magistrate if a dispensation is not granted, still a good proportion of them will not do so."
120 AO, Provincial Secretary, Registrar General's Office, Report Relating to Registration of Births, Marriages and Deaths in the Province of Ontario, Reports 42–51 (1911–20); *Casket*, 11 Apr. 1918.
121 Ibid.
122 J. Albert Foisy, *Le Catholicisme en Ontario* (Ottawa: Imprimerie Le Droit 1918), 48–9, 53.
123 ASV-DAC, 89.15, Thompson to Sbarretti, 8 Dec. 1905; 89.3 J.R. Teefy to Father Schaefer (re Falconbridge-Mulock), 5 June 1903; 89.4, Rohleder to Sbarretti, 8 Sept. 1904; 89.17, Castell Hopkins-Beatrice Bonner Case, 1905–06. Minehan is featured here in his opposition to O'Connor.
124 Ibid., 89, Mulock-Falconbridge Case, O'Connor to Sbarretti, 8 June 1903; 89.4, Rohleder to Sbarretti, 8 Sept. 1904; 89.4, Teefy to Sbarretti, 10 June 1906, 11 July 1906, tables included.
125 Ibid.
126 ARCAT, Roman Correspondence, draft of a letter from O'Connor to Gotti, 10 Feb. 1905, 8801. This is confirmed in Apostolic Delegate Papers, Donatus Sbaretti to O'Connor, 4 Dec. 1903.
127 Ibid., Roman Correspondence, Cardinal Gotti to O'Connor, 14 Sept. 1906, 8909, trans. from Latin.
128 Ibid., McNeil Papers, Christian Unity, Feb. 1921, 11.
129 United Church Archives, T.R. Robinson ed., *Report of the Social Survey Commission on Prostitution*, 9 Mar. 1914; theatres: *Register*, 7 Dec. 1905, 19 Feb. 1914, 25 Feb. 1915; motion pictures: *Register*, 26 Sept. 1918, 2 Dec. 1920.
130 ARCAT, Marriage Registers, passim; NPRC, confidential personnel files reveal practising Catholics of mixed marriages; ASAS, Register, 1914–94. Actual cases are confidential, but there are several men who entered the seminary and required proof that their parent's marriage was valid. Note in chap. 2 the case of Father Hugh Canning.

131 Devine, *Law of Christian Marriage*, 263.
132 Integrism: "The modernist crisis did usher in a reaction in the Church which, in some instances, led to heresy hunting, calumny, and persecution. This movement of extreme reaction is referred to as 'Integrism,' due to the over-zealous efforts on the part of those involved to protect the integrity of the Catholic faith." James C. Livingston, *Modern Christian Thought from the Enlightenment to the Present* (New York: Macmillan 1971), 292; Daly, *Transcendance and Immanence*, 8–12.
133 *Register*, 25 Apr. 1907, 2 Mar. 1911.
134 Clarke, "Piety, Nationalism and Fraternity," 485–96; Murray Nicolson, "Irish Tridentine Catholicism in Victorian Toronto: Vessel for Ethno-religious Persistence," CCHA, *Study Sessions* 50 (1983): 425–6.

CHAPTER FOUR

1 Excerpt from the Reverend H.F. Darnell, "The Maple," *Canadian Catholic Readers*, Fourth Book (Toronto: Copp Clark 1899), 11–12.
2 Murray W. Nicolson, "Irish Catholic Education in Victorian Toronto: An Ethnic Response to Urban Conformity," *Histoire sociale – Social History* 17 (Nov. 1984): 287.
3 For more information on the history and development of Catholic schools, consult Franklin Walker, *Catholic Education and Politics in Upper Canada* (Toronto: J.M. Dent 1955); Robert M. Stamp, *The Historical Background to Separate Schools in Ontario* (Toronto: Ministry of Education 1985); John Moir, "The Origins of the Separate School Question in Ontario," *Canadian Journal of Theology* 5, no. 2 (1959): 106–7; John Moir, *Church and State in Canada West* (Toronto: University of Toronto Press 1959); Robert Choquette, *L'Eglise Catholique dans l'Ontario francais du dix-neuvieme siecle* (Ottawa: Editions de l'Université d'Ottawa 1984); ARCAT, Charbonnel Papers, AA 04.07, Circular, 25 Apr. 1851; AA 04.09, Circular, 28 Dec. 1852; AA 04.10, Circular, 18 Mar. 1853; AB 01.01, Circular, 9 July 1853; Franklin Walker, *Catholic Education and Politics in Ontario* (Toronto: Federation of Catholic Educators Association 1964, repr. 1976); Robert Thomas Dixon, *Be A Teacher: A History of the Ontario English Catholic Teachers' Association, 1944–1994* (Toronto: OECTA 1994); Robert Stamp, *The Schools of Ontario, 1876–1976*, (Toronto: Ontario Historical Studies Series, University of Toronto Press 1982).
4 Nicolson, "Irish Catholic Education in Victorian Toronto," 296–7.
5 AO, RG 2, Ministry of Education, Separate School Board Inspector's Reports (hereafter ME, SSBIR), vol. 23, 1896; ACSJ, Separate School Board Reports, box 16, Annual Reports of Separate Schools in Charge of the Community of St Joseph, Toronto, 1895–1913.
6 AO, Ministry of Education, Separate School Board Reports, vol. 23, 1896; *Separate School Chronicle* 1 (May 1919), and 4 (Nov. 1921).

7 AO, ME, SSBIR, vol. 54, 1907. William Prendergast reported that most of the foreign children at St Patrick's school had little knowledge of English, and as a result few completed school through the fourth form.

8 Ibid.

9 AO, ME, SSBIR, vol. 48, 1905; vol. 50, 1906. In the latter Prendergast suggests that some inner-city teachers be transferred to the suburbs, where school enrolment was increasing.

10 Ibid., vol. 12, 1890.

11 *Register*, 22 July 1915; MSSBA, Roman Catholic Separate School Board Minutes, Lay Teachers, 1913–21.

12 Elizabeth M. Smyth, " 'Developing the powers of the youthful mind': The Evolution of Education for Young Women at St Joseph's Academy, Toronto, 1854–1911," CCHA, *Historical Studies* 60 (1993–94): 104. ASV-DAC, 179.2, Documenti vari – Statistiche sulle scuole elementari in Canada (1901–02), Sr M. Eucheria to Diomede Falconio, 23 July 1901.

13 Ibid., 111–12.

14 Sutherland, *Children in English-Canadian Society*, 157–9, 167; and Alison Prentice, "The Feminization of Teaching," in Susan M. Trofimenkoff and Alison Prentice, eds., *The Neglected Majority: Essays in Canadian Women's History* (Toronto: McClelland and Stewart 1977), 57–9, 64–5.

15 AO, ME, SSBIR, vol. 12, 1890; vol. 14, 1891; vol. 23, 1896; vol. 27, 1898. In the 1890s salaries for young female teachers with less than five years' experience varied from $225 to $300 per annum. This was well below the provincial average for public school teachers in urban areas, who made $382 in 1887 and $425 in 1897; see Stamp, *The Schools of Ontario*, app. 2, 279. In a letter to the premier in 1914, Archbishop McNeil admitted that "salaries of teaching sisters is below a living wage." ARCAT, McNeil Papers, Education, copy of a letter from McNeil to Premier Hearst, 2 Nov. 1914.

16 Walker, *Catholic Education*, 2:201–4. For additional information about the linguistic battles in Ottawa that precipitated the Gratton case upon which McMahon ruled, see Robert Choquette, *Language and Religion: A History of French-English Conflict in Ontario* (Ottawa: University of Ottawa Press 1975): 59–68.

17 AAK, Charles Gauthier Papers, Denis O'Connor to Gauthier, 16 Oct. 1905, 8 Mar. 1907; ARCAT, O'Connor Papers, Charles Gauthier to O'Connor, 7 Mar. 1907, and Draft of Provisions in Case of Separate School Teachers. Walker, *Catholic Education*, 2:207–20.

18 *Record*, 30 July 1904. AO, Sir James Pliny Whitney Papers, Inspector J.F. White to Whitney, 23 Mar. 1907, MU 3122; ARCAT, Other Collections, Canadian Catholic Union, MM01, box 1, Minute Book, 30 Nov. 1903.

19 *Record*, 11 Jan., 5 and 12 Apr. 1890. Walker, *Catholic Education*, 2:60–81. Brian Clarke, "Piety, Nationalism and Fraternity: The Rise of Catholic Voluntary Associations in Toronto, 1850–1895," PhD, University of Chi-

cago 1986, 485–96. ARCAT, John J. Lynch Papers, copy of letter from Lynch to Mr Mulligan, 27 Dec. 1887, and Lynch to Mr Curran, 27 Dec. 1887; Letterbook 6, 16 Feb. 1894; AAK, Cleary Papers, James Cleary to John Walsh, 12 Jan. 1890. *Register,* 22 Feb. 1894, stated that the clergy felt comfortable with a board elected by secret ballot.

20 AO, Whitney Papers, McEvay to Whitney, 15 Feb. 1907, MU 3122.

21 Ibid., 3 Apr. 1907, MU 3122.

22 *An Act Respecting the Qualification of Certain Teachers,* 7 Edward VII, 1907, chap. 52, 20 Apr. 1907. Walker, 2:221.

23 AO, ME, SSBIR, vol. 67, 1909.

24 Ibid., vol. 12, 1890; vol. 14, 1891; vol. 23, 1896; vol. 31, 1900; Stamp, *The Schools of Ontario,* 279.

25 *Register,* 5 July 1917, 26 July 1917, 9 Aug. 1917, 9 Jan. 1919. Stamp, *The Schools of Ontario,* 279. The average annual separate school salary reported to McNeil in 1913 for a male was $415, while a female was paid $286. ARCAT, McNeil Papers, Education, F. Hall to McNeil, 21 Aug. 1913.

26 ARCAT, McNeil Papers, Education, J.M. Bennet, Inspector of Separate Schools, to McNeil, 30 Mar. 192; Lynch Papers, AD 30.01, Daniel P. Cahill, To the Electors of the Separate Schools within St George's Ward, ca 1888.

27 AO, ME, SSBIR, vol. 40, 1903.

28 Ibid., vol. 61, 1908; vol. 67, 1909. St Anthony's, St Basil's, St Cecilia's, St Helen's, and St Joseph's schools were all praised for their new facilities or renovations. Prendergast reserved the highest praise for the new St Michael's School: "This is perhaps the best building belonging to the Board ... the classrooms are models of neatness and cleanliness; the walls are hung with well-chosen pictures, the window sills and stands with thriving house plants." In 1909 J.F. Power confirmed this appraisal, but added scathing condemnations of the conditions at St Patrick's School and St Joseph's High School. See also MSSBA, Minutes, 10 Dec. 1920; ARCAT, McNeil Papers, Education, Inspector J.F. Power to McNeil, 16 Apr. 1914.

29 ARCAT, Lynch Papers, AD 30.01, Daniel Cahill, "To the Electors of Separate Schools."

30 AO, ME, SSBIR, vol. 27, 1898; vol. 40, 1903. St Cecilia's and St Helen's bore the brunt of the criticism. For a broad appreciation of the reform movement for public health in schools, see Neil Sutherland, *Children in English-speaking Canada,* 40–2.

31 AO, ME, SSBIR, vol. 23, 1896.

32 Ibid., vol. 29, 1899.

33 Stamp, *The Schools of Ontario,* 280.

34 AO, ME, SSBIR, vol. 23, 1896.

35 Cases of overcrowding are legion: AO, Ministry of Education, Separate School Board Reports, vol. 12, 1890, St Paul's Boys, St Paul's Girls, St Pe-

ter's and St Mary's Girls; vol. 23, 1896, St Cecilia's, St Patrick's Boys, St Francis' Boys, St Peter's and St Ann's; vol. 31, 1900, St Cecilia's; vol. 67, 1909, St Peter's and St Patrick's; *Register*, 25 Nov. 1909; and ARCAT, McNeil Papers, Education, J.F. Power to McNeil, 16 Apr. 1914. Power complains of a general "overcrowding of primary classes, which leads to retardation and poor school work at the very outset of a child's school life."

36 ARCAT, McEvay Papers, Notes on Assessment, AE01.104; *Separate School Chronicle* 1 (Dec. 1919).

37 ARCAT, McNeil Papers, Education, J.P. Treacy to McNeil, 16 Apr. 1915.

38 Ibid., Report on School Attendance, 1919; *Register*, 28 Dec. 1916; ARCAT, McNeil Papers, Pastoral Letters, PC 25.05, Lenten Pastoral, "Christian Unity," Feb. 1921.

39 AO, ME, SSBIR, vol. 12, 1890.

40 Ibid., vol. 31, 1900, and St Francis's School, vol. 61, 1908.

41 Smyth, "Developing the Powers," 112.

42 AO, ME, SSBIR, vol. 40, 1903; ARCAT, McNeil Papers, Education, J.F. Power to McNeil, 16 Apr. 1914.

43 Stamp, *The Schools of Ontario*, 74–84; Sutherland, *Children in English-speaking Canada*, 172–201.

44 Stamp, *The Schools of Ontario*, 74.

45 AO, ME, SSBIR, vol. 12, 1890; *Register*, 25 Oct. 1894, 6 Dec. 1894, 31 Jan. 1895.

46 *Register*, 5 Dec. 1895. Reports filed by the separate school inspectors praised St John's prior to the Great War: AO, ME, SSBIR, 1898–1909. By 1915, however, J.J. Kelso, superintendent of Neglected and Dependent Children, found that the facilities were outdated and the agricultural training in need of expansion due to the larger number of rural boys living at the school: ARCAT, Brothers of Christian Schools Papers, J.J. Kelso to the Provincial Secretary, 26 Jan. 1915. For a short but readable study of Kelso and child relief in Ontario, see Andrew Jones and Leonard Rutman, *In the Children's Aid: J.J. Kelso and Child Welfare in Ontario* (Toronto: University of Toronto Press 1981).

47 *Register*, 18 May 1893, 6 Apr. 1893; ARCAT, Walsh Papers, AA 07.07, Circular on Blantyre Park, 2 July 1897; *Canadian Messenger of the Sacred Heart* 8 (June 1898): 233; NA, Sir John Thompson Papers, vol. 172, Father J.M. Cruise to Sir John Thompson, 7 Jan. 1893, 21541–3; *Register*, 28 and 22 Dec. 1898.

48 AO, Ministry of Education, Separate School Board Reports, vol. 12, 1890; *CWR*, 28 Dec. 1889. Walsh commended De La Salle High School for its strong insistence upon both religious and scientific education.

49 "A Day in the Junior Sixth Class," *St Joseph's Lilies* 3 (Mar. 1915); J. Hodgins, *The Establishment of Schools and Colleges in Ontario* (1910), 2:146;

ARCAT, McNeil Papers, Education, letter from Brother Rogatien of De La Salle to McNeil, 7 Apr. 1913; *Register*, 7 Sept. 1905, 21 July 1910, 15 Aug. 1912. ASV-DAC, 179.2, J.R. Teefy to Diomede Falconio, 29 July 1901.

50 ARCAT, O'Connor Papers, Education, Report on Toronto Separate School Board, 1904; *Register*, 22 June 1916.

51 AO, ME, SSBIR, vol. 61, 1908; ARCAT, McNeil Papers, Education, J.F. Power to McNeil, 16 Apr. 1914.

52 *Register*, 21 Oct. 1897, 3 Jan. 1907, 25 July 1907.

53 Mary Francis Mallon, *John Mallon of Brockton and Toronto (1836–1913)* (Toronto: Pro Familia Publishing 1990), 77.

54 ASV-DAC, 89.28, Thomas Mulvey to Donatus Sbarretti, 20 May 1908.

55 *Record*, 28 Aug. 1897. In 1910 these sentiments were repeated by the annual convention of the Ancient Order of Hibernians in Kingston. Provincial President Frank J. Walsh lamented that "Children of Irish parentage, surrounded by the environment of the Western Hemisphere, are too apt to forget the land of their forefathers." AO, C.J. Foy Papers, Eleventh Biennial Convention of the Ancient Order of Hibernians, Ontario, 23–5 Aug. 1910.

56 AO, ME, SSBIR, vol. 61, 1908. Prendergast said the same about St Mary's Industrial School.

57 *IC*, 17 July 1890; *Record*, 26 July 1890.

58 *Record*, 26 July 1890. In the 1890s there was a vigorous attempt by the department to inculcate patriotic values in the province's schools. Textbooks, courses, and school activities were redefined, with new emphasis placed on Canada and her role in the British Empire. Stamp, *The Schools of Ontario*, 32–7; Sutherland, *Children in English-Canadian Society*, 172, 202–15. Edison J. Quick, "The Development of Geography and History Curricula in the Elementary Schools of Ontario," EdD, University of Toronto 1967, 113, 123, 135, 145, 151–2. Alison Prentice, *The School Promoters: Education and Social Class in Mid-Nineteenth Century Upper Canada* (Toronto: McClelland and Stewart 1977), 66–87 passim.

59 *The Separate Public School Review* 1 (Nov. 1921): 1–2.

60 Neil McNeil, "A Need of the Day," *Cathedral Magazine* 3 (Oct. 1919): 2.

61 *Register*, 4 July 1895; MSSBA, Board Minutes, May 1899.

62 *CWR*, 19 Sept. 1891; *Register*, 24 Jan. 1907; *IC*, 13 June 1889. In the latter Walsh recommended the *St Basil's Hymn Book* for use in the city's separate schools.

63 A tradition dating back at least to Tertullian's eloquent claims, in the second century, that good Christians were, by their very nature, good citizens: see *Apology*, 30.1, 30.4–5, 32.1, 33.1–2.

64 ARCAT, McNeil Papers, AR 01.45a, undated.

65 C.J. Foy, "Catholic Education," *St Joseph's Lilies* 5 (Dec. 1915): 110.

66 James Butler, *Catechism* (Montreal: D.J. Sadlier and Company 1871), and Richard Gilmour, DD, *Bible History* (New York: Benzinger Brothers 1881). ASV-DAC, 179.2 and 179.4, Statistiche sulle scuole elementari, 1901–02. Reports indicate that the CSJs, Loretto Sisters, Christian Brothers, and Basilian Fathers all used these texts at their schools, frequently supplementing them with other catechisms and theological texts.

67 ARCAT, O'Connor Papers, Education, Results of the Diocesan Examinations on Christian Doctrine and Bible History, 1 Aug. 1902, 30 Jan. 1908; McEvay Papers, Education, Results of the Diocesan Examinations, 2 Feb. 1910, 15 May 1911; *Register*, 2 Feb. 1905, 14 Sept. 1905, 2 Sept. 1909, 18 Feb. 1909, 1 Sept. 1910.

68 ARCAT, McNeil Papers, Education, "Christian Doctrine," 17 Jan. 1914.

69 Ibid., Sister M. Ernestine, IVBM, Loretto Day School, to McNeil, 30 Aug. 1917; *Register*, 2 May 1918, 17 July 1919. After 1915 the *Register* ran a series of columns by Father Lancelot Minehan that offered in-depth exploration of questions featured in the Butler. Even the vociferous "Teresa" called for catechetical reform as early as 1899: *Register*, 2 Feb. 1899.

70 ARCAT, McNeil Papers, Education, McNeil to Roderick McEachen, 28 Oct. 1918, and J.C. Walsh, Ottawa Separate School Inspector, to McNeil, 28 Sept. 1922.

71 Ibid., draft of letter from McNeil to John Seath, 9 Sept. 1915, and John Seath to McNeil, 16 Sept. 1915; St Augustine's Seminary Papers, Semiannual Meeting of Bishops of Ontario, Minutes, 10 Oct. 1916; AAO, Toronto Correspondence, McNeil to Charles Gauthier, 6 Dec. 1913. It is interesting to note that the *Third Golden Rule Book* (Toronto: Macmillan 1918) was very fair when dealing with Catholics and their literature. Thomas More was praised for his act of defiance against the "cruel" King Henry VIII (16–18). By contrast, Gilmour's *Bible History* made unflattering comments about Protestant reformers; John Knox, for example, was referred to as "the ruffian of the Reformation" (296).

72 MSSBA, Board Minutes, Sept. 1886; AAK, Cleary Papers, Father George Northgraves to Cleary, 6 Apr. 1887, and Bishop Richard A. O'Connor to Cleary, 24 Mar. 1887; ARCAT, Walsh Papers, J.T. White to Walsh, 3 Oct. 1891, 23 Feb. 1895; Lynch Papers, Richard A. O'Connor to Lynch, 6 Feb. 1888.

73 A Catholic Teacher, *Sadlier's Dominion Fourth Reader* (Toronto: James A. Sadlier 1886), vii–x, 41–3, 193–4, 274–96; *Third Reader* (1886), 46–7.

74 Ibid., *Fourth Reader*, rev. ed. (nd). Given the historical selections in this revised text, it was published in the 1890s.

75 Nicolson, "Irish Education in Victorian Toronto," 298.

76 *Record*, 2 Sept. 1899; MSSBA, Board Meeting Minutes, 6 June 1899; AO, Ministry of Education, Separate School Board Reports, vol. 61, 1908;

vol. 67, 1909. The 1908 reports indicate for the first time whether or not schools were using unauthorized textbooks. Inspectors William Prendergast and J.F. Power asserted that no unauthorized texts were being used in Toronto's separate schools. See also Ontario, Department of Education, *Circular 14*, 1889–1920. Although each reader was authorized as early as 1899, *Circular 14* omits them until 1912.

77 *Register*, 24 Aug. 1899; AAO, Toronto Correspondence, Correspondance des civiles, 1893–1900, A.W. Thomas, Secretary-Treasurer of Copp Clark, to Archbishop Thomas Duhamel, 27 Jan. 1900.

78 *Record*, 2 Sept. 1899.

79 *Canadian Catholic Readers*, Third Book (Toronto: Copp Clark 1899), 220–3.

80 Ibid., 235–6.

81 Ibid., Fourth Book (1899), 257–9.

82 Ibid., 124; see also "Ye Mariners of England," 161; "Before Agincourt," 129–30; "Richard I In Palestine," 124–8; "Battle of Sedgemoor," 91–9; and "Waterloo," 230–2.

83 ARCAT, McEvay Papers, Charles Gauthier to Denis O'Connor, 28 Jan. 1908, and Gauthier to McEvay, 29 Jan. 1909.

84 AAO, Toronto Correspondence, Fergus McEvay to Thomas Duhamel, 27 Jan. 1909; McEvay to Duhamel, 29 Jan. 1909; and Gauthier Papers, Correspondence with Bishops, 1904–10, David Scollard to Gauthier, 30 Jan. 1909; ARCAT, McEvay Papers, David Scollard to McEvay, 29 Jan. 1909; Charles Gauthier to McEvay, 5 Feb. 1909; Narcisse Lorrain to McEvay, 2 Feb. 1909; and McEvay to P.S. Dowdall, 7 Feb. 1909.

85 ARCAT, McEvay Papers, H.L. Thompson, president of Copp Clark to McEvay, 6 May 1909.

86 Ibid., Thompson to McEvay, 27 May 1909. This letter indicates that Thompson had found potential buyers for the readers in western Canada, which would permit increased production and thereby reduce the unit price of the books to 62¢. When the bishops were unable to come up with extra funds and the first galleys proved inferior, the project collapsed. See ibid., J.T. Kidd to Gauthier, 20 July 1910, and Michael Fallon to McEvay, 22 Dec. 1910.

87 Ibid., Walsh Papers, George Ross, minister of Education, to Walsh, 11 Feb. 1890.

88 Ibid., McEvay Papers, Teefy to McEvay, 26 Feb. 1911.

89 Ibid., copy of letter from Michael O'Brien to John Seath, minister of Education, 15 Jan. 1909, and O'Brien to McEvay, 8 Mar. 1909.

90 Ibid., Gauthier to McEvay, 29 Jan. 1909.

91 AAK, Gauthier Papers, Education box, copy of letter from D.J. Scollard, secretary to meeting, to James Pliny Whitney, 20 Jan. 1909.

92 Ibid., copy of letter from Gauthier to Whitney, 4 Feb. 1909.

93 *Register*, 12 Aug. 1920.

94 Stamp, *The Schools of Ontario*, 93.
95 *The Ontario Reader,* Fourth Book (Toronto: T. Eaton Co. 1909), 1–2, 74–5,
   154–5, 358–62, 363–4. For the historical vignettes of Canada and the Empire see *The Ontario Reader,* Third Book (1909), 31–3, 61–4, 65–6, 84–5,
   109–10, 123–5, 179–80, 189–91, 192–3, 209–11, 215–21, 246–9, 301–6,
   307–9, 332–6; Fourth Book, 28–36, 37–8, 65–73, 95–6, 103–5, 105–8, 122–7,
   141, 143–8, 149–153, 170–2, 192–5, 202–3, 219–26, 227, 248–60, 302–24,
   369–71, 409.
96 AAK, Michael J. Spratt Papers, Bishop Michael Fallon to Spratt, 6 Dec.
   1916; ARCAT, McNeil Papers, Education, Fallon to McNeil, 6 Dec. 1916,
   and H.L. Thompson to McNeil, 19 Aug. 1918; *Canadian Catholic Corona*
   Readers, Third and Fourth Books, (Montreal: Ginn and Company 1931).
97 *Ontario Teacher's Manuals, History* (Toronto: Copp Clark 1915), 13.
98 Ibid., 13–14, 16–17, 52.
99 Quick, "The Development of Geography and History Curricula," 90–2,
   108–9, 135–6, 147–8, 150–1, 183–5, 195.
100 *CWR,* 4 Aug. 1888, 10 Oct. 1891; *IC,* 19 Nov. 1891; ARCAT, Lynch Papers,
   extract from the Minutes of Council on Public Instruction, 19 May 1875.
   Lynch had complained about Collier's histories. ARCAT, Walsh Papers,
   D.J. Sadlier to Walsh, 3 Aug. 1892.
101 MSSBA, Board Minutes, Sept. 1911, Dec. 1911.
102 A Catholic Teacher, *Outlines of Canadian History* (Toronto: James Sadlier
   1888), preface.
103 Ibid., 7–8. As early as 1899 Archbishop Walsh negotiated for the government's sanction of Sadlier's history text, without much success. ARCAT,
   Letterbook 6, Walsh to Bishop Thomas Dowling of Peterborough, 20 Dec.
   1889.
104 AAK, Cleary Papers, G.W. Ross to J.V. Cleary, 10 Oct. 1893. A reader in
   my possession was inscribed by its user at St Patrick's School in Toronto as well as her book list for the fourth form, which included *The*
   History of England and Canada, presumably by Arabella Buckley and
   James Robertson. The Toronto Separate School Board attempted to introduce a course in Irish history as early as 1904 in response to complaints from some older Catholics who felt that children knew little
   about their Irish heritage. In 1906, 250 Irish history texts, unauthorized
   by the Ministry of Education, were purchased, but nothing seems to
   have come of them except at De La Salle, where they were used as supplementary texts. By 1908 inspectors reported that no unauthorized
   texts were in use. MSSBA, Board Minutes, 4 Oct. 1904, 7 Mar. 1905,
   2 May 1905, 3 Oct. 1905, 6 Sept. 1905, 30 Jan. 1906; *Register,* 1 Feb. 1906;
   and AO, Separate School Reports, 1908.
105 Anabella Buckley and W.J. Robertson, *High School History of England and*
   Canada (Toronto: Copp Clark 1891), 121–3, 131, 141–2, 154, 214. George

M. Wrong, *The British Nation* (Toronto: George Morang 1904), 298. Fair treatment is also witnessed in *Ontario Public School History of England* (Toronto: Macmillan 1913), 123, 133–4, 138–42, 200, 284.

106 James K. McConica, "Kingsford and Whiggery in Canadian History," *Canadian Historical Review* 40 (June 1959): 113–15; Carl Berger, *The Writing of Canadian History*, 2nd ed. (Toronto: University of Toronto Press 1986), 32–3; Herbert Butterfield, *The Whig Interpretation of History* (London 1931); Kenneth N. Windsor, "Historical Writing in Canada to 1920," in Carl F. Klinck, ed., *Literary History of Canada: Canadian Literature in English* (Toronto: University of Toronto Press, 1965), 215, 220, 225, 230.

107 M. Brook Taylor, "The Writing of English-Canadian History in the Nineteenth Century," PhD, University of Toronto 1984, 258, 280–2, 308, 459–60.

108 Berger, *The Writing of Canadian History*, 11–13, 31–3, 38–9, 44–5; Windsor, "Historical Writing," 230–1, 233.

109 Robertson, *Public School History of England and Canada*, 280; *Ontario Public School History of Canada* (Toronto: Macmillan 1912), 259; Buckley and Robertson, *High School History of England and Canada*, 405; and George M. Wrong, *Ontario Public School History of Canada* (Toronto: Ryerson Press 1921), 354; William Grant, *Ontario High School History of Canada* (Toronto: T. Eaton Co. 1914), 407; W.H.P. Clement, *The History of the Dominion of Canada*, 2nd ed. (Toronto: William Briggs, Copp Clark, 1898), 341.

110 Ministry of Education, *Ontario School Geography* (Toronto: Educational Book Company 1910), 191, 60–1. These racist views were reiterated to potential teachers in the Normal School. The notebooks of Catholic student-teacher Margaret Lowe reveal that Normal School instruction included the categorization of racial types. MSSBA, Lesson Books and Scribblers of Margaret Lowe, Toronto Normal School, 1914–15.

111 *Register*, 15 Nov. 1894, and 4 July 1895.

112 MSSBA, Minutes of the Property Committee, 18 May 1915; Board Minutes, 3 Jan. 1919. *Register*, 16 Jan. 1902, 12 Feb. 1903, 17 Nov. 1910, 27 Apr. 1911, 19 June 1913. The school trustees, however, rejected a request that the Ensign be flown over schools on 12 July, on the grounds that they had too much respect for the flag: "The 12th of July was the death of the Irish union and patriotism. It will bring about the same evil here." *Register*, 11 Apr. 1907.

113 *Register*, 12 Apr. 1900; *Globe*, 24 May 1899.

114 Stamp, *The Schools of Ontario*, 35. Also see Robert Stamp, "Empire Day in the Schools of Ontario: The Training of Young Imperialists," *Journal of Canadian Studies* 8 (Aug. 1973): 32–42. *Ontario Teacher's Manuals, History* (Toronto: Copp Clark 1915), 75–77. There were Catholic cadet corps at St Mary's School and De La Salle. MSSBA, Board Minutes, 6 May 1912, 29 Aug. 1919, 30 Mar. 1920, 3 May 1921, 7 Mar. 1922. *Register*, 5 June 1919.

For Catholic schools in the context of the Great War, see *Register*, 15 Feb. 1917, 3 Feb. 1916, 14 June 1917.

115 ACSJ, *Annals of the Sisters of St Joseph, Toronto* 2 (1 Jan. 1916): 500.

116 *IC*, 2 Jan. 1890; Dean O'Malley, "Catholic Journalism in Schools and Colleges," *St Joseph's Lilies* 5 (Sept. 1916): 6; ibid. (Dec. 1916): 7; *Register*, 13 Feb. 1902.

117 Edmund McCorkell, *Henry Carr: Revolutionary* (Toronto: Griffin House 1969), 15; *Register*, 11 Jan. 1894, 9 Aug. 1894.

118 *Register*, 3 Jan. 1901, 18 Oct. 1900.

119 The *Register* made the link between higher education and serving material interests. It expected that higher education would facilitate the movement of Catholics into better jobs and thereby ensure that Catholics would never again be hewers of wood and drawers of water. *Register*, 19 May 1904, 8 Aug. 1907, 11 Sept. 1914, 31 Mar. 1910. In the latter Thomas O'Hagan warned: "Catholic young men should know their advancement lies in their own hands."

120 Ibid., 16 May 1918. ARCAT, McNeil Papers, galley proofs of an unpublished biography of McNeil, ca 1934; Jeanne R.M. Beck, "Henry Somerville and the Development of Catholic Social Thought in Canada," PhD, McMaster University 1977, 72–3.

121 McCorkell, *Henry Carr*, 15; NA, Charles Murphy Papers, vol. 36, "Memorial re: Ottawa University," 15003, 15010.

122 *Register*, 13 Sept. 1906, 20 Sept. 1906.

123 NA, Charles Murphy Papers, "Memorial re: Ottawa University," 7 Oct. 1901, vol. 36, 15003–10. The following spring the petitioners appealed to the Apostolic Delegate to compel the Oblates to convert the University of Ottawa into an English-speaking institution. Ibid., Petition to Diomede Falconio, 6 Mar. 1902, vol. 36, 14951–6. For more information on the language conflict at the University of Ottawa see Robert Choquette, *Language and Religion* (Ottawa: University of Ottawa Press 1975), 9–44.

124 Quoted in Choquette, *Language and Religion*, 19; Choquette, *La Foi: Gardienne de la Langue* (Montréal: Bellarmin 1987), 172–6 passim.

125 ARCAT, Apostolic Delegate Papers, DS16.09, Bishop Stagni to McNeil, 12 Aug. 1914; *Register*, 19 May 1904.

126 Choquette, *La Foi*, 184–5.

127 ARCAT, McNeil Papers, J.W. McIsaac to McNeil, 2 Feb. 1919. For financial losses at the University of Ottawa, see AAK, Spratt Papers, Bishop M.J. O'Brien of Peterborough to Spratt, 3 Nov. 1915.

128 Michael Power, "Fallon Versus Forster: The Struggle over Assumption College, 1919–1925," CCHA, *Historical Studies* 56 (1989): 49–66; Terence Fay, SJ, "The Jesuits and the Catholic University of Canada at Kingston," ibid., 58 (1991): 57–78; Michael Cottrell, "John Joseph Leddy and the Battle for the Soul of the Catholic Church in the West," ibid., 61 (1995): 41–51.

129 ARCAT, McNeil Papers, Education, F.R. Latchford to MacNeil, 5 Sept. 1913, "Facilities for Catholic Education," *Ontario Catholic Yearbook* (Toronto: Newman Club 1914), 99; *Register,* 11 Sept. 1913.

130 NA, James F. Kenney Papers, Diaries, vol. 7, file 21, 21 Feb. 1904. An earlier attempt by Catholic students to establish a clubhouse ended in temporary failure after the death of Archbishop McEvay, who had supported the proposal. NA, Kenney Papers, vol.7, file 23, Diaries, 16 Nov. 1908; *Register,* 10 Mar. 1910.

131 Laurence Shook, CSB, *Catholic Post-secondary Education in English-speaking Canada: A History* (Toronto: University of Toronto Press 1971), 142–5.

132 McCorkell, *Henry Carr,* 15, 20.

133 Ibid., 21–2; Shook, *Catholic Post-secondary Education,* 150–2.

134 Elizabeth Smyth, "'Not Vital for the College nor of Interest to the Canadian Hierarchy': The Establishment of Catholic Women's Colleges at the University of Toronto," paper prepared for the 75th annual meeting of the Canadian Historical Association, 1996.

135 Shook, *Catholic Post-secondary Education,* 155. Shook adds, however, that St Michael's was no pioneer in post-secondary co-education; the University of Toronto admitted women in 1884.

136 Editorial, *St Joseph's Lilies* 2 (Sept. 1913): 72.

137 *Register,* 19 June 1902, and NA, Kenney Papers, vol. 7, Diaries, 30 Oct. 1904.

138 *Register,* 8 June 1916, 28 Mar. 1920; ARCAT, McEvay Papers, Education, List of Catholic Men at the University of Toronto, 1910–11.

139 *Register,* 8 June 1916, 14 Mar. 1918, 8 Aug. 1918, 12 Sept. 1918; *Separate School Chronicle* 1 (Oct. 1919): 7.

140 *Register,* 31 Jan. 1919.

141 An examination of the addresses of Catholic students at the University of Toronto in 1910 reveals that native Torontonian students came, with few exceptions, from either wealthy sections of inner-city parishes or from suburban areas. This suggests a possible correlation between wealth and enrolment among Catholics. ARCAT, McEvay Papers, Education, Lists of Roman Catholic Students at the University of Toronto, 1910–11.

CHAPTER FIVE

1 J. Martin Galvin, "The Jubilee Riots in Toronto, 1875," CCHA, *Reports* 26 (1959): 93–108; and Mark G. McGowan, "'We Endure What We Cannot Cure': John Joseph Lynch and Roman Catholic-Protestant Relations in Toronto, 1864–1875," CSCH, *Papers* (1984): 89–111.

2 *Register,* 22 June 1911.

3 ARCAT, Holy Name Society Papers, Constitution, By-Laws and Pledge.

4 Timothy L. Smith, "Religion and Ethnicity in America," *American Historical Review* 83 (Sept. 1983): 1168; Timothy L. Smith, "Lay Initiative in the

Religious Life of American Immigrants, 1880–1950," in Tamara Hereven, ed., *Anonymous Americans: Explorations in 19th Century Social History* (Englewood Cliffs, NJ: Prentice-Hall 1974), 233, 236–8; Michael Banton, "Voluntary Associations," in David Sills, ed., *International Encyclopedia of the Social Sciences*, vol. 6 (New York: Macmillan and Free Press 1968), 357–60; and David Sills, "Voluntary Associations: Sociological Aspects," in Sills, ed., *International Encyclopedia of the Social Sciences*, 362–3.

5 Brian P. Clarke, *Piety and Nationalism: Lay Voluntary Associations and the Creation of an Irish-Catholic Community in Toronto, 1850–1895* (Montreal and Kingston: McGill-Queen's University Press 1993), 7.

6 Ibid., 199–223.

7 Ibid., 224–53. Clarke sees the efforts by these associations to retreat from offering a self-contained social life for the laity as the beginning of their demise. Once their aims and activities could be compartmentalized as only one among many options for lay social involvement, the *raison d'etre* for the nationalist society and its provision of a communal identity was gone. In addition, Catholic men were readily joining Church-based societies, demonstrating further that the Church itself, not the independent Catholic nationalist associations, was rapidly becoming "the salient feature of Irish-Catholic consciousness."

8 Fergus Macdonald, *The Catholic Church and the Secret Societies in the United States* (New York: Catholic Historical Association 1946), 2–3, 94–8, 115, 189. In 1738 Pope Clement XII condemned freemasonry in the bull *In Eminenti*, and Leo XIII reiterated the condemnation in his 1884 encyclical *Humanum Genis*. There seems to have been some concern that Catholics in Toronto might join forbidden societies. ARCAT, Letterbook 8, Father J.F. McBride to James J. Johns, 13 Feb. 1890; Letterbook 6, Archbishop John Walsh to all it may concern, 8 Apr. 1892; and Roman Correspondence, draft of letter from Archbishop Denis O'Connor to Cardinal Ledochowski, Aug. 1900.

9 *Rerum Novarum, Encyclical Letter of His Holiness Pope Leo XIII on the Condition of the Working Classes*, 15 May 1891 (Boston: Daughters of St Paul [1942]), para. 69, 73, 75, 78–80.

10 ARCAT, St Mary's Parish box, *St Mary's Hundred Birthdays*; *Catholic Record*, 18 Apr. 1891; *Register*, 18 Oct. 1900.

11 Clarke, Piety and Nationalism, 224–53. J.C. Beckett, *The Making of Modern Ireland, 1603–1923* (London: Faber and Faber 1966), chaps. 19–21. Gregory Kealey and Bryan Palmer, *Dreaming of What Might Be: The Knights of Labor in Ontario, 1880–1900* (Cambridge: Cambridge University Press 1982; repr. Toronto: New Hogtown Press 1987), 313–16.

12 Hereward Senior, *The Fenians in Canada* (Toronto: Macmillan 1978), 84–8; Gerald Stortz, "John Joseph Lynch, Archbishop of Toronto: A Biographical Study of Religious, Political and Social Commitment," PhD, University of Guelph 1980, 217–27.

13 ARCAT, Lynch Papers, William Lane to Archbishop Lynch, 11 May 1885; Lane to Lynch, 24 Apr. 1887; Lane to Lynch, 25 Apr. 1888; AAO, Diocese of Toronto file, 1848–1900, Father F.P. Rooney to Archbishop Duhamel, 7 Sept. 1889.

14 *Register*, 19 Mar. 1896; *Record*, 16 Aug. 1890; *IC*, 18 May 1882, 22 Mar. 1883, 25 June 1891, 1 Sept. 1892; and *CWR*, 10 Dec. 1887, 14 Jan. 1888. In the latter M.W.Casey calls for more Canadian nationalism in the face of what he sees as rule by "foreigners."

15 *IC*, 1 Sept. 1892. In 1889, at the Irish Catholic Benevolent Union convention in St Louis, Archbishop Cleary's speech to the delegates still possessed the same stinging vitriol of the nineteenth-century nationalists: "No Queen, no English rule, no bloody Balfour – (hisses) – no Governor General of Canada [Lansdowne] and no power on the face of God's world that can stamp Irish sentiments out of Irish hearts." *IC*, 12 Sept. 1889.

16 *Record*, 25 May 1895; *Detailed Report of the Inspector of Insurance and Registrar of Friendly Societies* (Toronto: L.K. Cameron, King's Printer 1906), C-135.

17 *Might's City Directories, 1895–1905* (Toronto: Might's 1895, 1900, 1905), 1736; *Record*, 27 Dec. 1890, 10 Jan. 1891. In 1895 the financial affairs of the Emerald Benevolent Association were so bad that, when it was proposed that the members' monthly assessment be increased to pay off the debt, the St Patrick's Women's Circle No. 1 withdrew from the association. *Record*, 14 Dec. 1895.

18 *Record*, 10 Jan. 1891, 21 Dec. 1895, 3 Oct. 1896, 29 Jan. 1898.

19 *Polk's City Directory* (1890), 1571; and *Might's City Directory* (1895), 1736; (1900), 1043.

20 AO, Charles J. Foy Papers, box 3, file 14, J.H. Barry to Foy, national vice-president, 2 Oct. 1915; and Presidential Report to the Officers and Delegates of the 13th Biennial Convention of the Ancient Order of Hibernians (Ontario), 10 Aug. 1914.

21 Ibid., Foy Papers, box 3, file 16, By-Laws of Ancient Order of Hibernians; and *IC*, 12 July 1900.

22 *Detailed Report of the Inspector of Insurance and Registrar of Friendly Societies, 1899* (Toronto: L.K. Cameron, Queen's Printer, 1900), C-134.

23 *Record*, 28 Nov. 1896; *Detailed Report of the Inspector of Insurance and Registrar of Friendly Societies, 1895* (Toronto: Warwick and Brothers 1895), C-139; *IC*, 22 May 1890.

24 *Record*, 9 Feb. 1895, 13 Nov. 1897.

25 AO, Foy Papers, box 3, file 16, Presidential Report, 10 Aug. 1914.

26 *Register*, 22 Mar. 1900; other reports of concerts appear on 19 Mar. 1903 and 25 Mar. 1915. At the latter Father Thomas F. Burke, CSP, defended

the people of Ireland against charges of disloyalty during the war. See also *Record*, 11 Apr. 1891, 5 Jan. 1895.

27 AO, Foy Papers, box 3, file 16, Eleventh Biennial Convention of the Ancient Order of Hibernians, 23–5 Aug. 1910, Report of Provincial President Frank J. Walsh.

28 Ibid., President's Report, 10 Aug. 1914.

29 ARCAT, Archbishop Fergus McEvay Papers, Frank Walsh to Fergus McEvay, 12 Mar. 1909; and *Register*, 20 Mar. 1902.

30 AAO, Toronto Correspondence, Archbishop Denis O'Connor to Archbishop Duhamel, 11 Feb. 1903.

31 AO, Foy Papers, box 3, file 16, President's Report, Eighth Biennial Convention of the Ancient Order of Hibernians, Aug. 1904; Eleventh Biennial Convention, 23–5 Aug. 1910; Thirteenth Biennial Convention , 10 Aug. 1914; and Proceedings of the Forty-Seventh National Convention, 1910. In 1904 there were 175 members in ladies' auxiliaries, or 11.1 per cent of the total membership.

32 Ibid., file 14, To the National Board of the Ancient Order of Hibernians in America from the County Board of Carleton County, Ontario, undated, unanimously adopted.

33 *Record*, 8 Apr. 1916.

34 Arthur Link, *Woodrow Wilson and the Progressive Era* (New York: Harper and Row 1954), 245–7, 251ff; William Leuchtenburg, *The Perils of Prosperity, 1914–1932* (Chicago: University of Chicago Press 1958), 43; and James Hennessey, SJ, *American Catholics* (New York: Oxford University Press 1981), 223–5.

35 *National Hibernian*, 15 Oct. 1914. For a brief account of the Hibernian position on the war in the United States, see Kerby A. Miller, *Emigrants and Exiles: Ireland and the Irish Exodus to North America* (New York: Oxford University Press 1985), 542–3; AO, Foy Papers, box 3, file 14, J.H. Barry to Foy, 2 Oct. 1915, and copy of letter from Thomas M. Malloy to Philip J. Sullivan, national secretary of AOH, 8 Feb. 1916.

36 AO, Foy Papers, box 3, file 14, T.D. O'Connor, Leeds County, to Foy, 26 Nov. 1914; Patrick O'Dowd, secretary, Wentworth County, to Foy, 10 Aug. 1915; To the National Body of the AOH in America from the County Board of Carleton County, ca 1914; letter from Division 3, AOH, Smith's Falls, to Foy, 3 Dec. 1914; letter from Thomas Malloy to Philip J. Sullivan, national secretary of AOH, 8 Feb. 1916; copy of motion from Division 1 AOH, Gananoque, 22 Nov. 1914; letter from J.H. Barry, Fredericton, to Foy, 2 Oct. 1915; John Hart, Victoria, BC, to Foy, 24 Oct. 1914; Hart to Foy, 24 Nov. 1914; telegram, Hart to Foy, 11 Dec. 1916; William Murray, Vancouver, to Foy, 26 Oct. 1914; and draft of letter from C.J. Foy to national president Joseph McLaughlin, Philadelphia, ca 1914. Although no letters

survive from Toronto divisions, other letters indicate that Ontario Hibernians were of the same mind on the issue of secession.

37 Ibid., Declaration to the Officers of the AOH of the Provinces of New Brunswick and Nova Scotia, ca 1915.

38 *New Freeman*, 29 July 1916, and *Boston Pilot*, 23 Sept. 1916.

39 Clarke, *Piety and Nationalism*, 62–96; *Women of Canada: Their Life and Work* (National Council of Women of Canada 1900; repr. 1975), 276–9, 282–9.

40 Ibid.; Edward Kelly, *The Story of St Paul's Parish, Toronto* (Toronto 1922), 252.

41 *Women of Canada*, 290–5; *Canadian Messenger of the Sacred Heart* 7 (Jan. 1897): 39.

42 CWR, 14 June 1890, 2 Apr. 1892; Kelly, *The Story of St Paul's*, 262–4; *Canadian Messenger of the Sacred Heart* 7 (Jan. 1897): 45–7.

43 Quoted in Brian Clarke, " 'To Bribe the Porters of Heaven': Poverty, Salvation and the St Vincent de Paul Society in Victorian Toronto," *Canadian Society of Church History Papers* (1983): 99–100. In sharp contrast, Murray Nicolson views the St Vincent de Paul Society as a vehicle for Catholic social action. Nicolson's interpretation is derived from observations of what the society did, as opposed to an examination of the philosophical and religious underpinnings of the society itself. Nicolson, "The Catholic Church and the Irish of Victorian Toronto," PhD, University of Guelph 1980, chap. 5.

44 NA, H.F. McIntosh Papers, Circular, St Vincent de Paul Society, Toronto, 13 Apr. 1882; Irene Ball, "History and Methods of the St Vincent de Paul Society," *St Joseph's Lilies* 8 (Sept. 1919): 88–93.

45 Clarke, *Piety and Nationalism*, 98–9.

46 Ibid., 104–5.

47 *Register*, 1 Aug. 1895; *Record*, 25 Dec. 1897; *Register*, 18 July 1918.

48 Clarke, *Piety and Nationalism*, 234–6.

49 M.J. Ripple, OP, *The Holy Name Society and Its Great National Convention* (New York: National Holy Name Headquarters 1925), 19–27; Kelly, *The Story of St Paul's Parish*, 265.

50 Ripple, *The Holy Name Society*, 17.

51 Kelly, *The Story of St Paul's*, 267; *Renewal* (Archdiocesan Union of Holy Name societies, 1966); ARCAT, Holy Name Society Papers, Constitutions and By-laws of Archdiocesan Union of Holy Name Societies of the Archdiocese of Toronto (ca 1936); and *Official Officer's Handbook* (New York: National Headquarters of the Holy Name Society 1940), 6; *Register*, 16 July 1908, 11 Dec. 1919.

52 Ripple, *The Holy Name Society*, 17.

53 Kelly, *The Story of St Paul's*, 265; *Register*, 24 Jan. 1907. Shortly after the first meeting at St Paul's in 1906, 180 men joined the new Holy Name Society at St Basil's Parish. Similarly, in 1909, the first meeting of the Holy Name Society at St Michael's Cathedral recorded 400 members. *Register*, 18 Jan. 1906, 11 Nov. 1909.

54 ARCAT, Holy Name Society Papers, Presidential and Executive Committee Report, 10 Feb. 1913.

55 Ibid., Parish boxes, Spiritual Statistics, 1916–18; Catholic Truth Society Papers, Holy Name Society Executive, 1918.

56 Ibid., Holy Name Society Papers, Presidential Report, 1913, 1916.

57 *Register*, 22 Jan. 1914, 24 Oct. 1918, 18 Sept. 1919; ARCAT, Holy Name Society Papers, Archdiocesan Holy Name Union, Executive, 1918.

58 ARCAT, Holy Name Society Papers, Holy Name Union, Executive, 1918.

59 Ibid., Minutes of Quarterly Meeting, 14 Feb. 1916.

60 Ibid.

61 Ibid., Secretary's Report, Minutes of Annual Meeting, 1916; Minutes of Fall Quarterly Meeting, 25 Sept. 1916; Minutes of Quarterly Meeting, 14 Feb. 1916; Minutes of Quarterly Meeting, 25 Nov. 1918; and Minutes of Quarterly Meeting, 14 Oct. 1920.

62 *Register*, 29 Mar. 1917.

63 ARCAT, Holy Name Society Papers, Holy Name Union Annual Meeting, 16 Mar. 1924. In 1915 the Holy Name Baseball League consisted of western, eastern, and central sections in order to accommodate the large number of teams from all areas of the city. *Register*, 13 May 1915, 23 Mar. 1916. In 1920 the hockey league had thirty teams in four divisions determined by age. *Register*, 8 Jan. 1920.

64 *Register*, 30 Apr. 1914, 1 Apr. 1915.

65 ARCAT, Holy Name Society Papers, Minutes of Quarterly Meeting, 14 Oct. 1920.

66 Ibid., Constitution and By-laws. In the American context the Holy Name Society was seen as developing "a clear-minded and noble citizenship." Good Catholicism and good citizenship were inclusive in a member's duties. Ripple, *The Holy Name Society*, 35–6.

67 ARCAT, Holy Name Society Papers, Meeting Minutes, 25 Nov. 1918; letter from F.R. Boylan to Archbishop McNeil, 12 Nov. 1917; and Secretary's Report, Minutes of Annual Meeting, 1916.

68 *Register*, 29 Mar. 1917, 22 Feb. 1917. St Paul's branch sent 515 men, St Cecilia's 221, and St Helen's 225. Eighteen branches in Toronto and area reported that at least 25 per cent of their members had enlisted by 1916. ARCAT, Holy Name Society Papers, Secretary's Report, 1916.

69 ARCAT, Holy Name Society Papers, Minutes of Meeting, 25 Nov. 1918. Duff Crerar, "In the Day of Battle: Canadian Catholic Chaplains in the Field, 1885–1945," CCHA, *Historical Studies* 61 (1995): 66.

70 Ripple, *The Holy Name Society*, 33–4.

71 *Register*, 22 June 1911. For background to the rioting during the Jubilee processions, see Galvin, "The Jubilee Riots," 93–107.

72 *Register*, 6, 13 June 1912.

73 Ibid., 5, 16 June 1913; and ARCAT, Holy Name Society Papers, program for Third Annual Rally, 1 June 1913. The program noted that a collection

for the St Vincent de Paul Society was taken along the parade route, and new memberships in the Holy Name Society were solicited.

74 *Register*, 11, 18 June 1914, 24 June 1915, 11 Nov. 1915, 24 June 1920, 1 July 1920, 23 June 1921; ARCAT, Holy Name Society Papers, Secretary's Report, 1916, and Wallace J. Baker to Archbishop McNeil, 16 May 1921. In his report of 1916 Francis Boylan remarked that the parade was suspended in 1916 on the suggestion of the clergy that, "with the Motherland convulsed in the throes of a fearful war in which Canada was playing a glorious part, ... a parade of thousands of men through the city streets would serve no good and would be conducive to the disapproval of public opinion."

75 *Register*, 10 July 1913.

76 Jeanne Ruth Merifield Beck, "Henry Somerville and the Development of Catholic Social Thought in Canada: Somerville's Role in the Archdiocese of Toronto, 1915–1943," PhD, McMaster University 1977, 70.

77 *Register*, 23 June 1921. From Eph. 2:19.

78 *Record*, 29 Nov. 1890. AO, Foy Papers, box 3, file 17, Official Convention Program, Catholic Mutual Benefit Association (hereafter CMBA), Montreal, 22 Aug. 1922.

79 *Record*, 6 Sept. 1890, 29 Nov. 1890; and AO, Foy Papers, box 2, file 5, CMBA of Canada, undated.

80 In 1907 there was a move in the Canadian branches of the association to introduce handshakes and ritual, which sparked opposition from some member bishops. AASB, Adélard Langevin Papers, Thomas Dowling, Bishop of Hamilton, to Adélard Langevin, Archbishop of St Boniface, 18 July 1907; and AAO, Charles Gauthier Papers, David J. Scollard, Bishop of Sault Ste Marie, to Charles Gauthier, Archbishop of Ottawa, 14 Aug. 1907.

81 *Canadian* 11 (Feb. 1905): 2; and *Record*, 29 Nov. 1890.

82 *Record*, as quoted in *Canadian* 10 (Aug. 1904): 6, and (Sept. 1904): 1. The religious nature of the society is reflected upon in *CWR*, 13 Sept. 1890, 15 Nov. 1890, 22 Nov. 1890, 13 Dec. 1890, 31 Jan. 1891, 21 Feb. 1891. Its charitable aims are evident in *Record*, 29 Nov. 1890.

83 *IC*, 23 Aug. 1888; *Register*, 7 Nov. 1895; *Record*, 28 Mar. 1891; *Toronto City Directory* (Toronto: R.L. Polk 1890); *Might's City Directory* (1895), 1735; (1900), 1043; (1905), 1135; (1910), 1465; (1915), 1842; (1920), 59. The estimate of membership in Toronto is based on dividing the total number of Ontario members (10,253) by branches (193) and multiplying the quotient (53.1) by the number of Toronto branches (8). In 1910 Holy Family Parish opened one of the largest branches in western Ontario, indicating that at least some Toronto churches had membership in excess of the provincial average. *Register*, 31 Mar. 1910.

84 *Record*, 4 Oct. 1890.

85 *Canadian* 10 (Aug. 1904): 1, and (Dec. 1905); and *Record*, 7 Feb. 1891.

86 *Record*, 29 Nov. 1890; and *Register*, 2 Nov. 1893. In 1890 the payments were $16 per annum for $2,000 and $8 per annum for $1,000. When Canadians created an insurance beneficiary separate from the American parent in 1892, Canadians no longer contributed to the American reserve fund, and reduced their premiums accordingly.

87 *Register*, 1 Mar. 1894.

88 In 1905 15/27 businessmen and 14/27 clerical workers had $2,000 claims, as compared to only 18/41 unskilled workers. In 1918, 11/22 businessmen and 2/19 unskilled workers had $2,000 claims.

89 ARCAT, John Walsh Papers, "Little Mary" of St John, NB, to Archbishop Walsh, 11 Oct. 1891. The author praised the work of the CMBA in Ontario, while expressing hope that the association could bind the Catholics of the Maritimes together.

90 *Record*, 24 Jan. 1891, 7 Feb. 1891, 16 May 1891, 6 June 1891, 3 Oct. 1891; CWR, 16 May 1891. The death rate in Canada was 7.7 per 1,000 members and in New York 10.4 per 1,000.

91 *Record*, 30 May 1891.

92 CWR, 16 May 1891; *Record*, 17 Oct. 1891; and IC, 12 (Nov. 1891). Opposition was recorded from Toronto (St Mary's No. 49), Montreal (No. 84), London (No. 4), Québec (St Patrick's No. 108), and Almonte, Ont. (No. 34).

93 IC, 12 Nov. 1891, 9 July 1891, 27 Aug. 1891; and *Record*, 18 Apr. 1891, 29 Aug. 1891.

94 IC, 27 Aug. 1891.

95 *Record*, 18 Apr. 1904.

96 Ibid., 16 May 1891.

97 Ibid., 5 Sept. 1891, 19 Sept. 1891, 12 Sept. 1891; IC, 3 Sept. 1891.

98 *Record*, 3 Oct. 1891; and St Michael's College Rare Book Room, Office of the President of the Grand Council of the CMBA of Canada, 3 Nov. 1892, filed with the *Canadian*. Anti-separatists even criticized the editor of *Record* for his pro-separatist stance and his "unworthy" insinuations against Americans. IC, 22 Oct. 1891.

99 IC, 1 Dec. 1892, 22 Dec. 1892; and CWR, 17 Sept. 1892, 22 Oct. 1892.

100 *Canadian* 11 (Sept. 1904): 5; and *Record*, 23 Oct. 1897. St Basil's No. 145 branch of the association invited guests to lecture on Canadian and religious themes. In 1897 George Ross, the minister of Education, spoke to the members on "The Formative Influences of Canadian History." *Record*, 13 Mar. 1897.

101 *Canadian* 10 (Sept. 1904): 2; 11 (Jan. 1905): 2; and 10 (Nov. 1904): 2.

102 Ibid., 25 (Oct. 1919): 2.

103 Ibid., 24 (June 1918), (Mar. 1918). For a retrospective view of the association's patriotism and the war, consult 24 (Dec. 1918).

104 Ibid., 24 (May 1918): 3.
105 Ibid., 24 (Oct. 1918); and AO, Foy Papers, box 2, file 2, Declaration and Agreement Relating to the Service in the Army or Navy and to Munitions Plant Employees.
106 *Canadian* 24 (May 1918), (Oct. 1918).
107 Ibid., 25 (May 1919); 14 (Dec. 1918); and AO, Foy Papers, box 2, file 2, copy of letter from James Brady, Halifax, to F.J. Curran, 14 July 1919.
108 *Canadian* 25 (June 1919), (July 1919). All $2,000 policies dating prior to 1907 were subject to a basic reduction of $180. Those purchased after Nov. 1907 were assessed this basic deduction minus $10 per year. Therefore, a young man who purchased his policy in 1913 faced a reduction of $110. A similar sliding scale to a minimum of $50 on $1,000 certificates was arranged.
109 AO, Foy Papers, box 2, file 2, copy of William F. Bernard's report to the CMBA Convention, 25 Aug. 1916. Plans were made to alter the constitution of the association immediately after the Quebec convention in 1916. See draft of letter from Charles J. Foy to unknown source, ca 1917. Financial troubles are discussed in *Register*, 5 Oct. 1916; Foy Papers, box 2, file 2, Department of Insurance, Ottawa, 25 July 1918, and notice from CMBA Grand President F.J. Curran, 2 Dec. 1918. See also *Canadian* 24 (Mar. 1918), (Feb. 1918).
110 AO, Foy Papers, box 2, file 9, Grand Council Meeting, Jan. 1922. St Mary's attracted 35 members but expelled 27.
111 *Canadian* 26 (Sept. 1920), 25 (Oct. 1919).
112 ARCAT, McNeil Papers, Leo Mallon to McNeil, 16 Dec. 1919; *Canadian* 26 (June 1920), (Nov. 1920).
113 The Knights of St John: *IC*, 5 Apr. 1888; *CWR*, 2 July 1892, 9 July 1892; *Register*, 11 June 1903, 24 Aug. 1911, 27 July 1912; *Record*, 9 Nov. 1895. Catholic Order of Foresters: *CWR*, 2 May 1891, 6 June 1891; *Record*, 1 May 1897, 14 Jan. 1899; *Register*, 20 Aug. 1903, 16 Nov. 1905, 7 Feb. 1912, 19 June 1913. ARCAT, McNeil Papers, AE15.08, *Catholic Foresters Companion* 8 (Oct. 1918).
114 *Knights of Columbus, Toronto Council 1388, Seventy-Fifth Anniversary, 1909–1984* (Toronto 1984). This commemorative brochure indicates that within its first year the membership of Council 1388 jumped from 131 to over 200. For regalia, see *American Catholic Quarterly* (Apr. 1884), and Christopher J. Kaufmann, *Faith and Fraternalism: The History of the Knights of Columbus, 1882–1982* (New York: Harper and Row 1982), 38–9.
115 Gérard Langlois, *L'Ordre des Knights of Columbus* (Quebec: Les Éditions du Cactus 1952), 38.
116 Kaufmann, *Faith and Fraternalism*, 36.
117 David Murray, *A Columbian Souvenir* (Quebec: Commercial Printing 1910), 2.

118 Kaufmann, *Faith and Fraternalism*, 9; Miller, *Emigrants and Exiles*, 534.

119 Kaufmann, *Faith and Fraternalism*, 17.

120 Ibid., xii–xiv.

121 Ibid., 16.

122 Quoted in ibid., 139; regarding patriotism see also Langlois, *L'Ordre des Knights of Columbus*, 17, and L'Abbé B. Poirier, *Histoire de la Chevalerie de Colomb* (Montreal: Valiquette 1943), 20, 33.

123 Kaufmann, *Faith and Fraternalism*, 116–17; Murray, *A Columbian Souvenir*, 6–7; and Pierre Vigeant, *Knights of Columbus: Que sont les Chevaliers de Colomb* (Montreal: L'Action National, ca 1951), 5.

124 Murray, *A Columbian Souvenir*, 6–7; Kaufmann, *Faith and Fraternalism*, 117; *Register*, 24 Sept. 1903; and Poirier, *Histoire de la Chevalerie*, 45.

125 ASV-DAC, 89.20, John Teefy to Donatus Sbarretti, 20 Aug. 1906.

126 ARCAT, Denis O'Connor Papers, William A. Macdonell, Bishop of Alexandria, to Denis O'Connor, 16 Sept. 1907; galley proofs of a biography of O'Connor, author unknown, AA01.01; and Francis A. O'Brien, *Life Work of a Saintly Prelate* (Kalamazoo: Augustinian Print 1914).

127 ARCAT, Knights of Columbus Papers, Edward Hearn, Supreme Knight, to Archbishop McEvay, 19 Feb. 1909; copy of letter from Father James T. Kidd to Edward Hearn, 24 Feb. 1909; and copy of letter from J.T. Kidd to Dr McGinnis, Seaforth, Ont.; *Register*, 25 Mar. 1909, 10 June 1909.

128 ARCAT, Knights of Columbus Papers, W.H. Leacock, District Deputy, Toronto, to Neil McNeil, 16 Mar. 1917. *Register*, 28 Apr. 1910.

129 Gregory S. Kealey and Bryan Palmer, "The Bonds of Unity: The Knights of Labor in Ontario, 1880–1900," *Histoire Sociale – Social History* 14 (Nov. 1981): 370, 372, 393, 395.

130 ARCAT, Other Collections, Canadian Catholic Union, file 1, Handbook, 1903–04.

131 Ibid.

132 Ibid., Annual Report of the Executive Committee, 1902–03, and Minute Book, 1903 to [1912].

133 *Register*, 7 July 1910.

134 Ibid., 5 Sept. 1919.

135 I.J.E. Daniel and D.A. Casey, *For God and Country: A History of the Knights of Columbus Catholic Army Huts* (Toronto 1922), 13.

136 Knights in Toronto were involved in a plethora of social, recreational, and charitable activities, including vaudeville nights, scholarship trusts for Catholic students, and strengthening the devotional and associational life of Catholic students at the University of Toronto. *Register*, 5 Feb. 1914, 18 Nov. 1920, 20 May 1909, 28 July 1910, 21 Sept. 1911.

137 ARCAT, Knights of Columbus Papers, Wallace Baker to McNeil, 9 Dec. 1912.

138 Ibid., Chart, "Canadianization of the Newcomer," 10 Feb. 1923.

139 Ibid., McNeil to District Deputy W.H. Leacock, 2 Mar. 1917, as quoted in letter from McNeil to Quebec District Deputy G.H. Boivin, MP, 17 Mar. 1917; AAM, Paul Bruchesi Papers, 225–104, McNeil to Bruchesi, 17 Mar. 1917, #917–1.

140 Ibid., Statement of Archbishops McNeil and Bruchési to the State Deputies of the Knights of Columbus in Canada, 3 Apr. 1917.

141 Ibid., L.J. Murray to McNeil, 28 Apr. 1917; George Boivin to McNeil, 12 May 1917, and Reverend George O'Toole, Cantly, Que., to McNeil, 10 May 1917.

142 Ibid., copy of letter from McNeil to Charles Fitzpatrick, 19 Sept. 1917, and copy of letter from George Boivin to J.L. Murray, 6 Sept. 1917.

143 Ibid.; and copy of letter from McNeil to Boivin, 2 Dec. 1916.

144 Daniel and Casey, *For God and Country*, intro.

145 *Register*, 8 Oct. 1914, 31 Dec. 1914, 6 Sept. 1917, 30 June 1917, 7 July 1917, 19 Sept. 1918, 26 Sept. 1918. For a more complete account of the K of C wartime activities, consult Daniel and Casey, *For God and Country*, chapter 6.

146 The co-operation was sometimes not appreciated by Catholic leaders. In 1920 reports that twenty-five Knights attended a meeting of the Masonic Order brought stiff condemnation from the *Register* and a demand that the Knights discipline these members. *Register*, 30 Sept. 1920, and *Toronto Star*, 27 Sept. 1920. Some French Canadians later condemned the order as a front for Catholic freemasonry and American assimilation. Langlois, *L'Ordre des Knights of Columbus*, 17, 20, 32, 64ff, 117–18; and Vigeant, *Knights of Columbus*, 4, 13, 20–1.

147 Kaufmann offers a similar observation for the American Knights in *Faith and Fraternalism*, 71.

148 One of the only scholarly studies of the CWL to date is Sheila Ross, " 'For God and Canada': The Early Years of the Catholic Women's League in Alberta," CCHA, *Historical Studies* 62 (1996): 89–108.

149 ARCAT, Roman Correspondence, Circular on the Cult of the Holy Family, 10 Dec. 1890, and Rules for the Pious Association for the Holy Family, 8 Jan. 1893; *Register*, 4 June 1914, 30 May 1918, 12 June 1919, 30 Dec. 1920 (Confraternity of Christian Mothers); *Women of Canada*, 291–5.

150 NA, Fanny Penfold Coffey Papers, ms history of the Catholic Women's League of Canada 1910–35.

151 Ross, "For God and Canada," 91–3.

152 Lina O'Neill, "Catholic Women's League in Canada," *St Joseph's Lilies* 8 (Mar. 1920): 73; and *Register*, 4 Dec. 1919.

153 Ibid.; Ross, "For God and Canada," 97.

154 O'Neill, "Catholic Women's League," 73.

155 NA, Coffey Papers, ms history of the Catholic Women's League.

156 ARCAT, Catholic Women's League Papers, letter from Bellelle Guerin to McNeil, 24 Oct. 1921. This was ratified by the Toronto-dominated national executive. *Register*, 9 June 1921.

157 NA, Coffey Papers, history of the CWL; Sister Ella Zinck, SOS, "Church and Immigration: The Sisters of Service, English Canada's First Missionary Congregation of Sisters, 1920–1930," CCHA, *Study Sessions* 43 (1976): 30–1.
158 O'Neill, "Catholic Women's League of Canada," 75–6.
159 NA, Canadian Fraternal Association Papers, W.C. Mikel to Citizens of Belleville, 18 July 1918; Associated Press report of CFA meeting, 25–6 July 1918; and Second Convention for "Better Understanding," Ottawa, 28 Nov. 1918.
160 *Register*, 18 May 1893.

CHAPTER SIX

1 *Register*, 8 Aug. 1901.
2 Gerald J. Stortz, "The Irish Catholic Press in Toronto, 1887–1892," *Canadian Journal of Communications* 10, no. 3 (1984): 36–7; and Stortz, "The Irish Catholic Press in Toronto, 1874–1887," CCHA, *Study Sessions* 47 (1980): 42, 51. "Patrick Boyle," *DCB* 13:106–8.
3 Paul Rutherford, *A Victorian Authority: The Daily Press in Late Nineteenth-Century Canada* (Toronto: University of Toronto Press 1982), 6–8.
4 Paul Rutherford, "The People's Press: The Emergence of the New Journalism in Canada, 1869–1899," *Canadian Historical Review* 56 (June 1975): 169–71, 190–1.
5 Daniel Connor, "The Irish Canadian: Image and Self-Image," MA, University of British Columbia 1976, 19–20, 11, 93–4.
6 *Register*, 31 Mar. 1921.
7 Edith Firth, ed., *Early Toronto Newspapers, 1793–1867* (Toronto: Baxter Publishing Company 1961), 5; and William Stewart Wallace, "The Periodical Literature of Upper Canada," *Canadian Historical Review* 12 (Mar. 1931): 14.
8 P.F. Cronin, "Early Catholic Journalism in Canada," CCHA, *Reports* 3 (1935): 33–5; Firth, *Early Toronto Newspapers*, 13; and AO, IC, preface to microfilm reel 19.
9 Elizabeth Hulse, *A Dictionary of Toronto Printers, Publishers, Booksellers and the Allied Trades, 1798–1900* (Toronto: Anson-Cartwright, 1982), 57.
10 Cronin, "Early Catholic," 37; and Firth, *Early Toronto Newspapers*, 27.
11 Firth, *Early Toronto Newspapers*, 48.
12 Cronin, "Early Catholic," 38.
13 Gerald J. Stortz, "The Irish Catholic Press in Toronto, 1887–1892," 28–9; Stortz, "The Irish Catholic Press in Toronto, 1874–1887," 42, 49. For a more extensive study of the political nature of the Irish press in Canada, see E.J. Doherty, "An Analysis of Social and Political Thought in the Irish Canadian Press in Upper Canada, 1858–1867," MA, University of Waterloo 1976.
14 IC, 6 Sept. 1888.

15 Quoted in ibid., 8 May 1888.
16 Ibid., 29 Dec. 1892.
17 Ibid., 4 Oct. 1888, 1 Jan. 1890, 10 May 1890, 29 May 1890, 12 June 1890, 26 Feb. 1891, 10 Mar. 1892, 29 Dec. 1892. NAC, Macdonald Papers, vol. 255, Frank Smith to Macdonald, 12 Aug. 1882, 1115481–7; Letterbook 23, Macdonald to Frank Smith, 30 July 1884, 41.
18 *The Canadian Newspaper Directory* (Montreal: A. McKim and Company 1892), 119.
19 CWR, 19 Feb. 1887.
20 Stortz, "The Irish Catholic Press in Toronto, 1887–1892," 28.
21 CWR, 23 Nov. 1889.
22 Ibid., 16 Feb. 1889.
23 *Canadian Newspaper Directory* (1892), 118; CWR, 4 Jan. 1890.
24 CWR, 19 Feb. 1887; NA, Macdonell Family Papers, vol. 42, Catholic Weekly Review Subscriptions, 1893, 36. This brief listing of 26 subscribers can be broken down into the following occupational classifications: professional, 2; business, 7; clerical, 8; skilled, 0; semi-skilled, 4; unskilled, 3; unknown, 2. Classifications are based on Peter Goheen, *Victorian Toronto, 1850–1900* (Chicago: University of Chicago Department of Geography, Research Paper no. 127, 1970), 229–30, and *Might's City of Toronto Directory* (Toronto: Might's 1892).
25 CWR, 18 Feb. 1888.
26 Ibid., 19 Feb. 1887; IC, 16 Jan. 1890, 5 June 1890; NA, Macdonell Family Papers, vol. 42, 19. Ledgers from A.C. Macdonell indicate the paper made donations to the Liberal-Conservative Association while he was on the *Review's* editorial staff. Moreover, Conservative Prime Minister John Thompson was an active subscriber to the *Review.* See NA, Sir John Thompson Papers, vol. 121, Douglas Stewart, CWR, to Thompson, 19 Jan. 1891, 14263.
27 CWR, 10 and 31 May 1890, 7 June 1890.
28 For the most comprehensive overview of the rivalry between the two papers, see Stortz, "The Irish Catholic Press in Toronto, 1887–1892," 30–41.
29 CWR, 24 Nov. 1888.
30 Ibid., 1 Dec. 1888. This was one of many notices to subscribers to pay their bills promptly.
31 Stortz, "The Irish Catholic Press in Toronto, 1887–1892," 42.
32 IC, 10 Jan. 1901, 20 June 1901, 27 June 1901; *Record*, 14 July 1900; and *Register*, 5 July 1900.
33 *Register*, 8 Aug. 1901, 15 Aug. 1901, 19 Sept. 1901.
34 Ibid., 8 Aug. 1901.
35 CWR, 17 Dec. 1892.
36 *Register*, 5 Jan. 1893.
37 Ibid. See Henry Carr, CSB, "The Very Reverend J.R. Teefy, CSB, LL.D.," CCHA, *Reports* 7 (1939): 85–95.

38 *CWR*, 19 Feb. 1887; clerical approval also came from Archbishop Walsh of Toronto, ibid., 22 Feb. 1890; and Bishop Cornelius O'Brien of Halifax, 16 Feb. 1889; see also Stortz, "The Irish Catholic Press in Toronto, 1874–1887," 44–5.

39 The *Register*'s editor-priests included J.R. Teefy, CSB (1893–94), Alfred E. Burke (1908–15), and Thomas O'Donnell (1918–24). The *Record*'s roster included founding editor George Northgraves, Father Lawrence Flannery, and James T. Foley.

40 ARCAT, Fergus Patrick McEvay Papers, Private Circular to the Clergy, 4 Apr. 1911; McEvay's clerical censorship took effect in 1908; Denis O'Connor Papers, O'Connor to P.F. Cronin, editor of the *Register*, 22 Mar. 1901; and Catholic Church Extension Society (CCES), Meeting Minutes Book, 1913.

41 ARCAT, *Catholic Register* Papers, 1898–99 file, list of shareholders. Patrick Boyle remained the printer for the journal, while J.D. Macdonell and A.C. Macdonell, formerly of the *Review*, handled accounts and legal matters respectively. *CWR*, 24 Dec. 1892, and *IC*, 22 Dec. 1892.

42 *Register*, 5 and 26 Jan. 1893, 2 and 9 Feb. 1893.

43 ARCAT, Archbishop John Walsh Papers, Director's Report of *Catholic Register* Printing and Publishing Company, 31 Dec. 1895.

44 *Canadian Newspaper Directory* (1899), 107; (1905), 108.

45 *Register*, 5 July 1900. The editors between 1893 and 1905 were, in order, Father J.R. Teefy, CSB, Mr F.P. Duffy, Mr J.C. Walsh, and Mr P.F. Cronin. *Register*, 30 Aug. 1894, 13 Sept. 1894.

46 Ibid., 26 Dec. 1901.

47 Ibid., 2 Jan. 1908, 22 Oct. 1908, 19 Feb. 1920. It is interesting to note that the paper carried advertisements for O'Keefe's Star Beer, a "non-intoxicant" with less than 1.25 per cent alcohol per volume. There was no advantage in insulting Eugene O'Keefe, the most generous Catholic philanthropist in the city; see 29 Oct. 1908.

48 *Canadian Newspaper Directory* (1919), 84; CCES, Meeting Minutes Book, 29.

49 John Moir, "A Vision Shared? *The Catholic Register* and Canadian Identity before World War I," in William Westfall and Louis Rousseau, eds., *Canadian Issues / Thèmes canadiens* 7 (1985): 356–66.

50 ARCAT, Catholic Truth Society Papers, "Results from an Inquiry among the Readers," 1920.

51 *Register*, 16 Sept. 1897, 21 Oct. 1897; NA, Sir Charles Tupper Papers, reel c-3206, A.E. Burke to Tupper, 8 Jan. 1896, 5329; and Burke to Tupper, 12 Nov. 1900, 6290. These letters confirm that Burke, future editor of the *Register*, was an active Conservative. Liberals identified the *Register* as a Tory sympathizer, except in 1904, when Charles Fitzpatrick boasted to Laurier that "we control every English Catholic paper in Ontario." NA, Laurier Papers, reel 815, Fitzpatrick to Laurier, 7 Sept. 1904, 89419; and

reel 760, Thomas Coffey, proprietor of the *Record*, to Charles Fitzpatrick, 5 Oct. 1898, 27056–7.

52 *Record*, 3 and 31 May 1890, 11 Jan. 1890.

53 Ibid., 18 Oct. 1902, 21 Mar. 1903.

54 NA, Laurier Papers, reel 779, Walter Boland to Laurier, 24 Sept. 1900, 49447; and vol. 33, John F. Coffey to Laurier, 14 Jan. 1897.

55 ARCAT, Catholic Truth Society Papers, "Results from an Inquiry," 1920.

56 *Record*, 28 Jan. 1915.

57 *Canadian Newspaper Directory* (1899), 75; (1919), 45.

58 CWR, 10 Dec. 1887. See also 19 Feb. 1887, 26 May 1888; IC, 26 Jan. 1888, 14 June 1888, 21 June 1888, 27 June 1901; *Register*, 18 Mar. 1909.

59 CWR, 8 June 1889, 19 Apr. 1890, 11 July 1891, 18 July 1891.

60 *Register*, 2 Feb. 1899, 18 May 1899, 29 June 1899. In June, for example, twelve editorial pieces were concerned with Canadian issues, and only two with Irish questions.

61 Ibid., 19 Jan. 1893, 3 May 1894, 4 July 1895, 8 Aug. 1895, 15 Aug. 1895, 5 Nov. 1896, 14 Dec. 1899.

62 IC, 12 July 1888, 1 Nov. 1888, 29 Nov. 1888, 8 Aug. 1889; CWR, 25 Jan. 1890, 8 Feb. 1890; *Record*, 8 Feb. 1890. For background consult Emmet Larkin, *The Roman Catholic Church in Ireland and the Fall of Parnell, 1888–1891* (Chapel Hill: University of North Carolina Press 1979), 24–5.

63 *Record*, 13 July 1901, 9 Feb. 1895. See also Stanley W. Horrall, "Canada and the Irish Question: A Study of the Canadian Response to Irish Home Rule, 1882–1893," MA, Carleton University 1966, 8–9, 22–3. ARCAT, Lynch Papers, AE 02.09, copy of letter from Lynch to Archbishop Thomas Connolly of Halifax, 1 Feb. 1866.

64 *Register*, 7 Oct. 1897.

65 *Record*, 7 Feb. 1891, 22 Mar. 1890, 16 Aug. 1890, 27 Sept. 1890, 9 Feb. 1895; CWR, 27 Apr. 1889, 5 Dec. 1891; IC, 4 Dec. 1890. The change of tone is evident in *Record*, 27 Dec. 1890, 29 Nov. 1891, 24 Jan. 1891, 4 Apr. 1891, 17 Oct. 1891; *Register*, 5 Jan. 1893; CWR, 27 Dec. 1890, 8 Aug. 1891; IC, 8 Oct. 1891.

66 Brian P. Clarke, "Piety, Nationalism and Fraternity: The Rise of Irish Catholic Voluntary Associations in Toronto, 1850–1895," PhD, University of Chicago 1986, chap. 8. For further background on Irish affairs consult Larkin, *The Roman Catholic Church*, 191–232; Joseph Lee, *The Modernisation of Irish Society, 1848–1918* (Dublin: Gill and McMillan 1973), 114–22; and J.C. Beckett, *The Making of Modern Ireland, 1603–1923* (London: Faber and Faber 1966; 2nd ed., 1981), 400–4.

67 *Register*, 11 May 1893; 1 and 15 Feb. 1894; 2 and 16 July, 10, 17, and 24 Sept. 1896. *Record*, 22 and 29 Aug. 1896, 26 Sept. 1896, 7 Nov. 1896, 1 May 1897.

68 Daniel C. Lyne, "Irish-Canadian Financial Contributions to the Home Rule Movement in the 1890s," *Studia Hibernica* 7 (1967): 188, 191–200,

204–6. David Shanahan, "The Irish Question in Canada: Ireland, The Irish and Canadian Politics, 1880–1922," PhD, Carleton University 1988, 230–42; and ARCAT, Walsh Papers, Circular, Collection for Irish Members of Parliament, 24 Jan. 1894.

69 *Register*, 29 Sept. 1904, 4 Dec. 1902, 1 Jan. 1903, 12 May 1904, 29 Sept. 1904; *Record*, 13 Sept. 1902, 11 Apr. 1903, 4 July 1903.

70 *Register*, 27 July 1905, 7 Dec. 1905, 16 May 1907, 30 May 1907, 5 Mar. 1908.

71 Ibid., 28 May 1914; 20, 27 Nov. 1913; and 11 Dec. 1913.

72 Ibid., 24 Sept. 1914; and *Record*, 8 Aug. 1914.

73 *Record*, 8 and 15 Aug. 1914; 5 Sept. 1914; 3, 10, 24 Oct. 1914; 21 Nov. 1914; *Register*, 6 May 1915.

74 *Register*, 4 May 1916.

75 *Record*, 6, 20 May 1916.

76 *Register*, 4 May 1916.

77 Bottigheimer, *Ireland and the Irish*, 227–8; and Joseph M. Curran, *The Birth of the Irish Free State, 1921–1923* (Alabama: University of Alabama Press 1980), 12–13.

78 *Register*, 11 May 1916, 18 May 1916.

79 *Register*, 1 June 1916. For more information on the rise of Sinn Fein see Charles Townshend, *The British Campaign in Ireland 1919–1921: The Development of Political and Military Policies* (Oxford: Oxford University Press 1975), 2–14.

80 *Register*, 22 June 1916.

81 *Record*, 27 May 1916.

82 Ibid., 3 June 1916.

83 For details of the division see Curran, *The Birth of the Irish Free State*, 14–22; Beckett, *The Making of Modern Ireland*, 435–45; Lee, *The Modernisation of Irish Society*, 156–63.

84 *Register*, 11 July 1918.

85 Ibid., 23 May 1918, 30 May 1918, 27 June 1918, 24 Oct. 1918.

86 Ibid., 17 June 1920.

87 *Record*, 10 Apr. 1920.

88 *Register*, 5 Aug. 1920, 18 July 1918, 5 Dec. 1918, 19 Dec. 1918, 20 Mar. 1919, 15 July 1920.

89 Ibid., 17 Mar. 1921.

90 Ibid., 5 Feb. 1920. The *Register* accused Wilson of being too timid when dealing with England. His failure to support Irish autonomy was condemned outright: 13 Mar. 1919, 1 May 1919.

91 Ibid., 1 May 1919; and *Record*, 3 Apr. 1920, 10 Apr. 1920.

92 *Record*, 31 Dec. 1921; *Register*, 14 July 1921.

93 *Register*, 5 May 1921; 1, 15 Jan. 1920.

94 Ibid., 17 Mar. 1921, 27 Jan. 1921; *Record*, 21 Feb. 1920, 3 Apr. 1920, 27 Nov. 1920. More pointed critiques of Lloyd George and Carson are made in

Register, 23 Dec. 1920, 27 Jan., 17 Feb., 2 June 1921; *Record*, 17 Jan., 16 Oct., 18 Sept. 1920. For a more in-depth study of the Irish revolt, see John A. Murphy, *Ireland in the Twentieth Century* (Dublin: Gill and MacMillan 1975), 1–26; Curran, *The Birth of the Irish Free State*, 23–63; and Townshend, *The British Campaign in Ireland*, 33–72.

95 *Record*, 10 Jan. 1920, 30 Oct. 1920; *Register*, 1 Sept. 1921. The Catholic press downplayed the violent acts committed by Sinn Fein, with whom they had come to sympathize after the collapse of John Redmond's Parliamentary Party. They outlined the ferocity of the British reprisals more than the activities of the Sinn Feiners themselves. *Register*, 7 Aug. 1919; *Record*, 3 Apr. 1920.

96 ARCAT, Catholic Truth Society Papers, "Results of an Inquiry," 1920.

97 *Record*, 16 Dec. 1922.

98 Ibid., 31 Dec. 1921, 16 Dec. 1922.

99 *Register*, 15 Dec. 1921, 5 Jan. 1922, 19 Jan. 1922, 22 June 1922. For more information on these editors consult *Register*, 20 Feb. 1993.

100 *Record*, 19 Aug. 1922; *Register*, 29 June 1922, 17 Aug. 1922.

101 *Register*, 20 July 1922, 31 Aug. 1922, 5 Oct. 1922, 2 Nov. 1922, 7 Dec. 1922, 5 Apr. 1923; *Record*, 4 Feb. 1922, 19 Aug. 1922, 2 Sept. 1922, 24 Dec. 1922.

102 Carl Berger, ed., *Imperialism and Nationalism, 1884–1914: A Conflict in Canadian Thought* (Toronto: Copp Clark 1969), 9–12, 63–5.

103 Raymond MacLean, "The Highland Catholic Tradition in Canada," in W. Stanford Reid, ed., *The Scottish Tradition in Canada* (Toronto: McClelland and Stewart 1976), 95, 111.

104 ARCAT, Lynch Papers, Bishop John Walsh to Lynch, 18 June 1887; copy of letter from Lynch to Cardinal Taschereau, 23 Apr. 1877; copy of letter from Lynch to Taschereau, 26 Apr. 1887; and Letterbook 5, copies of Lynch to Walsh, 15 June, 18 June 1887.

105 Ibid., Letterbook 4, copy of pastoral letter to all the Catholics in Toronto, 18 Feb. 1888.

106 CWR, 4 June 1887.

107 Ibid., 9 July 1887.

108 Ibid., 4 June 1892; IC on the same occasion criticized "slavish worship of any man or woman" and asserted that it entertained the same respect for Victoria as for "any excellent woman": 19 May 1892.

109 *Record*, 3 July 1897.

110 *Register*, 3 June 1897.

111 IC, 31 Jan. 1901; *Register*, 24 Jan. 1901; *Record*, 2 Feb. 1901.

112 *Record*, 17 Aug. 1901, 11 July 1903, 17 Sept. 1904; *Register*, 5 Apr. 1906. After Victoria's death Catholic archbishops and bishops petitioned Westminster to eliminate the anti-Catholic sections from the Coronation Oath. Unanimously supported by the Parliament of Canada, the hierarchy of Canada sent a letter to Cardinal Herbert Vaughan of Westminster, outlin-

ing their loyalty to Crown and Empire but adding their names to the long list of those wishing changes in the oath. They stated most fervently: "It is far from our desire to raise a religious controversy which might disturb the peace of the Empire; on the contrary, it is the love of peace, of a solid and lasting peace, founded on justice, that inspires our action." Both Catholic papers circulated in Toronto supported revision of the oath during Edward's reign, and subsequently during that of George v. AAO, Charles Gauthier Papers, Correspondence to Bishops, copy of "To His Eminence Cardinal Vaughan," 16 Mar. 1901; ARCAT, Denis O'Connor Papers, Cardinal Herbert Vaughan to O'Connor, 15 July 1901, and Archbishop Thomas Duhamel to O'Connor, 14 Oct. 1907; *Register* 18 July 1901, 30 June 1910; and *Record*, 2 Mar. 1901, 9 Mar. 1901, 26 July 1902.

113 *Register*, 12 May 1910.
114 *IC*, 26 Feb. 1891.
115 Ibid., 19 Feb. 1891, 2 July 1891, 5 May 1892.
116 Ibid., 24 Mar. 1892, 25 Oct. 1888, 10 Jan. 1889, 2 Oct. 1890, 5 Feb. 1891, 10 Dec. 1891, 28 Apr. 1892, 1 Sept. 1892.
117 *CWR*, 26 Jan. 1889, 9 Nov. 1889, 25 Oct. 1890.
118 David Gagan, *The Denison Family of Toronto, 1792–1925* (Toronto: University of Toronto Press 1973), 68–92; and Carl Berger, *The Sense of Power: Studies in the Ideas of Canadian Imperialism 1867–1914* (Toronto: University of Toronto Press 1970), 81, 134–5.
119 *CWR*, 14 Jan. 1888.
120 Ibid., 1 Sept. 1888, 11 July 1889.
121 Berger, *The Sense of Power*, 170–6; Robert Page, *The Boer War and Canadian Imperialism*, CHA Booklet no. 44 (Ottawa 1987), 17; Norman Penlington, *Canada and Imperialism, 1896–1899* (Toronto: University of Toronto Press 1965), 11, 198–225.
122 *CWR*, 18 May 1889.
123 Ibid., 25 Oct. 1890, 26 Jan., 17 Aug. 1889; *Record*, 22 Dec. 1900, 31 Dec. 1904; *Register*, 23 Mar. 1906, 4 Apr. 1912, 25 Jan. 1917, 8 Mar. 1917, 27 May 1920.
124 *Register*, 12, 19, 26 May 1898, 23, 30 June 1898, 28 July 1898, 10 Dec. 1898, 13, 20 July 1899, 24 Aug. 1899, 26 Oct. 1899, 25 May 1902, 7 May 1903; *Record*, 18 Nov. 1899, 9 Dec. 1899. *CWR*, 29 Dec. 1888, 26 Jan. 1889, 2 Feb. 1889, 25 Oct. 1890, 15 Nov. 1890.
125 *CWR*, 26 Jan. 1889.
126 Berger, *The Sense of Power*, 176; *Register*, 6 Sept. 1900.
127 *Register*, 10 Oct. 1912, 25 Feb. 1915, 29 Apr. 1915.
128 Ibid., 23 June 1904.
129 Ibid., 22 Mar. 1900.
130 Ibid., 6 Sept. 1900.
131 *Record*, 3 July 1897.

132 Ibid., 9 Apr. 1898, 3 July 1897, 9 Apr. 1898, 22 Apr. 1899.

133 *Register*, 26 Oct. 1899, 19 Oct. 1899, 28 Dec. 1899.

134 Ibid., 20 July 1899, 3 Aug. 1899, 17 Aug. 1899, 24 Aug. 1899, 31 Aug. 1899, 5 Oct. 1899.

135 Ibid., 10 Nov. 1899.

136 *Record*, 18 Nov. 1899, 25 Nov. 1899, 16 Dec. 1899, 24 Mar. 1900, 29 Sept. 1900, 9 Feb. 1901.

137 Catholic opposition to the war was certainly not consistent, although such consistency is suggested in Carman Miller, "A Preliminary Analysis of the Socio-economic Composition of Canada's South African Contingents," *Histoire sociale – Social History* 8 (Nov. 1975): 226, and his "English-Canadian Opposition to the South African War as seen through the Press," *Canadian Historical Review* 55 (Dec. 1974): 435–6. Miller's assumptions regarding Catholic participation are based neither on manuscript sources from Catholic archives nor on leading Ontario Catholic newspapers. The exploits of Father O'Leary, Catholic chaplain to the Canadian troops, in fact, are well documented in the *Register*, 1 Dec. 1899 and 3 Jan. 1901.

138 *Register*, 14 Dec. 1899, 2 Nov. 1899, 1 Dec. 1899.

139 Ibid., 28 Dec. 1899, 10 May, 15 Nov. 1900, 20 Dec. 1900, 3 Jan. 1901, 3 Oct. 1901. Carman Miller's statistics on Catholic participation in the war are misleading. He claims that only 12.2 per cent of the Canadian contingent was Catholic, although their percentage of the national population was 41.7 per cent. He also asserts that only 3 per cent of the contingent was French Canadian. Analysis of his own statistics would indicate that when the French Canadians (overwhelmingly Catholic) are deducted from the total percentage of Catholic participants, we are left with an English-speaking Catholic contingent constituting 9 per cent of the total. This figure would seem to indicate that English-speaking Catholics were well represented among the South African volunteers. Miller, "Canada's South African War Contingents," 223–5.

140 *Register*, 21 Dec. 1899.

141 Ibid., 6 Nov. 1902.

142 Ibid., 21 Aug. 1902; and *Record*, 26 July 1902, 12 Oct. 1902.

143 *Register*, 9 June 1904.

144 Ibid., 15 Oct. 1903, 23 Oct. 1903, 12 Nov. 1903, 19 Nov. 1903.

145 Ibid., 29 Oct. 1903, 23 Oct. 1903.

146 Ibid., 5 Nov. 1903.

147 NA, Charles Murphy Papers, vol. 10, Father James T. Foley to Murphy, 25 Mar. 1913, 4134–5. Similar sentiments are expressed in Foley to Murphy, 13 June 1913, 4137–44; Foley to Murphy, Liberal Circular No. 8, 4145–49; and Foley to Murphy, 17 Dec. 1913, 4158–61.

148 Ibid., vol. 16, Murphy to Wilfrid Laurier, 21 June 1913, 6508–9; and vol. 10, Foley to Murphy, 13 June 1913, 4143.

149 *Register*, 5 July 1917; and *Record*, 13 Feb. 1917.

150 *Register*, 31 Dec. 1903.

151 Reprinted in ibid., 30 Nov. 1905. Similar claims were made in the CWR, 27 Aug. 1892.

152 *Register*, 13 May 1897. Such ideas were repeated by the *Record*, 10 July 1915.

153 *Register*, 16 Oct. 1902. Some other patriotic editorials and reprints can be found in *IC*, 9 Oct. 1890, 25 June 1891, 1 Sept. 1892; CWR, 25 June 1887, 25 Oct. 1890; *Record*, 25 Oct. 1890, 25 Mar. 1899, 6 July 1901, 27 July 1901, 3 May 1902, 22 Aug. 1914, 10 July 1915; and *Register*, 20 July 1893, 30 July 1896, 5 Apr. 1900, 3 July 1902, 26 Mar. 1903, 20 July 1911.

154 *Register*, 4 July 1901.

155 *Record*, 20 Nov. 1920. *Register*, 8 July 1920, 7 July 1921. Early evidence appears in CWR, 26 Oct. 1889.

156 *Register*, 31 Mar. 1921.

157 Ibid., 14 Feb. 1901.

158 Helen Kernahan, "Why Canadians Should Love Canada," *St Joseph's Lilies* 8 (Dec. 1919): 122–4; M.L. Hart, "Things We Might Have," *St Joseph's Lilies* 1 (Sept. 1912): 10–11; NAC, Charles Murphy Papers, vol. 49, Speech, undated, 21716; *Record*, 29 Oct. 1898, 25 Mar. 1899, 22 Aug. 1914; *Register*, 16 Oct. 1902, 26 Mar. 1903, 13 Feb. 1908, 9 Oct. 1919, 1 Dec. 1921.

159 *Record*, 29 Oct. 1898.

160 Ibid., 16 Nov. 1895, 23 Mar. 1895, 25 Oct. 1902.

161 *Register*, 26 Mar. 1903.

162 *IC*, 3 Jan. 1889, 16 Apr. 1891; CWR, 28 Mar. 1891, 18 Apr. 1891, 2 Jan. 1892; *Record*, 8 Nov. 1890, 29 Nov. 1890, 22 Feb. 1896, 18 Dec. 1897, 29 Sept. 1900; and *Register*, 26 Sept. 1907. In civic politics criticism of a bigoted electorate continued into the twentieth century, especially during the failed campaign of John O'Neill for mayor in 1919. *Register*, 9 Jan. 1919.

163 *IC*, 18 Jan. 1891, 5 June 1890, 3 Jan. 1889.

164 *Register*, 24 May 1900. Similar claims had been made by Patrick Cronin's predecessors at the *Register*; see 23 May 1895.

165 *IC*, 3 Jan. 1889.

166 *Register*, 23 Dec. 1897, 19 Aug. 1897, 26 Aug. 1897, 30 Nov. 1911.

167 Ibid., 28 Dec. 1893, 23 Dec. 1897.

168 Ibid., 23 Dec. 1897.

169 *IC*, 14 Feb. 1889.

170 Ibid., 10 Oct. 1889; AAK, James Vincent Cleary Papers, Oliver Mowat to Cleary, 23 Sept. 1890.

171 *Register*, 16 Sept. 1897, 27 Jan. 1898. *Record*, 18 Dec. 1897.

172 *Record*, 22 Feb. 1896, 15 Sept. 1900. For more information on Catholic support for Macdonald see James R. Miller, " 'This saving remnant': Macdonald and the Catholic Vote in the 1891 Election," CCHA, *Study Sessions* 41 (1974): 33–52.
173 *Globe*, 9 May 1899; and NA, Laurier Papers, Peter Ryan to Laurier, 1 May 1899, reel 765, 33047; Thomas Mulvey to Laurier, 27 May 1899, reel 766, 33928–33; O.K. Fraser to Laurier, 31 July 1899, reel 767, 36119; copy of letter from Laurier to Fraser, 2 Aug. 1899, reel 767, 36120; Fraser to Laurier, 18 Aug. 1899, reel 768, 36623–4; and L.V. McBrady to Laurier, 12 May 1900, reel 776, 45483–9. In his letter McBrady assured Laurier that "Ontario Catholics have supported the Liberal party in the past, and will do so again, more convinced than ever that Liberalism stands for everything that is best and noblest in the interest of our Canada."
174 CWR, 28 Mar. 1891, 9 Jan. 1892; and IC, 14 Feb. 1889.
175 *Register*, 28 Feb. 1895, 20 Apr. 1893; *Record*, 6 July 1901.
176 Connor, "Irish Canadian Image," 100–4; IC, 3 Jan. 1889; *Record*, 13 May 1899.
177 *Register*, 14 May 1896, 28 Feb. 1895, 9 July 1896; NA, Sir John Thompson Papers, vol. 71, Frank Smith to Thompson, 15 Dec. 1887.
178 NA, Laurier Papers, reel 781, Thomas Coffey to Laurier, 5 Dec. 1900, 51451–3.
179 *Register*, 24 Oct. 1907.
180 Ibid., 14 May 1896, 14 Jan. 1904.
181 Joseph Schull, *Laurier: The First Canadian* (Toronto: Macmillan 1965), 328–9; Robert Craig Brown and Ramsay Cook, *Canada 1896–1921: A Nation Transformed* (Toronto: McClelland and Stewart 1974), 18.
182 *Register*, 9 July 1896, 16 July 1896.
183 Ibid., 14 Jan. 1904, 6 Oct. 1904; and NA, Charles Murphy Papers, vol. 16, file 77, copy of letter from Charles Murphy to Wilfrid Laurier, 23 Mar. 1915, enclosing "List of Ontario Counties in Which the Catholic Vote is the Determining Factor," 6529–33. Toronto South is listed as having 9,143 Catholic voters out of 43,956 total, or 20.8 per cent.
184 *Register*, 3 Nov. 1904, 10 Nov. 1904. Members were as follows: Liberals: Fitzpatrick (Quebec County); Power (Quebec West); Gallery (Ste Anne's, Montreal); Harty (Kingston); McCool (Nipissing); McColl (West Northumberland); Conmee (Thunder Bay); McIsaac (Antigonish); Costigan (Victoria); Johnston (Cape Breton); Hughes (Kings, PEI); Reilly (Victoria, BC). Conservatives: Monk (Jacques Cartier); Walsh (Huntingdon); Macdonell (South Toronto); and Daniel (St John). Macdonell was descended from the famous Highland Catholic family of Glengarry County. He resided with his family, including Brigadier General Archibald Hayes Macdonell, in St Helen's parish. He was a member of the original editorial staff of the *Catholic Weekly Review*, thereby helping to give it a more

Conservative sympathy. Macdonell incurred the wrath of the *Register* in 1905 when he was the only Catholic in Tory ranks to oppose the separate school provisions in Laurier's Autonomy Bill for the creation of Alberta and Saskatchewan. The *Register* warned him, "The experience not only of Canadian politics, but of Imperial politics, must convince him that party service has its limits and parliamentary freedom its field." *Register*, 4 May 1905.

185 Charles Humphries, *"Honest Enough to Be Bold": The Life and Times of James Pliny Whitney* (Toronto: OHSS, University of Toronto Press 1985), 47–9.

186 *Register*, 13 Mar. 1898. The Liberals included McKee (North Essex); Harty (Kingston); O'Keefe (Ottawa); and Evanturel (Prescott). Conservatives were Foy (South Toronto); Robillard (Russell); Lamarche (Nipissing); McDonald (Glengary); Wardell (Wentworth North); and McLaughlin (Stormont). For more information on Foy's success, see Roderick Lewis, *A Statistical History of All the Electoral Districts of the Province of Ontario since 1867* (Toronto: Baptist Johnston, Queen's Printer, nd), 265–6.

187 *Register*, 17 Jan. 1918, 25 Mar. 1920.

188 Ibid., 27 July 1922. See also 17 May 1894; *Record*, 15 Feb. 1896; *Globe*, 7 Feb. 1896.

189 *Register*, 13 Jan. 1898, 11 Aug. 1898, 13 Apr. 1911, 1 Mar. 1923.

190 *Register*, 5 May 1910.

191 Ibid.

192 Ibid., 13 Aug. 1896. Election results and percentages are calculated from figures in Joseph Schull, *Ontario since 1867* (Toronto: McClelland and Stewart 1978), 124–5, 232.

193 ARCAT, McEvay Papers, copy of letter from McEvay to Sir Wilfrid Laurier, 17 Feb. 1909; CWR, 9 Aug. 1890; *Register*, 7 July 1910. Several studies deal directly and indirectly with Toronto's sectarian tensions: Martin J. Galvin, "The Jubilee Riots in Toronto, 1875," CCHA, *Reports* 26 (1959): 93–107; Galvin, "Catholic-Protestant Relations in Ontario, 1864–1875"; Gregory Kealey, "The Orange Order in Toronto," in Kealey and P. Warrian, eds., *Essays in Canadian Working Class* (Toronto: McClelland and Stewart 1976), 13–34; Gregory Kealey, *Toronto Workers Respond to Industrial Capitalism* (Toronto: University of Toronto Press 1980), 98–123; Gerald J. Stortz, "Archbishop John Joseph Lynch and the Anglicans of Toronto," *Journal of the Canadian Church Historical Society* (1985).

194 *Record*, 17 Mar. 1917.

195 Berger, *The Sense of Power*, 6–9. Berger argues that Canadian imperialism has been misunderstood by Canadians, largely because definitions of it have been passed down by its critics. Berger recognizes imperialism as one form of Canadian nationalism. Imperialists, he asserts, merely sought Canadian greatness through an active role in the British Empire.

Critiques of Berger's position can be found in Douglas Cole, "Canada's Nationalistic Imperials," *Journal of Canadian Studies* 5 (Aug. 1970): 44–9; Robert J.D. Page, "Carl Berger and the Intellectual Origins of Canadian Imperialist Thought, 1867–1914," *Journal of Canadian Studies* 5 (Aug. 1970): 39–43.

196 NA, Charles Murphy Papers, vol. 49, Speech, undated, 21716.

CHAPTER SEVEN

1 ARCAT, Denis O'Connor Papers, Father J. Schweitzer, CR, to O'Connor, 12 Apr. 1907.

2 John Webster Grant, "The Reaction of WASP Churches to Non-WASP Immigrants," *Canadian Society of Church History Papers* (1968): 1–4.

3 "Opening Address," in F.C. Kelley, ed., *The First American Catholic Missionary Congress* (Chicago: J.S. Hyland 1909), 4.

4 Mason Wade, *The French Canadians*, vol. 1 (Toronto: Macmillan 1968), 580; *Register*, 15 Sept. 1910.

5 *Register*, 22 Feb. 1912.

6 George Daly, CSSR, *Catholic Problems in Western Canada* (Toronto: Macmillan 1921), 85. Similar statements are found in *Register*, 12 Nov. 1908, 18 Feb. 1909, 26 Feb. 1920.

7 *Register*, 14 May 1908; Murray Nicolson, "The Other Toronto: Irish Catholics in a Victorian City, 1850–1900," in Gilbert Stelter and Alan Artibise, eds., *The Canadian City* (Ottawa: Carleton University Press 1984), 341. Nicolson estimates that one-fifth of the Catholics in the city were "foreigners" by 1900. According to appropriate census data, his estimate for 1900 is far too liberal. Robert Harney, however, demonstrates that the Canadian census underestimated the seasonal variations in size of the Italian community. The census was taken in months when many Italian men were sojourning in other areas of Ontario, working on railways or in lumber camps. In the winter months hundreds of these migrant labourers ventured back to their home bases in Toronto. Harney, "Toronto's Little Italy," in Harney and J. Vincenza Scarpaci, eds., *Little Italies in North America* (Toronto: Multicultural History Society 1981), 46. For a statistical profile of declining levels of Irish immigration to Canada, see Kerby A. Miller, *Emigrants and Exiles: Ireland and the Irish Exodus to North America* (New York: Oxford University Press 1985), 569.

8 Robert Harney, "Chiaroscuro: Italians in Toronto, 1885–1915," *Italian Americana* 1, no. 2 (1975): 158. Harney considers the exoticism of the newcomers to both Catholics and Protestants in the city.

9 *Register*, 22 Aug. 1901, 16 Jan. 1913; *Sadlier's Catholic Almanac and Ordo* (New York: D.J. Sadlier 1890), 21–2. In 1892 a special mass was said at St Michael's Cathedral for the small Italian community. The celebrants

were Fathers Cruise and Coyle, both of whom could speak Italian. *CWR*, 9 Apr. 1892.

10 Roberto Perin, "Religion, Ethnicity and Identity: Placing the Immigrant within the Church," in Louis Rousseau and William Westfall, eds., "Religion / Culture," *Canadian Issues / Thèmes Canadiens* 7 (1984): 217.

11 *Register*, 16 Aug. 1894, 14 July 1904, 21 Mar. 1901, 6 Nov. 1902, 5 Mar. 1908. ARCAT, Archbishop Denis O'Connor Papers, letter from J. Schweitzer to O'Connor, 12 Apr. 1907. ASV-DAC, 89.22/2, Dean John L. Hand to Donatus Sbarretti, 13 Apr. 1908, and 89.17, Lancelot Minehan to Sbarretti, 12 Dec. 1905.

12 Harney, "Toronto's Little Italy," 42, 46–7; Zofia Shahrodi, "The Polish Community in Toronto in the Twentieth Century," in Robert Harney, ed., *Gathering Place: Peoples and Neighbourhoods of Toronto, 1834–1945* (Toronto: Multicultural History Society of Ontario 1985), 244; and Zoriana Yaworsky-Sokolsky, "The Beginnings of Ukrainian Settlement in Toronto 1891–1939," in ibid., 280–1.

13 ARCAT, Baptismal Registers, St Mary's and St Patrick's parishes, 1890, 1895, 1900, 1905, 1910, 1915, 1920.

14 Clermont Trudelle et Pierre Fortier, *Toronto se raconte: la paroisse du Sacré-Coeur* (Toronto: La Société d'histoire de Toronto 1987), 40.

15 CTA, Assessment Rolls, St David's Ward and St Thomas's Ward, 1891, and Wards 1 and 2, 1901, 1911, 1921.

16 *Christian Guardian*, 13 Oct. 1916. John Zucchi, "Church and Clergy and the Religious Life of Toronto's Italian Immigrants, 1900–1940," CCHA, *Study Sessions* 50 (1983): 537; UCA, Toronto Church Extension and Mission Union / Toronto Home Missions Council; Harney, "Chiaroscuro," 158–9; and Harney, "Toronto's Little Italy," 49.

17 *Register*, 11 June 1908. See Enrico Carlson-Cumbo, " 'Impediments to the harvest': The Limits of Methodist Proselytization of Toronto's Italian Immigrants, 1905–1925," in McGowan and Clarke, eds., *Catholics at the "Gathering Place": Historical Essays on the Archdiocese of Toronto, 1841–1991* (Toronto: CCHA 1993), 155–76.

18 *Register*, 3 Dec. 1908.

19 ARCAT, Neil McNeil Papers, draft of a circular letter, ca 1920; *Separate School Chronicle* 1 (1919).

20 *Ontario Catholic Year Book* (Toronto: Newman Club 1920), 54–5. The Italians held Our Lady of Mount Carmel, St Agnes, and St Clement's; the Poles worshipped at St Stanislaus Kostka and Nativity; Ukrainians established St Josaphat's; and the Maronite Syrians and others of the Melchite Rite shared Assumption Parish. See also *Register*, 13 Apr. 1911.

21 ARCAT, Roman Correspondence, James McGuigan to Sacred Congregation of the Council, ca 1949; Sacred Congregation of the Council to McGuigan, 26 Mar. 1949.

22 *Register,* 30 July 1908, 13 Apr. 1911.

23 Ibid., 26 Mar. 1914.

24 Ibid., 22 Jan. 1914. McNeil addressed 1,700 members of the city's Holy Name Society, demanding that offensive words regarding Italians be stricken from a Catholic's vocabulary.

25 Ibid., 25 May 1911; Harney, "Chiaroscuro," 158. Harney reports that some Italians in the city were also eager to learn English.

26 ARCAT, McNeil Papers, "National Unity and the School," 8 Feb. 1933; see also "Nations and Races, Wars and World Peace, Schools and Religion," 1932. Separate schools also became vehicles for promotion of the home mission movement, as children were urged to support Catholic efforts to thwart Protestant proselytism among Ukrainian Catholics. *Separate School Chronicle,* 1918.

27 AO, Ministry of Education Papers, Report of Separate School Board Inspector, Toronto, 1907.

28 *Separate School Chronicle* 2 (Dec. 1919).

29 Gerald Shaughnessy, SM, *Has the Immigrant Kept the Faith?* (New York: Macmillan 1925), 221, 267–8; Silvano Tomasi, "The Ethnic Church and Integration of Italian Immigrants in the United States," in Tomasi, ed., *The Italian Experience in the United States* (Staten Island: Centre for Migration Studies 1970), 185–92; Rudolph Vecoli, "Prelates and Peasants: Italian Immigrants and the Catholic Church," *Journal of Social History* 3 (July 1969): 220–1, 225, 259, 263; Victor Greene, "For God and Country: The Origins of Slavic Self-Consciousness in America," *Church History* 35 (Dec. 1966): 255–60. Robert Harney regards immigrant assimilation as the goal behind the establishment of ethnic parishes in Toronto: *Toronto: Canada's New Cosmopolite* (Toronto: Multicultural History Society of Ontario 1981), 5.

30 ARCAT, Our Lady of Mount Carmel Parish box, copy of letter from Fergus McEvay to Father Brick, 3 Aug. 1908; UCA, Mission Society of the Methodist Church, *Annual Reports,* 1905–06, 1906–07; *Register,* 11 June 1908.

31 Luigi Pautasso, "Archbishop Fergus P. McEvay and the Betterment of Toronto's Italians," *Italian Canadiana* 5 (1989): 71–5.

32 ARCAT, Carl Doglio File, Doglio to McEvay, 23 Sept. 1909; draft of letter from J.T. Kidd to Doglio, nd; Kidd to Doglio, 1 Mar. 1910; draft of letter from Fergus McEvay to Bishop of Rochester, 13 May 1910, 28 May 1910; Apostolic Delegate Papers, McEvay to Donatus Sbarretti, 28 May 1910; *Register,* 24 Sept. 1908, 15 Oct. 1908.

33 ARCAT, Joseph Longo File, copy of letter from McEvay to unnamed bishop, 5 Nov. 1909; Apostolic Delegate to McEvay, 8 Nov. 1909; and private letter from Apostolic Delegate to McEvay, 8 Nov. 1909.

34 John Zucchi, "Italian Hometown Settlements and the Development of an Italian Community in Toronto, 1875–1935," in Harney, ed., *Gathering Place*, 121; ARCAT, Our Lady of Mt Carmel Parish Papers, unsigned letter to Father Mohan, nd; Harney, "Toronto's Little Italy," 43; and Harney, "Chiaroscuro," 147.

35 ARCAT, Secretary's Report, Minutes of the Annual Meeting, 1916.

36 Ibid., Presidential and Executive Committee Report, 10 Feb. 1913; Minutes of Fall Quarterly Meeting, 25 Sept. 1916; Secretary's Report, Annual Meeting, 1916; Archdiocesan Holy Name Union, Executive, 1918; and *Register*, 19 Apr. 1917.

37 ARCAT, Holy Name Society Papers, Secretary's Report, Minutes of Annual Meeting, 1916; and Minutes of Fall Quarterly Meeting, 25 Sept. 1916. The executive report of 1918 put the Syrian membership at 21.

38 *Register*, 24 July 1919. ARCAT, Holy Name Society Papers, Secretary's Report, 1916, and Minutes of Annual Meeting, 16 Mar. 1924. The latter indicated at least one Polish branch had been founded since the end of the war. For numbers of immigrant members, see Archdiocesan Holy Name Union, Executive, 1918.

39 Zucchi, "Church and Clergy," 545–6.

40 ARCAT, Holy Name Society Papers, Fall Quarterly Meeting, 14 Oct. 1920.

41 Recent unpublished graduate work by Enrico Cumbo at the University of Toronto indicates that Italian popular religion itself was the greatest barrier to the Methodists, who never could fully comprehend the depth of the Italian Catholic spirituality.

42 ARCAT, O'Connor Papers, J. Schweitzer to Denis O'Connor, 12 Apr. 1907.

43 Zofia Shahrodi, "The Experience of Polish Catholics in the Archdiocese of Toronto, 1905–1935," in McGowan and Clarke, eds., *Catholics at the "Gathering Place,"* 144.

44 *Register*, 29 June 1911, 7 Sept. 1911; Shahrodi, "The Polish Community in Toronto in the Early Twentieth Century," 250–1; Shahrodi, "St Stanislaus' Parish: The Heart of Toronto Polonia," *Polyphony* 6 (Fall/Winter 1984): 27–8.

45 ARCAT, Ruthenian and Ukrainian Papers, Fergus McEvay to Donatus Sbarretti, 18 June 1910; St Stanislaus Parish box, J.T. Kidd to Joseph Hinzmann, 23 Jan. 1911.

46 Yaworsky-Sokolsky, "The Beginnings of Ukrainian Settlement in Toronto," 280, 286.

47 In 1919 Poles and Ukrainians were at war in Europe, which in part caused a breakdown of relations between Polish and Ukrainian Catholic immigrants in Toronto. Polish nationalists contested all other groups for control of parishes. To make matters worse, Father John Joseph Dekowski was appointed pastor of St Stanislaus in 1922, succeeding the be-

leagred Leonard Blum. Dekowski had been a chaplain in the Polish army that overran the Western Ukraine; this alienated him from the Ukrainian "latynnyky" (Roman Catholics) of the parish and precipitated the schism at St Stanislaus. Yaworsky-Sokolsky, "The Beginnings of Ukrainian Settlement in Toronto," 286–7.

48 ARCAT, St Stanislaus Parish box, L.N. Blum to Neil McNeil, 24 Jan. 1920; see also Elizabeth Kaminski, "St Stanislaus Parish," unpublished paper, Ontario Institute For Studies in Education 1978, 4–7.

49 ARCAT, St Stanislaus Parish box, copy of letter from departing parishioners to Blum, 9 Feb. 1920.

50 Ibid., copy, Rule and Regulations for St Stanislaus Kotska Parish Church, Toronto, Ont., ca 1920.

51 Yaworsky-Sokolsky, "The Beginnings of Ukrainian Settlement," 286; ARCAT, St Mary's Parish (Polish) Papers, Father Charles Bonner, St Cecila's Parish, to McNeil, 28 July 1920. Bonner informed the archbishop that: "The polish children are taught this polish language and history by a pole under the auspices of some anti catholic organization, in a protestant hall, where they occasionally hear anti-catholic remarks. Also I heard from one Russian schismatic laity and from one Pole of good character, that this anticatholic organization intends to buy the Russian Schismatic church ... on cor. Royce & Edwin Ave, in the center of the Polish settlement, and which is at present vacant, to be known as 'the Polish independent Church of Canada.'" Bonner added that the Polish clergy gave the people little sympathy or encouragement.

52 Shahrodi, "The Experience of Polish Catholics," 148. American examples are found in Greene, "For God and Country," 448–57; Timothy Smith, "Lay Initiative in the Religious Life of American Immigrants, 1880–1950," in Tamara Hereven, ed., *Anonymous Americans: Explorations in Nineteenth Century Social History* (Englewood Cliff: Prentice-Hall 1974), 238–40.

53 For the purposes of this chapter the author will refrain from using the term Ruthenian – now considered pejorative – and will use the title Ukrainian throughout except where the other is used in direct quotations.

54 Father Leo Sembratowicz was the temporary pastor for the community until the arrival of Yermy in 1911. ARCAT, Ruthenian and Ukrainian Papers, Alfred Sinnott, secretary of the Apostolic Delegation, to Archbishop Fergus McEvay, 14 Sept. 1910; St Josaphat's Parish Papers, James T. Kidd to Father Joseph Boyaczuk, 17 Feb. 1912. *The Official Catholic Directory* (New York: P.J. Kenedy and Sons 1912), 53, and (1911), 52.

55 *Register*, 23 Feb. 1911, 25 May 1911.

56 ARCAT, CCES Papers, Archbishop Paul Bruchesi of Montreal to Fergus McEvay, 13 June 1910; Father Achille Delaere to Paul Bruchesi, 7 June 1910.

57 Ibid., memorandum of Leo Sembratowicz, 22 Oct. 1909.

58 *Register*, 29 Feb. 1912; Yaworsky-Sokolsky, "The Beginnings," 280; ARCAT, Ruthenian and Ukrainian Papers, John T. Kidd to Bishop Ortynski, 25 Jan. 1912. Kidd's request was answered within the month with the promise of Boyarczuk's transfer to Toronto.

59 Yaworsky-Sokolsky, "The Beginnings," 292; *Register*, 16 Apr. 1914.

60 Tomasi, "The Ethnic Church," 186.

61 CCES Office, Toronto, Meeting Minutes Book, 2.

62 *Register*, 12 Nov. 1908.

63 ARCAT, McNeil Papers, "Bulletin on the Ruthenian Situation," 1916.

64 NA, Sir Charles Fitzpatrick Papers, vol. 13, copy of letter from Fergus P. McEvay to Sir Charles Fitzpatrick, 29 Dec. 1910, 5815; *Register*, 8 Apr. 1909.

65 Sermon by Michael Francis Fallon, in Francis C. Kelley, ed., *Official Report of the Second American Catholic Missionary Congress* (Chicago: J.S. Hyland 1914), 33–4.

66 *Register*, 18 Feb. 1909. Burke continued, "The other day we heard with amazed satisfaction, a great British Imperialist say: 'I admire the work of the Catholic Church in this grand Canadian member of the Empire. I hope for everything from it in the development of an ideal race and government. I would be delighted to see Canada Catholic and a model member of the Empire.' And may it be so."

67 NA, Sir Robert Borden Papers, *The Tunnel* by Alfred E. Burke, vol. 318, 188794–807; *Canadian* 10 (Dec. 1904): 5; and *St Joseph's Lilies* 1 (Dec. 1912): 12–13.

68 Francis C. Kelley, *The Bishop Jots It Down: An Autobiographical Strain on Memories by Francis C. Kelley* (New York: Harper Brothers 1939), 149; ARCAT, Alfred E. Burke File, "Fact Sheet on Alfred E. Burke."

69 Speech by Mary Hoskin, in Kelley, ed., *Report of the Second American Catholic Missionary Congress*, 282; *Register*, 16 Sept. 1909.

70 *Register*, 12 Nov. 1908.

71 Ibid., 20 May 1909.

72 Ibid., 24 June 1915. Burke's friendship with the English Jesuit Bernard Vaughan, and his accompaniment of Vaughan on a Canadian speaking tour, advocating vigorous imperial support in Canada, reaffirmed Burke's personal dedication to a Catholic and English-speaking Canada under the auspices of the Empire. *Register*, 22 Sept. 1910, 15 Dec. 1910, 7 Dec. 1911, 28 Dec. 1911; see also *Record*, 29 Jan. 1916.

73 Daly, *Catholic Problems in Western Canada*, 85; similar statements can be found in *Register*, 12 Nov. 1908, 18 Feb. 1909, 26 Feb. 1920.

74 CCES, *Annual Report*, 1917–18, 15; *Register*, 1 Apr. 1909, 5 May 1910.

75 Subcouncils included St Peter's, St Mary's, St Helen's, St Basil's, St Anthony's, St Ann's, and St Vincent de Paul parishes, and students at Lor-

etto Abbey Schools. *Register*, 12 Sept. 1912, 15 Apr. 1920; and CCES Office, Minutes Book, Report of the Women's Auxiliary, Apr. 1915, 47–50.

76 Alfred E. Burke, "The Need of a Missionary College," *The First American Catholic Missionary Congress*, 83. The exact number of Ukrainians in Canada by 1910 has been hotly disputed due to inaccuracies in identifying Ukrainian ethnicity in the census. Archives of the Sacred Congregation of the Propaganda Fide (PF), Oriental Rites Affairs, Rutini #31945, July 1912. This document estimates between 120,000 to 150,000. Vladimir Kaye, "Settlement and Colonization," and Paul Yuzyk "Religious Life," in Manoloy Lupul, ed., *A Heritage in Transition: Essays in the History of the Ukrainians in Canada* (Toronto: McClelland and Stewart 1982); ARCAT, Ruthenian and Ukrainian Papers, "Fact Sheet Submitted by Bishop Budka," 1919; or Alexis Barbizieux, *L'Eglise Catholique au Canada* (Québec: L'Action Sociale Catholique 1923), 72–8.

77 *Register*, 5 Sept. 1912.

78 RPA Delaere, CSSR, *Mémoire sur les tentatives de schisme et d'hérésie au milieu des Ruthènes de l'Ouest Canadien* (Québec: L'Action sociale 1908).

79 ARCAT, Ruthenian and Ukrainian Papers, "Memorial to the First Plenary Council," 1 Oct. 1909. Burke appealed to the Canadian hierarchy for the building of Ukrainian chapels, the recruitment of missionary priests, the founding of a Ukrainian Catholic paper, and the appointment of a Ukrainian Catholic bishop.

80 *Telegram*, 20 Sept. 1909.

81 Francis C. Kelley, *The Story Of Extension* (Chicago: Extension Society Press 1922), 163; *Register*, 24 Feb. 1910, 16 Sept. 1909; Delaere, *Mémoire sur les tentatives de schisme*.

82 *Register*, 7 Apr. 1911. Other attacks against Protestants, especially Presbyterians, can be found on 15 and 29 Apr., 20 May, 23 Sept., and 21 Oct. 1909; 13 Jan. 1910; and 23 Feb., 27 Apr., and 10 and 17 Aug. 1911.

83 CCES Papers, Minutes Book, 29.

84 Paul Yuzyk, *The Ukrainians in Manitoba* (Toronto: University of Toronto Press 1953), 73; *Register*, 16 Mar. 1911; Kelley, *The Story of Extension*, 164.

85 Prior to the Great War, Hungarians were served by Jule Pirot (Belgian), Father A. Conter (Belgian), Francis Woodcutter (German), Jean T.G. Vorst (Belgian), and Menyhért Érdujhelyi (Hungarian). See Martin Kovacs, "The Saskatchewan Era, 1885–1914," in N.F. Dreisziger, ed., *Struggle and Hope: The Hungarian Canadian Experience* (Toronto: McClelland and Stewart 1982), 61–93; and Pirot, *One Year's Fight for the True Faith in Saskatchewan*, 4–6; *Register*, 30 June 1910, 11 May 1911.

86 ARCAT, CCES Papers, Archbishop Paul Bruchési of Montreal to Fergus McEvay, 13 June 1910; Father Achille Delaere to Paul Bruchési, 7 June 1910.

87 *Register*, 19 Mar. 1914. The newspapers reported that there were fourteen candidates for the Eastern rite under the spiritual direction of the Reverend "Dr Radkiewicz" at St Augustine's Seminary in Scarborough.

88 *Register*, 31 May 1917; ARCAT, Ruthenian and Ukrainian Papers, "Fact Sheet submitted by Archbishop Budka," 1919; *The Official Catholic Directory* (New York: P.J. Kenedy and Sons, 1927, 1930).

89 Ibid.; Josephat Jean, "S.E. Adelard Langevin, Archévêque de St Boniface et les Ukrainiens," CCHA, *Reports* (1944–45): 103; ARCAT, CCES Papers, Father Boels to Archbishop Fergus McEvay, 13 Oct. 1909. ASV-DAC, 184.31, J. Sabourin to Joseph Poitras, 25 Jan. 1910; 184.22, Adelard Langevin to Cardinal Gotti, 25 Oct. 1909.

90 NA, Fitzpatrick Papers, vol. 13, copy of letter from McEvay to Louis N. Bégin, 27 Dec. 1910, 5816; see also *Register*, 31 Dec. 1908, 16 Sept. 1909.

91 NA, Fitzpatrick Papers, vol. 82, memorandum from Alfred E. Burke to the Duke of Norfolk, 6 Apr. 1909, 45453–7.

92 Ibid., vol. 82, Burke to Fitzpatrick, 9 Apr. 1909, 45458.

93 Quoted in *Register*, 3 Feb. 1910.

94 *Register*, 28 Apr. 1910.

95 ASV-DAC, 184.31, "Rapport de la Reunion de Quelques Pretres du Rite Ruthene," 4 Jan. 1910; *Register*, 3 Feb. 1910, 28 Apr. 1910. For Budka's comments see *Register*, 25 July 1918, 23 Jan. 1919; and *Kanadyskyi Rusyn*, 29 Jan. 1919.

96 See Mark G. McGowan, "The Harvesters Were Few: A Study of the Catholic Church Extension Society of Canada, French Canada, and the Ukrainian Question," unpublished graduate paper, University of Toronto 1983, 110–12; ARCAT, CCES Papers, "One of Our Needs For the Church in Canada," by Neil McNeil, 1926.

97 In 1923 Father George Daly made a detailed report on the Ukrainian missions to the Canadian bishops and recommended "THE GRADUAL, PRUDENT, SYSTEMATIC ABSORPTION OF RUTHENIAN CATHOLICS INTO THE LATIN CHURCH." ARCAT, Eparchy of Toronto Papers, "Confidential Report on the Ruthenian Problem in Canada," 1923. Also see Stella Hryniuk, "The Bishop Budka Controversy: A New Perspective," *Canadian Slavonic Papers* 23 (1981): 162; ARCAT, Ruthenian and Ukrainian Papers, Circular, 27 July 1914; copy of letter from a "Canadian Ukrainian" to the editor of *Saturday Night*, 22 Jan. 1919, and Thomas Murray to McNeil, 21 May 1921. For more detail on the treatment of Ukrainians in Canada during the war, see John H. Thompson and Frances Swyripa, eds., *Loyalties in Conflict: Ukrainians in Canada during the Great War* (Edmonton: Canadian Institute of Ukrainian Studies 1983).

98 CCES Office, Minutes Book, 17 Apr. 1912, 25; 4 Apr. 1915, 47–51; *Register*, 16 Jan. 1910, 28 Apr. 1910, 7 Aug. 1911.

99 ARCAT, McNeil Papers, Bulletin to Clergy, 8 Apr. 1916. Annual totals of the CCES pale in comparison to "Report on the Commission of Statistics," *Canada's Missionary Congress* (Toronto: Canadian Council of the Laymen's Missionary Movement 1909), 323; John S. Moir, " 'On the King's Business': The Rise and Fall of the Laymen's Missionary Movement in Canada," *Miscellanea Historiae Ecclesiasticae* 7 (Congrés de Bucarest, Aug. 1980): 327–8.

100 CCES Office, Minutes Book, 2 Apr. 1913, 28–30; NA, Fitzpatrick Papers, vol. 15, McNeil to Fitzpatrick, 8 Nov. 1913, 6540.

101 ARCAT, McNeil Papers, Bishop James Morrison to McNeil, 29 Jan. 1913; Bishop David Scollard to McNeil, 4 Feb. 1913; Auxiliary Bishop P.T. Ryan to McNeil, 26 Feb. 1913; James Gaffey, *Francis Clement Kelley and the American Catholic Dream*, vol. 1 (Besenville, Ill.: Heritage Foundation 1980), 96, 132, 136–7.

102 CCES Office, *Minutes*, 2 Apr. 1913, 22 Apr. 1913; NA, Fitzpatrick Papers, vol. 15, McNeil to Fitzpatrick, 8 Nov. 1913, 6540; ARCAT, Judge H.T. Kelly Papers, McNeil to Kelly, 27 Mar. 1915; copy of letter from Kelly to McNeil, 31 Mar. 1915.

103 Raymond Huel,"*Gestae Dei Per Francos*: The French Catholic Experience in Western Canada," in Benjamin Smillie, ed., *Visions of the New Jerusalem* (Edmonton: NeWest Press 1983), 39–54.

104 ARCAT, CCES Papers, Adelard Langevin to Fergus Patrick McEvay, 16 Jan. 1909.

105 AASB, Adelard Langevin Papers, copy of letter from Adelard Langevin to Archbishop L.N. Bégin of Quebec, 21 Aug. 1908; Langevin to Bégin, 20 Sept. 1909; copy of letter from Langevin to Father Thomas Dauson, OMI, 24 Oct. 1912; and Langevin on the CCES, 13 Jan. 1913.

106 Raymond Huel, "The Irish-French Conflict in Catholic Episcopal Nominations: The Western Sees and the Domination Within the Church," CCHA, *Study Sessions* 42 (1975): 51–70.

107 AASB, Langevin Papers, Langevin to Arthur Beliveau, 20 Sept. 1909.

108 ASV-DAC, 91.7/1, Adelard langevin to Pellegrino Stagni, 15 July 1911.

109 Ibid., 184.2, Langevin to Donatus Sbarretti, 10 June 1905; my trans. He may not have been far wrong in the potential disruption caused by the Eastern rite priests. Father J.T. Roche confided to Burke that he and Father Canning "considered ... the Ruthenian Rite ... a big advance over the Latin." Ibid., 184.18, Roche to Burke, 30 Aug. 1909.

110 AASB, Josaphat Jean Papers, Document 12, Langevin to Father Josaphat Jean, 4 Aug. 1913.

111 Ibid., Document 13, Jean to Langevin, 10 Aug. 1913; and Langevin Papers, Father A. Husson, OMI, 7 Mar. 1910, L34297.

112 ASV-DAC, 184.2, Langevin to Sbarretti, 10 June 1905, and Emile Légal to Sbarretti, 12 Mar. 1905. Also see 184.14, "Réponses au questionnaire," 11 June 1909.

113 Ibid., 184.21, Leo Sembratowicz to Sbarretti, 4 Nov. 1909.

114 Quoted in Pirot, *One Year's Fight for the True Faith in Saskatchewan*, 9; see also Martin L. Kovacs, "The Hungarian School Question," in Martin L. Kovacs, ed., *Ethnic Canadians, Culture and Education* (Regina: Canadian Plains Research Centre 1978), 341, 350; Huel, "*Gestae dei per Francos*," 42. Other references to the French Canadian vision in the west can be gleaned in Arthur I. Silver, "Some Quebec Attitudes in an Age of Imperialism," *Canadian Historical Review* 57 (Dec. 1976): 440–60; Robert Painchaud, "French Canadian Historiography and Franco-Canadian Settlement in Western Canada," *Canadian Historical Review* 59 (Dec. 1978): 447–66; and Raymond Huel, "French-speaking Bishops and the Cultural Mosaic in Western Canada," in Richard Allen, ed., *Religion and Society in the Prairie West* (Regina: Canadian Plains Research Centre 1978): 335–58.

115 *Register*, 24 June 1915; NAC, Charles Murphy Papers, vol. 9, Michael F. Fallon to Charles Murphy, 29 Apr. 1909, 3548–51.

116 ARCAT, McEvay Papers, copy of letter from McEvay to Cardinal DeLai of the Consistorial Congregation, Rome, 30 Apr. 1911.

117 ASV-DAC, 184.18, J.T. Roche to Burke, Aug. 1909.

118 AASB, Langevin Papers, A.E. Burke to Langevin, 3 Oct. 1909; Langevin to Burke, 12 Oct. 1909; and Burke to Langevin, 13 Apr. 1910.

119 *Register*, 1 Sept. 1910; AASB, Langevin Papers, copy of letter from Langevin to Burke, 16 Apr. 1910; Burke to Langevin, 16 July 1910. ASV-DAC, 184.21, Langevin to Sbarretti, 26 Nov. 1909; Sembratowicz to Burke, 17 Jan. 1910; Burke to Sbarretti, 5 Apr. 1910. See also L.P.A. Langevin, *Mémoire confidentiel sur la situation religieuse et statistique de la population catholique de l'archdiocese de St Boniface* (St Boniface, 18 May 1911).

120 Several of the suffragans expressed reservations when Langevin insisted that the Canadian bishops' collection for the Ukrainians be sent to St Boniface for distribution throughout the west. Bishop Pascal wanted to receive money directly but was afraid to differ openly with Langevin when McEvay suggested he press the issue. ARCAT, Ruthenian and Ukrainian Papers, Fergus McEvay to Bishop Richard O'Connor of Peterborough, 22 Nov. 1910. AASB, Langevin Papers, Father A. Husson to Langevin, 7 Mar. 1910.

121 Kelley, *The Bishop Jots It Down*, 146–7. NA, Charles Murphy Papers, vol. 4, file 19, copy of letter from Murphy to Paul Bruchési, 22 Aug. 1910, 1344–7. In the letter Murphy implies that Bruchési regards "Dr. Burke as a mischief-maker."

122 ARCAT, McNeil Papers, Bishop Ryan to McNeil, 26 Feb. 1913; further evidence noted in NA, Fitzpatrick Papers, vol. 82, memorandum from A.E. Burke to the Duke of Norfolk, 6 Apr. 1909, 45453–4; Burke to Fitzpatrick, 9 Apr. 1909, 45458.

123 *Register*, 4 July 1912; *Le Droit*, 9 Sept. 1913; and *Register*, 15 Sept. 1910, 18 Sept. 1913, 5 Mar. 1914, 24 June 1915, 30 Mar. 1916, 16 Sept. 1916. The

Apostolic Delegate, Pellegrino Stagni, demanded an end to the war between English and French Catholic newspapers. He ordered McNeil to
muzzle Burke on issues regarding French Canadian nationalism. ARCAT,
Apostolic Delegate's Correspondence, Stagni to McNeil, 18 Sept., 16 Oct.
1913.

124 *Register*, 26 Oct. 1916.

125 AAO, Charles H. Gauthier Papers, Apostolic Delegate to Gauthier, 11 Jan.
1908; Thomas Duhamel to Cardinal Gotti, *Propaganda Fide*, 2 Feb. 1908.

126 ASV-DAC, Pellegrino Stagni to Cardinal De Lai, Consistorial Congregation, Rome, 7964, 19 Sept. 1911.

127 AAO, Toronto Correspondence, Fergus McEvay to Charles Gauthier,
10 Feb. 1909; McEvay to O'Leary, 15 Apr. 1909.

128 ARCAT, Apostolic Delegate Papers, copy of letter from McEvay to Dona-
tus Sbarretti, 10 Mar. 1909; see also McEvay Papers, copy of letter from
Cardinal DeLai of the Consistorial Congregation to Donatus Sbarretti,
Apostolic Delegate, 17 Feb. 1909; and AAO, Toronto Correspondence,
McEvay to Gauthier, 15 Mar. 1909.

129 Ibid., McEvay Papers, Richard O'Connor to McEvay, 19 Mar. 1909.

130 Ibid., McEvay's statement to His Holiness the Pope accompanying Terna
for London Diocese, [Mar. 1909]; List of Terna, 25 Mar. 1909; and Apostolic Delegate Papers, copy of letter from McEvay to Donatus Sbarretti,
1 Apr. 1909.

131 Ibid., copy of letter from McEvay to O'Leary, 15 Apr. 1909; O'Leary to
McEvay, 20 May 1909, 9 July 1909. Scollard revealed that Gauthier also
had a major influence in promoting the candidature of Fallon, to the de-
light of the prelate from the Sault. AAO, Gauthier Papers, Bishops' Correspondence, Scollard to Gauthier, 30 Dec. 1909; NA, Charles Murphy
Papers, vol. 9, Michael Francis Fallon to Murphy, undated, 3576.

132 ASV-DAC, 19.10/1, Sbarretti to Merry del Val, 25 May 1909, 12 June 1909.
An excellent detailed analysis of the Fallon appointment is found in Pas-
quale Fiorino, "The Nomination of Bishop Fallon as Bishop of London,"
CCHA, *Historical Studies* 62 (1996): 33–46.

133 Robert Choquette, *La Foi: Gardienne de la langue en Ontario, 1900–1950*
(Montréal: Bellarmin 1987), 39–40.

134 ARCAT, McEvay Papers, David Scollard to McEvay, 10 Oct. 1910.

135 Ibid., CCES Papers, Alfred Burke to McEvay, 17 July 1909.

136 Ibid., McEvay Papers, Henry O'Leary to McEvay, 4 Nov. 1909. AASB,
Langevin Papers, Father A. Husson to Langevin, 7 Mar. 1910. This priest
revealed that Francis Kelley of American Extension asserted that Langevin's aims would be thwarted if he protested to Rome about the CCES.
Kelley added that Extension and the Anglo-Celtic bishops "are very
strong there [Rome]."

137 Barbizeaux, *L'Église Catholique*, 57.
138 ARCAT, McEvay Papers, copies of letters from McEvay to Gauthier, 18 Apr. 1911, 24 Apr. 1911. See Raymond Huel, "Mgr. Olivier-Elzéar Mathieu: Guardian of French Catholic Interests In Saskatchewan," *Revue de l'Université d'Ottawa* 42 (Sept. 1972): 384–5.
139 AAH, Edward McCarthy Papers, Pellegrino Stagni to McCarthy, 14, 15 Aug. 1912; McCarthy to Stagni (copy), 10 Aug. 1912. ASV-DAC, 91.7/1, Stagni to Cardinal De Lai, 20 Sept. 1911.
140 Huel, "The Irish-French Conflict," 57–9.
141 Ibid., 63–8.
142 ARCAT, McEvay Education Papers, Fallon to McEvay, 21 Jan. 1911.
143 *Register*, 15 Sept. 1910; Robert Choquette, *Language and Religion: A History of English-French Conflict in Ontario* (Ottawa: University of Ottawa Press 1975), 91.
144 *Register*, 15 Sept. 1910. NA, James Kenney Papers, vol. 8, file 7, copy of letter from Charles Murphy to Archbishop Bourne, 12 Sept. 1910; ARCAT, McNeil Papers, copy of letter from Fallon to Paul Bruchési, 27 July 1915.
145 Wade, *The French Canadians*, 582.
146 The bilingual schools issue is perhaps the most examined of any issue in the educational history of Ontario since 1900. Choquette, *Language and Religion*; Marilyn Barber, "The Ontario Schools Issue: Sources of Conflict," *Canadian Historical Review* 47 (Sept. 1966); Margaret Prang, "Clerics, Politicians, and the Bilingual Schools Issue in Ontario, 1910–1917," *Canadian Historical Review* 41 (Dec. 1960); C.B. Sissons, *Bilingual Schools in Canada* (Toronto: J.M. Dent and Sons 1917); Chad Gaffield, *Language, Schooling and Cultural Conflict: The Origins of the French Language Controversy in Ontario* (Montreal and Kingston: McGill-Queen's University Press 1987).
147 AO, James Pliny Whitney Papers, Fergus McEvay to Whitney, 15 Feb. 1910; and Whitney to McEvay, 9 Mar. 1910.
148 ARCAT, McNeil Papers, McNeil to Mr Whalen of the *Casket*, 6 Dec. 1913; *Register*, 14 Sept. 1916.
149 AO, Whitney Papers, Michael Fallon, bishop of London, to Whitney, 28 Dec. 1912; William Macdonell, bishop of Alexandria, to Whitney, Nov. 1912; and David Scollard, bishop of Sault Ste Marie, to Whitney, 21 Oct. 1912. Archbishop Charles Gauthier of Ottawa supported the government's initiatives but asked that the French-language training be expanded in bilingual schools that were almost exclusively attended by the French: Gauthier to Whitney, 24 Dec. 1912; ARCAT, McEvay Papers, copy of letter from Michael Fallon to Gauthier, 18 Aug. 1910.
150 Choquette, *Language and Religion*, 85. ARCAT, McNeil Papers, Fallon to Apostolic Delegate Pellegrino Stagni, 26 May 1913, 1–39. *Le Pays*, 10 Oct. 1910; *Ottawa Citizen*, 15 Oct. 1910; and *Ottawa Journal*, 14 Oct. 1910.

151 *Register,* 29 Sept. 1910, 20 Oct. 1910. Robert Stamp, *The Schools of Ontario 1876–1976* (Toronto: Ontario Historical Studies Series and University of Toronto Press 1982), 87–8. McEvay was more cautious, asking Fallon to clarify to his colleagues that he sought only to eliminate inefficient schools, not to wipe out the French language in the province. Referring to the latter point, he added, "It is true we can and often should urge the advantages of knowing English in this country. But having done this we should go no farther." ARCAT, McEvay Papers, McEvay to Fallon, 24 Jan. 1911.

152 *Register,* 27 Jan. 1910.

153 AO, Whitney Papers, quoted in letter from James Whitney to Alfred Burke, 3 July 1914.

154 J. Albert Foisey, *Le Catholicisme en Ontario, quelques statistiques* (Ottawa: Le Droit 1918), 53–8.

155 CCES Office, Minutes, 19 Nov. 1910, 23; NA, Sir Charles Fitzpatrick Papers, vol. 13, copy of letter from Louis Bégin to Burke, 4 Nov. 1910, 5736; and copy of letter from Joseph Archambault to Burke, 2 Nov. 1910, 5735.

156 NA, Fitzpatrick Papers, vol. 13, file 1910, copy of letter from Archbishop McEvay to Bégin, 27 Dec. 1910, 5823; copy of letter from Fergus McEvay, chancellor of Extension, to Louis N. Bégin, 27 Dec. 1910, 5814–19. In the former letter, he also defended his record of fairness to French Canadians and added that the bilingual schools issue was more the creation of the French Canadian nationalist press than of Ontario's English-speaking Catholics.

157 Huel, "*Gestae Dei Per Francos*: The French Catholic Experience," 39–54.

158 Jeanne Beck, "Henry Somerville and Social Reform: His Contribution to Canadian Catholic Social Thought," CCHA, *Study Sessions* 42 (1975): 96–103; Boyle, *Pioneer in Purple: The Life and Work of Archbishop Neil McNeil* (Montreal: Palm Publishers 1951), 125–38.

159 *Register,* 6 Apr. 1916, 6 July 1916, 4 Jan. 1917, 15 Jan. 1920, 9 Mar. 1922, 11 Mar. 1922, 25 Mar. 1926, 15 Dec. 1927. ARCAT, CCES Papers, Financial Reports, 1918–29; McNeil Papers, Bulletin to the Clergy, 8 Apr. 1916; "Can We Defend the Church?" 11 July 1920; Circular Letter, 1 Oct. 1924; Circular Letter, 15 Jan. 1926; and Records of Donations sent to the Ukrainian Diocese. Also Ruthenian and Ukrainian Papers,"Rapport de la quête spéciale pour les Ruthènes,"1924–26. Toronto was joined in its endeavours by the dioceses of Charlottetown, Antigonish, Halifax, Alexandria, and Hamilton. Toronto's donations to the Ukrainian eparchy were usually double what was donated by the Archdiocese of Quebec.

160 ARCAT, CCES Papers, Thomas O'Donnell to the bishops of the west, Dec. 1917; NA, Fitzpatrick Papers, vol. 26, Bishop Roy to Fitzpatrick, 20 Jan. 1920, 15197–8. ARCAT, McNeil Papers, J.E. Cloutier, president of ACFEO, to McNeil, 18 Feb. 1920; Archbishop Arthur Beliveau of St Boniface to McNeil, 27 Jan. 1919; Father L.N. Campeau to McNeil, 15 June 1917; and clipping, "The Language Question, by Archbishop McNeil," 14 Feb.

1920; Father James Athol Murray Papers, Father J.A. Murray to McNeil, 7 June 1916; Ruthenian and Ukrainian Papers, Father Ad. Sabourin to McNeil, 18 Dec. 1919; and AAK, Michael J. Spratt Papers, Minutes of the Meeting of the Archbishops of Canada, 27–30 Apr. 1919.

161 ARCAT, McNeil Papers, copy of letter from McNeil to Mr Whalen of the *Casket*, 6 Dec. 1913. *Register*, 5, 19, 26 Feb. 1920, 4 Mar. 1920. ARCAT, McNeil Papers, Speech of Bishop Henry O'Leary, "One of the Needs for the Church in Canada," 2 Jan. 1926.

162 It was reprinted in the *Register*, 26 Oct. 1916.

CHAPTER EIGHT

1 AAO, Toronto Correspondence, "Correspondance des Civiles, 1901–1919," Berta Wadham to Archbishop Charles Gauthier, 8 Oct. 1915; NA, National Personnel Records Centre (NPRC), Personnel file, Private Elmer Wadham, 144953; *A Historical Sketch of the Seventy-Seventh Battalion, C.E.F.* (Ottawa: War Publications 1926), 175.

2 *Toronto Star*, 26 Jan. 1918; ARCAT, Spiritual Statistics and Financial Records, St Ann's and St John's parishes.

3 Robert Matthew Bray, "The Canadian Patriotic Response to the Great War," PhD, York University 1977, vii–viii.

4 Carl Berger, *The Sense of Power* (Toronto: University of Toronto Press 1970), 259–65; Berger, *Imperialism and Nationalism, 1884–1914: A Conflict in Canadian Thought* (Toronto: Copp Clark 1969), 1–5, 9–12, 63–5; Bray, "The Canadian Patriotic Response," 21–3. Bray indicates that the Toronto *Globe* and the *Manitoba Free Press* were the only two dailies to take the position that the war was Canada's and that it was being fought for liberty and democracy.

5 *Catholic Register*, 20 Aug. 1914; ARCAT, Neil McNeil Papers, Education box, 1914 file.

6 *Register*, 27 Aug. 1914.

7 ARCAT, McNeil Papers, Circulars, 25 Aug. 1914; War box, 1914, Patriotic Fund pledge card no. 924.

8 *Register*, 31 Dec. 1914; ARCAT, War box, P.F. Stagni, Apostolic Delegate, to S.P. Matheson, Anglican Bishop of Rupert's Land, 15 Dec. 1914.

9 *Catholic Record*, 16 Jan. 1915; text of the sermon in *Register*, 7 Jan. 1915. During the discourse McNeil gave the Empire a glowing tribute: "Think of the extent of the British Empire; it makes us feel proud to belong even in part to this great Empire ... No one can say that the British Empire has used power immoderately to crush any people."

10 *Register*, 19 Nov. 1914; for announced masses see ARCAT, Holograph Collection, Document 19.62, Announcement Book for St Michael's Cathedral, Oct. 1915 to Dec. 1921, 92, 108, 188.

11 Military District 2 included the counties of Lincoln, Welland, Haldimand, Norfolk, Brant, Wentworth, Halton, Peel, York, Ontario, Gray, Dufferin,

and Simcoe, and the districts of Muskoka, Parry Sound, Algoma, and Nipissing (north of the Mattawa and French Rivers, including the townships of Ferris and Bonfield); see Barbara M. Wilson, *Ontario and the First World War* (Toronto: Champlain Society, University of Toronto Press 1977), xviii–xix.

12 ARCAT, St Helen's Parish box, Photos file, Honour Roll; NAC, RG 9 II B3, Militia and Defence, vol. 80, Canadian Expeditionary Force Nominal Roll, 126th Battalion.

13 *Register*, 18 May 1916; see also ARCAT, War box, Major F.K. Prowse to Neil McNeil, 22 Nov. 1916.

14 ARCAT, War box, FWGC 01.103, "Catholic Young Men 'SHUN!'"

15 Alfred E. Burke, "The Irishman's Place in the Empire," in J. Castell Hopkins, ed., *Empire Club Speeches, 1909–1910* (Toronto: Warwick Bros. and Rutter 1910), 225–32.

16 *Register*, 10 Sept. 1914.

17 *Register*, 20 Oct. 1914.

18 Ibid., 29 Oct. 1914, 21 Jan. 1915.

19 Ibid., 25 Feb. 1915. Catholics wanted to make clear to the rest of the Empire that the Irish troubles were over and that Irishmen in Ireland would loyally support Britain now that the Home Rule Bill had been passed.

20 Ibid., 18 Mar. 1915. See also *Record*, 2 Jan. 1915, 20 Feb. 1915, 10 July 1915.

21 *Register*, 5 Aug. 1915.

22 The Liberal ties to the *Record* are confirmed by NA, Sir Wilfrid Laurier Papers, reel 779, Walter Boland to Laurier, 24 Sept. 1900, 49447; vol. 33, John P. Coffey to Laurier, 14 June 1897; Charles Murphy Papers, vol. 10, James T. Foley to Charles Murphy, 25 Mar. 1913, 4134–5; Foley to Murphy, 13 June 1913, 4137–44; Foley to Murphy, Liberal Circular #8, 4145–9; *Record*, 21 Mar. 1903.

23 *Record*, 15 Aug. 1914. Its questioning of the imperial relationship is noted on 13 Feb. 1915, 8 July 1916, 4 Nov. 1916, 11 Nov. 1916, and 6 Jan. 1917.

24 Like the *Register*, the *Record* expressed the Church's belief that patriotism was a Christian virtue and that to die in battle for this reason assured the salvation of the soul. See 2 Jan. 1915, 20 Feb. 1915, 10 July 1915.

25 *Record*, 15 Aug. 1914, 22 Aug. 1914.

26 *Register*, 7 Dec. 1916.

27 ARCAT, Parish Records, Our Lady of Lourdes Parish, Report of Eleanor Moore, Secretary, Patriotic Association, 13 Nov. 1917.

28 *Register*, 20 July 1916.

29 *St Joseph's Lilies* 4 (June 1915): 87–8.

30 Archives of the Community of St Joseph, *Annals of the Sisters of St Joseph* 2 (Jan. 1916), 500.

31 *Register*, 3 Sept. 1914; *Record*, 8 Jan. 1916.

32 *Register*, 3 Sept. 1914.

33 Ibid.
34 *Record*, 8 Jan. 1916.
35 Robert Craig Brown and Donald Loveridge, "Unrequited Faith: Recruiting the CEF 1914–1918," *Révue Internationale d'Histoire Militaire* 51 (1982): 56–63. This article indicates that the number of recruits dropped dramatically after June 1916, largely because of inefficiency in the recruiting process and competition from a revitalized domestic industrial complex; Catholic contribution list in NA, RG 9 III C15, Militia and Defence, vol. 4673, memorandum re Religious Statistics.
36 Desmond Morton, *When Your Number's Up: The Canadian Soldier in the First World War* (Toronto: Vintage 1993), 279.
37 NA, RG 9 III C15, vol. 4673, Religious Statistics. All figures represent enlistment to the end of June 1916. RG 9 III C15, vol. 4636, C-O-3, O'Gorman file, memorandum from J.J. O'Gorman to the Joint Meeting of the Bishops and Archbishops of Canada, 4 Oct. 1917, 10–11. The latter figures on French Canadian enlistment are corroborated in J.L. Granatstein and J.M. Hitsman, *Broken Promises: A History of Conscription in Canada* (Toronto: Copp Clark Pitman 1985), 28.
38 *Register*, 22 Nov. 1917, 28 July 1918. The figures provided by the *Register* were derived from the total enlistment prior to 1 Oct. 1916. The reprint from the *Peterborough Daily Review* (28 July 1918) demonstrates that out of the 484,997 Catholics in Ontario reported in the 1911 census, 202,000 were French Canadians. Consequently, the majority of the Catholic volunteers from Ontario represented only about 282,997 English-speaking and ethnic Catholics in the province. The article also points out that Ontario's Catholics were by no means the most zealous in Canada. The Catholic population of Nova Scotia, New Brunswick, and Prince Edward Island had given about 2.83 per cent of its total to the CEF. Moreover, the *Record*, 8 Jan. 1916, estimated that the Catholics of Nova Scotia, who composed 28 per cent of the provincial population, accounted for 47 per cent of the recruits in the province.
39 *Register*, 28 Oct. 1915.
40 *Toronto Star*, 26 Jan. 1918; *Register*, 31 Jan. 1918; ARCAT, Parish boxes and Spiritual and Financial Statistics, St Anthony's, St Ann's, and St John's parishes. These statistics do not include the number of recruits from St Francis of Assisi or Holy Name parishes. By 1917 the former had a population of 2,653, and given the contributions of parishes of comparable size, St Francis's could have had as many as 300 to 600 volunteers. Holy Name, however, was smaller at about 1,300, and if the contributions of other parishes its size are any indication, this Danforth Avenue parish could have had at least 100 attestations. No records exist to verify these estimates, although the *Ontario Catholic Yearbook* (Toronto: Newman Club 1919), 96, speculated that 3,500 volunteers would be a modest estimate.

41 *Census of Canada,* 1911, 2:80.

42 J. Castell Hopkins, *The Province of Ontario in the War* (Toronto: Warwick Bros. and Rutter 1919), 28–9. Hopkins lists only 20.

43 *Register,* 3 Feb. 1916, 10 Feb. 1916, 26 Apr. 1917, 22 Feb. 1917. All these clubs reported high enlistment during the voluntary phase of the war. In Feb. 1917 F.R. Boylan, president of the Holy Name Union of Toronto, stated that 47 per cent of the membership of eleven city branches had enlisted. *Ontario Catholic Directory,1918,* 105, states that 50 per cent of the eligible members of the Newman Club at the University of Toronto had enlisted. For more information on the university's Catholic volunteers see *University of Toronto, Roll of Service, 1914–1918* (Toronto: University of Toronto Press 1921), 10, 17, 26, 37, 44, 47, 57, 85, 122.

44 NPRC, Personnel files, Private Charles H. Speyer, 249116, Hugh Patrick McGrath, 249140; *The Irish Canadian* ([Toronto]: 208th Irish Canadian Battalion 1917).

45 UTA, 67th Varsity Battery Association, B84–0010/003, Nominal Roll.

46 *Send Out the Army and the Navy,* diary of W.J. O'Brien, 89018, 15 Mar. 1915 to 9 May 1919; see 16 Jan. 1917. My sincerest thanks to James O'Brien, John O'Brien, and Father William O'Brien, CSB, who kindly who gave me copies of the diary and indispensable background information. NPRC, William J. O'Brien File, 89018.

47 SMCA, St Michael's College *Yearbook,* 1916, 51, and 1919, 58; St Michael's College War Memorial, "The Slype," and GABF, A-11, Henry Carr to Francis Forster, 11 June 1918.

48 SMCA, *Yearbook,* 1916, 53–4.

49 NA, RG 9 III C15, vol. 4656, Assistant Director Chaplain Service, Roman Catholic, Michael Fallon to Canon L.A. Sylvestre, 26 Sept. 1918; Sylvestre to Fallon, 28 Sept. 1918, 7 Nov. 1918.

50 NAC, RG 9 III C15, vol. 4220, 75th Canadian Infantry Battalion, Register of Recruits; RG 9 II B 3, vol. 80, 75th Battalion and Reinforcing Draft, Nominal Roll of Officers, Non-Commissioned Officers and Men, 1916. All statistics based on the Seventy-fifth were compiled by using only the names of the men who appeared on the official sailing list and the register of recruits. An earlier register, RG 9 III C15, vol. 4219, was examined but was found wanting in its correlation with the other two sources. Other units surveyed were located in RG 9 III C15, vol. 4650, Denominational Census #6, #7, and #8.

51

Church	% of 75th	% in Toronto
Roman Catholic	8.4	13.1
Methodist	9.8	19.2
Presbyterian	10.6	19.9
Church of England	67.1	31.1

Source: *Census of Canada,* 1911, 2:80.

52 Brown and Loveridge, "Unrequited Faith," 57; Desmond Morton, *Canada and War* (Toronto: Butterworths 1981), 60.

53 NAC, RG 24, Department of National Defence, vol. 1249, HQ-593-1-77, S.D. Chown to Lt-Col. Charles F. Winter, 28 Oct. 1915; J. Michael Bliss, "The Methodist Church and World War I," *Canadian Historical Review* 49 (Sept. 1968); John Webster Grant, *The Church in the Canadian Era* (Toronto: McGraw-Hill Ryerson 1972), 114.

54 G.W.L. Nicholson, *The Canadian Expeditionary Force, 1915–1918* (Ottawa: Queen's Printer 1964), 170–4; NPRC, Personnel file, Brig.-Gen. Archibald Hayes Macdonell; Desmond Morton, *A Peculiar Kind of Politics* (Toronto: University of Toronto Press 1982), 121–2. The *Record*, 13 Jan. 1917, stated, "He is regarded as one of the ablest officers ever connected with the local staff." The other general was J.H. Elmsley of St Basil's Parish, who was mentioned four times in dispatches and commanded the Canadian Expeditionary Force to Siberia. *Ontario Catholic Yearbook*,1919, 96.

55 *Toronto Star*, 26 Jan. 1918; ARCAT, Spiritual and Financial Statistics, St Paul's parish, 1917; *Register*, 30 Sept. 1915.

56 Edward Kelly, *The Story of St Paul's Parish* (Toronto 1922), 173–5, 311. A speech from the Holy Name Society of St Paul's to Dean J.L. Hand praised the cleric for helping to deliver 850 from the parish to the war effort.

57 ARCAT, Spiritual and Financial Statistics, St Helen's parish, M.J. Crottie to F.R. Boland, 13 Apr. 1917; *Register*, 30 Sept. 1915; the former deals with the voluntary contribution of St Helen's parish. Crottie admits that his list of volunteers was not started by the parish priest until mid-1915 and that the earliest recruits were not recorded. Considering that the *Register*, 22 Feb. 1917, reported that 225 men had enlisted from the parish, it is possible that the missing 44 men were either recruited in the first call to arms or were a clerical error.

58 Brown and Loveridge, "Unrequited Faith," 57; NPRC, Personnel files 27066, 27837, 8007,35577, 11493, 27313, 9564.

59 *Labour Gazette* 14 (Feb. 1914): 881–2; (May 1914): 1265–6; 15 (July 1915): 35–6; 14 (Sept. 1914): 359; (Oct. 1914): 451; (Dec. 1914): 666–7; 15 (Jan. 1915): 786–7.

60 Wilson, *Ontario and the First World War*, xxi.

61 NPRC, Personnel file, Pte Charles Wehrle, 35577; Canada, Department of Veterans' Affairs, Commonwealth War Graves Commission (CWGC), Burial Registers.

62 NAC, RG 24, vol. 1249, HQ 593–1–77, "Battalions 18–85, Question: What Is the Country of Your Birth?" and Nationalities from Attestation, 22 Aug. 1916.

63 Statistics are derived from NAC, RG 9 III C15, vol. 4220, 75th Canadian Infantry Battalion, Register of Recruits, and RG 9 II B 3, vol. 80, 75th Roll of Officers.

64 Wilson, *Ontario and the First World War*, lx; R. Craig Brown and Ramsay Cook, *Canada, 1896–1921: A Nation Transformed* (Toronto: McClelland and Stewart 1974), 239–41. In St Helen's parish 11 of the 46 men who attested during the third phase of enlistment (23.91 per cent) were skilled workers such as tailors, machinists, and moulders. All were in demand on the home front. Another 10 could have been classified as clerical, business, and professional. The situation differed in St Paul's, where only 12 per cent of the volunteers in this phase were skilled labourers. Unskilled and semi-skilled labourers, by far the largest groups in the parish, constituted the majority of volunteers in the third phase.

65 AAO, Toronto Correspondence, Correspondance des civiles, 1901–19, Berta Wadham to Archbishop Gauthier, 8 Oct. 1915.

66 NA, RG 9 III C15, vol. 4220. The statistical breakdown for units in Military District 2 are found in NAC RG 24, vol. 1249, HQ 593-1-77, Occupations, 18 June 1916.

67 *Labour Gazette* 15 (Nov. 1915): 559; (Dec. 1915): 688; 16 (Jan. 1916): 778–9; (Mar. 1916): 986; (Apr. 1916): 1084; (May 1916): 1184; (June 1916): 1278.

68 Brown and Loveridge, "Unrequited Faith," 60.

69 NPRC, Personnel file, Corporal ER, 11200.

70 Brown and Loveridge, "Unrequited Faith," 57. NAC, RG 9 III, vol. 4220, and RG 9 II B 3, vol. 80.

71 ARCAT, St Helen's Parish box, Photos file, St Helen's Church Honour Roll, 4 Apr. 1917.

72 NPRC, Personnel files: James Mitchell Cooney, 404303; Patrick Arthur, 681391; John Thomas, 405724; Cornelius Vincent, 404724.

73 AAO, Toronto Correspondence, Correspondance des civiles, 1901–19, Berta Wadham to Archbishop Gauthier, 8 Oct. 1915.

74 Morton, *When Your Number's Up*, 47–70 passim.

75 NPRC, Personnel file, William Edward Pennylegion, 862085.

76 ARCAT, War box, K.E. Morrow to McNeil, 22 Aug. 1918.

77 Ibid., Arthur O'Leary to McNeil, 18 Aug. 1918.

78 RG 9 II B3, vol. 80, #9 Stationary Hospital, and NPRC, Personnel files and attestation papers for personnel of #9. *Catholics of the Diocese of Antigonish and the Great War, 1914–1919* (Antigonish: St Francis Xavier University Press [1920]), 55–6.

79 NPRC, Attestation Papers, Margaret McEvoy.

80 Ibid., Aimee Mary Christie.

81 *St Joseph's Lilies* 4 (June 1915): 87–8; The first nurses to leave were Miss A. Doig, Miss N. Turner, Miss Christie, Miss McEvay, Miss E. Dunn, Miss F. Conlin, Miss McCallum, and Miss H. Schyll: ibid., 86.

82 NPRC, Attestation Papers, random sample of 34 men from the 208th Battalion. Recruitment appeared to taper off after May 1916. Files 1006727,

249466, 249664, 249710, 250000, 249396, 249416, 249459, 249654, 249641, 249764, 250015, 250048, 250083, 249275, 249383, 249836, 249140, 249508, Major SJM, 2490005, 249307, 249167, 249116, Lt MMW, 249254, 249575, 249751, 249414, 249056, 250121, 249176, 249780, 249114. NA, RG 9 II B3, vol 80, 208th Battalion, Nominal Roll of Officers, Non-Commissioned Officers, and Men.

83 ADP, Michael O'Brien Papers, W.J. O'Brien to Bishop O'Brien, 5 Sept. 1915, 5 Oct. 1915.

84 ARCAT, War box, Father Bernard S. Doyle to McNeil, 1 Mar. 1918; J. Pirot to McNeil, 27 Apr. 1917; Gilbert Sim to McNeil, 17 Jan. 1915; Lt D.F. Finney to McNeil, 17 Apr. 1916; NPRC, Personnel file, Gilbert A. Sim, 304354; NA, RG 9 III C15, vol. 4656, file ADCS (Assistant Director of Chaplain Services, RC), Father A. Sylvestre to McNeil, 23 July 1918. Catholic chaplains from Toronto included Melville Staley, William Kelly, William Terrence Kelly, Bernard Stephen Doyle, and Alfred E. Burke; NPRC, Personnel files; NAC, RG 9 III C15, vol. 4649, Biographies. Burke's adventures deserve note. He quit as editor of the *Catholic Register* to join the chaplaincy in an unspecified role. After a series of misadventures, including controversy over whether he was head of the Catholic chaplains, he was "struck off" the list of chaplains and forced to return to Canada. NA, RG 9 III C15, vol. 4643, C-O-3, O'Gorman, 11 Sept. 1917, 25 July 1917; vol. 4618, A.E. Burke, 1 May 1917.

85 *Register*, 30 Mar. 1916. Pte Frederick Fenton of Spadina Avenue was more sober in recollections printed in the *Register*, 24 June 1915.

86 NPRC, Personnel files, Frank J. Gorman, 669542, and Wilfrid J. O'Brien, 138931.

87 William O'Brien, CSB, transcripts of St Michael's College Honour Roll. SMCA, *Yearbook*, 1917, 49.

88 See Dennis Winter, *Death's Men: Soldiers of the Great War* (Harmondsworth: Penguin 1978), and Morton, *When Your Number's Up*, 181–206. NPRC, Personnel files, random sample of 91 recruits from St Helen's parish (under terms of Privacy Act and Access to Information Act).

89 NPRC, Personnel file, William Pennylegion, 862085.

90 ARCAT, War box, W.T.M. Kennedy to McNeil, 28 Mar. 1916; McNeil to Sir Thomas White, minister of Finance, 17 Feb. 1917.

91 *Star*, 4 Aug. 1916.

92 ARCAT, War box, McNeil to Thomas White, 17 Feb. 191?

93 *Register*, 8 Nov. 1917. Support from Father Minehan came in his column "Canada's Victory War Loan" in the *Register*, 22 Nov. 1917. He asked: "Shall teuton fiendishness which has robbed Europe of the flower of its manhood, wrecked the masterpieces of Christian civilization in wanton deviltry, strewn the ocean with the bones of non-combatants – men, women and children be allowed to emerge victorious in this long drawn-out struggle?"

94 ARCAT, McNeil Papers, AH07.84, McNeil to J.C. O'Connor, 12 Oct. 1918. McNeil published a circular in the same month to encourage the purchase of Victory Bonds: ARCAT, McNeil Papers, Circulars, 31 Oct. 1918; *Register*, 24 Oct. 1918.

95 *Register*, 25 Mar. 1915, 20 Jan. 1916, 27 Jan. 1916; *Record*, 20 Oct. 1915.

96 *Register*, 16 Nov. 1916.

97 *Record*, 8 Apr. 1916, 8 July 1916, 4 Nov. 1916, 11 Nov. 1916, 6 Jan. 1917, 3 Feb. 1917, 24 Feb. 1917, 31 Mar. 1917, 12 May 1917. The *Record* gave a rare glimpse of the effects of the war on families in its 29 July 1916 issue. The editor recounted the story of a young newlywed who died two days after receiving word that her husband had been killed in action. This was more the exception than the rule for the paper; the *Register*, by contrast, concentrated more on the local effects of the war, publishing weekly reports of the killed and wounded Catholics from the city. McNeil initiated this local thrust when he assumed the chancellorship of the CCES, the *Register's* owner. Once Burke was out of the way in 1915, McNeil appointed a new editorial staff, marking a dramatic shift to more local questions and liberalizing the paper by means of a "Life and Labour" column.

98 *Record*, 4 Dec. 1915.

99 ARCAT, McNeil Papers, Circulars, 21 June 1917; *Register*, 28 June 1917.

100 *Register*, 21 June 1917.

101 Ibid., and 28 June 1917.

102 Bray, "The Canadian Patriotic Response to the Great War," 351. Bray cites only one small paragraph in John Castell Hopkins, *Canadian Annual Review of Public Affairs, 1917* (Toronto: Canadian Annual Review 1918), 412, a source whose accuracy he has already questioned (20). J.L. Granatstein and J. Hitsman's *Broken Promises* makes no mention of the issue.

103 ARCAT, McNeil Papers, Circulars, 1917. War box, R.B. Bennett to McNeil, 21 Dec. 1916. Although the circular itself does not so indicate, the *Register*, 11 Jan. 1917, asserts that McNeil gave his official endorsement on 7 Jan. 1917. McNeil was not alone among the bishops in his support; Archbishop Paul Bruchesi of Montreal also requested that his flock co-operate with the registration. Morton, *Canada and War*, 69.

104 ARCAT, War box, John M. Godfrey to McNeil, 17 June 1917.

105 *Record*, 23 Dec. 1916.

106 *Register*, 11 Jan. 1917.

107 Ibid., 24 July 1917.

108 Ibid., 28 June 1917, 21 June 1917, 2 Aug. 1917.

109 Bray, "The Canadian Patriotic Response," vii–viii, 526–7.

110 J. Castell Hopkins, *Canada at War: A Record of Heroism and Achievement, 1914–1918* (Toronto: Canadian Annual Review 1919), 331; ARCAT, War box, rough notes, 1917.

111 *Star*, 22 Feb. 1916, 18 Aug. 1917, 19 Apr. 1918, and 22 Apr. 1918.

112 See Jeanne Beck,"Henry Somerville and Social Reform," CCHA, *Study Sessions* 42 (1975): 96–103; Gregory Baum, *Catholics and Canadian Socialism* (Toronto: James Lorimer 1980), 98, 122–3, 128–31.

113 *Register*, 23 Aug. 1917.

114 Ibid., 28 June 1917. Somerville grants that some of those opposing conscription may have done so out of conscience and on national grounds, while others may have done so for sectional reasons. He felt that the former were still rendering a national service, although he disagreed with their motives.

115 About one-fifth of the riding was Catholic. *Census of Canada*, 1911, 2:80. South Toronto, 43,956, of which 9,143 were Catholic: NA, Charles Murphy Papers, vol. 16, file 77, copy of letter from Murphy to Laurier, 23 Mar. 1915, 6533.

116 *Debates of the House of Commons*, 1917, vol. 3, 29 June 1917, 2848–9.

117 Ibid., 2854.

118 Berger, *The Sense of Power*, 171–3, 260–1; Berger, ed., *Imperialism and Nationalism*, 61; William L. Grant, "The Fallacy of Nationalism," *Empire Club Addresses, Delivered during the Session of 1911–1912* (Toronto: Warwick Bros. and Rutter 1913), 223–8.

119 ARCAT, McNeil Papers, AS07.03, J.S. McGinnis to McNeil, 15 Apr. 1918.

120 *Canadian* 26 (June 1918). The newsletter also gave specific details of how to register. The CMBA had members from coast to coast, but with concentrations in Ontario and Quebec.

121 *Record*, 26 May 1917.

122 Ibid., 7 July 1917.

123 Ibid., 30 June 1917.

124 Ibid., 28 July 1917. Editor J.T. Foley was candid to Liberal MP Charles Murphy that he was uncertain how obliged Canada was to help the imperial cause. He was equally confused about Canada's constitutional status after the war; he did not discount federation with the United States as a possibility. He also admitted that the intolerance of French Canadian nationalism was probably worse than even its harshest critic, Newton Wesley Rowell, feared. NAC, Charles Murphy Papers, vol. 10, J.T. Foley to Charles Murphy, 7 Jan. 1918, 4163–5.

125 *Star*, 3 Nov. 1917.

126 *Record*, 2 June 1917, 28 July 1917; *Register*, 26 Aug. 1915, 18 Nov. 1915, 20 Jan. 1916, 2 Aug. 1917, 25 Oct. 1917, 16 May 1918. In most of these articles the *Register* tended to praise the efforts of the clergy while condemning the positions of Henri Bourassa and many of the Nationalistes. Father O'Leary of St Joseph's parish warned McNeil that if the *Register* became too Conservative in its views and too intemperate in its criticism of Bourassa, it might lose Liberal readers, who, he felt, were the majority in Toronto. ARCAT, *Catholic Register* Papers, Arthur O'Leary to McNeil, 18 Nov. 1917.

127 ARCAT, McNeil Papers, AS13.02, A. Fitzpatrick to McNeil, 23 Oct. 1917; War box, S. Layhy to McNeil, 22 Feb. 1918.
128 Trans. by the *Register*, 2 May 1918.
129 *La Presse*, 19 Apr. 1918. ARCAT, McNeil Papers, AS13.08, J.A.H. Cameron to McNeil, 25 Apr. 1918; AH07.134, "A Pea Soup" to McNeil, 21 Apr. 1918; AH08.01, letter from Oswald Mayrand, managing editor of *La Presse*, to McNeil, 4 Jan. 1919. The latter commented: "Your broadminded views impressed me very deeply and what we first published, from you, last year ... was very much appreciated by our readers."
130 Granatstein and Hitsman, *Broken Promises*, 74.
131 Morrison's support for conscription is made clear in *Casket*, 4 Jan. 1917; ADL, Fallon Papers, Speeches, Statement of Bishop Fallon in Favour of Union Government, 6 Dec. 1917.
132 Hopkins, *Canada at War*, 331, recognizes the support of McNeil and Fallon. Robin Burns, "The Montreal Irish and the Great War," CCHA, *Historical Studies*, 52 (1985): 78–81. John English, *The Decline of Politics: The Conservatives and the Party System, 1901–1920* (Toronto: University of Toronto Press 1977), 200, shows that only five Catholics sat in the Union caucus, four of them English-speaking. This substantiates his claim that Catholics were disproportionately underrepresented.
133 *Register*, 13 Sept. 1917.
134 NA, Murphy Papers, vol. 23, Father Arthur O'Leary, St Joseph's Parish, to Charles Murphy, 20 Mar. 1918, 9915; for other statements of the same, see *Register*, 20 Dec. 1917, 27 Dec. 1917.
135 Brian Hogan, CSB, "The Guelph Novitiate Raid: Conscription, Censorship and Bigotry during the Great War," CCHA, *Study Sessions* 45 (1978): 57–80. *House of Commons Debates*, 2 Apr. 1919, 2:1218–59. In Toronto the raid's impact never extended beyond the press reports. The *Register* regarded it as merely the product of Orange bigotry and reprinted sympathetic articles from the *Mail and Empire*: 27 June 1918, 4 July 1918, 18 July 1918, 14 Aug. 1919.
136 ARCAT, Dollard Papers, James B. Dollard to McNeil, 3 Mar. 1918; McNeil Papers, Pamphlets, PC25.04.
137 *Register*, 7 Mar. 1918.
138 NA, RG 9, C III 15, vol. 4628, file CH-21, Thomas Peter Hussey File, Hussey to Wolsten Workman, 22 Nov. 1917.
139 *Register*, 16 Jan. 1919; Desmond Morton and Glenn Wright, *Winning the Second Battle: Canadian Veterans and the Return to Civilian Life, 1915–1930* (Toronto: University of Toronto Press 1987), 62.
140 I.J.E. Daniel and D.A. Casey, *For God and Country: A History of the Knights of Columbus Catholic Army Huts* (Toronto 1922), 17; *Register*, 22 Nov. 1917, 15 Aug. 1918.
141 Daniel, *For God and Country*, intro.

142 *Register*, 22 Nov. 1917, 13 Dec. 1917.

143 AAM, Bruchesi Papers, 732.256, Circular for Campaign, 15–23 Sept. 1918. It indicates that J.J. Leddy of Saskatoon and George Boivin of Montreal had joined Murray of Ontario on the national executive of the campaign.

144 ARCAT, War box, Circular to the Clergy, 25 Sept. 1918; *Ontario Catholic Yearbook* (Toronto: Newman Club 1920), 25.

145 *Register*, 12 Sept. 1918, 19 Sept. 1918, 3 Oct. 1918.

146 ARCAT, Knights of Columbus Papers, Colonel Dinnick's Speech for Catholic Army Huts Campaign, 29 Sept. 1918.

147 NA, RG 9 III C15, C-F-6 Fallon, M.F. Fallon to Lt-Col. the Rev. G.C. Workman, 19 Oct. 1918. Other key members of the Committee included G.A. Warburton of the YMCA, Col. W.S. Dinnnick, and Ralph Connable of Woolworths, all of whom were Protestant. See ARCAT, War box, List of Officers for Campaign, Oct. 2, 3, 4 1918.

148 *Ontario Catholic Yearbook* (1920), 25; the *Register* reported that the total after the initial campaign was $181,244.75. This included a $15,000 donation from city council. The *Register* also included supportive excerpts from Toronto dailies.

149 ARCAT, War box, copy of letter from McNeil to Ralph Connable, Woolworth Co., 10 Oct. 1918.

150 Daniel and Casey, *For God and Country*, 37. One patron offered his praise of one particular Hut in verse:

> Bread when you are hungry,
> Beer when you are dry;
> Bed when you are sleepy,
> And Heaven when you die.

151 Daniel and Casey, *For God and Country*, 203–4.

152 ARCAT, War box, 10 Jan. 1919; NA, FWSCCC Papers, McNeil to S.D. Chown, 20 Dec. 1918; Minutes of meeting held at Synod Office, Ottawa, 13 Feb. 1919.

153 ARCAT, Clergy files, Michael Moyna, Ministry of Militia, to McNeil, 18 July 1919; War box, Pietro Di Maria, Apostolic Delegate, to McNeil, 25 July 1919.

154 *Register*, 21 Nov. 1918.

Index